Lecture Notes in Computer Science 1345

Edited by G. Goos, J. Hartmanis and J. van Leeuwen

Advisory Board: W. Brauer   D. Gries   J. Stoer

Springer
Berlin
Heidelberg
New York
Barcelona
Budapest
Hong Kong
London
Milan
Paris
Santa Clara
Singapore
Tokyo

R.K. Shyamasundar   K. Ueda (Eds.)

Advances in Computing Science – ASIAN'97

Third Asian Computing Science Conference
Kathmandu, Nepal, December 9-11, 1997
Proceedings

Springer

Series Editors

Gerhard Goos, Karlsruhe University, Germany

Juris Hartmanis, Cornell University, NY, USA

Jan van Leeuwen, Utrecht University, The Netherlands

Volume Editors

R. K. Shyamasundar
Tata Institute of Fundamental Research
Bombay 400 005, India
E-mail: shyam@tcs.tifr.res.in

K. Ueda
Waseda University, Department of Information and Computer Science
3-4-1, Okubo, Shinjuku-ku, Tokyo 169, Japan
E-mail: ueda@ueda.info.waseda.ac.jp

Cataloging-in-Publication data applied for

Die Deutsche Bibliothek - CIP-Einheitsaufnahme

Advances in computing science : proceedings / ASIAN '97, Third
Asian Computing Science Conference, Kathmandu, Nepal, December
9 - 11, 1997. R. K. Shyamasundar ; K. Ueda (ed.). - Berlin ;
Heidelberg ; New York ; Barcelona ; Budapest ; Hong Kong ;
London ; Milan ; Paris ; Santa Clara ; Singapore ; Tokyo : Springer,
1997
   (Lecture notes in computer science ; Vol. 1345)
   ISBN 3-540-63875-X

CR Subject Classification (1991): D, C, F.1-2, I.6

ISSN 0302-9743
ISBN 3-540-63875-X Springer-Verlag Berlin Heidelberg New York

© Springer-Verlag Berlin Heidelberg 1997
Printed in Germany

Typesetting: Camera-ready by author
SPIN 10652647   06/3142 – 5 4 3 2 1 0   Printed on acid-free paper

Preface

This conference, ASIAN'97, is the third in a series of Asian Computing Science Conferences promoted to provide a world-class academic computer science forum for the regional research community. The inaugural conference was held in 1995 at the Asian Institute of Technology (AIT), Bangkok, Thailand in partnership with INRIA, France, and UNU/IIST, Macau. The logistic support for the series has been provided by these three partners ever since. The second conference was held in 1996 in Singapore, organized by the National University of Singapore (NUS). Their proceedings were published as Lecture Notes in Computer Science 1023 and 1179, respectively.

The basic strategy of the conference series has been (1) to select themes to provide a varying focus for the otherwise general conference on computing science and (2) to have eminent invited speakers. The themes of focus for this year are: Programming Languages and Compilation Technology, Formal Reasoning and Constraints, Real-Time Computing, and Network/Mobile Computing. Our keynote speaker is Michael Rabin (Harvard University and The Hebrew University of Jerusalem). The invited speakers are Nicholas Ayache (INRIA, Sophia Antipolis), and Randal R. Bryant (Carnegie Mellon University).

We received 94 submissions, a majority of them electronically, from 25 countries. Country-wise breakdown of papers is as follows: *Asia:* China (2), India (8), Israel (2), Japan (20), Korea (1), Macau (1), Malaysia (2), Philippines (1), Singapore (2), Taiwan (4), and Thailand (2). *Other Countries:* Australia (9), Belgium (1), Brazil (1), Canada (7), Finland (1), France (6), Germany (7), Italy (4), The Netherlands (1), Norway (3), Russia (1), UK (3), USA (4), Yugoslavia (1). The review process was conducted electronically over the Net. Almost all papers had three or more reviews. The program committee meeting was conducted electronically over a period of 10 days after circulating a summary of the reviews to all the PC members. The majority of the program committee members actively participated in the review process looking into the comments/suggestions of the reviewers, and made fresh reviews as and when needed. Finally, the program committee selected 24 regular papers and 10 poster papers.

We thank our keynote speaker and invited speakers for accepting our invitation to give talks and contribute papers or extended abstracts. The referees and the program committee members deserve a great deal of gratitude for their careful attention and response often at very short notice.

We are once again indebted to the main partners of the series, AIT, INRIA, and UNU/IIST. Our home departments Tata Institute of Fundamental Research (India) and Waseda University (Japan) provided valuable support. The support of the European Commission and NTT (Japan) is being requested. Organization of the conference has been coordinated by Kanchana Kanchanasut of AIT and Roland H. C. Yap of NUS through active support of the International Centre for Integrated Mountain Development (ICIMOD, Nepal), the Computer Association of Nepal, AIT Alumni Association Nepal Chapter, and the National University of Singapore. Thanks go to Alfred Hofmann of Springer-Verlag and his staff for bringing out the proceedings in time for the conference.

September 1997   R. K. Shyamasundar
                                                    Kazunori Ueda

Steering Committee

Dines Bjørner(UNU/IIST, Macau)
Shigeki Goto (Waseda Univ., Japan)
Joxan Jaffar (NUS, Singapore)
Gilles Kahn (INRIA, France)
Kanchana Kanchanasut (AIT, Thailand)
Jean-Jacques Lévy (INRIA, France)
R. K. Shyamasundar (TIFR Bombay, India)
Kazunori Ueda (Waseda Univ., Japan)

Program Committee

Arnie Azcarraga (De La Salle Univ., Philippines)
Gérard Berry (Ecole des Mines de Paris, France)
Manfred Broy (Tech. Univ. Munich, Germany)
Gihan Dias (Univ. Moratuwa, Sri Lanka)
Phan Minh Dung (AIT, Thailand)
Georges Gonthier (INRIA Rocquencourt, France)
Shigeki Goto (Waseda Univ., Japan)
Jan Friso Groote (CWI, Netherlands)
Nicolas Halbwachs (Vérimag, France)
Jieh Hsiang (National Taiwan Univ., Taiwan)
Gérard Huet (INRIA Rocquencourt, France)
Kanchana Kanchanasut (AIT, Thailand)
Deepak Kapur (SUNY Albany, USA)
Jimmy H. M. Lee (CUHK, Hongkong)
Chidchanok Lursinsap (Chula/AIT, Thailand)
Michael Maher (Griffith Univ., Australia)
Tatsuo Nakajima (JAIST, Japan)
Kesav V. Nori (TRC, India)
Catuscia Palamidessi (Pennsylvania State Univ., USA)
Amir Pnueli (Weizmann Inst., Israel)
Willem P. de Roever (Univ. Kiel, Germany)
Taisuke Sato (Tokyo Inst. Tech., Japan)
Natarajan Shankar (SRI, USA)
R. K. Shyamasundar, *Co-Chair* (TIFR Bombay, India)
Ambuj Singh (UCSB, USA)
John Staples (Univ. Queensland, Australia)
Yohanes Stefanus (Univ. Indonesia, Indonesia)
Doug Tygar (CMU, USA)
Kazunori Ueda, *Co-Chair* (Waseda Univ., Japan)
Martin Wirsing (Univ. Munich, Germany)
Nor Adnan Yahaya (Telekom Malaysia Berhad, Malaysia)
Roland H. C. Yap (NUS, Singapore)
Zhou Chaochen (UNU/IIST, Macau)

Local Arrangements

Pramod Pradhan, *Chairperson* (ICIMOD, Nepal)
Kanchana Kanchanasut (AIT, Thailand)
Suresh Regmi (CAN, Nepal)
Basanta Shrestha (ICIMOD, Nepal)
Sushil Pandey (ICIMOD, Nepal)

List of Referees

Atul Adya
Hassan Aït-Kaci
Thorsten Altenkirch
K. C. Anand
Duong Tuan Anh
Arvind
Arnulfo P. Azcarraga
Rana Barua
Ulrich Berger
Gérard Berry
Yves Bertot
Philippe Besnard
David Billington
Ahmed Bouajjani
Mark van den Brand
Manfred Broy
Luca Cardelli
Mats Carlsson
P. Caspi
Laiwan Chan
Philip Chan
Sharat Chandran
Bernard Chazelle
Chong-kan Chiu
Cristina Cornes
Nguyen Duong Dam
J. E. K. Dayao
D. M. Dhamdhere
Damien Doligez
Gilles Dowek
Phan Minh Dung
Herbert Ehler
Mike Ehrlich
Hugo Elbers
Thom Fruewirth
Maurizio Gabbrielli

Mordecai J. Golin
Georges Gonthier
Shigeki Goto
Jan Friso Groote
Philippe de Groote
Radu Grosu
Gopal Gupta
Masami Hagiya
Nicolas Halbwachs
Zahran Halim
Wang Hanpin
Ian Hayes
Kohei Honda
Jieh Hsiang
Guan-Shieng Huang
Zhiyi Huang
Gérard Huet
Dang Van Hung
Paul Jackson
Joxan Jaffar
Jerry James
Matthias Jantzen
Kazuki Joe
Laxmikant V. Kale
Kanchana Kanchanasut
K. V. Ravi Kanth
Deepak Kapur
P. Kearney
Uday Khedkar
Piotr Kosiuczenko
Yassine Lakhnech
Kwok-Yan Lam
Bernard Lang
Jimmy H. M. Lee
Raimondas Lencevicius
Ho-fung Leung

Yaw-Ren Lin
Bing Liu
Zhiming Liu
Kamal Lodaya
John Lui
Michael Maher
Luc Maranget
Monica Marcus
Kim Marriott
Viviana Mascardi
Bernd Meyer
Madhavan Mukund
Olaf Müller
Tatuso Nakajima
Hideyuki Nakashima
Peter Nickolas
Raymond Nickson
Kesav V. Nori
Kazuo Ohta
Catuscia Palamidessi
Hemant Pande
Paritosh K. Pandya
Rohit Parikh
L. M. Patnaik
Christine Paulin
Amir Pnueli
Andreas Podelski
Enrico Pontelli
Sunil Prabhakar
Wishnu Prasetya
Femke van Raamsdonk
Jaikumar Radhakrishnan
N. Raja
R. Ramanujam
S. Ramesh
Abhiram Ranade
M. R. K. Krishna Rao
P. V. S. Rao
Michel Raynal
Peter Robinson
Willem-Paul de Roever
François Rouaix
Sitvanit Ruah
Harald Ruess
Oliver Ruething
A. Sanyal

Taisuke Sato
Birgit Schieder
Pranab Sen
Tan Tiow Seng
Anil Seth
Elad Shahar
Natarajan Shankar
Etsuya Shibayama
Ofer Shtrichman
R. K. Shyamasundar
Friedemann Simon
Eli Singerman
Ambuj K. Singh
G. Sivakumar
Jan Smith
Ashok Sreenivas
John Staples
Gheorghe Stefanescu
Yohanes Stefanus
Bernhard Steffen
Harald Störrle
S. Sudrashan
Jefferson L. Tan
Owen Traynor
Hsieh-Chang Tu
Doug Tygar
Kazunori Ueda
M. Vidyasagar
Sundar Viswanathan
Razvan Voicu
Fer-Jan de Vries
Joost Warners
Pierre Weis
Martin Wirsing
Man Hon Wong
Daniel Wu
Xu Qiwen
Nor Adnan Yahaya
Roland H. C. Yap
Makoto Yokoo
Norihiko Yoshida
Brad Vander Zanden
Zhou Chaochen
Neng-Fa Zhou
Floriano Zini
Uri Zwick

Table of Contents

Keynote Address

Correctness of Programs and Protocols through Randomization 1
  Michael O. Rabin

Invited Lectures

Medical Image Analysis and Simulation 4
  Nicholas Ayache
Verification of Pipelined Microprocessors by Comparing Memory Execution
Sequences in Symbolic Simulation 18
  Randal E. Bryant, Miroslav N. Velev

Session 1

Rules for Abstraction 32
  Stephan Merz
Combining Z and Temporal Interval Logics for the Formalization of
Properties and Behaviors of Embedded Systems 46
  Robert Büssow, Wolfgang Grieskamp
Rules for Trace Consistent Reasoning 57
  R. Ramanujam

Session 2

Sensitivity Analysis of Real-Time Task Sets 72
  Sasikumar Punnekkat, Rob Davis, Alan Burns
Dynamic Multiprocessor Scheduling for Supporting Real-Time Constraints 83
  Shin-Mu Tseng, Y. H. Chin, Wei-Pang Yang
Heuristic Diff Acquiring in Lazy Release Consistency Model 98
  Zhiyi Huang, Wan-Ju Lei, Chengzheng Sun, Abdul Sattar

Session 3

Representation of Discretely Controlled Continuous Systems in Software-
Oriented Formal Analysis 110
  Tetsuya Mizutani, Shigeru Igarashi, Kohji Tomita, Masayuki Shio
A Generalized Framework for Reasoning with Multi-point Events 121
  R. Wetprasit, A. Sattar, L. Khatib
Implementing Constraint Retraction for Finite Domains 136
  Yan Georget, Philippe Codognet, Francesca Rossi

Session 4

INSTANCE: The Intermediate Storage Node Concept 151
  Thomas Plagemann, Vera Goebel

Checking Hybrid Automata for Linear Duration Invariants 166
  Li Xuandong, Dang Van Hung, Zheng Tao

Hierarchical Automata as Model for Statecharts 181
  Erich Mikk, Yassine Lakhnech, Michael Siegel

Session 5

Proof Discovery in LK System by Analogy 197
  Masateru Harao

Efficient Induction of Executable Logic Programs from Examples 212
  Nobuhiro Inuzuka, Hirohisa Seki, Hidenori Itoh

Automated Verification of Behavioural Properties of Prolog Programs ... 225
  B. Le Charlier, C. Leclère, S. Rossi, A. Cortesi

Session 6

Typing the Use of Resources in a Concurrent Calculus 239
  Gérard Boudol

An Imperative Language with Read/Write Type Modes 254
  Paul Roe

Efficient Goal Scheduling in a Concurrent Logic Language Using Type-
Based Dependency Analysis 268
  *Kazuhiko Ohno, Masahiko Ikawa, Masahiro Goshima, Shin-ichiro Mori,
  Hiroshi Nakashima, Shinji Tomita*

Session 7

An Analysis of Divisibility Orderings and Recursive Path Orderings 283
  Ryu Hasegawa

Share-Where Maintenance in Visual Algebraic Specifications 297
  T. B. Dinesh, Susan M. Üsküdarlı

A Fault Tolerant Broadcast Scheme in Star Graphs 312
  Satoshi Fujita

Session 8

Calculus of Classical Proofs I 321
   Ken-etsu Fujita

Tracing the Evaluation of Lazy Functional Languages: A Model and Its
Implementation 336
   Richard Watson, Eric Salzman

Basic Results in Automatic Transformations of Shared Memory Parallel
Programs into Sequential Programs 351
   Yosi Ben-Asher, Esti Stein

Posters

Recurrent Oscillatory Self-organizing Map: Adapting to Complex
Environmental Periodicities 367
   Mauri Kaipainen, Pantelis Papadopoulos, Pasi Karhu

Basic Binary Decision Diagram Operations for Image Processing 368
   C. Lursinsap, K. Kanchanasut, T. Siriboon

Adaptive Object Storage System for Mobile Computing Environments ... 371
   Tatsuo Nakajima

Structure of User Interface Module for Practical Internet Messages 373
   Morioka Tomohiko

Software Specification Using *LASS* 375
   Mihal Badonski, Mirjana Ivanović, Zoran Budimac

Nepi^2: A Two-Level Calculus for Network Programming Based on the
π-Calculus 377
   Eiichi Horita, Ken Mano

On Semantics of Reactive Rule-Based Systems 379
   Man Lin, Jacek Malec, Simin Nadjm-Tehrani

The Non-standard Semantics of Esterel 381
   Jean-Raymond Gagné, John Plaice

Hybrid Support for Lenient Implementation of Array-Comprehension 383
   Shigeru Kusakabe, Kentaro Inenaga, Makoto Amamiya

Solver for Hierarchical CSP Containing Several Constraint Types and
Multi-output Constraints 385
   Mouhssine Bouzoubaa

Author Index 387

Correctness of Programs and Protocols through Randomization

(Extended Abstract)

Michael O. Rabin

Harvard University and the Hebrew University of Jerusalem

The problem of proving the correctness of programs and protocols is long standing and of central importance. Numerous formal systems and logics were developed and are being used to tackle this difficult task. When it comes to involved protocols, the formal proofs of correctness, where possible, are hard and often require an understanding of the behavior of the protocol so deep as to amount to an informal proof of correctness. At the same time, there are instances of practically significant protocols which were for a long time accepted as being correct, until an attempt at a formal proof of correctness has actually uncovered an error. As is well known from practice, the difficulty of establishing the correctness of protocols usually arises out of the presence of concurrent actions and the complexity of attempting to follow the myriad of ways in which these actions may interleave to produce unintended behavior. In the case of security protocols, proving correctness involves delineation of all possible ways in which an adversary or corrupt participants may subvert the protocol.

We propose an alternate approach employing randomization. It is well known that in many cases, randomized algorithms and protocols for the solution of specific problems are considerably simpler as well as more efficient than the "classical" deterministic solutions. Also, for some important problems, one can prove that no deterministic solution exist. It is the relative simplicity of the randomized solutions that we propose to utilize for facilitating the task of proving their correctness. In methodological terms, what we do is to exchange the need to account for all possible behaviors of a protocol, with the task of proving that certain random variables (such as coin-tosses) employed in the randomized solution are independent. While the latter task may be subtle, it involves well known methods of probability theory and in most cases is not challenging even when dealing with problems that in the deterministic setting are very hard.

We shall demonstrate the efficacy of the randomized approach by dealing with two classical problems which are very important in their own right and which were the subject of hundreds of papers.

The first one is the Critical Section Problem. Processes $P_1, \cdots, P_n$ are computing concurrently. From time to time any one of the processes, say P_i, may need to enter a *critical section* C (say use a shared resource). It is required that while P_i is in C, no other process will enter the critical section. This requirement is defined as *mutual-exclusion*. A proper solution for this problem should also be deadlock free, i.e. that the attempt to insure mutual-exclusion will not result in a situation that none of of the processes wishing to enter the critical section can do so. In addition, it may be desirable that the solution impose some fair distribution of the accesses to C amongst the processes.

Clearly the processes $P_1, \cdots, P_n$ must communicate amongst themselves so as to avoid cohabitation of the critical section and to impose fair sharing. There are many models for the mode of communications that were proposed, and for each model several protocols were proposed and sometimes proved correct. We shall consider an important model suggested by L. Lamport. With every process P_i we associate a variable R[i], owned by P_i. This means that only P_i can update (write) $R[i]$, but every other P_j can read this variable. There is a natural justification for considering such an arrangement. Using these variables, Lamport gave a number of protocols achieving deadlock free and fair mutual exclusion. Lamport and many others gave formal correctness proofs for such protocols. The difficulty of this problem is highlighted by the fact that in some instances, errors were discovered despite correctness proofs.

A great deal of the challenge in proving correctness of protocols formulated in Lamport's model arises from the stringent semantics the he imposes on reads and writes of the variables $R[i]$. Namely, Lamport stipulates that a write or a read operation on $R[i]$ is not instantaneous but extends in time. Furthermore, if some P_j reads $R[i]$ while P_i updates that variable, the value returned to P_j may be arbitrary. Again, there are good reasons for such a stipulation.

An examination of the protocols for the Critical Section Problem in Lamport's model reveals that, absent the possible interference between write and read operations on the same owned variables, verification is quite straightforward. Thus we finesse the obstacle posed by the stringent write/read semantics, by introducing a new construct of a *faithful version* of an owned variable R[i]. The methodology is completely general and applies to any protocol or concurrent program written in Lamport's model.

Let $R[i]$ be a variable owned by P_i. We define a data structure $F(R[i])$ and two procedures $Write_i(F(R[i])$ and $Read(F(R[i]))$. The Write and Read procedures are randomized. The faithful version of $R[i]$ has the following strong properties.

If a process P_j executes $Read(F(R[i]))$ and this execution does not overlap in actual time an execution of $Write_i(F(R[i])$ by P_i, then the Read will return to P_j the value of $R[i]$ written by P_i in the latest execution of $Write_i(F(R[i])$ preceding the start of $Read(F(R[i]))$ by P_j.

If P_j's execution of $Read(F(R[i]))$ does overlap an execution of $Write_i(F(R[i])$ by P_i, then the Read will either return to P_j a value of $R[i]$ written by P_i between the start and end of the execution of $Read(F(R[i]))$, or return the value "undefined".

In summation: $Read(F(R[i]))$ will always return a correct value for $R[i]$, or else signal to P_j that an interference has occurred. Note that this is achieved under the stringent condition that for the memory cells comprising the faithful version $F(R[i])$ of $R[i]$, which are all owned by P_i, if a read by P_j overlaps in time with a write by P_i, then an arbitrary value may be returned.

Our methodology extends to an even more stringent semantics for the read/ write of a single cell. Namely, if two different processes P_j and P_k overlap in time in reading a cell $R[i]$ owned by P_i, then each reader may get a different arbitrary value. None of the existing protocols for the Critical Section Problem is true in this more stringent model. Our extended faithful version of owned variables takes care of this difficulty as well.

Time permitting, we shall also discuss the Byzantine Agreement Problem (BAP). This topic was introduced in a ground breaking paper by Lamport, Pease, and Shostack and the results we describe are by now classical. Still, they serve as an excellent illustration for the power of randomness when it comes to producing and proving the correctness of a solution to a difficult problem in distributed computing.

In a distributed system, we have n processes $P_1, \cdots, P_n$. Each process P_i has an initial value v_i and the processes want to agree, by a protocol involving rounds of exchanges of messages between pairs of processes (there is no broadcast!), on a common value v. The difficulty arises from the fact that up to $t < n/3$ of the processes may be "bad" and not follow the protocol. The identity of the bad processes is not known and may, in fact, be dynamically determined by an adversary. The conditions for BA are (1) In any execution of the protocol, all the good processes (of whom there are at least $n - t$) will always terminate with a common value. (2) If initially at least $n - t$ good processes P_i had $v_i = v$ for some v, then that v will be the common value under (1).

It is known that deterministic solutions for the BAP exist only if the distributed system is synchronous. Also, any deterministic BA protocol requires $t + 1$ rounds of exchanges of messages.

Enter randomization. By use of randomization in a special model for the BAP, we can achieve BA in an *asynchronous* distributed system in a *fixed number* of message rounds. Furthermore, whereas the proofs of correctness of deterministic protocols for BA are very hard, the correctness of the randomized version is easily established. We advocate randomized algorithms as a general approach to theoretical as well as practical protocol constructions.

Medical Image Analysis and Simulation

Nicholas Ayache

INRIA – EPIDAURE Project
06902 Sophia-Antipolis, France
ayache@sophia.inria.fr

Abstract. This article introduces the research field of digital image analysis and simulation applied to medicine.

Although the number of medical images produced in the world increases each year, their quantitative exploitation for diagnosis and therapy remains quite suboptimal.

This article reviews the potentialities offered by the research in digital image analysis and simulation, and presents a short survey of the state of the art.

1 Introduction

Millions of three-dimensional (3-D) and even four-dimensional (4-D) images of patients are produced every year all over the world to assess diagnosis and therapy. Most of them come from the following imaging modalities: Computed Tomography (CT), Magnetic Resonance (MR), Ultrasounds (US), and Nuclear Medicine (NM).

Medical images contain a lot of information on the internal geometry and on the functions of the human body. Unfortunately their current exploitation is usually purely qualitative. The observation is done in 2-D, on analogic supports (films), typically cross-section by cross-section, and one modality at a time.

Storing medical images in a digital format on the production site, and linking production sites together with high bandwidth networks has open a new era with the potential for a much more efficient and powerful exploitation of images.

We list in the next section the tremendous progress which could be made in the coming decade for a better and more reliable diagnosis and therapy of patients, with the help of automated medical image analysis and computer-assisted intervention.

Then we provide a list of current research issues in the field of medical image analysis, with pointers towards recent litterature before we conclude.

2 Improving Diagnosis and Therapy

2.1 Diagnosis

One of the major benefits of digital image analysis in terms of diagnosis is the introduction of **objective** and **quantitative 3-D measurements** in the images. These quantitative measurements cannot be extracted easily by hand from a succession of 2-D cross-sections. On the other hand, with adequate image processing tools, it should be possible to extract precisely the **size, location** and **texture** of specific **3-D anatomical** and **pathological structures**.

4-D images correspond to temporal sequences of moving organs, like the beating heart for instance. Here again, digital image analysis should provide a set of objective **motion parameters** to interpret quantitatively the motion, and establish quantified comparisons.

Even in terms of the *qualitative* evaluation of 3-D or 4-D images, digital image analysis should provide new modes of **visualization** more efficient than a purely 2-D static observation of chosen cross-sections. For instance one should aim at a realistic 3-D exploration on a powerful graphics workstation, both for static and dynamic organs, and from arbitrary dynamic viewpoints.

The presence of a network between connecting different production sites should allow to **fuse complementary multimodal images** together. For instance one should combine easily anatomical information from MR or CT images with functional information coming from NM images (SPECT or PET). Also, functional MR images could benefit from this type of image fusion.

Digital storage of medical images should also permit **temporal comparisons** between images taken at different times for the same patient, and automatically detect and measure any change.

Finally, digital image analysis should allow automatic **comparisons between patients**, as well as comparisons with a **digital anatomical atlas**. The objective could be either to retrieve similar anatomical structures or pathologies in large databases of medical images, or to detect significant differences with respect to "standard" anatomy.

2.2 Therapy

Once a diagnosis is established, medical images should again play an increasingly important role in the **preparation, control and validation of therapy**. This is true for most forms of therapy including radiotherapy, traditional surgery, video-surgery, interventional radiology, chimiotherapy...

In effect, the precise geometrical and physical information given by medical images should provide an accurate planning of care delivery. In most cases, **simulation** now appears as an intermediate stage between diagnosis and therapy itself. The idea is to build a model of a **virtual patient**, to simulate the result of the chosen therapy. Even more, medical gestures could be practiced in advance, either on a *standard* virtual patient on which it is possible to create as many artificial pathologies as desired, or on a virtual *template* of a real patient who must undergo a delicate intervention. **Surgery simulators** should become as common for surgeons as flight simulators for pilots.

During the intervention, **augmented reality** should allow pre-operative and per-operative images to be superimposed on the patient itself to provide useful additional information to the surgeon, typically the location of internal structures and/or pathologies. For instance the image of important vessels obtained from pre-operative MR angiography (MRA), could be superimposed on the video image of the patient, as if the patient was semi-transparent. Also per-operative 3-D Ultrasounds could allow the surgeon to "see" his endoscope, while navigating in delicate anatomical structures like brain, lungs, vertebra, etc. . .

Finally, it should be possible to **fuse images** taken **before** and **after therapy**, in order to assess quantitatively the differences.

3 State of the Art and Research Issues

Many of the problems addressed in the previous section are still open, and have generated an intense activity of research.

A good overview of the state of the art can be obtained from a selection of the chapters of the book *Computer Integrated Surgery* recently edited by Taylor, Lavallee, Burdea and Moesges [1], in a survey article by Pun, Gerig and Ratib [2], and in an article published by the author [3]. Also, the new participant to this field will be interested by a recent tutorial published by Acharya et al. [4] introducing the most popular biomedical imaging modalities currently in clinical use (CT, MR, Ultrasound, NM. . .).

In the sequel, and in order to present the state of the art in an organized manner, I tried to identify a set of "canonical" or "generic" scientific problems, which could be grouped under the terms **Segmentation, Visualisation, Registration, Morphometry and Atlases, Motion, Surgery Simulation** and **Medical Robotics**.

3.1 Segmentation

Segmentation is usually a first processing stage to extract regions or features of interest for another task (for instance visualisation, measurement, registration, motion analysis). There is no unique solution to this problem, but instead classes of tools (e.g. deformable models, scale-space analysis, mathematical morphology), which can often be combined together to reach a given goal. A general introduction to the topic was recently published in [5].

On the use of deformable models in medical image analysis, one should refer to the important survey written by McInerney and Terzopoulos [6], and the following references [7–9].

A lot of efforts are dedicated to scale-space analysis, as reports a recent tutorial written by B.M. Ter Haar Romeny [10]. This tutorial can be completed by articles on anisotropic diffusion in 3-D, [11–13]. Multiscale extraction of vessels is also an important topic discussed for instance in [14–16]. Cores are described by Pizer in [17].

Mathematical morphology is a powerful tool to segment images. Examples of its use with medical images can be found in [18]. Also, examples of segmentation techniques which combine image restoration, mathematical morphology and deformable models are given in [19].

MR images often require a bias field correction prior to any further processing. Recent publications on this topic are [20,21]. One should also consult [22] on the segmentation of dynamic MR breast images using a model of contrast enhancement.

Differential features can be extracted in 3-D images to characterize edges, crest lines, ridges, and extremal points. These features are often used for registration purposes. Recent references include (but see also references in the registation section): [23–26]. A thorough analysis of multi-scale extraction of differential features in 3-D images was done by Fidrich [27].

Finally, extracting iso-surfaces in original or segmented images can be performed with the marching cubes algorithm [28]. Alternatively, and after an edge extraction is performed, this can be done with a Delaunay triangulation [29]. The marching line algorithm is powerful to extract lines defined at the intersection of 2 iso-surfaces, with subvoxel accuracy [30].

3.2 Visualisation

Historically, visualisation used to be the most active research field in 3-D image processing. G. Herman published a survey on the 3-D display of volumetric images [31], which can be completed by a less recent survey on the basic algorithms and systems for image rendering published by Stytz et al. [32].

In general, visualization requires a preliminary *segmentation* stage (previous section). A spectacular illustration of the state of the art in rendering possibilities is presented on the "visible man" data by Hoehne's team in [33].

3.3 Registration

Registration (or matching) can be performed intra- or inter-patients, between mono- or multi-modal 3-D images. This leads to rigid or non-rigid, mono- or multimodal registration algorithms. Also, some methods are feature based (using for instance the results of a segmentation), others use the raw intensity data.

A review of medical image registration methods with a classification was written by van den Elsen [34]. Also, an excellent survey of registration methods for computer integrated surgery was written by S. Lavallee [35]. Quite recently, a comparison of algorithms based on a retrospective evaluation was published by J. West [36]. Many references can be found in these 3 articles.

Among rigid registration algorithms, one can separate methods using geometrical features like ridges and/or extremal points [23,24,37,38], and methods based on the minimization of a distance or correlation criterion: [39–44]. Recently, mutual information was introduced as a new measure to compare and register multimodal images: one can refer to the recent publications [45–47] and the references cited by these 2 articles.

The quantitative evaluation of the accuracy and robustness of rigid registration was studied by Pennec [48].

Finally, rigid registration can be computed between a 3-D image and a 2D projection including applications in virtual and augmented reality [41,49–53].

Non-rigid registration is a much more difficult problem. Recent references on non-rigid registration include (but see also the morphometry section) feature based methods [54–57] and methods based on the raw intensity of the images [58–60].

3.4 Morphometry and Atlases

Morphometry consists in studying the geometry of shapes, and in particular the extraction of quantitative parameters, the computation of average shapes and the measurement of variations around them.

The definition of statistics on shapes requires a specific formalism, because they usually involve differential manifolds which are not vector-space (e.g. lines, frames, oriented points, rotations,...). The interested reader should refer to the excellent book by C. Small [61] which makes an excellent presentation of the pioneering work of Kendall and Bookstein, and to the work of X. Pennec [62,63] who made significant extensions of the theory and experiments in 3-D.

Applications are related to the computation of quantitative anatomical atlases, and the analysis of inter-patient images. The references on these topics include the work of Thompson and Toga [64], A. Evans et al. [65], Bookstein[66], Dean et al. [67], Davatzikos et al. [68], Subsol et al.[69], Roberts et al. [70], Mangin et al. [71], Martin et al., [72,73], Cootes et al. [74], Szekely et al. [75], Andreasen et al. [76].

A European project called Biomorph, funded by BIOMED-II, currently develops morphometric techniques for measurement of the size and shape of cerebral structures, with applications to multiple sclerosis and schizophrenia [77].

They are also related to the actual construction of anatomical atlases [78,79] and also to indexation problems, in the sense that inter-patient comparisons can guide the selection of "similar" images in large databases of images [80].

3.5 Motion Analysis

Analyzing time series of 3-D medical images (i.e. 4-D images) is an important topic, especially for cardiac imaging. The objective is usually twofold: tracking the boundaries of some anatomical structure to estimate a displacement field, and quantifying the overall motion with a few objective and significant parameters.

On tracking, one can refer to the previously cited survey on deformable models [6], and also to feature-based methods, in particular methods using the curvature information along surface edges [81–84]. Some images have physical markers like in tagged MRI, or a local estimation of the velocity like in phase-contrast MRI. The physical principles of tagged MRI is well presented in [85]. Methods to recover the displacement of the tags are presented in [86,87], and its extrapolation to the whole image is presented in [88,89]. Methods adapted to phase-contrast MRI images are presented in [90,91].

On the quantitative analysis of the motion field, one can refer to methods using a modal decomposition [92,93], deformable parametric geometric models [94,95], 4-D continuous deformation models [96], or other approaches [97–99].

3.6 Surgery Simulation

A lot of research has focused on spring-mass methods, because of their simplicity of implementation and their relatively low computational complexity [100,101]. For example, [102] present a simulation of endoscopic surgery based on a surface spring-mass model. Although in this case the interactions are driven by instruments with sensors, no force feedback is used. The simulation environment at MERL [103] takes into account the volumetric nature of the organs with a deformation law derived from a spring-mass model. [104] have developed a model based on thin plates for endoscopic gall bladder surgery simulation.

Finite element models are less widely used due to the difficulty of their implementation and the large computing time. Nevertheless, [105] proposed a method for simulating features of the human eye with a complex behavior (large incompressible 3-D elastic deformations). Another example of eye surgery is given by [106], but still very far from real-time applications.

Reduction of computing time was studied by [107] using a condensation technique. With this method, the computation time required for the deformation of a volumetric model can be reduced to the computation time of a model only involving the surface nodes of the mesh. [108] described a technique for cutting linear elastic objects defined as finite element models. This technique was only applied to very simple two dimensional objects. One can also cite a method for free-form cutting in tomographic volume data [109] based on voxel operations for cutting and visualization.

In the Epidaure group at INRIA, we tried to integrate all the requirements for a realistic simulation. The static equations of the elastic model are solved by a modified finite element method which takes into account particular boundary conditions. The solution of these equations gives not only the deformed mesh but also the forces to be sent to a force feedback device according to the actual deformation. Finally, real-time interaction is possible thanks to a pre-processing of elementary deformations coupled with a speed-up algorithm. The linear elastic deformations, computed in real-time, give a first approximation of reality as reported in [110,111]. This linear model was then improved to introduce nonlinear biomechanical properties of soft tissues as reported in [112]. A good review of realistic soft tissue modeling in medical simulation can be found in [113].

3.7 Medical Robotics

Going from simulation to the actual performance of surgery or radiotherapy with a robot is also an active research area. For a flavor, the interested readers can consult the following recent publications involving robotics [114,115], as well as a number of chapters of the book [50].

4 Conclusion

In this article, I tried to present the increasing role of digital image processing and simulation in medicine. I presented a list of potential improvements for diagnosis and therapy of the patient. I listed the major research issues attached to this field, and made a short survey of the current state of the art.

A striking aspect of this research field is the combined work of applied mathematicians, computer scientists, physicists and physicians, as well as the broad range of computer-science fields involved: image processing, computer-vision, graphics, and robotics.

These research efforts will bring a revolution in medicine in the future.

5 Acknowledgments

I have been helped in the preparation of this document by several persons including S. Cotin, J. Declerck, H. Delingette, G. Malandain, G. Subsol, and J.P. Thirion. I wish to thank them very much for their help, as well as the constant and stimulating support of G. Kahn.

References

1. R. Taylor, S. Lavallee, G. Burdea, and R. Moesges, editors. *Computer Integrated Surgery*. MIT Press, 1995.
2. G. Gerig T. Pun and O. Ratib. Image Analysis and Computer Vision in Medicine. *Computerized Medical Imaging and Graphics*, 18(2):85–96, 1994.
3. N. Ayache. Medical computer vision, virtual reality and robotics. *Image and Vision Computing*, 13(4):295–313, 1995. promising research track.Also available at http://www.inria.fr/epidaure/personnel/ayache/ayache.html.
4. R. Acharya, R. Wasserman, J. Stevens, and C. Hinojosa. Biomedical Imaging modalities: a tutorial. *Computerized Medical Imaging and Graphics*, 19(1):3–25, 1995.
5. N. Ayache, P. Cinquin, I. Cohen, L. Cohen, F. Leitner, and O. Monga. Segmentation of complex 3D medical objects: a challenge and a requirement for computer assisted surgery planning and performing. In R. Taylor, S. Lavallee, G. Burdea, and R. Moesges, editors, *Computer Integrated Surgery*, pages 59–74. MIT Press, 1995.
6. Tim McInerney and Demetri Terzopoulos. Deformable Models in Medical Image Analysis: A Survey. *Medical Image Analysis*, 1(2):91–108, 1996.
7. W. Barrett and E. Mortensen. Fast, Accurate, and Reproducible Live-Wire Boundary Extraction. *Medical Image Analysis*, 1(4), 1997.
8. I. Cohen, L. D. Cohen, and N. Ayache. Using deformable surfaces to segment 3-D images and infer differential structures. *Computer Vision, Graphics and Image Processing: Image Understanding*, 56(2):242–263, 1992.
9. H. Delingette. General object reconstruction based on simplex meshes. Technical Report 3111, INRIA, February 1997.
10. B.M. Ter Haar Romeny. Introduction to scale-space theory: Multiscale geometric image analysis. Technical Report ICU-96-21, Utrecht University, September 1996. http://www.cv.ruu.nl/Conferences/ScaleSpace97.html.
11. G. Gerig, O. Kübler, R. Kikinis, and F.A. Jolesz. Nonlinear Anisotropic Filtering of MRI Data. *IEEE Transactions on medical imaging*, 11(2):221–232, 1992.

12. L.M. Florack, A.H. Salden, B.M. ter Harr Romeny, J.J. Koenderink, and M.A. Viergever. Nonlinear scale-space. *Image and Vision Computing*, 13(4):279–294, May 1995.

13. W.J. Niessen, K.L. Vincken, and M.A. Viergever. Comparison of multiscale representations for a linking-based image segmentation model. In *Proceedings of MMBIA*, pages 263–272, June 1996.

14. Th.M. Koller, G. Gerig, G. Székely, and D. Dettwiler. Multiscale detection of curvilinear structures in 2-D and 3-D image data. In IEEE, editor, *International Conference on Computer Vision (ICCV'95)*, pages 864–869, 1995.

15. C. Lorenz, I.C. Carlsen, T.M. Buzug, C. Fassnacht, and J. Weese. Multi-scale line segmentation with automatic estimation of width, contrast and tangential direction in 2d and 3d medical images. In J. Troccaz E. Grimson, R. Moesges, editor, *CVRMed-MRCAS: International Conference on medical computer vision, virtual reality, robotics and computer assisted surgery*, Grenoble, France, 1997. Springer-Verlag. Lecture Notes in Computer Science.

16. K. Krissian, G. Malandain, and N. Ayache. Directional anisotropic diffusion applied to segmentation of vessels in 3d images. In *First Conference on Scale-Space Theory in Computer Vision*, Utrecht, the Netherlands, July 1997.

17. S. Pizer, D. Eberly, B. Morse, and D. Fritsch. Zoom-invariant vision of figural shape: the mathematics of cores. Technical report, University of North Carolina, 1996. available through S. Pizer: pizer@cs.unc.edu.

18. K.H. Höhne and W. Hanson. Interactive 3-D segmentation of MRI and CT volumes using morphological operations. *Journal of Computer Assisted Tomography*, 16(2):285–294, March/April 1992.

19. T. Kapur, W.E.L. Grimson, W. Wells, and R. Kikinis. Segmentation of Brain Tissue from MR Images. *Medical Image Analysis*, 1(2):109–127, 1996.

20. W.M. Wells III, W.E.L. Grimson, R. Kikinis, and F.A. Jolesz. Adaptive segmentation of MRI data. In N. Ayache, editor, *First International conference on computer vision, virtual reality and robotics in medicine, CVRMed'95*, Nice, France, 1995. Springer-Verlag. Lecture Notes in Computer Science. To appear in IEEE Tr. on Medical Imaging.

21. R. Guillemaud and M. Brady. Enhancement of MR Images. In K. H. Höhne and R. Kikinis, editors, *Visualization in Biomedical Computing*, volume 1131 of *Lecture Notes in Computer Science*, Hamburg (Germany), September 1996. Springer.

22. P. Hayton, M. Brady, L. Tarassenko, and N. Moore. Analysis of dynamic MR breast images using a model of contrast enhancement. *Medical Image Analysis*, 1(3):207–224, 1997.

23. Petra A. van den Elsen J. B. Antoine Maintz and Max A. Viergever. Comparison of edge-based and ridge-based registration of CT and MR brain images. *Medical Image Analysis*, 1(2):151–161, 1996.

24. J-P Thirion. New feature points based on geometric invariants for 3d image registration. *International Journal of Computer Vision*, 18(2):121–137, May 1996.

25. D. Eberly, R. Gardner, B. Morse, S. Pizer, and C. Scharlach. Ridges for image analysis. *Mathematical Imaging and Vision*, 4:353–373, 1994.

26. O. Monga, S. Benayoun, and O. Faugeras. From partial derivatives of 3D volumetric images to ridge lines. In *IEEE Conf. on Computer Vision and Pattern Recognition, CVPR'92*, Urbana Champaign, 1992.

27. Márta Fidrich. Following feature lines across scale. In *First Conference on Scale-Space Theory in Computer Vision*, Utrecht, the Netherlands, July 1997.

28. Wiliam E. Lorensen and Harvey E. Cline. Marching cubes: A high resolution 3d surface reconstruction algorithm. *Computer Graphics*, 21(4), July 1987.

29. J-D. Boissonnat and B. Geiger. 3D reconstruction of complex shapes based on the delaunay triangulation. *Inria research report*, (1697), 1992.

30. J-P. Thirion and A. Gourdon. The 3d marching lines algorithm. *Graphical Models and Image Processing*, 58(6):503–509, November 1996.

31. G. Herman. 3-D Display: a survey from theory to applications. *Computerized Medical Imaging and Graphics*, 17(4):231–242, 1993.

32. M. Stytz, G. Frieder, and O. Frieder. Three-Dimensional Medical Imaging: Algorithms an Computer Systems. *ACM Computing Surveys*, 23(4), 1991.

33. T. Schiemann, J. Nutmann, U. Tiede, and K.H. Hoehne. Segmentation of the visible human for high quality volume based visualisation. *Medical Image Analysis*, 1(4), 1997.

34. P.A. van den Elsen, E.J.D. Pol, and M.A. Viergever. Medical image matching - a review with classification. *IEEE Engineering in Medicine and Biology*, 12(4):26–39, March 1993.

35. S. Lavallee. Registration for computer integrated surgery: methodology, state of the art. In R. Taylor, S. Lavallee, G. Burdea, and R. Moesges, editors, *Computer Integrated Surgery*, pages 77–97. MIT Press, 1995.

36. J. West and al. Comparison and evaluation of retrospective intermodality registration techniques. *Computer Assisted Tomography*, 1997. http://cswww.vuse.vanderbilt.edu/ image/registration.

37. P. van den Elsen, A.J.B. Maintz, E-J.D. Pol, and M.A. Viergever. Automatic Registration of CT and MR Brain Images using Correlation of Geometrical Features. *IEEE Trans. on Medical Imaging*, 14(2):384–396, June 1995.

38. A. Guéziec and N. Ayache. Smoothing and matching of 3−D-space curves. *Int. Journal of Computer Vision*, 12(1):79–104, 1994.

39. Colin Studholme, D. L. G. Hill, and D. J. Hawkes. Automated 3-D Registration of MR and CT Images of the Head. *Medical Image Analysis*, 1(2):91–108, 1996.

40. G. Malandain and S. Fernandez-Vidal. Physically based rigid registration of 3-d free-form objects: Aplication to medical imaging. Technical Report 2453, INRIA, Sophia-Antipolis, January 1995.

41. W.E.L. Grimson, G.J. Ettinger, S.J. White, P.L. Gleason, T. Lozano-Perez, W.M. Wells III, and R. Kikinis. Evaluating and validating an automated registration system for enhanced reality visualization in surgery. In N. Ayache, editor, *First International conference on computer vision, virtual reality and robotics in medicine, CVRMed'95*, Nice, France, 1995. Springer-Verlag. Lecture Notes in Computer Science. To appear in IEEE Tr. on Medical Imaging.

42. R.P. Woods, J.C. Mazziotta, and S.R. Cherry. MRI-PET registration with automated algorithm. *Journal of Computer Assisted Tomography*, 17(4):536–546, 1993.

43. H. Jiang, R. Robb, and K. Holton. A new approach to 3-D registration of multimodality medical images by surface matching. In *Visualization in Biomedical Computing*, volume 1808 of *SPIE proceedings series*, pages 196–213. SPIE, 1992.

44. C.A. Pelizzari and al. Accurate three-dimensional registration of CT, PET and/or MR images of the brain. *Journal of Computer Assisted Tomography*, 13(1):20–26, 1989.

45. W.M. Wells, P. Viola, Hideki Atsumi, Shin Nakajima, and Ron Kikinis. Multi-Modal Volume Registration by Maximization of Mutual Information. *Medical Image Analysis*, 1(1):35–51, 1996.

46. F. Maes, A. Collignon, D. Vandermeulen, G. Marchal, and P. Suetens. Multi-Modal Volume Registration by Maximization of Mutual Information. *IEEE Trans. on Medical Imaging*, 1997. in press.

47. D. Hill, C. Studholme, and D. Hawkes. Voxel similarity measures for automated image registration. In Richard A. Robb, editor, *Third Conf. Visualization in Biomedical Computing VBC'94*, october 1994.

48. X. Pennec and J.P. Thirion. A framework for uncertainty and validation of 3d registration methods based on points and frames. *Int. Journal of Computer Vision*, 1997. in press.

49. J. Feldmar, N. Ayache, and F. Betting. 3d-2d projective registration of free-form curves and surfaces. *Computer Vision and Image Understanding*, 65(3):403–424, 1997. Also INRIA Research Report Number H120, 1995.

50. R. Szeliski S. Lavallee and L. Brunie. Anatomy based registration of 3-d medical images, range images, x-ray projections, and 3-d models using octree splines. In R. Taylor, S. Lavallee, G. Burdea, and R. Moesges, editors, *Computer Integrated Surgery*, pages 115–143. MIT Press, 1995.

51. H. Fuchs, A. State, E. Pisano, W. Garrett, G. Hirota, M. Livingston, M. Whitton, and S. Pizer. Towards performing ultrasound-guided needle biopsies from within a head-mounted display. In K.H. Höhne and R. Kikinis, editors, *Visualization in Biomedical Computing VBC'96*, volume 1131 of *Lec. Notes in Computer Science*, pages 591–600, Hamburg, Germany, September 1996. Springer.

52. A. Colchester, J. Zhao, K. Holton-Tainter, C. Henri, N. Maitland, P. Roberts, C.Harris, and R. Evans. Develpment and preliminary evaluation of VISLAN, a surgical planning and guidance system using intra-operative video imaging. *Medical Image Analysis*, 1(1):73–90, 1996.

53. B. Geiger and R. Kikinis. Simulation of endoscopy. In *Computer Vision, Virtual Reality and Robotics in Medecine*, volume 905 of *Lecture Notes in Computer Science*, pages 277–281, 1995.

54. R. Szeliski and S. Lavallee. Matching 3-d anatomical surfaces with non-rigid deformations using octree-splines. *the International Journal of Computer Vision*, 18(2):171–186, 1996.

55. J. Declerck, G. Subsol, J. Ph. Thirion, and N. Ayache. Automatic retrieval of anatomical structures in 3D medical images. In N. Ayache, editor, *First International Conference on Computer Vision, Virtual Reality and Robotics in Medicine, CVRMed'95*, volume 905 of *Lecture Notes in Computer Science*, pages 153–162, Nice (France), April 1995. Springer Verlag. Electronic version: http://www.inria.fr/RRRT/RR-2485.html.

56. J. Declerck, J. Feldmar, M.L. Goris, and F. Betting. Automatic Registration and Alignment on a Template of Cardiac Stress & Rest SPECT Images. In *Mathematical Methods in Biomedical Image Analysis*, pages 212–221, June 1996. (Also INRIA Research Report # 2770).

57. J. Feldmar and N. Ayache. Rigid, affine and locally affine registration of free-form surfaces. *the International Journal of Computer Vision*, 18(2):99–119, 1996.

58. Gary E. Christensen, Michael I. Miller, and Michael Vannier. A 3d deformable magnetic resonance textbook based on elasticity. In *AAAI Spring Symposium Series: Applications of Computer Vision in Medical Image Processing*, pages 153–156, Standford University, March 1994.

59. J-P Thirion. Non-rigid matching using demons. In *Computer Vision and Pattern Recognition, CVPR'96*, San Francisco, California USA, June 1996.

60. M. Bro-Nielsen and C. Gramkow. Fast fluid registration of medical images. In K.H. Höhne and R. Kikinis, editors, *Visualization in Biomedical Computing VBC'96*, volume 1131 of *Lec. Notes in Computer Science*, pages 267–276, Hamburg, Germany, September 1996. Springer.

61. S. Small, editor. *The statistical theory of shape*. Springer, 1996.

62. X. Pennec. *L'incertitude dans les problèmes de reconnaissance et de recalage - Applications en imagerie médicale et biologie moléculaire (in French.* PhD thesis, Ecole Polytechnique and INRIA, 1996. Electronic version: http//www.inria.fr/epidaure/personnel/pennec/These.html.

63. X. Pennec and N. Ayache. Uniform distribution, distance and expectation problems for geometric features processing. *Journal of Mathematical Imaging and Vision*, 1997. in press.

64. P. Thompson and A.W. Toga. Visualization and Mapping of Anatomic Abnormailities Using a Probabilistic Brain Atlas Based on Random Fluid Transformations. *Medical Image Analysis*, 1(4), 1997.

65. A.C. Evans, S. Marrett, J. Torrescorzo, S. Ku, and L. Collins. MRI-PET correlation in three dimensions using a volume-of-interest (voi) atlas. *Journal of Cerebral Blood Flow Metabolism*, 11:A69–A78, 1991.

66. F. Bookstein. Landmarks methods for forms without landmarks: morphometrics of group differences in outline shape. *Medical Image Analysis*, 1(3):225–243, 1997.

67. D. Dean, P. Buckley, F. Bookstein, J. Kamath, D. Kwon, L. Friedman, and Ch. Lys. Three Dimensional MR-Based Morphometric Comparison of Schizophrenic and Normal Cerebral Ventricles. In Höhne, K.H. and Kikinis, R., editor, *Visualization in Biomedical Computing*, volume 1131 of *Lecture Notes in Computer Science*, pages 363–372, Hamburg (Germany), September 1996. Springer.

68. C. Davatzikos, M. Vaillant, S. Resnick, J.L. Prince, S. Letovsky, and R.N. Bryan. Morphological Analysis of Brain Structure Using Spatial Normalization. *Medical Image Analysis*, 1(4), 1997.

69. G. Subsol, J.-Ph. Thirion, and N. Ayache. Application of an Automatically Built 3D Morphometric Brain Atlas: Study of Cerebral Ventricle Shape. In K. H. Höhne and R. Kikinis, editors, *Visualization in Biomedical Computing*, volume 1131 of *Lecture Notes in Computer Science*, pages 373–382, Hamburg (Germany), September 1996. Springer.

70. G. Subsol, N. Roberts, M. Doran, and J. Ph. Thirion. Automatic Analysis of Cerebral Atrophy. *Magnetic Resonance Imaging*, September 1997.

71. J.F. Mangin, V. Frouin, I. Bloch, J. Régis, and Lòpez-Krahe J. From 3D Magnetic Resonance Images to Structural Representations of the Cortex Topography using Topology Preserving Deformations. *Journal of Mathematical Imaging and Vision*, 5:297–318, December 1995.

72. J. Martin, A. Pentland, and R. Kikinis. Shape Analysis of Brain Structures Using Physical and Experimental Modes. In *Computer Vision and Pattern Recognition*, pages 752–755, Seattle, Washington (USA), June 1994.

73. J. W. Martin. *Characterization of Neuropathological Shape Deformations*. PhD thesis, Massachusetts Institute of Technology, May 1995. Electronic version: http//splweb.bwh.harvard.edu:8000/pages/papers/martin/thesis.ps.Z.

74. T. F. Cootes, C. J. Taylor, D. H. Cooper, and J. Graham. Active Shape Models - Their Training and Application. *Computer Vision and Image Understanding*, 61(1):38–59, January 1995.

75. G. Székely, A. Kelemen, Ch. Brechbühler, and G. Gerig. Segmentation of 2-D and 3-D objects from MRI volume data using constrained elastic defromations of flexible Fourier contour and surface models. *Medical Image Analysis*, 1(1):19–34, March 1996.

76. N. C. Andreasen, S. Arndt, V. Swayze II, T. Cizadlo, M. Flaum, D. O'Leary, J. C. Ehrhardt, and W. T. C. Yuh. Thalamic Abnormalities in Schizophrenia

Visualized Through Magnetic Resonance Image Averaging. *Science*, 266:294–298, October 1994.

77. A. Colchester, G. Gerig, T. Crow, N. Ayache, and D. Vandermeulen. Biomorph: Development and validation of techniques for brain morphometry. Technical report, BIOMED2, European Project, 1996. available through A. Colchester: a.colchester@ukc.ac.uk.

78. K. Hoehne, M. Bomans, M. Riemer, R. Schubert, U. Tiede, and W. Lierse. A volume-based anatomical atlas. *IEEE Computer Graphics and Applications*, 12(4), 1992.

79. W. Nowinski, R. Bryan, and R. Raghavan, editors. *The electrical clinical brain atlas. Three-dimensional navigation of the human brain.* Thieme,N.Y., 1996.

80. A. Guimond, G. Subsol, and J.-Ph. Thirion. Automatic MRI Database Exploration and Applications. *International Journal on Pattern Recognition and Artificial Intelligence*, 1997. Accepted for publication.

81. S. Kumar and D. Goldgof. Automatic Tracking of SPAMM Grid and the Estimation of Deformation Parameters from Cardiac MR Images. In *IEEE Transactions on Medical Imaging*, pages 122–132, March 1994.

82. A. Amini and J. Duncan. Bending and Stretching Models for LV wall Motion Analysis from Curves and Surfaces. In *Image and Vision Computing*, volume 10, pages 418–430, August 1992.

83. S. Benayoun and N. Ayache. 3D motion analysis using differential geometry constraints. *Int. Journal of Computer Vision*, 1997. in press.

84. J.M. Gorce, D. Friboulet, and I. E. Magnin. Estimation of three-dimensional cardiac velocity fields:assessment of a differential method and application to 3-d ct data. *Medical Image Analysis*, 1(3):245–261, 1997.

85. E. McVeigh. MRI of myocardial function: motion tracking techniques. *Magnetic Resonance Imaging*, 1996.

86. D. Kraitchman, A. Young, C.N. Chang, and L. Axel. Semi-Automatic Tracking of Myocardial Motion in MR Tagged Images. *IEEE Transactions on Medical Imaging*, 14(3):422–433, September 1995.

87. M.A. Guttman, J.L. Prince, and E.R. McVeigh. Tag and Contour Detection in Tagged MR Images of the Left Ventricle. In *IEEE Transactions on Medical Imaging*, volume 13, pages 74–88, March 1994.

88. P. Radeva, A. Amini, J. Huang, and E. Marti. Deformable B-Solids and Implicit Snakes for Localization and Tracking of MRI-SPAMM Data. In *Mathematical Methods in Biomedical Image Analysis*, June 1996. also in a special issue of Computer Vision and Image Understanding, May 1997.

89. T.S. Denney Jr and J.L. Prince. 3D Displacement Field Reconstruction from Planar Tagged Cardiac MR Images. In *IEEE Workshop on Biomedical Image Analysis*, pages 51–60, June 1994.

90. F.G. Meyer, R. Todd Constable, A. Sinusas, and J. Duncan. Tracking Myocardial Deformation Using Spatially-Constrained Velocities. In Y. Bizais et al., editor, *Information Processing in Medical Imaging*, pages 177–188, 1995.

91. J.C. McEachen, F. Meyer, R. Constable, A. Nehorai, and J. Duncan. A recursive filter for phase velocity assisted shape-based tracking of cardiac non-rigid motion. In *IEEE Fifth International Conference on Computer Vision*, pages 653–658, June 1995.

92. C. Nastar and N. Ayache. Frequency-based nonrigid motion analysis: Application to 4 dimensional medical images. *IEEE Transaction on Pattern Analysis and Machine Intelligence (PAMI)*, 18(11):1067–1079, November 1996.

93. B. Horowitz and A. Pentland. Recovery of non–rigid motion and structure. In *IEEE Conf. on Computer Vision and Pattern Recognition, CVPR'91*, pages 325–330, Lahaina, Maui, Hawaii, June 1991.

94. J. Park, D. Metaxas, and L. Axel. Analysis of left ventricular motion based on volumetric deformable models and MRI-SPAMM. *Medical Image Analysis*, 1(1):53–71, March 1996.

95. E. Bardinet, L.D. Cohen, and N. Ayache. Tracking and motion analysis of the left ventricle with deformable superquadrics. *Medical Image Analysis*, 1(2):129–149, 1996. (also INRIA research report #2797).

96. J. Declerck, J. Feldmar, and N. Ayache. Definition of a 4D continuous polar transformation for the tracking and the analysis of LV motion. In J. Troccaz E. Grimson, R. Moesges, editor, *CVRMed-MRCAS: International Conference on medical computer vision, virtual reality, robotics and computer assisted surgery*, Grenoble, France, 1997. Springer-Verlag. Lecture Notes in Computer Science.

97. A. Young, D. Kraitchman, L. Dougherty, and L. Axel. Tracking and Finite Element Analysis of Stripe Deformation in Magnetic Resonance Tagging. *IEEE Transactions on Medical Imaging*, 14(3):413–421, September 1995.

98. E. McVeigh, M. Guttman, E. Poon, P. Chandrasekhar, C. Moore, E. Zerhouni, M. Solaiyappan, and P. Ann Heng. Visualization and Analysis of Functional Cardiac MRI data. In SPIE, editor, *Medical Imaging: Physiology and Function from Multidimensional Images*, volume 2168, 1994.

99. P. Shi, G. Robinson, A. Chakraborty, L. Staib, R. Constable, A. Sinusas, and J. Duncan. A Unified Framework to Assess Myocardial Function from 4D Images. In *Computer Vision, Virtual Reality and Robotics in Medicine*, volume 905 of *Lecture Notes in Computer Science*, pages 327–337. Springer-Verlag, April 1995.

100. R. Baumann and D. Glauser. Force Feedback for Virtual Reality based Minimally Invasive Surgery Simulator. In *Medecine Meets Virtual Reality*, volume 4, San Diego, CA, January 1996.

101. P. Meseure and C. Chaillou. Deformable Body Simulation with Adaptative Subdivision and Cuttings. In *Proceedings of the WSCG'97*, pages 361–370, February 1997.

102. U.G. Kuehnapfel and B. Neisius. CAD-Based Graphical Computer Simulation in Endoscopic Surgery. *End. Surg.*, 1:181–184, 1993.

103. S. Gibson, J. Samosky, A. Mor, C. Fyock, E. Grimson, T. Kanade, R. Kikinis, H. Lauer, N. McKenzie, S. Nakajima, H. Ohkami, R. Osborne, and A. Sawada. Simulating arthroscopic knee surgery using volumetric object representations, real-time volume rendering and haptic feedback . In *CVRMed-MRCAS: International Conference on medical computer vision, virtual reality, robotics and computer assisted surgery*, Lecture Notes in Computer Science, 1997.

104. S. A. Cover, N. F. Ezquerra, and J. F. O'Brien. Interactively Deformable Models for Surgery Simulation. *IEEE Computer Graphics and Applications*, pages 68–75, 1993.

105. M. A. Sagar, D. Bullivant, G. Mallinson, P. Hunter, and I. Hunter. A Virtual Environment and Model of the Eye for Surgical Simulation. In *Computer Graphics*, Annual Conference Series, pages 205–212, 1994.

106. Le Tallec, P. and Rahier, C. and Kaiss, A. Three Dimensional Incompressible Viscoelasticity in Large Strains. *Computer Methods in Apllied Mechanics and Engineering*, 109:233–258, 1993.

107. M. Bro-Nielsen and S. Cotin. Real-time Volumetric Deformable Models for Surgery Simulation using Finite Elements and Condensation. In *Proceedings of Eurographics'96 - Computer Forum*, volume 15, pages 57–66, 1996.

108. G. J. Song and N. P. Reddy. Tissue Cutting In Virtual Environment. In *Medecine Meets Virtual Reality IV*, pages 359–364. IOS Press, 1995.
109. B. Pflesser, U. Tiede, and Hoehne. Towards realistic visualization for surgery rehearsal. In *Computer Vision, Virtual Reality and Robotics in Medecine*, volume 905 of *Lecture Notes in Computer Science*, pages 487–491. Springer, April 1995.
110. S. Cotin, H. Delingette, J-M. Clément, V. Tassetti, J. Marescaux, and N. Ayache. Geometric and Physical Representations for a Simulator of Hepatic Surgery. In *Medecine Meets Virtual Reality IV*, Interactive Technology and the New Paradigm for Healthcare, pages 139–151. IOS Press, January 1996.
111. S. Cotin, H. Delingette, and N. Ayache. Real Time Volumetric Deformable Models for Surgery Simulation. In K. Hohne and R. Kikinis, editors, *Vizualisation in Biomedical Computing*, volume 1131 of *Lecture Notes in Computer Science*, pages 535–540. Springer, 1996.
112. S. Cotin, H. Delingette, and N. Ayache. Real-time non-linear elastic deformations of soft tissues for surgery simulation. Technical Report 0000, INRIA, March to appear.
113. H. Delingette. Towards realistic soft tissue modeling in medical simulation. *Proceedings of the IEEE*, March 1998. in press.
114. A. Schweikard, J. Adler, and J.C. Latombe. Motion planning in stereotaxic radiosurgery. IEEE. Trans. on robotics and automation, 1995.
115. C. Cutting, F. Bookstein, and R. Taylor. Applications of simulation, morphometrics and robotics in craniofacial surgery. In R. Taylor, S. Lavallee, G. Burdea, and R. Moesges, editors, *Computer Integrated Surgery*, pages 641–662. MIT Press, 1995.

Verification of Pipelined Microprocessors by Comparing Memory Execution Sequences in Symbolic Simulation[1]

Randal E. Bryant[‡, *]   **Miroslav N. Velev**[*]
randy.bryant@cs.cmu.edu   mvelev@ece.cmu.edu

[‡]School of Computer Science
[*]Department of Electrical and Computer Engineering
Carnegie Mellon University, Pittsburgh, PA 15213, U.S.A.

Abstract. This paper extends Burch and Dill's pipeline verification method [4] to the bit level. We introduce the idea of memory shadowing, a new technique for providing on-the-fly identical initial memory state to two different memory execution sequences. We also present an algorithm which compares the final states of two memories for equality. Memory shadowing and the comparison algorithm build on the Efficient Memory Model (EMM) [13], a behavioral memory model where the number of symbolic variables used to characterize the initial state of a memory is proportional to the number of distinct symbolic locations accessed. These techniques allow us to verify that a pipelined circuit has equivalent behavior to its unpipelined specification by simulating two memory execution sequences and comparing their final states. Experimental results show the potential of the new ideas.

Keywords: pipelined microprocessor verification, memory shadowing, Efficient Memory Model (EMM), circuit correspondence checking, symbolic simulation.

1. Introduction

We are extending Burch and Dill's pipeline verification method [4] to a bit-level circuit verification. The idea of a commutative diagram and an underlying abstraction function, used by Burch and Dill, is not new to verification. It has been introduced by Hoare [6] for verifying computations on abstract data types in software, and has been used by Bose and Fisher [1] to verify pipelined circuits. All these verification methods are based on comparing an implementation transformation F_{Impl} against a specification transformation F_{Spec}. The assumption is that the two transformations start from a pair of matching initial states - Q_{Impl} and Q_{Spec}, respectively - where the match is determined according to some abstraction function Abs (see Figure 1). The correctness criterion is that the two transformations should yield a pair of matching final states - Q'_{Impl} and Q'_{Spec}, respectively - where the match is determined by the same abstraction function. In other words, the abstraction function should make the diagram commute.

The Burch and Dill approach is conceptually elegant in the way it uses a symbolic simulation of the hardware design to automatically compute an abstraction function from the pipeline state to the user-visible state. Namely, starting from a general symbolic initial state Q_{Impl} they simulate a *flush* of the pipeline by stalling it for a sufficient number of cycles that will allow all partially executed instructions to complete. Then,

---

1. This research was supported in part by the SRC under contract 97-DC-068.

they consider the resulting state of the user-visible memory elements (e.g., the register file and the program counter) to be the matching state Q_{Spec}.

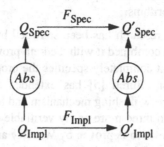

Figure 1. Commutative diagram for the correctness criterion.

Burch and Dill's implementation [4][5] of their method requires a high level abstract model of the implementation that still exposes relevant design issues, such as pipelining. They work on models that completely represent the control path of the processor, but hide the functional details of the data path by means of uninterpreted functions. Our implementation of Burch and Dill's method, presented in this paper, allows verification at the bit level.

By verifying at the bit level, we avoid the need to construct an abstracted model of the circuit. We can verify the actual hardware design, given a logic gate-level or register-transfer-level description. A naive implementation of Burch and Dill's method at the bit-level would require introducing a symbolic Boolean variable for every bit of register or memory state. This would lead to unacceptable complexity. Our paper overcomes this limitation by using the Efficient Memory Model (EMM) [13] to represent memory state.

The EMM is a behavioral memory model where the number of symbolic variables used to characterize the initial state of a memory is proportional to the number of distinct symbolic locations accessed, rather than to the size of the memory. It is based on the observation that a single execution sequence used in formal verification typically accesses only a limited number of distinct symbolic locations. Memory state is represented in the EMM by a list of entries encoding the relative history of memory operations. The list interacts with the rest of the circuit by means of a software interface developed as part of our symbolic simulator.

Burch and Dill also use a symbolic representation of memory arrays in their implementation [4]. They apply uninterpreted functions with equality, which allows them to introduce only a single symbolic variable to denote the initial state of the entire memory. Each *Write* or *Read* operation results in building a formula over the current state of the memory, so that the latest memory state reflects the sequence of memory writes. However, we need bit-level data for various memory locations in order to verify the data path. This requires our algorithms to introduce symbolic variables proportional to both the number of distinct symbolic memory locations accessed and to the number of data bits per location. Furthermore, we need the flexibility to include new symbolic memory locations as part of the initial memory state at any point in the verification process. Hence, the memory state in our case reflects the relative history of memory operations, rather than the sequence of writes. This difference will become clear as we present our algorithms.

An extensive body of research has been spawned by Burch and Dill's method. Sawada and Hunt [11] have combined it with theorem proving, assuming the availability of a set of invariants that completely specifies the properties of the pipelined processor in correct operation. Burch [5] has extended it to superscalar processor verification by proposing a new flushing mechanism and by decomposing the commutative diagram from [4] into three more easily verifiable commutative diagrams. The correctness of this decomposition is proven by Windley and Burch [14]. Jones, Seger, and Dill [8] propose the use of the pipeline as a specification for the correctness of its forwarding logic. They apply two specially designed instruction sequences that should yield identical behaviors and compare their effects on the register file. One of the sequences completely fills the pipeline with instructions and then flushes it with a sequence of NOPs, while the other consists of the same instructions but separated with as many NOPs as to avoid the exercising of the forwarding logic.

The contributions of this paper are: 1) the memory shadowing technique for ensuring identical initial memory state encountered by two different memory execution sequences; 2) an algorithm to compare the final states of two memories; 3) a methodology that extends Burch and Dill's pipeline verification method [4] to efficiently model the complete functionality of the data path at the bit level; and 4) experimental results that confirm the applicability of the new ideas.

We consider two forms of verification: 1) *Symbolic Trajectory Evaluation* (STE) [12], where one proves that a circuit satisfies a specification given as a temporal logic formula; and 2) *Correspondence checking*, where one proves a correspondence between two circuits by evaluating two execution sequences starting from a common initial state and showing that they yield identical final user-visible states, based on the commutative diagram of Figure 1. We propose using both forms as part of a four step approach for the verification of pipelined processors. The first step is to use STE to verify the transistor-level memory elements (both memory arrays and latches), independently from the rest of the circuit. Pandey and Bryant have combined symmetry reductions and STE to enable the verification of very large memory arrays at the transistor level [9][10]. The second step is to replace the memory arrays with EMMs for both the implementation and the specification circuits. The third step is to use STE to verify the non-pipelined specification circuit, which is assumed to support the same instruction set architecture and to have the same user-visible state as the pipelined processor. Our previous paper describes the use of the EMM in this context [13]. The fourth and last step is to perform correspondence checking between the pipelined processor and its specification. This step is the focus of the present work.

In the remainder of the paper, Section 2 summarizes Burch and Dill's pipeline verification method. Section 3 describes the symbolic domain used in our algorithms. Section 4 presents the assumptions, data structures, and algorithms of the EMM. The memory shadowing technique for providing on-the-fly identical initial memory state to two different execution sequences is explained in Section 5, which also presents an algorithm that compares for equality the states of two memory arrays. The verification methodology for correspondence checking by applying memory shadowing is described in Section 6. Experimental results are presented in Section 7. Finally, conclusions are made and future work is outlined in Section 8.

2. Burch and Dill's Pipeline Verification Method

For the purpose of verifying a pipelined processor, Burch and Dill [4] assume the availability of a specification non-pipelined circuit, which has user-visible state $U = \{0, 1\}^n$ and input state $I = \{0, 1\}^m$. The implementation (possibly pipelined) circuit is assumed to have the same user-visible and input state, although it can also have pipeline state $P = \{0, 1\}^k$. The combined user-visible and pipeline state of the implementation is then $U \times P$ and will be written in the form $\langle \vec{u}, \vec{p} \rangle$. Each of the circuits is characterized with its transition function: $\delta_I : I \times (U \times P) \rightarrow (U \times P)$ for the implementation, and $\delta_S : I \times U \rightarrow U$ for the specification.

Burch and Dill further assume that if the implementation is pipelined, it has or can be modified to include a stall input. When asserted, this input will prevent new instructions from entering the pipeline, while letting partially executed instructions advance and allowing the pipeline state to be flushed. The notation *Stall* will be used for the implementation's transition function when the stall input is asserted. It is also assumed that the two circuits support the same instruction set architecture and start from the same arbitrary initial user-visible state.

The method uses a *projection function*, $Proj : (U \times P) \rightarrow U$, which removes all but the the user-visible state from the implementation, and an *abstraction function*,

$$Abs(\langle \vec{u}, \vec{p} \rangle) \doteq Proj(Stall^l(\langle \vec{u}, \vec{p} \rangle)),$$

which maps the combined user-visible and pipeline state $\langle \vec{u}, \vec{p} \rangle$ of the implementation to its user-visible state. This is done by stalling the pipeline for as many cycles as its depth l, so that it can be flushed, and then stripping off all but the user-visible state. The correctness criterion expressed by Figure 1 is

$$\forall \vec{x}, \vec{u}, \vec{p} \ . \ Abs(\delta_I(\vec{x}, \langle \vec{u}, \vec{p} \rangle)) \stackrel{?}{=} \delta_S(\vec{x}, Abs(\langle \vec{u}, \vec{p} \rangle)), \tag{1}$$

where $\vec{x}$ is an input combination that allows the implementation and the specification to execute one cycle without stalling, i.e. to start executing one instruction (and to complete it in the case of the specification).

3. Symbolic Domain

We will consider three different domains - Boolean, address, and data - corresponding respectively to the control, address, and data information that can be applied at the inputs of a memory array. Symbolic variables will be introduced in each of the domains and will be used in expression generation. Address and data expressions will be represented by vectors of Boolean expressions having width n and w, respectively, for a memory with $N = 2^n$ locations, each holding a word consisting of w bits. The types **BExpr**, **AExpr**, and **DExpr** will denote respectively Boolean, address, and data expressions in the algorithms to be presented.

We will use the term *context* to refer to an assignment of values to the symbolic variables. A Boolean expression can be viewed as defining a set of contexts, namely those for which the expression evaluates to **true**.

The selection operator *ITE* (for "If-Then-Else"), when applied on three Boolean expressions, is defined as:

$$ITE(b, t, e) \doteq (b \wedge t) \vee (\neg b \wedge e). \tag{2}$$

Address comparison is then implemented as:

$$A1 = A2 \doteq \neg \bigvee_{i=1}^{n} A1_i \oplus A2_i, \tag{3}$$

while address selection $A1 \leftarrow ITE(b, A2, A3)$ is implemented by selecting the corresponding bits:

$$A1_i \leftarrow ITE_i(b, A2, A3) \doteq A1_i \leftarrow (b \wedge A2_i) \vee (\neg b \wedge A3_i), \quad i = 1, ..., n. \tag{4}$$

The definition of data operations is similar, but over vectors of width w.

We have used Ordered Binary Decision Diagrams (OBDDs) [3] to represent the Boolean expressions in our implementation. However, there is nothing about this work that intrinsically requires it to be OBDD based. Any canonical representation of Boolean expressions can be substituted.

4. Efficient Modeling of Memory Arrays

4.1 Overview

The assumption of the EMM [13] is that every memory array can be represented, possibly after the introduction of some extra logic, as a memory with only write and read ports, all of which have the same numbers of address and data bits (see Figure 2).

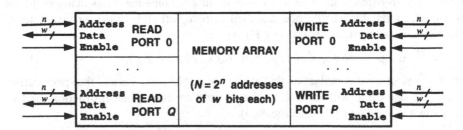

Figure 2. View of a memory array as an EMM.

A latch can be viewed as a memory array with a single address, so that it can be represented as an EMM with one write port and one read port, both of which have the same number of data bits and only one address input, which is identically connected to the same constant logic value, e.g., **true**.

The interaction of the memory array with the rest of the circuit is assumed to take place on the rising edge of a port Enable signal. In case of multiple port Enables having rising edges simultaneously, the resulting accesses to the memory array will be ordered according to the priority of the ports.

During symbolic simulation, the memory state is represented by a list containing entries of the form $\langle c, a, d \rangle$, where c is a Boolean expression denoting the set of contexts for which the entry is defined, a is an address expression denoting a memory location, and d is a data expression denoting the contents of this location. The context information is included for modeling memory systems where the *Write* and *Read* operations may be performed conditionally depending on the value of a control signal. Initially the list is empty.

The list interacts with the rest of the circuit by means of a software interface developed as part of the symbolic simulation engine. The interface monitors the port Enable lines. Should a rising edge occur at a port Enable, a *Write* or a *Read* operation will result, as determined by the type of the port. The Boolean expression c for the contexts of the memory operation will be formed as the condition for a rising edge on the port Enable. The operation will be performed if c is a non-zero Boolean expression. The Address and Data lines of the port will be scanned in order to obtain the address expression a and the data expression d, respectively. A *Write* operation completes with the insertion of the entry $\langle c, a, d \rangle$ in the list. A *Read* operation retrieves from the list a data expression rd that represents the data contents read from the memory at address a given the contexts c. The software interface completes the *Read* operation by asserting the Data lines of the port to the data expression $ITE(c, rd, d)$, i.e. to the retrieved data expression rd under the contexts c of the operation and to the old data expression d otherwise. The routines needed by the software interface for accessing the list are presented next.

4.2 Memory Support Operations

The list entries are kept in order from *head* (low priority) to *tail* (high priority). Intuitively, the entries towards the low priority end correspond to the initial state of the memory, while the ones at the high priority end represent recent memory updates, with the tail entry being the result of the latest memory *Write* operation. Entries may be inserted at either end, using procedures *InsertHead* and *InsertTail*, and may be deleted using procedure *Delete*.

The function *Valid*, when applied to a Boolean expression, returns **true** if the expression is valid, i.e. true for all contexts, and **false** otherwise. Note that in all of the algorithms, a Boolean expression cannot be used as a control decision in the code, since it will have a symbolic representation. On the other hand, we can make control decisions based on whether or not an expression is valid.

The function *GenDataExpr* generates a new data expression, whose variables are used to denote the initial state of memory locations that are read before ever being written.

4.3 Implementation of Memory *Read* and *Write* Operations

The *Write* operation, shown as a procedure in Figure 3, takes as arguments a memory list, a Boolean expression denoting the contexts for which the write should be performed, and address and data expressions denoting the memory location and its desired contents, respectively. As the code shows, it is implemented by simply inserting an element into the *tail* (high priority) end of the list, indicating that this entry should overwrite any other entries for this address. As an optimization, it removes any list elements that for all contexts are overwritten by this operation. Note that this optimization need not be performed, as will become apparent after the definition of the *Read* operation. We could safely leave any overwritten element in the list.

procedure *Write*(**List** *mem*, **BExpr** *c*, **AExpr** *a*, **DExpr** *d*)

/* Write data *d* to location *a* under contexts *c* */

    /* Optional optimization */

    for each ⟨*ec*, *ea*, *ed*⟩ **in** *mem* **do**

        if *Valid*(*ec* ⇒ [*c* ∧ *a*=*ea*]) **then**

            Delete(*mem*, ⟨*ec*, *ea*, *ed*⟩)

    /* Perform Write */

    InsertTail(*mem*, ⟨*c*, *a*, *d*⟩)

Figure 3. Implementation of the *Write* operation.

The *Read* operation is shown in Figure 4 as a function which, given a memory list, a Boolean expression denoting the contexts for which the read should be performed, and an address expression, returns a data expression indicating the contents of this location.

function *Read*(**List** *mem*, **BExpr** *c*, **AExpr** *a*): **DExpr**

/* Read from location *a* under contexts *c* */

    g ← *GenDataExpr*()

    return *ReadWithDefault*(*mem*, *c*, *a*, *g*)

function *ReadWithDefault*(**List** *mem*, **BExpr** *c*, **AExpr** *a*, **DExpr** *d*): **DExpr**

/* Read from location *a*, using *d* for contexts where no value found */

    rd ← *d*

    found ← **false**

    for each ⟨*ec*, *ea*, *ed*⟩ **in** *mem* from head to tail **do**

        match ← *ec* ∧ *a*=*ea*

        rd ← *ITE*(*match*, *ed*, *rd*)

        found ← *found* ∨ *match*

    if ¬*Valid*(*c* ⇒ *found*) **then**

        InsertHead(*mem*, ⟨*c*, *a*, *d*⟩)

    return *rd*

Figure 4. Implementation of the *Read* operation.

The main part of the *Read* operation is implemented with the function *ReadWith-Default*. The purpose of *ReadWithDefault* is to construct a data expression giving the contents of the memory location denoted by its argument address expression. It does this by scanning through the list from lowest to highest priority, adding a selection operator to the expression that chooses between the list element's data expression and the previously formed data expression, based on the match condition. It also generates a Boolean expression *found* indicating the contexts for which a matching list element has been encountered. *ReadWithDefault* has as its fourth argument a "default" data expression to be used when no matching list element is found. When this case arises, a new list element is inserted into the *head* (low priority) end of the list.

The *Read* operation is implemented by calling *ReadWithDefault* with a newly generated symbolic data expression g as the default. The contexts for which *ReadWith-Default* does not find a matching address in the list are those for which the addressed memory location has never been accessed by either a read or a write. The data expression g is then returned to indicate that the location may contain arbitrary data. By inserting the entry $\langle c, a, d \rangle$ into the list, we ensure that subsequent reads of this location will return the same expression. Note that computing and testing the validity of $c \Rightarrow found$ is optional. We could safely insert the list element unconditionally, although at an increased memory usage.

5. Comparing Memory Execution Sequences

In some applications, we wish to test whether two sequences of memory operations, which we will refer to as "A" and "B," yield identical behaviors. That is, we assume the two sequences start with matching initial memory states. For each externally visible *Read* operation in sequence A, its counterpart in sequence B must return the identical value. Furthermore, the final states resulting from the two sequences must match. To implement this, we require some mechanism for guaranteeing that consistent values are used for the initial contents of the two memories. In addition, we require an algorithm for comparing the contents of two memories.

5.1 Maintaining Consistent Initial States

If we were to execute the operations for the two sequences independently, we would generate different symbols to represent the initial memory contents, and hence we would not yield matching results. Even if we could "reset" our symbol generator, so that the execution sequence B used the same series of generated symbols as sequence A, there would be a mismatch if the two sequences access memory locations in a different order. Instead, we modify the *Read* operation to maintain a consistent initial state between the memory being operated on, and a "shadow" memory, as shown in Figure 5.

When executing the sequence A, we would use memory B as the shadow, and conversely when executing the sequence B, we would use memory A as the shadow. Note that the *Write* operations proceed as before. With this shadowing, any time a symbolic variable is assigned to represent the initial state of a memory location, the same symbol will be assigned to the same location and under the same context in both memories, thus enforcing the assumption that the two memories have matching initial states.

> **function** *ShadowRead*(**List** *mem*, **List** *shadow*, **BExpr** *c*, **AExpr** *a*): **DExpr**
> /* Read from location *a* under context *c* */
> /* Maintain consistency with shadow memory */
>   *g* ← *GenDataExpr*()
>   *ReadWithDefault*(*shadow, c, a, g*)
>   **return** *ReadWithDefault*(*mem, c, a, g*)

Figure 5. Implementation of the *Read* operation when initial state consistency between two memories must be maintained.

5.2 Comparing Final States

In comparing the contents of two memories, we can exploit the fact that only a small number of locations actually have defined values for any given context. Figure 6 shows function *CompareMem* which constructs a Boolean expression indicating the contexts for which two memories have matching contents. This code only checks the locations denoted by the set of address expressions occurring in the two lists. As a further optimization, it maintains a table *tested* to ensure that only one comparison is performed for each unique address expression.

> **function** *CompareMem*(**List** *MemA*, **List** *MemB*): **BExpr**
> /* Compare states of two memories */
>   *same* ← **true**
>   *tested* ← ∅
>   **for each** ⟨*ec, ea, ed*⟩ **in** *MemA* **do**
>   **if** (*ea* ∉ *tested*) **then**
>   *g* ← *GenDataExpr*()
>   *da* ← *ReadWithDefault*(*MemA, ec, ea, g*)
>   *db* ← *ReadWithDefault*(*MemB, ec, ea, g*)
>   *same* ← *same* ∧ (*da* =*db*)
>   *tested* ← *tested* ∪ {*ea*}
>   **for each** ⟨*ec, ea, ed*⟩ **in** *MemB* **do**
>   **if** (*ea* ∉ *tested*) **then**
>   *g* ← *GenDataExpr*()
>   *da* ← *ReadWithDefault*(*MemA, ec, ea, g*)
>   *db* ← *ReadWithDefault*(*MemB, ec, ea, g*)
>   *same* ← *same* ∧ (*da* =*db*)
>   *tested* ← *tested* ∪ {*ea*}
>   **return** *same*

Figure 6. Comparing states of two memories.

CompareMem compares matching locations in the two memories using the function *ReadWithDefault*, with a newly generated symbolic data expression g as the default value. This operation will add a list element and return a data expression dependent on g only when either some *Write* operation has been performed with context argument $c \neq$ **true**, or some *Write* operation was performed to one memory, without a counterpart for the other. By using the same, newly-generated symbol for a pair of accesses, we maintain consistency between the initial states of the two memories as well as the property that each memory location can have an arbitrary initial value.

5.3 Observation

One final subtlety about our comparison technique is worth noting. Normally two execution sequences will yield matching final memory states only if they perform identical *Write* operations, at least for the final writes to each memory location. Thus, if sequence A performs a write to some address a, one would expect sequence B to do likewise. Consider the case, however, where sequence A first reads from address a and then writes that value back to address a. Then location a is still in its initial state, and there is no need for sequence B to either read or write this location. Observe that our method wil correctly handle this case. In executing sequence A, we will add entries ⟨**true**, a, g⟩ to both lists. The *Write* operation in A may cause this entry to be replaced, but since it preserves the initial state of this location, the two memories will compare successfully.

The condition described above is also the reason why the list for memory A must be used as a shadow argument for the *Read* operations performed on memory B. Even though we have already evaluated the effect of all *Read* and *Write* operations by sequence A, sequence B may access memory locations never accessed by A. This is allowed as long as the accesses do not alter the values at these or any other memory locations.

On the other hand, suppose sequence A writes to address a without ever reading the initial state, while sequence B never reads or writes this address. Then the list for A will contain an entry with address a, while the list for B will not. Executing *ReadWithDefault(memB, a, g)* will return an expression involving g, which will not equal the expression returned by *ReadWithDefault(memA, a, g)*, and hence the mismatch will be detected.

6. Correspondence Checking by Applying Memory Shadowing

When applying memory shadowing, the EMM software interface uses function *ShadowRead* for performing reads, and procedure *Write* for performing writes. *ShadowRead* provides the two execution sequences with identical initial memory state by constructing it on-the-fly. We check the correctness criterion (1) of Burch and Dill's method by applying function *CompareMem* on all the user-visible memory elements. The universal quantification is done implicitly by using the same symbolic initial memory state and the same symbolic instruction for both execution sequences.

The steps of our methodology are:

1. Load the implementation (possibly pipelined) circuit and associate every memory element in it with empty original and shadow memory lists.

2. Cycle the implementation with a symbolic instruction.

3. Flush the implementation.

4. Swap the original and shadow memory lists for every memory element.

5. Flush the implementation.

6. Swap the implementation and the specification (non-pipelined) circuits by keeping the memory lists for every user-visible memory element.

7. Cycle the specification with the same symbolic instruction as used in Step 2.

8. Compare the original, mem_i, and the shadow, $shadow_i$, memory lists for every user-visible memory element i and let $equality_i \doteq CompareMem(mem_i, shadow_i)$, $i = 1, ..., u$, where u is the number of user-visible memory elements.

9. Form the Boolean expression for our correctness criterion:

$$legal\_instruction \Rightarrow \bigwedge_{i=1}^{u} equality_i, \qquad\qquad (5)$$

where $legal\_instruction$ is a Boolean expression for the symbolic instruction from Steps 2 and 7 to be legal.

It is also possible to traverse the commutative diagram with another sequence of circuit and memory swaps, i.e. to first flush the implementation, swap it with the specification, cycle the specification, swap it with the implementation, swap the memory lists, and perform Steps 2, 3, 8, and 9 from above. As expected, our experiments found that the two sequences of traversing the commutative diagram perform comparably in terms of CPU time and memory for our simple circuit presented next.

7. Experimental Results

We implemented all the correspondence checking routines, presented in this paper, within a tool [7] that supports the STE technique. Although correspondence checking and STE are two different forms of verification, as noted in Section 1, they have in common the use of a symbolic simulator and the EMM. This allows them to be applied on the same circuit descriptions, which can be in both gate-level and register-transfer-level form. Furthermore, gate-level circuits can be automatically generated from transistor-level circuits [2].

Experiments were performed on the pipelined addressable accumulator shown in Figure 7. The current instruction is specified by the inputs Addr, Clear, In, and Nop, where the last one indicates whether the instruction is a nop and is used for flushing the pipeline. The pipeline register Hold separates the execution and the write back stages of the processor. The control logic stores the previous address and compares it with the present one at the Addr input. In case of equality of the two addresses and a valid previous instruction (the Nop input was **false**), the control signal of the multiplexor is set so as to select the data output of the Hold register. Hence, data forwarding takes effect. For a more detailed description of the circuit (however without a Nop input) and its verification by STE, the reader is referred to [7] for the case of transistor-level memory elements, and to [13] for the case of EMM-replaced memory elements.

For all of the experiments, the dual-ported register file was removed from the circuit and replaced with an EMM. The software interface ensures that: 1) a *Read* operation takes place relative to phi1; and 2) a *Write* operation takes place relative to phi2, as long as the corresponding instruction was not a Nop - see the register file connections shown in Figure 7.(b).

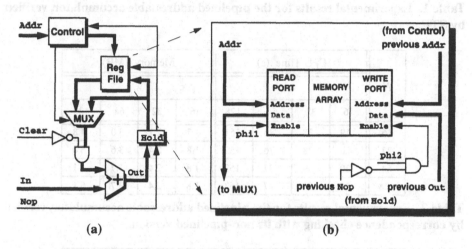

(a)   (b)

Figure 7. (a) The pipelined addressable accumulator; (b) the connections of its register file when replaced by an EMM. The thick lines indicate buses, while the thin ones are of a single bit.

The experiments were performed on an IBM RS/6000 43P-140 with a 233MHz PowerPC 604e microprocessor, having 512 MB of physical memory, and running AIX 4.1.5. Table 1 shows the results from the STE verification of the pipelined addressable accumulator. Table 2 - from the correspondence checking between the same circuit and its non-pipelined version (the specification circuit) by applying memory shadowing. Finally, Table 3 presents the results from the STE verification of the specification circuit. In all of the tables, N is the number of addresses and w is the number of data bits per address.

It can be observed that the results in Table 1 depend on N, while those in Tables 2 and 3 are almost constant with N. The reason is that for the experiments for Table 1, the RegFile and the Hold latch are initialized conditionally on the equality of the current and previous addresses, as opposed to unconditionally which is the case in the experiments for Tables 2 and 3. The idea is that these conditions will cancel the effect of the forwarding logic, and the output of the multiplexor will be simple (see [7] and [13] for details). However, when the RegFile and the Hold latch are read, the initialization conditions get conjuncted with the contents of every data bit. Hence, the BDDs get bigger, require more CPU time to process, and the results depend on N.

N	CPU Time (s)				Memory (MB)			
	w				w			
	16	32	64	128	16	32	64	128
16	33	65	129	259	1.8	2.4	3.5	5.8
32	38	75	147	300	2.2	2.4	3.5	5.8
64	51	99	200	402	2.2	3.2	5.1	9.0
128	83	163	324	661	2.3	3.3	5.2	9.2

Table 1. Experimental results for the pipelined addressable accumulator, verified by STE.

N	CPU Time (s)				Memory (MB)			
	w				w			
	16	32	64	128	16	32	64	128
16	19	38	75	151	1.7	2.1	3.0	4.8
32	20	38	76	152	1.8	2.4	3.6	6.0
64	20	39	77	153	1.8	2.4	3.7	6.1
128	20	39	77	153	1.8	2.4	3.7	6.1

Table 2. Experimental results for the pipelined addressable accumulator, verified by correspondence checking with its non-pipelined version.

N	CPU Time (s)				Memory (MB)			
	w				w			
	16	32	64	128	16	32	64	128
16	23	46	91	183	1.5	1.7	2.1	3.0
32	23	46	92	183	1.5	1.7	2.2	3.0
64	23	46	91	183	1.5	1.8	2.3	3.3
128	24	47	92	186	1.5	1.8	2.3	3.4

Table 3. Experimental results for the non-pipelined addressable accumulator, verified by STE.

8. Conclusions and Future Work

We are very encouraged by our results. Correspondence checking between the pipelined addressable accumulator and its non-pipelined version required CPU time and memory that are logarithmic with respect to N, and linear with respect to w. By comparing the sum of the entries in Tables 2 and 3 to their corresponding entry in Table 1, it can be concluded that for pipelined processors with sufficiently large memory state, it may take less CPU time and memory to verify an equivalent non-pipelined circuit and then to check it for correspondence to the pipelined one, than to directly verify the pipelined processor. Furthermore, when the pipelined processor is incrementally modified, it can directly be checked for correspondence to its non-pipelined version, assuming the latter is already verified, and the savings in CPU time and memory will be even greater.

Future work may focus on applying the memory shadowing methodology on real-life processors. Crucial for that will be techniques for resolving the conflicting orderings of variables generated by function *GenDataExpr*, when representing the initial state of the pipeline registers. Namely, some of the instruction bits may correspond to both the functional code in one class of instructions and to a part of an immediate data operand in another class. The variables generated in the former case, since used in the control of the processor, will require to be towards the front of the variable ordering. However, the ones generated in the latter case, since used in the data path, will be more efficiently placed around the end of the variable ordering.

References

[1]   S. Bose, and A. L. Fisher, "Verifying Pipelined Hardware Using Symbolic Logic Simulation," *International Conference on Computer Design*, October 1989, pp. 217-221.

[2]   R. E. Bryant, "Extraction of Gate Level Models from Transistor Circuits by Four-Valued Symbolic Analysis," *International Conference on Computer Aided Design*, November 1991, pp. 350-353.

[3]   R. E. Bryant, "Symbolic Boolean Manipulation with Ordered Binary-Decision Diagrams," *ACM Computing Serveys*, Vol. 24, No. 3 (September 1992), pp. 293-318.

[4]   J. R. Burch, and D. L. Dill, "Automated Verification of Pipelined Microprocessor Control," *CAV '94*, D. L. Dill, ed., LNCS 818, Springer-Verlag, June 1994, pp. 68-80.

[5]   J. R. Burch, "Techniques for Verifying Superscalar Microprocessors," *DAC '96*, June 1996, pp. 552-557.

[6]   C. A. R. Hoare, "Proof of Correctness of Data Representations," *Acta Informatica*, 1972, Vol.1, pp. 271-281.

[7]   A. Jain, "Formal Hardware Verification by Symbolic Trajectory Evaluation," Ph.D. thesis, Department of Electrical and Computer Engineering, Carnegie Mellon University, August 1997.

[8]   R. B. Jones, C.-J. H. Seger, and D. L. Dill, "Self-Consistency Checking," *FMCAD '96*, M. Srivas and A. Camilleri, eds., LNCS 1166, Springer-Verlag, November 1996, pp. 159-171.

[9]   M. Pandey, "Formal Verification of Memory Arrays," Ph.D. thesis, School of Computer Science, Carnegie Mellon University, May 1997.

[10] M. Pandey, and R. E. Bryant, "Exploiting Symmetry When Verifying Transistor-Level Circuits by Symbolic Trajectory Evaluation," *CAV '97*, O. Grumberg, ed., LNCS 1254, Springer-Verlag, June 1997, pp. 244-255.

[11] J. Sawada, and W. A. Hunt, Jr., "Trace Table Based Approach for Pipelined Microprocessor Verification," *CAV '97*, O. Grumberg, ed., LNCS 1254, Springer-Verlag, June 1997, pp. 364-375.

[12] C.-J. H. Seger, and R. E. Bryant, "Formal Verification by Symbolic Evaluation of Partially-Ordered Trajectories," *Formal Methods in System Design*, Vol. 6, No. 2 (March 1995), pp. 147-190.

[13] M. Velev, R. E. Bryant, and A. Jain, "Efficient Modeling of Memory Arrays in Symbolic Simulation," *CAV '97*, O. Grumberg, ed., LNCS 1254, Springer-Verlag, June 1997, pp. 388-399.

[14] P. J. Windley, and J. R. Burch, "Mechanically Checking a Lemma Used in an Automatic Verification Tool," *FMCAD '96*, M. Srivas and A. Camilleri, eds., LNCS 1166, Springer-Verlag, November 1996, pp. 362-376.

Rules for Abstraction

Stephan Merz*

Institut für Informatik, Universität München
merz@informatik.uni-muenchen.de

Abstract. Abstraction techniques for the verification of reactive systems promise to provide a theoretical basis for the integration of automatic and interactive proof techniques. In this paper, we give an account of homomorphic abstraction by studying a series of proof rules in Lamport's Temporal Logic of Actions. We believe that the main advantage of a logical formalization of abstraction is that it points towards more refined abstraction techniques. Specifically, we demonstrate two novel techniques that appear helpful in the verification of liveness properties over abstract models.

1 Verification by Abstraction

Machine assistance in the verification of reactive systems traditionally comes in two different forms: interactive theorem proving allows the verification of arbitrarily complex systems, but it requires a large amount of training and can be tedious, even with the help of sophisticated tactics. Model checking and similar techniques, on the other hand, integrate smoothly with traditional testing and debugging and are largely automatic, but they are usually limited to systems whose state space is finite and relatively small.

Abstraction techniques [5, 7, 10, 12, 16, 18, 22, 23] promise to integrate the two approaches: in a first step, the original system model Φ is reduced to a smaller model $\overline{\Phi}$. If Φ is large or infinite, this step will in general require interactive proof techniques. In a second step, the small system $\overline{\Phi}$ is analyzed using automatic tools.

The reduction from Φ to $\overline{\Phi}$ is based on the structure of Φ. For example, in an automata-based approach, one would compute the abstract automaton $\overline{\Phi}$ by abstracting the initial condition of Φ and each possible state transition. However, fairness conditions imposed on Φ are not as easily abstracted, and liveness properties are often considered hard to prove by abstraction.

The contribution of this paper is twofold: first, we re-examine the principles that underly abstraction techniques by stating a series of proof rules in Lamport's Temporal Logic of Actions TLA [14]. Although our exposition can be easily rephrased in terms of other formalisms, this choice is convenient because TLA distinguishes between the level of actions and temporal formulas, and these two

---

* This work was supported by a grant from the state of Bavaria (Bayerischer Habilitations-Förderpreis).

levels are respectively associated with automatic and interactive theorem proving in proofs by abstraction. The second contribution is a suggestion to generalize known abstraction techniques by making use of standard laws of temporal logic. In this way, it is possible to go beyond purely structural abstractions and consider entire runs of a system rather than just individual state transitions. We present two specific novel techniques that we have found useful for the verification of liveness properties by abstraction. These techniques allow much of the tedium usually associated with hand proofs (or interactive proofs) of liveness properties to be left to the model checker. Finally, our approach allows the principle of abstraction to be itself formalized within a proof system, rather than to be stated as a separate meta-rule.

The outline of this paper is as follows: Section 2 gives a short overview of TLA. Section 3 introduces the principal proof rules for abstraction, which are applied to an example in section 4. Section 5 discusses techniques to obtain better abstractions. Finally, section 6 summarizes the key points and compares with existing work.

2 The Temporal Logic of Actions

We begin with a short review of the logic TLA, concentrating on the concepts that we use in the remainder of this paper. TLA is defined more formally in [14, 2]. Specifications and properties of systems are expressed in TLA as *temporal formulas*, which are interpreted over infinite sequences of states. States assign values to state variables that represent individual system components.

Syntactically, TLA is a two-tiered formalism whose temporal formulas are defined on top of *actions* (transition formulas), interpreted over pairs of states, that describe state transitions. This separation of the transition level from the temporal level is deliberate; TLA proof rules aim at reducing temporal properties to action reasoning. The syntax of actions is that of standard first-order formulas, except that state variables may have primed as well as standard, unprimed occurrences, with the convention that a primed occurrence like x' refers to the value of x in the second state of the state pair. For example, the action $x' = x + 1$ is true of a pair $\langle s, t \rangle$ of states if the value of x at state t equals the value of x at s plus one. If v is a variable, we write UNCHANGED v for the action $v' = v$, and we use a similar convention for tuples of variables.

A *state predicate* is a transition formula that does not contain free primed variables; similarly, a *state function* is a term that contains only unprimed variables. If A is an action and v is a state function, then $[A]_v$ and $\langle A \rangle_v$ are abbreviations for $A \vee (v' = v)$ and $A \wedge (v' \neq v)$, where v' is obtained from v by priming all state variables. The state predicate ENABLED A is an abbreviation for the formula $\exists x'_1, \ldots, x'_n : A$, where $x'_1, \ldots, x'_n$ are all primed variables that occur free in A. Semantically, ENABLED A holds of state s iff there exists some state t such that A holds of the pair $\langle s, t \rangle$.

Temporal formulas are built from transition formulas using the connectives $\Box$ and $\exists$ in addition to ordinary first-order connectives. The $\Box$ operator is the usual "always" operator of temporal logic. The quantifier $\exists$ represents hiding; the formula $\exists x : F$ is true of a state sequence σ if there exists some state sequence τ such that F holds of τ and where all states of τ agree with the corresponding states of σ, except possibly for the valuation of the variable x. Standard abbreviations include $\Diamond F$ for $\neg\Box\neg F$ and weak and strong fairness, defined as

$$\text{WF}_v(A) \triangleq \Box\Diamond\neg\text{ENABLED } \langle A \rangle_v \vee \Box\Diamond\langle A \rangle_v$$

$$\text{SF}_v(A) \triangleq \Diamond\Box\neg\text{ENABLED } \langle A \rangle_v \vee \Box\Diamond\langle A \rangle_v$$

One distinguishing feature of TLA is that all temporal formulas are invariant under stuttering, that is, finite repetitions of identical states. For this reason, temporal formulas are restricted so that $\Box A$ is well-formed for an action A only if A is either a state predicate or if it is of the form $[B]_v$; the logic without this restriction is called "raw TLA" (RTLA) in [14]. Lamport [13] emphasizes the importance of stuttering-invariant specifications in the light of refinement. However, for the purposes of verification, it is often easier to work in the simpler logic RTLA, and we will do so in this paper. RTLA and TLA differ subtly in the precise semantics of the hiding operator $\exists$. Because our rules do not make essential use of quantification, they are sound for both versions of TLA.

3 Proof Rules for Abstraction

In this section we reconstruct the standard theory of verification by homomorphic abstraction in the context of TLA, introducing basic concepts and notations. Extensions of the standard theory will be presented in section 5.

3.1 Basic Principle

The overall principle that underlies homomorphic abstraction is to deduce some property P of a "concrete" system Φ from a proof of property Q for an "abstract" system $\overline{\Phi}$. The relation between the concrete and abstract state spaces is provided by an abstraction function h.

In TLA, specifications and properties are both represented by formulas, and implementation is implication. The state components of the concrete and abstract systems will be represented by different (tuples of) variables, say x for the concrete level and $\bar{x}$ for the abstract level, whose values at every state are related by the function h. (Variables that occur at both the abstract and the concrete level are implicitly left unabstracted.) The principle of abstraction proofs is reflected in the TLA proof rule

$$\frac{\begin{array}{c} \Phi \wedge \Box A \wedge \Box(\bar{x} = h(x)) \Rightarrow \overline{\Phi} \\ \overline{\Phi} \Rightarrow Q \\ Q \wedge \Box A \wedge \Box(\bar{x} = h(x)) \Rightarrow P \end{array}}{\Phi \wedge \Box A \Rightarrow P} \quad (\bar{x} \notin \mathit{Vars}(\Phi, A, P)) \tag{1}$$

The second premise of rule (1) asserts that the abstract system $\overline{\Phi}$ satisfies the abstract property Q. The first and third premises relate the abstract and concrete levels of description and assert that the abstract specification $\overline{\Phi}$ is an image of the concrete specification Φ under the function h, and that the concrete property P is a pre-image under h of the abstract property Q. The auxiliary formula $\Box A$, where A is a transition formula, can be used to represent the "context" of the concrete system. Typically, A will imply the next-state relation and pre-established invariants of the concrete system. Whereas rule (1) remains correct if all occurrences of $\Box A$ are erased, a suitable choice of A is usually essential to make the rule applicable in practice.

To prove the correctness of rule (1), we observe that its premises and propositional logic imply

$$\Phi \wedge \Box A \wedge \Box(\bar{x} = h(x)) \Rightarrow P$$

By standard quantifier rules and using the assumption that none of the abstract variables $\bar{x}$ occur in the concrete-level formulas Φ, A or P, we obtain

$$\Phi \wedge \Box A \wedge (\exists \bar{x} : \Box(\bar{x} = h(x))) \Rightarrow P$$

Finally, the conclusion of rule (1) follows from the tautology $\Box(h(x) = h(x))$, which implies the validity of the conjunct $\exists \bar{x} : \Box(\bar{x} = h(x))$.

3.2 Generic Abstractions

The second premise $\overline{\Phi} \Rightarrow Q$ of rule (1) concerns only the abstract system, and we expect to use automatic verification techniques in its proof. However, the other premises are also formulated as proof obligations in temporal logic, and it is not clear why they should be easier to prove than the conclusion $\Phi \Rightarrow P$ itself. It is here where we need to use the idea that the abstract and concrete levels are structurally related by the homomorphism h. In a logical setting, this means that the formulas at the two levels have similar shape.

Rule (1) suggests that it makes sense to define *two* kinds of abstractions: the abstract-level formula $\overline{\Phi}$ is weaker than its concrete-level counterpart Φ, whereas Q is stronger than P. Actually, this setup is a little more general than the definitions that are often found in the literature, which consider only weakening abstractions and require the properties P and Q at the abstract and concrete level to be identical. We believe that this added bit of generality can be useful and comes at no extra price.

Definition 1. Let h be a state function and A be an action.

1. For any action N, an action $\overline{N}^+$ (resp., $\overline{N}^-$) is called a *weakening (resp., strengthening) abstraction* of N w.r.t. h and A if the following formulas are valid:
$$A \wedge (\bar{x} = h(x)) \wedge (\bar{x}' = h(x)') \Rightarrow (N \Rightarrow \overline{N}^+) \quad \text{resp.}$$
$$A \wedge (\bar{x} = h(x)) \wedge (\bar{x}' = h(x)') \Rightarrow (\overline{N}^- \Rightarrow N)$$

2. For any temporal formula F, a temporal formula $\overline{F}^+$ (resp., $\overline{F}^-$) is called a *weakening (resp., strengthening) abstraction* of F w.r.t. h and A if the following formulas are valid:

$$\Box A \wedge \Box(\bar{x} = h(x)) \Rightarrow (F \Rightarrow \overline{F}^+) \quad \text{resp.}$$
$$\Box A \wedge \Box(\bar{x} = h(x)) \Rightarrow (\overline{F}^- \Rightarrow F)$$

Note that TRUE and FALSE are trivial abstractions of any formula. In general, a suitable choice of the auxiliary action A will be important to find good abstractions. Note also that there can be different abstractions of a given formula G, although the values at the concrete and abstract levels are functionally related. Therefore, our definition of a weakening abstraction subsumes the notion of "abstraction" as well as that of "approximation" from [5].

Using the notation of definition 1, we can rephrase rule (1), assuming that $\overline{\Phi}^+$ and $\overline{P}^-$ are weakening and strengthening abstractions of Φ and P:

$$\frac{\overline{\Phi}^+ \Rightarrow \overline{P}^-}{\Phi \Rightarrow P} \tag{2}$$

The idea of a homomorphic relationship between the concrete and abstract specifications implies that abstractions of complex systems can be obtained from abstractions of their components. This is made precise in the following theorem, which is proved by induction on the structure of temporal formulas.

Theorem 2. *Let F be a temporal or transition formula built from elementary actions R_i by the connectives of TLA such that no variables that occur free in A, $\bar{x} = h(x)$ or $\bar{x}' = h(x)'$ occur bound in F, and assume given weakening and strengthening abstractions $\overline{R_i}^+$ and $\overline{R_i}^-$ w.r.t. h and A for every R_i.*

1. *$\overline{F}^+$ is a weakening abstraction of F, where $\overline{F}^+$ denotes the formula obtained from F by replacing every positive (resp., negative) occurrence of R_i by $\overline{R_i}^+$ (resp., $\overline{R_i}^-$).*
2. *$\overline{F}^-$ is a strengthening abstraction of F, where $\overline{F}^-$ denotes the formula obtained from F by replacing every positive (resp., negative) occurrence of R_i by $\overline{R_i}^-$ (resp., $\overline{R_i}^+$).*

Theorem 2 asserts that one can build abstractions of complex formulas F given abstractions of elementary transition formulas. The abstractions obtained in this way have the same shape as F, except that the concrete actions R_i are replaced by their abstract counterparts $\overline{R_i}^+$ or $\overline{R_i}^-$. The decision which transition formulas should be regarded as elementary is left to the user; typically, one might consider the initial conditions and the individual actions of single processes as elementary.

Theorem 2 does not imply that ENABLED $\overline{G}$ is an abstraction of ENABLED G if $\overline{G}$ is an abstraction of G, because the ENABLED operator is defined by quantification over state variables. For example, FALSE is a weakening abstraction of G with respect to h and $\neg G$, but since $\neg G$ does not imply $\neg$ENABLED G, we may

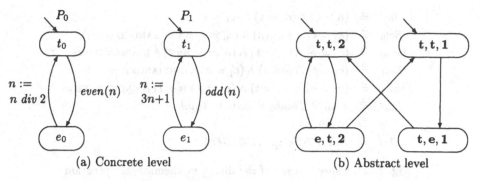

Fig. 1. The dining mathematicians

not conclude that ENABLED FALSE (which is again FALSE) is a weakening abstraction of ENABLED G w.r.t. $\neg G$. One can show that abstraction can be lifted over ENABLED provided that $A \wedge \text{ENABLED } G$ implies ENABLED $(G \wedge A \wedge (\bar{x}' = h(x)'))$. Although this side condition is frequently satisfied, it may be more practical to replace enabledness conditions by equivalent quantifier-free state predicates. This complication in abstracting enabledness predicates affects the abstract representation of concrete-level fairness conditions. Besides, A has both negative and positive occurrences in the formulas $\text{WF}_v(A)$ and $\text{SF}_v(A)$, and one would therefore have to find an abstraction $\overline{A}$ of A that is both weakening and strengthening in order to represent the concrete fairness conditions as $\text{WF}_{\overline{v}}(\overline{A})$ or $\text{SF}_{\overline{v}}(\overline{A})$. We will discuss issues of fairness and liveness under abstractions in section 5.

Rule (2) and theorem 2 suggest a methodology for verification by abstraction where automated verification techniques are used to reason about the abstract system and establish the premise of rule (2), whereas first-order theorem proving is used to verify abstractions of elementary transition formulas. Because the latter proof obligations do not involve temporal logic, their proof may benefit from well-developed theories for interactive theorem provers such as PVS [20] or Isabelle [21].

4   An Example

Let us illustrate our theory at the hand of a trivial example, the so-called "dining mathematicians" problem introduced in [7]. Figure 1(a) depicts the system, which consists of two processes P_0 and P_1 that communicate via the shared variable n. Both processes have a "thinking" state t_i and an "eating" state e_i; initially they are thinking. The variable n is initialized to some unspecified positive natural number. The purpose of the system is to ensure mutually exclusive access to the dining room for both processes without starvation. Process P_0 may eat only if n is even and it divides n by 2 when it resumes thinking. Process P_1 may eat only if n is odd and sets n to $3n + 1$ when it leaves the dining room.

Figure 2 contains a TLA specification of the dining mathematicians program, represented by the temporal formula DM. We wish to verify the following

$$
\begin{aligned}
Init &\triangleq (n > 0) \wedge (c_0 = t) \wedge (c_1 = t) \\
Eat_0 &\triangleq (c_0 = t) \wedge even(n) \wedge (c_0' = e) \wedge \text{UNCHANGED } \langle n, c_1 \rangle \\
Think_0 &\triangleq (c_0 = e) \wedge (c_0' = t) \wedge (n' = n \ div \ 2) \wedge \text{UNCHANGED } c_1 \\
Eat_1 &\triangleq (c_1 = t) \wedge odd(n) \wedge (c_1' = e) \wedge \text{UNCHANGED } \langle n, c_0 \rangle \\
Think_1 &\triangleq (c_1 = e) \wedge (c_1' = t) \wedge (n' = 3 * n + 1) \wedge \text{UNCHANGED } c_0 \\
Next &\triangleq Eat_0 \vee Think_0 \vee Eat_1 \vee Think_1 \\
v &\triangleq \langle c_0, c_1, n \rangle \\
DM &\triangleq Init \wedge \Box[Next]_v \wedge \Box\Diamond\langle Next \rangle_v
\end{aligned}
$$

Fig. 2. TLA specification of the dining mathematicians program

properties:

(Pos) $DM \Rightarrow \Box(n \in \mathbb{N}^+)$ $(Excl)$ $DM \Rightarrow \Box\neg(c_0 = e \wedge c_1 = e)$

$(Live_0)$ $DM \Rightarrow \Box\Diamond(c_0 = e)$ $(Live_1)$ $DM \Rightarrow \Box\Diamond(c_1 = e)$

The invariance properties (Pos) and $(Excl)$ assert that the shared variable n is a positive natural number[1] throughout any execution of the system specified by DM, and that the two processes never meet in the dining room. The liveness properties $(Live_0)$ and $(Live_1)$ assert starvation freedom for the two processes. We wish to establish all four properties by abstraction, following the method outlined in section 3. We replace the integer variable n of the concrete program by an abstract variable $\bar{n}$ that takes values from the set $\{0, 1, 2\}$ where 0 represents the natural number 0, and 1 and 2 represent any odd or even positive natural number. Formally, the abstraction function h is defined as

$$
h(n) \triangleq \text{if } n = 0 \text{ then } 0 \text{ elsif } odd(n) \text{ then } 1 \text{ else } 2
$$

We let the conjunction of the specification's next-state relation $[Next]_v$ and the predicate $n \in \mathbb{N}$ be the auxiliary transition formula A that defines the context of the abstraction. The theorem $DM \Rightarrow \Box(n \in \mathbb{N})$, which asserts the type correctness of program DM, can be established by a straightforward invariance proof, or even automatically by the type checker [15] of a typical interactive theorem prover.

Figure 3 contains an abstract version $\overline{DM}$ of the dining mathematicians program[2]. It has the same shape as the specification DM of figure 2, except that the elementary transition formulas have been replaced by abstract versions. Using an interactive theorem prover, these abstract formulas are quickly proved to be weakening abstractions[3] of their concrete counterparts with respect to h and A.

---

[1] We let $\mathbb{N}$ denote the set $\{0, 1, 2, \ldots\}$ of natural numbers and $\mathbb{N}^+$ denote the set $\mathbb{N} \setminus \{0\}$.

[2] We adopt the convention of writing multi-line conjunctions or disjunctions as lists bulleted with the connectives $\wedge$ and $\vee$.

[3] In this simple example, they are also strengthening abstractions of the concrete formulas (because the next-state relation is a conjunct of A), but this fact is not used in the verification.

$$\overline{Init} \triangleq (\bar{n} \in \{1, 2\}) \wedge (c_0 = t) \wedge (c_1 = t)$$

$$\overline{Eat_0} \triangleq (c_0 = t) \wedge (\bar{n} \in \{0, 2\}) \wedge (c_0' = e) \wedge \text{UNCHANGED } \langle \bar{n}, c_1 \rangle$$

$$\overline{Think_0} \triangleq \wedge (c_0 = e) \wedge (c_0' = t) \wedge \text{UNCHANGED } c_1$$
$$\wedge \vee (\bar{n} = 0) \wedge (\bar{n}' = 0)$$
$$\vee (\bar{n} = 1) \wedge (\bar{n}' \in \{0, 1, 2\})$$
$$\vee (\bar{n} = 2) \wedge (\bar{n}' \in \{1, 2\})$$

$$\overline{Eat_1} \triangleq (c_1 = t) \wedge (\bar{n} = 1) \wedge (c_1' = e) \wedge \text{UNCHANGED } \langle \bar{n}, c_0 \rangle$$

$$\overline{Think_1} \triangleq \wedge (c_1 = e) \wedge (c_1' = t) \wedge \text{UNCHANGED } c_0$$
$$\wedge \vee (\bar{n} \in \{0, 2\}) \wedge (\bar{n}' = 1)$$
$$\vee (\bar{n} = 1) \wedge (\bar{n}' = 2)$$

$$\overline{Next} \triangleq \overline{Eat_0} \vee \overline{Think_0} \vee \overline{Eat_1} \vee \overline{Think_1}$$

$$\bar{v} \triangleq \langle c_0, c_1, \bar{n} \rangle$$

$$\overline{DM} \triangleq \overline{Init} \wedge \Box[\overline{Next}]_{\bar{v}} \wedge \Box \Diamond \langle \overline{Next} \rangle_{\bar{v}}$$

Fig. 3. Abstract version of the dining mathematicians program

For example, the proof of

$$[Next]_v \wedge (n \in \mathbb{N}) \wedge (\bar{n} = h(n)) \wedge (\bar{n}' = h(n)') \Rightarrow (Think_1 \Rightarrow \overline{Think_1})$$

relies on the fact that $3n + 1$ is odd if n is an even integer and even otherwise. By theorem 2, it follows that $\overline{DM}$ is a weakening abstraction of DM.

Specification $\overline{DM}$ describes a finite-state system that can be analyzed by conventional model checkers. Its reachable state space is depicted in figure 1(b), where each state is labelled with the values of the state variables c_0, c_1, and $\bar{n}$. The following properties are easily read off the state transition diagram:

$$(\overline{Pos}) \quad \overline{DM} \Rightarrow \Box(\bar{n} \in \{1, 2\}) \qquad (\overline{Excl}) \quad \overline{DM} \Rightarrow \Box \neg(c_0 = e \wedge c_1 = e)$$
$$(\overline{Live_0}) \quad \overline{DM} \Rightarrow \Box \Diamond(c_0 = e)$$

From these properties and rule (2), we may conclude that properties *Pos*, *Excl*, and *Live_0* hold for the concrete specification *DM*. For example, $\bar{n} \in \{1, 2\}$ is a strengthening abstraction of $n \in \mathbb{N}^+$, and therefore $\Box(\bar{n} \in \{1, 2\})$ is a strengthening abstraction of $\Box(n \in \mathbb{N}^+)$.

Unfortunately, we cannot prove $\overline{DM} \Rightarrow \Box \Diamond(c_1 = e)$, which would imply property *Live_1* of starvation-freedom for process P_1, because of the cycle that connects the two left-hand states of figure 1(b). In fact, no finite-state homomorphic abstraction of specification *DM* allows a proof of property *Live_1*, because for every k there exists an execution of *DM* where P_0 eats k times in succession while P_1 has to wait. Techniques that allow homomorphic abstractions to be systematically improved, and which in particular allow a proof of property *Live_1*, will be discussed in section 5.

Let us emphasize that this example serves only as an illustration of the concepts of section 3. Automatic provers that employ techniques for invariant generation based on linear arithmetic [3, 4] can verify the three properties (*Pos*), (*Excl*), and (*Live_0*) without explicitly constructing an abstract version of *DM*.

5 Beyond Structural Abstractions

A useful abstraction function maps distinct concrete states to a single abstract state. This desired reduction of the size of the state space, however, does not come for free: first, it is likely to introduce cycles in the state graph of the abstract system that have no counterpart in the concrete system. Second, the concrete specification may contain subformulas that are too "fine-grained" and admit no useful abstraction. Technically, it may be impossible to find nontrivial strengthening abstractions for negative subformulas of the specification, such as the enabling conditions in fairness constraints. Both problems particularly affect the verification of liveness properties. In the first case, one can strengthen the abstract specification. In the second case, it may be helpful to weaken the concrete specification. Because TLA does not distinguish between specifications and properties, we may formally express both principles by the rule

$$\frac{\Phi \Rightarrow H \qquad \overline{\Phi}^+ \wedge \overline{H}^+ \Rightarrow \overline{P}^-}{\Phi \Rightarrow P} \tag{3}$$

In this rule, the temporal formula H, which represents either an auxiliary property or a weaker specification, is implied by the concrete specification Φ, and $\overline{P}^-$ is deduced from $\overline{\Phi}^+ \wedge \overline{H}^+$ instead of just $\overline{\Phi}^+$ as in (2). According to the general methodology of abstraction proofs, the premise $\Phi \Rightarrow H$ should be reduced to transition-level proof obligations by general principles. We will discuss two instances of rule (3) that we have found useful: one technique eliminates "false" cycles and the other one attempts to weaken fairness conditions in order to obtain stronger abstractions.

5.1 Strengthening by Well-Founded Orderings

If cycles in the abstract state graph cannot be broken with the help of a better abstraction function, it may still be possible to strengthen the abstract specification using an auxiliary liveness property of the concrete system. Liveness proofs are usually based on induction over a well-founded ordering $(S, \prec)$, a concept formalized in standard libraries of interactive theorem provers. The TLA formula

$$\Box(y \in S) \Rightarrow (\Box\Diamond\langle y' \prec y\rangle_y \Rightarrow \Box\Diamond\langle y' \not\prec y\rangle_y) \tag{4}$$

asserts that if y is always an element of S and if the value of y decreases infinitely often, then there have to be infinitely many steps that change y without decreasing it. If $\prec$ is a linear ordering, $\langle y' \not\prec y\rangle_y$ is of course equivalent to $\langle y \prec y'\rangle_y$. Formula (4) is valid if $(S, \prec)$ is well-founded. If $\overline{Decr}^-$ and $\overline{NonDecr}^+$ are strenghtening and weakening abstractions, respectively, of $\langle y' \prec y\rangle_y$ and $\langle y \not\prec y'\rangle_y$ with respect to h and $A \wedge (y \in S)$, we may use (4) and theorem 2 to obtain the instance

$$\frac{\Phi \Rightarrow \Box(y \in S) \qquad \overline{\Phi}^+ \wedge (\Box\Diamond\overline{Decr}^- \Rightarrow \Box\Diamond\overline{NonDecr}^+) \Rightarrow \overline{P}^-}{\Phi \Rightarrow P} \tag{5}$$

of rule (3). The first premise of (5) asserts an invariant of Φ that may be proved by standard invariant rules (perhaps even by type checking) or by another proof by abstraction. The second premise strengthens the abstract specification $\overline{\Phi}^+$ in order to establish the desired property.

We demonstrate rule (5) at the hand of the remaining liveness property $Live_1$ from the dining mathematicians example of section 4, choosing the well-founded ordering $(\mathbb{N}^+, <)$. We have already established the first premise of rule (5) as property Pos. Moreover, the only actions that change n are $Think_0$ and $Think_1$, and in fact $\overline{Think_0}$ and $\overline{Think_1}$ are strengthening and weakening abstractions, respectively, of $\langle n' < n \rangle_n$ and $\langle n < n' \rangle_n$ with respect to h and $A \wedge (n \in \mathbb{N}^+)$. Hence, to prove $Live_1$, it suffices to show

$$\overline{DM} \wedge (\Box \Diamond \overline{Think_0} \Rightarrow \Box \Diamond \overline{Think_1}) \Rightarrow \Box \Diamond (c_1 = \mathbf{e}) \tag{6}$$

The additional conjunct prohibits the abstract system to persistently cycle between the two left-hand states of figure 1(b), because any such execution would perform infinitely many $\overline{Think_0}$ actions, but only finitely many $\overline{Think_1}$ actions. In fact, decision procedures for linear-time temporal logic such as the model checking component of STeP [4] easily verify property (6).

5.2 Weakening Fairness

The lifting of abstractions to complex formulas as suggested by theorem 2 is a simple syntactic procedure and is therefore sensitive to the syntactic shape of a formula. If the concrete specification Φ contains both negative and positive occurrences of elementary subformulas, the lifting operation is not monotonic: a weaker formula at the concrete level may have a stronger abstraction with respect to a given mapping. Because enabledness conditions occur negatively in fairness conditions, it may be useful to weaken the fairness conditions of the concrete specification before constructing the abstraction.

Many specifications have an infinite state space because they are generic in some parameter. There will often be a fairness condition for each possible parameter value, that is, the TLA specification Φ contains conjuncts of the form $\forall x \in S : \mathrm{XF}_v(A(x))$, where XF denotes either SF or WF. Now suppose that we wish to verify a property of the form $\Phi \Rightarrow \forall x \in S : P(x)$. The first step in the proof is to introduce a fresh Skolem constant, say $\mathbf{x}$, and prove $\Phi \wedge (\mathbf{x} \in S) \Rightarrow P(\mathbf{x})$. Because of interaction between the subprocesses of the system, it will be impossible to prove this property from the process associated with $\mathbf{x}$ alone, so we have to distinguish between actions that concern $\mathbf{x}$ and actions of different processes. For the sake of simplicity, assume that it is not necessary to distinguish between individual parameter values other than $\mathbf{x}$, but that it is enough to consider the two-element abstract parameter domain that consists of $\mathbf{x}$ and a second constant $\mathbf{y}$ representing an arbitrary value different from $\mathbf{x}$.

An application of theorem 2 to compute abstractions for the fairness conditions of Φ requires strengthening abstractions of ENABLED $\langle A(y) \rangle_v$ for $y \in S \backslash \{\mathbf{x}\}$.

$$Init \triangleq \forall x \in P : \neg req[x] \land \neg granted[x]$$

$$R(x) \triangleq req'(x) \land \forall y \in P \setminus \{x\} : \text{UNCHANGED } \langle req[y], granted\rangle$$

$$G(x) \triangleq \land req(x) \land \text{UNCHANGED } req$$
$$\land \forall y \in P : \neg granted[y] \land (granted'[y] \Leftrightarrow (y = x))$$

$$F(x) \triangleq \land granted[x] \land \neg granted'[x] \land \neg req'[x]$$
$$\land \forall y \in P \setminus \{x\} : \text{UNCHANGED } \langle req[y], granted[y]\rangle$$

$$v \triangleq \langle req, granted\rangle$$

$$RM \triangleq \land Init \land \Box[\exists x \in P : R(x) \lor G(x) \lor F(x)]_v$$
$$\land \forall x \in P : \text{WF}_v(F(x)) \land \text{SF}_v(G(x))$$

Fig. 4. A simple resource manager

Unfortunately, we can no longer identify individual processes different from **x** in the abstract state space, and can therefore not compute a useful strengthening abstraction of these enabledness condition. Instead, we will have to use the trivial abstraction TRUE for the fairness conditions, and are likely to introduce deadlocks in the abstract specification. In such a situation we may use the TLA rule

$$\frac{N \land \neg(\exists z \in M : \langle A(z)\rangle_v) \land (y \in M)}{\Rightarrow (\text{ENABLED } \langle A(y)\rangle_v \Rightarrow (\text{ENABLED } \langle A(y)\rangle_v)')}{\Box N \land \forall y \in M : \text{XF}_v(A(y)) \Rightarrow \text{XF}_v(\exists y \in M : A(y))} \tag{7}$$

Rule (7) asserts that it is weaker to require fairness with respect to *some* action $A(y)$ than to require fairness of $A(y)$ for each individual value of y, provided that no action except $A(z)$ for some value of z can disable $A(y)$. It is therefore enough to find abstractions for $\text{ENABLED}(\exists y \in S \setminus \{x\} : A(y))$, that is, parameter values that map to the same abstract element need no longer be distinguished.

As a concrete, if trivial, example, consider the specification of a shared-variable resource manager shown in figure 4. The state of the system is encoded by two arrays *req* and *granted* indexed by a set P of processes. With each process are associated three actions: $R(x)$ and $F(x)$ represents process actions requesting and releasing the resource. The action $G(x)$ models the granting of the resource by the manager. Although the specification itself is overly simplistic, its syntactic shape is typical of shared-variable specifications.

Suppose that we wish to prove liveness for each process $x \in P$, which is expressed by the formula $RM \Rightarrow \forall x \in P : \Box(req[x] \Rightarrow \Diamond granted[x])$. As indicated above, we introduce a fresh Skolem constant **x** and try to prove

$$RM \land (\mathbf{x} \in P) \Rightarrow \Box(req[\mathbf{x}] \Rightarrow \Diamond granted[\mathbf{x}]) \tag{8}$$

By (7), whose antecedent (for both the F and the G actions) is easily seen to be satisfied, we may weaken RM to the specification

$$\land Init$$
$$\land \Box[R(\mathbf{x}) \lor G(\mathbf{x}) \lor F(\mathbf{x}) \lor \exists y \in P \setminus \{\mathbf{x}\} : R(y) \lor G(y) \lor F(y)]_v$$
$$\land \text{WF}_v(F(\mathbf{x})) \land \text{SF}_v(G(\mathbf{x}))$$
$$\land \text{WF}_v(\exists y \in P \setminus \{\mathbf{x}\} : F(y)) \land \text{SF}_v(\exists y \in P \setminus \{\mathbf{x}\} : G(y))$$

Applying theorem 2 to this weaker specification, we arrive at the abstract specification

$$\land \neg req[\mathbf{x}] \land \neg req[\mathbf{y}] \land \neg granted[\mathbf{x}] \land \neg granted[\mathbf{y}]$$
$$\land \; \Box[R(\mathbf{x}) \lor G(\mathbf{x}) \lor F(\mathbf{x}) \lor R(\mathbf{y}) \lor G(\mathbf{y}) \lor F(\mathbf{y})]_v$$
$$\land \; \mathrm{WF}_v(F(\mathbf{x})) \land \mathrm{SF}_v(G(\mathbf{x})) \land \mathrm{WF}_v(F(\mathbf{y})) \land \mathrm{SF}_v(G(\mathbf{y}))$$

from which (8) can be established automatically.

6 Conclusion

We have given a logical reconstruction of the principle of homomorphic abstraction, which has been widely investigated from both theoretical and practical points of view. The principle that underlies proofs by abstraction can be concisely expressed as a proof rule in temporal logic. For this to be useful in practice, it is essential that abstractions of complex systems can be composed from abstractions of their elementary constituents (theorem 2). In particular, one can build the abstraction from a syntactic description of the concrete program, without constructing its state graph.

The setting of temporal logic makes it natural to take entire system runs into account and to explore interactions between abstraction proofs and ordinary temporal reasoning. In this way, we are able to verify interesting liveness properties by abstraction. Nitsche and Wolper [19] have also addressed the preservation of liveness under abstractions and have obtained more specific results for a restricted class of homomorphisms.

We have used TLA in our exposition because its distinction between the transition and temporal levels of description is a good match for the methodology of abstraction that combines interactive theorem proving and model checking. Of course, our concrete results are not restricted to TLA. For example, rule (5) is easily reformulated in an automata-theoretic framework [23, 24], where one would add a Streett condition. Our rules also formalize the method suggested in [8] to strengthen abstract specifications by auxiliary properties in order to exclude unrealistic counter-examples reported by model checkers.

We have concentrated on homomorphic abstractions, the most widely considered abstraction method. It has been argued [7, 22] that it may be useful to consider more general relational instead of functional abstractions, possibly restricted to Galois connections as in the theory of abstract interpretation [6]. To some extent, this flexibility is already present in our approach because logical properties naturally form a lattice. The most useful generalization of our basic rule (1) in terms of an abstraction relation R seems to be the rule

$$\frac{\begin{array}{c} \Phi \land \Box A \;\Rightarrow\; \exists \bar{x} : \Box R(x, \bar{x}) \land \overline{\Phi} \\ \overline{\Phi} \;\Rightarrow\; Q \\ Q \land \Box A \land \Box R(x, \bar{x}) \;\Rightarrow\; P \end{array}}{\Phi \land \Box A \;\Rightarrow\; P} \qquad \bar{x} \notin Vars(P) \tag{9}$$

One could use auxiliary variables [1] to prove the first premise of (9). It remains to explore whether the additional complexity is justified in practice.

Throughout our exposition, we have assumed that the necessary abstractions are provided by the user. A useful abstraction methodology also has to assist in the actual construction of the abstractions. Graf and Saidi [9] propose to exploit powerful automatic proof procedures of the interactive verifier to heuristically compute sound, although perhaps not optimal, abstractions, and to improve these as necessary.

We have used our approach to verify a novel reader-writer algorithm developed at Siemens Corporate Research [11]. In that case study, we have found abstraction particularly helpful to establish liveness properties, which are notoriously tedious to prove in temporal logic and are traditionally considered hard to verify by abstraction. The concepts presented in this paper have been implemented in an embedding of TLA in the theorem prover Isabelle [17]. We are investigating the integration of a tableau prover for linear temporal logic into our Isabelle embedding.

Acknowledgement. Comments by Martín Abadi, Leslie Lamport, Olaf Müller, and the referees on earlier drafts of this paper have helped to clarify the exposition.

References

1. Martín Abadi and Leslie Lamport. The existence of refinement mappings. *Theoretical Computer Science*, 81(2):253–284, May 1991.
2. Martín Abadi and Stephan Merz. On TLA as a logic. In Manfred Broy, editor, *Deductive Program Design*, NATO ASI series F, pages 235–272. Springer-Verlag, Berlin, 1996.
3. S. Bensalem, Y. Lakhnech, and H. Saidi. Powerful techniques for the automatic generation of invariants. In Rajeev Alur and Thomas A. Henzinger, editors, *Computer Aided Verification: 8th International Conference*, volume 1102 of *Lecture Notes in Computer Science*, pages 323–335. Springer-Verlag, 1996.
4. Nikolaj Bjørner, Anca Browne, Edward Chang, Michael Colón, Arjun Kapur, Zohar Manna, Henny B. Sipma, and Tomás E. Uribe. STeP: deductive-algorithmic verification of reactive and real-time systems. In Rajeev Alur and Thomas A. Henzinger, editors, *Computer Aided Verification: 8th International Conference*, volume 1102 of *Lecture Notes in Computer Science*, pages 415–418. Springer-Verlag, 1996.
5. Edmund M. Clarke, Orna Grumberg, and David E. Long. Model checking and abstraction. *ACM Transactions on Programming Languages and Systems*, 16(5):1512–1542, September 1994. A preliminary version appeared in POPL 1992.
6. Patrick Cousot and Radhia Cousot. Abstract interpretation: A unified lattice model for static analysis of programs by construction or approximation of fixpoints. In *4th ACM Symposium on Principles of Programming Languages*, pages 238–252, Los Angeles, California, 1977. ACM Press.
7. Dennis Dams, Orna Grumberg, and Rob Gerth. Abstract interpretation of reactive systems: Abstractions preserving ∀CTL*, ∃CTL* and CTL*. In Ernst-Rüdiger Olderog, editor, *Programming Concepts, Methods, and Calculi (PROCOMET '94)*, pages 561–581, Amsterdam, 1994. IFIP Transactions, North Holland/Elsevier.
8. J. Dingel and T. Filkorn. Model checking for infinite state systems using data abstraction, assumption-commitment style reasoning and theorem proving. In *Computer-Aided Verification*, volume 939 of *Lecture Notes in Computer Science*, Berlin, 1995. Springer-Verlag.

9. Susanne Graf and Hassan Saidi. Construction of abstract state graphs with PVS. In Orna Grumberg, editor, *Computer Aided Verification: 9th International Conference*, volume 1254 of *Lecture Notes in Computer Science*, pages 72–83. Springer-Verlag, 1997.

10. Klaus Havelund and Natarajan Shankar. Experiments in theorem proving and model checking for protocol verification. In Marie-Claude Gaudel and Jim Woodcock, editors, *Formal Methods Europe*, pages 662–681, Berlin, March 1996. Springer-Verlag.

11. Hermann Hellwagner. Scalable readers/writers synchronization on shared-memory machines. Technical report, Siemens AG, ZFE ST SN 2, 1993.

12. Robert P. Kurshan. Analysis of discrete event coordination. In J.W. de Bakker, W.-P. de Roever, and G. Rozenberg, editors, *Proceedings REX Workshop on Stepwise Refinement of Distributed Systems: Models, Formalisms, Correctness*, volume 430 of *Lecture Notes in Computer Science*, pages 414–454. Springer-Verlag, May 1989.

13. Leslie Lamport. What good is temporal logic? In R. E. A. Mason, editor, *Information Processing 83: Proceedings of the IFIP 9th World Congress*, pages 657–668, Paris, September 1983. IFIP, North-Holland.

14. Leslie Lamport. The Temporal Logic of Actions. *ACM Transactions on Programming Languages and Systems*, 16(3):872–923, May 1994.

15. Leslie Lamport and Lawrence C. Paulson. Should your specification language be typed? Research Report 147, Digital Equipment Corporation, Systems Research Center, Palo Alto, California, May 1997.

16. Claire Loiseaux, Susanne Graf, Joseph Sifakis, Ahmed Bouajjani, and Saddek Bensalem. Property preserving abstractions for the verification of concurrent systems. *Formal Methods in System Design*, 6:11–44, 1995. A preliminary version appeared as Spectre technical report RTC40, Grenoble, France, 1993.

17. Stephan Merz. Isabelle/TLA. Available on the WWW at URL http://www4. informatik.tu-muenchen.de/~merz/isabelle/, 1997.

18. Olaf Müller and Tobias Nipkow. Combining model checking and deduction for I/O-automata. In *Tools and Algorithms for the Construction and Analysis of Systems*, volume 1019 of *Lecture Notes in Computer Science*, pages 1–16. Springer-Verlag, 1995.

19. Ulrich Nitsche and Pierre Wolper. Relative liveness and behavior abstraction. In *Principles of Distributed Computing*. ACM Press, 1997. to appear.

20. Sam Owre, John Rushby, Natarajan Shankar, and Friedrich von Henke. Formal verification for fault-tolerant architectures: Prolegomena to the design of PVS. *IEEE Transactions on Software Engineering*, 21(2):107–125, February 1995.

21. Lawrence C. Paulson. *Isabelle: A Generic Theorem Prover*, volume 828 of *Lecture Notes in Computer Science*. Springer-Verlag, Berlin, Heidelberg, 1994.

22. Joseph Sifakis. Property preserving homomorphisms of transition systems. In Edmund M. Clarke and Dexter Kozen, editors, *4th Workshop on Logics of Programs*, volume 164 of *Lecture Notes in Computer Science*, pages 458–473. Springer-Verlag, June 1983.

23. Bernhard Steffen, Kim G. Larsen, and Carsten Weise. A constraint oriented proof methodology based on modal transition systems. In *Tools and Algorithms for the Construction and Analysis of Systems*, volume 1019 of *Lecture Notes in Computer Science*, pages 17–40. Springer-Verlag, 1995.

24. Wolfgang Thomas. Automata on infinite objects. In Jan van Leeuwen, editor, *Handbook of Theoretical Computer Science, volume B: Formal Models and Semantics*, pages 133–194. Elsevier, Amsterdam, 1990.

Combining Z and Temporal Interval Logics for the Formalization of Properties and Behaviors of Embedded Systems

Robert Büssow and Wolfgang Grieskamp

Technische Universität Berlin,
Institut für Kommunikations- und Softwaretechnik
Sekr. FR5-13, Franklinstr. 28/29, D-10587 Berlin, Germany
E-mail: {buessow,wg}@cs.tu-berlin.de

Abstract. We describe a variant of discrete temporal interval logics which is embedded, and extends the Z notation. The resulting formalism, called $\mathcal{D}Z$, includes the usual set of operators known from interval logics together with a set of operators tailored for the operational description of deterministic process behavior. We apply our approach to the foundation of a combination of Statecharts and Z by giving a translation from a significant subset of Statecharts into $\mathcal{D}Z$.

1 Introduction

Applying formal techniques to the development of safety-critical embedded systems is promising, since the proper function of these systems is important enough to be worth possible extra effort induced by a formal approach. A method for applying formal techniques for embedded systems is currently developed in the context of our working area, the ESPRESS project[1]: a specification of a safety-critical system consists of a *model* described by a combination of Statecharts and Z and a set of *properties* (usual safety-critical requirements), which have to be a consequence of the model.

In this paper, we describe $\mathcal{D}Z$ ("Dynamic Z"), a moderate extension of Z by discrete temporal interval logics, which shall serve as a logical framework for a methodological approach as sketched above. $\mathcal{D}Z$ provides the usual set of operators known from interval logics together with operators tailored for the operational description of deterministic process behavior. Due to the combination of these operators with temporal interval logics, we get a framework in which behavior and properties of embedded systems can be described simultaneously.

An axiomatic framework based on temporal logics does not obviously support *concurrency*. We view concurrency conceptually as a situation where distinguishable *activities* compete for the access to restricted *resources* (let it be

---

[1] The ESPRESS project is a cooperation of industry and research institutes funded by the German ministry BMBF.

shared variables, channels, or whatsoever). Activities and resources can be modeled in $\mathcal{D}Z$ without a need for extending the language. We will show this for the case of shared variables with "racing".

We apply our approach by providing a sketch of a translation from a significant subset of Statemate-Statecharts into $\mathcal{D}Z$. The translation serves as a formalization of the semantics of this version of Statecharts; even more important, it defines a formal basis for relating Statecharts with temporal properties. For reasons of space, a complete and formal semantics of statecharts is not presented in this paper. In a next step – which will not be tackled in this paper – $\mathcal{D}Z$ is used for combining Statecharts and Z as a model oriented specification language as it is used in ESPRESS [2,1].

2 Integrating Temporal Interval Logics and Z

Z is a relative successful specification formalism based on set-theory and first order logic (cf. [13]). One restriction of Z is that though it is well suited for the specification of data, data-invariants and -transformation, it does not provide a mechanism for directly specifying invariants on *traces* of states. Consider, for example, the specification of an embedded system with a variable x with the requirement that x is less than zero in the beginning and then greater zero. This kind of property cannot be directly specified by invariants that refer only to single states as supported by Z.

By searching for concepts which fit to Z and which enable the descriptive specification of state traces, one naturally comes to some version of temporal logics. For $\mathcal{D}Z$, we have chosen *discrete temporal interval logics* [11,3]. In this logics, a property such as the above can be formulated as $\lceil x < 0 \rceil ^\frown \lceil x > 0 \rceil$. This formula looks similar to a regular expression or non-deterministic automaton, a concept software-engineers are used to. Moreover, interval logics allows to model not only properties but also operations by the finite traces they produce (for Z operations that would be traces of length 2).

2.1 Embedding of $\mathcal{D}Z$ in Z

$\mathcal{D}Z$ adds to Z the concepts of *dynamic values* and *dynamic schemata*. A dynamic value models a trace of elements of some type, and can be represented directly in Z. A dynamic schema bundles a collection of dynamic values which simultaneously satisfy a property given in temporal interval logics. Let as consider an example: the dynamic schema $S \mathbin{\widehat{=}} [\, x, y : \mathrm{dyn}\,\mathbb{Z} \mid (\lceil x > 0 \rceil ^\frown \lceil x < 0 \rceil) \wedge \lceil y \geq x \rceil \,]$ describes those dynamic values x and y (i.e. traces of integers) such that x is greater 0 up-to some state and less 0 after this state, whereas y is in each state greater or equal x. Hereby, dyn A is a normal Z set-constructor which denotes the set of traces of elements from some set A. For each binding $\sigma \in S$, $\sigma.x$ and $\sigma.y$ represent traces which are constraint as described above. By definition, the traces of the components of a binding of a dynamic schema have the same length.

Since dynamic schemata denote plain sets of bindings, they can be used wherever plain schemata can. For example, the schema expression $S \land [x, y : \text{dyn}\,Z \mid x = y]$ conjuncts the dynamic schema S with a plain schema, which enforces the dynamic values x and y to be equal as a whole, meaning pointwise equality of their traces. DZ allows to declare "types" of dynamic values. It therefore introduces one further construct, a dynamic set comprehension. For example, the set $X == \{x : \text{dyn}\,Z \mid \lceil x > 0\rceil \,\hat{}\, \lceil x < 0\rceil\}$ denotes a subset of $\text{dyn}\,Z$ where traces behave as described for the example above. With this definition of X, an alternate description for the above defined dynamic schema S would be $[x : X; \; y : \text{dyn}\,Z \mid \lceil y \geq x\rceil]$. This again is equivalent to $[x, y : \text{dyn}\,Z \mid x \in X \land \lceil y \geq x\rceil]$, as to be expected in a Z based framework.

2.2 Temporal Predicates of DZ

Temporal predicates are a superset of normal Z predicates: element test, conjunction, negation, universal quantification, and its derivatives.

State Observations. The *state* predicate $\lceil \phi \rceil$ is satisfied for those traces where the normal Z predicate ϕ is satisfied at each point. For example, $\lceil x > 0\rceil$ holds for traces of x such that for every point i in the trace, $x\,i > 0$ holds (representing the trace of x as a function $\mathbb{N} \nrightarrow Z$). In a state predicate a variable $x : \text{dyn}\,A$ denotes an element of type A. A second form of observing states is the *transition* predicate, which allows to relate observations at the beginning and the end of a trace: $\langle x' = x + 1 \rangle$ describes those traces, where in the last state the value of x is by one greater than in the first.

Length Constraints. A *length constraint* is denoted by the predicate $\ell\,\underline{R}\,e$, where e must denote a natural number, and $\underline{R}$ is some binary relation on natural numbers. For example, $\ell \leq 2$ describes those traces which length is less or equal 2. A special form of a length constraint is denoted as $\ell = \infty$, which holds for all traces of infinite length. For convenience, we can also annotate length constraints at other temporal predicates: $\lceil x \leq 0\rceil_{=1}$ abbreviates $\lceil x \leq 0\rceil \land \ell = 1$.

Chopping. The basic chopping operator of DZ is *overlapping chop*, $\delta_1\,;\,\delta_2$. It is satisfied for those traces which can be chopped at a state such that δ_1 holds up to this state and δ_2 holds from this state up-to the end. For example, $\lceil x > 0\rceil\,;\,\langle x' = x - 1 \rangle_{=2}$ describes those traces where x is constrained to be greater than zero in any state except the last, and in the last state its value is decremented by one compared to the previous state. The overlapping chop is actually our basic chop operator, and the normal chop known from interval logics, $\delta_1\,\hat{}\,\delta_2$, is a derived form, defined as $\delta_1\,;\,true_{=2}\,;\,\delta_2$.

Quantification. DZ entails the usual versions of existential and universal quantification of interval logics. For example, **everywhere** $(\ell > 1 \Rightarrow \langle x < x' \rangle)$ describes those traces where the value of x increases monotonically. In general, **everywhere** δ holds for traces such that for each sub-trace δ holds, and **somewhere** δ for traces such that there exists a sub-trace for which δ holds. The *repetition*, **repeat** δ, holds for traces such that $\delta\,;\,\delta\,;\,\ldots$ holds (one or more repetitions of δ).

Awaiting. The *await* operator, $?\lceil \phi \rceil$, allows to wait until a state predicate becomes true. For example, $?\lceil x > 0 \rceil$ describes those runs where x is not greater then 0 except of the last state; it equals to $\lceil \neg\, x > 0 \rceil \widehat{\,} \lceil x > 0 \rceil_{=1} \vee \lceil \neg\, x > 0 \rceil_{=\infty}$. Note that the disjunction is necessary in order to allow await to deadlock; chopping implies the existence of a finite chopping point.

Choice. The *guarded choice*, $\_ \rightarrow \_ \oplus \ldots \oplus \_ \rightarrow \_$, allows to choose a behavior on bases of the validity of some temporal predicate (the guard). For example, $?\lceil x > 0 \rceil \rightarrow \langle\!| x' = x - 1 |\!\rangle_{=2} \oplus ?\lceil x < 0 \rceil \rightarrow \langle\!| x' = x + 1 |\!\rangle_{=2}$ describes those traces where, after an initial segment, x is greater 0, and then is decremented by 1, or, otherwise, is less then 0 and is incremented. The choice gives priority to the path which can be first entered. If several paths can be entered at the same time, the choice uses some arbitrary but fixed priority; hence it doesn't introduces silent non-determinism.

Preemption. The *preemption*, $\_ \nearrow \_ \rightarrow \_ \oplus \ldots \oplus \_ \rightarrow \_$, is another form of the choice, which allows to express that a behavior is interrupted and continued with another behavior if a certain condition becomes true. For example, the temporal predicate **repeat** $(\langle\!| y' = 1 \text{ div } x |\!\rangle_{=2}) \nearrow ?\lceil x = 0 \rceil \rightarrow \delta$ describes a behavior where y is repeatedly computed by dividing 1 by the value of x in the previous state; however, if at some point x becomes zero, then this behavior is interrupted and instead continued with δ.

2.3 Semantics of $\mathcal{D}Z$

The set constructor for dynamic values is introduced by an ordinary Z declaration, $\text{dyn } A == \{f : \mathbb{N} \nrightarrow A \mid \forall i : \mathbb{N} \bullet i + 1 \in \text{dom } f \Rightarrow i \in \text{dom } f\}$.

We view a dynamic schema of the form $[\, x_1 : \text{dyn } A_1; \ \ldots; \ x_n : \text{dyn } A_n \mid \delta \,]$, where constraints induced by the declarations are already shifted to the property part. The semantics of a dynamic schema is defined by the function $[\![\delta]\!]^{\mathcal{D}} \Sigma$ (Figure 1), which translates a dynamic schema with a signature described by Σ and the property δ syntactically into a Z expression, denoting a set of bindings.[2] We emphasize the translation view in order to demonstrate that $\mathcal{D}Z$ is syntactic sugar. For example, $[\![[x = 0]]\!]^{\mathcal{D}} [x : \text{dyn } \mathbb{Z}]$ literally yields the set-expression $\{\sigma : [x : \text{dyn } \mathbb{Z}] \mid \text{points } \sigma \neq \emptyset \wedge (\forall i : \text{points } \sigma \bullet \langle x \Rightarrow \sigma.x\, i \rangle) \in [\![[x : \mathbb{Z}] \mid x = 0]\!])\}$.

In the definition of the translation, Σ represents a plain Z schema, $[\, x_1 : \text{dyn } A_1; \ \ldots; \ x_n : \text{dyn } A_n \mid \phi \,]$, which is initially constructed from the declaration part of the dynamic schema to be translated. With $\Sigma_\sim$ we denote Σ extended by a property which enforces the traces of all dynamic values to be of the same length. With $\Sigma_\downarrow$ we denote the flattening of Σ, such that all declarations $x_i : \text{dyn } A_i$ are replaced by $x_i : A_i$. $\Delta\Sigma$ is the schema operator as known from Z. The Z expression $\langle x_1 \Rightarrow e_1, \ldots, x_n \Rightarrow e_n \rangle$ denotes a binding. Given a binding $\sigma \in \Sigma_\sim$, then **points** σ yields the domain of the traces of the dynamic values (which is

---

[2] Alternatively, one could define the semantics as a set of traces of bindings, where each trace denotes a run of the system and each binding denotes a state in the trace. Nevertheless, this would make the definitions (e.g. 2.10) more complicate.

$$[\![\phi]\!]^{\mathcal{D}} \Sigma := \{\, \sigma : \Sigma_{\sim} \mid \text{points } \sigma \neq \varnothing \wedge (\forall i : \text{points } \sigma \bullet \quad (2.1)$$
$$\langle x_1 \Rrightarrow \sigma.x_1\, i, \ldots, x_n \Rrightarrow \sigma.x_n\, i \rangle \in [\,\Sigma_{\downarrow} \mid \phi\,])\}$$

$$[\![(\![\phi]\!])]\!]^{\mathcal{D}} \Sigma := \{\, \sigma : \Sigma_{\sim} \mid \text{points } \sigma \neq \varnothing \wedge \text{finite } \sigma \wedge \quad (2.2)$$
$$\langle x_1 \Rrightarrow \sigma.x_1\, 0, x_1' \Rrightarrow \sigma.x_1\, (\text{last } \sigma), \ldots,$$
$$x_n \Rrightarrow \sigma.x_n\, 0, x_n' \Rrightarrow \sigma.x_n\, (\text{last } \sigma) \rangle \in [\,\Delta\Sigma_{\downarrow} \mid \phi\,]\}$$

$$[\![\delta_1\, ;\, \delta_2]\!]^{\mathcal{D}} \Sigma := \{\, \sigma : \Sigma_{\sim} \mid (\exists i : \text{points } \sigma \bullet \quad (2.3)$$
$$\sigma[0\, ..\, i] \in [\![\delta_1]\!]^{\mathcal{D}} \Sigma \wedge \sigma[i\, ..] \in [\![\delta_2]\!]^{\mathcal{D}} \Sigma)\}$$

$$[\![\ell\, \underline{R}\, e]\!]^{\mathcal{D}} \Sigma := \{\, \sigma : \Sigma_{\sim} \mid \text{finite } \sigma \wedge \#(\text{points } \sigma)\, \underline{R}\, e\} \quad (2.4)$$

$$[\![\text{prefix } \delta]\!]^{\mathcal{D}} \Sigma := \{\, \sigma : \Sigma_{\sim} \mid \exists \sigma' : [\![\delta]\!]^{\mathcal{D}} \Sigma \bullet \quad (2.5)$$
$$\exists i : \text{points } \sigma' \bullet \sigma = \sigma'[0\, ..\, i]\}$$

$$[\![\delta_1 \wedge \delta_2]\!]^{\mathcal{D}} \Sigma := [\![\delta_1]\!]^{\mathcal{D}} \Sigma \cap [\![\delta_2]\!]^{\mathcal{D}} \Sigma \quad (2.6)$$

$$[\![\neg\, \delta]\!]^{\mathcal{D}} \Sigma := [\![true]\!]^{\mathcal{D}} \Sigma \setminus [\![\delta]\!]^{\mathcal{D}} \Sigma \quad (2.7)$$

$$[\![\forall s \bullet \delta]\!]^{\mathcal{D}} \Sigma := \{\, \sigma : \Sigma_{\sim} \mid \forall s \bullet (\sigma \setminus clashes) \in [\![\delta]\!]^{\mathcal{D}} (\Sigma \setminus clashes)\} \quad (2.8)$$

$$[\![true]\!]^{\mathcal{D}} \Sigma := \{\, \sigma : \Sigma_{\sim}\} \quad (2.9)$$

$$[\![e_1 \in e_2]\!]^{\mathcal{D}} \Sigma := \{\, \sigma : [\,\Sigma_{\sim} \mid e_1 \in e_2\,]\} \quad (2.10)$$

Fig. 1. Basic temporal predicates of $\mathcal{D}Z$

the same for any individual dynamic value), finite σ tells whether the traces are finite, and last σ yields the last index of the traces (which is only defined if finite σ holds). The notation $\sigma[i\, ..\, j]$ denotes the binding where all dynamic values are "sliced" from i to j, whereas $\sigma[i\, ..]$ denotes the tail starting from i.

In (2.8), s represents a "schema text" (a set of declarations). In our translation view, we just insert this text in the resulting expression. However, names introduced by s can shadow names from Σ; we have expressed this only informally by the phrase $\sigma \setminus clashes$ resp. $\Sigma \setminus clashes$, which remove components with clashing names from a binding resp. hide them in a schema. In (2.4), the expression e is just syntactically inserted; it cannot depend on names from Σ. In (2.10), by using $\Sigma_{\sim}$ in the position of schema inclusion, its declarations are bounded for e_1 and e_2.

In (2.5), an auxiliary predicate is introduced, which is not supposed to be visible on the user level, but allows to describe preemption and choice as a derived operator: prefix δ holds for those traces which are a prefix of the traces for which δ holds.

The derived forms of temporal predicates are summarized in Figure 2. We present only the special case of choice with two paths and preemption with one watchdog. In the guarded choice (2.18), the branch is taken which is able to proceed at first, i.e. the branch whose guard describes the shortest interval. $\delta_1 \wedge \neg\, \delta_2 \wedge$ prefix δ_2 ensures that δ_2 describes a longer interval than δ_1. Note that there has to be a prefix of δ_2 and thus δ_2 must not be false. A branch that is never taken is described by an infinite guard rather then a false guard. This

$$\ell = \infty \ \equiv \ \forall n : \mathbf{N} \bullet \neg \, \ell = n \tag{2.11}$$

$$\delta_{\underline{R}c} \ \equiv \ \delta \wedge \ell \, \underline{R} \, c \tag{2.12}$$

$$\delta_1 \ ^\frown \delta_2 \ \equiv \ \delta_1 \ ; \ true_{=2} \ ; \ \delta_2 \tag{2.13}$$

$$?\lceil \phi \rceil \ \equiv \ \lceil \neg \, \phi \rceil \ ^\frown \lceil \phi \rceil_{=1} \vee \lceil \neg \, \phi \rceil_{=\infty} \tag{2.14}$$

$$\text{somewhere } \delta \ \equiv \ true \ ; \ \delta \ ; \ true \tag{2.15}$$

$$\text{everywhere } \delta \ \equiv \ \neg \ \text{somewhere} \ \neg \ \delta \tag{2.16}$$

$$\text{repeat } \delta \ \equiv \ \delta \vee (\delta_{>0} \ ; \ \text{repeat } \delta) \tag{2.17}$$

$$\delta_1 \to \delta_1' \oplus \delta_2 \to \delta_2' \ \equiv \ (\delta_1 \wedge \neg \, \delta_2 \wedge \text{prefix } \delta_2) \ ; \ \delta_1' \ \vee \tag{2.18}$$
$$(\delta_2 \wedge \neg \, \delta_1 \wedge \text{prefix } \delta_1) \ ; \ \delta_2' \ \vee$$
$$(\delta_1 \wedge \delta_2) \ ; \ \delta_{oracle}'$$

$$\delta_1 \nearrow \delta_2 \to \delta_2' \ \equiv \ (\delta_1 \wedge \neg \, \delta_2 \wedge \text{prefix } \delta_2) \ \vee \tag{2.19}$$
$$(\text{prefix } \delta_1 \wedge \delta_2) \ ; \ \delta_2'$$

Fig. 2. Derived temporal predicates of $\mathcal{DZ}$

models the intended operational character of choice. In case that both ones can proceed at the same time, δ_{oracle}' defines that a fixed but arbitrary path δ_1' or δ_2' is taken; hence the choice does not introduce silent moves.

3 Concurrency

Concurrency can be characterized as a situation where distinguishable *activities* compete for the access to restricted *resources*. Such behavior is modeled in $\mathcal{DZ}$ without extending the language. We will illustrate this by the example of *shared variables* with *racing semantics*. With *racing* we denote the situation where two activities write to a shared variable at the same time; it is resolved in that only one write succeeds whereas the other is ignored. Racing already entails everything necessary to study the problem of concurrency in the framework of $\mathcal{DZ}$; more high-level concepts such as synchronous channels do not introduce additional problems.

In order to identify concurrent activities, we introduce the notion of a so-called *place*. A place is a "point in space" that identifies a concurrent activity. Places are represented in $\mathcal{DZ}$ by the given set place.

Shared variables are represented by a subset of dyn($[val : A; writers : \mathbf{P} \, place]$) (Figure 3). The field *val* represents the current value and the field *writers* the set of places writing to the shared variable. Every shared variable satisfies the constraint that there is never more then one writer and the value keeps persistent during writes. This invariant is defined by using dynamic set comprehension for the declaration of shared A.

The relation $x :=_p y$ models a write to a shared value x from place p with value y. A concurrent write operation is logically expressed as $\lceil x :=_p a \rceil \wedge \lceil x :=_p b \rceil$, with $p \neq q$, which is satisfied for those traces such that x has either the value a or the value b (provided that no other places then p and q do write).

$$SharedState[A] \triangleq [val : A; \; writers : \mathbb{P} \, place]$$
$$shared \; A == \{ \; x : \mathrm{dyn}(SharedState[A]) \; | \;$$
$$\lceil \#(x.writers) \le 1 \rceil \wedge$$
$$everywhere \; (\ell = 2 \Rightarrow \emptyset(x'.writers = \varnothing \Rightarrow x'.val = x.val) \}$$
$$\_ :=\_ \_[A] == \{ x : SharedState[A]; \; p : place; \; a : A \; | \;$$
$$\{p\} = x.writers \wedge x.val = a \vee \{p\} \ne x.writers \supset \varnothing \}$$

Fig. 3. Definition of Shared Variables in $\mathcal{D}Z$

Though we have defined what happens if a write action is performed, we have not described yet how unintended writes are *excluded*. Unwanted behavior has to be specified explicitly in an axiomatic framework – this is similar to plain Z where operation schemata have to include equalities such as $x' = x$ if x is supposed to keep its value. To model which places write or write not to a shared variable x, we use predicates such as $\lceil x.writers \cap ps = \varnothing \rceil$, where ps is a set of places that shall not write to x during a trace. The usage of such constraints will be tackled in more detail in the next Section.

4 Translating Statecharts to $\mathcal{D}Z$

Statecharts [5] are a graphical notation for hierarchical structured automatons, which have gained relative relevance in industrial applications. Statecharts and their semantics have been subject to a notably amount of research activities, leading to various syntactic and semantic variants (see [14]). Since the ESPRESS project aims at a tool environment which is centered around the Statemate tool [6], we consider the Statecharts semantics as implemented by Statemate and presented in [7]. Here, we are handling main statecharts' concepts as hierarchy, concurrency, and inter-level transitions whereas history connectors etc. are omitted.

4.1 Dealing with Inter-Level Transitions

The pathological problem when mapping Statecharts to some text-based language is to cope with the problem of inter-level transitions. These transitions cross several hierarchy levels, by leaving not only the direct source state but also enclosing super-states (a concept similar to exceptions), or by jumping directly into a sub-state of another state (a concept which has no direct counterpart in structured programming).

To cope with this problem, we normalize Statecharts prior to translation. The normalization cuts the transition at points where it crosses level-borders. At the cut-points, *connectors* are introduced, which are used to reconstruct inter-level transitions when composing states from their sub-states. This concept is similar to the *Unvollendete* introduced in [9]. Figure 4 shows an example. The transition labeled with G/A is partitioned into three sub-transitions, where the

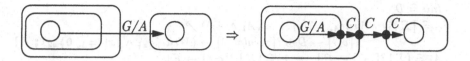

Fig. 4. Remove Inter-level Transitions

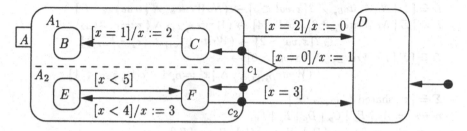

Fig. 5. Example Statechart

guard is assigned to the first transition. The connectors are all labeled with the same name C, which uniquely identifies them belonging to the same compound transition.

4.2 Outline of the Translation

Assuming the sketched normalization, we can treat the translation of states independent from their context. The basic strategy is illustrated by the Statechart in Figure 5, whose translation is given in Figure 6. Each state is represented by exactly one dynamic schema. Due to loops in the Statechart, the schema definitions are recursive. Nevertheless, the construction creates only tail-recursion, which can be replaced by terms build from the repeat operator. From the structure of the Statechart, additional declarations are induced. The schema Σ contains the data variables of the chart. In addition to the variable x, it declares event variables c_i which are used to realize the gluing of inter-level-transitions: whenever the first sub-transition of the cut of the transition is taken, the associated event c_i is generated; the remaining parts of the cut are guarded with the presence of this event, and will fire instantaneously until the target state is reached. Event variables themselves are represented as shared variables (Section 3) of a special type $trigger ::= \perp$ that has only one value ($\mathbb{E} ==$ shared $trigger$). $e?$ tests whether the event e is present ($e? \equiv e.writers \neq \varnothing$) and $e!_p$ emits it ($e!_p \equiv e :=_p \perp$), where p denotes a place.

In order to represent concurrent activities of the chart, the translation introduces for each state S that is a sub-state of an xor-state, a place S_p. Note that sub-states of an and-state (i.e. A_1, A_2) do not write variables and therefore do not need places. From the structure of the Statechart, we define the function $exclusive$, statically mapping each state-place to the set of state-places which definitively can not write when the given state is active, i.e. its neighboring states and their sub-states. This information can be used to derive whether and with whom racing can happen. The "schematic" schemata $NoWrite_p$ and

$Init \mathrel{\widehat{=}} D$

$A \mathrel{\widehat{=}} [\, \Sigma \mid (NoWrite_{A_p} \wedge ?\lceil c_1?\rceil \to (A_1 \wedge A_2)) \nearrow$

$\qquad\qquad ?\lceil c_2?\rceil \to D \oplus ?\lceil x.val = 2\rceil \to (Write_{p,\{x\}} \wedge \langle\!\langle x' :=_{A_p} 0\rangle\!\rangle_{=2})\,;\, D\,]$

$A_1 \mathrel{\widehat{=}} [\, \Sigma \mid ?\lceil c_2?\rceil \to C\,] \qquad A_2 \mathrel{\widehat{=}} [\, \Sigma \mid ?\lceil c_2?\rceil \to F\,]$

$B \mathrel{\widehat{=}} [\, \Sigma \mid NoWrite_{B_p}\,]$

$C \mathrel{\widehat{=}} [\, \Sigma \mid NoWrite_{C_p} \nearrow ?\lceil x.val = 1\rceil \to (Write_{C_p,\{x\}} \wedge \langle\!\langle x' :=_{C_p} 2\rangle\!\rangle_{=2})\,;\, B\,]$

$E \mathrel{\widehat{=}} [\, \Sigma \mid NoWrite_{E_p} \nearrow ?\lceil x.val < 5\rceil \to (NoWrite_{E_p} \wedge \langle\!\langle true\rangle\!\rangle_{=2}\,;\, F\,]$

$F \mathrel{\widehat{=}} [\, \Sigma \mid NoWrite_{F_p} \nearrow ?\lceil x.val < 4\rceil \to (Write_{F_p,\{x\}} \wedge \langle\!\langle x :=_{F_p} 3\rangle\!\rangle_{=2})\,;\, E$

$\qquad\qquad\qquad \oplus ?\lceil x.val = 2\rceil \to (Write_{C_p,\{c_2\}} \wedge \langle\!\langle c_2'!_{F_p}\rangle\!\rangle_{=2}))\,]$

$D \mathrel{\widehat{=}} [\, \Sigma \mid NoWrite_{D_p} \nearrow ?\lceil x.val = 0\rceil \to$

$\qquad\qquad\qquad (Write_{D_p,\{x,c_1\}} \wedge \langle\!\langle x' :=_{D_p} 1 \wedge c_1'!_{D_p}\rangle\!\rangle_{=2})\,;\, A\,]$

$\Sigma \mathrel{\widehat{=}} [\, x : \text{shared } \mathbb{Z};\ c_1, c_2 : \mathbb{E}\,]$

$place ::= A_p \mid B_p \mid C_p \mid D_p \mid E_p \mid F_p;$

$exclusive == \{A_p \mapsto \{D_p\}, B_p \mapsto \{C_p\}, C_p \mapsto \{B_p\},$

$\qquad\qquad D_p \mapsto \{A_p, B_p, C_p, E_p, F_p\}, E_p \mapsto \{F_p\}, F_p \mapsto \{E_p\}\}$

$NoWrite_p \mathrel{\widehat{=}} [\, \Sigma \mid (each\ v : \{x, c_1, c_2\} \bullet \lceil (\{p\} \cup exclusive\ p) \cap v.writers = \varnothing\rceil)\,]$

$Write_{p,vs} \mathrel{\widehat{=}} [\, \Sigma \mid NoWrite_p \,\widehat{}\, ((each\ v : \{x, c_1, c_2\} \setminus vs \bullet \lceil p \notin v.writers\rceil) \wedge$

$\qquad\qquad (each\ v : vs \bullet \lceil exclusive\ p \cap v.writers = \varnothing\rceil))_{=1}\,]$

Fig. 6. Naive Translation of the example Statechart

$Write_{p,vs}$ are used to model effects on variables during the activity of a state with place p. Besides resolving write conflicts, $Write$ and $NoWrite$ also prevent unintended writes.

The sketched translation is rather naive, since it does not perform any "optimizations" of the use of shared variables. Such an optimization can easily derive on base of the represented model, for which write operations racing is excluded, and can replace in such cases $x :=_p v$ by the predicate $x.val = v \wedge x.writers = \{p\}$. In the shown example, this could be done for the events and transition going from A to D and vice versa. More sophisticated techniques would base on theorem proving and take exclusive guards into consideration. A complete translation from Statemate Statecharts to $\mathcal{D}Z$ is out of scope of this paper. It can be found in an extended version.

5 Conclusion

Discussion and Related Work. We have presented $\mathcal{D}Z$, a framework which combines Z and discrete temporal interval logics for the formalization of properties as well as of behaviors of embedded systems. $\mathcal{D}Z$ is a moderate extension of Z, since it adds only a few new syntactic constructs, which can be explained as syntactic sugar for existing concepts of Z. As a consequence, we could relative easily extend the ESPRESS Z type checker, *ESZ*, to support $\mathcal{D}Z$[3]. Our integra-

---

[3] The *ESZ* type checker is downwards compatible to fUZZ, and will be become available in the middle of '97.

tion of Z with interval logics differs from similar approaches which base e.g. on the duration calculus [3,4], since we focus on a discrete time model, and support a tailored set of operators for the operational description of behavior, which is oriented towards notions of process algebras [8, e.g.]. We are currently restricted to external choice. By that, we can represent the semantics as a set of traces and avoid problems arising with silent moves. The restriction to a trace semantics also allows to mix "don't care" non-determinism as introduced by specification looseness and "don't know" non-determinism as a result of behavioral descriptions.

The Statechart translation yields a setting, where (theoretically) we can argue about propositions such as a Statechart implies a property given by a trace invariant. We hope that by extending an existing encoding of Z in a theorem prover such as Isabelle [10], it is possible to provide tool support for such propositions. Extending an encoding of Z to $\mathcal{D}Z$ should not be to hard, since $\mathcal{D}Z$ is a moderate extension of Z. However, developing the set of adequate theorems, to make such an encoding of $\mathcal{D}Z$ practical, will need a lot of further work.

As a side-effect, the translation of Statecharts provides a formalization of the semantics of Statecharts as found in the Statemate tool [7,6]. A main characteristic of this semantics is that actions that are performed in one step will not become visible before the next step, thereby avoiding the problem of global inconsistency. In contrast, the semantics presented e.g. in [12,9] allow transitions to immediately react upon emited events.

Future Work. $\mathcal{D}Z$ needs to be evaluated in case studies, which is currently done in the course of the ESPRESS project. These experiments shall give evidence about the applicability of discrete temporal interval logics for the specification of properties of embedded systems. We are currently studying an extension of $\mathcal{D}Z$ to the hybrid case, which bases on the model of phase transition systems. We need to further investigate if and how to represent internal choice; one possible direction is to adapt the notion of failure sets [8] to the framework of interval logics. Related is the problem of distinguishing "don't care" from "don't know" indeterminism, which probably needs to be done in the presence of internal choice. Last not least, we plan to extend the encoding of Z in Isabelle used in ESPRESS [10] to the case of $\mathcal{D}Z$, on the one hand to validate the model itself and to derive useful theorems, on the other hand to open possibilities for deduction based tool-support.

Acknowledgements. We would like to thank Frank Lattemann and Eckard Lehmann for the fruitful discussions on Z and interval logics, and Robert Geisler and Marcus Klar for the discussions about Z and Statecharts.

References

1. R. Büssow, R. Geisler, and M.Klar. Spezifikation eingebetteter Steuerungssysteme mit Z und Statecharts. In *Tagungsband zur 5. Fachtagung Entwurf komplexer Automatisierung ssysteme.* TU Braunschweig, 1997.

2. Robert Büssow, Heiko Dörr, Robert Geisler, Wolfgang Grieskamp, and Marcus Klar. μSZ – ein Ansatz zur systematischen Verbindung von Z und Statecharts. Technical Report TR 96-32, Technische Universität Berlin, 1996.

3. Z. Chaochen, C. A. R. Hoare, and A.P Ravn. A calculus of durations. *Information Processing Letters*, 40(5), 1991.

4. M. Engel. Specifying real-time systems with Z and the Duration Calculus. In J. Bowen and J. Hall, editors, *Z User Workshop, Cambridge 1994*, Workshops in Computing, pages 282–294. Springer-Verlag, Berlin, Heidelberg, New York, 1994.

5. David Harel. Statecharts: A visual formalism for complex systems. *Science of Computer Programming*, 8(3):231–274, June 1987.

6. David Harel, Hagi Lachover, Amnon Naamad, Amir Pnueli, Michal Politi, Rivi Sherman, Aharon Shtull-Trauring, and Mark Trakhtenbrot. Statemate: A working environment for the development of complex reactive systems. *IEEE Transactions on Software Engineering*, 16 No. 4, April 1990.

7. David Harel and Ammon Naamad. The statemate semantics of statecharts. Technical report, The Weizmann Institute of Science, October 1995.

8. C.A.R. Hoare. *Communicating Sequential Processes*. Prentice Hall, Eaglewood Cliffs, N.J., 1985.

9. C. Huizing, R. Gerth, and W. P. de Roever. Modelling statecharts behaviour in a fully abstract way. In *Proc. 13th CAAP*, volume 299 of *Lecture Notes in Computer Science*. Springer-Verlag, 1988.

10. Kolyang, Thomas Santen, and Burkhart Wolff. A structure preserving encoding of Z in Isabelle/HOL. In J. von Wright, J. Grundy, and J. Harrison, editors, *Theorem Proving in Higher-Order Logics*, number 1125 in Lecture Notes in Computer Science. Springer-Verlag, Berlin, Heidelberg, New York, 1996.

11. B. C. Moszkowski. *Reasoning about Digital Circuits*. PhD thesis, Stanford University, 1983. Tech. Report STAN-CS-83-970.

12. A. Pnueli and M. Shalev. What is in a step: On the semantics of statecharts. In Takayasu Ito and Albert R. Meyer, editors, *Theoretical Aspects of Computer Software*, pages 244–264, New York, September 1991. Springer-Verlag. Lecture Notes in Computer Science 526.

13. J. M. Spivey. *The Z Notation: A Reference Manual*. Prentice Hall International Series in Computer Science, 2nd edition, 1992.

14. Michael von der Beeck. A comparison of statecharts variants. In Langmaak, de Roever, and Vytopil, editors, *Formal Techniques in Real-Time and Fault-Tolerant Systems*, volume 863 of *Lecture Notes in Computer Science*, pages 128–148, 1994.

Rules for Trace Consistent Reasoning

R. Ramanujam

The Institute of Mathematical Sciences
C.I.T. campus
Madras 600 113
India

jam@imsc.ernet.in

ABSTRACT

Formulas of temporal logic which cannot distinguish between different inter-leavings of the same run are said to be *trace consistent*. So called partial-order methods can be applied for verification of such formulas, since checking such a property over an equivalence class of runs reduces to checking it for one repre-sentative.

In this paper, we present *inference rules* that typify this kind of reasoning. The rules lead us to a complete axiomatization of a linear time temporal logic, all formulas of which are trace consistent. The axiomatization is presented in a layered manner so that we can attempt to isolate the global reasoning required.

0 Introduction

In this paper, we study some aspects of *local reasoning* in the context of the Propositional Temporal Logic of Linear Time (PTL). Models for PTL are given by infinite runs (computations) of finite-state transition systems. For instance, the formula $\Box(p \supset \Diamond q)$ specifies the set of runs to be those such that every state along the run that satisfies the property p is eventually followed by a state that satisfies q. This has crucial implications for model checking, where we wish to check that every run of a given system satisfies a given formula: for a formula as above, we need to check every path issuing out of a node satisfying p and see if a node satisfying q is reachable. The use of next-time operators $\bigcirc$ in the formula can force this check along specific paths.

Such a view of PTL presents the models of formulas merely as finitely gener-ated infinite sequences. This hides the fact that the transition systems which generate these computations themselves often possess some structure, which could perhaps considerably cut down the paths to be checked. PTL is mainly used to reason about behaviours of distributed systems, and transition systems modelling distributed programs have the following structure:

- States of the system are given as tuples of *local* states. If there are n processes in the system, a global state is an n-tuple of local states.
- A typical transition of the system is of the form $(q_1, \ldots, q_n) \xrightarrow{a} (r_1, \ldots, r_n)$, where a is an action of the system. Suppose $\theta(a) \subseteq \{1, 2, \ldots, n\}$ is the set of processes (components) in the system that participate in the action a. It is then the case that for all $j \notin \theta(a)$, $q_j = r_j$.

In addition, if the processes communicate only via synchronization rather than message passing, the following additional property holds as well:

- If $(q_1, \ldots, q_n) \xrightarrow{a} (r_1, \ldots, r_n) \xrightarrow{b} (s_1, \ldots, s_n)$, and $\theta(a) \cap \theta(b) = \emptyset$, then there exists a global state $(t_1, \ldots, t_n)$ such that $(q_1, \ldots, q_n) \xrightarrow{b} (t_1, \ldots, t_n) \xrightarrow{a} (s_1, \ldots, s_n)$.

We can now use this structure to reason as follows: whenever we are checking a property *local* to a specific process i, we can 'skip' over transitions along any run in which i is not taking part. For instance, in the formula $\Box(p \supset \Diamond q)$, suppose that the propositions p and q refer only to the local variables of process 1. Now consider the parallel program (intuitively) given by the expression $(ac)^\omega \| (bc)^\omega$ whose behaviour is given as a pair of transition systems, $s_0 \xrightarrow{a} s_1 \xrightarrow{c} s_0$ and $t_0 \xrightarrow{b} t_1 \xrightarrow{c} t_0$. Assume that a is a local action of process 1, b that of 2 and c, a synchronization between them (perhaps the update of a shared variable). Clearly, there are infinitely many runs of the system starting at (s_0, t_0). Examples are runs on the words $(abc)^\omega$, $(bac)^\omega$, $(abcbac)^\omega$, $(abc)^{100}(bac)^{50}(abc)^\omega$ etc. However, the formula being considered cannot distinguish between all these runs, which are all different interleavings of the run on the word $(abc)^\omega$. Any of these runs satisfy this formula *iff* every one of these runs satisfy it. Thus checking the property on all runs reduces to checking it on any one of these runs.

Based on this observation, many *partial order methods* have been developed for speeding up verification of PTL formulas([V90], [KP92], [GW94]). In this approach, we define an equivalence relation on the set of runs so that to verify a property for an equivalence class of runs, it suffices to verify it for one run. However, this works only for those properties that are insensitive to interleavings, and it is only too easy to specify formulas in PTL which hold for some interleavings and not for others. For instance, in the system above, consider the formula $\Box(\lambda_c \supset \bigcirc \lambda_a)$, where the proposition λ_x denotes that the next transition of the run at that state is on action x. This singles out two runs, on the words $(abc)(abc)^\omega$ and $(bac)(abc)^\omega$, among the equivalence class of runs referred to. For such formulas, the methods suggested above for pruning the state space do not apply.

PTL formulas which cannot distinguish between different interleavings of the same run are called *equivalence robust* [P93], or *trace consistent*[T95]. Checking whether a given formula is trace consistent or not is decidable ([DGP95], [PWW96]), though of high complexity. In [R96c], we studied the alternative of considering stronger notions of satisfiability (and associated notions of validity) for PTL, where one asks whether there is an equivalence class of runs satisfying a formula, rather than a single such run. In this context, it is important to study trace consistent subsets of PTL, in which *every* formula, by choice, is trace consistent. When they can be identified syntactically as done with increasingly larger subsets in [T95], [T94] and [R96a], the structure of temporal connectives reflects the trace consistent reasoning involved. [TW97] presents an expressively complete logic where every formula is trace consistent.

While the papers mentioned above study trace consistency principally from the viewpoint of PTL satisfiability and model checking, in this paper, we take up the study from an *axiomatic* viewpoint. We believe that the insights gathered from deductive methods and model checking are both complementary and valuable. It has been argued that the major hopes for verification theory lie in combining deductive methods with model checking ([Ru96]). There is another motivation for the study of inference rules that involve trace consistent reasoning: they help us to isolate structurally those properties which we can reason about locally, componentwise in a distributed system, and those which must be analyzed globally. In this sense, this paper is a (modest) contribution to the theory of *compositional reasoning* about distributed systems.

For the study, we have chosen a simple model of distributed systems and a structurally straightforward subset of PTL, presented earlier in [R96a]. This choice of logical language and models has been so that we can focus on the issues peculiar to local reasoning which are already quite nontrivial. The global next-time modality is the major culprit in violation of trace consistency, and hence is replaced by a weaker, less global, next-time modality that preserves trace consistency. Otherwise, the logic is basically PTL for each agent and globally defined to be boolean combinations of located formulas : for instance $\alpha@i \wedge \beta@j$ (read α holds at i). The model is a distributed network consisting of a fixed finite number of sequential components that synchronize by performing common actions together. Each component is a finite state automaton, and when a common ("handshake") action is performed, it is a 'lock-step' transition involving several automata at once.

This is a simple set-up, but axiomatizing the valid formulas is already quite non-trivial. The reason for this is that we cannot simply have an axiom system for each agent, namely that for PTL, and globally use the propositional calculus. When a is a synchronization between 1 and 2, the formulas 'the next action of agent 1 is a', and 'a is henceforth never enabled for agent 2' are by themselves satisfiable, but their conjunction is not. Such synchronization can in fact be seen as a local liveness property : if agent 1 needs to synchronize with 2, eventually both do so. This requires an induction principle for the logic, quite distinct from that required for eventuality. (Note that this is a kind of fairness property we reason about *in* the logic, as opposed to those which we assume externally.)

Consider the standard induction rule of linear time temporal logic, which asserts that the eventuality modality steps through the successor modality. This rule is crucial for obtaining a complete axiomatization.

$$(Ind) \; \frac{\alpha \supset \bigcirc \alpha}{\alpha \supset \Box \alpha}$$

To verify that a property α holds at s henceforth, it suffices to show that it is an invariant (preserved by every transition) at any state reachable from s. Now, this is the sort of reasoning we need to do on the *global transition system* of the distributed program, and we may expect that a rule of the above form, where instead of α, we have a global invariant (maintained by global transitions) of the form $\bigwedge_k \alpha_k$ will do the job. However, the global $\bigcirc$ is crucially used in the premise above, and it is not as such available in trace consistent logics. This forms the central technical issue addressed in obtaining a complete axiomatization in this paper.

On the other hand, a 'local' version of the above rule, as given below, is sound, but too weak. The rule uses local premises, each saying that α_k is a local invariant, to conclude globally that their conjunction holds henceforth.

$$(Ind) \quad \frac{\vdash_k \alpha_k \supset \bigcirc \alpha_k}{(\bigwedge_k \alpha_k @k) \supset (\bigwedge_k \Box \alpha_k @k)}$$

Suppose we are at a global state $(s_1, \ldots, s_n)$ of a distributed program, and wish to assert that a property, say $\beta @i$ holds henceforth in Γ, the set of all global states of the program, reachable from this state. The formula $\bigwedge_k \alpha_k @k$ might well be an invariant in Γ, but applying the rule requires that $\alpha_k @k$ be a local invariant for each k. But this is too strong a requirement, since there may be local states satisfying $\alpha_k @k$ from which a transition to a local state satisfying $\neg \alpha_k @k$ may well be possible, except that they never form part of global states in Γ. Therefore, we go for a weaker premise, which involves a next-time modality less expressive than the global $\bigcirc$, but defines next-instants for groups of agents that synchronize.

$$(Ind) \quad \frac{(\bigwedge_k \alpha_k @k) \supset \bigwedge_{a \in \Sigma} [a] (\bigwedge_{i \in \theta(a)} \alpha_i @i)}{(\bigwedge_k \alpha_k @k) \supset (\bigwedge_k \Box \alpha_k @k)}$$

In fact, we will work with a logic where even such a restricted modality is not available globally, but we will get the same effect by an appropriately strengthened local next-state modality.

In [R96a], we have studied trace consistent logics with greater expressiveness than the one presented here, with present and past tense modalities. While we certainly need to study reasoning in these enriched logics, the basic difficulties in axiomatization are already present in the simpler logic studied here, so we content ourselves with it for this short presentation.

1 Preliminaries

We begin with the notion of a **distributed alphabet**. Fix a finite set of *locations* or *agents* $Loc = \{1, \ldots, n\}, n > 0$. A distributed alphabet is a tuple $\widetilde{\Sigma} = (\Sigma_1, \ldots, \Sigma_n)$, where each Σ_i is a finite nonempty set of *actions* of agent i. When an action a is in $\Sigma_i \cap \Sigma_j, i \neq j$, we think of it as a synchronization between i and j. Given a distributed alphabet $\widetilde{\Sigma}$, we often speak of the set

$\Sigma \stackrel{\text{def}}{=} \Sigma_1 \cup \ldots \cup \Sigma_n$ as the alphabet of the system. We also make implicit use of the associated function $\theta : \Sigma \to 2^{\{1,\ldots,n\}}$ defined by $\theta(a) \stackrel{\text{def}}{=} \{i \mid a \in \Sigma_i\}$. We will keep a fixed n and a fixed distributed alphabet for the discussion from now on.

The frames for our logics are networks of n transition systems over $\widetilde{\Sigma}$. As usual, a transition system over a finite nonempty alphabet Σ is a pair $T = (Q, \to)$, where Q is a **finite** set of states, $\to \subseteq Q \times \Sigma \times Q$ is the transition relation. We write $q \stackrel{a}{\to} q'$ to mean that $(q, a, q') \in \to$. A (finite or infinite) *run* from $q_0 \in Q$ is a sequence of transitions of the system: $q_0 \stackrel{a_0}{\to} q_1 \stackrel{a_1}{\to} \ldots$. Let R_T denote the set of runs of T.

Let $\widetilde{\Sigma} = (\Sigma_1, \ldots, \Sigma_n)$ be a distributed alphabet. A **system** over $\widetilde{\Sigma}$ is a tuple $\mathcal{T} = (T_1, \ldots, T_n)$, where $T_i = (Q_i, \to_i)$ is a transition system over Σ_i, for $i \in Loc$. The **product transition** relation of the system $\to \subseteq (Q_1 \times \ldots \times Q_n) \times \Sigma \times (Q_1 \times \ldots \times Q_n)$ is defined as usual : $(q_1, \ldots, q_n) \stackrel{a}{\to} (q'_1, \ldots, q'_n)$ iff $\forall i \in \theta(a) : q_i \stackrel{a}{\to}_i q'_i$, and $\forall j \notin \theta(a) : q_j = q'_j$. We can use the product transitions to define the *global runs* of $\mathcal{T}$, and the set of all global runs is denoted $R_{\mathcal{T}}$.

Given $\delta \in R_{\mathcal{T}}$, we can speak of the *i-projection* of δ, given by projecting down to the ith components of states and actions in Σ_i. (Essentially, erase all states not in Q_i, and all actions not in Σ_i.) It is easy to check that this gives us an element of R_{T_i}, and we will denote this by $\delta \lceil i$. Note that $\delta \lceil i$ can be finite even if δ is itself infinite.

We can now define an equivalence relation $\sim$ on runs of $\mathcal{T}$: $\delta \sim \delta'$ iff $\forall i, \delta \lceil i = \delta' \lceil i$. This equates different interleavings of the same run. We will denote the equivalence class of δ by $[\delta]$.

Below let δ be of the form $x_0 \stackrel{a_0}{\to} x_1 \stackrel{a_1}{\to} \ldots$ (finite or infinite). Similarly let $\delta' = y_0 \stackrel{b_0}{\to} y_1 \stackrel{b_1}{\to} \ldots$. By $\delta(0 \ldots m)$, we denote the initial segment $x_0 \stackrel{a_0}{\to} x_1 \stackrel{a_1}{\to} \ldots x_m$. We use the notation $x_m[j]$ to denote the jth component (local state) of the n-tuple in the mth instant.

We now define some special functions describing the views of agents at different points of global time and relating different agents' views.

The **local clock functions** $clock_{\delta,i}: \{0, 1, \ldots\} \to \{0, 1, \ldots\}$ are defined by: $clock_{\delta,i}(0) \stackrel{\text{def}}{=} 0$. $clock_{\delta,i}(k+1) \stackrel{\text{def}}{=} clock_{\delta,i}(k) + 1$, if $a_k \in \Sigma_i$, and $clock_{\delta,i}(k+1) \stackrel{\text{def}}{=} clock_{\delta,i}(k)$, otherwise. We will speak of global instants and i-local instants with the implicit assumption of their relationship as given by these functions.

Proposition 1.1 *Suppose $\delta \sim \delta'$. If $clock_{\delta,i}(k) = clock_{\delta',i}(l)$, then we have $\delta(0 \ldots k) \lceil i = \delta'(0 \ldots l) \lceil i$.*

Thus, at any local instant m for agent i, the set $\{\delta'(0 \ldots k) \mid \delta' \in [\delta], clock_{\delta',i}(k) = m\}$, represents the global i-view of the system.

While we have presented the programs here to be obtained by products of transition systems, the framework applies equally well to the class of n-variable programs introduced in [R96c]. We can think of each agent as managing a group of program variables, and a synchronization as an update of a shared variable. Further, we can weaken the product assumption to consider systems which are defined by global transitions that respect the forward diamond condition referred to in the previous section. However, we keep the more restricted presentation for the sake of uniformity with [R96a], where the logic was originally introduced.

2 The logics

2.1 The basic logic L_0

Let $P = (P_1, \ldots, P_n)$ be a tuple of countable sets of atomic propositions. We will speak of $p \in P_i$ as a proposition of agent i. We do not assume disjointness of P_i and P_j for distinct agents i and j, as there can be common meaningful propositions. ("Has terminated" is one such.) The **i-formulas** are defined as follows:

$$\Phi_i ::= p \in P_i \mid \neg \alpha \mid \alpha \vee \beta \mid \langle a \rangle \, \alpha, \; a \in \Sigma_i \mid \alpha \mathbf{U} \beta$$

The **global formulas** are defined from these using boolean combinations: (We use the convention that α, β etc denote local formulas, whereas ϕ, ϕ' etc are used for global formulas.)

$$L_0 ::= \alpha @ i, \; \alpha \in \Phi_i, \; i \in Loc \mid \neg \phi \mid \phi_1 \vee \phi_2$$

Note that there are no modalities at the global level, and that formulas in Φ_i cannot refer to any other agent j in the system. Further note that L_0 is parametrized by the distributed alphabet.

Typically linear time logics have an $\bigcirc$ modality rather than the action-indexed successor modality, as the successor state at any instant is unique in linear time models. Here, the main purpose of using $\langle a \rangle$ is to describe synchronizations. When we encounter a formula of the form $(\langle a \rangle \alpha) @ 1 \wedge (\langle a \rangle \beta) @ 2$, where $\{1, 2\} \subseteq \theta(a)$, we understand that there will be a future instant when $\alpha @ 1 \wedge \beta @ 2$ will hold.

A **frame** for the logic is a pair $F = (\mathcal{T}, \delta)$, where $\mathcal{T} = (T_1, \ldots, T_n)$ is a system over $\widetilde{\Sigma}$ and $\delta \in R_{\mathcal{T}}$ is an infinite run of system $\mathcal{T}$. A **model** is a pair $M = (F, V)$, where F is a frame, and $V = (V_1, \ldots, V_n), V_i : Q_i \to 2^{P_i}$ give the local valuations. Given a model M, we define its ith projection to be the tuple $M_i = ((T_i, \delta \lceil i), V_i)$.

We first define satisfaction of local formulas : $M_i, k \models_i \alpha$ denotes that the i-formula α is satisfied at (local) instant k for agent i. Below let $\delta \lceil i = q_0 \overset{a_0}{\to} q_1 \overset{a_1}{\to} \ldots$.

- $M_i, k \models_i p$ iff $p \in V_i(q_k)$.
- $M_i, k \models_i \neg \alpha$ iff $M_i, k \not\models_i \alpha$.
- $M_i, k \models_i \alpha \vee \beta$ iff $M_i, k \models_i \alpha$ or $M_i, k \models_i \beta$.
- $M_i, k \models_i \langle a \rangle \alpha$ iff q_{k+1} exists, $a_k = a$ and $M_i, k+1 \models_i \alpha$.
- $M_i, k \models_i \alpha \mathbf{U} \beta$ iff $\exists m$ such that $k \leq m, M_i, m \models_i \beta$ and for every $l : k \leq l < m : M_i, l \models_i \alpha$.

We now define the semantics of L_0 formulas. Since there are no global modalities, the formulas are not defined at every instant, but only at the initial state of the run.

- $M, 0 \models \alpha@i$ iff $M_i, 0 \models_i \alpha$.
- $M, 0 \models \neg\phi$ iff $M, 0 \not\models \phi$.
- $M, 0 \models \phi_1 \vee \phi_2$ iff $M, 0 \models \phi_1$ or $M, 0 \models \phi_2$.

As usual, we say that a formula ϕ is satisfiable if there exists a model M such that $M, 0 \models \phi$. A formula is valid if and only if its negation is not satisfiable.

2.2 The logic L_1

L_0 is a very simple logic, but expressively weak. Specifically, the fact that agents in the system *learn* about others' states on synchronization is not reflected in L_0-formulas. Indeed, the whole purpose of synchronizing is to exchange information, and hence we should be able to utilize this in reasoning. Below we propose an extension, where agents can "see" the local states of their partners in synchronization at the time they synchronize. Of course, this also means that they can see the other's future at that instant, and hence this gives a good deal of expressive power.

Formally, the logic L_1 is defined as follows:

$$\Psi_i ::= p \in P_i \mid \neg\alpha \mid \alpha \vee \beta \mid \langle a \rangle \phi, \ a \in \Sigma_i, \ AV(\phi) \subseteq \theta(a) \mid \alpha \mathbf{U} \beta$$

$$L_1 ::= \alpha@i, \ \alpha \in \Psi_i, \ i \in Loc \mid \neg\phi \mid \phi_1 \vee \phi_2$$

$AV(\phi)$, the *agent vocabulary* of ϕ, is the set of agents mentioned in ϕ, and is inductively defined in the obvious manner:

$$AV(\alpha@i) \stackrel{\text{def}}{=} \{i\}; \ AV(\neg\phi) \stackrel{\text{def}}{=} AV(\phi); \ AV(\phi_1 \vee \phi_2) \stackrel{\text{def}}{=} AV(\phi_1) \cup AV(\phi_2)$$

The semantics needs to be suitably changed. Below we give only those parts of the definition that require change. Fix a model $M = (F, V)$, where $F = (\mathcal{T}, \delta)$ and $\delta = x_0 \stackrel{a_0}{\to} x_1 \ldots$.

- $M_i, k \models_i \langle a \rangle \phi$ iff $\exists l: clock_i(l) = k, \ clock_i(l+1) = k+1, \ a_l = a$ and $M, l+1 \models \phi$.

Note that the expression $\exists l$ in the definition can be replaced by '$\exists$ a unique l'; this means that the formula $\langle a \rangle \phi$ implies its dual formula $[a]\phi$, as we would expect in linear time temporal logics.

- $M, k \models \alpha@i$ iff $M_i, clock_i(k) \models_i \alpha$.
- $M, k \models \neg\phi$ iff $M, k \not\models \phi$.
- $M, k \models \phi_1 \vee \phi_2$ iff $M, k \models \phi_1$ or $M, k \models \phi_2$.

In L_1, we not only have both local and global formulas in the syntax, but local formulas can refer to global formulas as well. Therefore, to avoid confusion, the reader is requested to note the following **Notational Conventions**: We will use α, β etc to refer to local formulas and ϕ, ϕ' etc denote global formulas. Let $a \in \Sigma_i$, and ϕ be a global formula. Then $\langle a \rangle \phi$ is an i-formula, and $(\langle a \rangle \phi)@i$ is a global formula, which we often abbreviate as $\langle a \rangle_i \phi$. We use $\bigcirc \phi$ to denote the i-formula $\bigvee_{a \in \Sigma_i} \langle a \rangle \phi$.

The i-formula $True_i$ is defined to be $p_0 \vee \neg p_0$, where p_0 is a fixed propositional letter in P_i. Now $True_i@i$ is a global formula. Let $a \in \Sigma$. The abbreviation $en_i(a)$ is used to denote the i-formula $\langle a \rangle (True_i@i)$. We further use the abbreviation $en_G(a)$ to denote the global formula $\bigwedge_{j \in \theta(a)} (en_j(a)@j)$. Note that $True_i@i$ is a valid formula, and that $en_i(a)$ asserts that the action a is enabled locally. The stronger assertion $en_G(a)$ says that a is enabled at the global state where it is asserted. We also define $dis_G(a) \stackrel{\text{def}}{=} \neg en_G(a)$, and $dis_i(a) \stackrel{\text{def}}{=} \neg en_i(a)$, to refer to disabled actions globally and locally.

Derived connectives and dual modalities $(\alpha \wedge \beta, \alpha \supset \beta, [a]\phi, \Diamond \alpha, \Box \alpha)$ are standard.

Note that global dependencies can be expressed nicely in this logic. For instance, suppose the distributed alphabet $\tilde{\Sigma}$ is such that $a \in \Sigma_1 \cap \Sigma_2, b \in \Sigma_2 \cap \Sigma_3$, $c \in \Sigma_3 \cap \Sigma_4$ and $p \in P_4$. Then a formula like $\langle a \rangle_1 \langle b \rangle_2 \langle c \rangle_3 p@4$ describes a sequence of dependent communications. In this manner one can 'walk down' the global run as in $TrPTL$ [T94]. The following propositions will be useful later on. The latter asserts that every formula of the logic L_1 is trace consistent.

Proposition 2.1 *Let $k \geq 0$ and $i \in \theta(a)$ such that $M, k \models (\langle a \rangle \phi)@i$. Let m be the least instant such that $m \geq k$ and $a_m = a$. Then $M, m + 1 \models \phi$.*

Proposition 2.2 *Consider models $M = (\mathcal{T}, \delta, V)$ and $M' = (\mathcal{T}, \delta', V)$, where $\delta \sim \delta' \in R_{\mathcal{T}}$. For any formula ϕ of L_1, $M, 0 \models \phi$ iff $M', 0 \models \phi$.*

3 Axiom system for L_1

We present the axiomatization only for the more expressive logic. The system is presented in a layered manner. We have one axiom system Ax_i for each agent i in the system, and in addition a global system Ax_g to reason about synchronization. We use the notation $\vdash_i \alpha$ to mean that the formula $\alpha \in \Psi_i$ is a theorem of system Ax_i. Similarly, $\vdash \phi$ means that ϕ is a theorem of the global system Ax_g. Both the systems use the theorems of each other recursively, and we refer to the combined system as AX.

Ax_i, **The axiom schemes for agent** i

($A0_i$) All the substitutional instances of the tautologies of PC

($A1_i$) $[a](\phi_1 \supset \phi_2) \supset ([a]\phi_1 \supset [a]\phi_2)$

($A2_i$) $en_i(a) \supset dis_i(b) \quad (a \neq b)$

($A3_i$) $\langle a \rangle \phi \supset [a]\phi$

($A4_i$) $\alpha \mathbf{U} \beta \equiv \beta \vee (\alpha \wedge \bigcirc(\alpha \mathbf{U}\beta)@i)$

Inference rules

$(MP_i)\ \dfrac{\alpha,\ \ \alpha \supset \beta}{\beta} \qquad (NG_i)\ \dfrac{\vdash \phi, AV(\phi) \subseteq \theta(a), a \in \Sigma_i}{[a]\phi}$

Before we proceed to present the global axiom system, some remarks are in order. As mentioned in Section 0, for eventuality, we need induction rules that step through the more expressive next-time modality in L_1. Moreover, when we are at a global state where agent i is waiting for a synchronization with agent j, eventually such a synchronization must occur, and this again necessitates a form of induction. Such rules add to the complexity of reasoning in the logic.

Ax_g, **Global axiom schemes**

($B0$) $(\neg \alpha)@i \equiv \neg \alpha @i$

($B1$) $(\alpha \vee \beta)@i \equiv (\alpha @i \vee \beta @i)$

($B2$) $\displaystyle\bigvee_{a \in \Sigma} en_G(a)$

($B3$) $en_G(a) \supset (([a]\phi)@i \supset \displaystyle\bigwedge_{j \in \theta(a)} ([a]\phi)@j) \quad a \in \Sigma_i$

Inference rules

$(MP)\ \dfrac{\alpha,\ \ \alpha \supset \beta}{\beta} \qquad (GG)\ \dfrac{\vdash_i \alpha}{\alpha @i}$

$(GM)\ \dfrac{\displaystyle\bigwedge_{i \in \theta(a)} \phi_i \supset \bigvee_{j \notin \theta(a)} \alpha_j @j}{\displaystyle\bigwedge_{i \in \theta(a)} (\langle a \rangle \phi_i)@i \supset \bigvee_{j \notin \theta(a)} \alpha_j @j}$

Below let ψ *be of the form* $\displaystyle\bigwedge_k \alpha_k @k$, *let* ψ_b *denote* $\displaystyle\bigwedge_{j \in \theta(b)} \alpha_j @j$.

$(Sy)\qquad \dfrac{\psi \supset dis_G(a) \quad a \in \Sigma_i}{\psi \wedge en_G(b) \supset ([b]\psi_b)@k \quad b \in \Sigma_k - \Sigma_i}{\psi \supset dis_i(a)@i}$

$(Ev)\qquad \dfrac{\psi \supset \alpha @i}{\psi \wedge en_G(b) \supset ([b]\psi_b)@k \quad b \in \Sigma}{\psi \supset (\Box \alpha)@i}$

Note that we do not have an analog of (A0) in Ax_g to derive tautologies, but "@-versions" of tautologies can be got as follows: for instance consider $p \supset \neg\neg p$, $p \in P_i$. This is a theorem of Ax_i, and hence by rule (GG), $(p \supset \neg\neg p)@i$ is derived. Now we use (B0) and (B1) to derive $(p@i \supset (\neg\neg p)@i)$. (B2) asserts that models are infinite runs of the system. (B3) says that at any global state when a is enabled (all the synchronizing agents being ready to perform a together), they must all agree on the global state resulting after the synchronization. The soundness of this axiom directly follows from Proposition 2.1.

The rule (GM) describes joint moves in the system. In particular, when an a-move is made, this leaves the states of agents outside $\theta(a)$ unchanged, and this is stated in (GM). This rule typifies the pattern of reasoning in a "true concurrency" based logic.

Note that the validity of premise $\psi \supset dis_G(a)$ in rule (Sy) *cannot* by itself give the conclusion $\psi \supset dis_i(a)@i$, despite such an appearance. The premise merely states that in all ψ-states, *some one* of the agents in $\theta(a)$ is unwilling to do an a, whereas the latter is an assertion that at ψ-states, the specific agent $i \in \theta(a)$ cannot decide on doing a, and hence implies that at ψ-states, no agent in $\theta(a)$ may commit to a as its next action. This does require the extra premise leading to an induction argument.

Theorem 3.1 *The combined system AX provides a sound and complete axiomatization of the valid formulas of L_1.*

The axioms are easily seen to be sound. Among the rules, checking that (Sy) preserves validity is worth remarking on. (Soundness of (Ev) follows similarly.) Assume ψ such that the premises of (Sy) are valid, but not the conclusion. Then there exists a model M based on a run $\delta = x_0 \overset{a_0}{\to} x_1 \overset{a_1}{\to} \ldots$ such that $M, 0 \models \psi \wedge en_i(a)@i$. By the semantics of the modality, there exists k such that $clock_i(k) = clock_i(0)$, $a_k = a$, and for all l such that $0 \leq l < k$, $a_l \notin \Sigma_i$. $M, k \models en_G(a)$.

Note that $M, 0 \models \psi$ and ψ is of the form $\bigwedge_j \alpha_j@j$. By the semantics of @-formulas, for every $j \notin \theta(a_0)$, $M, 1 \models \alpha_j@j$ as well. Now consider $j \in \theta(a_0)$. $M, 0 \models en_G(a_0)$ and by the validity of the premise, $M, 0 \models [a_0]\psi_{a_0}@j$. But then, by Proposition 2.1, $M, 1 \models \psi_{a_0}@j$ and hence $M, 1 \models \alpha_j@j$. Thus, we have shown that $M, 1 \models \psi$. Proceeding this way, we get $M, k \models \psi$, and by validity of premise, $M, k \models dis_G(a)$, contradicting the fact that $M, k \models en_G(a)$.

The crucial use of the enriched L_1 modality in the rules (Sy) and (Ev) should be noted. The formula $[b]\psi_b$ above is much stronger than the L_0 formula $\bigwedge_{j \in \theta(b)} ([b]\alpha_j)@j$. The latter form would also give a sound rule, but proves too weak to give completeness. With an infinitary version of the (Sy)-scheme, not in the sense of having infinitely many premises, but in parametrizing the rule by a number m (thus yielding one scheme for each m), we can obtain an axiomatization of L_0-valid formulas. Details can be found in [R96b].

4 Completeness

For technical convenience, assume that Ψ_i is enriched with $\bigcirc \alpha, \alpha \in \Psi_i$, where $\bigcirc \alpha$ is semantically equivalent to $\bigvee_{a \in \Sigma_i} \langle a \rangle \alpha@i$. Further assume that we have $en_i(a) \in \Psi_i$ for $a \in \Sigma_i$, and $en_G(a) \in L_1$, for $a \in \Sigma$, with $Voc(en_G(a)) = \theta(a)$.

We can define, for any L_1-formula ϕ and any $\alpha \in \Psi_i$, the sets of their subformulas $CL(\phi)$ and $CL_i(\alpha)$ by simultaneous induction in such a way that :

- $\phi \in CL(\phi)$ and $\alpha \in CL_i(\alpha)$.
- if $\alpha@i \in CL(\phi)$ then $\{\beta@i | \beta \in CL_i(\alpha)\} \subseteq CL(\phi)$.
- if $(\langle a \rangle \phi')@i \in CL(\phi)$ then $CL(\phi') \subseteq CL(\phi)$ and $\forall j \in \theta(a), en_j(a)@j \in CL(\phi)$.
- if $\langle a \rangle \phi' \in CL_i(\alpha)$ then $\{\langle a \rangle \beta@i, \beta | \beta@i \in CL(\phi')\} \subseteq CL_i(\alpha)$.
- if $\phi' \in CL(\phi)$ then $\neg\phi' \in CL(\phi)$; a similar condition holds for $CL_i(\alpha)$ and here $\neg\neg$ is treated as identity.
- if $\phi_1 \vee \phi_2 \in CL(\phi)$ then $\phi_1, \phi_2 \in CL(\phi)$.
- if $\beta_1 \vee \beta_2 \in CL_i(\alpha)$ then $\beta_1, \beta_2 \in CL_i(\alpha)$.
- if $\beta_1 \mathbf{U} \beta_2 \in CL_i(\alpha)$ then $\beta_1, \beta_2, \bigcirc(\beta_1 \mathbf{U} \beta_2) \in CL_i(\alpha)$.

It can be checked that $CL(\phi)$ is linear in the size of ϕ. Fix a formula $\phi_0 \in L_1$. We will refer to $CL(\phi_0)$ simply as CL. By CL_i, we refer to the union of sets $CL_i(\alpha)$, where $\alpha@i \in CL$. Let $X \subseteq CL$. By $X \lceil i$, we refer to the subset $\{\alpha \mid \alpha@i \in X\}$ of CL_i.

Call $A \subseteq CL_i$ an *i-atom* iff it is propositionally consistent, and satisfies the conditions :

- if both $en_i(a)$ and $en_i(b)$ are in A, then $a = b$.
- $\alpha \mathbf{U} \beta \in A$ iff ($\beta \in A$ or both α and $\bigcirc(\alpha \mathbf{U} \beta)$ are in A).

Call $X \subseteq CL$ an *atom* if and only if it is propositionally consistent, and:

- $en_G(a) \in X$ iff for every $i \in \theta(a)$, $en_i(a)@i \in X$.
- for every i, $X \lceil i$ is an i-atom.

Let AT denote the set of all atoms and AT_i denote the set of i-atoms.

For $X, Y \in AT$, define $X \overset{a}{\Rightarrow}' Y$ iff for every $i \in \theta(a)$, the following conditions hold : for every $\langle a \rangle \phi$ in CL_i, $(\langle a \rangle \phi)@i \in X$ iff $\phi \in Y$, and for every $\bigcirc \alpha$ in CL_i, $(\bigcirc \alpha)@i \in X$ iff $\alpha@i \in Y$, and for every $j \notin \theta(a)$, $X \lceil j = Y \lceil j$. This induces a relation on i-atoms: $A \overset{a}{\to}_i B$ iff there exist atoms X and Y such that $X \overset{a}{\Rightarrow}' Y, X \lceil i = A$ and $Y \lceil i = B$. We also say $a \in \Sigma$ is enabled at X if $en_G(a) \in X$.

Let $G \subseteq AT, \Rightarrow \subseteq \Rightarrow'$. Call the graph $(G, \Rightarrow)$ a *pseudo-model* for ϕ_0, if the following conditions hold :

1. There exists $X \in G$ such that $\phi_0 \in X$.
2. Every $X \in G$ has a successor in G.
3. Consider $X \in G$ and $a \in \Sigma$ such that $en_G(a) \in X$. Then there exists $Y \in G$ such that $X \overset{a}{\Rightarrow} Y$.
4. Consider $X \in G$ and $a \in \Sigma$ such that for some $i \in \theta(a)$, $en_i(a) \in X \lceil i$. Then there exists a sequence $X = X_0 \overset{b_0}{\Rightarrow} X_1 \ldots \overset{b_k}{\Rightarrow} X_k \overset{a}{\Rightarrow} Y$, $k \geq 0$.
5. Consider $X \in G$ such that for some i, $(\alpha \mathbf{U} \beta)@i \in X$. Then there exists a sequence $X = X_0 \overset{b_0}{\Rightarrow} X_1 \ldots \overset{b_k}{\Rightarrow} X_k$, $k \geq 0$ such that $\beta@i \in X_k$.

Lemma 4.1 *If ϕ_0 is AX-consistent, then there exists a pseudo-model for ϕ_0 in $(AT, \Rightarrow')$.*

Suppose the lemma holds. Then we can use the pesudo-model $(G, \Rightarrow)$ to construct an infinite atom-run $X_0 \overset{a_0}{\Rightarrow} X_1 \overset{a_1}{\Rightarrow} \ldots$ which has the following properties : $\phi_0 \in X_0$; whenever there exists $en_i(a) \in X_k \lceil i$ there exists an $l \geq k$ such that l is the next index after k with $a = a_l$; whenever there exists $(\alpha \mathbf{U} \beta)@i \in X_k$ there exists an $l \geq k$ such that $\beta@i \in X_l$ and for all $k \leq j < l$, $\alpha@i \in X_j$. Now consider $Q_i = \{X \lceil i | X \text{ occurs in the constructed infinite run}\}$. $Q_i \subseteq AT_i$. Consider the system defined by $\mathcal{T} \overset{\text{def}}{=} (T_1, \ldots, T_n)$, where $T_i = (Q_i, \rightarrow_i \cap (Q_i \times \Sigma_i \times Q_i))$. Clearly, $R_{\mathcal{T}}$ contains a run $\delta = Y_0 \overset{a_0}{\rightarrow} Y_1 \overset{a_1}{\rightarrow} \ldots$, where $Y_j = (X_j \lceil 1, \ldots, X_j \lceil n)$. Consider the model $M = ((\mathcal{T}, \delta), V)$, where for $A \in Q_i$, $V_i(A) \overset{\text{def}}{=} A \cap P_i$. We can then show by (double) induction that for every k and for every $\phi \in CL$, $M, k \models \phi$ if and only if $\phi \in X_k$. But then, since $\phi_0 \in X_0$, we get $M, 0 \models \phi_0$, and we have a model for the consistent formula ϕ_0 and completeness of AX is proved.

We now run through the proof of the lemma. Fix ϕ_0, a consistent formula. Consider $G \overset{\text{def}}{=} \{X \in AT | X \text{ is a maximal } AX\text{-consistent subset of } CL\}$.

For any finite set of formulas Z, $\overline{Z}$ denotes the conjunction of all formulas in Z. For $X \in G$, let X^i denote the conjunction of formulas in the i-atom $X \lceil i$. Clearly, because of rule (GG), X^i is a maximal Ax_i-consistent subset of CL_i. Further, for $X \in G$, let $\widehat{X}$ denote the conjunction $\bigwedge_k X^k@k$, and for $a \in \Sigma, X \in G$, let X^a denote $\bigwedge_{i \in \theta(a)} X^i@i$. We see, thanks to axioms (B0) and (B1) that $\vdash \overline{X} \equiv \widehat{X}$. For $X, Y \in G$ define $X \overset{a}{\Rightarrow} Y$ iff $\widehat{X} \wedge \bigwedge_{i \in \theta(a)} (\langle a \rangle Y^a)@i$ is consistent and for every $j \notin \theta(a), X \lceil j = Y \lceil j$. It is easy to check that every $X \in G$ is indeed an atom and that $\Rightarrow \subseteq \Rightarrow'$. The claim is that $H = (G, \Rightarrow)$ is a pseudo-model for ϕ_0.

The first two conditions for H being a pseudo-model for ϕ_0 are easily seen to be satisfied. ϕ_0 being a consistent formula and in CL, there exists a maximal consistent subset of CL containing ϕ_0. If we prove the third condition, the second one follows from global axiom (B2). Suppose there exists $X \in G$ and $a \in \Sigma$ such that a is enabled in X. Working within Ax_i, we can derive i-theorems of the form $\overline{X^i} \supset \langle a \rangle \widetilde{\Gamma_i}$, where Γ_i is a non-empty subset of G, and $\widetilde{\Gamma_i}$ denotes the disjunction of Y^a, $Y \in \Gamma_i$. We can then show that $\bigwedge_{i \in \theta(a)} (\langle a \rangle \widetilde{\Gamma_i})@i \wedge \bigwedge_{j \notin \theta(a)} X^j$ is consistent.

By rule (GM), we can show that there exists Y such that $\bigwedge_{i \in \theta(a)} Y^i@i \wedge \bigwedge_{j \notin \theta(a)} X^j$ is consistent. Now the union of i-formulas from Y, $i \in \theta(a)$, and j-formulas from X, $j \notin \theta(a)$ has been shown to be consistent and is a subset of CL. Hence there exists $Z \in G$ containing this subset, and by definition $X \overset{a}{\Rightarrow} Z$, as required.

To prove condition 4 above, suppose $X \in G$ and $en_i(a) \in X \lceil i$ for some i. Form the least subset of Γ of G such that $X \in \Gamma$, and if $X_1 \in \Gamma$ and there exists a path in $(G, \Rightarrow)$ from X_1 to some X_2 which involves no action in Σ_i, then $X_2 \in \Gamma$. If there exists $Z \in \Gamma$ such that a is enabled in Z, we are done. We claim that this is indeed the case, by showing a contradiction otherwise.

Define $\psi \stackrel{\text{def}}{=} \bigwedge_k Y_k@k$, where $Y_k = \bigvee_{Z \in \Gamma} Z^k$. By assumption and condition (3) for pseudo-models, for every $Z \in \Gamma$, we have $\vdash \overline{Z} \supset dis_G(a)$, and hence $\vdash \psi \supset dis_G(a)$. Suppose we can show that for each k and $b \in \Sigma_k - \Sigma_i$, the following formula is a theorem: $\vdash \psi \wedge en_G(b) \supset ([b]\psi_b)@k$. Then we get from rule (Sy) and the fact that $X \in \Gamma$ that $\overline{X} \supset dis_i(a)@i$, which contradicts the assumption that $en_i(a) \in X\lceil i$.

Now, suppose that the above formula is not a theorem for some k and b in $(\Sigma_k - \Sigma_i)$. Then $\psi \wedge en_G(b) \wedge (\langle b \rangle \neg \psi_b)@k$ is consistent. If $\tilde{\Gamma}$ denotes the disjunction of all atoms in Γ, we have $\vdash \tilde{\Gamma} \supset \psi$, and hence we find that for some $Z \in \Gamma, \overline{Z} \wedge en_G(b) \wedge (\langle b \rangle \neg \psi_b)@k$ is consistent. From this we can conclude that b is enabled in Z, and (using rule GM) that there is a b-successor of Z which is consistent with $\bigvee_{j \in \theta(b)} \neg Y_j@j$. But then this b-successor of Z must be an atom outside Γ. We thus have an atom Z' such that $Z \stackrel{b}{\Rightarrow} Z'$ where $Z' \notin \Gamma$. But then $Z \in \Gamma$, there is a (one-step) path from Z to Z' using $b \notin \Sigma_i$, and $Z' \notin \Gamma$, clearly contradicting the closure condition on Γ.

The proof that condition (5) holds is similar. This completes the proof of the lemma and establishes the completeness theorem for AX.

5 System Validity

The axiom system presented here is meant for establishing pure logical validities, in the sense that theorems are formulas valid in all runs of all systems. This is of theoretical interest, whereas in practice, we are more interested in **system validity** where we are concerned with formulas satisfied by all runs of a *given system*. We now show that the presented system AX is valid for system validity as well.

Let $\tilde{\Sigma} = (\Sigma_1, \ldots, \Sigma_n)$ be a distributed alphabet. By abuse of notation, we say a system over $\tilde{\Sigma}$ is a pair $S = (\mathcal{T}, V)$, where $\mathcal{T} = (T_1, \ldots, T_n)$, $T_i = (Q_i, \rightarrow_i)$ is a transition system over Σ_i, and $V = (V_1, \ldots, V_n)$, $V_i : Q_i \rightarrow 2^{P_i}$ give the local valuations. Let $R_{\mathcal{T}}$ denote the set of all infinite runs of $\mathcal{T}$. For an L_1 formula ϕ, we say $S \models \phi$ iff for every $\delta \in R_{\mathcal{T}}$, $M, 0 \models \phi$, where $M = (\mathcal{T}, \delta, V)$ is the associated model. Such a formula is said to be S-valid. For an i-formula α, we say $S \models_i \alpha$ iff $S \models \alpha@i$. Such an i-formula is said to be S_i-valid.

Theorem 5.1 *Let S be a given system. If α is a theorem of Ax_i, then $S \models_i \alpha$, and if ϕ is a theorem of Ax_g, we have $S \models \phi$.*

Fix a system S. It is easy that every axiom of Ax_i is S_i-valid, and every axiom of Ax_g is S-valid. To see that the inference rules of Ax_i preserve S_i-validity, first observe the following: let $\delta = x_0 \stackrel{a_0}{\rightarrow} x_1 \stackrel{a_1}{\rightarrow} \ldots$ be a run of S and M the associated model. Now, for any L_1 formula ϕ, and any $k \geq 0$, $M, k \models \phi$ iff $M', 0 \models \phi$, where M' is the model based on $\delta' = x_k \stackrel{a_k}{\rightarrow} x_{k+1} \stackrel{a_{k+1}}{\rightarrow} \ldots$. Now, consider rule NG_i

and assume that ϕ is S-valid, but that $[a]\phi$ is not S_i-valid. Let M be a model based on a run δ of S such that $M_i, 0 \models_i \langle a \rangle \neg \phi$. Let k be the first instant in δ such that $a_k = a$. Then, $M, k + 1 \models \neg \phi$. But then by the observation above, we can construct a run $\delta' = x_{k+1} \overset{a_{k+1}}{\to} \ldots$ such that the induced model $M', 0 \not\models \phi$. contradicting S-validity of ϕ, and we are done.

We now show that the rule GM preserves S-validity. For this first observe that if M is any model based on run $\delta = x_0 \overset{a_0}{\to} x_1 \ldots$ and $a \in \Sigma$ such that $M, 0 \models en_G(a)$, then there exists a run $\delta' = x_0 \overset{a}{\to} y_0 \overset{b_0}{\to} y_1 \ldots$ such that $\delta' \sim \delta$. This follows from the fact that we are considering product systems; if k is the earliest instant in δ such that $a_k = a$, then all the actions $a_j, j < k$ are 'independent' of a and hence can be 'commuted'. Now consider rule GM and suppose the premise is S-valid but the conclusion is not. Then there is a model M based on a run δ such that $M, 0 \models \bigwedge_{i \in \theta(a)} (\langle a \rangle \phi_i)@i \wedge \bigwedge_{j \notin \theta(a)} \neg \alpha_j @j$. Note that $M, 0 \models en_G(a)$, and by the observation above, we can consider the model M' based on the equivalent run δ'. By proposition 2.2 (trace consistency) the formula above is satisfied at instant 0 in M'. But then $M', 1 \models \bigwedge_{i \in \theta(a)} \phi_i \wedge \bigwedge_{j \notin \theta(a)} \neg \alpha_j @j$. We now consider the model M'' based on the run δ' but starting at 1, and this violates the S-validity of the premise, and we are done.

The other rules are proved to preserve S-validity in a similar fashion. Thus, the presented system is sound for S-validity. It is clear that as yet it is not complete for S-validity (since we need to add system dependent axioms capturing the given transition structure). Obtaining such a complete system poses an interesting question for future study.

Acknowledgement: I thank the anonymous referees for most helpful comments. Section 5 was added thanks to a referee's suggestion.

References

[DGP95] Diekert, V., Gastin, P. and Petit, A., "Rational and recognizable complex trace languages", *Information and Computation*, vol 116, #1, 1995, 134-153.

[GW94] Godefroid, P. and Wolper, P., "A partial approach to model checking", *Information and Computation*, vol 110, 1994, 305-326.

[KP92] Katz, S. and Peled, D., "Interleaving set temporal logic", *TCS*, vol. 73, #3, 1992, 21-43.

[P93] Peled, D., "All from one and one from all: on model checking using representatives", Proc. CAV, *LNCS 697*, 1993, 409-423..

[PWW96] Peled, D., Wilke, T. and Wolper, P., "An algorithmic approach to proving closure properties of ω-regular languages", Proc. CONCUR, *LNCS 1119*, 1996.

[R96a] Ramanujam, R., "Locally linear time temporal logic", *Proc. IEEE LICS*, 1996, 118-127.

[R96b] Ramanujam, R., "Axiomatization of a partial order based temporal logic", *Bericht Nr 9605*, Christian-Albrechts Universität Kiel, June 1996.

[R96c]   Ramanujam, R., "Trace consistency and inevitability", Proc. FST and TCS, *LNCS 1180*, 1996, 250-261.

[Ru96]   Rushby, J., "Mechanized formal methods: progress and prospects", Proc. FST and TCS, *LNCS 1180*, 1996, 43-51.

[T94]   Thiagarajan, P.S., "A trace based extension of propositional linear time temporal logic", *Proc. IEEE LICS*, 1994, 438-447.

[T95]   Thiagarajan, P.S., "A trace consistent subset of PTL", Proc. CONCUR, *LNCS 962*, 1995, 438-452.

[TW97]   Thiagarajan, P.S. and Walukiewicz, I., "An expressively complete linear time temporal logic for Mazurkiewicz traces", *Proc. IEEE LICS*, 1997.

[V90]   Valmari, A., "A stubborn attack on state explosion", Proc. CAV, *LNCS 531*, 1990, 156-165.

Sensitivity Analysis of Real-Time Task Sets

Sasikumar Punnekkat, Rob Davis and Alan Burns

Real-Time Systems Research Group
Department of Computer Science
University of York, UK
E-mail : {sasi,robd,burns}@cs.york.ac.uk

Abstract. Though schedulability analysis has matured to the point where it is now possible to analyse realistic systems, there is still a lack of flexibility as far as the designer is concerned. Feasibility tests often provide little or no indication of the changes in task timing characteristics required to achieve a feasible system, nor any indication of the extent to which the worst case execution times of tasks may be increased without causing deadlines to be missed (in the case of a feasible system). In practice, however, it is useful to know how sensitive system feasibility is to changes in task timing characteristics. We give a general approach to the sensitivity analysis of task sets, which aids system developers in incorporating changes to the system whilst ensuring that the schedulability guarantees remain intact.

1 Introduction

Typically, in the initial design of a real-time system, the application is decomposed into a set of tasks and resources which are assigned execution time budgets. During subsequent development, progressively more accurate estimates, measurements and analysis of worst case execution times(WCETs) become available. However, it is often the case that WCETs exceed the initial budgets, leading to an unschedulable system. Similarly, with an operational system, it may be necessary to add enhancements which cause the WCETs of certain tasks to increase or new tasks to be added. In both cases, the system developer has to determine if optimisation is needed and to focus effort on those tasks/resources where it will have the most benefit in terms of obtaining a schedulable system. Given the large cost of optimising code, both in the initial effort required, and in the inevitable loss of clarity and hence increased maintenance effort, it is important that unnecessary/arbitrary optimisation is avoided. This can be achieved by performing sensitivity analysis on task timing characteristics.

In systems which employ fixed priority preemptive scheduling, the designer not only has the basic responsibility to guarantee at design time that all the tasks will meet their corresponding deadlines, but also has to ensure the same during the entire period of evolution of the system. In other words, the designer has to ensure the robustness of schedulability guarantees. In this domain, by sensitivity analysis we refer to the study of the permissible changes to task or resource timing characteristics which lead to a schedulable system. This information is of great importance for the system designer, in locating and analysing the bottlenecks in the system related to schedulability and to incorporate necessary modifications or performance tuning.

2 Computational Model

The computational model assumed in this paper does not impose any restrictions on the priority assignment algorithm used. This could be Rate Monotonic, Deadline Monotonic or any other priority assignment algorithm. We assume that each task is assigned a unique priority and that a task can be immediately preempted by a higher priority task. At run time, the highest priority task from the set of runnable tasks is allocated processor time. We assume a set of n tasks, $(\tau_1, \tau_2, .., \tau_n)$ in which tasks are ordered according to the assigned priorities, where 1 denotes the highest priority and n denotes the lowest priority. Each task τ_i is assumed to have a minimum inter-arrival time T_i, worst case execution time (WCET) C_i and deadline D_i. Thus tasks arrival may be either periodic or sporadic. We assume that $D_i \leq T_i$ for $i = 1, 2, \ldots, n$. Each task τ_i may be blocked by lower priority tasks for at most B_i units of time as a result of the operation of the Priority Ceiling Protocol [7] (or a similar protocol). We use $hp(i)$ to denote the set of tasks with higher priorities than i, (viz., $\tau_1, \tau_2, .., \tau_{i-1}$). The feasibility of such a task set under a no-failure hypothesis can be evaluated using the response time analysis presented in [1]. Here the response time R_i of a task τ_i is expressed as the sum of its WCET C_i, worst case blocking B_i and interference I_i due to preemption by higher priority tasks. If we can find $R_i \epsilon [0, D_i)$, which satisfies the equation,

$$i.e., \quad R_i = C_i + B_i + \sum_{j \epsilon hp(i)} \left\lceil \frac{R_i}{T_j} \right\rceil C_j \tag{1}$$

then task τ_i is feasible. The smallest value of R_i which satisfies the above equation is the worst case response time of task τ_i. Solutions to above equation can be obtained using the following recurrence relation,

$$r_i^{n+1} = C_i + B_i + \sum_{j \epsilon hp(i)} \left\lceil \frac{r_i^n}{T_j} \right\rceil C_j \tag{2}$$

Iteration starts with $r_i^0 = C_i$. When $r_i^{n+1} = r_i^n$ we have found a minimum solution, that is R_i. If $r_i^{n+1} > D_i$, then task τ_i is infeasible, and hence iteration is terminated. Note that the highest priority task does not suffer from interference and the lowest priority task does not suffer any blocking.

We now discuss the models and analysis of the effects of perturbations in timing characteristics of real-time task sets which follow the above computational model.

3 Metrics and Models for Sensitivity Analysis

Since deadlines are a most important factor in real-time systems, it is natural to think of a measure related to deadlines and task response times for the purpose of sensitivity analysis. How about $D_i - R_i$, which is the maximum possible increase in the response time that task τ_i can afford, without sacrificing schedulability? Consider the following task set given in table 1. This task set is schedulable as per the computation time values given in column headed 'C'. Also we can see (from column headed 'D-R') that the response times of tasks τ_1, τ_2 and τ_3 can be increased by 10, 5 and 10 units respectively, before they become unschedulable. Now we make a very small modification in the task computation times as shown in column 'C^{new}'. Here we have increased the computation time of τ_1 by just 1 unit. But it can be seen that the response time of τ_2 increases by 3 units and that τ_3 becomes now unschedulable.

Task set							
P	T	C	D	R	D-R	C^{new}	R^{new}
1	20	10	20	10	10	11	11
2	50	15	50	45	5	15	48
3	100	10	100	90	10	100	UnS

Table 1. Non-linearity of Task Response Times

As this example shows, the task response times are not a linear function of their respective computation times. This is due to the complex way in which a task response time is related to tasks of higher priorities, their periods and computation times. This non-linearity of tasks means that a minor change in timing characteristics of even a single task could lead to a much bigger impact in the response times of some lower priority tasks. Hence $D_i - R_i$ is not a good metric for sensitivity analysis. Better choices for sensitivity analysis of fixed priority systems include the maximum permissible increase in the WCETs of tasks and resources (this value will be negative in the case of an unschedulable task), and the maximum permissible decrease in task periods and deadlines. As periods and deadlines are related to the environment and are usually fixed by the system requirements, we do not intent to perform sensitivity analysis on them. We focus mainly on metrics related to WCETs, since WCETs are implementation dependent and are amenable to changes. We will also show how sensitivity analysis can be applied to obtain maximum failure rates.

Common sensitivity metrics include [9]:

1. The maximum permissible change/percentage change in the WCET of a single task/resource which still results in a schedulable system.
2. The largest factor by which the WCET of each task in a group may be scaled and still result in a schedulable system.

3. The largest factor by which the WCET of every task and resource may be scaled and still result in a schedulable system.

4. The maximum permissible change/percentage change in the WCET of a module contained in one or more tasks and/or resources.

Lehoczky et al [5] have defined the *critical scaling factor* Δ^* as the largest possible scaling factor for task computation times, above which some task will miss its deadline at critical instant phasing, whereas the task set remains schedulable for all $\Delta \leq \Delta^*$. The utilization corresponding to Δ^* is called the *breakdown utilization* U^*. The threshold value of critical scaling factor under Rate Monotonic analysis is given by

$$\Delta^* = [\max_{1 \leq i \leq n} \min_{t \in S_i} \sum_{j=1}^{i} C_j \frac{\left\lceil \frac{t}{T_j} \right\rceil}{t}]^{-1}$$

where $S_i = \{k.T_j | j = 1, .., i; k = 1, .., \lfloor \frac{T_i}{T_j} \rfloor\}$ represent the scheduling points for task τ_i, the deadline of τ_i and the arrival times of tasks of priorities higher than i before the deadline of τ_i assuming a critical instant phasing. The difference between the task set utilization and its breakdown utilization can be used as a primary measure for the available room for increase in task computation time estimates.

Katcher et al [3] have used the above concept of breakdown utilization for evaluating and comparing different scheduling implementations. They use the term α (equivalent to the *critical scaling factor* Δ^*) to indicate the value such that when C for all tasks is replaced by αC, the task set is just schedulable. In other words, $\sum_{i=1}^{n} \frac{\alpha C_i}{T_i} = U^*$. However, there is no proper discussion on either α or methods for its calculation, since the main focus of their paper is not sensitivity analysis. Also the analytical results in this paper address only case where D=T.

Klein et al [4] have addressed one aspect of this problem under 'Technique 8: Calculating Growth by Increasing Resource Usage of All Events'. Here they first calculate the scaling factor for the lowest priority event by looking at each of the scheduling points in the interval $(R_n, D_n]$, computing an approximation to the scaling factor and testing schedulability after scaling the task computation times by that factor. This procedure is then repeated successively upwards till the highest priority event and the minimum among all the scale factors thus obtained gives the desired scaling factor applicable for the whole system. The procedure outlined in [4] does not include any formal reasoning or proof. Though it is mentioned that the procedure can be extended to the case of arbitrary deadlines, it seems to be highly cumbersome. Also it works under the assumption of rate monotonic priority assignment. This method could not be applied to task sets which are not schedulable, since it aims at obtaining the possible growth only, by assuming the starting value of scaling factors as 1. Moreover it is not very versatile, as it can provide only a single scaling factor applicable to all task computation times and blocking times.

Analysis given by Vestal in [9] allows the above mentioned four metrics to be calculated for systems where task deadlines are equal to their periods and blocking times are a linear combination of resource access times. The basic idea used here is to extend the exact characterization of the critical instant suggested by Lehoczky [5] by introducing a slack variable into each of the inequalities, in order to convert them to equalities and then solve the resulting equalities to obtain the value of this slack variable. These values of slack variable thus obtained could be used to derive upper bounds of the computation times of tasks. In the case of tasks composed of several modules, the computation time C_i is replaced with a linear combination of the computation times of individual modules and the analysis is extended to obtain the upper bounds for computation times of individual modules. Similar analysis is performed for deriving the upper bound for task delays due to blocking where the blocking times could be represented as a linear combination of computation times of modules. The calculation of a critical scaling factor Δ^* is also described.

Unfortunately, the above analysis [9] does not apply when task deadlines are greater than their periods. Also this method cannot be applied when blocking is a non-linear function of the individual computation times of critical sections, as is the case under the Priority Ceiling Protocol or Immediate Priority Ceiling Protocol. If K is the number of critical sections, $CS(k)$ is the worst-case computation time required for executing the k-th critical section and $usage(k, i)$ is a binary function defined by,

$$
usage(k, i) = \begin{cases} 1 & \text{if } k \text{ is used by at least one task with priority greater than or} \\ & \text{equal to } i, \text{ and at least one task with priority less than } i \\ 0 & \text{otherwise} \end{cases}
$$

Then the maximum blocking is given by,

$$
B_i = \max_{k=1}^{K}(usage(k, i)CS(k))
$$

which is not a linear function and hence an alternative approach is required.

Since using the worst case execution times for all tasks will lead to a rather pessimistic schedulability analysis, Yeraballi et al [10] advocate the use of average tasks' execution times obtained by statistical estimation techniques in conjunction with a knowledge of maximum permissible variance that can be tolerated. They provide a detailed procedure for finding the minimum common scale factor sf (equivalent to the critical scale factor Δ^*) by which the individual task execution times can be multiplied without affecting the schedulability of a schedulable task set. This procedure is based on utilizing the idle time at each priority level. The individual scale factors for each task found by this procedure assume that all higher priority tasks are also scaled using that factor. These individual scale factors seems to be of not much practical importance since all the higher priority tasks are scaled as well by this scale factor, hence it may be less than the maximum possible factor for that particular task individually. Also the procedure does not care about the schedulability of lower priority tasks. This paper discusses only the case where deadlines are less than or equal to periods. Blocking delays are not explicitly considered in their analysis.

4 An Improved Approach

Each of the sensitivity metrics described previously can be obtained by combining a binary search (branch and bound) with a slightly modified version of the response time schedulability test given in [1] [8].

For example, to find the maximum permissible change in the WCET of a single task τ_i, when all other task and resource WCETs remain the same, we proceed as follows: let M_i represent the maximum permissible execution time of task τ_i, which we seek using a binary search. The initial high and low bounds for M_i are D_i (as M_i cannot exceed the deadline of τ_i) and 0 respectively. The value of M_i chosen by the binary search is then substituted for the WCET, C_i, of task τ_i in the schedulability equations. Using this modified value, the response time test then determines if every task in the system is schedulable and thus whether the binary search should select a larger or smaller value of M_i to try next. The search continues until the largest value of M_i commensurate with a schedulable system is determined. The maximum permissible change in the WCET of τ_i is then simply M_i - C_i. Note, if $M_i = 0$, it means that the original task set is unschedulable and that removing task τ_i may still not be sufficient to obtain a schedulable system.

Similarly, to find the largest factor, Δ, by which the WCET of every task in a group may be scaled, we substitute ΔC_i for C_i in the schedulability equations for each task τ_i in the group. Δ is then varied using a binary search between 0 and $\max_{\forall \tau_i \in group} \frac{T_i}{C_i}$ (as the system cannot be schedulable with a utilisation > 1). Another upper bound for Δ is $\min_{\forall \tau_i \in group} \frac{D_i}{C_i}$ (as any higher value of Δ will result in at least the task with minimum value of $\frac{D_i}{C_i}$ to miss its deadline. So a combined upper bound of $\min(\max_{\forall \tau_i \in group} \frac{T_i}{C_i}, \min_{\forall \tau_i \in group} \frac{D_i}{C_i})$ will be ideal and will reduce the number of iterations needed for the binary search. The search is continued until the largest value of Δ commensurate with a schedulable system is found. Δ is then the largest value by which the WCET of every task in the group can be scaled and the system still be schedulable. Stated otherwise, the WCET of every task τ_i in the group may be simultaneously changed to ΔC_i and the system still be schedulable. Here one point to be noted is that since we are performing a binary search to find a real number, an appropriate criterion must be given to ensure that the algorithm terminates. This can be specified according to the required precision of Δ. In our examples we have calculated Δ with precision up to 4 decimal places.

Sensitivity analysis can be applied to resource WCETs in a similar manner, however, care must be taken to re-evaluate blocking times whenever the execution time of a resource is changed by the binary search. Finally, sensitivity analysis can be applied at the module level, where each task/resource comprises one or more modules and task/resource WCETs are a linear combination of module WCETs. In this case, the WCETs of the tasks and resources which are dependent on the module WCET being varied, must be re-evaluated along with blocking times before applying the response time schedulability test.

4.1 Example

In this section, we give an example of the output from a simple sensitivity analysis tool developed to incorporate the improved approach. A more extensive and realistic example is given in [6].

					Task set		
P	T	C	D	R	Max_et	%change	UnS
1	100	30	100	30	50	66.66%	4
2	175	35	175	65	65	85.71%	4
3	200	25	200	90	55	120%	4
4	300	30	300	150	90	200%	4

Table 2. Sensitivity Analysis (Under no faults assumption)

In Table 2, the column headed 'Max_et' gives the maximum permissible execution time for each task, given that all other task WCETs remain the same (i.e. at the value specified in the WCET column). The maximum permissible percentage change in a single task's WCET is given in the column headed '%Change'. Finally, the column headed 'UnS' gives the highest priority unschedulable task if Max_et is exceeded infinitesimally.

From the tabulated values (%Change and UnS), it is clear that task 1 is most critical to system schedulability, whilst task 4 is the least critical. With this task set the overall Δ^* is calculated as 1.253.

5 The Case of Unschedulable Task Sets

So far we have confined our analysis to cases where the original task set is schedulable. Now we examine a complimentary aspect of this problem, viz., is it relevant to perform a sensitivity analysis on a task set which is originally unschedulable? One motivation for performing sensitivity analysis of unschedulable task sets is to direct the optimisation efforts to critical tasks so that with the minimum effort the task set could be made schedulable. For this purpose we need to perform some sort of sensitivity analysis on a per-task basis. The nature of this analysis will be to scale down the computation times of individual tasks to arrive at the point where the task set becomes schedulable. Here the procedure for finding individual scaling factors may be quite different from the procedure adopted in the case of schedulable task sets. This is due to the fact that the task set need not become schedulable even if we reduce the computation time of a single task to 0! So this procedure will be applicable only in the case of task sets which are marginally unschedulable. If we find that by scaling down a single task does not result in schedulability, then we have to make the dual decisions of which tasks and by how much should they be scaled down.

Another motivating factor would be to assist in suggesting modifications in the speed and architecture of the target processor in order to make the task set schedulable. For this purpose we need to scale down all the task computation times simultaneously. Our definition of *degree of schedulability*, Δ^* as *the highest value such that when C for all tasks is replaced by Δ^*C, the task set is schedulable* remains unchanged in this case. But it should be noted that the value of Δ^* is less than one since the original task set is not schedulable.

In the case of originally unschedulable task sets, the binary search is performed with initial lower bound of Δ as 0 and the upper bound as 1. We continue the search till we arrive at the value of Δ above which the task set is just unschedulable. The original task set needs to be scaled down at least by such a Δ^*, in order to make it schedulable. In other words, $\frac{1}{\Delta^*}$ gives the minimum required scale factor for the processor speed to make the task set schedulable.

It should be noted that, the same procedure will be able to find the scale factor irrespective of whether original task set is schedulable or not, if we set the lower bound of Δ for binary search as 0 and the upper bound as $\min(\max_{\forall \tau_i \epsilon group} \frac{T_i}{C_i}, \min_{\forall \tau_i \epsilon group} \frac{D_i}{C_i})$. But our software tackles the problem with appropriate bounds separately depending on the schedulability of the original task set, in order to reduce the number of iterations required for the binary search.

We illustrate the scaling down procedure by an example task set given in table 3. The utilization of this task set is 1.14762 and tasks τ_2 and τ_3 are not schedulable. Our sensitivity analysis points out that by scaling down each of the task computation times to 78.86% of its original value, we can make the task set schedulable. The utilization of the scaled-down task set is only 0.905. Alternatively we can use a 1.268 times faster processor to achieve schedulability.

Task Set							
P	T	C	D	R	ΔC	R^{New}	%change
1	10000	6000	10000	6000	4732	4732	-21.1333%
2	15000	5000	15000	UnS	3944	8676	-21.12%
3	35000	7500	28000	UnS	5915	27999	-21.1333%
Δ^*=0.78863							

Table 3. Scaling Down of Unschedulable Task Sets

One minor point is worth noting here. It is obvious that the computation time of τ_3 could be increased to 5916 and the task set still will be able to meet all its deadlines. The reason why our procedure cannot achieve this precision is that, we are scaling all the task computation times by the same factor.

6 Sensitivity Analysis Under Faults

Burns et al [2] provided recurrence relations for feasibility analysis of tasks under different fault assumptions and fault recovery strategies. We can combine these feasibility tests with the sensitivity analysis outlined above, thus enabling the highest fault rate commensurate with a system remaining schedulable to be determined. Though the sensitivity analysis method described above works with task deadlines greater than periods, the FT-sensitivity analysis given below is restricted to deadlines less than or equal to periods. A prototype tool has been developed for evaluating the feasibility of task sets under a given failure hypothesis. This tool provides the system designer with the following information,

- Whether the task set is feasible, given a stated inter-arrival time between faults
  - if feasible, the margins as given in the above sensitivity analysis
  - if not feasible, which tasks are unschedulable
- The worst-case fault arrival rate which can be tolerated by the system assuming no change in execution times.

Assuming a given fault tolerance/checkpoint strategy, sensitivity analysis can be used to determine the worst-case fault rate which can be tolerated by the system. This is achieved via a binary search on the probable range of values of T_F. The starting values for the search are $Max_{\forall j}(C_j)$ (as faults at this rate or higher will continually disrupt attempts to recover the task) and $Max_{\forall j}(D_j)$ (since any larger value will imply only one fault within the maximum response time of any task). If the system is not feasible with $T_F = Max_{\forall j}(D_j)$, then it will not be feasible with faults occurring at any rate. While $T_F > T_i \forall i$, then the above approach is exact. Otherwise, faults may not affect the task with the maximum execution time - out of $hp(i) \cup i$ and hence the test will be sufficient but not necessary.

The FT-Sensitivity calculations are illustrated in table 4 using the same task set as in previous tables. For a given value of inter-fault arrival time ($T_F = 300$ in this case), our prototype tool analyses whether the task set is schedulable or not. The maximum percentage change possible in task execution times under this failure rate is also calculated. It can be seen that the %change values in table 4 are considerably lower than those obtained under non-fault tolerant case given in table 2. The worst-case fault arrival interval that can be tolerated is also evaluated.

Our analysis also enables the trade-off between fault arrival rate and the maximum permissible change in task execution times to be investigated. Fig.6 illustrates this using the same task set as given in table 4. These plots show the possible changes in the worst-case execution time of each tasks against different permissible values of interarrival time between faults. In case of our example the X-axis values begin with 275, since the task set is unschedulable below this value. The maximum X-axis value shown in the graph is 300, which is equal to $Max_{\forall j}(D_j)$, since the maximum permissible change in the WCET of any task

Task set							
P	T	C	D	R	Max_et	%change	UnS
1	100	30	100	60	37	23.33%	4
2	175	35	175	100	43	22.85%	4
3	200	25	200	155	36	44%	4
4	300	30	300	275	45	50%	4

Worst-case fault arrival interval tolerated = 275

Table 4. Sensitivity analysis with faults assumption

will remain the same for all higher values of T_F. We have also included the graph of Δ^* against different permissible values of T_F. So, for example if T_F=285 then task 1 could be changed by 10%, whereas for T_F=295 it could be changed by 20%.

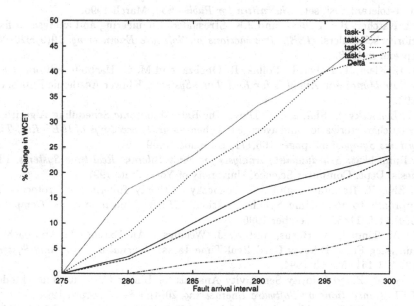

Fig. 1. Effect of fault arrival interval on %change of WCET

7   Summary

Embedding sensitivity analysis techniques in a schedulability analysis tool provides system developers with a powerful means of identifying possible bottlenecks in terms of tasks, resources or modules whose WCETs can increase very little before the system becomes unschedulable. Indeed, such information can be used to guide the development process as it may be desirable to develop such risky components first. Further, in the case of an unschedulable system, sensitivity analysis allows system developers to target optimisation effort where it will have most impact on system schedulability. It also allows developers to determine a system's sensitivity to faults in terms of the maximum fault rate which can be tolerated before faults lead to failures in timing or correctness. Due to the generic nature of our method, if necessary it could be easily adapted to find the possible changes in values of periods or deadlines, whilst keeping the computation times constant.

References

1. N. C. Audsley, A. Burns, M.F. Richardson, K. Tindell, and A.J. Wellings. Applying New Scheduling Theory to Static Priority Pre-emptive Scheduling. *Software Engineering Journal*, 8(5):284–292, September 1993.

2. A. Burns, R.I. Davis, and S. Punnekkat. Feasibility and Sensitivity Analysis of Fault-tolerant task sets. *Submitted for Publication*, March 1996.

3. D.I. Katcher, H. Arakawa, and J.K. Strosnider. Engineering and analysis of fixed priority schedulers. *IEEE Transactions on Software Engineering*, 19(9):920–934, September 1993.

4. M. H. Klein, T. Ralya, B. Pollak, R. Obebza, and M. G. Harbour, editors. *Guide to Rate Monotonic Analysis for Real-Time Systems*. Kluwer Academic Publishers, 1993.

5. J.P. Lehoczky, L. Sha, and Y. Ding. The Rate Monotonic Scheduling Algorithm - Exact characterization and average case behaviour. *Proceedings of IEEE Real-Time Systems Symposium*, pages 166,171, December 1989.

6. S. Punnekkat. *Schedulability Analysis for Fault Tolerant Real-time Systems*. PhD thesis, Dept. Computer Science, University of York, June 1997.

7. L. Sha, R. Rajkumar, and J.P. Lehoczky. Priority Inheritance Protocols: An Approach to Real-Time Synchronization. *IEEE Transactions on Computers*, 39(9):1175–1185, September 1990.

8. K. W. Tindell, A. Burns, and A. J. Wellings. An Extendible Approach for Analysing Fixed Priority Hard Real-Time Tasks. *Journal of Real-Time Systems*, 6(2):133–151, March 1994.

9. S. Vestal. Fixed Priority Sensitivity Analysis for Linear Compute Time Models. *IEEE Transactions on Software Engineering*, 20(4):308–317, April 1994.

10. R. Yerraballi, R. Mukkamala, K. Maly, and H.A. Wahab. Issues in Schedulability Analysis of Real-Time Systems. *Proceedings of Seventh Euromicro Workshop on Real-Time Systems*, pages 87–92, June 1995.

Dynamic Multiprocessor Scheduling for Supporting Real-Time Constraints

Shin-Mu Tseng[1] Y. H. Chin[2] and Wei-Pang Yang[1]

[1]Institute of Computer and Information Science, National Chiao Tung University,
Hsinchu, Taiwan, R.O.C., Email: tsm@dbsun1.cis.nctu.edu.tw
[2]Institute of Computer Science, National Tsing Hua University, Hsinchu, Taiwan, R.O.C.

Abstract. A real-time transaction carries the constraint that it must be completed before its assigned deadline. For some real-time applications, a successfully completed transaction may contribute a value to the system to reflect its profit. Satisfying both constraints of maximizing the totally obtained profits and minimizing the number of missed transactions simultaneously under various system conditions is a challenge. In this paper, we present a dynamic scheduling policy named Dynamic Processor Allocation (DPA) for scheduling value-based transactions in a multiprocessor real-time database system. The DPA policy allocates the processors to both of high-value transactions and urgent transactions dynamically by utilizing the statistical information of the system. Through simulation experiments, DPA is shown to deliver good performance in both maximizing the totally obtained profits and minimizing the number of missed transactions under various system environments. Hence, it resolves the drawbacks of the existing scheduling policies which can deliver good performance only at normal loads or at high loads.

1 Introduction

In a real-time database system (RTDBS), real-time transactions are associated with time constraints that must be satisfied. The time constraint of a transaction is normally expressed as a deadline before which the transaction must be completed. In recent years, a number of researches have been done on transaction scheduling in RTDBSs [1-6, 8-15, 18-19]. Most of them are focused on reducing the number of transactions that miss their deadlines [1-6, 8,10, 13-15, 18]. In many real-time applications, however, a transaction may assigned a value to reflect the profit the transaction contributes to the system if it is completed before the deadline. The main goal of the system shifts to maximizing the total values it receives from completed transactions. Minimizing the number of missed transactions becomes a secondary but still important concern. Satisfying both goals at the same time is a challenge.

For example, consider a stock trading system of an investment consulting company that allows customers to make orders of the stocks. Each customer may set a deadline to wait for the completion of the order transaction. The commission of the company is a percent (say 3%) of the dealt stock price for each transaction that is completed before its deadline. From the standpoint of a broker, this commission is the value of the transaction. The main goal of such a system is to maximize the total profits received from the dealt order transactions. Meanwhile, the number of missed transactions should also be kept as low as possible.

Studies on real-time value-based scheduling appeared in [9, 11-12, 19]. Huang *et al.* [11, 12] used a real-time database testbed to evaluate the performance of several representative scheduling algorithms and presented important results for scheduling value-based transactions. Haritsa *et al.* [9] made a detailed performance evaluation of various priority assignment policies and concurrency control protocols under different system environments through a simulation approach. Tseng *et al.* [19] considered value-based scheduling for transactions with dynamic values.

The motivation of this research is two-folded: 1) To improve the system performance, abundant processors are often equipped in an RTDBS to execute the transactions concurrently. However, most existing scheduling policies were designed for single processor systems. Consequently, it is difficult to meet both goals of minimizing the number of missed transaction and maximizing the total values simultaneously. A new scheduling policy that can utilize the benefits of multiprocessors to meet both goals mentioned above is needed. 2) The existing scheduling policies are not adaptive to changes of system loads. A certain policy can deliver good performance only at low loads or at high loads. For a real-time application in real-life like the stock trading system, however, the system loads are likely to change with time instead of staying still. Therefore, a dynamic scheduling policy that is adaptive to system loads is needed to maintain a steady performance for an RTDBS.

To our best knowledge, no work has been done on designing value-based scheduling policies that utilize the status information of a multiprocessor RTDBS to meet both goals of maximizing the totally obtained values and minimizing the number of missed transactions simultaneously under various system conditions. Haritsa *et al.* [9] considered a multiprocessor system in their simulation experiments, but the scheduling policies presented were basically the same as those for a single processor system and did not take into account the parallel property of a multiprocessor RTDBS. Tseng *et al.* [20] proposed a scheduling policy suitable for a multiprocessor RTDBS in which only the transaction information is used. The status information of the RTDBS, however, is not utilized to improve the scheduling.

In this paper, we present a dynamic scheduling policy, namely Dynamic Processor Allocation (DPA) policy, for scheduling value-based transactions in a multiprocessor RTDBS. The main property of DPA is it utilizes the information recording system status to allocate processors to both of urgent transactions and high-value transactions dynamically. In this way, both requirements of maximizing the total values and minimizing the number of missed transactions can be satisfied under various system loads. To verify the merits of DPA policy, a simulation model of an RTDBS is built and some experiments have been conducted to evaluate its performance. The experimental results show that DPA policy outperforms other scheduling policies in both maximizing the total values and minimizing the number of missed transactions under various system conditions.

The remainder of this article is organized as follows. Section 2 reviews previous work on value-based scheduling. Section 3 presents the proposed policy. Section 4 describes the simulation model and experimental results. Finally, a conclusion is made in Section 5.

2 Previous Work

A real-time scheduling policy consists of two main components, namely the priority assignment policy and concurrency control protocol. In the following, we briefly describe some typical priority assignment policies and concurrency control protocols proposed in previous work for scheduling value-based transactions.

2.1. Priority Assignment Policy

In the following discussion, the notations A_i, D_i, V_i and P_i are used to denote the arrival time, deadline, value and priority of transaction T_i, respectively. A Higher value of P_i represents a higher priority.

Earliest Deadline (ED): The principle of the ED policy is that a transaction having an earlier deadline should be given a higher priority. The priority assignment is $P_i = 1/D_i$. The ED policy focuses on completing transactions with urgent deadlines but ignores the values of transactions.

Highest Value (HV): The principle of the HV policy is to give a higher priority to the transaction having a higher value. The transaction priority assignment is $P_i = V_i$. In contrast to ED, HV focuses on completing transactions with high values. However, the urgency of transactions is not considered.

Value-Inflated Deadline (VD): The VD policy uses the priority assignment $P_i = V_i/D_i$. It considers both the value and deadline, and the absolute deadline is used in the priority assignment.

Value-Inflated Relative Deadline (VRD): The VRD policy uses the priority assignment $P_i = V_i / (D_i - A_i)$. The main difference between VRD and VD is that VRD uses the relative deadline $(D_i - A_i)$ instead of the absolute deadline.

In [9], the performance of the four priority assignment policies mentioned above were evaluated. When the transaction values are in uniform distribution, the simulation results indicate that the ED policy performs best under normal loads while the HV policy performs best under heavy loads. The VD policy behaves identically to HV, therefore we will not consider it in following discussions. On the whole, the VRD policy has the best performance. However, no one policy can deliver good performance steadily under various system loads.

2.2 Concurrency Control Protocol

A number of studies have shown that optimistic-based concurrency control protocols such as OPT-BC [16] and OPT-WAIT [8] perform better than lock-based ones such as 2PL-HP and 2PL-CR [2] in an RTDBS [8, 9, 12]. Therefore, we used OPT-BC for concurrency control in this work. Since our focus is on priority assignment policy, the OPT-BC protocol is not restated here for space limitations. Interested readers is referred to [16].

3 The Proposed Policy

3.1 Assumptions

When a transaction is submitted into the system, the arrival time, deadline, estimated execution time and value of the transaction are assigned and known to the scheduler. Moreover, the effective serviced time of a transaction is known to the scheduler. These assumptions are reasonable and have been used in various researches [2, 3, 10]. The processors in the RTDBS are assumed to share the common memory.

3.2 The DPA Policy

In order to maximize the total values and minimize the number of missed transactions, the key idea of DPA policy is to dynamically allocate the processors to both of high-value transactions and urgent transactions based on the status of an RTDBS. Figure 1 shows the diagram for DPA policy. Transactions arriving at the system enter the ready queue and wait to be scheduled by the *scheduler* for accessing the CPUs. The total CPUs are divided into two clusters by the *adjuster*: the H-cluster that executes the high-value transactions, and the U-cluster that executes the urgent transactions. The number of CPUs allocated to H-cluster or U-cluster is adjusted dynamically based on the system's status that is statistically measured dynamically. The main measured system status is the miss ratio, which is defined as (number of missed transactions/totally submitted transactions)* 100% and is recorded whenever a transaction is completed, either committed successfully or aborted due to missing deadline. Whenever the number of completed transactions reach a predefined count for an observed period, the adjuster will adjust the size of H-cluster and U-cluster based on the measured system status, with the aim to maintain good performance in both maximizing the total values and minimizing the number of missed transactions under various system conditions. In the following, we describe in details how to determine the degree of high-value or urgency for a transaction, and how the scheduler and adjuster work.

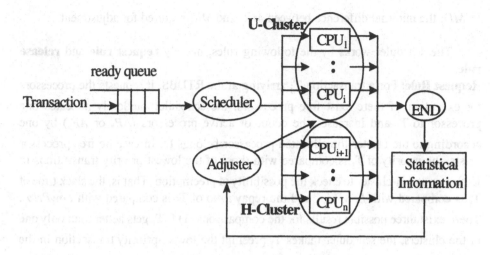

Figure 1. Diagram of DPA policy.

The degrees of urgency and high-value for a transaction T_i are measured by its slack time [3] S_i and *repay ratio* RP_i, respectively. S_i and RP_i are defined as D_i - (current_time + R_i) [3] and V_i/E_i, respectively, where R_i and E_i is the remaining execution time and estimated execution time of T_i, respectively. A transaction with a smaller slack time is more urgent, and a transaction with a larger repay ratio is expected to contribute a higher value to the system in a shorter required execution time. From the standpoint to reduce the number of missed transactions, the transactions with smaller slack time should be scheduled first, yielding the Least Slack (LS) policy [3]; while scheduling first the transactions with higher repay ratio, i.e., Highest Repay Ratio(HRR) policy, is more economical from the standpoint to maximize the total values. Therefore, there exist two priority assignment policies in the system: the LS policy for U-cluster and HRR policy for H-cluster.

Before introducing the principles of scheduler and adjuster, we describe first some working variables that are used in the system:
- NP: total number of processors in the system
- PL_h: limit of the number of processors allocated to H-cluster
- PL_u: limit of the number of processors allocated to U-cluster
- AP_h: current number of active processors in H-cluster at a given time
- AP_u: current number of active processors in U-cluster at a given time
- $LowPrio_h$: the lowest priority of transactions in H-cluster
- $LowPrio_u$: the lowest priority of transactions in U-cluster
- NT: number of transactions to be observed in an observed period
- MR_p: the miss ratio measured in previous observed period
- MR_c: the miss ratio measured in current observed period

• *MD*: the minimal difference between MR_p and MR_c required for adjustment

The scheduler works by the following rules, namely **request rule** and **release rule**.

Request Rule: For a transaction T_i arriving at the RTDBS, it requests the processors for execution. If there exist free processors, the scheduler randomly allocates one processor to T_i and increases the count of active processors (AP_h or AP_u) by one according to the cluster the allocated processor belongs to. In case no free processor exists, the priority of T_i is compared with those of the lowest-priority transactions in U-cluster and H-cluster to check the possibility of preemption. That is, the slack time of T_i is compared with $LowPrio_u$ and the repay ratio of T_i is compared with $LowPrio_h$. There exist three possible results for the comparisons: 1) If T_i gets better than only one of the clusters, the scheduler makes T_i preempt the lowest-priority transaction in the corresponding cluster, 2) If T_i gets better than both clusters, one cluster is chosen randomly to be preempted, 3) If T_i fails in both priority comparisons, T_i is inserted into the ready queue to wait for execution. In case 2, the reason for choosing randomly one cluster for preemption is to avoid biased results in selecting the preempted cluster.

Release Rule: Whenever a processor is released by a transaction, the count of active processors (AP_h or AP_u) is decreased by one according to the cluster the released processor belongs to. If the resulted count of active processors is smaller than the processor limit of the corresponding cluster (PL_h or PL_u), the scheduler chooses in the ready queue the highest-priority transaction for execution on the released processor based on the priority assignment policy of the corresponding cluster.

The adjuster plays an important role in DPA policy. Its principle is based on the observations made in [9, 19], which stated that urgency-flavored policies (like ED) perform best under normal system loads and value-flavored policies (like HV) perform best under overloaded conditions in both minimizing the miss ratio and maximizing the total values. Basically, a system is considered as overloaded if the miss ratio exceeds 20% [8, 9]. Hence, the principle of the adjuster is to adjust dynamically the size of H-cluster and U-cluster such that the scheduling results tend to be more urgency-flavored under normal loads and to be more value-flavored under overloaded conditions. Its rule is as follows:

Adjust Rule: Whenever a number of *NT* transactions are completed (either committed or aborted), an observed period is determined to be done and the miss ratio during this period, MR_c, is compared with that of previous observed period, MR_p. Let $w = (MR_c - MR_p)/ MR_p$, which indicates the increment ratio in miss ratio from previous observed period to current observed period. If $|w| < MD$, i.e., the difference between the miss ratios of the observed periods is small, no action is taken; otherwise, an adjustment will be made as follows based on the relationships between MR_c and MR_p:

Case 1: $MR_c > MR_p$ ($w > 0$)

If the system is under a normal load (i.e., $MR_c < 20\%$), the size of U-cluster is increased by a ratio of w, i.e., the new PL_u is set as $PL_u*(1 + w)$. The size of H-cluster is changed accordingly to be the number of remaining processors not allocated to U-cluster, i.e., $PL_h = NP - PL_u$. The reason for the adjustment in this way is based on the observation that the measured miss ratio is in an increasing trend under a normal system load. Under this condition, allocating more processors to the urgent transactions will help reduce the miss ratio and thus increase the total values. On the other hand, if the system is overloaded (i.e., $MR_c < 20\%$), the size of U-cluster is decreased by a ratio of w, i.e., the new PL_u is set as $PL_u*(1- w)$, and the size of H-cluster is set as the number of remaining processors. This adjustment is due to the fact that allocating more processors to the high-value transactions will help reduce the miss ratio and thus increase the total values under an overloaded condition.

Case 2: $MR_c < MR_p$ ($w < 0$)

The adjustment is similar to that of Case 1. If the system is under a normal load, the size of U-cluster is decreased by a ratio of $|w|$, i.e., the new PL_u is set as $PL_u*(1- |w|)$. On the other hand, if the system is overloaded, the size of U-cluster is increased by a ratio of $|w|$. The size of H-cluster is changed accordingly to be the number of remaining processors.

After the adjuster has completed the adjustment in current period, another new observed period is started. If an adjustment is made on the size of U-cluster and H-cluster, the value of MR_p is replaced by that of MR_c.

4 Performance Evaluation

To evaluate the performance of DPA, a real-time database simulation model was developed using *SimPack* simulation package [7]. The simulation model, workload parameters, and assumptions are similar to those in [9] to make the results compatible.

4.1 Simulation Model

We assume a closed queuing model of a single-site database system, which consists of multiple CPUs sharing the common memory and a memory-resident database. A preemptive-resume policy is used for competing the CPUs. Transactions arrive in a Poisson stream and each transaction is associated with an arrival time, a deadline, a value, and an estimated execution time. A transaction will request a sequence of read and write operations. Whenever a CPU is free, the transaction with the highest priority in the ready queue is selected for execution by the underlying priority assignment policy. The concurrency control is done by OPT-BC protocol, which always grants the access requests of a transaction and the validation of data consistency is deferred at the committed time of a transaction. When a transaction reaches the commit point, it is committed and the transactions conflicting with it are restarted. A transaction follows the same access sets if it is restarted, and transactions which miss the deadlines are eliminated immediately.

We assume that the cost of executing the scheduler is negligible because it is very small as compared to the time needed to access a data item [18]. The cost of executing concurrency control operations is assumed to be included in the CPU time needed to access a data item [3].

4.2 Workload Model

Table 1 lists the workload model parameters used. Parameter *db_size* determines the number of pages in the database, which is assumed to be resident in main memory. Parameter *tran_size* represents the average number of pages accessed by a transaction, which is the mean of a uniform distribution varying between 0.5 * *tran_size* and 1.5 * *tran_size*. The accessed pages are uniformly distributed over the database. Parameter *page_cpu* determines the CPU time needed to access a data page. Parameter *write_prob* determines the probability that a page read by a transaction will also be updated. The parameter used to model the load of the system is *arrival_rate*, which specifies the mean rate of transaction arrivals and has a Poisson distribution (i.e., the inter-arrival time of transactions is in exponential distribution with mean 1/arrival_rate). Parameter *reatart_delay* gives the delayed time to restart a transaction. The deadline of a transaction T_i is assigned as

$$D_i = A_i + SF_i * R_{max}$$

where R_{max} is the required resource time for the largest transaction in the workload (i.e., the transaction with size equal to 1.5 * *tran_size*), and SF_i is a slack factor that controls the tightness or looseness of the deadlines and varies uniformly over the range set by the parameters *min_slack* and *max_slack*. The values of transactions are distributed uniformly between 0.5 and 1.5 times the value of *mean_value*. Parameter *NT* determines the number of transactions to be observed in an observed period, and parameter *MD* is the minimal difference between miss ratios of observed periods required for making an adjustment in H-cluster and U-cluster.

Table 1. Workload parameters and base values

Parameter	Description	Value
db_size	Number of pages in database	1000 Pages
tran_size	Average pages accessed/transaction	20 Pages
arrival_rate	Rate of transaction arrivals	25 - 150 trs/sec
page_cpu	CPU time for accessing a data page	10 ms
write_prob	Write probability for accessed pages	0.25
restart_delay	Time delay to restart a transaction	5 ms
min_slack	Minimum slack factor	2
max_slack	Maximum slack factor	4
mean_value	Mean value of transactions	100
NP	Total number of processors	10
NT	Number of observed transactions in a period	100
MD	Minimal difference in miss ratio for adjustment	0.05 (5%)

4.3 Parameter Settings and Performance Metrics

A batch means method [17] was used for statistical analysis of the experimental results. We ran the simulation with the same parameters for 30 different random number seeds, and at least 1000 transactions are executed at each run. The averaged results over the 30 runs reached 90% confidence intervals whose endpoints were within 5% of the point estimate.

The main performance metrics used here are *MissRatio* and *LossRatio*, which are defined as

*MissRatio = (number of transactions missing the deadlines) / (total number of submitted transactions) * 100%*

and

*LossRatio = (totally offered values - totally obtained values) / (totally offered values) * 100%*

where the *offered value* indicates the value assigned to a transaction by the application when the transaction is submitted. This metric measures how much values is lost in the ratio of the totally offered values from the submitted transactions. Smaller values in the *LossRatio* and *MissRatio* represent the better performance. In the conducted experiments, the compared scheduling policies are ED, HV, VRD and DPA, and the concurrency control protocol used is OPT-BC.

4.4 Experimental Results

Experiment 1: Effects of Increased Loads

This experiment evaluates the performance of the tested policies under an RTDBS whose loads increase with time. We generate continuous periods of transaction arrivals with *arrival_rate* varied from 25 transactions/sec (denoted as trs/sec) to 150 trs/sec. For each period of transaction arrivals, 2000 transactions are generated. The system load resulting in a *MissRatio* less than 20% is considered as a normal load, while the one resulting in a *MissRatio* higher than 20% is considered as a high load (i.e., overloaded condition). The parameters are set as in Table 1.Meanwhile, PL_h and PL_u are set equally as 5 and MR_p is set as 0.2 initially. This setting is to balance the initial size of U-cluster and H-cluster. Figures 2a and 2b show the *MissRatio* and *LossRatio* results for each period, respectively. The following observations were made from the experimental results. For both *MissRatio* and *LossRatio*, the performance order for the tested policies is ED > DPA > VRD > HV (i.e., ED performs best and HV performs worst) at light loads (less than 35 trs/sec), DPA > ED > VRD > HV at normal loads, and DPA > HV > VRD > ED at high loads. The performance order for ED, HV and VRD indicates that the urgency-flavored scheduling policies (like ED) perform very well at normal loads but performs poorly at high loads, while the value-flavored scheduling policies (like HV) behaves conversely. This matches the results reported in [9].

The DPA policy performs best at almost all loads in both *MissRatio* and *LossRatio*, except that it performs slightly worse than ED at light loads. The excellent performance of DPA is due to its dynamic allocation of the processors to both of urgent transactions and high-repay-ratio transactions based on the system's status. The experimental results show that, when the system loads increase within the range of normal loads, DPA increases the size of U-cluster gradually based on the detection of increase in miss ratio for the observed periods. This adjustment results in an urgency-flavored scheduling, with a small percent of processors are still allocated to high-repay-ratio transactions. Hence, both of *MissRatio* and *LossRatio* can be kept as low as possible. When the system loads increase within the range of high loads, however, DPA decreases the size of U-cluster quickly based on the detection of sharp increase in miss ratio for the observed periods. Consequently, the resulted scheduling is value-flavored such that low *MissRatio* and *LossRatio* can still be maintained under high loads.

The above observations imply that using the same scheduling policy for all processors (i.e., all processors are allocated to a fixed type of transactions) can not deliver low *MissRatio* and low *LossRatio* simultaneously under various system loads. The right policy should be a hybrid and dynamic policy like DPA that allocates the processors to both high-value transactions and urgent transactions dynamically based on the status of the system.

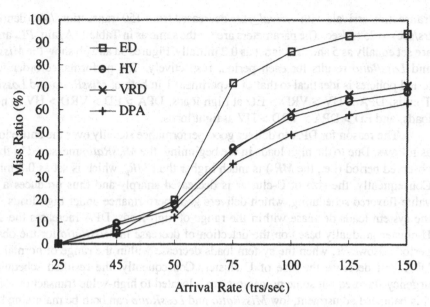

Figure 2a. *MissRatio* for increased loads.

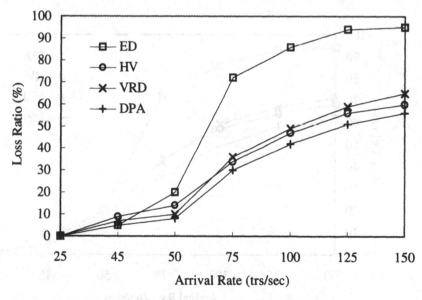

Figure 2b. *LossRatio* for increased loads.

Experiment 2: Effects of Decreased Loads

This experiment evaluates the performance of the tested policies under an RTDBS whose loads decrease with time. As in Experiment 1, we generate continuous periods of transaction arrivals with *arrival_rate* decreased from 150 transactions/sec (denoted as trs/sec) to 25 trs/sec. The parameters are set the same as in Table 1. Again, PL_h and PL_u are set equally as 5 and MR_p is set as 0.2 initially. Figures 3a and 3b show the *MissRatio* and *LossRatio* results for each period, respectively. The performance order for the tested policies is identical to that of Experiment 1 in both of *MissRatio* and *LossRatio*. That is, DPA > HV > VRD > ED at high loads, DPA > ED > VRD > HV at normal loads, and ED > DPA > VRD > HV at light loads.

The reason for DPA to deliver good performance steadily over the entire loads is as follows. Due to the high loads in the beginning, the *MissRatio* measured in the first observed period (i.e., the MR_c) is much higher than MR_p, which is set as 0.2 initially. Consequently, the size of U-cluster is decreased sharply and thus produces a high-value-flavored scheduling, which delivers good performance under high loads. When the system loads decrease within the range of high loads, DPA increases the size of U-cluster gradually based on the detection of decrease in *MissRatio* for the observed periods. However, when the system loads decrease within the range of normal loads, DPA will decrease the size of U-cluster. Consequently, the resulted scheduling is urgency-flavored but some processors are allocated to high-value transactions. Due to this balanced adjustment, low *MissRatio* and *LossRatio* can both be maintained under normal loads. Therefore, DPA is shown to deliver good performance steadily under decreasing loads.

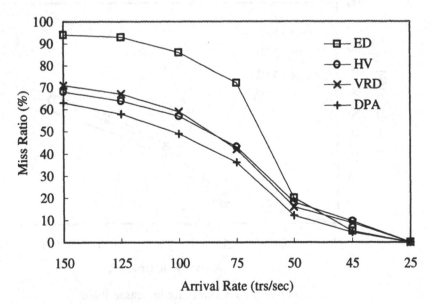

Figure 3a. *MissRatio* for decreased loads.

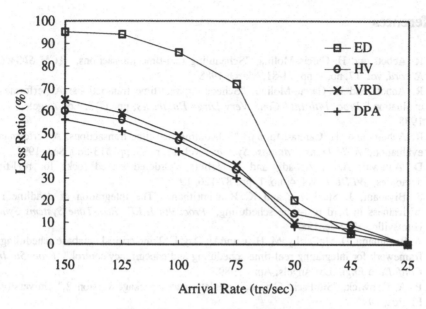

Figure 3b. *LossRatio* for decreased loads.

5. Conclusions

We have proposed a dynamic scheduling policy, namely Dynamic Processor Allocation (DPA) policy, for supporting real-time constraints of transactions in a multiprocessor RTDBS. The main property of DPA is it utilizes the information recording system status to allocate processors to both of urgent transactions and high-value transactions dynamically. To our best knowledge, this is the first work in presenting a dynamic approach for scheduling transactions in a multiprocessor RTDBS such as to meet both real-time and value constraints under various system conditions.

The simulation experiments show that DPA policy produces a urgency-flavored scheduling under normal system loads and switches to a high-value-flavored scheduling under overloaded conditions, no matter the loads is in increasing or decreasing trend. Therefore, DPA can maintain good performance in both of maximizing the total values and minimizing the miss ratio under various system loads, unlike other scheduling policies that can deliver good performance only at low loads or at high loads. An important lesson from this study is that using only a fixed scheduling policy for all processors in a multiprocessor RTDBS is not sufficient. The right scheduling policy should be a hybrid and dynamic one like DPA that allocates the processors to both of high-value transactions and urgent transactions dynamically by utilizing the information recording the status of the system.

References

1. R. Abbott and H. Garcia-Molina, "Scheduling real-time transactions," *ACM SIGMOD Record*, vol. 17, no. 1, pp. 71-81, March 1988.
2. R. Abbott and H. Garcia-Molina, "Scheduling real-time transactions: A performance evaluation," *Proc. 14th Int'l Conf. Very Large Databases*, pp. 1-12, Los Angeles, Aug. 1988.
3. R. Abbott and H. Garcia-Molina, "Scheduling real-time transactions: A performance evaluation," *ACM Trans. Database Systems*, vol. 17, no. 3, pp. 513-560, Sep. 1992.
4. D. Agrawal, A. E. Abbadi, and R. Jeffers, "Ordered shared locks for real-time databases," *VLDB J.*, vol. 4, no. 1, pp. 87-126, 1995.
5. S. Biyabani, J. Stankovic, and K. Ramamritham, "The integration of deadline and criticalness in hard real-time scheduling," *Proc. 9th IEEE Real-Time Systems Symp.*, Huntsville, AL, Dec. 1988.
6. A. Buchmann, D. McCarthy, M. Hsu, and U. Dayal, "Time-critical database scheduling: A framework for integrating real-time scheduling and concurrency control," *Proc. 5th Int'l Conf. Data Engi.*, Los Angels, Apr. 1989.
7. P. A. Fishwick, "SimPack: C-based simulation tool package version 2," University of Florida, 1992.
8. J. R. Haritsa, M. J. Carey, and M. Livny, "Dynamic real-time optimistic concurrency control," *Proc. 11th IEEE Real-Time Systems Symp.*, pp. 94-103, Orlando, Florida, Dec. 1990.
9. J. R. Haritsa, M. J. Carey, and M. Livny, "Value-based scheduling in real-time database systems," *VLDB J.*, vol. 2, no. 2, pp. 117-152, 1993.
10. D. Hong, T. Johnson, and S. Chakravarthy, "Real-time transaction scheduling: a cost conscious approach," *Proc. ACM Int'l Conf. Management Data*, pp. 197-206, Washington, DC, May, 1993.
11. J. Huang, J. Stankovic, D. Towsley, and K. Ramaritham, "Experimental evaluation of real-time transaction processing," *Proc. 10th IEEE Real-Time Systems Symp..*, pp. 144-153, Santa Monica, CA, Dec. 1989.
12. J. Huang and J. Stankovic, "Concurrency control in real-time database systems: optimistic scheme vs. two-phase locking," *COINS Technical Report 90-66*, University of Massachusetts, Amherst, MA, 1990.
13. E. Jensen, C. Locke, and H. Tokuda, "A time-driven scheduling model for real-time operating systems," *Proc. 6th IEEE Real-Time Systems Symp.*, pp. 112-122, Dec. 1985.
14. Y. Lin and S. H. Son, "Concurrency control in real-time database systems by dynamic adjustment of serialization order," *Proc. 11th IEEE Real-Time Systems Symp.*, Orlando, Florida, Dec. 1990.
15. J. Lee and S. H. Son, "Using dynamic adjustment of serialization order for real-time database systems," *Proc. 14th IEEE Real-Time Systems Symp.*, pp. 66-75, Raleigh-Durham, N.C. , Dec. 1993.
16. D. Menasce and T. Nakanishi, "Optimistic vs. pessimistic concurrency control mechanisms in database management systems," Information Systems, vol. 7, no. 1, pp. 13-27, 1982.
17. R. Sargent, "Statistical analysis of simulation output data," *Proc. 4th Ann. Symp. Simulation Computer Systems*, pp. 39-50, Aug. 1976.
18. S. M. Tseng and Y. H. Chin, "Prescheduling policy for real-time concurrency control: a performance evaluation," *Journal of Systems Integration*, vol. 3 , no. 3, pp. 23-42, 1993.

19. S. M. Tseng, Y. H. Chin, and W. P. Yang, "Scheduling real-time transactions with dynamic values: a performance evaluation," *Proc. 2nd Int'l Workshop Real-Time Computing Systems and Applications*, pp. 60-67, Tokyo, Japan, Oct. 1995.

20. S. M. Tseng, Y. H. Chin, and W. P. Yang, "An adaptive value-based scheduling policy for multiprocessor real-time database systems," *Proc.8th Int'l Conf. Database and Expert Systems Applications*, pp. 254 - 259, France, Sep. 1997.

Heuristic Diff Acquiring in Lazy Release Consistency Model

Zhiyi Huang, Wan-Ju Lei, Chengzheng Sun, and Abdul Sattar

Knowledge Representation and Reasoning Unit
School of Computing & Information Technology
Griffith University, Nathan, Qld 4111, Australia
Email:{hzy,wlei,scz,sattar}@cit.gu.edu.au

Abstract. *This paper presents a Heuristic Diff Acquiring (HDA) protocol in Lazy Release Consistency (LRC) based distributed shared memory (DSM) systems. Based on the run-time detection of associations between locks and data, the HDA can selectively piggy-back useful page diffs in a lock grant message. By adopting the novel HDA protocol, an improved LRC model has been implemented, and the experimental results have been collected and analyzed. First, we introduce the Lazy Diff Acquiring (LDA) and Eager Diff Acquiring (EDA) protocols in the LRC based DSM systems. Second, we discuss the impact of LDA and EDA on the performance of the LRC-based DSM systems. Third, we propose the idea and implementation of the HDA protocol. Finally, we present and analyze the experimental results. From the experimental results, we conclude the HDA protocol can significantly improve the performance of LRC model.*

Key Words: Distributed Shared Memory, Lazy Release Consistency, Eager Release Consistency

1 Introduction

Distributed Shared Memory (DSM) systems have been rapidly developed since last decade, with various kinds of memory consistency models proposed and implemented, such as Sequential Consistency (SC) [9, 10], Eager Release Consistency (ERC) [5], Entry Consistency (EC) [4], and Lazy Release Consistency (LRC) [7]. This sort of systems provides a virtual shared memory for the users on networks of workstations. So these systems can allow shared memory parallel programs to execute on networks of workstations. Through the improvement of protocols [2, 8], some optimized models, e.g., the LRC model, can support some parallel numerical computing applications efficiently [7, 11].

Even though the Lazy Release Consistency (LRC) is currently the up-to-date consistency model, its performance is still not satisfactory for some Artificial Intelligence applications [6]. The reason is that, comparing with an equivalent message passing program, the overhead to maintain the shared memory consistency of a shared memory parallel program is still very high because of the numerous messages. More improvements should and can be done on it in order to further decrease the number of messages. For example, the Lazy Diff Acquiring (LDA) in LRC can sometimes lead to more number of messages than the Eager Diff Acquiring (EDA), as will be explained in Section 3. If we can accurately predict which updates will be definitely acquired by some process and thus should be eagerly sent to that process, we can pack those updates in one message package, instead of several packages as in LDA. In this way, we can decrease the times of updates transfer. Based on this idea, a novel Heuristic Diff Acquiring (HDA) protocol is proposed in the paper, which can decide which updates should be eagerly acquired and which should not. From the experimental results, the HDA can significantly decrease the number of messages and increase the performance of the LRC-based DSM systems.

The organization of the rest of this paper is as follows. Section 2 gives an introduction to the LRC model, the Lazy Diff Acquiring (LDA) protocol, and the Eager Diff Acquiring (EDA) protocol. Section 3 discusses the impact of LDA and EDA on LRC model. Section 4 presents the heuristic protocol HDA. Section 5 presents and analyzes the experimental results. Finally, we conclude in Section 6.

2 Lazy Release Consistency model

The LRC model is proposed in [7]. Based on the LRC model, a DSM system—TreadMarks [1] has been implemented on standard Unix systems such as SunOS and Ultrix.

2.1 Lazy Release Consistency

LRC is an improvement of Eager Release Consistency (ERC) [5]. Both of them require mutual exclusion of accesses to a variable if there is at least one *write* operation among the accesses [5]. They permit a process to delay making its updates to shared data visible to other processes until certain synchronization accesses occur. Therefore, the time for making the shared memory consistent is actually the same as the time of mutual exclusion. The following are the conditions of ERC model.

Definition 1. Conditions for Eager Release Consistency

- Before an ordinary **read** or **write** access is allowed to perform with respect to any other process, all previous **acquire** accesses must be performed, and
- before a **release** access is allowed to perform with respect to any other process, all previous ordinary **read** and **write** accesses must be performed, and
- **sync** accesses are sequentially consistent with respect to one another.

The difference between ERC and LRC is that ERC requires ordinary *read* or *write* accesses to be performed globally at the next release of a lock, whereas LRC requires only that ordinary *read* or *write* accesses be performed with respect to some processes which acquire the released lock. The following are the conditions of LRC model.

Definition 2. Conditions for Lazy Release Consistency

- Before an ordinary **read** or **write** access is allowed to perform with respect to another process, all previous **acquire** accesses must be performed *with respect to that other process*, and
- before a **release** access is allowed to perform with respect to any other process, all previous ordinary **read** and **write** accesses must be performed *with respect to that other process*, and
- **sync** accesses are sequentially consistent with respect to one another.

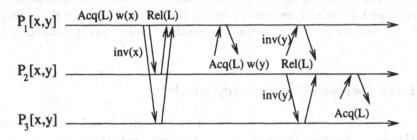

Fig. 1. Eager Release Consistency

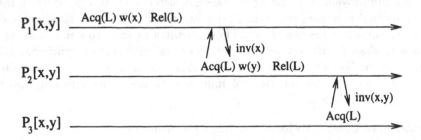

Fig. 2. Lazy Release Consistency

Fig. 1 and Fig. 2 are used to illustrate the difference between ERC and LRC. In Fig. 1, when P_1 calls Rel(L), it sends the invalidation of x immediately to other processes, such as P_2 and P_3. So does P_2 when it calls Rel(L). In Fig. 2, when P_1 calls Rel(L), there is no message passing from P_1 to other processes. Only when P_2 calls Acq(L) is the invalidation of x sent from P_1 to P_2. So is the invalidation of x and y when P_3 calls Acq(L). If a process does not acquire the lock L, it will not get the invalidation of x or y. Therefore, the expense for passing the invalidation of x and y is saved. Compared with ERC, the delay of invalidation can greatly reduce the number of data transfer messages and better performance is achieved in LRC.

2.2 Lazy Diff Acquiring (LDA) protocol

The LRC in TreadMarks [1] adopts a LDA protocol to achieve page fault processing, in which page *diff*, instead of the whole page, is used to renew a dirty copy. When a write access to a valid page is first performed, a *twin* of the page is created and stored in system space. A comparison of the *twin* and a later version of the page is used to create a *diff*, which is a run-length encoding of the differences between the two versions. The *diff* can then be used to update other processes' copies of the page.

Example 1. Shared memory access pattern (1)

```
P1                      P2
...                     ...
Acquire(1);             Acquire(1);
write(x);               read(x);
write(y);               read(y);
...                     ...
Release(1);             Release(1);
...                     ...
```

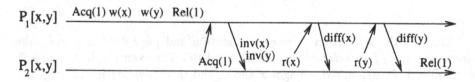

Fig. 3. The message passing in Example 1 under LDA

To understand how the LDA protocol passes messages, we consider the program in Example 1. Fig. 3 illustrates the message passing between two processes P_1 and P_2. In the example both P_1 and P_2 will access page x and y. Suppose P_1 gets the lock 1 first. When P_1 releases lock 1, there is no message passing between the two processes. Then when P_2 acquires the lock 1, the invalidation of x and y are sent from P_1 to P_2. In LDA, only when P_2 accesses x or y and page fault occurs, is the $diff$ of x or y acquired from P_1 by P_2. Since the $diff$ of a page is acquired only when the page is accessed, we call this protocol *Lazy Diff Acquiring* (LDA).

From above description, the LDA protocol is divided into four stages:

1. lock releasing of P_1, prepare for *write notices* (invalidation message).
2. lock acquiring of P_2, acquire *write notices* and invalidate the updated pages.
3. *diff* acquiring of P_2, when an invalidated page is accessed for the first time the *diff* is acquired.
4. *diff* performing of P_2, the *diff* is received and performed on the page.

Example 2. Shared memory access pattern (2)

```
P1                        P2
...                       ...
Acquire(0);               Acquire(1);
write(y);                 read(x);
Release(0);               Release(1);
...                       ...
Acquire(1);
write(x);
Release(1);
...
```

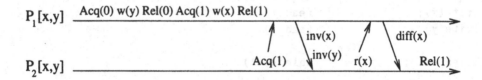

Fig. 4. The message passing in Example 2 under LDA

Through the separation of page invalidation and page *diff* acquiring, the unnecessary *diff* transfer can be avoided in LRC. For example, in Example 2, even though P_1 has updated pages x and y, and their invalidation message has been sent to P_2, P_2 only accesses page x and thus only the *diff* of x is acquired by P_2. As a result, only the *diff* of x is transfered from P_1 to P_2, even though both x and y are invalid in P_2. The message passing between P_1 and P_2 are illustrated in Fig. 4.

2.3 Eager Diff Acquiring (EDA) protocol

In LRC, we can also adopt an EDA protocol. To understand how the EDA protocol passes messages, we again consider Example 1 in previous section. Fig. 5 illustrates the message passing between two processes. Suppose P_1 gets the lock 1 first. When P_1 releases lock 1, there is no message passing between the two processes. Then when P_2 acquires the lock 1, the invalidation of x and y is sent from P_1 to P_2. And at the same time, the *diffs* of x and y are appended to the invalidation message and sent eagerly from P_1 to P_2. Therefore, when P_2

accesses x or y and page fault occurs, P_2 need not acquire $diffs$ again from P_1. Since the $diff$ is acquired eagerly when the invalidation of a page is sent, we call this protocol *Eager Diff Acquiring* (EDA).

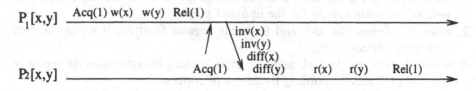

Fig. 5. The message passing in Example 1 under EDA

From above description, the EDA protocol is divided into three stages:

1. lock releasing of P_1, prepare for *write notices*.
2. lock acquiring of P_2, acquire *write notices* and $diffs$ and invalidate the updated pages.
3. $diff$ performing of P_2, the $diffs$ are performed on the invalidated pages.

Through the combination of invalidation and $diff$ messages, the number of $diff$ acquiring can be decreased in EDA at some situations. For example, in Fig. 5, by integrating the $diffs$ of x and y into the invalidation message, the number of messages between P_1 and P_2 is only 2, instead of 6 in Fig. 3.

However, EDA may cause unnecessary $diff$ transfer between processes at other situations. In Example 2, if we adopt EDA, the $diffs$ of x and y will be sent eagerly from P_1 to P_2, as illustrated in Fig. 6. But obviously the transfer of y's $diff$ is not necessary since P_2 will not access page y. Therefore, even though the number of messages may be decreased, the unnecessary data transfer will be increased in EDA.

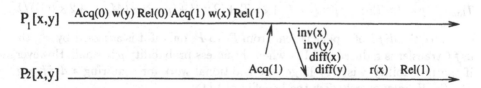

Fig. 6. The message passing in Example 2 under EDA

Then, which one is better, LDA or EDA? At what situations?

3 LDA vs. EDA

We will analyze theoretically at what situations LDA (or EDA) is better than EDA (or LDA) in this section.

Let us consider two processes P_1 and P_2. Suppose P_1 gets a lock first, P_2 waits and then gets the same lock after P_1 releases it. According to LDA protocol, the behavior of the two processes is as below:

1. when P_2 acquires the lock, it sends a message to P_1 to ask for the lock as well as the *write notices* for the updated pages.
2. after P_1 releases the lock and finds the request from P_2, it sends the lock and *write notices* to P_2.
3. when P_2 receives the lock and the *write notices*, it invalidates its copies of the updated pages according to the *write notices*.
4. when P_2 accesses an invalid page, it sends a message to ask for the *diff* of the page from P_1.
5. when P_1 receives the message, it produces the *diff* of the page and sends the *diff* back to P_2.
6. when P_2 receives the *diff*, it performs the *diff* on the page and continues execution.

From above description, we should note that the invalid page copies in P_2 are not made consistent with their up-to-date ones in P_1 unless they are accessed by P_2. Suppose, the number of invalid pages is N, the probability for P_2 to access the invalid pages is p, the average time for making *diff* of a page is T_{md}, the average time for performing *diff* on a page is T_{pd}, the message header has H bits, the *diff* of a page has M_{diff} bits, the bandwidth of the network is B, the system time to send a message is T_{ss}, and the system time for receiving a message is T_{sr}. To simplify the formula, let

$$T_d = T_{md} + T_{pd}$$

$$T_s = T_{ss} + T_{sr}$$

Then the time for making the memory consistent between the two processes is:

$$T_{lazy} = p \times N \times T_d + 2 \times p \times N \times T_s + 2 \times T_s + (2 \times H + (p \times N \times (M_{diff} + 2 \times H)))/B$$

Since the *diff* of a page is sent from P_1 to P_2 only if it is accessed by P_2, the *diff* transfer is reduced in LDA when the access probability p is small. However, if the probability p is very large, the additional work for acquiring a *diff*, e.g, T_s, T_d, H, may overshadow the benefits of LDA.

Now let us consider the time cost for EDA. According to the EDA protocol, the behavior of the two processes is as below:

1. when P_2 acquires the lock, it sends a message to P_1 to ask for the lock as well as the *write notices* and *diffs* for the updated pages.
2. after P_1 releases the lock and finds the request from P_2, it produces the *diffs* of the updated pages, then sends the lock, *write notices* and *diffs* to P_2.
3. when P_2 receives the lock, the *write notices* and *diffs*, it performs the *diffs* on its invalid copies according to the *write notices*.

Therefore, when P_2 acquires a lock from P_1 it gets the invalidation as well as the $diffs$ immediately from P_1. Fig. 5 illustrates the message passing in EDA. The time for making the memory consistent between the two processes in this eager protocol is:

$$T_{eager} = N \times T_d + 2 \times T_s + (H + (N \times M_{diff} + H))/B$$

In the following we discuss which protocol is better in terms of the time when some conditions are applied. We have the following formula deduction:

$$T_{eager} - T_{lazy} =$$

$$(1-p) \times N \times T_d - 2 \times p \times N \times T_s + ((1-p) \times N \times M_{diff} - 2 \times p \times N \times H)/B$$

If N is very small, there is not much difference between the two protocols. So we mainly discuss the situation when N is very large.

If p is very large, say, equals to 1, the above formula becomes:

$$T_{eager} - T_{lazy} = -2 \times N \times (T_s + H/B) < 0$$

In another words, if the pages updated by P_1 are most likely accessed by P_2, then the eager protocol is better than the lazy one.

If p is small, and if we want to let the lazy protocol be the better one, the following inequality should be satisfied:

$$T_{eager} - T_{lazy} =$$

$$(1-p) \times N \times T_d - 2 \times p \times N \times T_s + ((1-p) \times N \times M_{diff} - 2 \times p \times N \times H)/B > 0$$

In terms of above formula, the following relation among the different factors should be satisfied:

$$T_s < 0.5 \times ((1/p - 1) \times T_d + ((1/p - 1) \times M_{diff} - 2 \times H)/B)$$

For a concrete computer network, T_s, T_d, H, B are constant, the variables which can influence the inequality are p and M_{diff}. If p is small, the above inequality is easy to be satisfied, so the lazy one is better; otherwise, the eager one may be better. When p is small, M_{diff} may play an important role in the inequality. If M_{diff} is large, the inequality is easy to be satisfied and the lazy one is better; otherwise, if M_{diff} is small, the eager one may be better.

In a nutshell, if the access probability p is large, the EDA is usually better; if p is small and M_{diff} is also small, the EDA may still be the better one; otherwise, the LDA is better. In terms of these principles, the HDA protocol is proposed to improve the performance of LRC model.

4 Heuristic Diff Acquiring

From above analysis we know that there are preferred situations for either LDA or EDA. The most important factor is the access probability. If we know this probability we can use either LDA or EDA to achieve the best performance.

The idea of HDA in this paper is that we can get some hints about the probability from the user's programs. Normally a programmer uses lock to guard shared data and the same lock guards the same block of data. For example, a programmer uses lock L_i to guard the data in $page_i$. When process P_1 and P_2 access $page_i$, both of them will first acquire the lock L_i and then access $page_i$. Therefore, we conclude that when two or more processes use the same lock, it gives us a hint that they will very likely access the pages previously guarded by the lock. The probability of accessing these pages is normally very high. According to above analysis, if we use EDA for the pages previously guarded by the lock, we can save more time than using LDA. In Example 1, the lock 1 is used to guard page x and y. So when a process acquires lock 1, it will very likely access both page x and y. In HDA, the $diffs$ of x and y will be sent eagerly after lock 1 is acquired. The $diffs$ of other pages will still be sent lazily as in LDA.

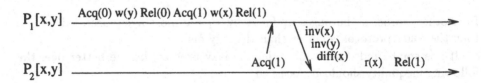

Fig. 7. The message passing in Example 2 under HDA

Based on above assumption, we proposed the HDA protocol. In HDA, we maintain a *page identifier list* for each lock. The pages in the list are previously guarded by the lock. Initially the list is empty. After a process acquires a lock, we begin to record the updated page identifiers in the list until the process releases the lock. That is, during the period between the acquiring and the release of the lock, if the process updates a page, the page's identifier is recorded into the *page identifier list* of the lock. When the lock is acquired by other processes, the $diffs$ of the pages in the *page identifier list* of the lock are created and sent eagerly to the other processes. For example, in Example 1, P_1 will record the identifiers of pages x and y into the *page identifier list* of lock 1 since it will update x and y between acquiring and release of lock 1. Then when P_2 acquires lock 1, the $diffs$ of x and y are sent from P_1 to P_2 eagerly. The message passing between them are the same as in Fig. 5. However, in Example 2, P_1 will record the identifier of x into the *page identifier list* of lock 1 and the identifier of y into the *page identifier list* of lock 0. When P_2 acquires lock 1, only the $diff$ of x is sent eagerly from P_1 to P_2 (the invalidation of y is also sent to ensure the correctness of HDA). The message passing between P_1 and P_2 are illustrated in Fig. 7. From the figure we find, the HDA decreases the number of messages comparing with the LDA, and it avoids useless $diff$ transfer comparing with the EDA.

From above examples, we can discover that HDA can take advantage of both LDA and EDA. In addition, the HDA requires neither programmer annotation nor compiler support. The hints are acquired automatically from the program by the system without much extra overhead (only keeping and recording a *page identifier list* for each lock). If the lock hints about the page accesses are accurate, HDA can greatly decrease the number of messages and avoid unnecessary $diff$ transfer in LRC. From the experimental results, our assumption about lock hints is correct at most situations.

5 Experimental results

This section presents an evaluation of HDA and LDA protocols. The protocols are implemented in the TreadMarks distributed shared memory system [1]. The experimental environment consists of 8 SGI workstations running IRIX Release 5.3. They are connected by Ethernet.

We used 4 applications in this experiment: *TSP, QS, Water, BT*, in which *TSP, QS, Water* are provided by TreadMarks research group. All the programs are written in C language and linked with TreadMarks library. *TSP* is the Traveling Salesman Problem, which finds the minimum cost path that starts at a designated city, passes through every other city exactly once, and returns to the original city. *QS* is a recursive sorting algorithm that operates by repeatedly partitioning an unsorted input list into a pair of unsorted sublists, such that all of the elements in one of the sublists are strictly greater than the elements of the other, and then recursively invoking itself on the two unsorted sublists. *BT* is an algorithm that creates a binary tree. *Water* is a molecular dynamics simulation. Each time-step, the intra- and inter-molecular forces incident on a molecule are computed. These applications are elaborately selected and representative in either numerical computing, e.g., *Water, QS*, or AI computing, e.g., *TSP, BT*.

In the following table, the item *Time* is the total running time of an application program; the *Total Data* is the sum of total message data; the *Diff Data* is the sum of total $diff$ data; the *Diff Miss* is the number of $diff$s acquired when a page fault occurs; the *Mesgs* is the number of messages;

From the results in Table 1, we conclude that:

- The HDA outperforms LDA for every applications. The maximum decrease of running time is 45.1% (TSP), and the minimum decrease is 3.3% (Water).
- the number of messages in HDA has been significantly decreased compared with LDA. The maximum decrease is 47.5% (TSP), and the minimum decrease is 3.6% (Water).
- the *Diff Miss* in HDA has been significantly reduced compared with LDA.
- the total data transferred in HDA is normally smaller than that in LDA because more messages in LDA cause more extra data transfer.

– there is no significant change of total $diff$ data between LDA and HDA. This suggests that the HDA does not send useless $diff$ data eagerly. So HDA can accurately send the useful $diff$s by using the detected lock-data associations.

– the performance of EDA is normally the worst except the TSP (the reason for this exception is, in TSP every process almost accesses every page of shared memory and therefore TSP is in favour of the eager protocol). The EDA normally causes a large amount of data transferred among processes, even though the number of messages and $diff$ misses is reduced.

application	protocol	Time (secs)	Total Data (bytes)	Diff Data (bytes)	Diff Miss	Mesgs
TSP	LDA	15.86	1267683	448958	1029	2846
	EDA	6.39	1250486	456163	7	734
	HDA	8.70	1292737	463896	384	1494
QS	LDA	20.09	10153006	6100023	3152	10432
	EDA	42.08	30329884	26549451	165	6707
	HDA	13.36	9332272	5577086	1053	5936
BT	LDA	82.92	39511375	8921228	27587	96979
	EDA	83.34	44205921	13536620	451	43505
	HDA	69.71	39148835	8761972	6681	53925
Water	LDA	32.59	11717602	9980061	4508	24495
	EDA	40.49	17806563	16013484	2402	20461
	HDA	31.53	11879024	9980913	4033	23606

Table 1. Performance Statistics for applications

6 Conclusions

This paper discussed the advantages and disadvantages of LDA and EDA protocols in LRC model. Based on the discussion, we proposed a HDA protocol which can take advantage of both LDA and EDA. The HDA is based on an **assumption** that *when a process is going to access a lock it will access the pages previously guarded by the lock*. So the associations between locks and data are built up at run-time, and the $diff$s of the pages previously guarded by the lock are acquired eagerly in HDA. In this way the number of messages is decreased significantly in HDA. From the experimental results, the HDA protocol can significantly improve the performance of the LRC model. In the future, some compile-time analysis will be adopted to further optimize the detection of associations between locks and data. Based on the HDA protocol, further research will be done on consistency models to facilitate the AI applications [6] as well as numerical applications in DSM.

Acknowledgments

The authors would like to thank members of Knowledge Representation and Reasoning Unit, especially Krishna Rao for their constructive suggestions to this work. We are grateful to Prof. Willy Zwaenepoel and TreadMarks research group for their valuable support. We also thank the anonymous referees for their comments. The research is supported by an ARC(Australian Research Council) large grant(A49601731), an ARC small grant and a NCGSS grant by Griffith University.

References

1. C.Amza, et al: "TreadMarks: Shared memory computing on networks of workstations," *IEEE Computer*, 29(2):18-28, February 1996.
2. C. Amza, A.L. Cox, S. Dwarkadas, and W. Zwaenepoel: "Software DSM Protocols that Adapt between Single Writer and Multiple Writer," *In Proc. of the Third High Performance Computer Architecture Conference*, pp. 261-271, Feb. 1997.
3. J.K. Bennett, et al: "Munin: Distributed shared memory based on type-specific memory coherence," *In Proceedings of the Second ACM SIGPLAN Symposium on Principles & Practice of Parallel Programming*, Pages 168-176, March 1990.
4. B.N. Bershad, et al: "The Midway Distributed Shared Memory System," *Proc. IEEE COMPCON Conf.*, IEEE, pp528-537, 1993.
5. K. Gharachorloo, et al: "Memory consistency and event ordering in scalable shared memory multiprocessors," *In Proc. of the 17th Annual International Symposium on Computer Architecture*, pp15-26, May 1990.
6. Zhiyi Huang, Chengzheng Sun, Abdul Sattar, and Wanzu Lei: "Parallel Logic Programming on Distributed Shared Memory System," *In Proc. of the IEEE International Conference on Intelligent Processing Systems*, Oct., 1997.
7. P. Keleher: "Lazy Release Consistency for Distributed Shared Memory," *Ph.D. Thesis*, Rice Univ., 1995.
8. P. Keleher, A.L. Cox, S. Dwarkadas, and W. Zwaenepoel: "An Evaluation of Software-Based Release Consistent Protocols," *Journal of Parallel and Distributed Computing, Special Issue on Distributed Shared Memory*, Vol. 29, pp.126-141, Oct. 1995.
9. L. Lamport: "How to make a multiprocessor computer that correctly executes multiprocess programs," *IEEE Transactions on Computers*, 28(9):690-691, September 1979.
10. K.Li, P.Hudak: "Memory Coherence in Shared Virtual Memory Systems," *ACM Trans. on Computer Systems*, Vol. 7, pp321-359, Nov. 1989.
11. H. Lu, S. Dwarkadas, A.L. Cox, and W. Zwaenepoel: "Message Passing Versus Distributed Shared Memory on Networks of Workstations," *In Proc. of Supercomputing '95*, Dec. 1995.

Representation of Discretely Controlled Continuous Systems in Software-Oriented Formal Analysis *

Tetsuya Mizutani[1], Shigeru Igarashi[1], Kohji Tomita[2] and Masayuki Shio[1]

[1] Institute of Information Science, University of Tsukuba
[2] Mechanical Engineering Laboratory, AIST, MITI
Tsukuba, JAPAN 305

Abstract. We have already introduced and demonstrated a new formalism SOFA to analyze and verify programs that control discretely certain continuously physical or other external systems, based on the analytical semantics. Using this formalism, program specifications and its behavior can be not only expressed easily but also directly translated into the conventional mathematics including differential equations. We obtain the actual rational time value when the next action from an observation time will rise, so that verification can be easier and more precise. Other verification systems, for example the verification diagram for reactive system, do not treat realtime system explicitly, so that they do not formulated various physical phenomena straightforward. Some examples, the leaking gas burner model and the autonomous vehicle control system, etc., will be represented, analyzed and verified formally.

1 Introduction

In this paper we demonstrate the formalism SOFA [14] based on the formal analysis FA[24] and the analytical semantics [9, 10, 11] for analyzing physical phenomena or external systems that are changing continuously but controlled by discrete actions of programs. Basically, our formalism is to analyze through investigating a wake-up time of the next action after an *observation time*. We obtain the actual value of time when the next action will rise, and additionally, differential equations can be treated directly because of the sake of FA, so that analysis and verification of these controlling phenomena, especially nonlinear ones, can be made easier and more precise.

In [14], we have shown a model that a car is merging at a T junction on a road. It is a control system of vehicles in which the position of each vehicle changes continuously but actions 'braking' and 'accelerating' are discrete. The movements of cars are given as second differential equations such as

$$\ddot{y} = a \ ,$$

* This work was supported in part by the Grant-in-Aid for the Scientific Research of Ministry of Education, Science and Culture (Nos. 06302013 and 09680322) and also by Fuji Xerox.

$$\ddot{x}_{n+1} = -b \ ,$$

etc., where y and x_{n+1} are the positions of the cars. A condition that the merging car does not crash others has been proved in SOFA.

Dekker's solution [2, 5, 8, 21] can be also easily formulated and analyzed in SOFA. Its component processes have critical sections. It has three good properties as mutually exclusive, starvation-free and deadlock-free. In [15], using the envelope theory, which is constructed from lattice theory with the special closure concept called *envelope* and also handles actual rational time values explicitly, not only we have verified that the program is starvation-free, but also we have obtained the maximum time for each process to wait. In SOFA, the same properties can be shown in the similar manner. For example, we can express a program specification that "the control of process 1 stays at its own critical section between 90 [s] and 120 [s]" as

$$\neg CS_1 \supset \lceil CS_1 \rceil + 90 < CS_1; \neg CS_1 < \lceil CS_1 \rceil + 120$$

and a property that "the control of process 1 arrives at the CS before 0.7 [s] or between 90 [s] and 124.1 [s] after the starting point" as

$$Start \supset \lceil CS_1 \rceil < \lceil \neg Start \rceil + 0.7 \vee \lceil \neg Start \rceil + 90 \leq \lceil CS_1 \rceil \leq \lceil \neg Start \rceil + 124.1$$

in SOFA, both of which are very similar to those in the envelope theory.

Related to this work, many systems to verify realtime systems have been proposed. The well-known systems are temporal logic [16, 17, 18], the interval temporal logic [23], the verification diagram for reactive system [3, 19], TCSP [6], the duration calculi [4, 28], the hybrid automaton [1, 20] and so on. Temporal logic formulates problems on partially ordered time, so concurrent systems are usually considered not as multi-CPU models but as "interleaving" models. Additionally, most variations of the logic, and also the verification diagram, do not deal with actual time values directly. The linear hybrid automaton deals with the "linear hybrid systems" which are similar to our object, but does (piecewise) linear external phenomena only. Manna and Pnueli's system [18] gives a similar idea to the ν-conversion based on the analytic semantics, but it is too complicated to verify parallel programs. Moreover, these systems except duration calculi cannot treat neither actual time value nor continuously changing objects. The locomorphism [13, 22] based on the ν-conversion is a generalization of equivalence of programs [7] which treats parallel program system easily and precisely. The tense arithmetic [12, 25] is our first approach to actual examples of the physical time problems, so it is another base of SOFA.

In section 2, we will introduce syntax and semantics of SOFA, the latter of which is interpreted by formulas of FA. Some examples will be demonstrated in section 3. In this section, we will formulate the leaking gas burner and water level controller, and additionally, the preview lateral vehicle control system, which is actually implemented, will be considered. Conclusions and discussions will be found in section 4.

2 Syntax and Semantics

2.1 Syntax

We start from the formal system FA. (Our symbolism here slightly differs from the original.) In this paper, we only explain (finite) types and abstracts. The brackets [ ] after an expression indicate occurrences of symbols.

Definition 1. 0 is a type. If $\tau_1, \cdots, \tau_n$ are types, then $\tau = [\tau_1, \cdots, \tau_n]$ is also. Type [0] is called type **1**. □

Type 0 indicates an object of a rational number. An object of type $[\tau_1, \cdots, \tau_n]$ is a relation among those of types $\tau_1, \cdots, \tau_n$. A real number is of type **1**, since it is represented by a Dedekind cut of rationals.

Definition 2. If $A[\xi_1, \cdots, \xi_n]$ is a formula (arithmetical in the original FA), $\xi_1, \cdots, \xi_n$ are of type $\tau_1, \cdots, \tau_n$ respectively, and $\varphi_1, \cdots, \varphi_n$ are new distinct bound variables of type $\tau_1, \cdots, \tau_n$, then $\{\varphi_1, \cdots, \varphi_n\}A[\varphi_1, \cdots, \varphi_n]$ is an *abstract* of type $[\tau_1, \cdots, \tau_n]$. □

An abstract $\{\varphi_1, \cdots, \varphi_n\}A[\varphi_1, \cdots, \varphi_n]$ means the set $\{\varphi_1, \cdots, \varphi_n | A[\varphi_1, \cdots, \varphi_n]\}$, i.e., the truth set of A.

In SOFA, certain free variables are specified as program variables, external variables and time. t denotes the variable expressing time. Propositional symbols $\alpha, \beta, \gamma, \cdots$, called *spurs*, each of which is a generalization of schedulers of processes, and *program labels* $L, M, \cdots$ are added to FA as atomic formulas, whose truth changes with time. Spurs and labels are called *time symbols*.

The following operators for formulas are introduced.

Definition 3. For a formula F, $\lceil F \rceil$ is a term, which is called *wake-up* of F. It intuitively means the earliest time when F wakes up (after an observation time). □

Definition 4. For formulas F_1 and F_2, $F_1; F_2$ is a term to mean the earliest wake-up $\lceil F_2 \rceil$ after $\lceil F_1 \rceil$ (after an observation time).

The precedence of this operator is stronger than that of logical connectives. □

In the present paper, $\lceil \ \rceil$ and ; are not nested.

2.2 Interpretation of SOFA Formulas

Each formula of SOFA is interpreted as a formula of FA in which a rational r standing for the observation time is contained. In order to describe changes of values of program variables and external variables, and also, truth of time symbols, higher type variables are introduced.

Definition 5. For each program variable (external variable) x of type τ, the new variable $\hat{x}$ of type $[0, \tau]$ is introduced to denote a function that maps time r onto the value of the original x at r. For a time symbol P, the variable $\hat{P}$ of type $\mathbf{1}$ is also introduced. It must be noted that $\hat{P}(r)$ is a formula of FA. □

Definition 6. Let $Q^{\geq 0}$ be the set of nonnegative rationals and $r \in Q^{\geq 0}$. The translation $\sim$ of a term into that in FA is defined as follows.

$$\widetilde{t}^{\,r} = r \ .$$
$$\widetilde{a}^{\,r} = \hat{a}(r) \ . \qquad a \text{ is a program variable.}$$
$$\widetilde{x}^{\,r} = \hat{x}(r) \ . \qquad x \text{ is an external variable.}$$
$$\widetilde{w}^{\,r} = w \ . \qquad w \text{ is a constant or a variable except}$$
$$\qquad\qquad\qquad\qquad a \text{ program or external variable.}$$
$$\widetilde{s_1 + s_2}^{\,r} = \widetilde{s_1}^{\,r} + \widetilde{s_2}^{\,r} \ .$$
$$\widetilde{s_1 \cdot s_2}^{\,r} = \widetilde{s_1}^{\,r} \cdot \widetilde{s_2}^{\,r} \ .$$
$$\widetilde{s_1 - s_2}^{\,r} = \widetilde{s_1}^{\,r} - \widetilde{s_2}^{\,r} \ .$$
$$\widetilde{s_1/s_2}^{\,r} = \widetilde{s_1}^{\,r}/\widetilde{s_2}^{\,r} \ . \qquad s_1 \text{ and } s_2 \text{ are terms.}$$
$$\widetilde{[F]}^{\,r} = r * F \ .$$
$$\widetilde{F_1;\ F_2}^{\,r} = (r * F_1) * F_2 \ .$$

(* is defined in definition 8 below.) □

Definition 7. The translation $\sharp$ of a formula into that in FA is defined as follows.

$$\alpha_r^{\sharp} \ \text{is} \ \hat{\alpha}(r) \ .$$
$$L_r^{\sharp} \ \text{is} \ \hat{L}(r) \ .$$
$$(s_1 = s_2)_r^{\sharp} \ \text{is} \ \widetilde{s_1}^{\,r} = \widetilde{s_2}^{\,r} \ .$$
$$(s_1 < s_2)_r^{\sharp} \ \text{is} \ \widetilde{s_1}^{\,r} < \widetilde{s_2}^{\,r} \ .$$
$$(\neg F)_r^{\sharp} \ \text{is} \ \neg(F_r^{\sharp}) \ .$$
$$(F_1 \wedge F_2)_r^{\sharp} \ \text{is} \ (F_{1r}^{\sharp}) \wedge (F_{2r}^{\sharp}) \ .$$
$$(\forall z F)_r^{\sharp} \ \text{is} \ \forall z(F_r^{\sharp}) \ .$$

□

Definition 8. For a formula F and a term s of FA, $s * F$ is defined as follows.

$$s * F = a \ \equiv \ \forall u(s < u \wedge F_u^{\sharp} \supset a \leq u)$$
$$\wedge \forall v(\forall u(s < u \wedge F_u^{\sharp} \supset v \leq u) \supset v \leq a)) \ .$$

$s * F$ is $\inf\{u | s < u, F_u^{\sharp}\}$ and intuitively means the earliest time value when F holds, or "wakes up", after the time represented by s. If F_1 never holds after s, then $s * F_1 \neq a$ for any a; so is $(s * F_1) * F_2$ also. □

It must be noted that we analyse continuous systems on the rational time values rather than real ones for the sake of the mathematical simplicity.

2.3 Program Restrictions

Definition 9. An increasing rational sequence $\{t_i\}_{i=0,1,2,\cdots}$ is *discrete* if it is finite or it contains arbitrarily large rationals. □

Definition 10. A function $f : Q^{\geq 0} \to X$, X is an arbitrary set, is called a *piece-wise continuous function* if and only if $f(t) = g_i(t)$ for $t_i < t \leq t_{i+1}$ for some continuous functions $g_i(t)$ of t and a discrete sequence $\{t_i\}_{i=0,1,2,\cdots}$. □

Definition 11. For a variable ξ of type 1, the *characteristic function* maps t onto 1 if $\xi(t)$ holds and 0 otherwise. □

Definition 12. (Restrictions of a Program.)

For a label L, the characteristic function of $\hat{L}$ is a step function, and $\{t_i|\hat{\alpha}(t_i)\}$ is discrete for a spur α. For each program variable a (external variable x), $\hat{a}$ ($\hat{x}$) is a left continuous step function (a piece-wise continuous function). Additionally, $\hat{x}$ is continuous, that is, if $\hat{x}$ is $\{g_i\}_{i=0,1,2,\cdots}$, $g_i(t_{i+1}) = g_{i+1}(t_{i+1})$ each i. □

The following proposition, which is easily proved from FA and the program restrictions, is very convenient for the verification of programs.

Notation 13. For a formula F, $F[t + 0]$ is an abbreviation of

$$\forall \varepsilon > 0 \exists \delta (0 < \delta < \varepsilon \wedge F[t + \delta]) .$$

□

Proposition 14. *Let r be an observation time and u greater than r. If $r * A = u$, then*

$$\begin{cases} A[u + 0] & \text{if } A \text{ is a formula , and} \\ \quad A[u] & \text{if } A \text{ is a spur .} \end{cases}$$

□

2.4 Spurs and Program Axioms

In this paper, we consider a multi-CPU parallel program system in which each process has its own CPU. So, we associate distinct spurs as the schedulers with processes. Program labels are supposed to be exclusive each other process-wise.

We express a program interfering with some external objects by some *program axioms* each of which represents one action step. Each program axiom may contain a spur, a current program label (or program stage), some next labels, conditions and actions (possibly with time conditions). Additionally, we axiomatize the *axiom of conservation* [9] that the values of program variables and truth of labels, i.e., the positions of locations, are kept unchanged as long as no action is performed.

3 Examples

3.1 Leaking Gus Burner

We consider the gas burner problem [1, 4, 28] whose requirement is that the total leaking time is not more than 1/20 of the elapsed time if the system is observed for more than or equal to 60 [s].

In SOFA, the requirement can be expressed as

$$d \geq 60 \supset \lceil x = x_0 \rceil + d \leq (x = x_0); (20(x - x_0) = d) , \qquad (1)$$

where x is the total amount of time when the gas is leaking from the starting period, d a free variable indicating the length of an observation duration and x_0 also free meaning the value of x at the first timing of the observation duration.

Program and Analysis The program in [1, 4, 28] can be expressed in SOFA as

$$Stop \supset Leak; Stop \leq \lceil Leak \rceil + 1 , \qquad (2)$$

$$Leak \supset \lceil Stop \rceil + 30 \leq Stop; Leak \qquad (3)$$

and

$$\dot{x} = a , \qquad (4)$$

where $Stop \equiv a = 0$ and $Leak \equiv a = 1$.

Let us suppose that r is an observation time and t_1 is greater than or equal to r satisfying $x = x_0$. We have

$$d \geq 60 \supset t_1 + d \leq t_1 * (20(x - x_0) = d) \qquad (5)$$

and

$$\hat{x}(t_1) = x_0 \qquad (6)$$

from (1). Let $t_2 \geq t_1$ be satisfying that $20(x - x_0) = d$, i.e., $20(\hat{x}(t_2) - \hat{x}(t_1)) = d$. Then $t_1 + d \leq t_2$. Additionally, $\hat{x}$ is an increasing function from (4). Therefore,

$$d \geq 60 \supset 20(\hat{x}(t_1 + d) - \hat{x}(t_1)) \leq d . \qquad (7)$$

Let s_i and l_i be duration lengths of the i-th states of $Stop$ and $Leak$, respectively. From (2), if the control stays in the i-th state of $Stop$ at time r, then

$$r + l_i \leq r + 1 , \qquad (8)$$

hence, $l_i \leq 1$. Similarly, we also have $30 \leq s_i$ from (3). Since the worst case is $l_i = 1$ and $r_i = 30$, the worst duration whose length is greater than 60 is that the 1-second-leakages happen three times and 30-second-stoppings twice. In this case, the total leaking time ratio is 3/63, which satisfies (7), therefore (1).

3.2 Water Level Controller

Let us consider a water level controller [1, 28]. A water level in a tank is controlled through a controller, which continuously senses the water level, and opens and closes a tap with a delay of 2 [s]. When the tap is open, the level falls by 2 [in] per second. When the tap is closed, the level rises by 1 [in] per second. To keep the water level, expressed y, between 1 and 12 [in], the controller turns off the tap if the level is lower than or equal to l, and on if the level higher than or equal to h.

Program The program axioms of the water level controller are as follows.

$$Shut \supset \lceil y = h \rceil + 2 = \lceil Open \rceil \ , \tag{9}$$

$$Open \supset \lceil y = l \rceil + 2 = \lceil Shut \rceil \ , \tag{10}$$

$$\dot{y} = a \tag{11}$$

and

$$1 \leq y \leq 12 \ , \tag{12}$$

where $Shut \equiv a = 1$ and $Open \equiv a = -2$. Suppose that the initial value of y is between $l \leq y \leq h$.

Analysis Let us analyze the control system and solve the values of l and h. From (9) and (11), we have

$$\hat{y}(r) = r + C_0 \supset r * (y = h) + 2 = r * (\dot{y} = -2) \tag{13}$$

at time r provided that $\hat{a}(r) = 1$. Let t_1 be $r * (y = h)$. So we have $\hat{y}(t_1) = h$ from proposition 14. The value $\hat{y}(t_1 + 2)$ is less than or equal to 12 from (12). Hence, $\hat{y}(t_1 + 2) - \hat{y}(t_1) = 2 \leq 12 - h$ since $\dot{y} = 1$. Then we have $h \leq 10$. On the other hand, we have $h \geq 1$ since $\hat{y}(t_1) \geq 1$. Additionally, it holds that $h + 2 \geq l$ since the value of y at $t_1 + 2$ must be greater than or equal to l, or otherwise, the value becomes less than 1 from (10) and the fact that $\dot{y} = -2$ after $t_1 + 2$. In the same manner, we have $5 \leq l \leq 12$ and $l - 4 \leq h$ from (10). Therefore, the solution is $3 \leq h \leq 10$ and $5 \leq l \leq 12$.

3.3 Vehicle Steering Control Algorithm

We will introduce a preview lateral control algorithm for a vehicle [27], and represent the specifications of the system on SOFA [26].

Preview Lateral Control Algorithm First, we briefly explain the algorithm
for a vehicle with machine vision to drive along an intended path given as a
reference line on the road. The steering angle for the lateral control is decided
by the following three steps. At First, the vehicle detects the reference line in
the field of view ahead from a video image in the x-y coordinate system. The
coordinate system is fixed to the vehicle so that the position of the vehicle is the
origin and its heading is zero. Then, it finds a cubic curve that approximates the
line. The cubic curve has the following form:

$$y = Ax^3 + Bx^2 .$$

Finally, the steering angle s is determined with a coefficient of the cubic curve
by

$$s = \arctan 2lB ,$$

where l is the wheelbase of the vehicle.

If a vehicle drives with a steering angle s at a speed v, then the dynamics of
the vehicle in the simplest form can be expressed by

$$
\begin{aligned}
\dot{x} &= v\cos\theta , \\
\dot{y} &= v\sin\theta \text{ and} \\
\dot{\theta} &= \frac{v}{l}\tan s .
\end{aligned}
\tag{14}
$$

With the dynamics, when the vehicle moves on a circular arc, the radius is
$l/(\tan s)$. If the vehicle is at a position (X_i, Y_i) with a heading Θ_i and drives
with a steering angle s, then after a period T, the new position and heading of
the vehicle can, therefore, be represented by

$$
\begin{aligned}
X_{i+1} &= X_i + \Delta X(\Theta_i, s, T) , \\
Y_{i+1} &= Y_i + \Delta Y(\Theta_i, s, T) \text{ and} \\
\Theta_{i+1} &= \Theta_i + \Delta\Theta(\Theta_i, s, T) .
\end{aligned}
$$

Here, the functions $\Delta X, \Delta y$, and $\Delta\Theta$, are expressed as follows:

$$
\begin{aligned}
\Delta X(\Theta, s, T) &= \Delta x \cos\Theta - \Delta y \sin\Theta , \\
\Delta Y(\Theta, s, T) &= \Delta x \sin\Theta + \Delta y \cos\Theta \text{ and} \\
\Delta\Theta(\Theta, s, T) &= \Delta\theta ,
\end{aligned}
$$

where, $\Delta x, \Delta y$, and $\Delta\theta$ represent increments in the x coordinate, the y coordinate, and the heading, and expressed as follows.

$$
\begin{aligned}
\Delta x &= r\sin\Delta\theta , \\
\Delta y &= r(1 - \cos\Delta\theta) \text{ and} \\
\Delta\theta &= \frac{vT}{r} ,
\end{aligned}
$$

where

$$r = \frac{l}{\tan s}.$$

Representation We consider to represent the control system in SOFA.

vehicle movement.

$$X = a \wedge Y = b \wedge \Theta = c \wedge s = d \wedge \lceil \alpha \rceil - t = u \supset$$
$$\lceil \alpha \rceil = \alpha \; ; (\; X = a + \Delta X(c, \; d, \; u) \wedge$$
$$Y = b + \Delta X(c, \; d, \; u) \wedge$$
$$\Theta = c + \Delta \Theta(c, \; d, \; u) \;) \; .$$

In this case, another representation is possible using the differential equations explicitly:

$$\dot{X} = \; v \cos \Theta \; ,$$
$$\dot{Y} = v \sin \Theta \; \text{and}$$
$$\dot{\Theta} = \; \frac{v}{l} \tan s \; .$$

position of the reference line. If the vehicle is located at a position X, Y with a heading Θ, and the reference line, detected by the vision system, is expressed as $y = px + q$, then p and q are decided as follows:

$$p = - \tan \Theta \wedge q = -Y/\cos \Theta \; .$$

control period. The constant control period is denoted by

$$\alpha ; \alpha - \lceil \alpha \rceil = T \; .$$

steering angle. Since the change of the steering angle is at the time of the next spur, the change is represented by

$$\lceil \alpha \rceil = \alpha ; (\; s = calc(p, q) \;) \; .$$

It is a problem to obtain a sufficient condition with the representation that the vehicle will drive along the reference line after some time in the future. Driving along the (straight) reference line can be expressed implicitly using the variable p and q. The problem is, therefore, modified to find some condition C that p and q must satisfy, and with the condition p and q approach closely enough 0 in the future.

To formally give the condition, we need to use a valuation function V, which is a continuous function of p and q. We assume V satisfies $V(x, y) \geq 0$ and $V(x, y) = 0 \equiv x = y = 0$. In the following we would like to state that if p and q satisfy D, then the value of V will decrease. If V have the following three properties, it can be shown that both p and q converge to 0.

1. $C(p, q) \supset \forall u(\lceil \neg D(p, q) \rceil \neq u)$,
2. $\alpha \wedge D(p, q) \wedge V(p, q) = a \supset \lceil \alpha \rceil = \alpha ; (V(p, q) < a)$,
3. $C(p, q) \supset \forall \varepsilon > 0(\exists u(\lceil V(p, q) < \varepsilon \rceil = u))$.

4 Conclusions and Discussions

We have demonstrated SOFA which explicitly deals with the rational time. As can be seen in the examples of section 3, the proof (and its verification formalism) is easy and intuitive, for the conventional mathematics is used directly.

Comparing with the other verification systems, for example, the verification diagram for reactive system, which does not treat realtime system explicitly, SOFA deals with rational time and the differential equations on it directly, so that various physical phenomena can be formulated more easily and straightforward.

The leaking gas burner model and the water level control model are (piecewise) linear, of which we can very easily translated to nonlinear ones for changing the differential equations (4) and (11) for second ones.

In the example of the preview lateral vehicle control system, we made some strong assumptions. For example, we assumed that the control period is constant. It was used to make the analysis simple, not for the representation itself. Though we can easily simulate the movement of the vehicle [26] for the sake of those simplifications, the model is still too complex to analyze completely. It is one of our future work.

References

1. Alur, R., Courcoubetis, C., Halbwachs, N., Henzinger, T. A., Ho, P. -H., Nicollin, X., Olivero, A., Sifakis, J. and Yovine, S. : The algorithmic analysis of hybrid systems, *Theoretical Computer Science*, **138** (1995), pp. 3–34.
2. Ben-Ari, M. : *Principles of concurrent programming*, Prentice-Hall International, 1982.
3. Browne, I. A., Manna, Z. and Sipma, H., B. : Hierarchical verification using verification diagrams, *Concurrency and Parallelism, Programming, Networking, and Security, Lecture notes in computer science*, **1179** (1996), pp. 276–286.
4. Chaochen, Z. : Duration calculi: an overview, *International Institute for Software Technology, The United Nations University, UNI/IIST Report*, **10** (1993).
5. E. W. Dijkstra : Co-operating sequential process, *Programming Languages* (1968), pp, 43–112.
6. Hoare, C. A. R. : *Communicating Sequential Processes*, Prentice-Hall International (1985).
7. Igarashi, S. : An axiomatic approach to the equivalence problems of algorithms with applications, *Rep. Comp. Centre Univ. Tokyo*, **1** (1968), pp. 1-101.
8. Igarashi, S. : Verification of programs, *Journal of Information Processing Society of Japan*, **19** (1978), pp. 1003–1010 (in Japanese).
9. Igarashi, S. : The ν-conversion and an analytic semantics, in Mason, R. E. A. (ed.), *Inf. Proc. 83* (1983), pp. 769–774 .
10. Igarashi, S., Mizutani, T. and Tsuji, T. : An analytical semantics of parallel program processes represented by ν-conversion., *TENSOR, N. S.*, **45** (1987), pp. 222-228.
11. Igarashi, S., Mizutani, T. and Tsuji, T. : Specifications of parallel program processes in analytical semantics., *TENSOR, N. S.*, **45** (1987), pp. 240-244.

12. Igarashi, S., Tsuji, T., Mizutani, T. and Haraguchi, T. : Experiments on Computerized Piano Accompaniment, *Proceedings of the 1993 International Computer Music Conference* (1993), pp. 415–417 .

13. Igarashi, S., Mizutani, T., Tsuji, T. and Hosono, C.: On locomorphism in analytical equivalence theory, in Jones, N. D., Hagiya, M. and Sato, M. eds., *Logic, Language and Computation: Festschrift in Honor of Satoru Takasu, Lecture notes in computer science,* **792** (1994), pp. 173–187.

14. Igarashi, S., Mizutani, T., Shirogane, T. and Shio, M. : Formal analysis for continuous systems controlled by programs, *Concurrency and Parallelism, Programming, Networking, and Security, Lecture notes in computer science,* **1179** (1996), pp. 347–348.

15. Igarashi, S., Shio, M., Shirogane, T. and Mizutani, T. : Formal verification and evaluation of execution time in the envelope theory, *Concurrency and Parallelism, Programming, Networking, and Security, Lecture notes in computer science,* **1179** (1996), pp. 299–308.

16. Kröger, F. : *Temporal logic of programs*, Springer-Verlag (1987).

17. Lamport, L. : What good is temporal logic?, in R. E. A. Mason (ed.), *Inf. Proc. 83* (1983), pp. 657–668.

18. Manna, Z. and Pnueli, A. : Completing the temporal picture, *Theor. Comp. Sci,* **83** (1991), pp. 97-130.

19. Manna, Z. and Pnueli, A. : *The temporal logic for reactive and concurrent systems : specification,* Springer-Verlag (1992).

20. Majumdar, R. and Shyamasundar, R. K. : design of controllers for linear hybrid systems, *Concurrency and Parallelism, Programming, Networking, and Security, Lecture notes in computer science,* **1179** (1996), pp. 309–320.

21. Mizutani, T., Hosono, C. and Igarashi, S. : Verification of programs using ν-definable acts, *Computer Software,* **2** (1985), pp. 529–538 (in Japanese).

22. Mizutani, T., Igarashi, S. and Tsuji, T. : An analytical equivalence theory of computer programs, *Proceedings of International Symposium on Structures in Mathematical Theories* (1990), pp. 199–204 .

23. Moszkowski, B. C. : *Executing temporal logic programs*, Cambridge Univ. Press (1986).

24. Takeuti, G. : *Two applications of logic to mathematics*, Princeton University Press (1978).

25. Tomita, K., Tsuji, T. and Igarashi, S. : Analysis of a software/hardware system by tense arithmetic, in Jones, N. D., Hagiya, M. and Sato, M. eds., *Logic, Language and Computation: Festschrift in Honor of Satoru Takasu, Lecture notes in computer science,* **792** (1994), pp. 188–205.

26. Tomita, K., Igarashi, S., Hosono, C., Mizutani, T. and Tsugawa, S. : Representations of autonomous realtime systems, *The 4th International Conference of Tensor Society on Differential Geometry and its Applications,* Tsukuba, 1996. (*TENSOR, N.S.,* submitted to.)

27. Tsugawa, S. and Murata, S. : Steering control algorithm for autonomous vehicle, *Proc. Japan-U.S.A. Symposium on Flexible Automation* (1990), 143–146.

28. Xuandong, L. and Hung, D. V. : Checking linear duration invariants by linear programming, *Concurrency and Parallelism, Programming, Networking, and Security, Lecture notes in computer science,* **1179** (1996), pp. 321–330.

A Generalised Framework for Reasoning with Multi-point Events

R. Wetprasit[1] and A. Sattar[1] and L. Khatib[2]

[1] Knowledge Representation and Reasoning Unit
School of Computing and Information Technology, Griffith University,
NATHAN, Brisbane, 4111 AUSTRALIA
[2] Computer Science Program, Florida Institute of Technology,
150 W. University Blvd., Melbourne, Fl. 32901, USA

Abstract. Allen's Interval Algebra (IA) and Vilain and Kautz's Point Algebra (PA) consider an *interval* and a *point* as basic temporal entities (i.e., *events*) respectively. However, in many real world situations we often need to deal with recurring events that include multiple points, multiple intervals or combinations of points and intervals. Recently, we presented a *multiple-point event* (MPE) framework to represent relations over recurring point events and showed that it can handle pointisable interval relations (SIA). We also showed that computing a minimal MPE network is a polynomial solvable problem. However, the MPE framework cannot correctly capture the relation between three points called a *discontinuous point relation* and this has not been satisfactorily addressed in the literature. In this paper, we extend MPE to a general framework that is expressive enough to represent discontinuous point relations and other complex situations which are relationships between single events (i.e., point-interval, and interval-interval relations), and clusters of events (i.e., recurring point-point and interval-interval relations). Further we developed a path-consistency algorithm for computing the minimal network for a generalised MPE network and improved our earlier path-consistency algorithm for MPE networks. We then present an analysis of experimental results on the implementation of these algorithms.

1 Introduction

Ability to reason with temporal information is an essential component of intelligent systems such as planning, scheduling and medical diagnosis. Allen's *Interval Algebra* [1] and Vilain & Kautz's *Point Algebra* [17] are two well known formalisms to represent and reason with temporal information. As a time point can also be seen as an infinitesimal time interval, interval algebra (IA) is strictly more expressive than point algebra (PA). From the computational point of view, point algebra has an advantage over interval algebra as most of the computational issues in IA are intractable. The intractability of IA and tractability of PA can be explained from the fact that there are only three basic PA relations (namely, $\{<, >, =\}$) whereas there are thirteen basic IA relations (namely, $\{before\ (<), after\ (>), equal\ (=),\ during\ (d), contains\ (di),\ over$-$laps\ (o),\ overlapped$-$by\ (oi),\ meets\ (m), met$-$by\ (mi), starts\ (s),\ started$-$by\ (si),\ finishes\ (f),\ finished$-$by\ (fi)\}$). Motivated by the computational advantages of PA, a subclass of IA called *pointisable interval algebra* (SIA) [14] was proposed. SIA relations are a subset of IA relations that contains only those relations that can be represented as relations between interval endpoints. Even though the number of allowed relations for SIA is small, they are important and useful in real world applications [15].

Both IA and PA consider events as unique occurrences and are not concerned with events that occur repeatedly. However, the repeated occurrence of events is a common phenomena in many applications such as electronic recording of cardiac cycles in medical diagnosis [4], reasoning with patient medical histories [2], and personal scheduling [13]. Ladkin [5] and Morris, Shoaff and Khatib [10, 3] proposed to deal with such temporal information in terms of sets of interval events that occur more than once, called *non-convex intervals* (NCIs). In this formalism, an event is an ordered sequence of subevents and each subevent is an interval event. In our recent paper [18], we proposed a point-based approach (called the *multi-point event* (MPE) framework) to handle recurring events where the subevent is either a point event or an endpoint (starting or ending) of an interval event. The MPE formalism has both expressive power (can handle both point and interval events) and computational efficiency.

Example 1. A patient suspected of having disease A had symptoms progressing in three phases: I, II, and III. During each phase, the patient experienced a period of fever and a period of chilling, with chilling starting before fever. During the three phases six temperature recordings were made, separated by fixed time periods. Of the six temperatures measured, the second and the sixth measures were normal and a significant high fever was found in the third measure.

Illustration: Given the above history, the knowledge can be represented as three different multi-point events: MPE 1 represents the six different temperature samples considered as point subevents, MPE 2 and MPE 3 represent the three periods of chilling and fever respectively. The information about the relationship between pairs of subevents is incomplete. For instance, between periods of chilling and fever we only know that the start point of chilling was before fever. In this case, the possible relation between each pair of chilling and fever subintervals is $\{<, o, m, fi, di\}$ which is an SIA class relation. When we model an interval as pair of ordered point subevents, the above relation can be represented by a multi-point event relation which is the translation of SIA to a point relation between the subinterval endpoints. MPE differs from SIA in that a repeating sequence of SIA relations are captured in a single MPE relation. For example the three SIA relations representing the three periods of chilling and fever can be represented as a single MPE relation between MPE 2 and MPE 3.

The MPE framework presented in [18] can handle this situation efficiently. The problem of finding minimal relations between pairs of MPEs was shown to have polynomial time complexity and an algorithm FEASIBLE_MPE was proposed for finding a minimal MPE network with *only* feasible set of relations between each pair of MPEs from the given input MPE network.

However, there is a class of point relations that the MPE model cannot represent as well as PA. This is the *discontinuous point relation*, e.g., *point A is either before both points P and Q, or after both points P and Q, but not between those two points*, given that P is before Q. Main reason for the inability of MPE framework in representing this relation is that the relation between two MPEs is given by a matrix corresponding to a conjunction of relations between the subevents of the two MPEs, while discontinuous point relation needs two matrices corresponding to two possibilities: (a) A is before both P and Q or (b) after both P and Q. See Section 3 for more details.

In this paper, we generalise the MPE framework by allowing multiple matrices (corresponding to various possibilites) in representing a relation between two MPEs. This ensures that the generalised MPE framework (GMPE, henceforth) is expressive enough to represent (1) discontinuous relations among recurring point events, (2) the full set of relations from IA, and (3) all recurring event relations either interval-based or point-based. Inherently, the problem of finding minimal relations between pairs of MPEs is computationally intractable. In view of this, we present an approximation algorithm for this problem.

The rest of the paper is organized into three main parts. The first part introduces the generalised MPE framework and gives an algorithm for reasoning with GMPE networks. The second part provides an improved version of the FEASIBLE_MPE algorithm given in [18], by eliminating some redundant computations. The third part discusses the implementation of our algorithms in C on Sun Creator 3D-2000 and the experimental results obtained.

2 Reasoning with Temporal Constraint Networks

Temporal reasoning problems can be formulated as *constraint satisfaction problems* [9]—sometimes called *Constraint Networks*. Temporal events (i.e., intervals, points, non-convex intervals, multi-point events) are represented by nodes, and *relations* between two events are represented as labelled arcs. Since incomplete information on the occurrences of events is allowed, the relation between a pair of events is a disjunction of possible basic relations. When obtaining more constraint(s), the reasoner has to determine the consistency of all assertions correctly. For instance, in Example 1 if we later know that in phase II the patient was treated resulting in no fever occurring after chilling, the relation between the second subinterval of chilling and the second subinterval of fever is restricted to $\{fi, di\}$, hence $\{<, o, m\}$ becomes infeasible. Therefore, the fundamental reasoning tasks for temporal constraint problems are:

1. considering whether the given qualitative information is *consistent*, i.e., whether there exists an *assignment* of real numbers to all variables such that all corresponding constraints are satisfied;
2. finding *a consistent scenario* or atomic labelled network that satisfies all constraints; and
3. finding a *minimal network* in which all infeasible relations are removed, or, in other words, finding the deductive consequences of the given information.

Deciding consistency reduces the problem to either task 2 or task 3. While backtracking based algorithms were used for solving task 2, path-consistency algorithms were applied to task 3. Essentially, path-consistency algorithms repeatedly tighten constraints on a third arc using the constraints on the other two consecutive arcs by computing the following *triangular operation*:

$$C_{i,j} \leftarrow C_{i,j} \times (C_{i,k} \circ C_{k,j})$$

where $C_{i,j}$ is a constraint on node i to j. The composition operation, $\circ$, expresses the transmitted constraint from node i to j via k. The intersection, $\times$, removes atoms from the current relation of arc (i, j) that are not included in the induced $C_{i,j}$. The algorithm performs the triangular operations on all possible triangles until the network is stable or until some constraint becomes empty indicating an inconsistent network.

In the next section, we introduce an extension of traditional point algebra to a more complex constraint network, MPE, in which a variable represents a set of related point-subevents. A domain is a tuple of real values on the time line on which those subevents take place.

3 Generalised Multi-Point Event Framework

A *multi-point event* (MPE), I, of size n is a collection of n totally ordered point subevents $\{I_1 < ... < I_i < I_{i+1} < ... < I_n\}$. An *MPE network* of k variables is a binary constraint network representing k MPEs where arcs are labelled with relations between pairs of MPEs. The *domain* of each variable is a set of n-tuples: $\{(x_1, ..., x_n) | x_i < x_{i+1}$ and $x_i \in$ REAL$\}$, and an *instantiation* of a node is one such n-tuple.

An MPE relation between two MPEs, I of size n and J of size m, is represented by an $n \times m$ matrix of point relations: $\{\emptyset, <, \leq, =, >, \geq, \neq, ?\}$, a so called *MPE matrix*. '?' represents $\{<, >, =\}$ or no constraint between two points. The ith row of the matrix represents the ith point of I and the jth column represents the jth point of J. If a matrix A represents a relation from MPE I to J of size m and n respectively, the element $A_{i,j}$ indicates the relation between subevent I_i of MPE I and subevent J_j of MPE J. The conjunction of elements of the matrix A represents a relation from I to J, denoted by IAJ.

$$IAJ \equiv ((I_1 r_{1,1} J_1) \wedge ... \wedge (I_1 r_{1,n} J_n) \wedge (I_2 r_{2,1} J_1) \wedge ... \wedge (I_2 r_{2,n} J_n) \wedge (I_m r_{m,1} J_1) \wedge ... \wedge (I_m r_{m,n} J_n)).$$

where $r_{i,j}$ is the relation from I_i to J_j.

An MPE network is *consistent* if there is an instantiation such that all MPE relations are satisfied. A *consistent scenario* is a consistent MPE network in which each arc is labelled with a matrix of atomic relations. The MPE operations defined over a *pair* of matrices are shown in Table 1. The symbols $+$, $\times$, $\bar{}$, $\circ$, and $\tilde{}$ correspond to union, intersection, complement, composition and inverse operators of two point relations [17], respectively.

In our earlier paper [18], we proposed a polynomial algorithm for deciding consistency and computing the minimal MPE network based on a path-consistency algorithm and proved that an MPE framework is expressive enough to handle SIA relations.

However, the MPE framework cannot handle the relation between three point subevents called *discontinuous point relation*. An example of such a relation is *point I_1 is either before or after point J_1 and J_2, but not in between them*, given J_1 is before J_2. Since the domain of point events is on a linear time line, this 3-point relation implies a

Union	$C = A \oplus B$ iff $C_{i,j} = A_{i,j} + B_{i,j}$
Intersection	$C = A \otimes B$ iff $C_{i,j} = A_{i,j} \times B_{i,j}$
Complement	$C = \hat{A}$ iff $C_{i,j} = {}^{\sim}A_{i,j}$
Inverse	$C = \breve{A}$ iff $C_{i,j} = {}^{\sim}A_{j,i}$
Composition	$C = A \odot B$ iff $C_{i,j} = \prod_{k=1}^{r}(A_{i,k} \circ B_{k,j})$
	$\quad = A_{i,1} \circ B_{1,j} \times A_{i,2} \circ B_{2,j} \times ... \times A_{i,r} \circ B_{r,j}$
	$\forall\, i,j\ (1 \leq i \leq n, 1 \leq j \leq m)$

Table 1. The Matrix Operations

gap between J_1 and J_2, and that I_1 is not permitted in between J_1 and J_2. The closest we can express this as an MPE relation is

$$(I_1 \neq J_1) \wedge (I_1 \neq J_2)$$

which can be simplified as

$$((I_1 < J_1) \vee (I_1 > J_1)) \wedge ((I_1 < J_2) \vee (I_1 > J_2))$$

This is an undesired interpretation as it includes $J_1 \leq I_1 \leq J_2$. To avoid using a ternary constraint to represent the discontinuous relation (as we know that $J_1 < J_2$), we represent such a relation by exploiting the fact that the events are *ordered*. We generalise the MPE framework (GMPE) to allow the disjunction of sets of relations between different pairs of subevents. This facilitates the following representation of the above discontinuous point relation:

$$((I_1 < J_1) \wedge (I_1 < J_2)) \vee ((I_1 > J_1) \wedge (I_1 > J_2)).$$

This disjunction can be captured in a matrix-based representation as a set of matrices, in this case two matrices. Each matrix corresponds to a disjunct.

Formally, a GMPE relation $\mathcal{A}$ between MPE I to J is a set of MPE matrices $\mathcal{A} = \{A^1, A^2, ..., A^M\}$, where each A^i represents a possible relation between MPE I to J, and M is a finite number indicating the number of matrices. The intersection of two GMPE relations is simply a set theoretic operation of two sets of matrices. The inverse and composition distribute over the set union. Therefore, the inverse of a GMPE relation is the union of the inverse of each matrix. The composition of GMPE $\mathcal{A}$ with M matrices and $\mathcal{B}$ with N matrices is $\mathcal{A} \odot \mathcal{B} = \bigcup_{p=1}^{M} \bigcup_{q=1}^{N} A^p \odot B^q$ while operator $\odot$ is defined in Table 1. A GMPE network is *consistent* if there is an instantiation that satisfies each single matrix of atomic relations labelling each arc.

Example 2. Given three MPEs: I, J, and K, all of size 2 with following relations:

i) Relation between MPEs: I and J

I_1 is before or after J_1 and J_2 but not in between J_1 and J_2

I_2 is after J_1 and I_2 is before or equal J_2

ii) Relation between MPEs: J and K

J_1 is not equal K_1, J_2 is after K_1, and both J_1 and J_2 are before K_2

From i) and ii), the constraints between I,J and J,K are

$$C_{IJ} = \begin{bmatrix} < & < \\ > & \leq \end{bmatrix} \begin{bmatrix} > & > \\ > & \leq \end{bmatrix}$$

$$C_{JK} = \begin{bmatrix} \neq & < \\ > & < \end{bmatrix}$$

However, the second matrix of C_{IJ} is inconsistent under condition $I_i < I_{i+1}$. Therefore, the relation between I and K is

$$C_{IK} = C_{IJ} \odot C_{JK} = \begin{bmatrix} < & < \\ > & \leq \end{bmatrix} \odot \begin{bmatrix} \neq & < \\ > & < \end{bmatrix} = \begin{bmatrix} ? & < \\ ? & < \end{bmatrix}$$

There are a finite number of consistent scenarios. One of them is shown below, while a possible consistent instantiation is $I \leftarrow\; <2,5>, J \leftarrow\; <4,7> K \leftarrow\; <1,8>$.

4 From Interval Relations to GMPE

In this section, we demonstrate how to accommodate the full set of IA relations using a GMPE framework. We initially explain why the MPE framework is sufficient to represent a small subset of IA called SIA [15]. Then we give an example of *disjointedness of interval relations* which, as van Beek claimed, cannot be handled by point algebra in the same way as SIA.

Van Beek provided a systematic method to enumerate SIA relations into conjunctions of point relations between pairs of interval endpoints. The interval relation *I is during J or I starts J* is an example of SIA and can be translated to a point-based representation as shown below:

$$((I_1 \geq J_1) \wedge (I_1 < J_2) \wedge (I_2 > J_1) \wedge (I_2 < J_2))$$

where I_1 and I_2 represent the start and end points of interval I. and J_1 and J_2 represent the start and end points of interval J. We know that the start point of an interval must be before the end point. As this interval relation is not discontinuous this implies a continuous relation between all endpoints. Thus, by representing the start and end points of each interval as an MPE, we can represent this relation in an MPE framework, as one MPE matrix. Even though this can be achieved in traditional point algebra by representing each endpoint as an individual point event, the implicit ordinal relationship between the start and end of an interval must be represented as well. This results in a larger knowledge base and requires more operations to be performed than in the MPE framework. This causes significant effects when dealing with non-convex intervals especially when the number of subintervals is large.

A general example of disjointedness of interval relations is *Interval I is either before or after Interval J*. This relation contains two discontinuous point relations among:

(I_1, J_1, J_2) and (I_2, J_1, J_2). From the representation of the discontinuous point relation described in the previous section, we have the relations between pairs of interval endpoints as follows:

$$((I_1 < J_1) \wedge (I_1 < J_2) \wedge (I_2 < J_1) \wedge (I_2 < J_2)) \vee ((I_1 > J_1) \wedge (I_1 > J_2) \wedge (I_2 > J_1) \wedge (I_2 > J_2))$$

which is denoted in a GMPE relation as:

$$C_{IJ} = \begin{bmatrix} < & < \\ < & < \end{bmatrix} \begin{bmatrix} > & > \\ > & > \end{bmatrix}$$

Theorem 3. *The GMPE network can represent all possible relations between MPEs of various sizes, non-convex intervals (NCIs) and full IA relations when translated into an equivalent GMPE representation.*

Allen's interval algebra has been an influential framework for representing and reasoning with time-dependent information. However, it is well known that the reasoning problems in IA are intractable. Since GMPE networks can represent full IA relations, the reasoning problems for GMPE are intractable as well. In view of this, we focus on the design of a polynomial, *approximate*, path-consistency algorithm for computing the minimal GMPE network.

5   Reasoning with a GMPE Network

As mentioned above, the major tasks for reasoning with temporal constraint networks are finding all feasible relation labels on a network and finding a consistent scenario of that network. In this section, we present an algorithm for computing feasible relations in a GMPE network based on a path-consistency algorithm. It is known that path-consistency algorithms are not complete, but they have been successfully used in computing approximate minimal networks that often yield the desired results[1]. Moreover, path-consistency is an excellent preprocessor for pruning search space in backtracking methods for computing a consistent scenario [6, 7].

We propose a path-consistency algorithm for GMPE in which a triangular operation is used which involves the composition and intersection operations over two sets of matrices. The algorithm PC_GMPE, given below, repeatedly propagates the operations through the network until stability or inconsistency is detected. When checking the path-consistency of the networks, we always enforce path-consistency between two MPEs, more precisely, we check all possible length two paths among all subevents of two MPEs[2].

Whenever a matrix is updated, we call the procedure Canonical_Conv which converts the matrix to it's canonical form, defined as follows:

---

[1] Checking arc-consistency is not necessary here as the domain of each variable is infinite (i.e., real numbers) where any pair of variables can be instantiated by arbitrary values to satisfy the constraint.

[2] This step is not necessary for MPE/GMPE networks obtained from (by translating) a SIA or IA.

Definition 4. An MPE matrix representing a relation between two MPEs is in *canonical form* if the path-consistency conditions [8] are satisfied such that every element is checked with all of it's neighbours (above, below, right, and left).

The variable Q_Point in the Canonical_Conv procedure represents the indices of the elements in the matrix that were changed by triangular operation. Therefore, converting into canonical form only requires four point compositions for each changed element, thus it is a linear time operation. The call to Canonical_Conv (with the set of all indices of the matrix) occurs before propagation, and enforces all asserted matrices to be in canonical form.

Procedure *Canonical_Conv(A, Q_Point)*
Input: *A* is a matrix relation to be converted into canonical form and
Q_Point is a queue of indices of previously updated elements in *A*.
Output: The canonical form of matrix *A*.

    While Q_Point is not empty
        Remove $< i, j >$ from Q_Point
        Check the path-consistency of all neighbouring elements of $A_{i,j}$
        If any neighbour of $A_{i,j}$ is empty then signal matrix relation contradiction
        If any neighbour of $A_{i,j}$ is updated
            Put its index into Q_Point
            Mark that element changed for further propagation

Algorithm *PC_GMPE*
Input: A *GMPE* network represented as a matrix *C* where entry C_{IJ} is the label on the arc from nodes *I* to *J*.
Each C_{IJ} is a set of matrix relations $R(I,J)^i$
Output: A path-consistent GMPE network
Variable: Q_MPE is a queue of tuples $< I, K, J >$ corresponding to length two paths,
Temp is a set of matrices of size $n \times m$ for matrix $R(I,K)^i$ of size $n \times o$ and matrix $R(K,J)^j$ of size $o \times m$,
QP is a set of queues, elements of each queue QP^k are tuples $< r, s >$ which correspond to indexes of matrix
begin
    Perform Canonical_Conv on each input matrix
    $Q\_MPE := \{(I,K,J) \mid 1 \le I < J \le k, 1 \le K \le k, K \ne I, J\}$
    While Q_MPE is not empty do
        select and delete a path (I, K, J) from Q_MPE
        Temp $:= R(I,K) \odot R(K,J)$ /* Composite over two sets of matrices */
        Mark all elements of R(I,J) unchanged
        MatricesIntersect(R(I,J),Temp,QP)
        If any QP^i is not empty then begin
            For each QP^i that is not empty do
                Canonical_Conv($R(I,J)^i, QP^i$)
            $Q\_MPE := Q\_MPE \cup \{(I,J,K), (K,I,J) \mid 1 \le K \le k, K \ne I, J\}$
    end
end

Procedure *MatricesIntersect(I, J: sets of same size matrices, Q: a set of queues)*
Variable: *T* is a set of matrices with the same size as matrices in *I* or *J*, initialise each matrix element to empty set
begin
    $i := 1, j := 1, t := 1$
    $nI :=$ number of matrices in *I*, $nJ :=$ number of matrices in *J*
    Repeat
        $T^t := I^i \otimes J^j$ /* intersection of two matrices */
        If any element(s) of T^t is empty then begin
            $j := j + 1$
            If $(j > nJ$ and $i < nI)$ then
                begin $i := i + 1, j := 1$ end
            elseif $(j > nJ$ and $i = nI)$ then
                $i := i + 1$
        end
        else begin
            If $T^t_{r,s} \ne I^i_{r,s}$ then begin
                Mark $T^t_{r,s}$ changed
                $Q^i := Q^i \cup < r, s >$

```
                     end
             i := i + 1, t := t + 1, j := 1
          end
    Until    i > nI
    If any element of T¹ is empty then Signal Contradiction
    else I := T
end
```

Theorem 5. *The time complexity of the Algorithm PC_GMPE is $O(n^5 k^3 M^3)$, where k is the number of MPEs in the input GMPE network, n is the maximum size (number of subevents) of MPEs in the input network and M is the maximum number of matrices labelling an arc in the input network.*

6 Improved Results for MPE Networks

In this section, we improve the results of our earlier paper [18] on MPE networks in two ways: (1) the efficiency of the path consistency algorithm is improved by eliminating some redundant computations and (2) the time complexity of the algorithm for finding forbidden subgraphs is shown to be $O(n^2 k^4)$ rather than $O(n^4 k^4)$, where k is the number of MPEs in the input network and n is the maximum number of subevents in an MPE.

The main processing cost of the path-consistency routine is checking consistency for all length two paths by performing triangular operations, which involves the composition of two matrices defined in Table 1. Our previous version of PC_MPE performs matrix compositions involving all elements in the matrix. However, we observed that it only needs to perform compositions involving the most recently changed elements. We mark the changed elements after performing a triangular operation and use this marking in the next loop to perform the composition only on the marked elements. This results in reduction of time complexity from $O(n^5 k^3)$ to $O(n^3 k^3)$.

For GMPE and MPE networks, the path-consistency checking can only compute the approximate minimal network. To obtain the correct minimal MPE network, we need to remove the infeasible relation existing in each *forbidden MPE subgraph* [18]. A subgraph consists of four MPEs with specific relations corresponding to arcs as described in Figure 1. Procedure FIND_SUBGRAPHS_MPE initially searches through all $O(n^2 k^2)$ relations between subevents to find '$\neq$' relation(s) in the path-consistent MPE network. For each '$\neq$' relation, the procedure finds subevents S_s and T_t from $O(k)$ matrices each with n relations within the vth and wth rows. Thus, at this step the time complexity for searching is $O(nk)$. In removing '$=$' from relation between subevent S_s and T_t, there are $O(nk)$ possibilities for S_s and T_t. This nested loop requires $O(n^2 k^2)$ time complexity. However, we observed that since all pairs of subevents in the same MPE are defined to be ordered ($I_i < I_{i+1}$), the infeasible relation existing in a forbidden subgraph must be from different MPEs within the subgraph. The complexity of this step is reduced to $O(k^2)$. Therefore, the complexity for FIND_SUBGRAPHS_MPE becomes $O(n^2 k^4)$ in the worst case.

Algorithm *FEASIBLE_MPE*
Input: A *MPE* network represented as a matrix C where entry C_{IJ} is the label on the arc from nodes I to J.
Each C_{IJ} is a matrix relation $R(I,J)$, where an entry of $R(I,J)$ is the relation between point in MPEs I and J
Output: The set of feasible relations for C_{IJ}, $I, J = 1, 2, .., k$
    PC_MPE
    FIND_SUBGRAPHS_MPE

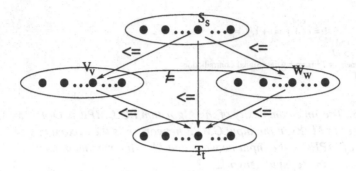

Fig. 1. A forbidden MPE subgraph

Procedure *PC_MPE*
Variable: *Q_Point* is a queue of tuples $< r, s >$ which correspond to indexes of matrix
begin
      Perform Canonical_Conv on each input matrix
      $Q\_MPE := \{(I,K,J) \mid 1 \leq I < J \leq k, 1 \leq K \leq k, K \neq I, J\}$
      Mark each element of all matrices changed
      While *Q_MPE* is not empty do
          select and delete a path (I,K,J) from *Q_MPE*
          For each row r in $R(I,K)$ that contains changed element(s)
          /* Changed elements in $R(K,J)$ are considered when checking path (K,J,I) */
              For $c = 1$ to SIZE(J)
                 Temp $:= R(I,J)_{r,c} \times \prod_{l \in C_r}(R(I,K)_{r,l} \circ R(K,J)_{l,c})$
                 /* $C_r = \{x: R(I,K)_{r,x}$ is marked changed$\}$
                 If Temp = 0 then Signal Contradiction
                 If $(R(I,J)_{r,c} \neq$ Temp) then
                    $R(I,J)_{r,c} = $ Temp
                    mark $R(I,J)_{r,c}$ changed and other elements of $R(I,J)$ unchanged
                    place $< r, c >$ on *Q_Point*
          If *Q_Point* is not empty   /* some elements in $R(I,J)$ have been changed */
               Canonical_Conv($R(I,J)$,*Q_Point*)
               $Q\_MPE := Q\_MPE \cup \{(I,J,K), (J,I,K) \mid 1 \leq K \leq k, K \neq I, J\}$
end

Procedure *FIND_SUBGRAPHS_MPE*
begin
      For each matrix relation such that $R(V,W)_{v,w} = \{\neq\}$ and $(1 \leq V < W \leq k, 1 \leq v, w \leq n)$ do
          Initialise I, J to empty set
          For each MPE M, N $(1 \leq M, N \leq k, M, N \neq V, W)$ do
              Find a set I of points M_m such that $R(V,M)_{v,m} = \{\geq\}$ and $R(W,M)_{w,m} = \{\geq\}$
              If I is not empty then
                  Find a set J of points N_n such that $R(V,N)_{v,n} = \{\leq\}$ and $R(W,N)_{w,n} = \{\leq\}$
          For each $S_s \in I$ do
              For each $T_t \in J$ do
                 If $S \neq T$ then $R(S,T)_{s,t} := \{<\}$
end

Theorem 6. *The algorithm FEASIBLE_MPE correctly finds all feasible relations for the network of k MPEs, each node contains at most n point subevents with a run time of $O(max(n^3k^3, n^2k^4))$.*

Theoretically, we can construct a corresponding PA network from an MPE (but not a GMPE) network by considering each subevent as individual point event. However, this results in losing connectivity in multi-point events. The extra number of relations required in the PA network is equal to the number of ordinal relationships between subevents from the same MPE. These relations are implicitly represented in the MPE approach. Therefore, in theory, MPE has better performance than PA, as shown in [18]. The complexity of computing the corresponding minimal PA network proposed in [15] is $O(max(n^3k^3, n^4k^4))$, in worst case.

7 Experimental Study

7.1 MPE

In Section 3, we described the MPE as a set of point subevents that occur in a linear order. When relations between a pair of MPEs are restricted to be represented by one matrix, then the network becomes a special case of GMPE. We also presented the FEASIBLE_MPE algorithm for finding all feasible MPE relations based on the path-consistency approach. The network resulting from the algorithm is a minimal MPE in which all labels are feasible, i.e., it is a globally consistent network. As mentioned earlier, there are two approaches to handle the proposed minimal problem: modelling relations in a MPE network, and representing each point subevent as individual traditional point events. Intuitively, by omitting the computation of implicit relations among subevents, our approach should yield better performance especially when the numbers of subevents are large.

Our preliminary study was motivated by the fact that SIA relations can be represented by a conjunction of relations between interval endpoints. Consequently, without losing information, an SIA network can be interpreted in terms of a corresponding MPE network. In our experimental study, we generated networks of 3 to 15 nodes whose labels were randomly chosen from SIA relations. We experimented on different degrees of nodes d. Thus, the total number of labelled arcs in a network was $kd/2$, where k is number of intervals in the network[3]. Using the SIA enumeration as presented in [15], we converted the labels into MPE relations where each MPE is restricted to two point subevents: the start and end points of an interval.[4] These small-size random networks, varying d from $d = k - 1$ (which is a complete graph) to $d = k/8$, took no more than 0.02 seconds[5]. Moreover, as shown in Figure 2, the difference between numbers of initial labelled arcs has little effect on execution time. This is possibly due to the effect of only performing compositions of changed elements or to the sizes of the networks being too small to detect a difference.

We are currently designing more experiments to evaluate the above two approaches. We intend to generate large-size consistent MPE networks by adding a randomly generated consistent scenario into a random MPE network. The performance of these approaches will be evaluated with respect to the size of the various MPEs.

---

[3] In Section 5 and 6, k denotes the number of MPEs in the network. Here each interval event corresponds to a two point MPE, so k is indeed representing the number of multi-point events.

[4] The simple PA composition table is stored and no heuristic was applied in our MPE implementation.

[5] With $d = k - 1$ and greater than 9 intervals, and $d = 3k/4$ and greater than 12 intervals, the networks are inconsistent so no information is shown in Figure 2. This is consistent to Fig.6 in [6].

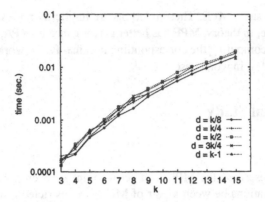

Fig. 2. Effect of degree of nodes on average time (sec.) of FEASIBLE_MPE algorithm for small-size random MPE networks

7.2 GMPE

We have shown earlier that a full IA network can be translated into an equivalent GMPE network. The GMPE framework also has an advantage over IA concerning expressiveness (i.e., it can represent relations over events that happen sequentially without losing connectivity).

To evaluate the GMPE approach, we adopted the $S(k, d)$ random model [16, 11], informally described in [6], to generate IA networks which are then converted into equivalent GMPE networks. An $S(k, d)$ instance is obtained by initially generating a k-interval network with an average degree of nodes d. The labels of arcs are randomly chosen from the full set of interval relations. The second step is to construct a consistent instance of the network, i.e., generating a "solution" of size k by randomly picking k intervals represented as pairs of real numbers, and then identifying consistent relations between pairs of these intervals. We then merge together these two networks to ensure that we have a consistent network.

We implemented the PC_GMPE algorithm, which takes a GMPE network (equivalent to the IA network generated by $S(k, d)$) as input and then computes an approximate minimal GMPE network as output. We found that the number of matrices assigned to arcs significantly affects the time and space complexity, e.g., the composition of two arcs with n and m matrices results in $n \times m$ matrices. Therefore, instead of converting each atomic IA relation into one corresponding matrix, we considered maximum subsets of SIA that cover the label. For example, if an arc IK is labelled with { $>$,=,d,o,s,f,fi,di,oi,si }, this is transformed into three MPE matrices which are equivalent to {$>$} {di,oi,si} {=,d,o,s,f,fi}. After finishing each triangular operation, we remove any redundant relation. The composition and intersection operations are the major factors contributing to the time cost of the algorithms. We used two techniques to reduce the number of these operations: *skipping* and *ordering* introduced in [16].

The main idea of skipping is that if the composition of two consecutive arcs does not constrain the arc that completes the triangle, we skip the computation of that path. For instance, we skip the computation of the above IK arc when there is any KJ arc that has the relation '<' or '*di*' in its label, e.g., {<,o,m} or {di,o,fi} as the composition results in "no information."

The ordering of paths in a path-consistency check also affects the number of calls to the triangular operations. If the composition yields a small number of relations, the intersection will be faster in removing infeasible relations than the case when composition yields a large number of relations. This ordering will eventually affect the number of calls to the triangular operations. When using IA networks as test cases, we ordered arcs according to the sum of the weights of atomic relations as discussed in [16].

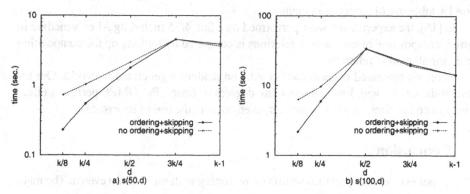

Fig. 3. Effect of heuristics on Average time (sec.) of PC_GMPE algorithm

Our implementation results for large-sized consistent networks, $S(k, p)$ when $k = 50$ and $k = 100$, are shown in Figure 3a and Figure 3b. As indicated in these figures, the degrees of nodes make a difference in the performance of PC_GMPE. For lower degrees of nodes, with and without ordering or skipping, the performance sharply improved in comparison to the networks with higher degrees of nodes. This is because low degree generated networks are labelled with a large number of single matrices with atomic elements (corresponding to the absence of arcs in the random network). Therefore, the number of matrices for composition and intersection operations is reduced. However, for lower degree problems there was still a marked improvement when ordering and skipping were employed. In contrast, the ordering and skipping techniques do not have much effect on moderate to high degrees of nodes. In fact, for complete graphs, ordering and skipping can cause worse performance due to the preprocessing of all arcs to calculate and order their weights and determine if they need skipping during propagation. Ordering and skipping produce better performance for lower degrees of nodes because there are a smaller number of relations to be assigned weights.

8 Related Implementations of Temporal Reasoning

While there have been extensive studies on the theoretical foundations of representation and reasoning with time-dependent information, very few attempts have been made to develop practical temporal reasoning systems.

Temporal Utility Package (TUP) [4] includes the implementation of IA relations as conjunctions of end-point relations and an applies these in a time varying medical domain. In TUP, information about events is stored as relations between the absolute times of the start and end points. However, the system can only handle atomic IA relations between events. Sets of atomic IA relations are not allowed.

In another diagnosis related temporal reasoning system [12], 1-convex and 2-convex relations are used. These relations are subclasses of the pointisable relations or SIA.

There are other experimental works using randomly generated IA networks reported in the literature. In [7], finding path-consistent IA networks of size 3 to 30 took between 2 and 5 seconds when using a SUN SparcStation 20 with the upper triangular composition IA table (64 MB) stored in memory.

In [16], the experiments were performed on a Sun 4/25 including Allen's method in which composition of non-atomic relations is computed by looking up the composition table for all atomic relations.

Here, we presented experimental results on randomly generated networks. Our results indicate that with low and moderate degrees of nodes, PC_GMPE performs effectively in comparison to Allen's method, even without the use of heuristics.

9 Conclusion

This paper extends our previous results on reasoning with multi-point events. The main contributions are:

- A generalisation of an MPE based approach to create a GMPE network. The generalised MPE approach provides high expressiveness to capture:
  - the *discontinuous point relations* which have not been investigated in the literature,
  - single event relations represented by full IA, and
  - recurring events as sequences of intervals and/or points.
- An improved algorithm for finding a minimal MPE network. Given the network of k MPEs, each node containing at most n point subevents, the basic version we proposed in [18] has $O(max(n^5k^3, n^4k^4))$ time complexity. The enhanced FEASIBLE_MPE algorithm requires $O(max(n^3k^3, n^2k^4))$ time in the worst case.
- The implementation of algorithms for finding a minimal MPE network (FEASIBLE_MPE) and a path-consistent GMPE network (PC_GMPE). In comparison to other experimental studies, our preliminary results are encouraging and have potential for further study regarding implementation and applications in real world situations such as medical diagnosis and patient history.

Acknowledgment

We would like to thank Bernhard Nebel for his network generator used in this paper, Peter van Beek for early discussion about disjointedness relations, Matthew Beaumont for his assistance in implementation of our algorithms, M.R.K. Krishna Rao for his help in improving the presentation, and John Thornton for his continuing fruitful discussion. Finally, thanks to the anonymous reviewers for their constructive criticism.

References

1. J. Allen. Maintaining knowledge about temporal intervals. *Communication of the ACM*, 26(11):832–843, 1983.
2. M.G. Kahn, J.C. Ferguson, E.H. Shortliffe, and L.M. Fagan. Representation and use of temporal information in oncocin - cancer therapy planning program. In M.K. Chytil and R. Engelbrecht, editors, *Medical Expert Systems: Using Personal Computers*, pages 35–44. Sigma press, Cheshire, 1987.
3. L. al Khatib. *Reasoning with Non-Convex Time Intervals*. PhD thesis, Florida Institute of Technology, Melbourne, Florida, 1994.
4. I.S. Kohane. *Temporal Reasoning in Medical Expert Systems*. PhD thesis, MIT Laboratory for Computer Science, Technical Report TR-389, Cambridge, 1987.
5. P. Ladkin. Time representation: A taxonomy of interval relations. In *Proceedings of AAAI-86*, pages 360–366, San Mateo: Morgan Kaufman, 1986.
6. P. Ladkin and A. Reinefeld. Effective solution of qualitative interval constraint problems. *Artificial Intelligence*, 57(1):105–124, 1992.
7. P. Ladkin and A. Reinefeld. Fast algebraic methods for interval constraint problems. *Annals of Mathematics and Artificial Intelligence, to appear*, 1996.
8. A.K. Mackworth. Consistency in networks of relations. *Artificial Intelligence*, 8:99–118, 1977.
9. A.K. Mackworth. Constraint satisfaction. Technical report, 85-15, Department of Computer Science, University of British Columbia, Vancouver, B.C., Canada, 1985.
10. R. Morris, W. Shoaff, and L. Khatib. Path consistency in a network of non-convex intervals. In *Proceedings of the 13th International Joint Conference on Artificial Intelligence (IJCAI-93)*, pages 650–655, Chamberey, France, 1993.
11. B. Nebel. Solving hard qualitative temporal reasoning problems: Evaluating the efficiency of using the ord-horn class. *Constraints*, 1:175–190, 1997.
12. K. Nökel. Temporally distributed symptoms in technical diagnosis. *Lecture Notes in Artificial Intelligence*, 517, 1991.
13. M. Poesio and R.J. Brachman. Metric constraints for maintaining appointments: Dates and repeated activities. In *Proceedings in AAAI-91*, pages 253–259, Anaheim, CA, 1991.
14. P. van Beek. Exact and approximate reasoning about qualitative temporal relations. Technical report, TR-90-29, University of Alberta, Edmonton, Alberta, Canada, 1990.
15. P. van Beek and R. Cohen. Exact and approximate reasoning about temporal relations. *Computational Intelligence*, 6:132–144, 1990.
16. P. van Beek and D.W. Manchak. The design and an experimental analysis of algorithms for temporal reasoning. *Journal of AI Research*, 4:1–18, 1996.
17. M. Vilain and H. Kautz. Constraint propagation algorithms for temporal reasoning. In *Proceedings of AAAI-86*, pages 377–382, San Mateo, 1986. Morgan Kaufman.
18. R. Wetprasit, A. Sattar, and L. Khatib. Reasoning with multi-point events. In *Lecture Notes in Artificial Intelligence 1081; Advances in AI, Proceedings of the eleventh biennial conference on Artificial Intelligence*, pages 26–40, Toronto, Ontario, Ca, 1996. Springer. The extended abstract published in Proceedings of TIME-96 workshop, pages 36-38, Florida, 1996. IEEE.

Implementing Constraint Retraction for Finite Domains

Yan Georget, Philippe Codognet
INRIA-Rocquencourt, BP 105, 78153 Le Chesnay, France
{Yan.Georget,Philippe.Codognet}@inria.fr

Francesca Rossi
Università di Pisa, Dipartimento di Informatica, Corso Italia 40,
56100 Pisa, Italy
rossi@di.unipi.it

Abstract. Constraint retraction, while being certainly a very convenient feature in many situations, is usually not provided in current constraint programming environments. In this paper we describe how constraint retraction can be incorporated in the FD constraint solver and we evaluate its behavior within the clp(FD) system. Experimental results on usual benchmarks and also on classes of problems of increasing connectivity show that in almost all cases the use of our retraction algorithm provides great speed-up with respect to standard methods while not slowing down the clp(FD) system when no retraction is performed.

1 Introduction

In Constraint Programming, each computation consists of a monotonic accumulation of constraints. However, it is clear that the possibility of removing constraints could be very useful in many applications, especially those requiring some level of interaction between the system and the user. We have adressed in a previous paper [5] the necessity and basic notions for considering *constraint retraction* as a basic feature of Constraint Programming systems, and we have already discussed the need for incrementality. In fact, the hope is to get an incremental algorithm which is able to keep as much as possible of the computation already done, redoing only the subcomputations directly depending on the deleted constraint.

The present paper extends and adapts traditional propagation techniques to selectively delete, from the current constraint set, a constraint and all its consequences on affected variables, while maintaining the rest of the problem untouched. It is important to note that we do not want a *justification-based* method that would compute and keep explicitly the dependencies between constraints resulting from consistency checking and domain reduction in a TMS [7] or ATMS style [6]. This has been proposed in CLP by [3] and [9] and developed in [8], in the Concurrent Constraint framework by [4], in the CSP framework by [17, 12], and for Hierarchical CLP in [14]. However all those methods have the drawback to slow down the constraint propagation while computing the dependencies and are therefore costly when no retraction is used. We rather define a specialized scheme where one has to determine the pertinent subgraph to modify upon constraint retraction only, in a manner close to [15]. In this way the classical forward phase of constraint solving is left untouched.

We propose in this paper an algorithm which is more general than that of [5] and handles all constraints that can be written in the FD system. We also propose a variant of this algorithm and prove the correctness of both versions. But the main contribution of this paper is the implementation of both algorithms within the clp(FD) system, a finite domain constraint logic language developed at INRIA [2], which tries to keep as much as possible of the original datastructures and efficiency. Preliminary experimental results, on both real-life and general classes of problems, are very encouraging, since they show that this way of achieving constraint retraction is much more efficient than recomputing from scratch.

The paper is organized as follows. Section 2 describes the FD constraint system, and Section 3 formalizes the usual propagation performed in it. Then Section 4 gives two deletion algorithms and shows their correctness, while Section 5 details implementation issues and the necessary changes to the clp(FD) system to perform constraint retraction. Section 6 gives a performance evaluation of the retraction algorithms on various examples, and Section 7 concludes the paper by summarizing its results.

2   The FD Constraint System

The FD constraint system has been extensively used in many CLP and CC programming systems, initially cc(FD) [20], then clp(FD) [2], later AKL(FD) [1] and Sictus Prolog version 3. Its popularity comes from the fact that it provides the user with the full range of arithmetic and symbolic constraints while being very simple and efficient to handle at the implementation level. FD is based on a single *primitive constraint* by which complex constraints are defined. Each constraint is thought of as a set of propagation rules describing how the domain of each variable is related to the domain of other variables, i.e., rules for describing node and (partial) arc consistency propagation [13, 18].

Definition 1 (Domain). A *domain* in FD is a subset of $0..\infty$ where ∞ is a particular integer denoting the greatest value that a variable can take. Let $\mathcal{D}$ be the set of all the domains.

Definition 2 (Constraint). If $\mathcal{V}$ is a set of variables, a *constraint* is a formula of the form X in r where $X \in \mathcal{V}$ and r is a syntactic domain (range) defined by Table 1.

Intuitively, a constraint X in r enforces X to belong to the range denoted by r. When an X in r constraint uses an indexical on another variable Y (for example, dom(Y) or min(Y)), it becomes *store-sensitive* and must be checked

```
c ::= X in r

r ::= t₁..t₂          (interval)
      {t}             (singleton)
      R               (range parameter)
      dom(Y)          (indexical domain)
      r₁ : r₂         (union)
      r₁ & r₂         (intersection)
      -r              (complementation)
      r + ct          (pointwise addition)
      r - ct          (pointwise subtraction)
      r * ct          (pointwise multiplication)
      r / ct          (pointwise division)

t ::= min(Y)          (indexical term min)
      max(Y)          (indexical term max)
      val(Y)          (delayed value)
      ct              (constant term)
      t₁+t₂ | t₁-t₂ | t₁*t₂ | t₁/<t₂ | t₁/>t₂   (integer operations)

ct ::= C              (term parameter)
       n | infinity   (greatest value)
       ct₁+ct₂ | ct₁-ct₂ | ct₁*ct₂ | ct₁/<ct₂ | ct₁/>ct₂
```

Table 1. Syntax of X in r constraints.

each time the domain of Y is updated. This is how consistency checking and domain reduction is achieved.

Complex constraints such as linear equation or inequations, as well as symbolic constraints can be defined in terms of the FD constraint system, see [2]. For instance, the constraint $X \leq Y$, is translated as follows:

$$X \leq Y \quad \equiv \quad \text{X in } 0..\max(Y) \ \wedge \ \text{Y in } \min(X)..\infty$$

Observe that this translation has also an operational flavour, and specifies, for a given n-ary constraint, how a variable domain has to be updated in terms of the other variables. For example, in the FD constraint X in 0..max(Y), whenever the largest value of the domain of Y changes (that is, decreases), the domain of X gets reduced. If instead the domain of Y changes but its largest value remains the same, then the domain of X does not change. One can therefore consider those primitive X in r constraints as a low-level language in which the propagation scheme can be expressed. Indeed, one can express in the constraint definition (that is, the translation of a high-level user constraint into a set of primitive constraints) the propagation scheme chosen to solve the constraint, such as forward-checking, full or partial look-ahead, depending on the use of **val**, **dom** or **min/max** indexical terms.

Definition 3 (Environment,Store). An *environment* is a function from $\mathcal{V}$ to $\mathcal{D}$. $E(X)$, will also be written D_X. E^∞ represent the environment where each variable has the domain $0..\infty$. We write $E \subseteq E'$ if $\forall x \in \mathcal{V}, E(x) \subseteq E'(x)$. It is obvious that $\forall E, E \subseteq E^\infty$. A *store* σ is a pair (C, E) where C is a set of constraints and E an environment.

Definition 4 (Dependencies, Well-formedness). Let c be a constraint of the form X in r. X is called the *constrained variable* of c, written $cv(c)$. We write $V(c)$ for the set of variables on which c depends (i.e. appearing in the indexical range r). Given a set of constraints S, we write $C(X)$ for the set of all constraints depending on X (i.e. $C(X) = \{c' \in S / X \in V(c')\}$). The set of constraint S is *well-formed* if $(\exists c \in C(X)/Y = cv(c)) \Rightarrow (\exists c' \in C(Y)/X = cv(c'))$. A store is *well-formed* if its set of constraint is well-formed.

An important remark is that a store derived from high-level ('user') constraints by the standard translation scheme of the clp(FD) library is always well-formed.

Definition 5 (Static, inactive constraint). A constraint c is *static* if $V(c) = \emptyset$. A constraint is *inactive* if its range computation gives $0..\infty$ in every environment. Let c be a constraint, c' is an inactive constraint associated to c if c' is inactive and $V(c') = V(c)$.

This notion of inactive constraints is needed to model the implementation of constraint retraction that we will see later. We can now define the notion of equivalence between sets of constraints that we need in our framework.

Definition 6 ($\equiv$). We write $C_1 \equiv C_2$ if $C_1 - (C_1 \cap C_2)$ and $C_2 - (C_1 \cap C_2)$ contain only inactive constraints. We also write $(C_1, E_1) \equiv (C_2, E_2)$ if $C_1 \equiv C_2$ and $E_1 = E_2$.

One can easily show that $\equiv$ (both among constraint sets and among stores) is an equivalence relation.

Definition 7 (Static domain). Let C be a set of constraints and X a variable. Let $R = \{r \mid c = (X \text{ in } r) \in C,$ and c *is static* $\}$. $D_X^S = \bigcap_{r \in R} r$ is called the *static domain* of X according to C.

3 Constraint addition

The classical use of FD constraints is within programming languages like CLP [11] and CC [16], which are intrinsically monotonic: the only change that can occur in the global constraint store is the addition of some new constraints during the computation, which corresponds to consistency checking in CSPs (see [18] for details on this issue). Let us rephrase this operation in our framework.

> **Algorithm** *Add*
>   **input** constraint set C, store σ
>   **output** store σ'

```
1.   push C
2.   while stack not empty do
3.       c := pop
4.       let c = X in r
5.       compute r in the current store
6.       if D_X ≠ D_X ∩ r then
7.           D_X = D_X ∩ r
8.           push C(X)
```

As shown in [5], algorithm *Add* always terminates. Moreover it has a complexity comparable with classical arc-consistency algorithms, ranging from AC-3 [13] to AC-5 [19] depending on the type of constraints (i.e., the type of indexical terms) used. Obviously less complex than the latest optimal consistency algorithms such as AC-7 or the soon-to-come AC-8, this incremental constraint addition and consistency checking algorithm is very efficient in practice, see for instance its performance evaluation in [2]. Algorithm *Add* defines an operator over stores, and in the following, we will not distinguish the algorithm from the corresponding operator, and we will write: $\sigma' = Add(C)(\sigma)$. There are a few properties obviously satisfied by algorithm *Add*:

Proposition 8 (Order independence). For any store σ, $Add(C_2)(Add(C_1)(\sigma)) = Add(C_1 \cup C_2)(\sigma)$.

Proposition 9 (Intensivity). If $Add(C_1)(C_2, E) = (C_1 \cup C_2, E')$ then $E' \subseteq E$; moreover, if $Add(C_1)(\emptyset, E) = (C_1, E'')$ then $E' \subseteq E''$.

In this paper we assume ranges to be monotonic, which means that when environments are larges, also ranges are so. This allows us to prove the following property.

Proposition 10 (Monotonicity). $(\forall i \in \{1,2\}\ Add(C)(D, E_i) = (C \cup D, E'_i)) \Rightarrow (E_1 \subseteq E_2 \Rightarrow E'_1 \subseteq E'_2)$.

Proposition 11 (Idempotence). $C_2 \subseteq C_1 \Rightarrow Add(C_1)(C_2, E) = Add(C_1)(\emptyset, E)$

We can now define the fundamental notion of partial arc-consistency, which is the state in which stores are usually kept in the FD constraint system:

Definition 12 (Partial arc-consistency). $\sigma = (C, E)$ is *partially arc-consistent* if $Add(C)(C, E) = (C, E)$.

Note that this condition coincides with $Add(C)(\emptyset, E) = (C, E)$.

Proposition 13. $Add(C)(\emptyset, E)$ is a partially arc-consistent store.

The following proposition shows that partial arc-consistency corresponds to the intuitive notion of a state where all the domain reductions have been made:

Proposition 14. (C, E) is partially arc-consistent $\Leftrightarrow \forall(X\ in\ r) \in C, D_X \subseteq r$. As a corollary: $\forall X, D_X \subseteq D_X^S$.

4 Constraint retraction

In this section, we will define a general scheme for constraint retraction algorithms, and we will give sufficient conditions for the correctness of all algorithms following this scheme. Then, we will describe two concrete (and implemented) retraction algorithms which are instances of the scheme and prove that they are correct.

4.1 Generic retraction algorithms and their correctness

Let $\sigma = (C, E) = Add(C)(\emptyset, E^{\infty})$ and $\sigma_1 = (C_1, E_1) = Add(C \cup \{c\})(\emptyset, E^{\infty})$ be two stores. By Proposition 13, both σ and σ_1 are partially arc-consistent; also, $\sigma_1 = Add(c)(\sigma)$. In the following sections, we will consider two algorithms for constraint retraction, their purpose being to retract constraint c, and thus to build environment E from E_1. Each algorithm $Del_i(c)$ (for $i = 1, 2$) consists of two phases (enlargement and then reduction) and has basically the following structure $Del(c) = Enlargement(c)$; $Add(S')$ where S' is a subset of the given set of constraints. Let $\sigma_2 = (C_2, E_2) = Enlargement(c)(\sigma_1)$ and $\sigma_3 = (C_3, E_3) = Add(S')(\sigma_2)$, then we will write $\sigma_3 = Del(c)(\sigma_1)$. Then we will say that algorithm Del is correct if it returns a store which is the same as that before the addition of c, that is, if $C_3 \equiv C$ and $E_3 = E$. We will now prove that the following three lemmas are sufficient for correctness.

Lemma 15. $C_2 \equiv C$. That is, after the enlargement step, we have, modulo $\equiv$, the initial constraint set without the retracted contraint.

Lemma 16. $E \subseteq E_2$. That is, after the enlargement step, the domain of each variable has been enlarged or has remained the same. Hence, no solution has been lost.

Lemma 17. $Add(S')(\sigma_2) = Add(C_2)(\sigma_2)$. That is, we do not have to consider the whole constraint graph to achieve partial arc-consistency after the enlargement step.

Proposition 18. $C_3 \equiv C$.

Proof: $(C_3, E_3) = Add(S')(C_2, E_2) = Add(C_2)(C_2, E_2)$ by Lemma 17. Therefore $C_3 = C_2$. By Lemma 15, $C_2 \equiv C$. Finally, $C_3 \equiv C$.

Proposition 19. $E_3 = E$.

Proof:
$\supseteq$ $(C_3, E_3) = Add(C_2)(C_2, E_2) = Add(C_2)(\emptyset, E_2)$, by Proposition 11. By Lemma 15, $C_2 \equiv C$, thus $(C_3, E_3) \equiv Add(C)(\emptyset, E_2)$. Moreover, (C, E) is partially arc-consistent, thus $(C, E) = Add(C)(\emptyset, E)$. By Lemma 16, $E \subseteq E_2$, thus, by Proposition 10, $E \subseteq E_3$.

$\subseteq$ $(C_3, E_3) = Add(C_2)(C_2, E_2)$ thus, by Proposition 8, $(C_3, E_3) = Add(C_2)(C_3, E_3)$. In the previous proof we had $C_3 = C_2$, thus $(C_3, E_3) = Add(C_2)(C_2, E_3) = Add(C_2)(\emptyset, E_3)$ by Proposition 11. By Lemma 15, $C_2 \equiv C$ thus $(C_3, E_3) \equiv Add(C)(\emptyset, E_3)$. But $(C, E) = Add(C)(\emptyset, E^\infty)$ and $E_3 \subseteq E^\infty$, thus, by Proposition 10, $E_3 \subseteq E$.

Thus we have proved that Lemmas 15, 16, and 17 are sufficient for the correctness of any algorithm following the scheme above. Once correctness has been established, the following result is obvious.

Proposition 20. σ_3 is partially arc-consistent.

4.2 The first retraction algorithm: Del_1

The idea of this concrete retraction algorithm, which we will call Del_1, is to enlarge the domains to their static values. Each time a domain has been enlarged, we mark the corresponding variable. Thanks to deactivate[1] we keep the store well-formed. A less general version of this algorithm has been presented in [5].

Algorithm Del_1
    input constraint c, store $(C \cup \{c\}, E_1)$
    output store σ_3

---

1. $S := \emptyset$; $S' := \emptyset$
2. let $c = X$ in r
3. deactivate c
4. enlarge X
5. while $S \neq \emptyset$ do
6. $c' :=$ pop from S
7.   let $c' = Y$ in r'
8.   if c' is active and Y is not marked then
9.   enlarge Y
10.   push $\{c'' \in C(Y)/cv(c'')$ is marked$\}$ in S'
11. Add S'

enlarge $X =$
1. mark X
2. if $D_X \neq D_X^S$ then
3. $D_X := D_X^S$
4.   push $c(X)$ in S

It is easy to see that algorithm Del_1 terminates. To prove its correctness, it is sufficient to prove that the three lemmas of the previous section hold:

— Proof of Lemma 15 ($C_2 \equiv C$): Let c' be the inactive constraint associated to c. $C_2 =$ deactivate$(c)(C \cup \{c\}) = C \cup \{c'\}$. Thus $C_2 \equiv C$.

---

[1] deactivate$(c)(C \cup \{c\}) = C \cup \{c'\}$ where c' is an inactive constraint associated to c.

- Proof of Lemma 16 ($E \subseteq E_2$): For each variable, we note: D its domain according to σ, D_1 its domain according to σ_1, D_2 its domain according to σ_2 and D^S its static domain according to C_2. Each variable reduced by $Add(c)$ will be marked by $Del_1(c)$: it is obvious that $D_1 \subset D \Rightarrow D_1 \neq D^S$ and we get the result by induction. Consider a marked variable: $D_2 = D^S \supseteq D$. Consider a non marked variable, it has not been reduced by $Add(c)$, thus: $D_2 = D_1 = D$.

- Proof of Lemma 17 ($Add(S')(\sigma_2) = Add(C_2)(\sigma_2)$): Let C' be the set of the static constraints over the enlarged variables and C'' the set of the constraints over the non-enlarged variables. The store is well-formed thus S' contains all the non-static constraints that constrain the enlarged variables. Thus $C_2 = S' \cup C' \cup C''$.

$$Add(C_2)(\sigma_2) = Add(S')(Add(C')(Add(C'')(\sigma_2))) \text{ by Proposition 8}$$
$$= Add(S')(Add(C')(\sigma_2))$$
$$= Add(S')(\sigma_2).$$

4.3 The second retraction algorithm: Del_2

Consider a constraint, say $c' = Y$ in r', from the stack S. We would like to enlarge the domain of Y to $D_Y := D_Y^S \cap r'$ rather than to $D_Y := D_Y^S$. In fact, enlarging Y to a smaller domain might amount to reconsider a smaller part of the constraint hypergraph during the retraction phase and therefore avoid useless work. However, the variables appearing in the range r' might be not yet enlarged, and this could lead to wrong results, as in the following example[2]. Consider the following constraints:

```
X in 0..1, Y in 0..1, Z in 0..1,
c₁: X in 0..max(Y)*max(Z),
c₂: Y in 0..max(X)*max(Z),
c₃: Z in 0..0.
```

Applying algorithm Add will instantiate all variables to 0. Consider now the deletion of constraint c_3. Since Z appears in the range of c_1, the domain of variable X has to be considered for enlarging. Algorithm Del_1 would enlarge it to its static domain, that is, 0..1. On the contrary, by using the assignment $D_X := D_X^S \cap r$, X would not be enlarged, since the current value of r is 0..0 due to the fact that the domain of Y has not been enlarged yet. The same reasoning holds also for c_2, thus even Y will not be enlarged. This is obviously wrong, since the deletion of c_3 should restore the initial domains (0..1) for all variables.

The solution to this problem is to delay the enlargement of the domain of Y until these variables are enlarged. This is technically done by pushing c' in a second stack S''. This achieves the classical freeze and wake up mechanism that is used for delayed goals in Prolog or suspended processes in Concurrent Logic Languages. In the case of cycles, S may be empty whereas S'' still contains

---

[2] We are indebted to Pascal Van Hentenryck for pointing out this example to us.

delayed constraints. In this case we just pop a constraint from S'' and enlarge its constrained variable to its static domain.

Algorithm Del_2
      input constraint c, store $(C \cup \{c\}, E_1)$
      output store σ_3

---

1. $S := \emptyset$; $S' := \emptyset$; $S'' := \emptyset$
2.   **let** $c = X$ **in** r
3.   **deactivate** c
4.   **enlarge** X
5.   **while** $S \neq \emptyset$ **or** $S'' \neq \emptyset$ **do**
6.   **if** $S \neq \emptyset$ **then**
7. $c' :=$ pop from S
8.   **let** $c' = Y$ **in** r'
9.   **if** c' is active and Y is not marked **then**
10. $\mathcal{F} := \{Z \in V(c) \mid Z$ is not marked$\}$
11.   **if** $\mathcal{F} \neq \emptyset$ **then**
12.   **forall** $Z \in \mathcal{F}$
13.   mark Z as freezing c'
14.   push c' in S''
15.   **else**
16.   **enlarge&reduce** Y, r'
17.   **propagate** Y
18.   push $\{c'' \in C(Y) \mid cv(c'')$ is marked$\}$ in S'
19.   **else**
20. $c' :=$ pop from S''
21.   **let** $c' = Y$ **in** r'
22.   **if** c' is active and Y is not marked **then**
23.   **enlarge** Y
24.   **propagate** Y
25.   push $\{c'' \in C(Y) \mid cv(c'')$ is marked$\}$ in S'
26. **Add** S'

enlarge&reduce X, r =	propagate X =
1. mark X	1. **forall** c frozen by $X \mid c$ is active
2. compute r in the store	2. **let** $c = Y$ **in** r
3. **if** $D_X \neq D_X^S \cap r$ **then**	3. $\mathcal{F} := \{Z \in V(c) \mid Z$ is not marked$\}$
4. $D_X := D_X^S \cap r$	4. **if** Y is not marked and $\mathcal{F} = \emptyset$ **then**
5. push $C(X)$ in S	5. push c from S'' to S

Algorithm Del_2 always terminates. As we did for Del_1, to prove the correctness of Del_2 it is sufficient to prove the three lemmas. Actually, we will only prove the second lemma, since the same proofs as in Section 4.2 hold for the first and third lemmas:

- Proof of Lemma 16 ($E \subseteq E_2$): For each constrained variable, we note r its range and we keep the same notations as before for the domains. Each variable reduced by $Add(c)$ will be marked by $Del_2(c)$: it is obvious that $D_1 \subset D \Rightarrow D_1 \neq D^S \cap r$ and we get the result by induction. During the computation, Z marked $\Rightarrow D \subseteq D_2$:

- If Z is enlarged by **enlarge** then, by the same reasoning as before $D \subseteq D_2$.
- If Z is enlarged by **enlarge&reduce**, $\{T \in V(r)/T \text{ is not marked}\} = \emptyset$, thus, by induction, $\forall T \in V(r), D_T \subseteq D_{2,T}$. The ranges are monotonic thus $r_\sigma \subseteq r$ (we still write r for the computation of the range in the current store). Thus $D \subseteq D^S \cap r_\sigma \subseteq D^S \cap r = D_2$.

Consider a marked variable: $D_2 \supseteq D$. Consider a non marked variable, it has not been reduced by $Add(c)$, thus: $D_2 = D_1 = D$.

5 Implementation

We first recall the implementation of clp(FD), and then we describe the changes needed to perform constraint retraction. Figure 1 summarizes the data structures currently used to manage X in r constraints (for more details, the reader should refer to [2]).

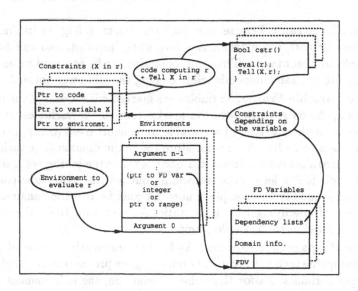

Fig. 1. Data structures for FD constraints

The three most important data structures right now are:

1. The Constraint Frame: A constraint frame is created for every constraint. The information recorded in a constraint frame are: the pointer to the associated argument frame, the address of the FD variable that is constrained, and the address of the associated code.

2. The FD Variable Frame: The frame associated to an FD variable X is divided into two main parts: the domain recording the range and the size of the range (number of elements currently present), and the constraints depending on X (i.e. several lists of pointers to constraint frames). These two parts are not modified at the same time. Chains are created when the constraints are *installed* whereas the domain can be updated during execution. Several distinct chains are used (constraints depending on $\min(X)$, ...) in order to avoid useless propagation. For instance, it is useless to reexecute a constraint depending on $\min(X)$ when only $\max(X)$ is modified.

3. The Propagation Queue: The propagation phase consists of awaking and executing a set of constraints that could themselves enrich this set by new constraints. We maintain an explicit propagation queue. A simple optimization consists in avoiding to enqueue all constraints but only a pair $< X, mask >$ where X is the updated variable (which has caused the propagation) and $mask$ is a bit-mask of dependency lists to awake.

In describing some of the details of the implementations of the two deletion algorithms, we recall that our purpose was to keep the data structures as close as possible to the above ones. Here are the changes made to implement Del_1:

1. The Constraint Frame: For each constraint, a flag, in its frame, tells if it is active or not. A constraint is active when installed, and can be deactivated thanks to **deactivate**. Thus the constraint has be replaced by an inactive constraint with the same dependencies, keeping the store well-formed.

2. The Variable Frame: Variables are marked with a date, thus it is easy, by increasing the date, to remove the marks from all the variables. It is useful because we want the marking of a variable to be short-lived (disappearing after the termination of Del_1). We do not store the static domain of a variable, but the static constraints constraining it. Hence, we save the storage of a second bit vector. It is obviously less space-consuming but a little more time-consuming. Here we had to modify the compiler: now the code for a static constraint starts with a keyword specifying that it is static. At execution time, the constraint (address) is stored in the variable frame.

3. The Propagation Queues: As for the propagation phase of Add, the enlargement queue is coded through variables, more precisely S is coded through the enlarged variables. As for the domain reduction, the enlargement does not check if a domain has changed but how it changed. Thus we can optimize the propagation step.

And here are the changes made to the data structures in order to implement Del_2:

1. The Constraint Frame: Because of the delay mechanism, we need, for each constraint, the list of the variables appearing in its range: see line 10 of Del_2 and line 3 of **propagate**. Therefore we had to modify the compiler: now the code for a constraint starts with a list of keywords specifying the list of its variables. Then, at execution time, these informations are stored in the constraint frame.

2. The Variable Frame: Because of line 1 of propagate, we need the list of the frozen constraints in the variable frame. Contrary to the dependency chains, this list is updated during the execution. More precisely, it is updated by line 13 of Del_2.

3. The Propagation Queues: The changes concern the enlargement queue: it is split into S and S''. Both are coded through variables: S is coded through the enlarged variables while S'' is coded through the freezing variables. Note that we have implemented a strategy that consists in popping first constraints that are unfrozen, that is, we do not actually have to move constraints from S'' to S as it is suggested by line 5 of propagate.

6 Performance Results

Our purpose was to implement the constraint retraction with no slow-down of the FD engine. The comparison of the performances of the three systems (the current one and the two sytems with constraint retraction) shows that **the slow-down is indeed less than 5% in all cases.** For that reason, we won't distinguish these timings in the considered benchmarks.

We would have liked to compare our results to those of justification-based methods, but the few examples given are either very simple [12], randomly generated [17] or confidential [8]. We have rather considered classical CLP problems (the alpha puzzle and a resource allocation problem) and two pedagogical generic ones to show the behavior of the algorithms.

It is obvious that, the more the problem to be solved is sparse, the less propagation will be needed, and the smaller the part involved in the retraction algorithm will be. Thus the connectivity of the problem influences the performance of the retraction algorithms, whose main advantage is the possibility of not having to consider the whole problem again. For this reason we have developed a class of problems with a varying connectivity, so that we will see at which level of connectivity it is no longer convenient to use the incremental retraction algorithms described in this paper. **generic1(N,D)** is a problem with

D	$Add(C \cup c)$	$Add(C)$	$Del_1(c)$	$Del_2(c)$	$Add(C)/Del_1(c)$
0	110	100	0	0	∞
100	110	110	30	30	3.67
200	160	170	90	90	1.89
400	360	370	320	360	1.16
600	690	720	680	720	1.06
800	1140	1180	1190	1270	0.99

Table 2. generic1(1000,D) (on a sun4, in milliseconds)

$6N$ variables and $18N + 2D - 1$ constraints: it consists of N small graphs of 6 variables and 18 constraints; D of these graphs are connected together, and one of them has another constraint, c, that will be retracted. The complete results with $N = 1000$ (and D varying) are given in Table 2 where by $Add(C \cup c)$ we mean the time to solve the initial problem, by $Add(C)$ the time to restart from scratch without c, by $Del_i(c)$ the time to retract, via Del_i, constraint c from the initial problem, and by $Add(C)/Del_1(c)$ the speedup obtained by using the first retraction algorithm (the fastest one for this example). The results show that it is worth using the constraint retraction algorithms in almost all cases, since the speedup is less than 1 only when the graph is almost fully connected (D = 800).

Then, we have developed a class of problems for which it is worth using the delay mechanism: **generic2(N)** is a problem with N variables and $3N - 1$ constraints. The constraint graph is chain-shaped, each variable is constrained by a static constraint and it is connected to the next variable by two constraints. The first variable has got another constraint c that we will be retracted. With $N = 10000$, $Add(C \cup c)$ is solved within **240ms**, $Add(C)$ is solved within **110ms**, $Del_1(c)$ is solved within **120ms** while $Del_2(c)$ is solve within **0ms**. It shows that, as expected, it is worth using the delay mechanism in that case.

The numbers beside each word are the total of the values (from 1 to 26) assigned to the letters in the word. Find the value of each letter under the equations:

BALLET	45 GLEE	66 POLKA	59 SONG	61
CELLO	43 JAZZ	58 QUARTET	50 SOPRANO	82
CONCERT	74 LYRE	47 SAXOPHONE	134 THEME	72
FLUTE	30 OBOE	53 SCALE	51 VIOLIN	100
FUGUE	50 OPERA	65 SOLO	37 WALTZ	34

Table 3. alpha

Let us now study a problem called **alpha**: this is a well-known puzzle from rec.puzzle newsgroup, used as a classical benchmark for CLP systems with finite domains. Table 3 gives a description of the problem. **alpha** involves 26 variables, 20 linear equations and 325 disequations. Instead, **beta** is a similar problem where we have BAND 46, BLUES 66, DOUBLEBASS 113, and TUBA 25 instead of BALLET 45 and OBOE 53. Thus **beta** can be obtained from **alpha** by removing two equations and adding four. **beta** involves 26 variables, 22 linear equations and 325 disequations. **alpha** is solved within **3300 ms**, **beta** is solved from scratch within **20000 ms** but it is solved within **30 ms** starting from **alpha** and using either Del_1 or Del_2. The speedup ((alpha + beta)/(alpha + Del_1)) obtained by using the first retraction algorithm for solving alpha and beta is thus equal to **6.99**.

Let us finally consider a more "real-life" problem taken from [10]. It is a resource allocation problem, where one has to assign attendants (hostesses and stewards) to ten flights, searching for an optimal solution that minimizes the sum of all attendants on all flights. This problem can be described with 200 boolean variables, 30 integer variables and 350 constraints. An optimal solution is found in **38030ms**. Assume now that a certain steward (in our experimentation, the first one) cannot work on the first flight. It defines another problem. One can restart the computation from scratch, another optimal solution is found in **25580 ms**. But it is more efficient to retract the instantiation constraints (those due to the labeling of the variables), as the same optimal solution is found in **12390ms** only, more than twice as fast as restarting from scratch.

7 Future work

Our experiments show that it is possible to efficiently implement constraint retraction without any slowdown of the FD engine, and in most cases with significant speed-up with respect to a naive algorithm which would achieve retraction by recomputing the desired store from scratch. Of course, we now need to experiment with more real-life problems to definitely assess our results.

The retraction operation that we proposed in this paper is a low-level mechanism. We can already imagine two ways of using it. As a high-level primitive, it allows the user to interact with the solver by removing some constraints; at a lower level, it allows the programmer to do local search and thus to implement complex strategies instead of simple backtrack. Of course there is still a lot of work to be done to make these two scenarios a reality.

References

1. B. Carlson, M. Carlsson and S. Janson. Finite Domain Constraints in AKL(FD). *Proc. ILPS'94*, MIT Press, 1994.
2. P. Codognet and D. Diaz. Compiling Constraints in clp(FD). *JLP*, 1996.
3. P. Codognet, F. Fages and T. Sola. A meta-level compiler for CLP(FD) and its combination with IB. In *CLP : Selected Research*, A. Colmerauer, F. Benhamou (Eds.), MIT Press, 1993.
4. P. Codognet and F. Rossi. NMCC Programming: Constraint Enforcement and Retraction in CC Programming. *Proc. ICLP'95*, MIT Press, 1995.
5. P. Codognet, D. Diaz and F. Rossi. Constraint Retraction in FD. *16th Conf. on Foundations of Software Technology and Theoretical Computer Science* , Springer-Verlag, LNCS 1116, 1996.
6. J. de Kleer. An assumption-based truth maintenance system. *Artificial Intelligence* 28, 1986.
7. J. Doyle. A Truth Maintenance System. Artificial Intelligence, vol. 12, 1979.
8. F. Fages, J. Fowler and T. Sola. A reactive CLP Scheme *Proc. ICLP'95*, Tokyo, 1995.

9. W. S. Havens. Intelligent Backtracking in the Echidna Constraint Logic Programming System. Research Rep. CSS-IS TR 92-12, Simon Fraser University, Vancouver, Canada, 1992.
10. ILOG SA. The Ilog Solver White Paper, April 1997.
11. J. Jaffar and J.L. Lassez. Constraint Logic Programming. *Proc. POPL*, ACM Press, 1987.
12. N. Jussien and P. Boizumault. Maintien de Déduction pour la Relaxation de Contraintes. *Proc. of JFPLC'96*, Clermont-Ferrand, 1996.
13. A.K. Mackworth. Consistency in networks of relations. Artificial Intelligence, vol.8, n.1, 1977.
14. F. Menezes, P. Barahona and P. Codognet. An Incremental Hierarchical Constraint Solver. In *proceedings of PPCP'93*, Newport, USA, April 93.
15. B. Neveu and P. Berlandier. Maintaining Arc Consistency through Constraint Retraction. *Proc. TAI94*, IEEE Press.
16. V.A. Saraswat. *Concurrent Constraint Programming*. MIT Press, 1993.
17. T. Schiex and Gérard Verfaillie. Nogood Recording for Static and Dynamic Constraint Satisfaction Problems. *International Journal of Artificial Intelligence Tools*, 1994.
18. E. Tsang. *Foundations of Constraint Satisfaction*. Academic Press, 1993.
19. P. Van Hentenryck, Y. Deville and C-M. Teng. A generic arc-consistency algorithm and its specializations. *Artificial Intelligence 57 (1992)*, pp 291-321.
20. P. Van Hentenryck, V. Saraswat and Y. Deville. Constraint processing in cc(FD). In *Constraint Programming : Basics and Trends*, A. Podelski (Ed.), LNCS 910, Springer Verlag 1995.

INSTANCE: The Intermediate Storage Node Concept

Thomas Plagemann and Vera Goebel
University of Oslo, Center for Technology at Kjeller (UNIK)
Granaveien 33, P.O. Box 70, N-2007 Kjeller
{plagemann, goebel}@unik.no

Abstract

The objective of the INSTANCE (Intermediate Storage Node Concept) project is to support asynchronous communication in server-based systems, like World-Wide Web and Video-on-Demand, more efficiently by a new structure for server-based systems. The proposed approach will lead to a structure that is capable to support concurrently a higher number of clients with lower costs (compared to traditional approaches). Servers, which are called *intermediate storage nodes* in INSTANCE, are seen as a vehicle to transfer information in asynchronous mode from provider to consumer. The protocol stack is drastically reduced at the server - in analogy to intermediate network nodes. The *Integrated Layer Processing* principle is applied to the handling of data management system, application, and the remaining communication protocol.

1 Introduction

The availability of multimedia personal computers and workstations, internet services, and high-speed network services has drastically increased the use of distributed multimedia applications for commercial, private, and other purposes. The world-wide web (WWW), distance education, video conferencing, video-on-demand (VoD), and multimedia mail are examples of such applications. Seen from the users point of view, these distributed applications can support two types of communication: *synchronous* and *asynchronous*.

Synchronous communication is often also called realtime communication, because information is exchanged between users in realtime. Obviously, synchronous communication requires that all users are using the distributed application at the same time, but they do not have to be in the same location. In other words, synchronous communication overcomes geographical separations between users. Famous examples for such applications are traditional telephony and video conferencing.

In *asynchronous communication*, information exchange between users is performed indirectly and does not require that all users are using the application at the same time. Information that should be exchanged is not directly transferred to the recipients. Instead, it is transferred from the information provider to the system and is stored on a server. Consequently, systems that support asynchronous communication are often called *server-based systems*. Afterwards, the information is either delivered from the server to the clients (i.e., information consumer) or it is actively retrieved from the clients. WWW, VoD, and file systems are well known examples for server-based systems, that overcome geographical and timely separations.

The objective of the INSTANCE (Intermediate Storage Node Concept) project is to support asynchronous communication more efficiently by a new structure for server-based systems. There is a general consensus, that servers that have to satisfy multiple concurrent consumer requests are the bottleneck in asynchronous communication. The relationship *server-information provider* is not considered harmless in most application domains. Consequently, most research activities in this area are concerned with the management and storage of information at a server or the transfer of information from the server to the consumers. In INSTANCE, we are starting with a different point of view on the problem: Instead of concentrating on the *server-consumer* relationship, we consider the *provider-consumer* relationship as the starting point. Servers, which are called *intermediate storage nodes* in INSTANCE, represent only a vehicle to transfer information in asynchronous mode from *provider* to *consumer*. This unusual and abstract view leads us to an important analogy: *intermediate nodes in networks*. In the OSI reference model, end-systems have to handle all seven protocol layers, while intermediate systems - or nodes - have only to handle the three lowest layers. The major part of the computation power is needed to handle the end-system protocols. Thus, servers might have to handle in heterogeneous networks only the lowest three layers and in homogeneous networks only the lowest two layers. The advantage of this approach is that the CPU intensive end-to-end protocol handling can be reduced to a minimum at the intermediate storage node. This decreases the load at the server and more clients can be concurrently served with the same hardware resources.

An important element in INSTANCE is the application of the *Integrated Layer Processing* (ILP) principle introduced in [7]. Obviously, some form of data management and application at the intermediate storage node is necessary. Traditionally, data management and application are performed on top of the highest protocol layer. The integrated processing of data management, application, and communication protocols will lead to performance improvements, because multiple optimizations are possible:

(1) The number of expensive copy operations to transfer data between the subsystems can be decreased. Furthermore, the number of context switches can be reduced.

(2) Redundancy in data management systems and communication protocols can be minimized. For example, buffer management, flow control, and error handling are often performed by data management systems and communication protocols.

(3) Functions in the subsystems can be adapted to optimize the server performance, like size of protocol data units (PDUs) and storage block sizes as well as Quality-of-Service (QoS) management[1].

The INSTANCE approach distinctly differs from existing server-based systems. Therefore, it is our main goal in this paper to identify the bottlenecks of current solutions and to explain the basic idea and approach of INSTANCE. In particular, the following section 2 presents a bottleneck analysis of server-based systems and recent approaches to improve the situation. In section 3, we explain the architectural principle of IN-STANCE. Section 4 describes the data handling aspect, and section 5 presents a simple analytical evaluation of the INSTANCE approach. The conclusions in section 6 summarize the current state and future work of the INSTANCE project.

2 Bottlenecks in Server-Based Systems

In all server-based systems, multiple clients (or consumers) retrieve via a network data from a server. Obviously, these systems are inherently centralized systems, with all known disadvantages of centralized approaches: the server represents a single point of failure and determines the scaleability of the systems, because it is the performance bottleneck.

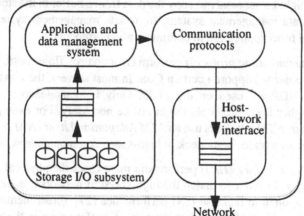

Figure 1:   Critical path in server-based systems

Before we take a closer look at this bottleneck, we briefly illustrate that todays available commercial networks and PCs (or workstations) are able to handle the workload in such systems with the example of a VoD system. For instance, MPEG-2 compressed video streams require approximately 4 Mbit/s for studio quality and 20 Mbit/s for HDTV quality [15]; both can be handled by modern PCs with commercial ATM adapter cards. The challenge of VoD systems lies in the server design, i.e., how to support a large number of viewers at reasonable costs [15]. The critical path in servers is illustrated in Figure 1 and includes the following elements:

- The *storage I/O subsystem* is responsible for durable storage and retrieval of digital video on secondary (and tertiary) storage media. Hard disks are a very popular

---

1. QoS management in data management systems and the coordination with QoS management in distributed multimedia systems is a central research issue in the OMODIS project [12] at UNIK. The close coordination between INSTANCE and OMODIS promises distinct synergetic effects.

storage devices, but commercial hard disks as they are used for workstations offer only an I/O throughput below 10 Mbyte/s. Buddhikot [4] points out that "a well known way to increase the effective storage throughput is to operate a large number of disks in parallel (an organization often called a disk array) and physically distribute (stripe) the data over the disks". However, the probability of disk failure increases with the number of disks. Therefore, different error handling mechanisms, i.e., redundancy mechanisms, are introduced in the various RAID (Redundant Array of Inexpensive Disks) levels [5]. Chen and Towsley [6] report a maximal throughput of approximately 90 Mbytes/s in a RAID system level 5 with 64 disks.

• *Application and data management system* handle requests from clients, manage the retrieval from the storage subsystem including buffering, and pass the data to the communication protocols. The data management system maintains mostly a simple data model, e.g., a file system. Depending on the implementation of the entire system, it might be necessary to copy the data from a buffer in the storage subsystem to the data management system, from data management system to the application, and from application to communication protocols.

• *End-to-end communication protocols* perform error control, flow control and other functions in order to support a certain QoS. In most servers, the transport protocols TCP or UDP are used on top of IP. Only in homogeneous networks, network and higher layer protocols might not be necessary. For example, VoD systems with pure ATM networks use an *ATM Adaptation Layer* (AAL). Software protocols represent a major bottleneck in high-speed communications.

• The *host-network interface (HNI)* performs in most cases the physical layer and the data link layer. In order to match the high-speed of networks, three different techniques are applied to increase HNI performance [27]: direct memory access (DMA) support for more efficient data movement, buffer space on the adapter to minimize number of copy operations, and protocol support on the adapter.

Communication Protocols	Datagram	Request-Response	Reliable Message	UDP/IP
Data link protocol	32 (33%)	36 (23%)	56 (44%)	37 (16%)
Transport protocol	6 (6%)	25 (16%)	31 (24%)	50 (21%)
Buffer management	30 (31%)	52 (43%)	27 (21%)	60 (26%)
Context switching	29 (30%)	41 (27%)	13 (10%)	87 (37%)
Total	97	154	127	234

Table 1: Send and receive overhead in microseconds for a one-word message using different communication protocols (percentage of total latency) [27]

An overview of the general communication overhead, i.e., for communication protocols and host network interfaces, is summarized in Table 1 [27]. The conclusion from this table is clear, the bottleneck lies in the software elements. In particular, more than 80% of the total latency of UDP/IP is consumed by the transport protocol, buffer management, and context switching.

There is a considerable amount of research projects aiming at improving the performance of VoD servers. We divide them into three groups:

- *Parallel storage systems and distribution of the server functionality over multiple nodes*: Example projects include MARS [4], Server Array [1], Continuous Media Storage Server [14], Tobagi et al. [30], the Image Server System [29], and the EL-VIRA Video Server [26].

- *Optimization of communication protocols via flexibility*: Flexible light-weight (transport) protocols such as XTPX [16], HSTP [8], and TP++ [10] enable the transport user to select a retransmission strategy. The systems HOPS [13] and Virtual Protocols [18] allow to combine fine granular building blocks to protocols that comprise the functionality of the OSI layers three up to seven. ADAPTIVE [3], F-CSS ([28] and [32]), and Da CaPo ([20] and [21]) additionally support mapping of application requirements onto protocol functionality.

- *New operating system mechanisms and abstractions*: I/O intensive applications are supported via direct device-to-device data movement in the container shipping mechanism [19] and in the Scout operating system [17]. Further techniques to minimize the number of copy operations are presented in the Alloc stream facility [24], the Tenex system [2], Accent [25], DASH [31], and Fbufs [9]. The Server Operating System project [23] at MIT combines these approaches with ILP.

From the above mentioned projects, the Server Operating System project at MIT is most similar to INSTANCE, because it reduces the number of necessary copy operations and applies ILP for protocol handling. However, the full protocol stack, i.e., TCP/IP, is handled and no coordination and optimization between data management system, application and communication protocols is performed.

3 Architectural Principals of INSTANCE

In the INSTANCE project, we propose a different approach to increase efficiency of servers by omitting higher-layer protocols and applying an extended form of the ILP in the intermediate storage node concept.

3.1 Omitting Higher-Layer Protocols

Instead of classifying server-based systems as people-to-system systems [11], we regard server-based systems as asynchronous people-to-people communication and consider the server as an intermediate storage node (see Figure 2). End-systems have to handle all seven protocol layers in the OSI reference model and all four protocol layers in the internet protocol suite, while intermediate systems - or nodes - have only to handle the three lowest layers. As shown in the previous chapter, the bottleneck in communication is located in transport and higher layer protocols, which will be referred to as end-to-end protocols in the rest of this paper.

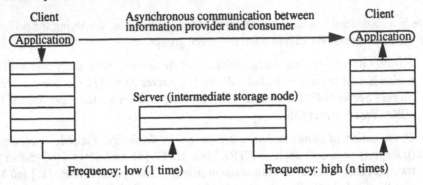

Figure 2: Protocol handling in the intermediate storage node concept

Current server-based systems see an end-to-end relationship between server and client. Consequently, servers have to handle end-to-end protocols when satisfying a request from a client. Data management system and application are placed on top of the end-to-end protocols. Opposed to this approach, INSTANCE regards a server as an intermediate storage node. Thus, servers might have to handle in heterogeneous networks only the lowest three layers and in homogeneous networks only the lowest two layers. The advantage of this approach is that the CPU intensive end-to-end protocol handling is not necessary - respectively reduced to a minimum - at the intermediate storage node. This results in a reduced load of CPU and system bus or in other words, more consumers (clients) can be served with the same hardware resources.

3.2 Integrated Layer Processing

Obviously, both data management system and application are necessary on the intermediate storage node. In the traditional approach, both represent applications or service users from the viewpoint of communication systems. However, the integration of data management system, application, and end-to-end communication protocols allows several optimizations. In particular, data management system and end-to-end protocols perform error handling and flow control. Furthermore, buffers and their management are necessary in data management system, application, and communication protocols. Figure 3 compares a layered approach for servers and the ILP in INSTANCE.

The integrated optimization and processing of data management system, application, and protocols promises to remove redundant functionality, the number of copy operations, and the number of context switches. Furthermore, it allows to adapt data block sizes and *protocol data unit* (PDU) size, i.e., to apply a form of *Application Level Framing* (ALF) Principle [7].

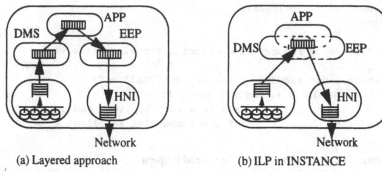

(a) Layered approach (b) ILP in INSTANCE

DMS: Data management system, APP: Application, EEP: End-to-end protocols,
HNI: Host-network interface

Figure 3: Different server implementations

Let us consider a simple example to illustrate this statement: The information provider
downloads a movie onto the intermediate storage node. The transport protocol that is
used for this operation includes a type of forward error correction that is also appropriate for the storage subsystem, and the size of the transport protocol units is coordinated
with the disk block size. The incoming network packets are directly stored on the storage subsystem. The data management system has to keep track of relationships
between network packets, disk location, and movies. Requests from consumers are
handled by application and data management system, as a result the network packets
are read in appropriate order from disk, the network and transport destination address
are adjusted in each packet, and the packets are sent to the consumer. Errors - except
long bursts of errors - can be corrected with the redundant forward error correction
information.

4 Data Handling in INSTANCE

In this section, we describe more detailed how data is handeled in INSTANCE with respect to two aspects: first, the layered architecture of servers, and second, segmentation
and encapsulation of application data. Our discussion emphasizes on the crucial read
situation, i.e, serving a client request.

4.1 Layering and Data Movements

The general task of servers is to accept requests from clients, perform the associated operation and return the result to the client. Figure 4 shows the skeleton of a C program
that roughly sketches how read requests from clients are handled in a simple VoD application on the UNIX operating system. Main task is to read chuncks from a video file
and send them to the client by writing them to a socket.

```
char buffer [BUFSIZE];
int n;
....
/* incoming request from client_a for video file vf_1 */
....
while ((n = read(vf_1, buffer, BUFSIZE)) > 0)
        sendto(s_a, buffer, BUFSIZE);
                            /* s_a is a socket, i.e., end-point */
                            /* of the connection to client_a */
....
```

Figure 4:   Handling a Client Read Request

In a traditional operating system like UNIX, these simple read and send operations within the application initiate multiple operations within different subsystems (or layers) of the system. The read system call initiates the file system to copy the corresponding block from disk into a file system buffer and afterwards to copy the data into the buffer of the application. The first activity of the send system call is to copy the contents of the application buffer into a buffer of the socket layer. Depending on the type of buffer structure (plain m_buf or clustered m_buf) there is a logical copy or physical copy from socket layer to protocol layer [22]. Afterwards, the protocol layer (traditionally TCP/IP or UDP/IP) processes the data, i.e., generates a PDU; and copies the PDU to the network interface.

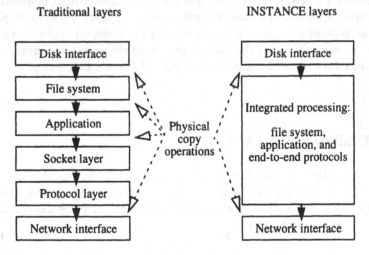

Figure 5: Layered server architectures

In contrast, INSTANCE requires only one copy operation to transfer a disk block to the buffer that is shared by file system, application, and protocol; and one copy operation to move the PDU to the network interface. Figure 5 compares the layers and number of copy operations in INSTANCE and traditional solutions. The integrated processing of file system, application and protocols is facilitated by the fact that the network PDUs that are generated by the information provider are stored directly on the disk of the server.

4.2 Segmentation and Encapsulation

The layering principle in communication protocols is closely coupled with nested encapsulation of data into PDUs of various layers. In case of the simple application above, using TCP/IP as transport and network protocols, the chuncks of the video file are passed from application to socket layer. Furthermore, they are handled in the protocol layer. The transport protocol TCP extends each chunck with 24 bytes *protocol control information* (PCI). This tranport PDU is passed to IP and extended with a 24 byte IP header.

In INSTANCE, we obviously do not use TCP/IP, instead we are using the flexible communication subsystem Da CaPo [21] to handle the necessary end-to-end protocol tasks. Nevertheless, PCI is also added from Da CaPo to the application data elements. At the information providers site, the application data, e.g., a video clip is segmented into fixed size chunks. The chunk size is coordinated with (a) the *maximum tranfer unit* (MTU) of the network, (b) the size of logical blocks in the file system, and (c) the size of the physical disk blocks.[2] Let us illustrate this with a concrete example: assuming that the Da CaPo protocol adds 48 bytes PCI, and the MTU size of the network to be used (Ethernet) is 1500 bytes, the logical block size of the file system is 4 Kbytes, and the physical block size is 1 Kbyte, we obviously would select a PDU size of 1 Kbyte. Thus, the sending application is segmenting the video clip into 976 byte large data elements.

Errors that might occur during transmission (or caused by a damaged disk in a disk array) are handled with forward error correcting codes. In the case of our example, the sending protocol entity at the information provider site is generating out of three PDUs one 1 Kbyte large PDU with parity information.

Figure 6 illustrates the different phases of segmentation, encapsulation, etc. when the information provider writes on the server and when the consumer reads information from the server. During the write operation, the information provider is segmenting the video clip into chuncks of 976 bytes and forwards the ownership of the buffer to the communication protocol. The protocol in turn adds 48 bytes of control information, sends the packet to the server, and generates a parity PDU out of three PDUs. The server receives 1 Kbyte large PDUs and stores them directly onto disk. In case of a disk array with striping unit 1Kbyte, the PDUs are distributed over four disks. Thus, it is assured that the *parity* PDU is stored on a different disk than the three related *data* PDUs. This approach enables to compensate disk errors with the parity PDU.

To fulfill a read request, the server reads blocks, i.e., PDUs, from disk and passes the ownership of the corresponding buffer to the protocol. The protocol in turn updates the address information in each PDU and writes them to the network interface. The information consumer receives the PDUs, removes the PCI, eventually corrects errors with the parity PDU, and reassambles the application object.

---

2. In case of a disk array, the striping unit depends on application characteristics, physical disk block size, and PDU size.

Information provider:

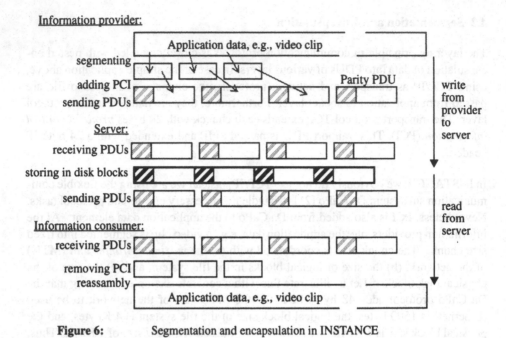

Figure 6: Segmentation and encapsulation in INSTANCE

5 Simple Analytic Evaluation

In order to get an idea about the possible performance of INSTANCE, we analyze in this section the time that a server needs to read data from disk, handle the application, end-to-end protocols, and to send the data to the network. In the following, we call this time *read-send delay* (RSD). Furthermore, we analyze the additional storage space that is necessary to accomodate PCIs and parity PDUs on disk.

5.1 Read-Send Delay

The main components of the RSD in traditional solutions are: (1) latency to read a block into a file system buffer, (2) copy the data into an application buffer (denoted d_copy), (3) copy the data into a buffer of the socket layer and forward the ownership of the data to the protocol layer (denoted d_socket), (4) protocol processing (denoted d_prot), (5) and moving the data onto the host network interface. The RSD in INSTANCE comprises latency to read a block into a file system buffer, processing of a minimized protocol that mainly updates the addresses in the PDUs (denoted d_addr), and moving of data onto the host-network interface. The data movements from disk to file system and from protocol layer to host network interface are necessary for both approaches. Thus, the remaining operations determine the difference in RSD for INSTANCE and the traditional case. The delay caused by these remaining operations is called core-RSD. However, the

INSTANCE server has to read and send more data because of the redundancy in the forward error coded data and the PCI[3]. This affects mainly two copy operations. We assume that the corresponding increase of RSD in INSTANCE is propotional to the amount of redundancy in the data (denoted red)[4]. Thus, the reduction of RSD in INSTANCE compared to the traditional approach is given by equation (C1):

$$\text{RSD reduction} = d\_copy + d\_socket + d\_prot - (d\_addr + 2 \cdot red \cdot d\_copy) \quad \text{(C1)}$$

Obviously, the values for all these factors are heavily dependent of the particular system, i.e., hardware and operating system that is used. In order to get an idea about possible RSD reduction in real systems, we use the experimental analysis results of the TCP/IP protocol implementation on a SparcStation 1 from Papadopoulus and Parulkar [22]. They report the following average delays for handling a 1 Kbyte block: d_copy = 130µs, d_socket = 280µs, and d_prot = 443µs. Furthermore, we estimate that d_addr corresponds to 1/4 of d_copy. Based on the assumption that the relationships between d_socket, d_prot, and d_copy will also be the same in faster systems, i.e., d_socket = $2.15 \cdot d\_copy$ and d_prot = $3.41 \cdot d\_copy$, we calculate the core-RSD according to (C2) and (C3):

$$\text{traditional core-RSD} = 6.56 \cdot d\_copy \quad \text{(C2)}$$

$$\text{INSTANCE core-RSD} = \frac{1}{4} \cdot d\_copy + 2 \cdot red \cdot d\_copy \quad \text{(C3)}$$

Figure 7 illustrates four curves: for the traditional core-RSD and three for INSTANCE core-RSD (with red = 1, red = 1/2, and red = 1/4); d_copy ranges from 50 µs to 130 µs. The curves are based on experimental results described in [22] and two assumptions that are not experimentally verified. Therefore, the particular values in Figure 7 do probably not describe the exact performance of an INSTANCE implementation, but they demonstrate that RSD can be drastically reduced in INSTANCE (even in the case of high red). This in turn implies that INSTANCE requires much less of the crucial server resources CPU and bus to fulfill a client request. Thus, more client requests can be handled in parallel by the server.

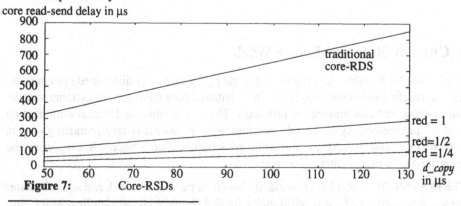

Figure 7: Core-RSDs

---

3. The overhead caused by the PCI is only relevant for the read operation.
4. red is measured as the relation of number of parity PDUs to number of data PDUs.

5.2 Storage Space Requirements

All incoming PDUs are stored from the server directly onto disk. Thus, the disk has to accommodate application data plus PCIs and parity PDUs. With respect to traditional solutions, parity PDUs and PCIs can be seen as overhead. This overhead can be determined as follows:

$$\text{overhead in \%} = \frac{\text{PCI\_size}}{\text{chunk\_size}} \cdot 100 + red \cdot 100 \qquad (C4)$$

Figure 8 illustrates the percentage of application data of the entire data (i.e., application data, PCIs, and parity PDUs) for different chunck sizes. The PCI size is for all four curves 48 bytes, but *red* can have different values, e.g., 0, 0.25, 0.5, or 1.

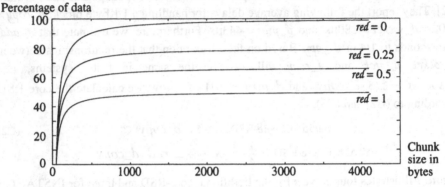

Figure 8: Storage space requirements for different headers and payload sizes

RAID systems generate parity information to correct disk errors. If the partity PDUs in INSTANCE are used for both kinds of errors - network errors and disk errors - then *red* can be set to zero, because the parity information is needed anyway and represents no additional overhead. In this case, more than 95% (for chunk sizes of 1 Kbytes and larger) of the data is application data. That means, we have quite small disk space overhead in INSTANCE (5% or less).

6 Current State and Future Work

The INSTANCE project investigates a central problem area of distributed systems, and tries to redefine the boundaries between distributed data management systems, operating systems, and communication protocols. The combination and mutual optimization of data management systems and communication protocols is very promising to gain performance improvements for distributed systems. Furthermore, it simplyfies the integrated QoS management in servers.

The INSTANCE project has been mainly based on the authors work and several master theses. Since June 1997, it is additionally funded from the Norwegian Research Council with a doctoral fellowship. Thus, current work and intermediate results are concerned with the appropriate software environment, tools, and building blocks of

INSTANCE. The micro-kernel operating system Chorus is used for the experimental studies, because of its modularity and realtime properties (to support guaranteed QoS). From the networking point, we consider two environments for the investigation of the intermediate storage node concept:

- *Heterogeneous networks*: Network layer PDUs might be stored directly - without handling them by the higher layer protocols - before writing them on disk. Correspondingly, during a read operation, network PDUs are retrieved from disk and forwarded with the new network and transport destination addresses to the link layer. The experimental studies for this environment are based on the protocol configuration tool Da CaPo, a video file system, buffer management algorithms for multimedia, scheduling support for QoS in Chorus, all being developed in master theses at UNIK.

- *Pure ATM networks*: The storage devices are directly attached to an ATM switch and ATM cells are stored on disks. The Virtual Path Identifier (VPI) and the Virtual Circuit Identifier (VCI) might be used to stripe a stream of ATM cells over several disks. Specialized hardware support is necessary to realize such a system. Currently, it is not realistic to implement such a system for us. Thus, we will study possible performance advantages with the help of simulation.

The design of appropriate protocols, e.g., forward error correction is our next step in INSTANCE. Furthermore, we are going to investigate the following questions:

- For which types and sizes of application objects is this approach appropriate?

- For which application scenarios and different write & read patterns (e.g., VoD and joint editing) is INSTANCE appropriate?

Acknowledgements: We would like to thank the anonymous reviewers for their helpful comments and suggestions.

7 References

[1]   Bernhardt, C., Biersack, E.: "The Server Array: A Scalable Video Server Architecture", in: Effelsberg, W., Spaniol, O., Danthine, A., Ferrari, D. (Editors), "High-Speed Networking for Multimedia Applications", Kluwer Publishers, Amsterdam, The Netherlands, March 1996

[2]   Bobrow, D.G., et. al: "Tenex, A Paged Time Sharing System for the PDP-10", in: The Communications of the ACM, Vol 15, No. 3, March 1972, pp 135-143

[3]   Box, D. F., Schmidt, D. C., Suda, T.: "ADAPTIVE - An Object-Oriented Framework for Flexible and Adaptive Communication Protocols", Proceedings of 4th IFIP conference on high performance networking, hpn 92, Liege, Belgium, December 1992

[4]   Buddhikot M. M., Parulkar, G. M., Cox, J. R.: "Design of a large scale multimedia storage server", in: Computer Networks and ISDN Systems, Vol. 27, 1994, pp. 503-517

[5]   Chen, P. C., Lee, E. K., Gibson, G. A., Katz, R. H., Patterson, D. A.: "RAID: High-Performance, Reliable Secondary Storage", in: ACM Computing Surveys, 1994, pp. 145-185

[6]   Chen, S., Towsley, D.: "A Performance Evaluation of RAID Architectures", http://www-net.cs.umass.edu/papers.html, Technical Report, 1994

[7]   Clark, D. D., Tennehouse, D. L.: "Architectural Considerations for a new Generation of Protocols", ACM SIGCOMM'90, September 1990, pp. 200-208

[8]   Cohn, M.: "High Speed Transport Protocol (HSTP)", Contribution to ISO/IEC JTC1 SC6/WG4, September 1991

[9]   Druschel, P., Peterson, L.: "Fbufs: A High-Bandwidth Cross-Domain Transfer Facility", Proceeding of 14th Symposium on Operating System Principles, ACM Press, New York, pp. 189-202

[10]   Feldmeier, D. C.: "An Overview of the TP++ Transport Protocol Project", in: Tantawy, A. (Editor): "High Performance Communication", January 1993

[11]   Fluckinger, F.: "Understanding Networked Multimedia", Prentice Hall, 1995

[12]   Goebel, V., Plagemann, T., Berre, A.-J., Nygård, M.: OMODIS - Object-Oriented Modeling and Database Support for Distributed Systems, Norwegian Computer Science Conference NIK'96 (Norsk Informatikkonferanse), Alta Norway, November 1996, pp.7-18

[13]   Haas, Z.: "A Protocol Structure for High-Speed Communication over Broadband ISDN", in: IEEE Network Magazine, January 1991, pp. 64-70

[14]   Lougher, P., Shephard, D.: "The Design of a Storage for Contionous Media", The Computer Journal, Vol. 36, No. 1, 1993, pp. 32-42

[15]   Lu, G.: "Communication and Computing for Distributed Multimedia Systems", Artech House Publishers, 1996

[16]   Metzler, B., Miloucheva, I.: "Specification of the Broadband Transport Protocol XTPX", CEC Deliverable R2060/TUB/CIO/DS/P001/b2, February 1993

[17]   Montz, A. B., Mosberger, D., O'Malley, S. W., Peterson, L. L., Proebsting, T. A., Hartman, J. H.: "Scout: A communications-oriented operating system", Technical Report 94-20, Department of Computer Science, University of Arizona, June 1994

[18]   O'Malley S., Peterson L.: "A Higly Layered Architecture for High-Speed Networks", in: Johnston, M. J. (Editor): "Protocols for for High-Speed Networks, II", Elsvier Science Publisher B.V. (North Holland), November 1990, pp. 141-156

[19]   Pasquale, J., Anderson, E., Muller, P. K.,: "Container Shipping - Operating System Support for I/O-Intensive Applications", IEEE Computer, Vol. 27, No. 3, March 1994, pp. 84-93

[20]   Plagemann, T., Plattner, B., Vogt, M., Walter, T.: "A Model for Dynamic Configuration of Light-Weight Protocols", in: Proceedings of IEEE Third Workshop on Future Trends of Distributed Computing Systems, Taipei, Taiwan, April 1992, pp. 100-107

[21] Plagemann, T.: "A Framework for Dynamic Protocol Configuration", VDF Hochschulverlag AG an der ETH Zuerich (ISBN 3 7281 2334 X), Januar 1996

[22] Papadopoulos, C., Parulkar, G.: "Experimental Evaluation of SunOS IPC and TCP/IP Protocol," ACM/IEEE Transactions on Networking, Vol. 1, No. 2, April 1993, pp. 199--216

[23] Kaashoek, M. F., Engler, D. R., Ganger, G. R., Wallach, D. A.: "Server Operating Systems", 1996 SIGOPS European Workshop, Ireland, September 1996, pp. 141-148

[24] Krieger, O., Stumm, M. Unrau, R.: "The Alloc Stream Facility - A Redesign of Application Level Stream I/O", IEEE Computer, Vol. 27, No. 3, March 1994, pp. 75-82

[25] Rashid, R., Robertson, G.: "Accent: A Communication-Oriented Network Operating System Kernel", Proc. 8th Symposium on Operating System Principles", ACM Press, New York, 1981, pp. 64-85

[26] Sandstå, O., Langørgen, S., Midtstraum, R.,: "Design and Implementation of the Elvira Video Server", Norwegian Computer Science Conference NIK'96 (Norsk Informatikkonferanse), Alta Norway, November 1996, pp. 259-270

[27] Steenkiste, P.: "A Systematic Approach to Host Interface Design for High-Speed Networks", IEEE Computer, Vol. 27, No. 3, March 1994, pp. 47-57

[28] Stiller, B.: "Flexible Protocol Configuration Support for a Service Integrated Commmunication System" (in German), Vol. 10, No. 306, Düsseldorf, Germany: VDI, 16, February 1994

[29] Tierney, B. L., Johnston, W. E., Herzog, H., Hoo, G., Jin, G., Lee, J., Chen, L. T., Rotem, D.: "The Image Server System: A High-Speed Parallel Distributed Data Server", Technical Report, Lawrence Berkely Laboratory, LBL-36002, 1994

[30] Tobagi, F., Pang, J., Baird, R., Gang, M.: "Streaming RAID - A Disk Array Management System for Video Files", Proceedings of ACM Multimedia'93, August 1993, pp. 393-400

[31] Tzou, S.-Z., Anderson, D. P.: "The Performance of Message -Passing Using Restricted Virtual Memory Remapping", Software - Practise and Experience, Vol. 21, No. 3, March 1991, pp. 251-267

[32] Zitterbart, M., Stiller, B., Tantawy, A.: "A Model for Flexible High-Performance Communication Subsystems", IEEE Journal on Selected Areas in Communications, Vol. 11, No. 4, May 1993, pp. 507-518

Checking Hybrid Automata for
Linear Duration Invariants

Li Xuandong*, Dang Van Hung**, and Zheng Tao***

International Institute for Software Technology
The United Nations University, P.O.Box 3058, Macau
email: {lxd, dvh, zt}@iist.unu.edu

Abstract. In this paper, we consider the problem of checking hybrid systems modelled by hybrid automata for a class of real-time properties represented by *linear duration invariants*, which are constructed from linear inequalities of integrated durations of system states. Based on linear programming, an algorithm is developed for solving the problem for a class of hybrid automata.
Keywords: Real-time and Hybrid Systems, Model-Checking, Duration Calculus, Linear Programming.

1 Introduction

A hybrid system consists of a discrete component and a continuous component. Since the methods to analyse the discrete components are different from the methods to analyse the continuous components, and since the interface between the two components is complicated, it is very difficult to analyse hybrid systems. Therefore, very often, one has to restrict oneself to some smaller class of hybrid systems so that the problems of concern can be solved efficiently. One of the classes of hybrid systems that has received a great deal of attention in the literature is the class of linear hybrid systems [1,2].

A linear hybrid system can be modelled by a linear hybrid automaton [1]. Informally, a hybrid automaton is a conventional automaton extended with a set of variables, which are used to model the state of the continuous component of hybrid systems and are assumed to be piecewise linear functions of time. The states of the automaton called *locations* are assigned with a change rate for each variable, such as $\dot{x} = w$ (x is a variable, w is a real number), and the transitions of the automaton are labelled with constraints on the variables such as $a \leq x \leq b$ and /or with reset actions such as $x := c$ (x is a variable, a, b, and c are real numbers). The automaton starts at one of the initial locations with all variables

---

* On leave from Department of Computer Science, Nanjing University, Nanjing 210093, P.R.China. Partly supported by National NSF of China. email: lxd@nju.edu.cn

** On leave from the Institute of Information Technology, Nghia Do, TuLiem, Hanoi, Vietnam.

*** On leave from Department of Computer Science, Nanjing University, Nanjing 210093, P.R.China. Partly supported by National NSF of China. email: zt@nju.edu.cn

initialised to their initial values. As time progresses, the values of all variables change continuously according to the rate associated with the current location. At any time, the system can change its current location from s to s' provided that there is a transition ρ from s to s' whose labelling conditions are satisfied by the current value of the variables. With a location change by a transition ρ, all the variables are reset to the new value accordingly by the reset actions labelled on ρ. Transitions are assumed to be instantaneous.

Let us consider an example of a water-level monitor in [1]. The water level in a tank is controlled through a monitor, which continuously senses the water level and turns a pump on and off. The water level changes as a piecewise-linear function of time. When the pump is off, the water level falls by two inches per second; when the pump is on, the water level rises by one inch per second. Suppose that initially the water level is one inch and the pump is on. The requirement for the monitor is that the water level should be kept in between one and 12 inches. There is a delay of two seconds from the time that the monitor signals to change the status of the pump to the time that the change becomes effective. Thus the monitor must signal to turn the pump on (off) at least two seconds before the water level falls to 1 inch (reaches 12 inches). The system is modelled by the hybrid automaton depicted in Figure 1. The automaton has four locations. In the locations s_1 and s_2, the pump is on; in the locations s_3 and s_4, the pump is off. The variable y is used to model the water-level, and x is used to specify the delays: whenever the control is in location s_2 or s_4, the value of x indicates how long the signal to switch the pump off or on has been sent.

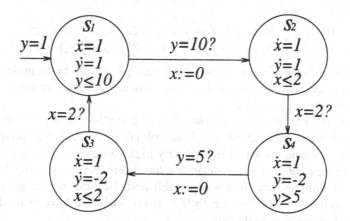

Fig. 1. A hybrid automaton modelling a water-level monitor

In this paper, we are concerned by the problem of checking automatically a linear hybrid automaton for a real time property, which is expressed by *linear duration invariants*. Linear duration invariants [4] are constructed from linear inequalities of integrated durations of system states. They form an important class of Duration Calculus (DC) [3] formulas. In DC, states are modelled as Boolean functions from reals (representing continuous time) to $\{0,1\}$, where 1 denotes state presence, and 0 denotes state absence. For a state S, the interval variable $\int S$ of DC is a function from bounded and closed intervals to reals which stands for the accumulated presence time (duration) of state S over the intervals, and is defined formally by $\int S[a,b] \hat{=} \int_a^b S(t)dt$, where $[a,b]$ ($b \geq a$) is a bounded interval of time. A linear duration invariant $\mathcal{D}$ in DC is of the form

$$T \geq \int 1 \geq t \Rightarrow \bigwedge_{j=1}^{k} (\sum_{i=1}^{n} c_{ij} \int S_i \leq M_j),$$

where T, t, c_{ij}, M_j are real numbers (T may be ∞).

The meaning of a linear duration invariant $\mathcal{D}$ is that: if the system is observed for an interval of time satisfying the premise of $\mathcal{D}$, then the duration of the system states must satisfy the consequence of $\mathcal{D}$. It turns out that many real-time properties can be written as a linear duration invariant.

For example, the requirement of the water-level monitor, which is that the monitor must keeps the water level in between 1 and 12 inches, can be expressed by linear duration invariants as well. We know that when the control is in locations s_1 or s_2, the water level rises 1 inch per second, and when the control is in locations s_3 or s_4, the water level falls by 2 inch per second. Furthermore, for an interval $[0,t]$, the accumulated time that the system stays in s_1 or s_2 is $\int s_1 + \int s_2$, and the accumulated time that the system stays in s_3 or s_4 is $\int s_3 + \int s_4$. Therefore, the water level at time t, given that at the beginning the water level is one inch, is $1 + \int s_1 + \int s_2 - 2(\int s_3 + \int s_4)$. Hence, the requirement for the water-level monitor can be described by the following linear duration invariants

$$0 \leq \int 1 \leq \infty \Rightarrow 1 + \int s_1 + \int s_2 - 2(\int s_3 + \int s_4) \leq 12;$$
$$0 \leq \int 1 \leq \infty \Rightarrow 1 + \int s_1 + \int s_2 - 2(\int s_3 + \int s_4) \geq 1.$$

Now, the problem we are concerned in this paper can be formulated as follows. Given a hybrid automaton A, given a linear duration invariant $\mathcal{D}$, decide efficiently whether A satisfy $\mathcal{D}$.

The problem has attracted a great deal of attention. In [6], the problem for a subclass of integration graph has been solved by using mixed integer/linear programming techniques which inherit very high complexity. In [4], the problem for a simple class of real time automata has been solved by using linear programming techniques, which is well established. Because of the advantages of the approach of [4] in comparison to the others, in [9] we have generalised it to a subclass of timed automata [5].

In this paper, by developing the techniques in [4,9] further, we show that by linear programming techniques the problem can be solved totally for a well-formed subclass of linear hybrid automata.

The paper is organised as follows. In the next section, we introduce the notion of hybrid regular expressions to express the behaviour of hybrid automata. Our model-checking algorithm is presented in Section 3. The last section is the conclusion of the paper.

2 Hybrid Regular Expressions

A traditional way to express the behaviour of an automaton is to use regular expressions. In this section, we extend the traditional regular expressions with time constraints and use them as a language to describe the behaviour of linear hybrid systems. The extended notation will be called *Hybrid Regular Expression* (HRE). While a regular expression over a set of states (alphabet) is a finite representation of a (infinite) set of sequences of states, an HRE will be a finite representation of a set of timed sequences of states.

Let V be a finite set, R^+ be the set of nonnegative real numbers. Each element of V is called a location. A finite sequence $(s_1, t_1)\char94(s_2, t_2)\char94 \ldots \char94(s_m, t_m)$ of elements in $V \times R^+$ is called a timed sequence over V. In this paper, we use $\char94$ to denote the concatenation of the sequences. The occurrence time $\tau(\sigma)$ of a timed sequence $\sigma = (s_1, t_1)\char94(s_2, t_2)\char94 \ldots \char94(s_m, t_m)$ over V is defined by $\tau(\sigma) = \sum_{i=1}^{m} t_i$.

A timed sequence $(s_1, t_1)\char94(s_2, t_2)\char94 \ldots \char94(s_m, t_m)$ represents a behaviour of a system that the system starts at the state s_1, stays there for t_1 time units, then changes to s_2 and stays in s_2 for t_2 time units, and so on. The values $t_1, t_2, \ldots$ have to satisfy some time constraints enforced by the system. These time constraints must be incorporate into the finite representation of the system behaviours. By incorporating time constraints into regular expressions, we get hybrid regular expressions.

An HRE $\mathcal{R}$ and the language $\mathcal{L}(\mathcal{R})$ represented by $\mathcal{R}$ over a finite set V of states are defined recursively as follows.

Definition 1.

1. ε is an HRE, and $\mathcal{L}(\varepsilon) = \{\varepsilon\}$.
2. Let $v_1, v_2, \ldots, v_m \in V$ ($m \geq 1$), and Δ be a set of linear inequalities on $\lambda_1, \lambda_2, \ldots, \lambda_m$ of the form $a \leq c_1\lambda_1 + c_2\lambda_2 + \ldots + c_m\lambda_m \leq b$, where a, b, and c_i ($1 \leq i \leq m$) are real numbers. Then $(v_1\char94 v_2\char94 \ldots \char94 v_m, \Delta)$ is an HRE, and

$$\mathcal{L}((v_1\char94 v_2\char94 \ldots \char94 v_m, \Delta)) =$$
$$\left\{ (v_1, t_1)\char94(v_2, t_2)\char94 \ldots \char94(v_m, t_m) \;\middle|\; \begin{array}{l} t_1, \ldots, t_m \geq 0 \text{ such that for all} \\ a \leq \sum_{i=1}^{m} c_i\lambda_i \leq b \in \Delta, \; a \leq \sum_{i=1}^{m} c_i t_i \leq b \end{array} \right\}.$$

When $\Delta = \phi$, $(v_1\char94 v_2\char94 \ldots \char94 v_m, \Delta)$ is taken to be $v_1\char94 v_2\char94 \ldots \char94 v_m$.

3. If $\mathcal{R}_1$ and $\mathcal{R}_2$ are HREs, then $\mathcal{R}_1\char94\mathcal{R}_2$ is an HRE, and

$$\mathcal{L}(\mathcal{R}_1\char94\mathcal{R}_2) = \{\sigma_1\char94\sigma_2 \mid \sigma_1 \in \mathcal{L}(\mathcal{R}_1), \; \sigma_2 \in \mathcal{L}(\mathcal{R}_2)\}.$$

4. If $\mathcal{R}_1$ and $\mathcal{R}_2$ are HREs, then $\mathcal{R}_1 \oplus \mathcal{R}_2$ is an HRE, and

$$\mathcal{L}(\mathcal{R}_1 \oplus \mathcal{R}_2) = \mathcal{L}(\mathcal{R}_1) \cup \mathcal{L}(\mathcal{R}_2).$$

5. If $\mathcal{R}$ is an HRE, then $\mathcal{R}^*$ is an HRE, and

$$\mathcal{L}(\mathcal{R}^*) = \{\sigma_1\char94 \ldots \char94\sigma_m \mid m \geq 0 \text{ and } \bigwedge_{i=1}^{m} (\sigma_i \in \mathcal{L}(\mathcal{R}))\},$$

where $\sigma_1\char94 \ldots \char94\sigma_m \hat{=} \epsilon$ when $m = 0$.

6. If $\mathcal{R}$ is an HRE, $a \in R^+, b \in R^+ \cup \{\infty\}, a \leq b$, and $b > 0$, then $(\mathcal{R}, [a, b])$ is an HRE (when $b = \infty$, $(\mathcal{R}, [a, b])$ is taken to be $(\mathcal{R}, [a, \infty)))$, and

$$\mathcal{L}((\mathcal{R}, [a, b])) = \{\sigma \mid \sigma \in \mathcal{L}(\mathcal{R}) \text{ and } a \leq \tau(\sigma) \leq b\}.$$

□

Although the traditional regular expressions are powerful enough to describe the behaviour of finite automata, it is not the case for HREs to describe the behaviour of all linear hybrid automata. The reason is that the constraints for continuous variables (occurring in Δ) can be put for a fixed finite sequence of states only. Nevertheless, it is simple and powerful enough to express the real-time behaviour of many hybrid systems encountered in practice.

For example, the behaviour of the linear hybrid automaton (Fig. 1) modelling the water level monitor in the introduction can be represented by the following HRE $\mathcal{R}_w$:

$$\mathcal{R}_w = \varepsilon \oplus (s_1, [0, 9]) \oplus (s_1, [9, 9])\hat{\ }(s_2, [0, 2]) \oplus \mathcal{R}_1$$
$$\oplus \mathcal{R}_2\hat{\ }\mathcal{R}_3^*\hat{\ }((s_4, [0, 2]) \oplus \mathcal{R}_4 \oplus \mathcal{R}_5 \oplus \mathcal{R}_6)$$

where

$$\mathcal{R}_1 = (s_1\hat{\ }s_2\hat{\ }s_3, \{\lambda_1 = 9, \ \lambda_2 = 2, \ 2\lambda_3 - \lambda_2 \leq 5\})$$
$$\mathcal{R}_2 = (s_1\hat{\ }s_2\hat{\ }s_3, \{\lambda_1 = 9, \ \lambda_2 = 2, \ 2\lambda_3 - \lambda_2 = 5\})$$
$$\mathcal{R}_3 = (s_4\hat{\ }s_1\hat{\ }s_2\hat{\ }s_3, \{\lambda_1 = 2, \ \lambda_2 - 2\lambda_1 = 5, \ \lambda_3 = 2, \ 2\lambda_4 - \lambda_3 = 5\})$$
$$\mathcal{R}_4 = (s_4\hat{\ }s_1, \{\lambda_1 = 2, \ \lambda_2 - 2\lambda_1 \leq 5\})$$
$$\mathcal{R}_5 = (s_4\hat{\ }s_1\hat{\ }s_2, \{\lambda_1 = 2, \ \lambda_2 - 2\lambda_1 = 5, \ 0 \leq \lambda_3 \leq 2\})$$
$$\mathcal{R}_6 = (s_4\hat{\ }s_1\hat{\ }s_2\hat{\ }s_3,$$
$$\{\lambda_1 = 2, \ \lambda_2 - 2\lambda_1 = 5, \ \lambda_3 = 2, \ -5 \leq \lambda_3 - 2\lambda_4\}) \ .$$

Since HREs form a very simple formalism to model hybrid systems, hopefully many problems are decidable for the class of hybrid systems defined by HREs. In next section, we show that checking an HRE for a linear duration invariant is decidable for the class, and we will give an efficient algorithm for solving the problem. In the rest of this section, we give some concepts concerning HREs that will be used for presenting our algorithms.

Definition 2. For an HRE $\mathcal{R}$, the *sub-expressions* of $\mathcal{R}$ are defined recursively by:

1. $\mathcal{R}$ is a sub-expression of $\mathcal{R}$.
2. If $\mathcal{R} = \mathcal{R}_1\hat{\ }\mathcal{R}_2$ or $\mathcal{R} = \mathcal{R}_1 \oplus \mathcal{R}_2$, where $\mathcal{R}_1$ and $\mathcal{R}_2$ are HREs, then all the sub-expressions of $\mathcal{R}_1$ and $\mathcal{R}_2$ are sub-expressions of $\mathcal{R}$.
3. If $\mathcal{R} = \mathcal{R}_1^*$ or $\mathcal{R} = (\mathcal{R}_1, [a, b])$, where $\mathcal{R}_1$ is an HRE, then all the sub-expressions of $\mathcal{R}_1$ are sub-expressions of $\mathcal{R}$. □

For an HRE $\mathcal{R}$, if $\mathcal{L}(\mathcal{R}) = \phi$, then $\mathcal{R}$ is said to be *empty*. For example,

$$((e_1\hat{\ }e_2, \{3 \leq \lambda_1 \leq 4, 4.5 \leq \lambda_2 \leq 5\}), [4, 7])$$

is an empty HRE. For an empty HRE $\mathcal{R}_1$ and for an HRE $\mathcal{R}$, it follows from the definition of HREs that

$$\mathcal{L}(\mathcal{R}_1 \hat{} \mathcal{R}) = \mathcal{L}(\mathcal{R} \hat{} \mathcal{R}_1) = \phi,$$
$$\mathcal{L}(\mathcal{R}_1 \oplus \mathcal{R}) = \mathcal{L}(\mathcal{R} \oplus \mathcal{R}_1) = \mathcal{L}(\mathcal{R}),$$
$$\mathcal{L}(\mathcal{R}_1^*) = \{\varepsilon\}, \text{ and } \mathcal{L}(\mathcal{R}_1, [a, b]) = \phi.$$

Furthermore, for an HRE $\mathcal{R}$, it is not difficult to give an efficient algorithm for checking the emptiness of $\mathcal{R}$. Therefore, if $\mathcal{R}$ is not an empty HRE, we can find out an HRE $\mathcal{R}'$ efficiently such that there is no empty sub-expression in $\mathcal{R}'$ and that $\mathcal{L}(\mathcal{R}) = \mathcal{L}(\mathcal{R}')$. For the simplicity, from now on, unless otherwise stated, we assume that all HREs under consideration are not empty and do not have any empty sub-expression.

A *simple* HRE is an HRE in which there is no occurrence of the combinators * (repetition) and $\oplus$ (union). From Definition 1, any simple HRE $\mathcal{R}$ can be rewritten as a simple HRE $\mathcal{R}'$ of the form $(v_1 \hat{} v_2 \hat{} \ldots \hat{} v_m, \Delta)$ such that $\mathcal{L}(\mathcal{R}) = \mathcal{L}(\mathcal{R}')$. For example, the simple HRE

$$(u \hat{} v, \{a \le c_1 \lambda_1 + c_2 \lambda_2 \le b\}) \hat{} (s, \{d \le c_1 \lambda_1 \le e\})$$

can be rewritten as

$$(u \hat{} v \hat{} s, \{a \le c_1 \lambda_1 + c_2 \lambda_2 + 0\lambda_3 \le b, d \le 0\lambda_1 + 0\lambda_2 + c_3 \lambda_3 \le e\}) .$$

Therefore, from now on, we assume that any simple HRE is of the form

$$(v_1 \hat{} v_2 \hat{} \ldots \hat{} v_m, \Delta),$$

where Δ is a finite set of linear inequalities of the form $a \le \sum_{i=1}^m c_i \lambda_i \le b$.

By a *normal form* we mean an HRE of the form

$$\mathcal{R}_1 \oplus \mathcal{R}_2 \oplus \ldots \oplus \mathcal{R}_m ,$$

where $\mathcal{R}_j$s are simple HREs.

3 Checking Hybrid Regular Expressions for Linear Duration Invariants

As mentioned in the introduction of the paper, linear duration invariants form an important class of DC formulas for specifying the requirement of real-time and hybrid systems. A linear duration invariant $\mathcal{D}$ is of the form

$$T \ge \int 1 \ge t \Rightarrow \bigwedge_{j=1}^k (\sum_{i=1}^n c_{ij} \int S_i \le M_j),$$

where T, t, c_{ij}, M_j are real numbers (T may be ∞), S_is are predicates over V.

For a location $v \in V$, for a predicate S over V, let $v \Rightarrow S$ denote that S holds during the system stays at v. For a timed sequence

$$\sigma = (v_1, t_1) \hat{} (v_2, t_2) \hat{} \ldots \hat{} (v_m, t_m) ,$$

the integrated duration of state S_i, i.e. the value of $\int S_i$, can be calculated as

$$\int S_i = \sum_{u \in \alpha_i} t_u \,,$$

where $\alpha_i \hat{=} \{u \mid (1 \leq u \leq m) \wedge (v_u \Rightarrow S_i)\}$. Consequently,

$$\int 1 = \sum_{u=1}^{m} t_u \,,$$

as $\{u \mid (1 \leq u \leq m) \wedge (v_u \Rightarrow 1)\} = \{1, 2, \ldots, m\}$.

Definition 3. A time sequence $\sigma = (v_1, t_1)\hat{\ }(v_2, t_2)\hat{\ } \ldots \hat{\ }(v_m, t_m)$ over V satisfies a linear duration invariant $\mathcal{D}$ iff $\bigwedge_{j=1}^{k}(\sum_{i=1}^{n} c_{ij}(\sum_{u \in \alpha_i} t_u) \leq M_j)$ when $T \geq \sum_{u=1}^{m} t_u \geq t$. An HRE $\mathcal{R}$ satisfies a linear duration invariant $\mathcal{D}$, denoted by $\mathcal{R} \models \mathcal{D}$, iff any timed sequences $\sigma \in \mathcal{L}(\mathcal{R})$ satisfies $\mathcal{D}$. $\qquad\square$

In this section, we will give an algorithm for checking HREs for linear duration invariants.

3.1 Basic Idea

Let $\mathcal{R}$ be a simple HRE

$$\mathcal{R} = (\langle v_1, \lambda_1 \rangle\hat{\ }\langle v_2, \lambda_2 \rangle\hat{\ } \ldots \hat{\ }\langle v_m, \lambda_m \rangle, \Delta) \,.$$

From the definition of HREs, every $\sigma \in \mathcal{L}(\mathcal{R})$ is of the form

$$(v_1, t_1)\hat{\ }(v_2, t_2)\hat{\ } \ldots \hat{\ }(v_m, t_m) \,,$$

where $t_1, t_2, \ldots, t_m$ satisfy the group of linear inequalities represented by Δ. Denoting this group of linear inequalities by C_1, the problem of checking $\mathcal{R} \models \mathcal{D}$ is then equivalent to the problem of finding the maximum value of the linear function

$$\sum_{i=1}^{n} c_{ij}(\sum_{u \in \alpha_i} t_u)$$

subject to the linear constraints C_1 and C_2 and checking whether it is not greater than M_j for all $j = 1, \ldots, k$, where C_2 denotes the inequality

$$t \leq t_1 + t_2 + \ldots + t_m \leq T \,.$$

The latters are linear programming problems.

Let $\mathcal{N} = \mathcal{R}_1 \oplus \mathcal{R}_2 \oplus \ldots \oplus \mathcal{R}_m$ be a normal form. Hence, each $\mathcal{R}_i$ $(1 \leq i \leq m)$ is a simple HRE. Since, by Definition 3,

$$\mathcal{N} \models \mathcal{D} \Leftrightarrow \bigwedge_{i=1}^{m} \mathcal{R}_i \models \mathcal{D} \,,$$

the problem of checking $\mathcal{N}$ for $\mathcal{D}$ can be solved by solving m linear programming problems $\mathcal{R}_i \models \mathcal{D}$, $i = 1, 2, \ldots, m$.

Therefore, for a general HRE $\mathcal{R}$, for a linear duration invariant $\mathcal{D}$, if we can effectively find a normal form $\mathcal{N}$ such that $\mathcal{R} \models \mathcal{D}$ if and only if $\mathcal{N} \models \mathcal{D}$, then we can check $\mathcal{R} \models \mathcal{D}$ effectively. Based on this idea, in the following subsections, we will give an algorithm to check an HRE $\mathcal{R}$ for a linear duration invariant $\mathcal{D}$. Without loss of generality, throughout the following subsections, let $\mathcal{D}$ be

$$ t \le \int 1 \le T \Rightarrow \sum_{i=1}^{n} c_i \int S_i \le M , $$

and for any $\sigma = (v_1, t_1)\,\hat{}\,(v_2, t_2)\,\hat{}\, \ldots \,\hat{}\,(v_m, t_m) \in \mathcal{L}(\mathcal{R})$, let $\theta(\sigma, \mathcal{D})$ be the value of $\sum_{i=1}^{n} c_i \int S_i$ evaluated over σ,

$$ \theta(\sigma, \mathcal{D}) = \sum_{i=1}^{n} c_i \big(\sum_{u \in \alpha_i} t_u \big), $$

where $\alpha_i = \{u \mid (1 \le u \le m) \wedge (v_u \Rightarrow S_i)\}$.

For any simple HRE $\mathcal{R}$, let $M_\tau(\mathcal{R})$ $(m_\tau(\mathcal{R}))$ denote the supremum (infimum) of the set $\{\tau(\sigma) \mid \sigma \in \mathcal{L}(\mathcal{R})\}$. $M_\tau(\mathcal{R})$ $(m_\tau(\mathcal{R}))$ can be calculated by finding the maximal (minimal) value of the linear objective function $t_1 + t_2 + \ldots + t_m$ subject to the group of linear inequalities $C1$ associated with $\mathcal{R}$, which is a classical linear programming problem. If $m_\tau(\mathcal{R}) = 0$, $\mathcal{R}$ is said to be a *zero-simple* HRE; otherwise $\mathcal{R}$ is said to be a *nonzero-simple* HRE.

For any nonzero-simple HRE $\mathcal{R}$, let $M_\theta(\mathcal{R})$ denote the supremum of the set

$$ \{\theta(\sigma, \mathcal{D}) \mid \sigma \in \mathcal{L}(\mathcal{R})\} . $$

Similarly to $M_\tau(\mathcal{R})$, $M_\theta(\mathcal{R})$ can be calculated effectively by finding the maximal value of the linear objective function $\sum_{i=1}^{n} c_i (\sum_{u \in \alpha_i} t_u)$ subject to the group of linear inequalities $C1$.

For a real number x, let $\lfloor x \rfloor$ denote the floor of x. For an HRE $\mathcal{R}$, let $\mathcal{R}^j$ denote the j-repetition of $\mathcal{R}$

$$ \mathcal{R}^j = \underbrace{\mathcal{R}\,\hat{}\,\mathcal{R}\,\hat{}\, \ldots \,\hat{}\,\mathcal{R}}_{j}, \ \mathcal{R}^0 = \varepsilon . $$

3.2 Foundations of the Model-Checking Algorithm

The basic idea of our algorithm for checking an HRE for a linear duration invariant $\mathcal{D}$, is to find out a normal form $\mathcal{N}$ such that $\mathcal{R} \models \mathcal{D}$ if and only if $\mathcal{N} \models \mathcal{D}$. In the following, we first introduce the concept *contexts* for describing this idea formally, then give several lemmas and theorems as the foundations of the algorithm.

Let $\mathcal{R}$ be an HRE, and $\mathcal{R}_1$ be a sub-expression of $\mathcal{R}$. Replacing an occurrence of $\mathcal{R}_1$ in $\mathcal{R}$ with a letter X, we obtain a *context* of X. Any context $\mathcal{C}(X)$ of X, is associated with two real numbers $\varphi(\mathcal{C}(X))$ and $\omega(\mathcal{C}(X))$, which specify a lower bound and a upper bound of the constraints on the occurrence time enforced by the context on the variable X. If the context does not enforce any time constraint on X then $\varphi(\mathcal{C}(X)) = 0$ and $\omega(\mathcal{C}(X)) = \infty$.

Definition 4. A context $C(X)$ of X, $\varphi(C(X))$ and $\omega(C(X))$ are defined recursively as:

1. X is a context of X, and $\varphi(X) = 0$ and $\omega(X) = \infty$ (no additional constraint).
2. If $C_1(X)$ is a context of X and $\mathcal{R}$ is an HRE, then $C(X) = C_1(X)^\wedge\mathcal{R}$ and $C(X) = \mathcal{R}^\wedge C_1(X)$ are contexts of X, and

$$\varphi(C(X)) = \varphi(C_1(X)), \, \omega(C(X)) = \omega(C_1(X))$$

(no additional constraint).
3. If $C_1(X)$ is a context of X and $\mathcal{R}$ is an HRE, then $C(X) = C_1(X) \oplus \mathcal{R}$ and $C(X) = \mathcal{R} \oplus C_1(X)$ are contexts of X, and

$$\varphi(C(X)) = \varphi(C_1(X)), \, \omega(C(X)) = \omega(C_1(X))$$

(no additional constraint).
4. If $C_1(X)$ is a context of X, then $C(X) = C_1(X)^*$ is a context of X, and

$$\varphi(C(X)) = \varphi(C_1(X)), \, \omega(C(X)) = \omega(C_1(X))$$

(no additional constraint).
5. If $C_1(X)$ is a context of X, $a \in R^+, b \in R^+ \cup \{\infty\}, b > 0$, and $a \leq b$, then $C(X) = (C_1(X), [a, b])$ is a context of X, and

$$\varphi(C(X)) = \max(\varphi(C_1(X)), a), \, \omega(C(X)) = \min(\omega(C_1(X)), b)$$

(additional constraint enforced by $[a, b]$). □

For any context $C(X)$, replacing X in $C(X)$ with an HRE, say $\mathcal{R}$, we obtain an HRE, denoted by $C(\mathcal{R})$.

A *finite* HRE is an HRE in which there is no occurrence of the combinator * (repetition). By Definition 1, it is not difficult to prove that for any HRE $\mathcal{R}$, distributing $^\wedge$ over $\oplus$, and $[a, b]$ over $\oplus$, we obtain a normal form $\mathcal{R}'$ such that $\mathcal{L}(\mathcal{R}) = \mathcal{L}(\mathcal{R}')$. For example, for a finite HRE

$$\mathcal{R} = (((v_1{}^\wedge v_2, \Delta_1) \oplus (v_3{}^\wedge v_4, \Delta_2))^\wedge(v_5{}^\wedge v_6, \Delta_3), [a, b]),$$

distributing $^\wedge$ over $\oplus$, and $[a, b]$ over $\oplus$, we get a normal form

$$\mathcal{R}' = ((v_1{}^\wedge v_2, \Delta_1)^\wedge(v_5{}^\wedge v_6, \Delta_3), [a, b]) \oplus ((v_3{}^\wedge v_4, \Delta_1)^\wedge(v_5{}^\wedge v_6, \Delta_3), [a, b]),$$

such that $\mathcal{L}(\mathcal{R}) = \mathcal{L}(\mathcal{R}')$. Hence, for an HRE $\mathcal{R}$ and a linear duration invariant $\mathcal{D}$, we attempt to find a normal form $\mathcal{N}$ such that $\mathcal{L}(\mathcal{R}) \models \mathcal{D}$ if and only if $\mathcal{L}(\mathcal{N}) \models \mathcal{D}$ by the following procedure:

Step 0. Let $\mathcal{R}' := \mathcal{R}$.
Step 1. For $\mathcal{R}'$, distributing $^\wedge$ over $\oplus$, and $[a, b]$ over $\oplus$, we obtain $\mathcal{Q}$. If $\mathcal{Q}$ is a normal form, then we are done.
Step 2. For a sub-expression $\mathcal{Q}_S$ of $\mathcal{Q}$ which is of the form $\mathcal{Q}_S = \mathcal{Q}_1{}^*$, replacing an occurrence of $\mathcal{Q}_S$ in $\mathcal{Q}$ with X, we obtain a context $C_{\mathcal{Q}}(X)$ such that $\mathcal{R}' = C_{\mathcal{Q}}(\mathcal{Q}_S)$.

Step 3. Finding a finite HRE Q'_S such that $C_Q(Q_S) \models D$ iff $C_Q(Q'_S) \models D$. Let $R' := C_Q(Q'_S)$, and go to Step 1. □

Obviously the procedure is correct. The problem is how to find Q'_S in Step 3. The following lemmas and theorems will help to solve that problem.

Let $C(X)$ be a context.

Lemma 1. Let R and R' be HREs. If for any $\sigma \in L(R)$, there is $\sigma' \in L(R')$ such that $\tau(\sigma) = \tau(\sigma')$ and $\theta(\sigma, D) \leq \theta(\sigma', D)$, then $C(R') \models D$ implies $C(R) \models D$. □

Lemma 2. Suppose $\omega(C(X)) = \infty$, and R be a nonzero-simple HRE R such that $M_\theta(R) \leq 0$. Then for any real number N_t, for any $\sigma \in L(C(R^*))$ such that $\tau(\sigma) \geq N_t$, there is $\sigma' \in L(C(\oplus_{j=0}^p R^j)$ such that

$$\tau(\sigma') \geq N_t \quad \text{and} \quad \theta(\sigma, D) \leq \theta(\sigma', D),$$

where $p = (\lfloor h/m_\tau(R) \rfloor + 1)$, and $h = \max(\varphi(C(X), N_t)$. □

Lemma 3. Suppose $\omega(C(X)) = \infty$, and R be a nonzero-simple HRE such that $M_\theta(R) > 0$. Then for any nonnegative real numbers N_t and M_r, there is $\sigma \in L(C(R^*))$ such that $\tau(\sigma) \geq N_t$ and $\theta(\sigma, D) > M_r$. □

Lemma 4. Suppose R be a nonzero-simple HRE, and $T \neq \infty$. Then for any $\sigma \in L(C(R^*))$, $\tau(\sigma) \leq T$ implies $\sigma \in L(C(\oplus_{j=0}^p R^j))$, where $p = \lfloor T/m_\tau(R) \rfloor + 1$. □

Lemma 5. Suppose R be a nonzero-simple HRE, $a \in R^+, b \in R^+ \cup \{\infty\}, a \leq b$, and $b > 0$. Then

$$L((C(\oplus_{j=0}^p R^j), [a, b])) \supseteq L((C(R^*), [a, b])),$$

where $p = \lfloor b/m_\tau(R) \rfloor + 1$. □

Lemma 6. Let R be a nonzero-simple HRE. Then $L(C(\oplus_{j=0}^p R^j)) \supseteq L(C(R^*))$, where $p = \lfloor \omega(C(X))/m_\tau(R) \rfloor + 1$. □

These lemmas can be proved by induction on the structure of context. For the details of their proofs, readers are referred to [10]. From these lemmas, we can prove the following theorems.

Theorem 1. Let R_1 and R_2 be HREs. Then

$$C((R_1 \oplus R_2)^*) \models D \quad \text{iff} \quad C((R_1^*)\hat{\ }(R_2^*)) \models D.$$

Proof. By Definition 1, $L((R_1^*)\hat{\ }(R_2^*)) \subseteq L((R_1 \oplus R_2)^*)$. From Lemma 1, the half of the claim follows, i.e.

$$C((R_1 \oplus R_2)^*) \models D \quad \text{implies} \quad C((R_1^*)\hat{\ }(R_2^*)) \models D,$$

The other half can be proved as follows. For any $\sigma_1 \in \mathcal{L}(\mathcal{R}_1)$ and $\sigma_2 \in \mathcal{L}(\mathcal{R}_2)$, since $\tau(\sigma_1\hat{\ }\sigma_2) = \tau(\sigma_1) + \tau(\sigma_2)$ and $\theta(\sigma_1\hat{\ }\sigma_2, \mathcal{D}) = \theta(\sigma_1, \mathcal{D}) + \theta(\sigma_2, \mathcal{D})$, we have $\tau(\sigma_1\hat{\ }\sigma_2) = \tau(\sigma_2\hat{\ }\sigma_1)$ and $\theta(\sigma_1\hat{\ }\sigma_2, \mathcal{D}) = \theta(\sigma_2\hat{\ }\sigma_1, \mathcal{D})$. Therefore, any $\sigma \in \mathcal{L}(\mathcal{C}((\mathcal{R}_1 \oplus \mathcal{R}_2)^*))$ can be permuted into $\sigma' \in \mathcal{L}(\mathcal{C}((\mathcal{R}_1{}^*)\hat{\ }(\mathcal{R}_2{}^*)))$. Hence, from Lemma 1, the result follows. $\qquad\square$

Theorem 2. Let $\mathcal{R}$ be a zero-simple HRE, $\mathcal{R} = (v_1\hat{\ }v_2\hat{\ } \ldots \hat{\ }v_m, \Delta)$. Let Δ' be the set $\{0 \le \sum_{i=1}^m c_i\lambda_i \mid 0 \le \sum_{i=1}^m c_i\lambda_i \le b \in \Delta \wedge \exists j \cdot (1 \le j \le m \wedge c_j < 0)\}$, and $\mathcal{R}' = (v_1\hat{\ }v_2\hat{\ } \ldots \hat{\ }v_m, \Delta')$. Then $\mathcal{C}(\mathcal{R}^*) \models \mathcal{D}$ iff $\mathcal{C}(\mathcal{R}') \models \mathcal{D}$.

Proof. Before the proof, we should note that by the definition of zero-simple HREs, $\tau(\mathcal{R}) = 0$ implies that for any inequality $a \le c_1\lambda_1 + c_2\lambda_2 + \ldots + c_m\lambda_m \le b$ in Δ, $a \le 0$ and $b \ge 0$.

The half of the claim that $\mathcal{C}(\mathcal{R}') \models \mathcal{D}$ implies $\mathcal{C}(\mathcal{R}^*) \models \mathcal{D}$, is explained as follows. By Definition 1, any $\sigma \in \mathcal{L}(\mathcal{R}^*)$ is of the form $\sigma_1\hat{\ }\sigma_2\hat{\ } \ldots \hat{\ }\sigma_n$, where

$$\sigma_i = (v_1, t_{i1})\hat{\ }(v_2, t_{i2})\hat{\ } \ldots \hat{\ }(v_m, t_{im}) \in \mathcal{L}(\mathcal{A}) \quad (i = 1, 2, \ldots, n).$$

For any j $(1 \le j \le m)$, let $t'_j = t_{1j} + t_{2j} + \ldots + t_{nj}$, and let

$$\sigma' = (v_1, t'_1)\hat{\ }(v_2, t'_2)\hat{\ } \ldots \hat{\ }(v_m, t'_m).$$

Since for any i $(1 \le i \le n)$, $t_{i1}, t_{i2}, \ldots, t_{im}$ satisfy Δ, $t'_1, t'_2, \ldots, t'_m$ satisfy Δ' as well. It follows that $\sigma' \in \mathcal{L}(\mathcal{R}')$. Since $\theta(\sigma, \mathcal{D}) = \theta(\sigma', \mathcal{D})$ and $\tau(\sigma) = \tau(\sigma')$, the first half of the claim follows from Lemma 1.

The other half of the claim, i.e. $\mathcal{C}(\mathcal{R}^*) \models \mathcal{D}$ implies $\mathcal{C}(\mathcal{R}') \models \mathcal{D}$, can be proved as follows. For any $\sigma' = (v_1, t_1)\hat{\ }(v_2, t_2)\hat{\ } \ldots \hat{\ }(v_m, t_m) \in \mathcal{L}(\mathcal{R}')$, since $t_1, t_2, \ldots, t_m$ satisfy Δ', for any $0 \le \sum_{i=1}^m c_i\lambda_i \le b \in \Delta$, we have $\sum_{i=1}^m c_i t_i \ge 0$. Because for each inequality $a \le c_1\lambda_1 + c_2\lambda_2 + \ldots + c_m\lambda_m \le b$ in Δ, $a \le 0$ and $b \ge 0$, and because Δ is a finite set, we can choose a natural number p such that for any inequality $a \le c_1\lambda_1 + c_2\lambda_2 + \ldots + c_m\lambda_m \le b \in \Delta$,

$$a \le \frac{c_1 t_1 + c_2 t_2 + \ldots + c_m t_m}{p} \le b.$$

For each i $(1 \le i \le m)$, let $b_i = t_i/p$, and let $\sigma_b = (v_1, b_1)\hat{\ }(v_2, b_2)\hat{\ } \ldots \hat{\ }(v_m, b_m)$. Obviously, $\sigma \in \mathcal{L}(\mathcal{R})$. Let

$$\sigma = \underbrace{\sigma_b\hat{\ }\sigma_b\hat{\ } \ldots \hat{\ }\sigma_b}_{p}.$$

It follows that $\sigma \in \mathcal{L}(\mathcal{R}^*)$. Since $\theta(\sigma, \mathcal{D}) = \theta(\sigma', \mathcal{D})$ and $\tau(\sigma) = \tau(\sigma')$, by Lemma 1, $\mathcal{C}(\mathcal{R}^*) \models \mathcal{D}$ implies $\mathcal{C}(\mathcal{R}') \models \mathcal{D}$. $\qquad\square$

Theorem 3. Suppose $\omega(\mathcal{C}(X)) = \infty$, $T = \infty$, and $\mathcal{R}$ be a nonzero-simple HRE such that $M_\theta(\mathcal{R}) > 0$. Then $\mathcal{C}(\mathcal{R}^*) \not\models \mathcal{D}$.

Proof. The theorem follows immediately from Lemma 3. $\qquad\square$

Theorem 4. Suppose $\omega(\mathcal{C}(X)) = \infty$, $T = \infty$, and $\mathcal{R}$ be a nonzero-simple HRE such that $M_\theta(\mathcal{R}) \leq 0$. Then $\mathcal{C}(\mathcal{R}^*) \models \mathcal{D}$ iff $\mathcal{C}(\oplus_{j=0}^p \mathcal{R}^j) \models \mathcal{D}$, where $p = (\lfloor h/m_\tau(\mathcal{R}) \rfloor + 1)$, $h = \max(\varphi(\mathcal{C}(X), t)$.

Proof. By Definition 1, $\mathcal{L}(\mathcal{R}^*) \supseteq \mathcal{L}(\oplus_{j=0}^p \mathcal{R}^j)$ holds, which by Lemma 1 implies a half of the claim, i.e. $\mathcal{C}(\mathcal{R}^*) \models \mathcal{D}$ implies $\mathcal{C}(\oplus_{j=0}^p \mathcal{R}^j) \models \mathcal{D}$. The other half is straightforward from Lemma 2. □

Theorem 5. Suppose $\omega(\mathcal{C}(X)) \neq \infty$ or $T \neq \infty$, and $\mathcal{R}$ be a nonzero-simple HRE. Then $\mathcal{C}(\mathcal{R}^*) \models \mathcal{D}$ iff $\mathcal{C}(\oplus_{j=0}^p \mathcal{R}^j) \models \mathcal{D}$, where $p = (\lfloor h/m_\tau(\mathcal{R}) \rfloor + 1)$, $h = \min(\omega(\mathcal{C}(X), T)$.

Proof. One half of the claim, i.e. $\mathcal{C}(\mathcal{R}^*) \models \mathcal{D}$ implies $\mathcal{C}(\oplus_{j=0}^p \mathcal{R}^j) \models \mathcal{D}$ is exactly the same as the proof of Theorem 4. The other half of the claim is a direct consequence of Lemmas 4 and 6. □

3.3 The Model-Checking Algorithm

Based on the theorems given in section 3.1, the algorithm to check an HRE $\mathcal{R}$ for a linear duration invariant $\mathcal{D}$ is now described as follows.

Step 0. Let $\mathcal{R}' := \mathcal{R}$.

Step 1. For $\mathcal{R}'$, distributing $\hat{\ }$ over $\oplus$, and $[a, b]$ over $\oplus$, we obtain $\mathcal{Q}$.

Step 2. Finding a sub-expression $\mathcal{Q}_S$ of $\mathcal{Q}$ which has one of the following three forms:

1. $\mathcal{Q}_S = (\mathcal{R}_1 \oplus \mathcal{R}_2 \oplus \ldots \oplus \mathcal{R}_k)^*$ $(k \geq 2)$, where every $\mathcal{R}_i$ $(1 \leq i \leq m)$ is a simple HRE.
2. $\mathcal{Q}_S = \mathcal{R}_1^*$, where $\mathcal{R}_1$ is a nonzero-simple HRE.
3. $\mathcal{Q}_S = \mathcal{R}_1^*$, where $\mathcal{R}_1$ is a zero-simple HRE.

If such $\mathcal{Q}_S$ could not be found, goto Step 6 (note that it is not difficult to prove that if we can not find out such a $\mathcal{Q}_S$, then $\mathcal{Q}$ is a normal form); otherwise replacing the occurrence of $\mathcal{Q}_S$ in $\mathcal{Q}$ with X, we get a context $\mathcal{C}_Q(X)$ such that $\mathcal{Q} = \mathcal{C}_Q(\mathcal{Q}_S)$. Then, if $\mathcal{Q}_S$ has the first form, goto Step 3; if $\mathcal{Q}_S$ has second form, goto Step 4; if $\mathcal{Q}_S$ has the third form, goto Step 5.

Step 3. By Theorem 2, we transform $\mathcal{Q}$ into $\mathcal{Q}' = \mathcal{C}_Q((\mathcal{R}_1)^* \hat{\ } (\mathcal{R}_2)^* \hat{\ } \ldots \hat{\ } (\mathcal{R}_m)^*)$. Thus, let $\mathcal{R}' := \mathcal{Q}'$, and goto Step 1.

Step 4. We first calculate $\omega(\mathcal{C}_Q(X))$ and $M_\theta(\mathcal{R}_1)$. If $\omega(\mathcal{C}_Q(X)) \neq \infty$ or $T \neq \infty$, then by Theorem 5, we transform $\mathcal{Q}$ into $\mathcal{Q}' = \mathcal{C}_Q(\oplus_{j=0}^p \mathcal{R}_1^j)$, where $p = (\lfloor h/m_\tau(\mathcal{R}_1) \rfloor + 1)$, and $h = \min(\omega(\mathcal{C}_Q(X), T)$. Therefore, let $\mathcal{R}' := \mathcal{Q}'$, and goto Step 1.

Otherwise, $\omega(\mathcal{C}_Q(X)) = \infty$ and $T = \infty$. If $M_\theta(\mathcal{R}_1) > 0$, then by Theorem 3, we conclude $\mathcal{C}_Q(\mathcal{R}_1^*) \not\models \mathcal{D}$ and exit. Otherwise, by Theorem 4, we transform $\mathcal{Q}$ into $\mathcal{Q}' = \mathcal{C}_Q(\oplus_{j=0}^p \mathcal{R}_1^j)$, where $p = (\lfloor h/m_\tau(\mathcal{R}_1) \rfloor + 1)$, and $h = \max(\varphi(\mathcal{C}_Q(X), t)$. Let $\mathcal{R}' := \mathcal{Q}'$, and goto Step 1.

Step 5. By Theorem 2, we transform $\mathcal{Q}$ into $\mathcal{Q}' = \mathcal{C}_Q(\mathcal{R}_1')$, where $\mathcal{R}_1'$ is the simple HRE defined from $\mathcal{R}_1$ in Theorem 2. Let $\mathcal{R}' := \mathcal{Q}'$, and goto Step 1.

Step 6. Since Q is a normal form now, we check $Q \models D$ by linear programming. If $Q \models D$, then $R \models D$; otherwise $R \not\models D$.

□

To illustrate how the algorithm works, we apply it to check the water level monitor for its requirement. The behaviour of the water level monitor is represented by the HRE R_w given in Section 2:

$$R_w = \varepsilon \oplus (s_1, [0, 9]) \oplus (s_1, [9, 9])\,\hat{}\,(s_2, [0, 2]) \oplus R_1$$
$$\oplus R_2\,\hat{}\,R_3^*\,\hat{}\,((s_4, [0, 2]) \oplus R_4 \oplus R_5 \oplus R_6)$$

where

$$R_1 = (s_1\,\hat{}\,s_2\,\hat{}\,s_3, \{\lambda_1 = 9,\ \lambda_2 = 2,\ 2\lambda_3 - \lambda_2 \le 5\})$$
$$R_2 = (s_1\,\hat{}\,s_2\,\hat{}\,s_3, \{\lambda_1 = 9,\ \lambda_2 = 2,\ 2\lambda_3 - \lambda_2 = 5\})$$
$$R_3 = (s_4\,\hat{}\,s_1\,\hat{}\,s_2\,\hat{}\,s_3, \{\lambda_1 = 2,\ \lambda_2 - 2\lambda_1 = 5,\ \lambda_3 = 2,\ 2\lambda_4 - \lambda_3 = 5\})$$
$$R_4 = (s_4\,\hat{}\,s_1, \{\lambda_1 = 2,\ \lambda_2 - 2\lambda_1 \le 5\})$$
$$R_5 = (s_4\,\hat{}\,s_1\,\hat{}\,s_2, \{\lambda_1 = 2,\ \lambda_2 - 2\lambda_1 = 5,\ 0 \le \lambda_3 \le 2\})$$
$$R_6 = (s_4\,\hat{}\,s_1\,\hat{}\,s_2\,\hat{}\,s_3,$$
$$\{\lambda_1 = 2,\ \lambda_2 - 2\lambda_1 = 5,\ \lambda_3 = 2,\ -5 \le \lambda_3 - 2\lambda_4\}).$$

and the requirement of the system is represented by the linear duration invariants given in the introduction of the paper:

$$0 \le \int 1 \le \infty \Rightarrow \int s_1 + \int s_2 - 2\int s_3 - 2\int s_4 \le 11$$
$$0 \le \int 1 \le \infty \Rightarrow -\int s_1 - \int s_2 + 2\int s_3 + 2\int s_4 \le 0.$$

Let $R_w = R_{w1} \oplus R_{w2}$, where $R_{w1} = \varepsilon \oplus (s_1, [0, 9]) \oplus (s_1, [9, 9])\,\hat{}\,(s_2, [0, 2]) \oplus R_1$ and $R_{w2} = R_2\,\hat{}\,R_3^*\,\hat{}\,((s_4, [0, 2]) \oplus R_4 \oplus R_5 \oplus R_6)$. Since for a linear duration invariant D, $R_w \models D$ if and only if $R_{w1} \models D$ and $R_{w2} \models D$, we can solve the problem by checking R_{w1} and R_{w2} for the requirement separately. Because R_{w1} is a simple HRE, checking R_{w1} for the requirement is easy and is omitted here.

In the following, let us check R_{w2} for the linear duration invariant

$$0 \le \int 1 \le \infty \Rightarrow \int s_1 + \int s_2 - 2\int s_3 - 2\int s_4 \le 11.$$

Starting from Step 0, let $R' := R_{w2}$. At Step 1, for R', distributing $\hat{}$ over $\oplus$ and $[a, b]$ over $\oplus$, we obtain $Q = R'$. At Step 2, choose $Q_S = R_3^*$, and

$$C_Q(X) = R_2\,\hat{}\,X\,\hat{}\,((s_4, [0, 2]) \oplus R_4 \oplus R_5 \oplus R_6).$$

Since Q_S has the 2th form, Step 4 should be the following one. By calculating $\omega(C_Q(X))$ and $M_\theta(R_3)$ we found that $\omega(C_Q(X)) = \infty$, $T = \infty$, and $M_\theta(A) \le 0$. By Theorem 4, we transform Q into $Q' = C_Q(\oplus_{j=0}^p R_3^j)$, where p is defined in Theorem 4. By a trivial calculation, $p = 1$ and $Q' = C_Q(\varepsilon \oplus R_3)$. Let

$$R' := R_2\,\hat{}\,(\varepsilon \oplus R_3)\,\hat{}\,((s_4, [0, 2]) \oplus R_4 \oplus R_5 \oplus R_6),$$

and goto Step 1 for repetition. At Step 1, for $\mathcal{R}'$, distributing $\hat{}$ over $\oplus$ and $[a, b]$ over $\oplus$, we obtain

$$\mathcal{Q} = \mathcal{R}_2\hat{}(s_4, [0, 2]) \oplus \mathcal{R}_2\hat{}\mathcal{R}_4 \oplus \mathcal{R}_2\hat{}\mathcal{R}_5 \oplus \mathcal{R}_2\hat{}\mathcal{R}_6 \oplus \mathcal{R}_2\hat{}\mathcal{R}_3\hat{}(s_4, [0, 2])$$
$$\oplus \mathcal{R}_2\hat{}\mathcal{R}_3\hat{}\mathcal{R}_4 \oplus \mathcal{R}_2\hat{}\mathcal{R}_3\hat{}\mathcal{R}_5 \oplus \mathcal{R}_2\hat{}\mathcal{R}_3\hat{}\mathcal{R}_6 .$$

At Step 2, Since $\mathcal{Q}$ is a normal form, $\mathcal{Q}_S$ cannot be found, and hence, Step 6 is taken as the last one. To perform Step 6, we have to solve the following eight linear programming problems.

Pr. No	Objective function	Constraints
1	$t_1 + t_2 - 2t_3 - 2t_4$	$t_1 = 9$, $t_2 = 2$, $t_3 = 3.5$, $0 \leq t_4 \leq 2$
2	$t_1 + t_2 - 2t_3 - 2t_4$ $+t_5$	$t_1 = 9$, $t_2 = 2$, $t_3 = 3.5$, $t_4 = 2$, $0 \leq t_5 \leq 9$
3	$t_1 + t_2 - 2t_3 - 2t_4$ $+t_5 + t_6$	$t_1 = 9$, $t_2 = 2$, $t_3 = 3.5$, $t_4 = 2$, $t_5 = 9$, $0 \leq t_6 \leq 2$
4	$t_1 + t_2 - 2t_3 - 2t_4$ $+t_5 + t_6 - 2t_7$	$t_1 = 9$, $t_2 = 2$, $t_3 = 3.5$, $t_4 = 2$, $t_5 = 9$, $t_6 = 2$, $0 \leq t_7 \leq 3.5$
5	$t_1 + t_2 - 2t_3 - 2t_4$ $+t_5 + t_6 - 2t_7 - 2t_8$	$t_1 = 9$, $t_2 = 2$, $t_3 = 3.5$, $t_4 = 2$, $t_5 = 9$, $t_6 = 2$, $t_7 = 3.5$, $0 \leq t_8 \leq 2$
6	$t_1 + t_2 - 2t_3 - 2t_4$ $+t_5 + t_6 - 2t_7 - 2t_8$ $+t_9$	$t_1 = 9$, $t_2 = 2$, $t_3 = 3.5$, $t_4 = 2$, $t_5 = 9$, $t_6 = 2$, $t_7 = 3.5$, $t_8 = 2$, $0 \leq t_9 \leq 9$
7	$t_1 + t_2 - 2t_3 - 2t_4$ $+t_5 + t_6 - 2t_7 - 2t_8$ $+t_9 + t_{10}$	$t_1 = 9$, $t_2 = 2$, $t_3 = 3.5$, $t_4 = 2$, $t_5 = 9$, $t_6 = 2$, $t_7 = 3.5$, $t_8 = 2$, $t_9 = 9$, $0 \leq t_{10} \leq 2$
8	$t_1 + t_2 - 2t_3 - 2t_4$ $+t_5 + t_6 - 2t_7 - 2t_8$ $+t_9 + t_{10} - 2t_{11}$	$t_1 = 9$, $t_2 = 2$, $t_3 = 3.5$, $t_4 = 2$, $t_5 = 9$, $t_6 = 2$, $t_7 = 3.5$, $t_8 = 2$, $t_9 = 9$, $t_{10} = 2$, $0 \leq t_{11} \leq 3.5$

We have solved these linear problems and found that for each one, the maximal value of the objective function is not greater than 11. Thus, we can conclude that one part of the requirement is satisfied by the system.

Similarly, we can check for the other part of the requirement, and conclude that the water-level monitor keeps the water-level between 1 and 12 inches.

4 Conclusion

We have presented our algorithm for checking a hybrid system whose behaviour is represented by an HRE, for a linear duration invariant. Our algorithm transforms the problem into a finite number of linear programming problems. Since the resulting linear programming problems are independent from each others, and since the programming problems can be solved efficiently, our algorithm when it can be applied gives an efficient way to solve the model checking problem.

The model checking problem for hybrid real time systems in general is very difficult. Even for a well-formed class of hybrid systems – the class of linear hybrid automata – the problem is still undecidable in general. HREs define a subclass of linear hybrid automata for which the problem can be solved efficiently. It should be noticed that the subclass defined by HREs is not comparable with the class of linear hybrid systems defined in [6]. Thus, theoretically the paper gives a new result for the decidability of the model checking problem.

Currently, a model checking tool based on the algorithms presented in this paper and in our previous ones is being developed. Hopefully, the tool will display more clearly the advantages of our approach.

References

1. R. Alur, C. Courcoubetis, N. Halbwachs, T.A. Henzinger, P.-H.Ho, X. Nicollin, A. Olivero, J. Sifakis, S. Yovine. The algorithmic analysis of hybrid systems. In *Theoretical Computer Science*, 138(1995), pp.3-34.
2. Thomas A. Henzinger. The theory of hybrid automata. In *Proceedings of the 11th Annual IEEE Symposium on Logic in Computer Science (LICS 1996)*, pp. 278-292.
3. Zhou Chaochen, C.A.R. Hoare, A.P. Ravn. A Calculus of Durations. In *Information Processing Letter*, 40, 5, 1991, pp.269-276.
4. Zhou Chaochen, Zhang Jingzhong, Yang Lu and Li Xiaoshan. Linear Duration Invariants. In *Formal Techniques in Real-Time and Fault-Tolerant Systems, LNCS 863*, pp.88-109.
5. Rajeev Alur, David L. Dill. A theory of timed automata. In *Theoretical Computer Science*, 126(1994), pp.183-235.
6. Y. Kesten, A. Pnueli, J. Sifakis, S. Yovine. Integration Graphs: A Class of Decidable Hybrid Systems. In *Hybrid System, LNCS 736*, pp.179-208.
7. S.C. Kleene. Representation of Events in Nerve Nets and Finite Automata. In *Automata Studies*, C.Shannon and J. McCarthy (eds.), Princeton Univ. Press, Princeton, NJ, 1956, pp.3-41.
8. J.U. Skakkebæk and N. Shankar. Towards a Duration Calculus proof assistant in PVS. In *Formal Techniques in Real-Time and Fault-Tolerant Systems, LNCS 863*, pp.660-697.
9. Li Xuandong, Dang Van Hung. Checking Linear Duration Invariants by Linear Programming. In *Concurrence and Parallelism, Programming, Networking, and Security, LNCS 1179*, pp.321-332.
10. Li Xuandong, Dang Van Hung, Zheng Tao. Checking Hybrid Automata for Linear Duration Invariants. Research report 109, UNU/IIST, P.O.Box 3058, Macau, June 1997.

Hierarchical Automata as Model for Statecharts
(Extended Abstract)

Erich Mikk[1], Yassine Lakhnech[1] and Michael Siegel[2]

[1] Christian-Albrechts-Universität zu Kiel
Institut für Informatik und Praktische Mathematik
Preußerstr. 1-9, D24105 Kiel, Germany
[2] Weizmann Institute of Science
Department of Applied Mathematics and Computer Science
76100 Rehovot, Israel

Abstract. Statecharts are a very rich graphical specification formalism supported by the commercial tool STATEMATE. Statecharts comprises powerful concepts such as interlevel transitions, multiple-source/multiple-target transitions, priority amongst transitions and simultaneous execution of maximal non-conflicting sets of transitions. Every add-on tool which is supposed to be linked with the STATEMATE tool have to deal with the rather involved semantics of these concepts. We propose *extended hierarchical automata* as an intermediate format to facilitate the linking of new tools to the STATEMATE environment, whose main idea is to devise a simple formalism with a more restricted syntax than statecharts which nevertheless allows to capture the richer formalism. We define the format, give operational semantics to it, and translate statecharts to it.

1 Introduction

Statecharts are a very rich graphical specification formalism supported by the commercial tool STATEMATE[3]. Statecharts comprises powerful concepts such as interlevel transitions, multiple-source/multiple-target transitions, priority amongst transitions and simultaneous execution of maximal non-conflicting sets of transitions [HN96]. Every add-on tool, such as code generators, test suite generators, simulators, model checkers, etc., which are supposed to be linked with the STATEMATE tool have to deal with the rather involved semantics of these concepts.

In this paper we suggest *extended hierarchical automata* (EHA) as an intermediate format to facilitate the linking of new tools to the STATEMATE environment. The EHA formalism uses single-source/single-target transitions as in usual automata (no interlevel transitions are admitted) and has a simple priority concept which facilitates computing the next step of an EHA when compared to statecharts. So, the main idea is to devise a simple formalism with a more restricted syntax than statecharts which nevertheless allows to capture the richer formalism. Extended hierarchical automata, which are related to the Argos language [Mar91], come with a simple operational semantics which simplifies the implementation of tools for this formalism.

---

[3] STATEMATE is provided by iLogix: http://www.ilogix.com/company/company.htm

In the current paper we introduce the concept and semantics of EHA and explain the translation of statecharts into EHA. This translation can be used as a generic front-end for the implementation of various tools for the statecharts formalism as supported by the STATEMATE environment.

Before formulating such an intermediate format, its semantics and a translation of statecharts into this format we need to fix a certain semantics for statecharts itself. Since we are interested in add-on tools for STATEMATE we base our work on the recent Harel&Naamad semantics [HN96] which we formalized in [MLPS97].

The main technical problem is to devise a simple formalism which is nevertheless capable to model interlevel transitions. Interlevel transitions (possibly with multiple sources/multiple targets) are transitions which do not respect the hierarchy of states, i.e. those that cross borderlines of states. They can be understood as a powerful goto mechanism which allows to arbitrary movement of control across the state hierarchy. The price of interlevel transitions is their intricate semantics in particular in combination with the priority mechanism as supported by STATEMATE. Interlevel transitions spoil in general a clean decomposition of a system into subsystems (since "dangling" transitions without source or target result) and thus denies a structural operational semantics for statecharts. A rather complicated continuation semantics for statecharts with interlevel transitions can be found in [Hui91].

These semantical problems, amongst others, caused the investigation of other graphical and hierarchical formalisms, such as Argos [Mar91, Mar92], Spec-Charts [NVG91], Modecharts [JM94], and RSML [LHHR94] which forbid the explicit use of interlevel transitions and thereby gain elegant structural operation semantics (SOS). Argos even supports an encoding to simulate the effect of interlevel transitions. The encoding exploits the non-preemptive interrupt mechanism of Argos as well as the synchronicity of input/output events. This encoding does not work for the statecharts formalism as implemented in STATEMATE since it is neither perfectly synchronous (generated events can only be sensed in the next step of the system) nor does it support non-preemptive interrupts (its priority mechanism forbids simultaneous execution of transitions which depart from states which are related in the state hierarchy). After introducing extended hierarchical automata and the translation of statecharts into this formalism we give a more detailed comparison between Argos and our approach in Section 4.

The two main side conditions for the definition of the intermediate format are that it must be as simple as possible but also remain close to the original statecharts formalism. The latter facilitates the actual translation of statecharts into this format (e.g. using a perfectly synchronous formalism will considerably complicate the translation) as well as the correctness proof of the translation. As a result of remaining close to the statecharts formalism the EHA format explains completely formal yet simple to grasp the semantical phenomena of statecharts. These features make EHA a good candidate as intermediate format when implementing new tools for statecharts. So far we have used EHA in the implementation of a compiler from statecharts to Promela, the input language of the SPIN model-checker [Hol91, Hol97].

The paper is organized as follows. In Section 2 we define hierarchical automata and give descriptive style semantics to them. Section 3 introduces the extended version of hierarchical automata, which allows for modeling interlevel transitions. A simple operational semantics is given for EHA which is shown to be compatible with the descriptional one. In Section 4 we translate statecharts with interlevel transitions to extended hierarchical automata.

2 Hierarchical automata

In this section we define the class of hierarchical automata (HA) that consists of parallel and hierarchical composition of sequential automata. HA resemble statecharts without interlevel transitions.

2.1 Introduction to hierarchical automata

A hierarchical automaton is built as parallel and/or hierarchical composition of sequential automata. HA have maximal parallelism semantics, i.e. parallel automata execute their transitions synchronously. Such a set of synchronously firing transitions constitutes a step (cf. [HN96]). As in statecharts the communication medium are events which are broadcasted instantaneously within the hierarchical automaton. A step consumes input events and produces output events which are inputs for the next step. Hierarchical composition means mapping states of a sequential automaton to another automaton or parallel composition of automata. If a state s of some automaton is mapped to automaton A, then we refer to A as the *sub-automaton* of s. We also say, that s *is refined by* A and that s is a *parent* of A.

The idea is that the parent state may delegate its step to its sub-automata. If a state does not have an internal structure we call it a *basic state*. Taking a transition means to leave the source state and enter the target state of the transition; if the source and the target are non-basic states then taking the transition affects the sub-structures of the source and the target as well: together with the source state all sub-states of the source are left and when a target is entered then the initial states of the target's sub-automata are entered.

Besides communication via events, statecharts support synchronization of concurrent components by state references to parallel components. Transitions are guarded by events and such state references. The guard is true if the event is available (i.e. provided by the environment or generated in the previous step) and the state references refer to states that are currently active. Since hierarchical automata are meant to model statecharts, we add this feature to hierarchical automata, too. Transition labels in hierarchical automata are pairs of trigger and action part. On the trigger part, we allow for propositions over event and state names. On the action part we allow for generation of events.

Example 1. Running example. We use state transition diagrams to visualize hierarchical automata. We use boxes to denote states, initial states are indicated by double boxes. Transitions are labeled arrows. Sequential automata are surrounded by a dashed line.

The hierarchical structure is indicated by dotted lines. If a state is mapped to more than one sequential automata then they are meant to run in parallel.

The hierarchical automata in Figure 1 depicts a model of a TV-set (this example is inspired by [HdR91]). The root automaton *TV* may be in states *ON* or *OFF*. State *OFF* is refined to automaton *POWER* and state *ON* is refined to the parallel composition of automata *IMAGE* and *SOUND*. Whenever the *TV* automaton is in the state *ON*, both *SOUND* and *IMAGE* are considered active; since *ON* and *OFF* are exclusive the system can never be in one of the states of *POWER* when *TV* is in state *ON*. The system changes its state upon reception of events from the environment, e.g., the event *on* initiates the state change from *OFF* to *ON*, which implies deactivation of *POWER* and activation of *IMAGE* and *SOUND*.

However, this specification is not quite what we would expect from a TV-set. The state *DISCONNECTED* is meant to model that the TV-set is not plugged in and only after the event *in* we should expect some activity from the system. Indeed, as described above we can constrain the transition from *OFF* to *ON* by a condition restricting its enabledness only to configurations where *STANDBY* is active. But we would like to have more, e.g., when being in *TV.ON* (we use the dot notation to select states of automata) upon receiving event *out* we would like to go straight to the sub-state *DISCONNECTED*. In extended hierarchical automata we provide the facility to explicitly specify such target-states of transitions.

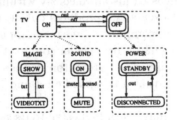

Fig. 1. Running example: TV-set as hierarchical automata

2.2 Definition of hierarchical automata

Definition 1. *Sequential automaton A is a 4-tuple* (Σ, s_0, L, δ) *where* Σ *is the set of states of A, s_0 is the initial state of A, L is the set of transition labels of A (we will be more specific about labels later),* $\delta \subseteq \Sigma \times L \times \Sigma$ *is the transition relation.*

Sequential automata can be parallely and hierarchically composed to build hierarchical automata. We assume that sequential automata participating in a hierarchical automaton have mutually disjoint sets of states. We introduce the notion of *composition function* that applies parallel and hierarchical composition to sequential automata.

Definition 2. *Given a finite set* $F = \{A_1, \ldots, A_n\}$ *of sequential automata with mutually distinct state spaces* Σ_{A_i}. *We call* $\gamma : \bigcup_{A \in F} \Sigma_A \to \mathbb{P}(F)$ *a composition function on F iff*

– There exists a unique root automaton: $\exists_1 A \in F.A \notin \bigcup ran(\gamma)$, denoted by γ_{root},
– Every non-root automaton has exactly one ancestor state:
$\bigcup ran(\gamma) = F \setminus \{\gamma_{root}\}$,
and $\forall A \in F \setminus \{\gamma_{root}\}.\exists_1 s \in \bigcup_{A' \in F \setminus \{A\}} \Sigma_{A'}.A \in \gamma(s)$,
– The composition function contains no cycles:
$\forall S \subseteq \bigcup_{A \in F} \Sigma_A.\exists s \in S.S \cap \bigcup_{A \in \gamma(s)} \Sigma_A = \emptyset$.

If $| \gamma(s) | = 1$ then s is refined to a single automaton, if $| \gamma(s) | > 1$ then s is refined to a parallel composition of automata. Otherwise, $\gamma(s) = \emptyset$, and we call s a *basic state* (denoted by $Basic_\gamma(s)$).

Example 2. The composition function in Figure 1 is

$$\gamma = \{OFF \mapsto \{POWER\}, ON \mapsto \{SOUND, IMAGE\}\}$$
$$\cup \{s \mapsto \emptyset \mid s \in \{SHOW, VIDEOTXT, SOUND.ON,$$
$$MUTE, STANDBY, DISCONNECTED\}\}.$$

Definition 3. *A hierarchical automaton HA is given by a triple* (F, E, γ) *where* $F = \{A_1, \ldots, A_n\}$ *is a set of sequential automata with mutually distinct state spaces, E is a set of events, and γ a composition function on F.*

A label l in a sequential automaton $A \in F$ is a tuple (ex, ac), where ex is a proposition over event and state names (constant *true*, primitive events and/or states connected with $\wedge, \vee, \neg$) and $ac \subseteq E$ is a set of event names. Models of ex are tuples (C, E), where C is a set of states and E is a set of events: $(C, E) \subseteq \bigcup_{A \in F} \Sigma_A \times E$.

Example 3. The hierarchical automata depicted in Figure 1 is given by the following triple: $(\{TV, IMAGE, SOUND, POWER\}, \{in, out, on, off, txt, mute, sound\}, \gamma)$, where γ is the composition function as in Example 2.

We associate selector functions with transitions: if $(s, l, s') \in \delta_A$ then $source(s, l, s') = s$, $target(s, l, s') = s'$ and $label(s, l, s') = l$; *Source*, *Target* and *Label* denote the usual extension to sets of transitions. We also associate selector functions with labels: if $(ex, ac) \in L_A$ then $expr(ex, ac) = ex$ and $action(ex, ac) = ac$ and respectively *Expr*, *Action* for sets of labels.

2.3 Semantics of hierarchical automata

We describe the semantics of HA along the lines of the statecharts semantics given in [HN96]. We associate a Kripke structure to a hierarchical automaton. First we need some preliminary definitions.

Definition 4. *A composition function* γ *on* $F = \{A_1, \ldots, A_n\}$ *induces a successor function* $\chi : \bigcup_{A \in F} \Sigma_A \to \mathbb{P}(\bigcup_{A \in F} \Sigma_A)$ *defined by*

$$\chi(s) = \{s' \mid \exists A \in F.A \in \gamma(s) \wedge s' \in \Sigma_A\},$$

thus, $s' \in \chi(s)$ iff s' is a state of the direct sub-automaton of s.

We denote by χ^+ and χ^* the *irreflexive*, resp. *reflexive transitive closure* of χ. Furthermore, χ induces an irreflexive *partial order* on states: $s \prec s'$ iff $s \in \chi^+(s')$. We say s is the *parent* of s' (denoted by $parent(s') = s$) iff $s' \in \chi(s)$ and s is an *ancestor* of s' (denoted by $ancestor(s, s')$) iff $s' \in \chi^+(s)$.

A *configuration* describes which states of sequential automata of an hierarchical automaton are simultaneously active.

Definition 5. Given a hierarchical automaton $HA = (F, E, \gamma)$. A set $C \subseteq \bigcup_{A \in F} \Sigma_A$ is a *configuration* of HA iff

- Exactly one state of the root automaton γ_{root} is in the configuration: $\exists_1 s \in \Sigma_{\gamma_{root}}.s \in C$,
- Downward closure: $s \in C \land A \in \gamma(s) \Rightarrow \exists_1 s_i \in \Sigma_A.s_i \in C$.

The set of all configurations is denoted by $Conf(\gamma)$. Note, configurations are also upward closed: $s \in C \land (\exists s'.s \in \chi(s') \Rightarrow s' \in C)$.

For the rest of this section let $HA = (F, E, \gamma)$ be a hierarchical automaton and consider a configuration C of HA and a set E of events. A transition (s, l, s') of $A \in F$ is called *enabled in* (C, E), if s is *active in* C, i.e. $s \in C$, and $(C, E) \models expr(l)$. Let $ET_{(C,E)}$ denote the set of enabled transitions in (C, E). Then, we call an automaton A of F *enabled in* (C, E), if there exists a transition (s, l, s') of A which is in $ET_{(C,E)}$. Given transitions t_1 and t_2, we say that t_2 *has higher priority than* t_1, if $source(t1) \prec source(t2)$.

An execution step of HA in (C, E) consists of synchronously firing all the transitions in a so-called *maximal non-conflicting set of transitions* [HN96], i.e. a set of transitions in which every enabled automaton contributes by exactly one transition unless it has an ancestor enabled automaton. Let $trs \subseteq ET_{(C,E)}$ be a set of enabled transitions in (C, E). A set $trs \subseteq ET_{(C,E)}$ is *maximal and non-conflicting* iff

1. $| trs \cap \delta_A | \leqslant 1$ for all $A \in F$, i.e. every automaton can contribute at most one transition,
2. $\forall t \in ET_{(C,E)}.t \in trs$ iff there does not exist $t' \in ET_{(C,E)}$ with higher priority, i.e. an automaton must contribute a transition to trs if there is no higher priority transition.

Let $HPT_{(C,E)}$ denote the set of all transitions which are maximal and non-conflicting in (C, E).

Though, we do not define the semantics of statecharts in this paper, it is not difficult to see that the notion of maximal non-conflicting sets as by Harel&Naamad in [HN96] and formalization due to [MLPS97] coincides with the definition above.

Example 4. Assume a configuration $C = \{TV.ON, IMAGE.SHOW, SOUND.ON\}$ and $E = \{off, txt, mute\}$. Then transitions emerging from $TV.ON, IMAGE.SHOW$ and $SOUND.ON$ are enabled, but the set of maximal non-conflicting transitions consists of a singleton set containing solely the transition from $TV.ON$ to $TV.OFF$.

Definition 6. The semantics of HA is a Kripke structure $\mathbf{K} = (S, s_0, \xrightarrow{STEP})$ where

- $S = Conf(\gamma) \times \mathbb{P}(E)$ is the set of states of **K**,
- $s_0 \in S$, where $s_0 = (C_0, \emptyset)$ is the initial state of **K**, where C_0 is defined as follows. Let $\gamma_{root} = (\Sigma, s_o, L, \delta)$ and $\Sigma_0 = \bigcup_{A \in F} s_{0_A}$ (Σ_0 is the set of all initial states of automata in F), then $C_0 = (\chi \mid_{\Sigma_0})^*(s_0)$.
- $\xrightarrow{STEP} \subseteq S \times S$ is the transition relation of **K**, where $(C, E) \xrightarrow{STEP} (C', E')$ iff there exists a maximal non-conflicting set $trs \in HPT_{(C,E)}$, or if $HPT_{(C,E)} = \emptyset$ then $trs = \emptyset$, such that

$$C' = (C \setminus \chi^*(Source(trs))) \cup Target(trs) \cup (\chi^+(Target(trs)) \cap \bigcup_{A \in F} s_{0_A})$$

and $E' = Action(Label(trs))$.

Proposition 7. *Given a hierarchical automaton $HA = (F, E, \gamma)$ and its semantics $\mathbf{K} = (\mathbf{S}, s_0, \xrightarrow{STEP})$. Let (C, E) be a state of $\mathbf{K}$, let trs be a maximum non-conflicting set $trs \in HPT_{(C,E)}$ and let*

$$C' = (C \setminus \chi^*(Source(trs))) \cup Target(trs) \cup (\chi^+(Target(trs)) \cap \bigcup_{A \in F} s_{0_A}).$$

Then C' is a configuration: $C' \in Conf(\gamma)$.

The proof is by induction over the cardinality of subsets of $HPT_{(C,E)}$. This proposition explains that the transition relation is well-defined.

3 Extended hierarchical automata

The operational semantics of statecharts as described in [HN96] and formalized in [MLPS97] is rather involved. This intricacy is mainly caused by the complicated interplay of interlevel transitions and the priority rule of statecharts.

Harel considers interlevel transitions as important concept of the language [Har87]: "... as our methods does not necessarily advocate layer-by-layer development; it is more flexible and encourages interlevel connections too, whenever appropriate." Hence we will not rule them out, instead we present an approach which allows to describe interlevel transitions but nevertheless has simple operational semantics. Since the priority concept of statecharts is very simple in case of non-interlevel transitions, we investigate a reformulation of interlevel transitions which allows to handle them just as ordinary transitions w.r.t. the priority concept.

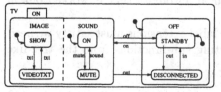 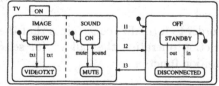

Fig. 2. Statechart with interlevel transition (left) and its desired extension.

Consider the left statecharts in Figure 2. Transitions from $TV.ON$ to $DISCONNECTED$, from $TV.ON$ to $STANDBY$ and from $STANDBY$ to $TV.ON$ are interlevel transitions. If any one of those is taken then not only the source state is exited but also the parent of each source state and entering a state means that the parent state is entered, too. Our idea is to lift those transitions to the uppermost states that are exited and entered when that transition is taken. This is done in the right statechart in Figure 2. Now we have to preserve information to restrict enabledness of those transitions: we extend labels by a set of state names, which were the original states of the transition; we call this extension *source restriction*. Furthermore, we have to preserve the information needed to determine the target states: we add another label extension td (which we call *target determinator*) that is a set of states that were entered originally. Hence label extensions in the right statecharts are as follows: $sr(l1) = \emptyset$, $td(l1) = \{STANDBY\}$, $sr(l2) = \emptyset$, $td(l2) = \{DISCONNECTED\}$, $sr(l3) = \{STANDBY\}$, $td(l3) = \{SHOW, SOUND.ON\}$. The trigger part is taken over unchanged from the corresponding transitions on the left. In the sequel we apply this idea to hierarchical automata.

Example 5. Note, that the specification in Figure 2 more faithfully reflects a conventional TV-set than the hierarchical automaton in Figure 1. Now there is a clear distinction between two groups of events the are responsible for switching in and out and for power supply: the events *on* and *off* switch between active mode and the standby mode, whereas *in* and *out* switch between a plugged-in and plugged-out TV-set. With this particular hierarchy of states the improved specification became possible only with interlevel transitions.

Note, the source restriction extension can already be expressed in HA and statecharts my means of state references in the trigger part of transitions. But target determinator extension has no counterpart in statecharts and HA. Statecharts don't need it due to the presence of interlevel transitions which can explicitly enter the correct target configuration. In this section we work out details of such extension on hierarchical automata. In Section 4 we give a translation from statecharts to extended hierarchical automata.

Another problem with the present semantics is that its descriptional style does not provide algorithmic insight, how one execution step can be computed, i.e., basically how to find a maximal non-conflicting set of transitions. We are looking for an operational description that allows to say for each enabled transition how it participates in a current step. Hence we need conditions on how transitions synchronize within one step in a priority preserving manner. This results in the operational semantics for extended hierarchical automata that is worked out in the sequel.

In order to formalize constraints that the label extensions must satisfy we need a restriction operation that allows for selecting sub-functions from the tree-like composition function.

Definition 8. Given a composition function γ on the finite set $F = \{A_1, \ldots, A_n\}$ of sequential automata. *Restriction* of γ to state s is a composition function $\gamma \mid_s$

defined as domain restriction to sub-states of s: $\gamma \mid_{\chi^{\bullet}(s)}$. The restriction is extended pointwise to sets of states.

Definition 9. *An extended hierarchical automata EHA is a 3-tuple* (F, E, γ), *where* $F = \{A_1, \ldots, A_n\}$ *is a set of sequential automata with mutually distinct state spaces,* E *is a set of events, and* γ *a composition function on* F.

Labels of the sequential automata are extended as follows: the label l of transition (s, l, s') in the automaton $A \in F$ is a 4-tuple (sr, ex, ac, td), where $sr \in Conf(\gamma \mid_s)$, $td \in Conf(\gamma \mid_{s'})$, and as before ex is a proposition guarding the transition, and ac is a set of generated events.

Given $EHA = (F, E, \gamma)$, the restriction of the composition function to states of some $A \in F$ yields an extended hierarchical automaton $EHA_A = (F_A, E_A, \gamma_A)$ by defining: $F_A = F \setminus \{A_i \mid \Sigma_{A_i} \cap \chi^*(\Sigma_A) = \emptyset\}$, $E_A = E$, $\gamma_A = \gamma \mid_{\chi^{\bullet}(\Sigma_A)}$. So the composition function γ can be seen as assigning EHA (or possibly a parallel composition of EHA) an internal structure to states; state s is refined by (the parallel composition of) EHA_{A_i}, for $A_i \in \gamma(s)$. This view suggests to define the semantics of extended hierarchical automata inductively over the composition function which is the main composition of EHA.

3.1 Semantics of extended hierarchical automata.

In the following let $EHA = (F, E, \gamma)$ be an extended hierarchical automaton. The semantics of EHA is the Kripke structure $\mathbf{K} = (\mathbf{Ss_0}, \xrightarrow{STEP})$ given in definition Definition 6, however with a step relation as defined in the sequel. In the sequel we refer to states of $\mathbf{K}$ as *status*.

Let (C, E) be a status of $\mathbf{K}$. A transition $t = (s, (sr, ex, ac, td), s')$ of an automata $A \in F$ is *enabled* in the status (C, E) (denoted by $enabled_{(C, E)}(t)$) iff $s \in C$, $sr \subseteq C$ and $(C, E) \models ex$.

The step relation. We define the step relation using inference rules. We distinguish between extended hierarchical automata 1) interacting with the environment by receiving events from environment and suppling generated events to the environment (open system approach) and 2) not interacting with the environment (closed system approach). The left rule is for closed systems. The right rule is for open systems, where the environment is allowed to add events after each step.

CLOSED SYSTEMS: OPEN SYSTEMS:

$$\frac{\gamma_{root} :: (C, E) \to (C', E')}{(C, E) \xrightarrow{STEP} (C', E')} \qquad \frac{\gamma_{root} :: (C, E) \to (C', E') \wedge E' \subseteq E''}{(C, E) \xrightarrow{STEP} (C', E'')}$$

These rules establish relation $\xrightarrow{STEP}$ based on relation $\to$; the latter is defined by inference rules given below. An inference in our rule system is denoted by $A :: (C, E) \to (C', E')$, where $A \in F$ is a sequential automaton; (C, E) is a status of the hierarchical automaton EHA, and $C' \in Conf(\gamma \mid_{\Sigma_A})$ (i.e. a configuration of an EHA which has A as root automaton) and $E' \subseteq E$.

Progress rule. If there is an enabled transition an active sequential automaton takes it.

$$\frac{\{s\} = C \cap \Sigma_A \quad \exists\, tr \in \delta_A . enabled_{(C,\,E)}(tr) \wedge tr = (s, (sr, ex, ac, td), s')}{A :: (C, E) \to (\{s'\} \cup td, ac)}$$

Stuttering rule. If an active sequential automaton does not have an enabled transition and the active state is a basic state then the automaton stutters and consumes events.

$$\frac{\{s\} = C \cap \Sigma_A \quad Basic_\gamma(s) \quad \forall\, tr \in \delta_A . tr = (s, l, s') \Rightarrow \neg\, enabled_{(C,\,E)}(tr)}{A :: (C, E) \to (\{s\}, \emptyset)}$$

Composition rule. This rule explains how an automaton delegates its step to its sub-automata: if it does not have an enabled transition then its step collects the results of steps performed by its sub-automata. Note, that if the active state is refined into a parallel composition then the components are executed simultaneously and they do not interfere during the step.

$$\frac{\begin{array}{l} \{s\} = C \cap \Sigma_A \\ \forall\, tr \in \delta_A . tr = (s, l, s') \Rightarrow \neg\, enabled_{(C,\,E)}(tr) \\ \gamma(s) = \{A_1, \dots, A_m\} \neq \emptyset \\ A_1 :: (C, E) \to (C'_1, E'_1) \\ \dots \\ A_m :: (C, E) \to (C'_m, E'_m) \end{array}}{A :: (C, E) \to (\{s\} \cup C'_1 \cup \dots \cup C'_m, E'_1 \cup \dots \cup E'_m)}$$

The next proposition explains that the transition relation is well-defined.

Proposition 10. *Given an extended hierarchical automaton* $EHA = (F, E, \gamma)$ *and its semantics* $\mathbf{K} = (\mathbf{S}, \mathbf{s_0}, \overset{STEP}{\longrightarrow})$. *Let* (C, E) *be a state of* $\mathbf{K}$ *and let* (C', E') *be such that* $(C, E) \overset{STEP}{\longrightarrow} (C', E')$. *Then* C' *is a configuration, i.e.* $C' \in Conf(\gamma)$.

This result implies that the semantics treats situations of non-determinism (one automaton may have more than one enabled transition) correctly: every automaton contributes at most one transition to each step of the overall extended hierarchical automaton. That in case of non-determinism all enabled transitions of an automaton (which are in conflict with each other) can contribute to the step relation is immediately evident from the existential quantification in the *progress rule*.

Furthermore, proposition 10 implies that in case of a hierarchical conflict (the source of one transition is an ancestor of the source of another transition) only one transition contributes to the current step. It is not difficult to see from the definition of the semantics, that this is the transition whose source is higher in the state hierarchy; this is in accordance with the priority rule in statecharts.

Note, that not every application of the progress or stuttering rule might contribute to the step relation, but only those that are collected by the composition rule. These superfluous inferences can be avoided by the following traversing strategy through the state hierarchy: beginning in the root we move downwards in the composition function if the current active automaton doesn't have an enabled transition; the downward movement ends if the progress or the stutter rule applies. An application of the progress rule stops further inferences in sub-components.

4 The relationship between statecharts and extended hierarchical automata

Now we describe how a sub-dialect of statecharts can be translated to extended hierarchical automata. We deal with a sub-dialect of statecharts, where transition labels are restricted as follows:

- only boolean combinations of predicates *in(st)* are allowed in expression *Cond*; informally, predicate *in(st)* is true iff *st* belongs to the current configuration of the system;
- the only effect of actions is the generation of events.

Since the correspondence between the state hierarchy of statecharts and composition function of hierarchical automata is straightforward, we focus on motivating how transitions of extended hierarchical automata can be used to model interlevel transitions of statecharts.

4.1 Transitions in statecharts

Syntax of transitions. The syntax of transitions in statecharts as supported by STATEMATE goes far beyond labeled arrows from one state to another. But our interest is the intermediate language that Harel&Naamad use to give semantics to statecharts: in [HN96] transitions of statecharts are transformed into what is called "full compound transitions" (full CT's). The purpose of full CT's is to collect labeling information that is spread over transition segments and to compute in advance sub-configurations to be entered when the transition is taken.

We briefly recall the full CT's below; a formal definition can be found in [MLPS97]. A full CT begins in a set of states and ends in a set of states. The transition can be taken only if its source states belong to the current configuration and if it is taken all target states are entered simultaneously. Only subsets of configurations may form source and target sets of transitions. The target set of states forms a sub-configuration below the scope of the transition.

Transition scope. Harel&Naamad associate *scope* to every full CT: "The scope of a full CT *tr* is the lowest OR-state in the hierarchy of states that is a proper common ancestor of all the sources and targets of *tr*." When a transition is taken then the scope is the lowest state in the state hierarchy that is an ancestor of sources and targets of the transition, but is not affected by taking the transition:

the scope has two direct sub-states that are roots of the configuration that are exited and entered, resp..

Assume a transition tr, its scope sc and a status (C, E). Let $Uexit$ and $Uenter$ be direct sub-states of the scope such that $source(tr) \subseteq \chi^*(Uexit)$ and $target(tr) \subseteq \chi^*(Uexit)$. We call $Uexit$ and $Uenter$ the *uppermost states that are exited, resp. entered*, when tr is taken. Let $exit_{(C,E)}$ denote the states which are exited when the transition is taken: $exit_{(C,E)}(tr) = C \cap \chi^*(Uexit)$. Let C' be a configuration below $Uenter$, i.e. $C' \in Conf(\gamma \mid_{Uenter})$, such that $target(tr) \subseteq C'$. This is the configuration to be entered and we denote it with $enter_{(C,E)}(tr) = C'$.

Example 6. Consider the statechart in Figure 3 and its counterpart in full CT's language. The scope of the full CT leading from $SHOW$ to $VIDEOTXT$ (denoted by "$SHOW \rightarrow VIDEOTXT$") is the state $IMAGE$, the scope of the full CT $STANDBY \rightarrow \{SOUND.ON, IMAGE.SHOW\}$ is the state TV and the scope of $TV.ON \rightarrow DISCONNECTED$ is TV as well. We compute the enter and exit states of the transitions $t_1 = STANDBY \rightarrow \{SOUND.ON, IMAGE.SHOW\}$ and $t_2 = STANDBY \rightarrow DISCONNECTED$ w.r.t. status (C, E), where $C = \{TV, OFF, STANDBY\}$ and $E = \{on, out\}$:

$$exit_{(C,E)}(t_1) = \{OFF, STANDBY\}$$
$$enter_{(C,E)}(t_1) = \{TV.ON, IMAGE, SOUND, SHOW, SOUND.ON\}$$
$$exit_{(C,E)}(t_2) = \{STANDBY\}$$
$$enter_{(C,E)}(t_2) = \{DISCONNECTED\}$$

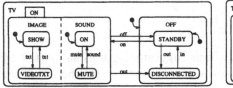 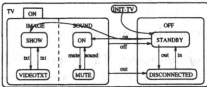

Fig. 3. Statechart with interlevel transition (left) and its counterpart in full CT's language (right).

Step relation. Like in hierarchical automata a maximal set of non-conflicting transitions must be taken simultaneously, which forms the step. Here, non-conflicting means that the set of transitions respects non-determinism and priorities. The maximality requirement ensures that an enabled non-conflicting transition is taken. Harel&Naamad use scope to compare transitions in order to decide on conflicts, i.e. either non-determinism or priority scheduling. Details can be found in [MLPS97].

Example 7. Let the statechart Figure 3 be in the same status as in the previous example: (C, E), where $C = \{TV, OFF, STANDBY\}$ and $E = \{on, out\}$. Then the full CT's departing from $STANDBY$ are in conflict because $STANDBY$ and OFF would be exited if any of them would be taken. For deciding whether it is a priority or non-determinism situation we have to compare their scopes: we have a priority conflict since their scopes are different and one scope is an ancestor of the other. Since the scope of $STANDBY \rightarrow \{SOUND.ON, IMAGE.SHOW\}$ is higher in the state hierarchy (TV is an ancestor of OFF) the priority is given to it.

4.2 Modeling statecharts' transitions in extended hierarchical automata

Given a statechart SC we translate it into an extended hierarchical automaton EHA. Assume that the state hierarchy is translated into the composition function γ. This translation induces a bijection ν which maps states of the statecharts to states of the sequential automata of EHA. The function ν also extends to sets of states.

Given a transition tr in a statechart. We associate with tr its scope denoted by $scope$. Let $Uexit$ and $Uenter$ be the uppermost states that are exited and entered, resp., when the transition is taken. We translate tr into a transition htr in an extended hierarchical automaton as follows:

- The source of htr is the state that corresponds to $Uexit$: $source(htr) = \nu(Uexit)$,
- The target state off htr is constructed in a similar way: $target(htr) = \nu(Uenter)$,
- The source restriction of htr is the original source set of tr: $sr(htr) = \nu(source(tr))$ (note, that $source(tr)$ may be a set of states); this is a valid entity as source restriction, because the original source set $source(tr)$ is a subset of the sub-configuration below $Uexit$ (property of full CT's language);
- The target determinator is constructed in a similar way: $td(tr) = \nu(target(htr))$; this is a valid entity as target determinator, because $target(tr)$ forms a sub-configuration below $Uenter$ (property of full CT's language);
- The triggering expression of htr becomes a conjunction of event and condition of tr.
- The action part of htr becomes the action part of tr.

Example 8. As seen in Figure 4 the composition function is deduced directly from the statechart in Figure 3. We omit the source restriction and target determinator labels where they are empty. The labels $l0$ to $l4$ are as follows.

- $l0$: $sr(l0) = \emptyset, td(l0) = \{STANDBY\}, expr(l0) = true$,
- $l1$: $sr(l1) = \emptyset, td(l1) = \{STANDBY\}, expr(l1) = off$,
- $l2$: $sr(l2) = \emptyset, td(l2) = \{DISCONNECTED\}, expr(l2) = out$,
- $l3$: $sr(l3) = \{STANDBY\}, td(l3) = \{SHOW, SOUND.ON\}, expr(l3) = on$.

4.3 Comparison with Argos

Rather than using explicit references to source/target configurations as in the advocated approach, Maraninchi [Mar91, Mar92] suggests an encoding of interlevel transitions by means of specific communication pattern between states in the state

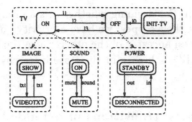

Fig. 4. Extended hierarchical automaton.

hierarchy. A transition $tr = (s, (sr, ex, ac, td), s')$ in an EHA can be modeled in Argos as follows: first, all states mentioned in the source restriction sr inform state s (by issuing designated events which are unique to the modeling of this transition) that the system currently resides in a configuration where transition tr is considered enabled. These designated events (one for each state mentioned in sr) are sensed as input trigger in the corresponding Argos transition departing from s. Upon entering state s' a further unique event is broadcasted which is used to enter the target configuration described by td.

As mentioned in the introduction this encoding requires a non-preemptive interrupt mechanism (otherwise the states in sr could not inform state s about the current sub-configuration) as well as perfect synchronicity of input/output events. Perfect synchronicity is needed since otherwise the chain reaction "informing s about the current configuration", "performing the transition" and "enforcing the correct target configuration" would not be performed atomically which means that the encoding would not be faithful. Due to the fact that different interrupt mechanisms are employed in statecharts and Argos as well as different assumptions are made about synchronicity of events the translation of statecharts into Argos as intermediate format is rather cumbersome.

However, it is worth noting that the underlying idea how to simulate interlevel transitions are quite similar in Argos and EHA. While we explicitly recall the relevant state information in the respective transition guards, Argos encodes this information by introducing unique communication events for the simulation of each interlevel transition (so the explicit state reference is shifted into the unique identification of sub-configurations by means of sets of communication events).

5 Conclusion, applications and future work

We introduced extended hierarchical automata (EHA) as intermediate format for the implementation of add-on tools for statecharts as supported by STATEMATE. The EHA allow for a simple syntax yet advanced enough to deal with interlevel transitions; we described a translation from statecharts to EHA. A fairly simple operational semantics to EHA was given; through the translation the operational semantics describes the semantics of statecharts as well. The operational semantics of EHA was shown to have the same properties as the Harel&Naamad semantics of statecharts (a maximal non-conflicting set of transitions fires in one step). In the full paper we will show that the semantics of a statechart coincides with the semantics of the corresponding extended hierarchical automata.

Translation of statecharts into extended hierarchical automata removes a number of obstacles when translating statecharts to other languages, e.g., to input languages of model-checkers:

- multiple sources and multiple targets of a transition are eliminated,
- interlevel transitions are eliminated,
- there is no need to associate scopes to transitions,
- priorities are made explicit,

By this we obtain a simple procedure for computing maximal non-conflicting sets of enabled transitions in statecharts.

A useful application of the advocated intermediate format is that it directly implies a compilation schema of statecharts to input languages of transition system based model-checkers. Now its is possible to define a translation such that the size of the code is linear in the size of the statecharts, hence the compiler faithfully passes the structure of the statechart to the model-checker (provided the target system has primitives like sequential and parallel composition, and conditional choice).

This paper does not cover our work [MHLS97] on how extended hierarchical automata are translated to the input language of the SPIN verification system ([Hol91, Hol97]) which allows for simulation and linear temporal logic model-checking. We implemented a partial order reduction technique in our compiler which lead to sequential code and made the partial order reduction technique in SPIN obsolete for our code. Our experiments supported our hypothesis that the sequential code performs better in time and space than the parallel code combined with partial order reduction as implemented in SPIN [HP94]. As a case study we verified safety properties expressed in linear temporal logic of a statecharts model of the production cell [LL95]. Further experiments will show where limits and possible trade-offs are.

Further applications of the format are in, e.g. simulators of statecharts, code generators, and test sequence generators.

We will also use our approach to translate statecharts to symbolic model-checking tools and investigate how BDD-based techniques perform on model-checking statecharts (cf. [HK94]).

Acknowledgment. We thank Amir Pnueli, Carsta Petersohn and Willem-Paul de Roever for helpful comments and suggestions relating to this work. We also thank the referees for pointing us to related work on this topic and other suggestions. The work of E. Mikk is partially supported by *Technologiestiftung Schleswig-Holstein* within the CATI project.

References

[Har87]   D. Harel. Statecharts: A Visual Formalism for Complex Systems. *Science of Computer Programming*, 8:231–274, 1987.

[HdR91]   C. Huizing and W.-P. de Roever. Introduction to design choices in the semantics of Statecharts. *Information Processing Letters*, 37:205–213, February 1991.

[HK94]   J. Helbig and P. Kelb. An OBDD–Representation of Statecharts. In *Proc. of the European Design and Test Conference EDAC'94*, pages 142–149, 1994.

[HN96]   D. Harel and A. Naamad. The STATEMATE semantics of statecharts. *ACM Transactions on Software Engineering and Methodology*, 5(4):293–333, Oct 1996.

[Hol91]   G.J. Holzmann. *Design and Validation of Computer Protocols*. Prentice-Hall, Englewood Cliffs, New Jersey, 1991.

[Hol97]   G.J. Holzmann. The Model Checker Spin. *IEEE Trans. on Software Engineering*, 23(5):279–295, May 1997. Special issue on Formal Methods in Software Practice.

[HP94]   G.J. Holzmann and D. Peled. An improvement in formal verification. In *Proc. FORTE94*, Berne, Switzerland, October 1994.

[Hui91]   C. Huizing. *Semantics of reactive systems: comparision and full abstraction*. PhD thesis, Technical University Eindhoven, 1991.

[JM94]   F. Jahanian and A. Mok. Modechart: a specification language for real-time systems. *IEEE Transactions of Software Engineering*, 20(12):933–947, December 1994.

[LHHR94] N.G. Leveson, M.P.E. Heimdahl, H. Hildreth, and J.D. Reese. Requirements Specification for Process-Control Systems. *IEEE Trans. Soft Eng*, 20(9):684–707, September 1994.

[LL95]   C. Lewerentz and T. Lindner. *Formal Development of Reactive Systems: Case Study Production Cell*. Number 891 in LNCS. Springer Verlag, 1995.

[Mar91]   F. Maraninchi. The Argos language: Graphical Representation of Automata and Description of Reactive Systems. In *IEEE Workshop on Visual Languages*, Oct 1991.

[Mar92]   F. Maraninchi. Operational and Compositional Semantics of Synchronous Automaton Compositions. In *CONCUR'92*, number 630 in Lecture Notes in Computer Science, pages 550–564. Springer-Verlag, 1992.

[MHLS97] E. Mikk, G. J. Holzmann, Y. Lakhnech, and M. Siegel. Implementing Statecharts in Promela/SPIN. Technical report, Manuscript, 1997.

[MLPS97] E. Mikk, Y. Lakhnech, C. Petersohn, and M. Siegel. On formal semantics of Statecharts as supported by STATEMATE. In *2nd BCS-FACS Northern Formal Methods Workshop*. Springer-Verlag, July 97.

[NVG91]   S. Narayan, F. Vahid, and D. D. Gajski. System Specification and Synthesis with the SpecCharts Language. In *Proceedings, 1991 IEEE International Conference on Computer-Aided Design (ICCAD '91)*, pages 266–269, November 11-14 1991.

Proof Discovery in LK System by Analogy

Masateru Harao*

Department of Artificial Intelligence
Kyushu Institute of Technology, Iizuka 820, Japan
e-mail harao@dumbo.ai.kyutech.ac.jp Phone&Fax Int+81-948-29-7612

Abstract. In this paper, a schema guided model of proof discovery by analogy in theorem proving under the concept such that *similar problems have similar proofs* is proposed. A proof discovery system for LK inference system is formulated by considering it as a general reasoning system which is close to our thinking process. At first, a schema and a proof schema which describe the types of formulas and proofs are formulated as higher order terms. Next, the similarities of formulas and proofs are defined by means of the realizability by schemata and proof schema. Finally, a unification based procedure of discovering an LK proof for any given sequent is presented, and the implemented system is overviewed.

1 Introduction

By *proof discovery* , we mean here a certain reasoning mechanism to find out a goal in the huge and complex problem space as human beings do. It is pointed out that the mechanisms such that abduction, induction and analogy act important roles in the thinking process of human beings such as scientific discovery [16, 25, 26] and lots of researches concerning such reasoning systems have been reported until now [9, 10, 19]. General theorem provers which have been constructed based on resolution are simple and easy to implement [8, 21], but their proof processes are very remote from our thinking process [22]. On the other hand, LK inference system provides us a general reasoning mechanism which is able to realize wide scientific problems in the close way to our thinking process.

When we have obtained certain results or proofs once, we generalize and store them in some manner so as to be reused [15, 16]. If a new problem is given, then we check the similarity with the problems which have already been solved. If some similarity is recognized, then we can produce its solution invoking the similarity. Lots of researches from this viewpoint have been reported [2, 3, 4, 11, 18, 28]. The generalized knowledge is sometimes called the *schema* and the reasoning using schema is called the *schema guided problem solving* [6, 18]. The purpose of this paper is to establish a proof discovery system for LK inference system by

* This work was supported in part by the Japanese Ministry of Education,Grant-in-aid for scientific research(A)07308027,scientific research(C)07680405 and Inamori Foundation in 1996

introducing analogy as heuristics in the schema guided framework which works such that *similar problems have similar proofs* .

In Section 2, we give a general model of proof discovery system by focusing on LK inference system. In section 3, the similarity of formulas is defined based on the syntactical feature of the formulas and is formulated by means of the concept schema which is defined as the higher order formulas. The problems concerning schema construction procedure, schema base and so on are discussed. In Section 4, the proof schema of proofs is defined and by introducing the term representation of proofs, their expressions as terms is presented. The similarity of proofs and the production of proofs are discussed using proof shema. In Section 5, the implemented proof discovery system is overviewed.

2 Formalization of a Proof Discovery System

2.1 A schema guided model of proof discovery

The proof discovery system proposed here is sketched in Fig. 1, where Δ is a set of problems and Γ is the background knowledge which is assumed to hold in the object problems. In the case of inference systems, Γ consists of axioms and inference rules.

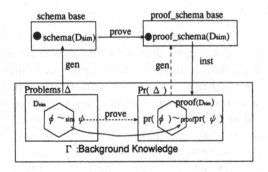

Fig. 1. Schema guided model of proof discovery system

We introduce a similarity relation on Δ under a certain measure of similarity *sim* such that $\sim_{sim} \subseteq \Delta \times \Delta$, where $\varphi \sim_{sim} \psi$ denotes that formulas $\varphi, \psi \in \Delta$ are similar with respect to *sim*. A set of formulas which are similar under the similarity relation $\sim_{sim}$ which contains φ by $D_{sim}^{(\varphi)}$ or simply D_{sim} if no confusion arises.

A proof of a formula of the LK inference system is given as a derivation from *premises* to the formula. We call a derivation from *axioms* a *complete proof* and a derivation from *hypotheses* a *partial proof*. For a formula φ, we denote a complete proof of φ and the set of all complete proofs of a formula φ by $pr(\varphi)$ and $Pr(\varphi)$, respectively. For a given set of formulas D, the set of all complete proofs of D is denoted by $Pr(D) = \cup_{\varphi \in D} Pr(\varphi)$. By *proof*, we denote a certain derivation structure which is standard in some sense for a set D_{sim}. A derivation of $\psi \in D_{sim}$ which is constructed according to a proof structure *proof* is denoted by $proof(\psi)$, and may be a partial proof. For a set of formulas D, we let $proof(D) = \{proof(\psi) \in Pr(D) \mid \psi \in D\}$. A similarity relation $\approx_{proof}$ on $Pr(\Delta)$ induced from *proof* means that if $pr(\varphi) \approx_{proof} pr(\psi)$,then $pr(\varphi)$ and $pr(\psi)$ are constructed using a common proof structure *proof*. When we emphasize that $pr(\varphi)$ is obtained by completing a partial proof $proof(\varphi)$, we denoted it by $pr_{proof}(\varphi)$.

A *schema* for a set of formulas D_{sim} denoted by $schema(D_{sim})$ is defined as a higher order formula which realizes each element of D_{sim} as its instance. A *schema base* is a collection of schemata. We extend this concept of schema to the proofs. A schema of proofs $pr(D_{sim})$ denoted by $schema(pr(D_{sim}))$ is a higher order expression which realizes each element of $pr(D_{sim})$ as its instance. Especially, the schema of $proof(D_{sim})$ is denoted by $schema(proof(D_{sim}))$.

Let Φ be $schema(D_{sim})$. A proof of Φ which is constructed according to a proof structure *proof* is denoted by $proof(\Phi)$. If $proof(\Phi) = schema(proof(D_{sim}))$ holds, then it is also a schema of $proof(D_{sim})$, and is denoted by $proof\_\Phi$. A proof schema $proof\_\Phi$ is designed so that a proof of $\psi \in D_{sim}$ such that $pr_{proof}(\psi)$ can be generated by completing the partial proof $proof(\psi)$ which is obtained by instantiating the $proof\_\Phi$. We denote the procedures schema construction, proof and instantiation in Fig. 1 by *gen*, *prove* and *inst*, respectively.

2.2 Representation of formulas

We use here the typed λ terms of $\lambda_\rightarrow$[2] as the description language since it is adequate to describe both formulas and their proofs in the same framework [12], and is suitable to formulate the proposed schema guided model. We assume that the definitions and notations of λ calculus due to the usual one [1]. Every term is assigned a type, and a term t of type α is denoted as $t : \alpha$. A term having the Boolean type o is called a *formula*. Here, the logical constants $\wedge, \vee, \supset$ and $\sim$ are defined as the terms of types $o \rightarrow o \rightarrow o$ and $o \rightarrow o$, respectively. Especially, $\forall$ and $\exists$ are expressed using the constants Π and Σ of type $(\iota \rightarrow o) \rightarrow o$ exhibiting *product* and *sum* ,respectively [24].

Let p be a predicate of type $\iota \rightarrow o$. For $p(x) : o$, its abstraction is expressed as $\lambda x.p(x) : \iota \rightarrow o$. Especially, the λ abstraction of $\forall x.p(x)$ and $\exists x.p(x)$ are interpreted as $\Pi\lambda x : \iota.p(x) = \forall(\lambda x.p(x))$ and $\Sigma\lambda x : \iota.p(x) = \exists(\lambda x.p(x))$[3]. A predicate variable P of type $\iota \rightarrow \cdots \rightarrow o$ is called a *schema variable* and a formula containing some schema variables a *schema*.

Definition 1. Let Φ and ψ be any terms. Then we say that Φ *realizes* ψ if there exists some sequence of terms $\psi_1, \cdots, \psi_k (k \geq 1)$ such that $\Phi\psi_1 \cdots \psi_k = \psi$, and

---

[2] The *simple theory of type* defined based on the functional type constructor $\rightarrow$.

[3] We denote them also as $\lambda x.(\forall x.p(x))$ and $\lambda x.(\exists x.p(x))$ if no confusion arises.

we denote it by $\Phi :\succ \psi$. We say that a schema Φ realizes a set of formulas D if $\Phi :\succ \varphi$ for all $\varphi \in D$.

It is easy to see that the relation $:\succ$ is a partial order relation on Δ. We assume hereafter that this partial order relation $:\succ$ is defined in the formula set Δ. It is noted that this relation $:\succ$ also holds among schemata.

2.3 LK inference system as reasoning system

A sequent is a expression such that $\Gamma \Rightarrow \Theta$, where Γ and Θ are set of formulas. If $\Gamma = \{L_1, \cdots, L_m\}$ and $\Theta = \{R_1, \cdots, R_n\}$, then a sequent $\Gamma \Rightarrow \Theta$ is semantically interpreted as the formula $L_1 \wedge \cdots \wedge L_m \supset R_1 \vee \cdots \vee R_n$. The LK inference system consists of the inference rules on sequents given in Fig. 2 and is known to be complete and sound for the first order logic [7], and its proving process is very close to our thinking process. The inference rules of the LK system are given as in Fig. 2. A LK proof is a transformation of a given sequent

$$\frac{A,B,\Gamma\Rightarrow\Theta}{A\wedge B,\Gamma\Rightarrow\Theta}(and\_L) \qquad \frac{\Gamma\Rightarrow A,\Theta \quad \Gamma\Rightarrow B,\Theta}{\Gamma\Rightarrow A\wedge B,\Theta}(and\_R) \qquad \frac{A,\Gamma\Rightarrow\Theta \quad B,\Gamma\Rightarrow\Theta}{A\vee B,\Gamma\Rightarrow\Theta}(or\_L)$$

$$\frac{\Gamma\Rightarrow\Theta,A,B}{\Gamma\Rightarrow\Theta,A\vee B}(or\_R) \qquad \frac{\Gamma\Rightarrow\Theta,A \quad B,\gamma\Rightarrow\Theta}{\Gamma,A\supset B\Rightarrow\Theta}(imp\_L) \qquad \frac{\Gamma,A\Rightarrow B,\Theta}{\Gamma\Rightarrow A\supset B,\Theta}(imp\_R)$$

$$\frac{A[x:=t],\Gamma\Rightarrow\Theta}{\forall x.A,\Gamma\Rightarrow\Theta}(all\_L) \qquad \frac{\Gamma\Rightarrow\Theta,A[x:=y]}{\Gamma\Rightarrow\Theta,\forall x.A}(all\_R)^* \qquad \frac{A[x:=y],\Gamma\Rightarrow\Theta}{\exists x.A,\Gamma\Rightarrow\Theta}(some\_L)^*$$

$$\frac{\Gamma\Rightarrow\Theta,A[x:=t]}{\Gamma\Rightarrow\Theta,\exists x.A}(some\_R) \qquad \frac{\Gamma\Rightarrow\Theta}{A,\Gamma\Rightarrow\Theta}(thin\_L) \qquad \frac{\Gamma\Rightarrow\Theta}{\Gamma\Rightarrow\Theta,A}(thin\_R)$$

$$\frac{\Gamma\Rightarrow\Theta,A}{\sim A,\Gamma\Rightarrow\Theta}(not\_L) \qquad \frac{\Gamma,A\Rightarrow\Theta}{\Gamma\Rightarrow\sim A,\Theta}(not\_R) \qquad \frac{A,\Pi\Rightarrow\Delta \quad \Gamma\Rightarrow\Theta,A}{\Gamma,\Pi\Rightarrow\Theta,\Delta}(cut)$$

Fig. 2. Inference rules of LK system (∗: eigenvariable condition)

to the axioms in the form $A \Rightarrow A$[4] by applying the inference rules to the sequent nondeterministically and can be represented by the proof figure. An example of LK proof of the following sequent φ is shown in Fig. 3.In the case of partial proofs, some of the premise sequents are not axiom sequents, i.e., *hypotheses*.
$$\varphi := \lceil \Rightarrow (p(a) \vee q(b)) \wedge \forall x.(p(x) \supset q(x)) \supset \exists x.q(x) \rfloor$$

3 Similarity under Schemata

3.1 Similarity of formulas

The key problem in analogical reasoning is to formalize the similarity relation $\sim_{sim}$ in some formal way so that if $\varphi \sim_{sim} \psi$ then $pr(\varphi) \approx_{proof} pr(\psi)$ holds

---

[4] In general, an axiom is a sequent of $\Gamma \Rightarrow \Theta$ such that $A \in \Gamma$ and $A \in \Theta$.

$$\frac{\displaystyle \frac{\displaystyle \frac{q(a) \Rightarrow q(a)}{q(a) \Rightarrow \exists x.q(x)} \, (some\_R)}{\displaystyle \frac{p(a) \Rightarrow p(a) \quad q(a) \Rightarrow \exists x.q(x)}{p(a), p(a) \supset q(a) \Rightarrow \exists x.q(x)} \, (imp\_L)}{p(a), \forall x.(p(x) \supset q(x)) \Rightarrow \exists x.q(x)} \, (all\_L)}{}$$

$$\frac{\displaystyle \frac{q(b) \Rightarrow q(b)}{q(b) \Rightarrow \exists x.q(x)} \, (some\_R)}{q(b), \forall x.(p(x) \supset q(x)) \Rightarrow \exists x.q(x)} \, (thin\_L)$$

$$\frac{p(a) \vee q(b), \forall x.(p(x) \supset q(x)) \Rightarrow \exists x.q(x)}{} \, (or\_L)$$

$$\frac{(p(a) \vee q(b)) \wedge \forall x.(p(x) \supset q(x)) \Rightarrow \exists x.q(x)}{\Rightarrow (p(a) \vee q(b)) \wedge \forall x.(p(x) \supset q(x)) \supset \exists x.q(x)} \, \begin{array}{l} (and\_L) \\ (imp\_R) \end{array}$$

Fig. 3. LK proof figure of φ

for some proof structure *proof*. A tree representation of a *formula/proof* is a tree whose nodes are labeled with the *logical connectives/inference rules* or *atomic formulas/sequents* in case of leaves. We define the similarity among *formulas/proofs* by the similarity of their tree structures. As we can observe from Fig. 3, we can construct a proof of a formula by applying the inference rules according to its tree structure. Then the tree structure of the obtained proof may be similar to the one of the formula. The main difference between them is the appearance of structure rules of the LK system[5]. If we use such proving strategy, we can obtain similar proofs from similar formulas. This is the intuitive idea of formalizing the mechanism such that *similar formulas have similar proofs*.

In order to formalize the similarity among the formulas, we use the schemata defined as higher order formulas. A schema for a set of formulas D is constructed by fixing the common tree parts and by abstracting the disagreement parts as schema variables. Let us observe this using the formulas φ, η and ξ defined as follows[6].

$$\varphi = \supset (\wedge(\vee(p(a), q(b)), \forall x.[\supset (p(x), q(x))], \exists x.q(x))$$
$$\eta = \supset (\wedge(\vee(\supset (p(a), r(a)), \wedge(s(b), t(b))),$$
$$\forall x.[\supset (\supset (p(x), r(x)), \wedge(s(x), t(x))), \exists x.[\wedge(s(x), t(x))]])$$
$$\xi = \supset (\wedge(\vee(\wedge(p(a), r(a)), \wedge(q(b), r(b)), \forall x.[\supset (r(x), q(x))], \exists x.q(x))]$$

The tree representations of φ, η, ξ are shown in Fig. 4. By abstracting the disagreement subformulas[7] to schema variables. The following Φ_1, Φ_2 and Φ_3 are the examples of schemata.

$$\Phi_1 = ((P(a) \vee Q(b)) \wedge \forall x.(P(x) \supset Q(x))) \supset \exists x.Q(x)),$$
$$\Phi_2 = ((\Omega(a) \vee \Psi(b)) \wedge \forall x.(P(x) \supset Q(x))) \supset \exists x.Q(x)),$$
$$\Phi_3 = ((P_1 \vee P_2) \wedge \forall x.(P_3 \supset P_4)) \supset \exists x.P_5),$$

where Ω, Ψ, P and Q are schema variables of type $\iota \to o$ and P_1, P_2, P_3, P_4 and P_5 are ones of type o, respectively. Here Φ_2 and Φ_3 realize $\{\varphi, \eta, \xi\}$

---

[5] Structure rules appear in proofs, but don't appear in formulas.

[6] We express formulas in the prefix forms, since the relation between formulas and their proofs become clearer.

[7] The parts which are surrounded by rectangles in the tree representations of formulas.

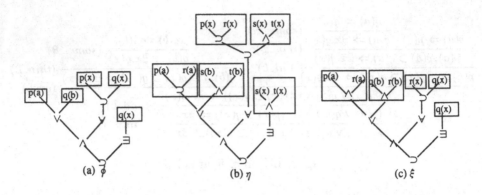

Fig. 4. Tree representation of formulas and their similarity

and Φ_1 realizes $\{\varphi\}$. We denote the set of formulas realized by a schema Φ as $D_\Phi = \{\varphi \in \Delta \mid \Phi :\succ \varphi\}$. Based on this idea, we define the similarity relation of formulas $\sim_\Phi$ as follows.

Definition 2. Let Φ be any schema. Then, formulas φ and ψ are similar under the schema Φ, denoted by $\varphi \sim_\Phi \psi$, if $\Phi :\succ \varphi$ and $\Phi :\succ \psi$ or $\varphi = \psi$.

Proposition 3. If Φ is a schema, then $\sim_\Phi$ is an equivalence relation. $\qquad\square$

Proposition 4. Let Φ_1 and Φ_2 be schemata such that $\Phi_2 :\succ \Phi_1$. Then it holds for the similarity relations $\sim_{\Phi_1}$ and $\sim_{\Phi_2}$ that $\sim_{\Phi_1} \subseteq \sim_{\Phi_2}$. $\qquad\square$

For instance, it holds among the schemata Φ_1, Φ_2 and Φ_3 the relations such that $\Phi_3 :\succ \Phi_2 :\succ \Phi_1$, and $\sim_{\Phi_1} \subseteq \sim_{\Phi_2} \subseteq \sim_{\Phi_3}$. This ordering $:\succ$ is useful in constructing the schema base in the hierarchical structure.

3.2 Schema construction

We assume that a standard formula, called a *guiding formula*, whose complete proof has already been obtained is given for each D_{sim}. For a given guiding formula $\varphi \in D_{sim}$, we decide a *context* of D_{sim}, denoted by $cxt[D]$, as the common subformula corresponding to the trunk of the syntax tree representations of these formulas. For $D = \{\varphi, \eta, \xi\}$, $cxt[\varphi, \psi, \xi]$ is given as follows:

$$cxt[\varphi, \eta, \xi] = \supset (\wedge(\vee(P_1, P_2), \forall x.(\supset (P_3, P_4)), \exists x.P_5)),$$

where P_1, P_2, P_3, P_4, P_5 are schema variables of type o corresponding to subformulas at disagreement part. In the previous example, Φ_3 corresponds to the schema $cxt[D]$ for $\{\varphi, \eta, \xi\}$. Any formulas which have the context $cxt[\varphi, \psi, \xi]$ can be realized by applying moderate formulas to P_i's. By specifying the subformulas corresponding to P_i's of $cxt[D]$ precisely, we can construct the more refined schemata. A schema is called a *complete schema* if its complete proof exists. According to the ordering $:\succ$, we introduce the following 3 schema classes.

1. *Type1 schema*: A complete schema which is a refinement of $cxt[D]$.
2. *Type2 schema*: A schema with hypotheses which is a refinement of $cxt[D]$.
3. *Type3 Schema*: A schema which corresponds to $cxt[D]$.

The problem of constructing a type 2 schema belongs to the *anti-unification* or *generalization* of typed λ terms [5, 13]. The main difference with other generalization is the use of guiding formula. In order to formalize the syntactical similarity of formulas, the generalization procedure proposed here is designed based on the imitation rule of the higher order unification [17, 27]. We sketch it briefly using an example.

Example 1. [**Schema construction by generalization**]
1. Let $D = \{\varphi, \eta, \xi\}$ and let φ be its guiding formula.
2. Obtain $cxt[D]$ from the guiding formula φ of D.
$$cxt[D] = (\supset (\wedge(\vee(P_1, P_2), \forall x.(\supset (P_3, P_4))), \exists x.P_5)).$$
3. Examine whether each formula of D can be adjusted to the form having the $cxt[D]$ as their common prenex (*context adjustment*).
$$\varphi = \supset (\wedge(\vee(\underline{p(a)}, \underline{q(b)}), \forall x.[\supset (\underline{p(x)}, \underline{q(x)})], \exists x.\underline{q(x)}))$$
$$\eta = \supset (\wedge(\vee(\supset (\underline{p(a)}, r(a)), \wedge(s(b), t(b))),$$
$$\forall x[\supset (\supset (\underline{p(x)}, r(x)), \wedge(s(x), t(x)))])\exists x.[\wedge(s(x), t(x))])$$
$$\xi = \supset (\wedge(\vee(\wedge(\underline{p(a)}, r(a)), \wedge(\underline{q(b)}, r(b))), \forall x.[\supset (\underline{r(x)}, \underline{q(x)})], \exists x.\underline{q(x)})))$$
4. If all of the formulas of D are not adjustable to $cxt[D]$, then this generalization for D fails, else the components corresponding to P_i's are checked if some of them are the same or not[8] (*Generation of disagreement components*). The disagreement parts of $\{\varphi, \eta, \xi\}$ are given as follows.
$$\begin{cases} p(a) \rightleftharpoons (\supset (p(a), r(a))) \rightleftharpoons (\wedge(p(a), r(a))), & q(b) \rightleftharpoons (s(b), t(b)) \rightleftharpoons (q(b), r(b)), \\ p(x) \rightleftharpoons (p(x), r(x)) \rightleftharpoons r(x), & q(x) \rightleftharpoons (s(x), t(x)) \rightleftharpoons q(x) \end{cases}$$
5. If they disagree, then we introduce different schema variables. For the disagreement set $\{p(a) \rightleftharpoons (\supset (p(a), r(a))) \rightleftharpoons (\wedge(p(a), r(a)))\}$, we have the following *form adjustment* :
$$\{(\lambda x.p(x))(a) \rightleftharpoons (\lambda x.(\supset (p(x), r(x)))(a) \rightleftharpoons (\lambda x.(\wedge(p(x), r(x)))(a)\}.$$
From this correspondence, a generalization of them is given as $\Omega(a)$, where $\Omega : \iota \to o$. It is noted that the obtained generalization is not the form of a simple predicate variable such that $\Omega : o$, but the formula $\Omega(a)$ having "a" as its argument.
6. Finally, we get $gen(\varphi, \eta, \xi)$ as the following:
$$\lambda.\Phi_2 = \lambda\Omega\lambda\Psi\lambda P\lambda Q.[\supset (\wedge(\vee(\Omega(a), \Psi(b)), \forall x.(\supset (P(x), Q(x)))), \exists x.Q(x))],$$
where $P : \iota \to o$, $Q : \iota \to o$, $\Psi : \iota \to o$, $\Omega : \iota \to o$, and ι. □

Proposition 5. Let Φ be a schema for D obtained by the generalization procedure gen, then it holds that $\varphi_1 \sim_\Phi \varphi_2$ for any $\varphi_1, \varphi_2 \in D$.

---

[8] This procedure is essentially the same to the first order case.

3.3 Schema base and similarity check

For a substitution $\theta = \{P := \psi\}$, we denote $\Phi\theta = (\lambda P.\Phi)\psi$ also by $(\lambda.\Phi)\theta$ if no confusion arises. Since $\varphi \sim_\Phi \psi$ if $\Phi\theta_1 = \varphi$ and $\Phi\theta_2 = \psi$ for some substitutions θ_1 and θ_2, the similarity check of formulas is reduced to the matching problem of schemata and formulas. We observe this by an example, and the details should be referred to other articles[17, 27].

Example 2. [**Matching**] Let Φ and ψ be a schema and a formula to be matched.

$$\Phi = ((P(a) \vee Q(b)) \wedge \forall x.(P(x) \supset Q(x)) \supset \exists x.Q(x)).$$
$$\psi = ((h(a) \supset g(a)) \vee (h(b) \wedge g(b)))) \wedge \forall x.(h(x) \supset g(x))$$
$$\supset (\lambda x.(h(x) \wedge g(x))) \supset \exists x.(h(x) \wedge g(x))).$$

By the higher order matching algorithm, we have the matchings θ such that
$$\theta = \{P := \lambda x.(h(x) \supset g(x)), Q := \lambda x.(h(x) \wedge g(x))\}. \qquad \Box$$

As for the validity of the realized formulas, we have the following properties according to the *predicate substitution theorem* [14].

Proposition 6. Let Φ be a complete schema. Then a formula ψ such that $\Phi :\succ \psi$ is a valid formula. $\qquad \Box$

Corollary 7. Let $\Phi(P_1, \cdots, P_n)$ be a type 1 schema with schema variables $P_1, \cdots, P_n$. Then the following formula $[\lambda P_1 \cdots \lambda P_n.\Phi(P_1, \cdots, P_n)](\psi_1) \cdots (\psi_n)$ is valid for any formulas $\psi_1, \cdots, \psi_n$ of the same types to $P_1, \cdots, P_n$. $\qquad \Box$

It is noted that a type 2 schema (and therefore type 3 schema) is not always a complete schema and the provability of its instances depends on the proof structure.

4 Proof and Proof Schema

4.1 Term representation of proofs

We have observed that both formulas and their proofs can be represented by tree structure. Such tree representations can be expressed as terms by considering the labels assigned to nodes as functions. Here, we consider a proof to be a mapping from premise sequents $(\Gamma_1 \Rightarrow \Delta_1), \cdots, (\Gamma_n \Rightarrow \Delta_n)$ to a conclusion sequent $\Gamma \Rightarrow \Delta$. Here, we consider the set of all proofs of $(\Gamma \Rightarrow \Delta)$ such that $pr(\Gamma \Rightarrow \Delta)$ as the *proof type* of $(\Gamma \Rightarrow \Delta)$. Then each inference rule can be interpreted as a mapping having a proof type from premise types to conclusion types. Hence, the proof from premise sequent $(\Gamma_1 \Rightarrow \Delta_1), \cdots, (\Gamma_n \Rightarrow \Delta_n)$ to a conclusion sequent $\Gamma \Rightarrow \Delta$ can be represented as a term having the proof type as follows.

$$Pr(\Gamma_1 \Rightarrow \Delta_1) \to \cdots \to Pr(\Gamma_n \Rightarrow \Delta_n) \to Pr(\Gamma \Rightarrow \Delta).$$

Examples of proof types of some LK inference rules are given in next, where Π means the general product and the notations such as $\Pi A : o.P$ can be interpreted as $\forall A : o.P$ [12].

$$sequent : *, \qquad o : * \qquad pr : sequent \to *.$$
$$axiom \; : \Pi A : o.Pr(A \Rightarrow A).$$
$$or\_L \quad : \Pi A : o\Pi B : o.Pr(A, \Gamma \Rightarrow \Theta) \to Pr(B, \Gamma \Rightarrow \Theta) \to Pr(A \vee B, \Gamma \Rightarrow \Theta).$$
$$and\_L \; : \Pi A : o\Pi B : o.Pr(A, B, \Gamma \Rightarrow \Theta) \to Pr(A \wedge B, \Gamma \Rightarrow \Theta).$$
$$imp\_L \; : \Pi A : o\Pi B : o.Pr(\Gamma \Rightarrow \Theta, A) \to Pr(B, \Gamma \Rightarrow \Theta) \to Pr(\Gamma, A \supset B, \Rightarrow \Theta).$$
$$all\_L \quad : \Pi A : o.Pr(A[x := t], \Gamma \Rightarrow \Theta) \to Pr(\forall x.A, \Gamma \Rightarrow \Theta).$$
$$some\_L : \Pi A : o.Pr(A[x := y], \Gamma \Rightarrow \Theta) \to Pr(\exists x.A, \Gamma \Rightarrow \Theta).$$
$$thin\_L \; : \Pi A : o.Pr(\Gamma \Rightarrow \Theta) \to Pr(A, \Gamma \Rightarrow \Theta).$$

The term expression of $proof(\varphi)$ and its proof type given in Fig. 3 is expressed by combining these inference rules as follows.

$$Pr(\Rightarrow \varphi) : \; \Pi p : o\Pi q : o\Pi a : \iota\Pi b : \iota.Pr[p(a) \Rightarrow p(a)] \to Pr[q(a) \Rightarrow q(a)]$$
$$\to Pr[q(b) \Rightarrow q(b)] \to Pr[(p(a) \vee q(b)) \wedge \forall x.(p(x) \supset q(x)) \supset \exists x.q(x)]$$
$$pr(\varphi) = [(imp\_R)((and\_L)((or\_L)((all\_L)((imp\_L)(axiom(p(a)))$$
$$((some\_R)(axiom(q(a)))))((thin\_L)((some\_R)(axiom(q(b)))))))]$$

The parts of $axiom(p(a)), axiom(q(a))$ and $axiom(q(b))$ of $pr(\varphi)$ represent the proofs of sequents of $p(a) \Rightarrow p(a), q(a) \Rightarrow q(a)$ and $q(b) \Rightarrow q(b)$, respectively. When some sequent $p \Rightarrow q$ is not axiom, we consider it as hypothesis and denote its proof by $ph(p \Rightarrow q)$. A proof term whose inputs are axioms is called a *complete proof term*, and otherwise it is called *incomplete proof term* or *proof term with hypotheses*.

4.2 Proof schemata and similarity of proofs

The procedure *prove* is to construct a proof of schemata under a proof structure *proof* of its guiding formula. We call the proof of a schema Φ of D under a proof structure *proof* a *proof schema* of Φ, and a schema having complete proof a *complete proof schema*. The proof figure and term representation of schema Φ_2 are given in Fig. 5, respectively. The procedure *gen* can be also considered as the procedure to form a proof of schema from proofs $proof(D)$ and the proof schema constructed from $proof(D)$ using *gen* is denoted by $gen(proof(D))$. Since the derivation structure of $proof(\Phi)$ and $gen(proof(D))$ are both same to $proof$, we have the following property.

Lemma 8. Let Φ be a schema of D under the guiding formula φ, and *gen* be the schema construction procedure. Then it holds the following relation.

$$proof(\Phi) = proof(gen(D)) = gen(proof(D)) = schema(proof(D)).\square$$

The proof of a schema Φ, i.e., $proof(\Phi)$ which satisfies Lemma 8 is denoted by $proof\_\Phi$. According to this property, we can get a proof of ψ which is similar with φ by instantiating $proof\_\Phi$.

$$\cfrac{\cfrac{\Omega(a) \Rightarrow P(a) \quad \cfrac{Q(a) \Rightarrow Q(a)}{Q(a) \Rightarrow \exists x.Q(x)} \; (some\_R)}{\cfrac{\Omega(a), P(a) \supset Q(a) \Rightarrow \exists x.Q(x)}{\Omega(a), \forall x.(P(x) \supset Q(x)) \Rightarrow \exists x.Q(x)} \; (all\_L)} \; (imp\_L) \qquad \cfrac{\cfrac{\Psi(b) \Rightarrow Q(b)}{\Psi(b) \Rightarrow \exists x.Q(x)} \; (some\_R)}{\Psi(b), \forall x.(P(x) \supset Q(x)) \Rightarrow \exists x.Q(x)} \; (thin\_L)}{\cfrac{\cfrac{\Omega(a) \lor \Psi(b), \forall x.(P(x) \supset Q(x)) \Rightarrow \exists x.Q(x)}{(\Omega(a) \lor \Psi(b)) \land \forall x.(P(x) \supset Q(x)) \Rightarrow \exists x.q(x)} \; (and\_L)}{\Rightarrow (\Omega(a) \lor \Psi(b)) \land \forall x.(P(x) \supset Q(x)) \supset \exists x.Q(x)} \; (imp\_R)} \; (or\_L)}$$

$$proof\_\Phi_2 = \lambda P \lambda Q \lambda \Omega \lambda \Psi.(imp\_R)((and\_L)((or\_L)((all\_L)((imp\_L)(ph(\Omega(a) \Rightarrow P(a)))$$
$$((some\_R)(axiom(Q(a))))))))((thin\_L)((some\_R)(ph(\Psi(b) \Rightarrow Q(b)))))))$$

Fig. 5. LK proof figure of Φ_2

We extend the relation $:\!\succ$ on *formulas/schemata* into *proofs/proof_schemata* such that $proof\_\Phi :\!\succ proof(\psi)$ if $(proof\_\Phi)\theta_1 \cdots \theta_n :\!\succ proof(\psi)$ for some substitutions $\theta_1, \cdots, \theta_n$. From the definition of the *prove* procedure, we have the following property.

Theorem 9. Let Φ and ψ be any schema and a formula such that $\Phi :\!\succ \psi$ and let *proof* be a proof structure used in *prove*. Then it holds the relation such that $proof\_\Phi :\!\succ proof(\psi)$.

Proof. Since $\Phi :\!\succ \psi$, there exists a matching θ such that $(\lambda.\Phi)\theta = \psi$. We form a proof of ψ by applying θ into $proof\_\Phi$. From Lemma 8, $(\lambda.proof\_\Phi)\theta$ gives $proof(\psi)$. $\qquad\square$

Corollary 10. Let Φ be a complete schema and let $proof\_\Phi$ be a complete proof schema of Φ. Then for any ψ such that $\Phi :\!\succ \psi$, there exists a complete proof $proof(\psi)$.

We define a similarity relation $\approx_{proof}$ of proofs as follows.

Definition 11. Let $proof\_\Phi$ be a proof schema of a schema Φ, and let $pr^*(\varphi)$ be any (partial) proof of φ. Then the similarity relation $\approx_{proof\_\Phi}$ between (partial) proofs is defined as follows.

$pr^*(\varphi) \approx_{proof\_\Phi} pr^*(\psi)$ if $proof\_\Phi :\!\succ pr^*(\varphi)$ and $proof\_\Phi :\!\succ pr^*(\psi)$. $\qquad\square$

Theorem 12. Let Φ be a schema for a set of formulas D and let $proof\_\Phi$ be a proof schema of Φ. Then there exist (partial)proofs for any $\varphi, \psi \in D$ such that $pr^*(\varphi) \approx_{proof\_\Phi} pr^*(\psi)$.

Proof. Since Φ is a schema of D, it holds that $\varphi \sim_\Phi \psi$. Let θ_1 and θ_2 be matchings such that $(\lambda.\Phi)\theta_1 = \varphi$ and $(\lambda.\Phi)\theta_2 = \psi$. The applications of θ_1 and θ_2 to $proof\_\Phi$ produce the (partial) proofs of φ and ψ from definition of *schema_Φ* such that $proof(\varphi) = (\lambda.proof\_\Phi)\theta_1$ and $proof(\psi) = (\lambda.proof\_\Phi)\theta_2$. By taking $pr^*(\varphi) = proof(\varphi)$ and $pr^*(\psi) = proof(\psi)$, we have (partial) proofs $pr^*(\varphi)$ and $pr^*(\psi)$ which are similar under $proof\_\Phi$. This means that $pr^*(\varphi) \approx_{proof} pr^*(\psi)$. $\qquad\square$

For given a type 2 schema Φ, we can get a partial proof of a formula $\psi \in D$ such that $\Phi\theta = \psi$ as $(proof\_\Phi)\theta = proof(\psi)$. If all of the hypotheses of $proof(\psi)$ are valid, then ψ is valid and a complete proof $pr_{proof}(\psi)$ can be obtained. The converse statement does not hold in general, that is, some complete proofs using a proof structure other than $proof$ may exist.

4.3 Proof derivation by instantiation

We discuus in this section to construct a complete proof according to the results of previous section. Let us consider the case of type 2 schemata. Let $ph(seq_1),...,ph(seq_k)$ be the hypotheses of $proof\_\Phi$ having schema variables $P_1,\cdots,P_n$. We replace each proof hypothesis $ph(seq_i)$ with variable X_i and denote the partial proof which contain $X_1,...,X_k$ by $\lambda X_1...\lambda X_k.proof\_\Phi$. The partial proof obtained from $proof\_\Phi$ by the instantiation of θ is given as $[\lambda.(\lambda X \cdots \lambda Y.proof\_\Phi)]\theta^9$, and the partial proofs of the hypotheses become $(\lambda.seq_1)\theta,\cdots,(\lambda.seq_k)\theta^{10}$. If no confusion arises, we denote $(\lambda.seq_k)\theta$ simply as $(\lambda.X_i)\theta$, and so on.

Thus the proving of the original formula is reduced to the proving of the hypotheses of $(\lambda.\Phi)\theta$. Let the *size* of a sequent be the total number of logical symbols[11]. Then the sizes of premises are smaller than the one of original formula. Therefore we can say that the proving of hypotheses becomes much simpler than the one of the original formula.

When some complete proof of $(\lambda.X_i)\theta$ for each i,i=1,...,k can be obtained as $pr((\lambda.X_i)\theta)$, then a complete proof can be obtained as follows.

$$([\lambda.(\lambda X \cdots \lambda Y.proof\_\Phi)]\theta)(pr((\lambda.X)\theta)) \cdots (pr((\lambda.Y)\theta)).$$

We denote the proof of ψ constructed using the schema $proof\_\Phi$ as $proof(\psi)$ $(= pr^*(\psi))$ and its complete proof obtained by proving its hypotheses as $pr_{proof}(\psi)$.

Theorem 13. Let Φ be a type 2 schema and let $X_1,\cdots,X_k$ be the hypotheses of $proof\_\Phi$. If there exist some complete proofs of $X_1,...,X_k$ such that $(pr((\lambda.X_1)\theta)),\cdots,(pr((\lambda.X_k)\theta))$ for θ, then a complete proof of $\psi = \Phi\theta$ is given as follows.

$$pr_{proof}(\psi) = ([\lambda.(\lambda X_1 \cdots \lambda X_k.proof\_\Phi)]\theta)(pr((\lambda.X_1)\theta)) \cdots (pr((\lambda.X_k)\theta)). \qquad \Box$$

The proof discovery by analogy which we propose in this paper is designed based on the property stated in Theorem 13, and we sketch it briefly in the next example.

Example 3. Let us consider the proof derivation from type 2 schema Φ_2. The hypotheses of $proof\_\Phi_2$ correspond to the underlined parts shown in Fig. 5. By

---

[9] This is the abbreviation for $[\lambda P_1 \cdots P_n.(\lambda X \cdots \lambda Y.proof\_\Phi)]\theta$, where $P_1 \cdots P_n$ are the schema variables in Φ.

[10] $\lambda.seq_i$ is the abbreviation for $\lambda P_1 \cdots P_n.seq_i$, where $P_1 \cdots P_n$ are the schema variables which appear in seq_i.

[11] If the same symbol occurs repeatedly, each occurrence is counted.

replacing $ph(\Omega(a) \Rightarrow P(a))$ by X, $ph(\Psi(b) \Rightarrow Q(b))$ by Y, the term representation of the partial proof $proof\_\Phi_2$ is given as follows.

$$\lambda.[\lambda X \lambda Y.proof\_\Phi_2] = \lambda P \lambda Q \lambda \Omega \lambda \Psi.[\lambda X \lambda Y.(imp\_R)((and\_L)((or\_L)((all\_L)((imp\_L)$$
$$(X)((some\_R)(axiom(Q(a))))))((thin\_L)((some\_R)(Y)))))].$$

Let θ and σ be the matchings of Φ_2 with η and ξ such that

$$\theta = \left\{ \begin{array}{l} \Omega := \lambda y.(\wedge(s(y), t(y))), \ \Psi := \lambda y.(\wedge(s(y), t(y))), \\ P := \lambda y.(\wedge(s(y), t(y))), \ Q := \lambda y.(\wedge(s(y), t(y))) \end{array} \right\},$$

$$\sigma = \left\{ \begin{array}{l} \Omega := \lambda y.(\wedge(s(y), t(y))), \ \Psi := \lambda y.(\wedge(q(y), r(y))), \\ P := \lambda y.(\supset (p(y), q(y))), \ Q := \lambda y.q(y) \end{array} \right\}.$$

Then the (partial) proofs of η and ξ under the schema $proof\_\Phi_2$ are given as follows.

$$pr^*(\eta) = (\lambda \Omega \lambda \Psi \lambda P \lambda Q.[\lambda X \lambda Y.proof\_\Phi_2])\theta$$
$$= (imp\_R)((and\_L)((or\_L)((all\_L)((imp\_L)(X)$$
$$((some\_R)(axiom(\wedge(s(a), t(a)))))))((thin\_L)((some\_R)(Y)))))$$
$$pr^*(\xi) = (\lambda \Omega \lambda \Psi \lambda P \lambda Q.[\lambda X \lambda Y.proof\_\Phi_2])\sigma$$
$$= (imp\_R)((and\_L)((or\_L)((all\_L)((imp\_L)(X)((some\_R)(axiom(q(a))))))$$
$$((thin\_L)((some\_R)(Y))))))).$$

It holds that $pr^*(\eta) \approx_{proof} pr^*(\xi)$. Since the hypotheses of $pr^*(\xi)$ are $ph((\lambda.X)\theta)$ $= axiom(\supset (p(a), r(a)))$ and $pr((\lambda.Y)\theta) = axiom(\wedge(s(b), t(b)))$, $pr^*(\eta)$ is a complete proof. On the other hand, the hypotheses of $pr^*(\xi)$ are $ph((\lambda.X)\sigma) =$ $ph((\wedge(p(a), r(a)) \Rightarrow p(a))$ and $ph((\lambda.Y)\sigma) = ph((\wedge(q(b), r(b)) \Rightarrow q(b))))$, $pr^*(\xi)$ is a partial proof. By proving these hypotheses, we have their complete proofs such that

$$pr((\lambda.X)\sigma) = (and\_L)((thin\_L)(axiom(p(a)))),$$
$$pr((\lambda.Y)\sigma) = (and\_L)((thin\_L)(axiom(q(b)))).$$

Therefore, a complete proof of ξ is obtained as follows.

$$pr_{proof}(\xi) = ((\lambda \Omega \lambda \Psi \lambda P \lambda Q.[\lambda X \lambda Y.proof\_\Phi_2])]\sigma)(pr((\lambda.X)\sigma))(pr((\lambda.Y)\sigma))$$
$$= [\lambda X \lambda Y.(proof\_\Phi_2)]((thin\_L)(axiom(p(a))))$$
$$(and\_L)((thin\_L)(axiom(q(b))))$$
$$= (imp\_R)((and\_L)((or\_L)((all\_L)((imp\_L)((and\_L)((thin\_L)$$
$$(axiom(p(a)))))((some\_R)(axiom((q(a)))))))))((thin\_L)$$
$$((some\_R)((and\_L)(thin\_L)(axiom(q(b))))))).$$

This proof generation corresponds to the proof discovery of formula ξ by analogy with φ. $\qquad\square$

5 Overview of an LK Proof Discovery System

An LK proof discovery system PDSYS has been implemented under the proposed formalization using the theorem prover Isabelle [23]. The PDSYS is composed of the sub-systems,*Inference System* DINA_thy,*Proof Control System*Tactic,*Schema Base System*PS_BASE,*Guiding Problem Base*Guide and *Visual Interface*Visual.

DINA_thy is a inference system of PDSYS constructed by extending the LK.thy of Isabelle [23] by adding schema_tacs. Tactic consists of the search procedure of schema base for input formulas,and the proof production procedure according to schema_tacs. It has also the functions to construct a schema from guiding formulas and to manage the *schema base/guiding formula base*. PS_BASE is a *schema base* for PDSYS. In present, 43 schemata which are considered as standard are stored. Guide is a *guiding formula base* which consists of formulas whose proofs have already been obtained. This Guide system constructs a schema according to the generalization procedure. In present, 10 guiding formulas are stored. Visual is the user interface to display formulas and proof figures obtained by the PDSYS.

PDSYS works as follows. After invoking the system,input a formula ξ as goal;

- ngoal DIANA_thy "|- ξ";

By ngoal command, PDSYS checks the syntax of input formula ξ, and makes the initial setting for display. After this, it displays the goal sequent. Next we check the schema base.

- by (schema_tac);

By schema_tac, PDSYS searches a schema having the goal ξ as its instance. **If** there exists such a schema, **then** it returns an available schema name as *rule name* and shows the hypotheses to be proved further, **else** it asks to search guiding formulas.

- by (const_tac);

By (const_tac), PDSYS checks its hypotheses are provable or not. **If** hypotheses are all provable, **then** it returns a comment check clear, **else** it asks to search guiding formula.

- by (proof_tac);

By (proof_tac), PDSYS completes the total proof of ξ and displays the proof figure of obtained $pr_{proof}(\xi)$ in the form shown in Fig. 6. The proof figure at each proof step can also be displayed.

- search guiding problem(y/n);

If no available schema exists or hypothesis check failed, then PDSYS checks if there exists some similar guiding formula with ξ. **If** some similar guiding formula exists, **then** it construct a new schema and store it into schema base, **else** ξ is not provable by PDSYS.

6 Discussions

In this paper, we have proposed a schema guided model for proof discovery by focusing on LK inference system, and have formulated this model in the framework of higher order formulas. A unification based proof discovery procedure has been presented, and PDSYS which is implemented according to the proposed

$$\dfrac{[pr((\lambda.X)\sigma)]}{\dfrac{\dfrac{(p(a)\wedge r(a))\Rightarrow p(a)}{\dfrac{(p(a)\wedge r(a)),p(a)\supset q(a)\Rightarrow \exists x.q(x)}{(p(a)\wedge r(a)),\forall x.(p(x)\supset q(x))\Rightarrow \exists x.q(x)}\,(all\_L)}\quad \dfrac{q(a)\Rightarrow q(a)}{q(a)\Rightarrow \exists x.q(x)}\,(some\_R)}{}}$$

$$\dfrac{[pr((\lambda.Y)\sigma)]}{\dfrac{\dfrac{(q(b)\wedge r(b))\Rightarrow q(b)}{\dfrac{(q(b)\wedge r(b))\Rightarrow \exists x.q(x)}{(q(b)\wedge r(b)),\forall x.(p(x)\supset q(x))\Rightarrow \exists x.q(x)}\,(thin\_L)}\,(some\_R)}{}}$$

Combined proof figure:

$$\dfrac{(p(a)\wedge r(a)),\forall x.(p(x)\supset q(x))\Rightarrow \exists x.q(x)\qquad (q(b)\wedge r(b)),\forall x.(p(x)\supset q(x))\Rightarrow \exists x.q(x)}{\dfrac{(p(a)\wedge r(a))\vee (q(b)\wedge r(b)),\forall x.(p(x)\supset q(x))\Rightarrow \exists x.q(x)}{\dfrac{((p(a)\wedge r(a))\vee (q(b)\wedge r(b)))\wedge \forall x.(p(x)\supset q(x))\Rightarrow \exists x.q(x)}{\Rightarrow ((p(a)\wedge r(a))\vee (q(b)\wedge r(b)))\wedge \forall x.(p(x)\supset q(x))\supset \exists x.q(x)}\,(imp\_R)}\,(and\_L)}\,(or\_L)$$

$$\dfrac{\dfrac{p(a)\Rightarrow p(a)}{\dfrac{p(a),r(a)\Rightarrow p(a)}{p(a)\wedge r(a)\Rightarrow p(a)}\,and\_L}\,thin\_L}{\text{(a)}[pr((\lambda..X)\sigma)]}\qquad \dfrac{\dfrac{q(b)\Rightarrow q(b)}{\dfrac{q(b),r(b)\Rightarrow q(b)}{q(b)\wedge r(b)\Rightarrow q(b)}\,and\_L}\,thin_L}{\text{(b)}[pr((\lambda.Y)\sigma)]}$$

Fig. 6. Proof figure of ξ

framework using Isabelle is overviewed. Through this investigation, it has been assured that the proposed system works as desired for simple examples. As the application of this proof discovery system, we can consider the problems such as program derivation, mathematical proof discovery, CAI, and so on. In order to develop this model further, it is necessary to discuss the following problems.

The most important procedure in the schema guided system is the parts of matching and generalization. The higher order unification/generalization provides us very powerful mechanism, but it becomes very complex. By considering such tradeoff, we should design some effective procedure according to the property of the target problem.

The schema base should be built so as to cover the problem space. On the other hand,the increase of schemata makes the search process very complex. The introduction of hierarchical structure into schema base may be a useful method for solving it.

In present, the logical equivalences of formulas are not taken into account in our system. Further,a proof obtained by the proposed method is not always optimum. How to improve such defects is an important problem to be solved.

Acknowledgement

I would like to thank Dr.Koichi Hirata for his helpful discussion and Keizo Yamada for the improvement of our PDSYS. I am also grateful to the anonymous refrees for their useful comments.

References

1. H. Barendregt: *Introduction to Generalized Type Systems*, Proc. of 3rd International Conference on Theoretical Computer Science, 1–37 (1989).
2. B. Brock, S. Cooper and W. Pierce: *Analogical Reasoning and Proof Discovery*, LNCS **310** 454–468 (1988).

3. M. R. Donat and L. A. Wallen: *Learning and Applying Generalized Solutions using Higher Order Resolution*, LNCS **310**, 41–60 (1988).
4. G. Evans: *A Program for the Solution of Geometric Analogy Intelligence Test Questions*, in Minsky (ed.): *Semantic Information Processing*, MIT Press, 271–353 (1968).
5. C. Feng and S. Muggleton: *A Note on Least General Generalization in Higher Order Logic*, Proc. of 1st Workshop on Inductive Logic Programming (1992).
6. P. Flener: *Logic Program Synthesis from Incomplete Information*, Kluwer Academic Press (1995).
7. J. H. Gallier: *Logic for Computer Science*, John Wiely & Sons (1987).
8. N. J. Genesereth and N. J. Nilson: *Logical Foundation of Artificial Intelligence*, Morgan Kaufman Pub. (1987).
9. R. Greiner: *Learning by Understanding Analogy*, Proc. of 1st Intern. Workshop on Analogical Reasoning (1987).
10. M. Haraguchi and S. Arikawa: *A Formulation of Analogical Reasoning and Its Realization*, J. of JSAI **1**, 132–139 (1986) (in Japanese).
11. M. Harao: *LK Theorem Proving by Analogy*, Proc. of PRICAI'92, 714–720 (1992).
12. R. Harper, F. Honsell and G.Plotokin: *A Framework for Defining Logics*, Proc. of Symposium on Logic in Computer Science, 194–204 (1987).
13. R. W. Hasker: *The Replay of Program Derivations*, PhD Thesis of the University of Illinois (1995).
14. S. Hayasi: *Mathematical logic*, Corona Publisher (1989) (in Japanese).
15. D. H. Helman (ed.): *Analogical Reasoning*, Kluwer Academic Publishers (1988).
16. J. H. Holland, K. J. Holyoak, R. E. Nisbett and P. R. Thagard: *Process of Inference, Learning, and Discovery*, The MIT Press (1986).
17. G. P. Huet: *A Unification Algorithm for Typed λ-Calculus*, Theoretical Computer Science **1**, 27–57 (1975).
18. G. Huet and B. Lang: *Proving and Applying Program Transformations Expressed with Second Order Patterns*, Acta Informatica **11**, 31–55 (1978).
19. K. Inoue: *Principles of Abduction*, J. of JSAI **7**, 48–59 (1991) (in Japanese).
20. S. Kedar-Cabelli: *Analogy from a Unified Perspective*, in [15].
21. J. W. Lloyd: *Foundations of Logic Programming*, Springer Verlag (1984).
22. D. Miller and A. Felty: *An Integration of Resolution and Natural Deduction Theorem Proving*, Proc. of the AAAI'86, 198–202 (1986).
23. L. C. Paulson: *Isabelle*, LNCS **828** (1988).
24. F. Pfenning: *Types in Logic Programming*, The MIT Press (1992).
25. G. Polya: *Induction and Analogy in Mathematics*, Princeton University Press (1953).
26. K. R. Popper: *The logic of Scientific Discovery*, Basic Book Inc. (1959).
27. W. Snyder and J. Gallier: *Higher Order Unification Revised*, J. of Symbolic Computation **8**, 101–140 (1989).
28. T. B. de la Tour and R. Caferra: *Proof Analogy in Interactive Theorem Proving*, Proc. IJCAI'87, 95–99 (1989).

Efficient Induction of Executable Logic Programs from Examples

Nobuhiro Inuzuka, Hirohisa Seki and Hidenori Itoh

Department of Intelligence and Computer Science,
Nagoya Institute of Technology
Gokiso-cho, Showa-ku, Nagoya 466, Japan
e-mail: {inuzuka,seki,itoh}@ics.nitech.ac.jp

Abstract. Some inductive logic programming (ILP) systems use determinate literals to efficiently induce logic programs. A determinate literal is a literal that does not distinguish positive examples from negative examples, but produces information in variables introduced by the literal. The concept of determinate literals, however, is not reflected by the concept of input/output mode of predicate attributes properly, and so a system using determinate literals may induce inconsistent logic programs with predicate mode or inexecutable programs. The paper extends the concept of determinate literals and proposes input and output determinate literals. These literals function as pre-processor and post-processor against other literals. The paper also describes an implementation of the method and experimentations.

1 Introduction

Inductive logic programming (ILP) is recently attracted by Machine Learning researchers. It aims to induce logic programs that derive given positive examples and no negative ones. It has advantage in expressive power of predicate logic and essential utility of background knowledge. Applying ILP systems to assist programming, or semi-automatic programming from examples, is a recent topic in ILP.

Efficiency of induction is critical. We are concerned for both efficiency of time cost and sample cost or of necessary examples to induce. Some bottom-up ILP systems, such as LOPSTER[8], CRUSTACEAN[1, 2], TIM[6] and MRI[4, 5], induce programs efficiently from a small number of examples. These ILP systems, however, induce only a very restricted class of programs. In general top-down ILP systems, such as FOIL[12, 13] and Progol[10], induce a larger class of programs. FOIL uses determinate literals for efficient induction. FOIL-I[7], a successor of FOIL, which is refined to induce from small sample sets, uses determinate literal more essentially.

To apply ILP for automatic programming, one of the most important things is executability of programs. Executability is not logical property, but essential for practical use of ILP. Programs induced have to be executable on a standard

Prolog system. Some concepts investigated in ILP researches are not considered from this point. In this paper, we redefine the concept of determinate literals considering executability, and propose an ILP algorithm for executable logic programs without loss of efficiency.

2 Preliminary definitions and a generic top-down ILP algorithm

Input to ILP algorithm consists of *background knowledge* and *examples*. Background knowledge is a set of Horn clauses, or clauses with at most one positive literal and zero or more negative ones. Examples are ground atoms with a predicate called a target predicate. We assume that every target predicate p has an *intended interpretation* M_p^I. A *positive (negative) example* of p is an example that is(is not) in M_p^I. A sample set of p is a pair of sets (E^+, E^-), where E^+ (E^-) is a set of some positive(negative) examples of p. The target predicate is not appeared in background knowledge. An ILP system is expected to output a logic program H which satisfies that

$$B \cup H \models e^+ \text{ for every } e^+ \in E^+, \text{ and } B \cup H \not\models e^- \text{ for every } e^- \in E^-.$$

B and H are assumed not to include any function symbols.

Figure 1 shows a generic top-down ILP algorithm[3], which is a greedy method based on coverage of examples by clauses.

```
1   Initialization
2       theory := a null program
3       remaining := a set of positive examples of R

4   While remaining is not empty
5       clause := 'R(A, B, ···) ←'
6       While clause covers a negative example of R
7           Find a literal L
8           Add L to the body of clause
9       EndWhile
10      Add clause to theory
11      Remove positive examples covered by clause from remaining
12  EndWhile
```

Fig. 1. A generic top-down ILP algorithm

We will prepare definitions for discussions. Some of definitions are borrowed from [9]. A *definite clause* is a clause with exactly one positive literal and zero or more negative literals. A *head* of a definite clause is only the positive literal of it. A *goal* is a clause consisting of only negative literals. Let us consider an atom a with a target predicate and a definite clause $c = h \leftarrow b_1, \cdots b_n$ with a head which has the target predicate. If $a = h\theta$ for the most general substitution θ, $c(a)$ denotes $\leftarrow b_1\theta, \cdots, b_n\theta$, where a is an example. We call $c(a)$ a *goal form* of a by c. When c is a clause $h \leftarrow b_1, \cdots, b_n$ and l is a literal, (c, l) denotes a clause $h \leftarrow b_1, \cdots, b_n, l$.

Let us consider a ground substitution $\theta = \{v_1/t_1, \cdots, v_n/t_n\}$, and a goal clause g. If $g\theta$ is ground and $\{v_1, \cdots v_n\}$ includes only variables appeared in g, we call θ an *answer substitution* of g. If θ is an answer substitution and $B \cup \{g\theta\} \vdash \square$, then we call $g\theta$ a *correct answer* of g wrt B, and θ a *correct answer substitution* of the answer, where B is a background knowledge.

Each predicate has a mode. The concept of mode is not a logical concept. It distinguishes arguments into input and output when we regard a predicate as a calculation device.

There is a mode function m_p for a predicate p to be called a *mode function of predicate*. m_p is a function from $\{1, \cdots, n\}$ to $\{-, +\}$, where n is the arity of p. If $m_p(i)$ is $+$ it means that i-th argument has to be assigned a constant. In the case that $m_p(i) = -$, i-th argument may be ground or variable and should be ground after the predicate is called. For example a predicate $\text{pred}(A, B)$, which calculates $B = A - 1$ from A, should have a mode function that $m_{\text{pred}}(1) = +$ and $m_{\text{pred}}(2) = -$. We denote this mode function by $\text{pred}(+, -)$. We assume that a predicate may have more than one mode function and the mode functions are given for each predicates.

Here we sort out the concept of executability. Let us consider an atom $a = p(t_1, \cdots, t_n)$, where p has a mode function m_p. If every term t_i such that $m_p(i) = +$ is ground we say that the atom a is *consistent with the mode*. We assume that for every consistent atom a with the mode, a standard Prolog system can find a correct answer of $\leftarrow a$ with respect to background knowledge. This is reasonable if mode functions are given appropriately.

Let us consider a clause $c = h \leftarrow b_1, \cdots, b_n$ whose head has a predicate p with a mode function m_p. We denote a clause $h \leftarrow b_1, \cdots, b_i$ $(i \leq n)$ by $c^{(i)}$. A preliminary concept, executable up to i-th literal, is defined as follows.

1. c is executable up to 0th literal wrt any atom.
2. c is executable up to i-th literal wrt an atom a if
   (a) c is executable up to $(i-1)$-th literal wrt a, and
   (b) $b_i\theta$ is consistent with the mode for every correct answer $c^{(i-1)}(a)\theta$ of $c^{(i-1)}(a)$.

We say that $c = h \leftarrow b_1, \cdots, b_n$ is executable if c is executable up to n-th literal wrt every consistent atom with the mode, the atom which has the same predicate with h.

3   Efficient induction using determinate literals

Determinate literals are originally used in a bottom-up ILP system GOLEM[11] and used in many ILP systems, such as FOIL[12, 13]. We use determinate literals in the sense of FOIL, but give the detail for the discussions.

Let B be a background knowledge, c a definite clause with a target predicate p in its head, and (E^+, E^-) be a sample set. We call a literal l a *determinate literal* of c wrt (E^+, E^-) and B if

1. l has at least one variable not appeared in c,
2. for every example $e^+ \in E^+$ and for every correct answer $c(e^+)\theta$ of a goal form $c(e^+)$ of e^+ by c, there is exactly one correct answer of $(c,l)(e^+)\theta$ wrt B, and
3. for every example $e^- \in E^-$ and for every correct answer $c(e^-)\theta$ of a goal form $c(e^-)$ of e^- by c, there is at most one correct answer of $(c,l)(e^-)\theta$ wrt B.

For example, if we consider a clause

$$c = \mathsf{append}(A, B, C) \leftarrow \mathsf{component}(A, D, E)$$

and examples

$$E^+ = \{\ e_1^+ = \mathsf{append}([a, b], [c], [a, b, c]), e_2^+ = \mathsf{append}([a], [b, c], [a, b, c]),$$
$$e_3^+ = \mathsf{append}([\,], [a, b], [a, b])\ \},\ \text{and}$$
$$E^- = \{\ e_1^- = \mathsf{append}([a, c], [b], [a, b, c]), e_2^- = \mathsf{append}([a], [\,], [\,])\ \},$$

then goal forms of the examples by c,

$$c(e_1^+) = \leftarrow \mathsf{component}([a, b], D, E),\quad c(e_2^+) = \leftarrow \mathsf{component}([a], D, E),$$
$$c(e_1^-) = \leftarrow \mathsf{component}([a, c], D, E),\quad c(e_2^-) = \leftarrow \mathsf{component}([a], D, E)$$

have correct answers with substitutions $\theta_1^+ = \{D/a, E/[b]\}$, $\theta_2^+ = \{D/a, E/[\,]\}$, $\theta_1^- = \{D/a, E/[c]\}$, and $\theta_2^- = \{D/a, E/[\,]\}$, respectively, and $c(e_3^+)$ does not, where background knowledge is shown in Table 1.   If we add a literal $l = \mathsf{component}(C, F, G)$, which introduces two new variables F and G, to c then

$$(c,l)(e_1^+)\theta_1^+ = \leftarrow \mathsf{component}([a, b], a, [b]), \mathsf{component}([a, b, c], F, G)$$

has exactly one correct answer

$$\leftarrow \mathsf{component}([a, b], a, [b]), \mathsf{component}([a, b, c], a, [b, c]),$$

and each of $(c,l)(e_2^+)\theta_2^+$ and $(c,l)(e_1^-)\theta_1^-$ also has one, and $(c,l)(e_2^-)\theta_2^-$ does not. Hence l is a determinate literal of c wrt (E^+, E^-) and B.

FOIL uses determinate literals to complete its evaluation method. It evaluates literals to be added to a clause using an information-based function *Gain*. A

Table 1. background knowledge used in the paper

component$(+, -, -)$	— component$([A|B], A, B)$
composite$(+, +, -)$	— composite$(A, B, [A|B])$
eq$(+, +)$	— eq(A, A)
succ$(+, -)$	— succ$(A, B) \leftarrow B$ is $A + 1$
pred$(+, -)$	— pred$(A, B) \leftarrow B$ is $A - 1$
null$(-)$	— null$([\,])$
zero$(-)$	— zero(0)

literal is given a good evaluation if a clause with the literal is true for a large part of positive examples and for a small part of negative ones. A determinate literal is, however, useful even if it does not exclude negative examples because it produces information as values of new variables introduced by the determinate literal. Because of this reason, FOIL primarily takes determinate literals.

A successor of FOIL, FOIL-I[7] separates a search procedure of clauses into two stages, appending determinate literals and appending other literals. We can give the following proposition for an explanation of this procedure.

Proposition 1 *For a definite clause c, a literal l, a determinate literal d wrt a set of positive example E^+, and a positive example $e^+ \in E^+$, if $(c,l)(e^+)$ has a correct answer $(c,l)(e^+)\theta$ then $((c,d),l)(e^+)$ has a correct answer $((c,d),l)(e^+)\theta'$, where d and l do not have common variables not appeared in c and $\theta' = \theta\rho$.*

This means that if an example is not excluded by l it is not excluded by d and l. Hence determinate literals can be exchanged with others only in a direction, from the tail side to the head side. We call this property *left commutativity of determinate literals*. To add a determinate literal before a literal does not change any coverage by them. Generating and adding all of determinate literals to a clause at first is efficient to search clauses.

4 Problems in Determinate literals

Determinate literals are defined by a logical property of predicates, but some predicates have non-logical property. Arithmetic predicates are defined with the restriction that some arguments should be ground.

Let us consider a target relation plus(A, B, C) with a mode plus$(+, +, -)$, which is true when $A + B = C$. Imagine an induction of it using a predicate pred$(+, -)$, zero$(-)$ and eq$(+, +)$. After a clause,

$$\text{plus}(A, B, C) \leftarrow \text{zero}(A), \text{eq}(B, C),$$

is found, the following two literals, $\mathsf{pred}(A,D)$ and $\mathsf{pred}(C,E)$, are found to be determinate literals of an initial clause '$\mathsf{plus}(A,B,C) \leftarrow$', and they makes the following clause.

$$\mathsf{plus}(A,B,C) \leftarrow \mathsf{pred}(A,D), \mathsf{pred}(C,E)$$

From this clause the following clause,

$$\mathsf{plus}(A,B,C) \leftarrow \mathsf{pred}(A,D), \mathsf{pred}(C,E), \mathsf{plus}(D,B,E) \qquad (1)$$

can be induced, but this clause is not executable. Indeed it is not executable up to the 2nd literal wrt a consistent atom $\mathsf{plus}(2,3,C)$ with the mode.

FOIL can take mode declarations for predicates. FOIL version 6, however, induces the clauses above with the background knowledge **zero**, **eq** and **pred** and appropriate mode declarations. FOIL uses mode declaration to prune search space, but does not pay attention for executability.

In order to avoid this problem we can apply a mode restriction. In addition to the definition of mode functions of predicates we will give mode functions for clauses.

A definite clause has a mode function, a *mode function of clause*. A mode function m_c of a definite clause c is a mapping from a set of all variables appeared in c to $\{+, -\}$. If $m_c(x_i)$ is $+$ it means that the variable x_i will be bound when every variable in an input argument of the head predicate of c is bound and the clause c is called. In the case that $m_c(x_i) = -$ variable x_i may not be bound.

A mode function of a definite clause c is defined as follows.

1. If c consists of only a head literal $p(x_1, \cdots, x_n)$ and m_p is a mode function of a predicate p, a mode function of c is defined as follows.

$$m_c(x_i) = m_p(i)$$

2. If c has a mode function m_c, a predicate p has a mode function m_p, and they satisfy the following condition, a literal $l = p(x_1, \cdots, x_m)$ can be appended to the body of clause c, where m is the arity of p.

$$m_c(x_i) = + \text{ if } m_p(i) = +, \text{ for } i = 1, \cdots, m \qquad (2)$$

Then the new clause $c' = (c,l)$ has a mode function $m_{c'}$ defined by

$$m_{c'}(x) = \begin{cases} + & ; x \in \{x_1, \cdots, x_m\} \\ m_c(x) & ; \text{otherwise} \end{cases}$$

Condition (2) is called a mode restriction.

Let us turn back the example of plus. From the definition above a clause $c = \mathsf{plus}(A,B,C) \leftarrow$ takes a mode function of clause defined by $m_c(A) = +, m_c(B) = +$, and $m_c(C) = -$, which is denoted by $c(+A, +B, -C)$. The determinate literal $l_1 = \mathsf{pred}(A,D)$ can be appended to c, and the resulted clause $c' = (c,l_1)$ has a mode function $c'(+A, +B, -C, +D)$. $l_2 = \mathsf{pred}(C,E)$, however, can not be appended because $m_{\text{pred}}(1) = +$ but $m_{c'}(C) = -$ where the variable C is in the position 1 in l_2.

This does not immediately means that an ILP system using this mode restriction fails to induce the definition of plus, but it makes difficult to induce it. Progol[10] has a mode language to restrict clauses to be induced. The mode language does not allow to induce clauses including inconsistent literals with the mode. Hence, Progol does not induce Clause (1), but does not also induce the intended clause from ground examples (It induces the intended clause from a set of examples that includes non-ground examples)

5 Extended determinate literals

To treat determinate literals properly we need to introduce new concepts *input determinate literals* and *output determinate literals*. These concepts are joint-concepts of determinate literal and mode restriction.

A literal $l = p(x_1, \cdots, x_n)$ is an *input determinate literal* of a definite clause c wrt examples (E^+, E^-) and a background knowledge B if

1. l is a determinate literal of c wrt (E^+, E^-) and B, and
2. $m_c(x_i) = +$ if $m_p(i) = +$, for $i = 1, \cdots, n$.

A literal $l = p(x_1, \cdots, x_n)$ is an *output determinate literal* of a definite clause c wrt examples (E^+, E^-) and a background knowledge B if

1. l is a determinate literal of c wrt (E^+, E^-) and B, and
2. $m_c(x_i) = -$ if $m_p(i) = -$ for $i = 1, \cdots, n$.

The conditions of input/output determinate literals are also regarded as mode restrictions to append to clauses. It means that a literal can be appended if it is an input/output determinate literal. A mode function of a clause appended by input/output literal should be redefined.

Let us consider a definite clause c which has a mode function m_c, and a literal $l = p(x_1, \cdots, x_n)$. If l is an input determinate literal of c or an output determinate literal of c, the literal can be appended to c, and the clause $c' = (c, l)$ appended has a mode function $m_{c'}$ defined as follows.

1. In the case that l is an input determinate literal,

$$m_{c'}(x) = \begin{cases} + & ; x \in \{x_1, \cdots, x_n\} \\ m_c(x) & ; \text{otherwise} \end{cases}$$

2. In the case that l is an output determinate literal,

$$m_{c'}(x) = \begin{cases} - & ; x \in \{x_1, \cdots, x_n\} \\ m_c(x) & ; \text{otherwise} \end{cases}$$

With the above mode restriction $l_1 = \mathsf{succ}(E, C')$, which is the same meaning in the logical sense with $\mathsf{pred}(C, E)$ but different in its mode, is an output determinate literal of $c = \mathsf{plus}(A, B, C) \leftarrow$, because $m_{\mathsf{succ}}(2) = -$ and $m_c(C') = -$ where C is in the place 2 of the literal. Similarly $l_2 = \mathsf{pred}(A, D)$ is an input determinate literal. The clause, $c' = ((c, l_2), l_1)$ is

$$c' = \mathsf{plus}(A, B, C) \leftarrow \mathsf{pred}(A, D), \mathsf{succ}(E, C),$$

and finally the following clause is induced.

$$\mathsf{plus}(A, B, C) \leftarrow \mathsf{pred}(A, D), \mathsf{succ}(E, C), \mathsf{plus}(D, B, E).$$

Let us consider executability of a definite clause $c = h \leftarrow b_1, \cdots, b_n$. We can see the following proposition.

Proposition 2
(A) *If b_i is an (non-determinate) literal that satisfies the mode restriction (2) wrt $c_1 = h \leftarrow b_1, \cdots, b_{i-1}$ and c_1 is executable then $(c_1, b_i) = h \leftarrow b_1, \cdots, b_i$ is also executable.*
(B) *If b_i is an input determinate literal of a clause $c_1 = h \leftarrow b_1, \cdots, b_{i-1}$ and c_1 is executable then $(c_1, b_i) = h \leftarrow b_1, \cdots, b_i$ is also executable.*

For executability of output determinate literals, we need definitions. Let us consider a clause $c = h \leftarrow b_1, \cdots, b_m, d_1, \cdots, d_n$, where d_i is an output determinate literal of a clause $h \leftarrow b_1, \cdots, b_m, d_{i+1}, \cdots, d_n$. To define a executability of output determinate literals, we prepare a preliminary concept. Let $s = d_1, \cdots, d_n$ be a sequence of output determinate literals of c.

1. *s is executable up to 0th output determinate literal* wrt any substitution.
2. *s is executable up to i-th output determinate literal* wrt a ground substitution θ if
   (a) *s is executable up to $(i-1)$-th output determinate literal wrt θ, and*
   (b) *$d_i\theta\rho$ is consistent with the mode for every correct answer $\leftarrow d_1\theta\rho, \cdots, d_{i-1}\theta\rho$ of $\leftarrow d_1\theta, \cdots, d_{i-1}\theta$.*

s is executable wrt V if s is executable up to n-th output determinate literal wrt any ground substitution that substitutes every variable in V.

Proposition 3 *Let $c = h \leftarrow b_1, \cdots, b_m, d_1, \cdots, d_n$ be a clause, where d_i is an output determinate literal of a clause $h \leftarrow b_1, \cdots, b_m, d_{i+1}, \cdots, d_n$. V is a set of variables.*
(A) *If $d_{i+1}, \cdots, d_n$ is executable wrt V, then $d_i, d_{i+1}, \cdots, d_n$ is executable wrt $V - V_O \cup V_I$, where V_I (V_O) is a set of variables at input (output) arguments of d_i.*
(B) *If $c' = h \leftarrow b_1, \cdots, b_m$ is executable and $d_1, \cdots, d_n$ is executable wrt a set of variables that appear in c', then c is also executable.*

Find a clause that covers no negative examples

1   **Repeat until** c is too complex or c covers no negative examples
2   Insert all input determinate literals at inserting point of c.
3   Insert all output determinate literals at inserting point of c.
4   Insert an appropriate literal at inserting point of c.

Fig. 2. A search algorithm of clauses

Considering Proposition 3 the following clause is executable, the clause in which an output determinate literal succ(E,C) is put into the proper position for its executability.

$$\mathsf{plus}(A, B, C) \leftarrow \mathsf{pred}(A, D), \mathsf{plus}(D, B, E), \mathsf{succ}(E, C).$$

6   Implementation

We implemented a FOIL-like top-down ILP system with the method of input/output determinate literals. The system obeys the algorithm shown in Figure 1. To find a clause our system uses an algorithm(Figure 2) which including the mechanism that have been explained.

It starts a search with adding all possible input determinate literals and output determinate literals. All of the literals are inserted at a particular point. Form Proposition 3 we can see that output determinate literals should be inserted to the point that is right of all input determinate literals and non-determinate literals and left of all output determinate literals. We call the point an *inserting point*. Inserting there keeps an order of literals to hold executability of clauses induced.

Input/output determinate literals are generated by enumeration and checked. Predicates that have at least one output variables are candidates of determinate literals. If the predicate has k input variables and n variables are appeared in clause, the number of candidates is at most the permutations of n things taken k at a time. Each candidate is checked according with the definition, that is, whether there is only a correct answer for each examples.

7   Examples and Experiments

Table 2 shows some of target predicates that our top-down ILP system correctly induce. The system is implemented on SICStus Prolog version 2.1 based on the mechanism that have been explained. It also shows sample sets with which the system induces predicates. We can see that predicates are induced using relatively small sample sets.

target predicates	positive examples	negative examples
member(+, +)	(c,[b,a,c]), (b,[b,c])	(c,[a,b]), ([],[c,a,b])
last(+, −)	(c,[c]), (a,[c,b,a])	(a,[c,b]), (c,[c,a,b]), ([],[c])
length(+, −)	([],0), ([a,b],2])	([],2), ([b,a],1), ([a,b,c],0)
nth(+, +, −) or nth(+, −, +)	([c,a],1,c), ([c,a,b],3,b)	([b],0,a), ([c,a,b],3,c) ([c,a,b],1,[])
plus(+, +, −)	(0,5,5), (3,1,4), (0,0,0)	(0,0,1), (1,4,4), (4,2,5)
append(+, +, −)	([a],[b,b],[a,b,b]) ([],[b,b,b],[b,b,b]) ([a,a],[b],[a,a,b])	([],[b],[b,b]), ([],[b],[]) ([a],[a,a],[a,a]) ([b],[a,a],[a,a,a])

Table 2. Target predicates and examples

Table 3 shows a comparisons of results of induction by a system using the mechanism for determinate literals(A) and a normal top-down system(B). The results shows that the system (A) induced predicate before visiting much fewer nodes than the system (B). The system (B) fails to induce some predicates. There are two lines for the predicate nth. These are different in their mode. The predicate nth of the first line has mode nth(+, +, −), and the second one has nth(+, −, +). Program (3) for the former one and Program (4) for the latter one are correctly affected by their mode as follows.

$$\begin{cases} \mathsf{nth}(A,B,C) \leftarrow \mathsf{component}(A,D,E), \mathsf{pred}(B,F), \mathsf{eq}(D,C), \mathsf{zero}(F) \\ \mathsf{nth}(A,B,C) \leftarrow \mathsf{component}(A,D,E), \mathsf{pred}(B,F), \mathsf{nth}(E,F,C) \end{cases} \quad (3)$$

$$\begin{cases} \mathsf{nth}(A,B,C) \leftarrow \mathsf{component}(A,D,E), \mathsf{eq}(D,C), \mathsf{zero}(F), \mathsf{succ}(F,B) \\ \mathsf{nth}(A,B,C) \leftarrow \mathsf{component}(A,D,E), \mathsf{nth}(E,F,C), \mathsf{succ}(F,B) \end{cases} \quad (4)$$

System logs tell that the fails of the system (B) for the predicates are caused because literals not included by correct programs are visited first and they lead to lengthy but consistent program with examples. That is because determinate literals are not always added before others in the system (B).

8   Conclusions

This paper has given an method to properly treat determinate literals. By the method executable programs are induced with efficiency. The results also shows that the system with this method makes possible to induce programs from relatively small sample sets, i.e. the system requires small sample cost. The time cost to generate determinate literals is the same as to generate other literals. This means that the time cost of this algorithm does not exceed the time cost of a naive one. The result in Table 3 shows that total time of our algorithm is smaller than the naive one. Difference between time spent by the two algorithm

predicates	(A)		(B)	
	T	N	T	N
member	0.6	7	0.8	27
last	0.6	11	1.0	42
length	0.7	12	5.6	170
nth(+,+,−)	1.6	27	3.8	130
nth(+,−,+)	1.6	21	-	-
plus	19.5	444	-	-
append	7.7	130	-	-

(A) : A system with determinate literal process

(B) : A system without determinate literal process

T : Runtime(seconds) of the systems

N : The number of nodes visited while inducing

Table 3. Induction of predicates

is gained for target predicates that need relatively large time. We can observe the same thing also in the number of nodes visited in algorithms.

In the paper we gave an order of literals in programs. The order is to hold executability. There is another factor to give orders. An order may cause efficiency of execution of programs. This point has not been discussed in the paper. This should be a subject in the future works.

References

1. David W. Aha, Stephen Lapointe, Charles X. Ling, and Stan Matwin, "Inverting implication with small training sets", In *Proc. of 7th European Conf. on Machine Learning, LNAI*, **784**, Springer-Verlag, pp 31–48, 1994.
2. David W. Aha, Stephane Lapointe, Charles X. Ling, and Stan Matwin, "Learning recursive relations with randomly selected small training sets", In *Proc. of 11th Int'l Conf. on Machine Learning*, pp 12–18. Morgan Kaufmann, 1994.
3. Francesco Bergadano and Daniele Gunetti. "Inductive Logic Programming — From Machine Learning to Software Engineering", MIT Press, 1996.
4. Mitsue Furusawa, Nobuhiro Inuzuka, Hirohisa Seki and Hidenori Itoh. "Bottom-up induction of logic programs with more than one recursive clause" to appear in Proc. IJCAI97 Workshop Frontiers of Inductive Logic Programming, Nagoya, 1997.
5. Mitsue Furusawa, Nobuhiro Inuzuka, Hirohisa Seki and Hidenori Itoh. "Induction of logic programs with more than one recursive clause by analyzing saturations", to appear in Proceedings of 7th Int'l Inductive Logic Programming Workshop (ILP97), LNAI seriese, Springer Verlag, Prague, 1997.
6. Peter Idestam-Almquist. "Efficient Induction of Recursive Definitions by Structural Analysis of Saturations", *Proc. of 5th Int'l Workshop on Inductive Logic Programming*, pp 77–94, 1995.
7. Nobuhiro Inuzuka, Masakage Kamo, Naohiro Ishii, Hirohisa Seki and Hidenori Itoh. "Top-down Induction of Logic Programs from Incomplete Samples", In *Proc. 6th Int'l Inductive Logic Programming Workshop*, pp 119–136, 1996.

8. Stephan Lapointe and Stan Matwin, "Sub-unification: a tool for efficient induction of recursive programs", In *Proc. of 9th Int'l Conf. on Machine Learning.* Aberdeen, Morgan Kaufmann, pp 273–281, 1992.

9. John W. Lloyd. "Foundation of Logic Programming", Second, Extended Edition, Springer-Verlag, 1993.

10. Stephen Muggleton, "Inverse entailment and progol", *New Generation Computing*, **3+4** pp 245–286, 1995.

11. Stephen Muggleton and Cao Feng, "Efficient induction in logic programs", In S. Muggleton, editor, *Inductive Logic Programming*, pp 281–298. Academic Press, 1992.

12. J.R. Quinlan. Learning logical definitions from relations. *Machine Learning*, **5**, pp. 239–266, 1990.

13. J.R. Quinlan and R.M. Cameron-Jones. "FOIL: A midterm report", In P. Brazdil, editor, *Proc. 6th European Conf. Machine Learning, LNAI*, **667**, Springer-Verlag, pp 3–20, 1993.

A   Proofs of propositions

A.1   Proof of proposition 1

Proposition 1 *For a definite clause c, a literal l, a determinate literal d wrt a set of positive example E^+, and a positive example $e^+ \in E^+$, if $(c,l)(e^+)$ has a correct answer $(c,l)(e^+)\theta_1$ then $((c,d),l)(e^+)$ has a correct answer $((c,d),l)(e^+)\theta$, where d and l do not have common variables not appeared in c and $\theta' = \theta\rho$.*

(proof) When $(c,l)(e^+)\theta_1$ is a correct answer of $(c,l)(e^+)$ wrt B, there is a substitution θ' that $c(e^+)\theta'_1$ is a correct answer of $c(e^+)$ by Lemma 1. Hence $(c,d)(e^+)\theta'_1$ has the exactly one correct answer denoted by $(c,d)(e^+)\theta_2$ because d is a determinate literal of c wrt B, where $\theta_2 = \theta'_1\sigma$ for a ground substitution σ for a variable newly appeared in d. As a result $((c,d),l)(e^+)$ has a correct answer $((c,d),l)(e^+)\theta$ by Lemma 2, where θ satisfies the condition in Lemma 2. There exists such θ because d and l do not have common variables not appeared in c.

Lemma 1 *For a goal $g =\leftarrow b_1, \cdots, b_n$ and a literal l, if $(g,l) =\leftarrow b_1, \cdots, b_n, l$ has a correct answer $(g,l)\theta$ wrt a background knowledge B then $g\theta'$ is a correct answer of g wrt B, where θ' is a substitution that substitute only variables appeared in g in the same way as θ.*

Lemma 2 *For a goal $g =\leftarrow b_1, \cdots, b_n$ and literals l_1, l_2, if $(g,l_1)\theta_1$ and $(g,l_2)\theta_2$ are correct answers of (g,l_1) and (g,l_2), respectively, and there is a substitutions θ, ρ_1 and ρ_2 that $\theta = \theta_1 \cdot \rho_1 = \theta_2 \cdot \rho_2$, then $((g,l_1),l_2)\theta$ is a correct answer of $((g,l_1),l_2)$.*

A.2   Proof of proposition 2

Proposition 2

(A) *If b_i is an (non-determinate) literal that satisfies the mode restriction (2) wrt $c_1 = h \leftarrow b_1, \cdots, b_{i-1}$ and c_1 is executable then $(c_1,b_i) = h \leftarrow b_1, \cdots, b_i$ is also executable.*

(B) *If b_i is an input determinate literal of a clause $c_1 = h \leftarrow b_1, \cdots, b_{i-1}$ and c_1 is executable then $(c_1, b_i) = h \leftarrow b_1, \cdots, b_i$ is also executable.*

(proof) (A) and (B) are proven in the same way. By the definition of executability the fact that c_1 is executable means that (c_1, b_i) is executable up to $(i-1)$-th literal. Every variable of b_i in an input argument of a predicate of b_i is appeared in c_1 because the mode restriction. Hence $b_1\theta$ is consistent with the mode for any correct answer substitution θ of $c_1(a)$, because $c_1(a)\theta$ is ground. As a result (c_1, b_i) is executable.

A.3 Proof of proposition 3

Proposition 3 *Let $c = h \leftarrow b_1, \cdots, b_m, d_1, \cdots, d_n$ be a clause, where d_i is an output determinate literal of a clause $h \leftarrow b_1, \cdots, b_m, d_{i+1}, \cdots, d_n$. V is a set of variables.*
(A) If $d_{i+1}, \cdots, d_n$ is executable wrt V, then $d_i, d_{i+1}, \cdots, d_n$ is executable wrt $V - V_O \cup V_I$, where V_I (V_O) is a set of variables at input (output) arguments of d_i.
(B) If $c' = h \leftarrow b_1, \cdots, b_m$ is executable and $d_1, \cdots, d_n$ is executable wrt a set of variables that appear in c', then c is also executable.

(proof) (A) It is trivial that $d_i\theta$ is consistent with the mode for every ground substitution that substitute every variable in $V - V_O \cup V_I$, and so $V - V_O \cup V_I$ is executable up to 1st output determinate literal. Every correct answer substitution of $\leftarrow d_i$ substitute all of variables in V. This yields executability of s wrt V.
(B) c is executable up to m-th literal. Every correct answer substitution of $c'(a)$ for a consistent atom with the mode, the atom which has the same predicate with the head of c, is a substitution that substitute every variable appear in c'. This yields that c is executable up to k-th literal ($m < k \leq n + m$) by the mathematical induction.

Automated Verification of Behavioural Properties of Prolog Programs

B. Le Charlier[1] and C. Leclère[1] and S. Rossi[2] and A. Cortesi[3]

[1] Institut d'Informatique, 21 rue Grandgagnage, B-5000 Namur, Belgium
e-mail: {ble,clc}@info.fundp.ac.be
[2] Dip. di Matematica, via Belzoni 7, 35131 Padova, Italy
e-mail: sabina@math.unipd.it
[3] Dip. di Matematica e Informatica, via Torino 155, 30173 Venezia, Italy
e-mail: cortesi@dsi.unive.it

Abstract. Program verification is a crucial issue in the field of program development, compilation and debugging. In this paper, we present an analyser for Prolog which aims at verifying whether the execution of a program behaves according to a given specification (behavioural assumptions). The analyser is based on the methodology of abstract interpretation. A novel notion of abstract sequence is introduced, that includes an over-approximatimation of successful inputs (this is useful to detect mutual exclusion of clauses), and expresses size relation information between successful inputs and the corresponding outputs, together with cardinality information in terms of input argument sizes.

Keywords: Program Verification, Static Analysis, Logic Programming, Prolog.

1 Introduction

Declarative languages have received great attention in the last years, as they allow the programmer to focus on the description of the problem to be solved while ignoring low level implementation details. Nevertheless, the implementation of declarative languages remains a delicate issue. Very often, languages include additional "impure" features which are intended to improve the efficiency of the programs but do not respect their declarative nature. This is what happens in logic programming with Prolog, where a number of these "impure" features arise, e.g., the incomplete (depth-first) search rule, the non logical negation by failure, the non-logical test predicates like **var**, and the cut.

Many static analysis techniques have been proposed in the literature to improve on this situation. Some analyses aim at optimizing programs automatically, relieving the programmer from using impure control features [8, 18]. Other analyses are designed to verify that a non declarative implementation of a program does behave according to its declarative meaning [6, 9]. These analyses may also be useful to transform a first (declaratively but not operationally correct) version of a program into a both declaratively and operationally correct program.

In this paper, we describe an analyser for Prolog programs which aims at verifying whether the concrete execution of a program behaves according to a given specification consisting of a set of behavioural assumptions. The analyser is based on the methodology of abstract interpretation [5, 14]: it can be seen as an online approximation of (sets of) concrete program executions. However, instead of performing a fixpoint computation, the analyser makes use of declarations on allowed program executions (*behaviours*) provided by the user. Therefore, the emphasis here is not on the analysis of substitution properties, like modes, sharing and types, that can be automatically inherited from previous works [14], but on the automatic verification of assumptions like the number of solutions, or the size relations between input and output arguments.

Our analyser is built upon the notion of *abstract sequence* [2, 3, 12]. Abstract sequences describe pairs $\langle \theta, S \rangle$, where θ is a substitution and S is the sequence of answer substitutions resulting from executing a program (a procedure, a clause, etc.) with input substitution θ. In this paper, we revisit this notion so that

- the new notion includes an over-approximatimation of successful inputs: this is useful to detect mutual exclusion of clauses,
- it allows to express size relation information between successful inputs and the corresponding outputs,
- it allows to express cardinality information in terms of input argument sizes.

Basically, the new notion of abstract sequence is more "relational", since it may relate the number of solutions and the size of output terms to the size of input terms in full generality. For instance, it may relate the input and output sizes of the same [4] term without requiring any invariance under instantiation.

This paper presents the main features of our analyser which uses abstract sequences for computing non trivial information on size relations and cardinality. The interested reader may found more details and correctness proofs in [10]. The practical implementation of the analyser (which is still under progress) is based on the generic system *GAIA* [14] and on the polyhedron library described in [19] to manipulate size information.

The paper is organized as follows. Section 2 provides an overview of the analyser. Section 3 recalls some basic concepts. Section 4 illustrates our domain of abstract sequences. Section 5 describes the analyser. Section 6 discusses the implementation of two abstract operations. Section 7 concludes the paper.

2   Overview of the Analyser

In this section, we introduce the main functionalities of the analyser by discussing a simple example. Consider the Prolog procedure `select/3` depicted below.

```
select(X, L, LS):- L=[H|T], H=X, LS=T, list(T).
select(X, L, LS):- L=[H|T], LS=[H|TS], select(X, T, TS).
```

Declaratively, it defines a relation between three terms[5] X, L, and LS that holds

---

[4] i.e., bound to the same program variable.

[5] We use roman letters to denote the values to which program variables are instantiated. Syntactic objects are denoted by typewriter characters.

if and only if the terms L and LS are lists and LS is obtained by removing one occurrence of X from L. Our analyser is not aimed at verifying this (informal) declarative specification. Instead, it checks a number of operational properties which ensure that the program execution of this program actually computes the specified relation, provided that the procedure is "declaratively" correct (and its operational specification guarantees such correctness). We assume one particular and reasonable class of input calls, i.e., calls such that X and LS are *distinct* variables and L is any ground term (not necessarily a list). For this class of input calls, the user has to provide a description of the expected behaviour of the procedure by means of an abstract sequence B and a size expression se. The abstract sequence B is a tuple $\langle \beta_{in}, \beta_{ref}, \beta_{out}, E_{ref\_out}, E_{sol} \rangle$, where

1. β_{in} is an abstract substitution describing the above class of input calls;
2. β_{ref} is an abstract substitution describing an over approximation of the successful input calls, i.e., those that produce at least one solution: in our example, β_{ref} states that L is a non empty ground list;
3. β_{out} is an abstract substitution describing an over approximation of the set of outputs corresponding to the successful calls: in our example, β_{out} states that X is a ground term and LS is a ground list;
4. E_{ref_out} describes a relation between the size of the terms of a successful call and the size of the terms returned by the call: in our example, E_{ref_out} states that the input length of L is equal to the output length of LS plus 1;
5. E_{sol} describes a relation between the size of the terms occurring in a successful call and the number of solutions returned by the call: in our example, E_{sol} states that the number of solutions is equal to the input length of L.

The size expression se is a positive integer expression over the formal parameters of the procedure denoting the size of the corresponding input terms; this expression must decrease strictly through recursive calls. In our example, se is equal to L representing the input length of L, denoted by $\|L\|$.

Starting from B and se, the analyser computes a number of abstract sequences, one for every prefix of the body of every clause, one for every clause, and, finally, one for the complete procedure. In our example, the analyser computes an abstract sequence B_1 for the first clause, expressing that for the specified class of input calls, the first clause succeeds if and only if L is a non empty list, and it succeeds exactly once. The derivation of this information is possible because the analyser is able to detect that the unification L=[H|T] succeeds if and only if L is of the form $[t_1|t_2]$ (not necessarily a list) and that both unifications H=X and LS=T surely succeed since X and LS are free and do not share. B_1 is obtained by combining this information with the abstract sequence that describes the behaviour of the procedure list/1. The latter states that, for ground calls, the literal succeeds only for lists, and it succeeds exactly once.

The second clause of select/3 is treated similarly. Only the recursive call deserves a special treatment. First, the analyser infers that the recursive call will be executed at most once and, in fact, exactly once when L is of the form $[t_1|t_2]$. It also infers that X and TS are distinct variables and that T is ground and strictly smaller than L with respect to the norm $\| \cdot \|$. Thus, it can be assumed by induction that the recursive call satisfies the conditions provided by the user through the abstract sequence B. The analyser deduces that the recursive call succeeds only if T is a *non-empty* list and that it returns a number of solutions equal to the length of T. It also infers that X is ground and that TS is a ground list whose size is the same as the size of T minus 1. Putting all pieces together, the analyser computes the abstract sequence B_2 for the second clause, which states that the second clause succeeds only for a list L of at least two elements and that the output size of LS is equal to the size of L minus 1, i.e., $\|L\| - 1$; moreover, the number of solution is also equal to $\|L\| - 1$.

The last step for the analyser is to combine the abstract sequences B_1 and B_2 to get a new abstract sequence B_{out} describing the behaviour of the whole procedure. Once again, a careful analysis is necessary to get the most precise result. When L is a list of at least two elements, the first clause succeeds once and the second one succeeds $\|L\| - 1$ times. Thus, the procedure succeeds $\|L\|$ times. Otherwise, when the length of L is equal to 1, the second clause fails and the first one succeeds exactly once. Thus, in both cases the procedure succeeds $\|L\|$ times. Hence, putting the abstract sequences B_1 and B_2 together, the analyser is able to reconstruct exactly the information provided by the user, which is automatically verified to be correct.

3 Preliminaries

The reader is assumed to be familiar with the basic concepts of logic programming and abstract interpretation [5, 17]. We denote by T the set of all terms, and for any set of indices I, we denote by T^I the set of all tuples of terms $\langle t_i \rangle_{i \in I}$. A size measure (or norm) is a function $\| \cdot \| : T \to \mathbf{N}$. Here, we refer to the list-length measure defined for any term t by $\|t\| = 1 + \|t_2\|$ if t is of the form $[t_1 | t_2]$ and $\|t\| = 0$ otherwise. The *disjoint union* of two (possibly non disjoint) sets A and B is an arbitrarily set $A + B$ in which the elements of A (resp. B) can be identified. Formally, $A + B$ is equipped with two injections functions in_A and in_B such that: for any set C and for any pair of functions $f_A : A \to C$ and $f_B : B \to C$, there exists a unique function $f : A + B \to C$ with $f_A = f \circ in_A$ and $f_B = f \circ in_B$ (the symbol $\circ$ is the usual function composition). We denote the function f by $f_A + f_B$. For any set V, we denote by $\mathbf{Exp}_V$ the set of all integer linear expressions with variables in V. An element $se \in \mathbf{Exp}_{\{X_1, \ldots, X_m\}}$ can also be seen as a function from $\mathbf{N}^m$ to $\mathbf{N}$. The value of $se(\langle n_1, \ldots, n_m \rangle)$ is obtained by evaluating the expression se where each X_i is replaced by n_i.

Programs are assumed to be normalized as follows. A *(normalized) program* P is a non empty set of procedures pr. A procedure is a non empty sequence of clauses c. Each clause has the form $h: -g$ where the head h is of the form $p(X_1, \ldots, X_n)$ and p is a predicate symbol of arity n, whereas the body g is a possibly empty sequence of literals. A literal l is either a built-in of the form $X_{i_1} = X_{i_2}$, or a built-in of the form $X_{i_1} = f(X_{i_2}, \ldots, X_{i_n})$ where f is a functor of arity $n - 1$, or an atom $p(X_{i_1}, \ldots, X_{i_n})$. The variables occurring in a literal are

all distinct; all clauses of a procedure have exactly the same head. We denote by
$\mathcal{P}$ the set of all predicate symbols occurring in the program P. Variables used
in the clauses are called *program variables* and are denoted by $X_1, \ldots, X_i, \ldots$.

A *(program) substitution* θ is a finite set $\{X_{i_1}/t_1, \ldots, X_{i_n}/t_n\}$ where variables $X_{i_1}, \ldots, X_{i_n}$ are distinct program variables and the t_i's are terms. The
domain of θ, denoted by $dom(\theta)$, is the set of variables $\{X_{i_1}, \ldots, X_{i_n}\}$. Variables occurring in $t_1, \ldots, t_n$ are taken from the set of *standard variables* which is
disjoint from the set of program variables. A *standard substitution* σ is a substitution in the usual sense which only uses standard variables. The application of
a standard substitution σ to a program substitution $\theta = \{X_{i_1}/t_1, \ldots, X_{i_n}/t_n\}$ is
the program substitution $\theta\sigma = \{X_{i_1}/t_1\sigma, \ldots, X_{i_n}/t_n\sigma\}$. We say that θ_1 is *more
general* than θ_2, noted $\theta_2 \leq \theta_1$, iff there exists σ such that $\theta_2 = \theta_1\sigma$. $mgu(t_1, t_2)$
denotes the set of standard substitutions that are a most general unifier of t_1
and t_2. The *restriction* of θ to a set of variables D, denoted by $\theta_{/D}$, is such that
$dom(\theta_{/D}) = D$ and $X_i\theta = X_i(\theta_{/D})$, for all $X_i \in D$. A *(program) substitution
sequence* S is a *finite* sequence $< \theta_1, \ldots, \theta_n >$ of (program) substitutions with
the same domain. We denote by $< >$ the empty sequence and by $Subst(S)$ the
set of all substitutions in S. The symbol $::$ denotes the sequence concatenation.

Our analyser refers to the concrete semantics of Prolog programs presented
in [13], which has been proven equivalent to Prolog operational semantics in [11].
The concrete semantics for a program P is a total function from the set of pairs
$\langle \theta, p \rangle$, where $p \in \mathcal{P}$ has arity n and $dom(\theta) = \{X_1, \ldots, X_n\}$, to the set of substitution sequences. The fact that $\langle \theta, p \rangle$ is mapped to the sequence S is denoted by
$\langle \theta, p \rangle \longmapsto S$. Here, this means that the execution of $p(X_1, \ldots, X_n)\theta$ terminates
and produces the (finite, possibly empty) sequence of answer substitutions S.

4 Abstract Domains

In this section, we describe the abstract objects used by the analyser, namely,
abstract substitutions, *abstract sequences* and *behaviours*.

Abstract Substitutions. Our domain of *abstract substitutions* is an instantiation
of the generic domain $\mathbf{Pat}(\Re)$ [4]. Here, we give only an informal presentation of
it and we refer the reader to our previous papers [14, 4] for more details.
An abstract substitution β with domain $\{X_1, \ldots, X_n\}$ describes a set of program substitutions with the same domain giving information not only about the
terms to which $X_1, \ldots, X_n$ are bound, but also about some subterms of them.
The terms described in β are denoted by indices from a set I. We say that β is an
abstract substitution over I. The following properties of terms are captured: the
pattern, which specifies the main functor of a term as well as the subterms that
are its arguments; the *mode* (e.g., **ground**, **var**); the *type* (e.g., **list**); and the
possible sharing with other subterms. We donote by $Cc(\beta)$ the set of all substitutions described by β, by $\bot$ the abstract substitution describing the empty set,
i.e., $Cc(\bot) = \emptyset$, and by $\mathbf{DECOMP}(\theta, \beta)$ the set of all tuples of terms $\langle t_i \rangle_{i \in I}$ respecting the term properties described in β and such that $\theta = \{X_1/t_{i_1}, \ldots, X_n/t_{i_n}\}$
(if $i_1, \ldots, i_n$ denote the terms bound to $X_1, \ldots, X_n$, respectively).

As an example, consider the abstract substitutions β_{in}, β_{ref}, β_{out} informally described in Section 2. They can be represented as follows. The terms bound to the formal parameters X, L and LS are denoted by indices 1, 2 and 3, respectively, whereas the subterms of L in β_{ref} and β_{out} are denoted by indices 4 and 5, in

β_{in} : X$_1$/var(1), X$_2$/ground(2), X$_3$/var(3), noshare(1,3)
β_{ref} : X$_1$/var(1), X$_2$/[ground(4)|ground_list(5)](2), X$_3$/var(3), noshare(1,3)
β_{out} : X$_1$/ground(1), X$_2$/[ground(4)|ground_list(5)](2), X$_3$/ground_list(3)

Abstract Sequences. We formally describe here our domain of *abstract sequences* which is substantially more elaborate than the similar notion used in [12, 13]. An abstract sequence B is a tuple $\langle \beta_{in}, \beta_{ref}, \beta_{out}, E_{ref\_out}, E_{sol} \rangle$. The first element β_{in} is the input abstract substitution; β_{ref} is a refinement of β_{in} approximating the set of concrete substitutions in $Cc(\beta_{in})$ that surely succeeds (i.e., whose execution produces at least one result); β_{out} approximates output information about variable instantiation. E_{ref_out} represents size relations between the output and the input arguments (we refer to β_{ref} for the input) whereas E_{sol} expresses the number of solutions in terms of the input argument sizes. The size components E_{ref_out} and E_{sol} are abstract objects representing tuples of natural numbers.

In this paper, we assume that a size component E over a set of indices I is a system of linear equations and inequations over $\mathbf{Exp}_I$. It represents the set of all tuples of natural numbers $\langle n_i \rangle_{i \in I} \in \mathbf{N}^I$ which are solutions of E. We denote by $Cc(E)$ this set. In order to distinguish indices of I, considered as variables, from integer coefficient and constants, when writing elements of $\mathbf{Exp}_I$, we wrap up each element i of I into the symbol $\mathbf{sz}(i)$. If f is a function from one set of indices to another one, such that $f(i) = i'$ and $f(j) = j'$, the expression $\mathbf{sz}(f(i)) = \mathbf{sz}(f(j)) + 1$ stands for the syntactical equation $\mathbf{sz}(i') = \mathbf{sz}(j') + 1$.

In the following definition, the symbol *sol* denotes a special index representing the number of substitutions belonging to the approximated sequences.

Definition 1 (Abstract Sequence). An *abstract sequence* B is either $\perp$ or a tuple of the form $\langle \beta_{in}, \beta_{ref}, \beta_{out}, E_{ref\_out}, E_{sol} \rangle$ where

- β_{in} is an abstract substitution over I_{in};
- β_{ref} is an abstract substitution over I_{ref} with $dom(\beta_{ref}) = dom(\beta_{in})$ and $Cc(\beta_{ref}) \subseteq Cc(\beta_{in})$;
- β_{out} is an abstract substitution over I_{out} with $dom(\beta_{out}) \supseteq dom(\beta_{in})$;
- E_{ref_out} is a size component over $I_{ref} + I_{out}$;
- E_{sol} is a size component over $I_{ref} + \{sol\}$;
- for all $\theta' \in Cc(\beta_{out})$, $\exists \theta \in Cc(\beta_{ref})$ such that $\theta'_{/dom(\beta_{ref})} \le \theta$.

The abstract sequence B represents the set of all pairs $\langle \theta, S \rangle$, noted $Cc(B)$, such that $\theta \in Cc(\beta_{in})$, S is a sequence of substitutions with $Subst(S) \subseteq Cc(\beta_{out})$ and

- if $S \ne <\ >$ then $\theta \in Cc(\beta_{ref})$;
- $\forall \theta' \in Subst(S)$, if $\langle t_i \rangle_{i \in I_{ref}} \in \mathbf{DECOMP}(\theta, \beta_{ref})$ and $\langle s_i \rangle_{i \in I_{out}} \in \mathbf{DECOMP}(\theta', \beta_{out})$ then $\langle \|t_i\| \rangle_{i \in I_{ref}} + \langle \|s_i\| \rangle_{i \in I_{out}} \in Cc(E_{ref\_out})$;

- if $\langle t_i \rangle_{i \in I_{ref}} \in \texttt{DECOMP}(\theta, \beta_{ref})$ then $\langle \|t_i\| \rangle_{i \in I_{ref}} + \{sol \mapsto |S|\} \in Cc(E_{sol})$.

Consider the abstract substitutions β_{in}, β_{ref}, and β_{out} described above where $I_{ref} = I_{out} = \{1, 2, 3, 4, 5\}$. Let $in_{ref} : I_{ref} \rightarrow I_{ref} + I_{out}$, $in_{out} : I_{out} \rightarrow I_{ref} + I_{out}$ and $in_{sol} : I_{ref} \rightarrow I_{ref} + \{sol\}$ be injection functions. The behaviour for the procedure $\texttt{select}/3$ described in Section 2 can be expressed in terms of the abstract sequence $B = \langle \beta_{in}, \beta_{ref}, \beta_{out}, E_{ref\_out}, E_{sol} \rangle$ where $E_{ref\_out} = \{sz(in_{ref}(2)) = sz(in_{out}(3)) + 1\}$ and $E_{sol} = \{sol = sz(in_{sol}(2))\}$.

Behaviours. A behaviour for a procedure is a formalization of its behavioural properties provided by the user. Formally, a *behaviour* Beh_p for a procedure p/n is a finite set of pairs $\{\langle B_1, se_1 \rangle, \ldots, \langle B_m, se_m \rangle\}$ where for all $k \in \{1, \ldots, m\}$, $B_k = \langle \beta_{in}^k, \beta_{ref}^k, \beta_{out}^k, E_{ref\_out}^k, E_{sol}^k \rangle$ is an abstract sequence with $dom(\beta_{in}^k) = dom(\beta_{ref}^k) = dom(\beta_{out}^k) = \{X_1, \ldots, X_n\}$, and se_k is a positive linear expression from $\mathbf{Exp}_{\{X_1, \ldots, X_n\}}$. As an example, the behaviour for $\texttt{select}/3$ described in Section 2 is simply $\{\langle B, X_2 \rangle\}$ where B is the abstract sequence defined above. In the following, we assume that a set of behaviours $SBeh$ for a program P contains exactly one behaviour Beh_p for each procedure name $p \in \mathcal{P}$.

Definition 2 (Consistency). We say that a set of behaviours $SBeh$ for a program P is *consistent with respect to the concrete semantics of* P iff for all $p \in \mathcal{P}$ and $\langle B, se \rangle \in Beh_p$, the execution of the procedure p called with a substitution θ described by the input of B terminates and $\langle \theta, p \rangle \mapsto S$ implies $\langle \theta, S \rangle \in Cc(B)$.

5 The Analyser

The analyser follows the standard top-down verification technique: for a given program, it analyses each procedure; for each procedure, it analyses each clause; for each clause, it analyses each atom such that if an atom is a procedure call, then it looks up the behaviour to infer information about its execution. The algorithm of the analyser is depicted in the Appendix. We specify here its main operations. To simplify the presentation, we assume that programs contain no mutually recursive procedures. We discuss this point below.

The analysis of a program P with a set of behaviours $SBeh$ returns a boolean value *success*. If *success* is true, then the program satisfies the set of behaviours $SBeh$ and, in particular, every procedure call (allowed by $SBeh$) terminates. Otherwise, if *success* is false then the analyser is not able to infer whether the program is correct with respect to the set of behaviours $SBeh$.

The analyser computes the glb-closure of the set of behaviours $SBeh$ through the function $\texttt{MAKE\_SAT}$. This is useful when analysing an atom which is a procedure call: in that case, a look-up to such a set is performed. Formally, $\texttt{MAKE\_SAT}(SBeh)$ returns a family $sat = \langle sat_p \rangle_{p \in \mathcal{P}}$ of sets of abstract sequences such that for all $p \in \mathcal{P}$, sat_p is the smallest set containing $\{B \mid \exists se : \langle B, se \rangle \in Beh_p\}$ which is closed under greatest lower bound. The results of the analysis of clauses in a same procedure are "concatenated" through the operation $\texttt{CONC}$ (see Section 6).

The analysis of a clause $c \equiv p(X_1, \ldots, X_n) \; : - \; l_1, \ldots, l_s.$ with respect to $\langle B, se \rangle \in Beh_p$ consists in the following steps:

1. extending the input substitution β_{in} of B to an abstract sequence B_0 on all the variables in the clause through the operation **EXTC**;
2. computing B_k from B_{k-1} and l_k ($k \in \{1, \ldots, s\}$);
3. restricting B_s to the variables in the head of c through the operation **RESTRC**.

Each B_k is computed from B_{k-1} and l_k by

1. restricting the domain of the output abstract substitution β_{out} of B_{k-1} to the variables $X_{i_1}, \ldots, X_{i_n}$ of l_k and renaming them into $X_1, \ldots, X_n$ through the operation **RESTRG**;
2. executing the literal l_k with β_{inter}^k which returns an abstract sequence B_{aux}^k;
3. propagating this result on B_{k-1} by computing $B_k = \texttt{EXTGS}(l_k, B_{k-1}, B_{aux}^k)$.

The execution of l_k with β_{inter}^k depends on the form of l_k.

1. If l_k is a built-in of the form $X_{i_1} = X_{i_2}$ then $B_{aux}^k = \texttt{UNIF\_VAR}(\beta_{inter}^k)$ (see Section 6).
2. If l_k is of the form $X_{i_1} = f(X_{i_2}, \ldots, X_{i_n})$ then $B_{aux}^k = \texttt{UNIF\_FUNC}(\beta_{inter}^k, f)$. This operation is defined similarly to the previous one.
3. If l_k is a non-recursive call $q(X_{i_1}, \ldots, X_{i_m})$ (i.e., $q \neq p$) then the analyser looks at sat, the glb-closed set of behaviours, to find an abstract sequence general enough to give information about this call.
4. If l_k is a recursive call $p(X_{i_1}, \ldots, X_{i_n})$ then the analyser checks whether the size of the arguments decreases through operation $\texttt{CHECK\_TERM}(l_k, B_{k-1}, se)$, i.e., it checks whether for all $\langle \theta, S \rangle \in Cc(B_{k-1})$ and for all $\theta' \in Subst(S)$, $se(\langle \|X_{i_1}\theta'\|, \ldots, \|X_{i_n}\theta'\| \rangle) < se(\langle \|X_1\theta\|, \ldots, \|X_n\theta\| \rangle)$.

Mutual Recursion. Mutual recursion is treated by extending the termination test to all mutual recursive procedures (above, such a test is applied only to recursive procedures). Mutual recursive procedures are found out by a first-stage analysis which returns all pairs $(\langle p, B_p, se_p \rangle, \langle q, B_q, se_q \rangle)$ with $\langle B_p, se_p \rangle \in Beh_p$ and $\langle B_q, se_q \rangle \in Beh_q$, describing possibly mutual recursive calls.

Theorem 3 (Correctness [10]). *Let P be a program and $SBeh$ be a set of behaviours for P. The analyser called with P and $SBeh$ as inputs returns a boolean value* success *as output such that if* success *is true, then $SBeh$ is consistent with respect to the concrete semantics of the program P.*

Proof. (sketch) In order to prove the theorem, we introduce the notion of *procedure call allowed by SBeh* which is a tuple $t = \langle \theta, B, se, p \rangle$ such that $p \in \mathcal{P}$, $\langle B, se \rangle \in Beh_p$ and θ is described by the input abstract substitution of B. We also introduce a *well-founded relation* on the set of all the allowed procedure calls as follows: for any allowed procedure calls $t = \langle \theta, B, se, p \rangle$ and $t' = \langle \theta', B', se', p' \rangle$, $t < t'$ iff either the procedure p' is used in the definition of p or t' is a (mutually) recursive call that may be reached during the execution of t. In the second case,

we also require that the "size" of θ' is (strictly) smaller than the "size" of θ, i.e.,
$$se_{p'}(\langle \|X_{i_1}\theta'\|, \ldots, \|X_{i_m}\theta'\|\rangle) < se_p(\langle \|X_1\theta\|, \ldots, \|X_n\theta\|\rangle).$$
The proof is done by induction on the ordering on allowed procedure calls: we assume that $SBeh$ correctly describes the executions of all procedure calls t' such that $t' < t$ and that these executions terminate and we prove that the execution of t terminates and is correcly described by $SBeh$. $\square$

6 Abstract Operations

In this section we describe the implementation of two main operations, namely UNIF_VAR and CONC. For a complete description of the operations used by the analyser and the corresponding correctness proofs, the reader is referred to [10].

Unification Operation. The unification operation UNIF_VAR is used for executing built-ins of the form $X_i = X_j$ with an input abstract substitution β. It returns an abstract sequence $B' = \langle \beta'_{in}, \beta'_{ref}, \beta'_{out}, E'_{ref\_out}, E'_{sol} \rangle$. The principle of the implementation is the following: first, we (re)use the operation UNIF_VAR$_{old}$ [14] to compute the abstract result of the execution of $X_i = X_j$ called with β; then we refine β to the set of $\theta \in Cc(\beta)$ for which the unification succeeds through operation REF$_{ref}$; finally, we derive constraints between the input and argument sizes as well as constraints on the number of solutions. Below, we state the specifications of the operations UNIF_VAR$_{old}$ and REF$_{ref}$ whereas we detail the implementation of UNIF_VAR.

UNIF_VAR$_{old}(\beta) = \langle \beta_{out}, ss, sf, tr, U \rangle$. This operation is similar [6] to the one defined in [14]. Given an abstract substitution β with $dom(\beta) = \{X_1, X_2\}$, it returns an abstract substitution β_{out} describing the unification of $X_1\theta$ and $X_2\theta$ for all $\theta \in Cc(\beta)$; two boolean values ss and sf specifying whether sure success or sure failure can be inferred at the abstract level, a so-called *structural mapping* tr between the indices of β and the indices of β_{out} representing corresponding terms before and after the unification, and a set of indices U representing the set of terms in θ whose norm is not affected by the instantiation.

REF$_{ref}(\beta_1, \beta_2, tr) = \langle \beta', tr' \rangle$. This operation takes as inputs two abstract substitutions β_1 and β_2 and a structural mapping tr between the indices of β_1 and β_2. It refines the abstract substitution β_1 by keeping substitutions in $Cc(\beta_1)$ that have at least an instance in $Cc(\beta_2)$. It returns an abstract substitution β' and a structural mapping tr' between the indices of β' and β_2 such that β' is at least as precise as β_1 and $\theta_k \in Cc(\beta_k)$ $(k = 1, 2)$ with $\theta_2 \leq \theta_1$ implies $\theta_1 \in Cc(\beta')$.

UNIF_VAR$(\beta) = B'$. Let β be an abstract substitution with $dom(\beta) = \{X_1, X_2\}$ and $\langle \beta_{out}, tr, ss, sf, U \rangle =$ UNIF_VAR$_{old}(\beta)$. B' is defined as follows.

---

[6] Actually, the signature in [14] of this operation is UNIF_VAR$(\beta) = \beta'$, as there was no need there to export sure success/failure information. Adapting that definition to our purposes is straightforward (see [13]). That's why we call it simply UNIF_VAR$_{old}$.

$$
\begin{aligned}
\beta'_{in} &= \beta \\
\beta'_{out} &= \beta_{out} \\
\langle \beta'_{ref}, tr_{ref\_out} \rangle &= \langle \beta'_{in}, tr \rangle && \text{if } ss \\
& \quad\ \langle \bot, undef \rangle && \text{if } sf \\
& \quad\ \mathtt{REF}_{ref}(\beta'_{in}, \beta'_{out}, tr) && \text{if } \neg ss \text{ and } \neg sf \\
E'_{ref\_out} &= \bot && \text{if } sf \\
& \quad\ \{ \mathtt{sz}(in_{ref}(i)) = \mathtt{sz}(in_{out}(tr_{ref\_out}(i))) : \\
& \qquad\ i \in tr_{in\_ref}(U) \} && \text{otherwise} \\
E'_{sol} &= \{sol = 1\} && \text{if } ss \\
& \quad\ \bot && \text{if } sf \\
& \quad\ \{0 \le sol, sol \le 1\} && \text{if } \neg ss \text{ and } \neg sf.
\end{aligned}
$$

where tr_{in_ref} is a canonical inclusion, and the following commutative diagram is satisfied by tr_{in_ref}, tr_{ref_out} and the injection functions in_{ref} and in_{out}.

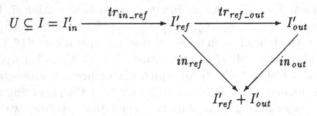

The accuracy of this operation may be improved in practice by using a reexecution strategy [15]: we may repeatedly apply $\mathtt{UNIF\_VAR}_{old}$ and $\mathtt{REF}_{ref}$ to β'_{ref} until sure success or sure failure is inferred or β'_{ref} stabilizes.

Concatenation Operation. The concatenation operation $\mathtt{CONC}$ is the counterpart for abstract sequences of the operation $\mathtt{UNION}$, used in [14], which simply collects information provided by two abstract substitutions into a single one. In fact, $\mathtt{CONC}$ differs from $\mathtt{UNION}$ only for the computation of the number of solutions to a procedure which is the sum of the numbers of solutions of its clauses, not an "upper bound" of them. To obtain a good precision, we detect mutual exclusion of clauses [2, 13] by computing the greatest lower bound of the β_{ref} component of the two abstract sequences. If it is $\bot$, then the clauses are exclusive: in this case, we only collect the numbers of solutions of the two clauses. Otherwise, we compute the sum of the numbers of solutions for the greatest lower bound only. The implementation of $\mathtt{CONC}$ uses special operations, namely $tr^>(E)$ and $tr^<(E)$, to manipulate size components (see [16]). If E is a size component over a set of indices I and $tr : I \to I'$ is a (possibly partial) function, then $tr^>(E)$ returns E' over I' such that $(n_i)_{i \in I} \in Cc(E)$ and $n_i = n'_{tr(i)}$ $(\forall i \in dom(tr))$ imply $(n'_i)_{i \in I'} \in Cc(E')$. Analogously, if E is as above and $tr : I' \to I$, then $tr^<(E)$ returns E' over I' such that $(n_i)_{i \in I} \in Cc(E)$ and $n_{tr(i)} = n'_i$ $(\forall i \in dom(tr))$ imply $(n'_i)_{i \in I'} \in Cc(E')$. The following auxiliary operations are also used.

$\mathtt{LUB}(\beta_1, \beta_2)$ returns a triplet $\langle \beta', tr_1, tr_2 \rangle$ where $\beta' = \beta_1 \sqcup \beta_2$ and tr_k are two structural mappings between β' and β_k, i.e., $tr_k : I' \to I_k$ $(k = 1, 2)$.

EXT_LUB(β_1, β_2) is an extension of the previous operation returning an additional boolean value st (standing for "strict union") such that $st = true$ implies that $Cc(\beta') = Cc(\beta_1) \cup Cc(\beta_2)$.

GLB(β_1, β_2) returns the triplet $\langle \beta', tr_1, tr_2 \rangle$ where $\beta' = \beta_1 \sqcap \beta_2$ and tr_k are two structural mappings between β_k and β', i.e., $tr_k : I_k \to I'$ ($k = 1, 2$).

SUM$_{sol}(E_1, E_2)$ returns a size component E' satisfying the following relation: if E_k ($k = 1, 2$) are two size components over $I + \{sol\}$ then E' is a size component over over $I + \{sol\}$ such that $(n_i^k)_{i \in I + \{sol\}} \in Cc(E_k)$ ($k = 1, 2$), $n_i^1 = n_i^2 = n_i$ ($i \in I$) and $n_{sol} = n_{sol}^1 + n_{sol}^2$ imply $(n_i)_{i \in I + \{sol\}} \in Cc(E')$.

Now we are in position to describe the implementation of **CONC**. Let $B_k = \langle \beta_{in}, \beta_{ref}^k, \beta_{out}^k, E_{ref\_out}^k, E_{sol}^k \rangle$ ($k = 1, 2$) be two abstract sequences. **CONC**(B_1, B_2) returns an abstract sequence B' such that $\langle \theta, S_1 \rangle \in Cc(B_1)$ and $\langle \theta, S_2 \rangle \in Cc(B_2)$ imply $\langle \theta, S_1 :: S_2 \rangle \in Cc(B')$. B' can be implemented as follows[7].

$$\beta'_{in} = \beta_{in}$$
$$\langle \beta'_{ref}, tr_{ref}^1, tr_{ref}^2, st \rangle = \textbf{EXT\_LUB}(\beta_{ref}^1, \beta_{ref}^2)$$
$$\langle \beta'_{out}, tr_{out}^1, tr_{out}^2 \rangle = \textbf{LUB}(\beta_{out}^1, \beta_{out}^2)$$
$$E'_{ref\_out} = (tr_{ref}^1 + tr_{out}^1)^< (E_{ref\_out}^1) \sqcup (tr_{ref}^2 + tr_{out}^2)^< (E_{ref\_out}^2)$$

$$E'_{sol} = \begin{cases} \begin{aligned} &(tr_{ref}^1 + \{sol \mapsto sol\})^< (E_{sol}^1) \sqcup \\ &(tr_{ref}^2 + \{sol \mapsto sol\})^< (E_{sol}^2) \sqcup & \text{if } st \\ &(tr_{int} + \{sol \mapsto sol\})^< (\textbf{SUM}_{sol}(\overline{E}_{sol}^1, \overline{E}_{sol}^2)) \end{aligned} \\[2ex] \begin{aligned} &(tr_{ref}^1 + \{sol \mapsto sol\})^< (E_{sol}^1) \sqcup \\ &(tr_{ref}^2 + \{sol \mapsto sol\})^< (E_{sol}^2) \sqcup & \text{if } \neg st. \\ &(tr_{int} + \{sol \mapsto sol\})^< (\textbf{SUM}_{sol}(\overline{E}_{sol}^1, \overline{E}_{sol}^2)) \sqcup \\ &tr_{sol}^> (\{sol = 0\}) \end{aligned} \end{cases}$$

where $\langle \beta_{int}, tr_{int}^1, tr_{int}^2 \rangle = \textbf{GLB}(\beta_{ref}^1, \beta_{ref}^2)$, $\overline{E}_{sol}^k = (tr_{int}^k + \{sol \mapsto sol\})^> (E_{sol}^k)$ ($k = 1, 2$), $tr_{sol} : \{sol\} \to I'_{ref} + \{sol\}$ is the canonical injection and the structural mappings tr_{ref}^k, tr_{int}^k, tr_{int} satisfy the commutative diagram below.

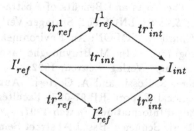

---

[7] The least upper bound operator $\sqcup$ between (in)equation systems is implemented as convex union (see [19]).

7 Conclusion

The analyser presented in this paper may apply to any kind of Prolog program (without dynamic predicates such as **assert** and **retract**). To cite some of its applications, it could be integrated in a programming environment to check correctness of Prolog programs and/or to derive efficient Prolog programs from purely logic descriptions. In particular, it may be integrated in the FOLON environment [6, 9] which was developed for supporting the automatable aspects of Deville's methodology for logic program construction [7]. Our system could support the automatable aspects of other works on verification, e.g., [1]. Moreover, since the information provided by the user is certified by the system, it can be used by a compiler to optimize the object code. Finally, since it may verify precise relations between the size of the arguments and the number of solutions to a procedure, it can be used as a basis for an automatic complexity analysis. This is the main topic of future work.

References

1. K.R. Apt. *From Logic Programming to Prolog*. Prentice Hall, 1997.
2. C. Braem, B. Le Charlier, S. Modard, and P. Van Hentenryck. Cardinality Analysis of Prolog. In M. Bruynooghe, editor, *Proc. of the International Logic Programming Symposium (ILPS'94)*, Ithaca NY, USA, November 1994. MIT Press.
3. A. Cortesi, B. Le Charlier, and S. Rossi. Specification-Based Automatic Verification of Logic Programs. In *Logic Program Synthesis and Transformation. Proceedings of the 6th International Workshop, LOPSTR'96*, volume 1207 of *LNCS*. Springer Verlag, August 1996.
4. A. Cortesi, B. Le Charlier, and P. Van Hentenryck. Combination of Abstract Domains for Logic Programming. In *Proc. of the 21th ACM Symposium on Principles of Programming Languages (POPL'94)*, Portland, Oregon, January 1994.
5. P. Cousot and R. Cousot. Abstract Interpretation Frameworks. *Journal of Logic and Computation*, 2(4):511–547, 1992.
6. P. De Boeck and B. Le Charlier. Static Type Analysis of Prolog Procedures for Ensuring Correctness. In *PLILP'90*, LNCS 456, Springer-Verlag, pages 222–237, Linköping, Sweden, 1990.
7. Y. Deville. *Logic Programming: Systematic Program Development*. MIT Press, 1990.
8. Thomas W. Getzinger. The Costs and Benefits of Abstract Interpretation-driven Prolog Optimization. In *SAS'94*, LNCS 864, Springer-Verlag, pages 1–25, 1994.
9. J. Henrard and B. Le Charlier. FOLON: An Environment for Declarative Construction of Logic Programs. In M. Bruynooghe and M. Wirsing, editors, *PLILP'92*, LNCS 631, Springer-Verlag, Leuven, 1992.
10. B. Le Charlier, C. Leclère, S. Rossi, and A. Cortesi. Automated Verification of Prolog Programs. Technical Report RP-97-003, Facultés Universitaires Notre-Dame de la Paix, Institut d'Informatique, March 1997.
11. B. Le Charlier and S. Rossi. Sequence-Based Abstract Semantics of Prolog. Technical Report RR-96-001, Facultés Universitaires Notre-Dame de la Paix, Institut d'Informatique, February 1996.

12. B. Le Charlier, S. Rossi, and P. Van Hentenryck. An Abstract Interpretation Framework Which Accurately Handles Prolog Search-Rule and the Cut. In M. Bruynooghe, editor, *ILPS'94*, Ithaca NY, USA, November 1994. MIT Press.

13. B. Le Charlier, S. Rossi, and P. Van Hentenryck. Sequence-Based Abstract Interpretation of Prolog. Technical Report RR-97-001, Facultés Universitaires Notre-Dame de la Paix, Institut d'Informatique, January 1997.

14. B. Le Charlier and P. Van Hentenryck. Experimental Evaluation of a Generic Abstract Interpretation Algorithm for Prolog. *ACM Transactions on Programming Languages and Systems (TOPLAS)*, 16(1):35–101, January 1994.

15. B. Le Charlier and P. Van Hentenryck. Reexecution in Abstract Interpretation of Prolog. *Acta Informatica*, 32:209–253, 1995.

16. C. Leclère and B. Le Charlier. Two Dual Abstract Operations to Duplicate, Eliminate, Equalize, Introduce and Rename Place-Holders Occurring Inside Abstract Descriptions. Technical Report RP-96-028, University of Namur, Belgium, 1996.

17. J.W. Lloyd. *Foundations of Logic Programming*. Springer Series: Symbolic Computation–Artificial Intelligence. Springer-Verlag, second edition, 1987.

18. P. Van Roy. 1983–1993 : The Wonder Years of Sequential Prolog Implementation. *Journal of Logic Programming*, 19/20:385–441, 1994.

19. D. K. Wilde. A Library for Doing Polyhedral Operations. Technical Report No. 785, IRISA, Rennes Cedex-France, 1993.

A The Algorithm of the Analyser

This appendix contains the implementation of the three main procedures of our analyser, namely **analyse_program**, **analyse_procedure** and **analyse_clause**.

PROCEDURE analyze_program$(P, SBeh) =$
    $success := true$
    $sat := $ **MAKE_SAT**$(SBeh)$
    for all $p \in \mathcal{P}$, **for all** $\langle B, se \rangle \in Beh_p$
       $success := success \wedge$ **analyse_procedure**(p, B, se)
    return $success.$

PROCEDURE analyze_procedure$(p, B, se) =$
    for $k := 1$ **to** r **do**
       $\langle success_k, B_k \rangle :=$ **analyze_clause**(c_k, B, se)
    if there exists $k \in \{1, \ldots, r\}$ **such that** $\neg success_k,$
    then $success := false$
    else $B_{out} :=$ **CONC**$(B_1, \ldots, B_r)$
           $success := (B_{out} \leq B)$
    return $success.$

PROCEDURE analyze_clause$(c, B) =$
    $\beta_{in} := input(B)$
    $B_0 :=$ **EXTC**(c, β_{in})
    for $k := 1$ **to** s **do**
       $\beta_{inter}^k :=$ **RESTRG**(l_k, B_{k-1})
       if $l_k \equiv X_{i_1} = X_{i_2}$ **then** $B_{aux}^k :=$ **UNIF_VAR**(β_{inter}^k)
       if $l_k \equiv X_{i_1} = f(X_{i_2}, \ldots, X_{i_m})$ **then** $B_{aux}^k :=$ **UNIF_FUNC**(β_{inter}^k, f)
       if $l_k \equiv q(X_{i_1}, \ldots, X_{i_m})$ **and** $q \neq p$ **then**
                 $\langle B_{aux}^k, success_k \rangle :=$ **LOOK_UP**$(\beta_{inter}^k, q, sat)$
       if $l_k \equiv p(X_{i_1}, \ldots, X_{i_m})$ **then**
                 $\langle B_{aux}^k, success_k' \rangle :=$ **LOOK_UP**$(\beta_{inter}^k, q, sat)$
                 $success_k := success_k' \wedge$ **CHECK_TERM**(l_k, B_{k-1}, se)
       $B_k :=$ **EXTGS**$(l_k, B_{k-1}, B_{aux}^k)$
    if there exists k **such that**
       either $l_k \equiv q(X_{i_1}, \ldots, X_{i_m}) \wedge \neg success_k$
       or $l_k \equiv p(X_{i_1}, \ldots, X_{i_n}) \wedge (\neg success_k \vee \beta_{inter}^k \not\leq \beta_{in})$
    then $success = false$
    else $success = true$ **and** $B_{out} =$ **RESTRC**(c, B_s)
    return$\langle success, B_{out} \rangle.$

Typing the Use of Resources in a Concurrent Calculus

(extended abstract)

Gérard Boudol

INRIA Sophia-Antipolis, BP 93
06902 SOPHIA ANTIPOLIS CEDEX, FRANCE

Abstract

We introduce a new type system for the blue calculus – a variant of the π-calculus that directly contains the λ-calculus. Our notion of type is built upon a combination of Curry-Church simple types and Hennessy-Milner logic with recursion. We interpret a modality $\langle u \rangle \tau$ as the type of a process offering a resource of type τ on the name u. In the typing system this is used in a kind of logical cut rule, ensuring that a message to the name u will meet a corresponding offer. We show that our calculus is type safe, that is, types are preserved along the computations.

1. Introduction

This work is concerned with the issue of typing in distributed systems. The relevance of types and type systems in computer science has been recognized since the very beginning of the programming activity. Types provide a valuable tool for software development, offering support for modular construction, early error detection and fast debugging, and also for guiding compiler optimization and reasoning about programs. A large amount of work has been done on the topic of typing programs, but it is fair to say that almost the totality of this work concerned sequential and functional programming. Our aim is to contribute to the study of type systems in distributed programming.

Types usually express quite rough information about program pieces, like being a function from integers to boolean, but still this is enough to guarantee some *safety* properties: indeed, one of the most important features of any type system is Curry's *subject reduction property*, that guarantees that no type error can occur at run-time. Concerns with safety properties arose in the area of concurrent computing, and more specifically of operating systems, where one

This work has been partially supported by the INDO-FRENCH CENTRE FOR THE PROMOTION OF ADVANCED RESEARCH, Research Project 1502-1, and by FRANCE TÉLÉCOM, CTI-CNET 95-1B-182, Modélisation de Systèmes Mobiles.

typically wants to avoid deadlocks, starvation, and the like. Even if nowadays the meaning of "safety" has somehow broadened with the advent of distributed and mobile computing, the task of ensuring such properties by statically checking programs has remained largely unexplored (we will comment on some recent attempts below). This task certainly requires using new methods, with respect to the traditional functional approach. For instance, in systems of concurrent objects, one would like to avoid the so-called "message-not-understood" error, but it is clearly not enough to record the methods' names (and types) in the type of an object, because the services it offers may not be uniformly available. In other words, we seek a way of specifying that a piece of program interacts with its environment in a manner that varies in time, and of formally checking that the program conforms to a specified "protocol". The need for expressing such temporal properties is stressed by Nierstrasz in [17] for instance.

The notion of type we propose is built upon a variant of Milner's π-calculus [15,16]. To illustrate the matter, let us use the paradigmatic example of a "one-slot buffer", offering alternately the put and get operations to store and deliver a value. In the π-calculus, this can be modelled as the process

$$\text{Buff} = \text{rec } x.\text{put}(v)\text{get}(r)(\bar{r}v \mid \bar{x})$$

where $\text{rec } x.P$ can be taken either as a primitive construct for recursively defined processes, or defined by means of the replication construct, namely $\text{rec } x.P = (\nu x)(!x()P \mid \bar{x})$. Then Buff is a process that first performs an input of the value v on the channel put, next gets on the channel get the name r of a return channel, on which the value is sent by emitting the message $\bar{r}v$, while the message $\bar{x}$ recursively calls the buffer process. The calculus we use is *asynchronous* in the sense that emitting a message does not block anything. The Buff process can be "typed" in a sense. More precisely, this process is *well-formed* if we assume that put is a channel of *sort* $\text{Ch}(\tau)$ – that is the kind of channels carrying values of type τ – and get is of sort $\text{Ch}(\text{Ch}(\tau))$. This kind of "typing" for π-terms allows us to rule out a program like (Buff $\mid \overline{\text{put}}\,xy \mid \overline{\text{get}}$) for instance, thus preventing some run-time errors (see [16]). However, we cannot exclude the processes $(\nu\text{put,get})(\text{Buff} \mid \overline{\text{get}}\,s)$, or $(\nu\text{put,get})(\text{Buff} \mid \overline{\text{put}}\,x \mid \overline{\text{put}}\,y)$, while intuitively we should, because both are deadlocked systems: since the channels put and get are restricted to be *local* by the "new" construct (ν), none of these two processes can ever conform to the protocol imposed by Buff.

In [5] we introduced a calculus, called π^*, or *the blue calculus*, which is a direct extension of both the π and the λ calculi, and we also designed a simple type system that encompasses both Curry's type discipline and Milner's sorting [16]. We made some notational modifications with respect to Milner's π-calculus: we regard an input $u(x_1, \ldots, x_n)P$ as a "resource located at u", where the resource is an abstraction, written $R = (\lambda x_1)\ldots(\lambda x_n)P$, and we call such an input a *declaration*, now written $\langle u \Leftarrow R \rangle$. As in the PICT programming language of Pierce and Turner [19,21], or the JOIN calculus of Fournet and Gonthier [7], we restrict replication to input processes, and we write $!u(x_1, \ldots, x_n)P$ as

$\langle u = (\lambda x_1)\ldots(\lambda x_n)P\rangle$. The main novelty is that in the blue calculus an abstraction is a first-class process, and correspondingly one is allowed to apply any process to a name. Then a message $\bar{u}v_1\cdots v_k$ is in fact the application of the name u to a series of [pointers to] arguments. More generally, we can define the λ-calculus application (MN) as (def $v = N$ in Mv), using the derived construct

$$(\text{def } u = R \text{ in } P) = (\nu u)(\langle u = R\rangle \mid P)$$

Regarding sorts and types, it is easy to see that, assuming a constant ok which is the only type for π-processes, a sort $\text{Ch}(\tau_1,\ldots,\tau_n)$ is nothing else than the type $(\tau_1 \to \cdots(\tau_n \to ok)\cdots)$ of a function taking a series of arguments and returning a process. In this way we provide a unified view of λ-calculus types and π-calculus sorts (see [5] for more details).

However, the type system of [5] does not guarantee very much, as far as the behavioural properties are concerned. For instance, although the λ-terms possess their usual types, like for instance $\mathbf{2} : (\tau \to \tau) \to (\tau \to \tau)$ where $\mathbf{2} = (\lambda f)(\lambda x)f(fx)$, we get as well some oddities: for example, even though $(\nu y)((\mathbf{2}y)z \mid \langle y \Leftarrow (\lambda x)x\rangle)$ is well-typed, evaluating this term results in $(\nu y)(yz)$, which is a deadlock. We should use here a more "resource conscious" type system, taking inspiration from Girard's Linear Logic [8]. In the type system we introduce in this paper, linearity constraints will be taken into account, using the style of Girard's "Logique Unifiée" (LU) [9].

Clearly, this is not enough to solve a problem as simple as the one posed by the buffer process. Here we must express some temporal properties into the types, to state for instance that a get can only follow a put. There is a standard way to do that in concurrency theory, which is to use Hennessy-Milner Logic HML [10], and more generally HML with recursion [13], since we want to specify recursive behaviours. We have noted that a declaration $\langle u \Leftarrow R\rangle$ is a synonym of "input on the u channel". Therefore it is natural to assign to such a term a type that says that an "input action" is performed on u, after which we get something of type σ, if this is the type of the resource. We denote this type $\langle u\rangle\sigma$, as usual. Then $P : \langle u\rangle\sigma$ means "P offers on the name u a resource of type σ". We only use a fragment of HML, without negation, for our purpose is to design a type system, not a proof system – which usually is related to some bisimilarity, and thus does not enjoy the subject reduction property (then our work contrasts with [3,13,14] for instance).

The notion of type we propose for processes, which previously was limited to just ok, is not only enriched with modal types $\langle u\rangle\sigma$ and recursion $\mu\xi.\tau$, but also with a kind of conjunction, denoted $\tau \otimes \sigma$ as the tensor product of linear logic, to type a system made of parallel components. Then for instance a type of the buffer process, written in blue style, is, assuming that the type of its content is τ and the type of the return channel is $\tau \to \sigma$:

$\text{rec}\,x.\langle\text{put} \Leftarrow (\lambda v)\langle\text{get} \Leftarrow (\lambda r)(rv \mid x)\rangle\rangle : \mu\xi.\langle\text{put}\rangle(\tau \to \langle\text{get}\rangle((\tau \to \sigma) \to (\sigma \otimes \xi)))$

To conclude this introduction, let us explain what is the difficulty in proving the type safety property (i.e. subject reduction) for our calculus: the type system tries to discover in a distributed program a possible sequentialisation of the messages that are sent to a given name, ensuring that there is an execution which is compatible with the "protocol" imposed on that name. For instance, a type inference for

$$(\text{Buff} \mid ((\text{get}\, r \mid \text{put}\, x) \mid \text{put}\, y))$$

will assume that $\text{put}\, x$ is first performed, then $\text{get}\, r$, and finally $\text{put}\, y$. Then in order to type a term one has to choose a particular decomposition of it. However, since we describe *asynchronous*, non-deterministic systems, where messages arrive from anywhere, without any predictable order, any possible execution should be, as far as typing is concerned, as good as the one chosen by the system. In other words, we have to show that a "distributed redex", that is a pair of remote subterms $\langle u \Leftarrow R \rangle$ and $u v_1 \cdots v_k$ of a typable system can always be turned, without disturbing the typing of the whole system, into a typable "local redex" $(\langle u \Leftarrow R \rangle \mid u v_1 \cdots v_k)$ (the typing of which can be transformed, by a kind of cut elimination, into a typing of $R v_1 \cdots v_k$). This is not so easy, because typing is *not* compatible with "chemical" transformations [4], allowing the components of a parallel system to freely move.

Related Work

The idea of using trace languages as types is not new. For instance, Abramsky, Gay and Nagarajan [1] developed a semantic framework for types, namely interaction categories, based on this idea. Regular trace expressions were also advocated by Nierstrasz in [18] as a possible candidate for providing an appropriate notion of type for concurrent objects. Here, by focusing on a type system and the subject reduction property, we make a further step in the specialization of the general notion of specification into that of type.

Some systems that enrich in a way the notion of sort, using traces, or more generally graphs, were recently proposed [12,20,22], with various aims. Kobayashi, for instance, proposes in [12] to enrich the typing context with some information about the ordering of the use of (linear) channel names, in order to achieve a deadlock-freedom property. This is somehow similar to the nesting of modalities in our system, though obviously, using ordering constraints one cannot cope with recursive agents that repeatedly offer communication on the same name. Yoshida' system [22] is perhaps closer to ours, in the sense that it provides meaningful types for π-terms – not just *ok*. The graph types of Yoshida look a bit more general than our modal types, since in a graph a node (similar to a modality) can be preceded by several independent nodes. A difference is that our system uses fairly standard means to deal with communication – or more generally interaction – namely a form of the logical cut rule. All sorting systems for the π-calculus I know (including the typing system of [5], which was designed to generalize Milner's sorting) miss such a relation between the transformation of typings – typically cut elimination – and computing – say by exchanging messages (with an exception regarding linear channels in [11]).

2. The Calculus

To define the terms of our calculus, we assume given a denumerable set $\mathcal{N}$ of names, ranged over by u, v, $w \ldots$, and we distinguish two kinds of names: (λ)-variables x, y, $z \ldots \in \mathcal{X}$ and references p, q, $r \ldots \in \mathcal{R}$. That is, $\mathcal{N}$ is the disjoint union of the two denumerable subsets $\mathcal{X}$ and $\mathcal{R}$. Then the syntax of the calculus is given by the following grammar:

$$P, Q, R \ldots ::= u \mid (\lambda x)P \mid (Px) \mid (\text{def } D \text{ in } P) \mid$$
$$(P \mid Q) \mid (\nu r)P \mid \langle r \Leftarrow R \rangle$$

where D is a sequence of definitions $x_1 = R_1, \ldots, x_n = R_n$. For convenience we allow a definition to be empty, regarding $(\text{def in } P)$ as identical to P. As usual, we abbreviate a sequence of abstractions $(\lambda x_1) \cdots (\lambda x_n)P$ into $(\lambda x_1 \ldots x_n)P$, and we write $Pz_1 \cdots z_n$ for a sequence of applications $(\cdots (Pz_1) \cdots z_n)$. In particular, we call $uz_1 \cdots z_n$ a *message* – this is an "asynchronous output" in π. We sometimes add some parentheses, writing for instance $((\lambda x)P)z$ or $((\nu r)P)z$. We denote by $\text{def}(D)$ the set of variables defined by D; these are bound in $(\text{def } D \text{ in } P)$. The constructs $(\lambda x)P$ and $(\nu r)P$ also act as binders for the names x and r respectively. We denote by $\text{fn}(P)$ the set of free names of P. The operation of substituting the name v for u in P, denoted $[v/u]P$, is only defined if u and v are of the same kind; as usual, this operation may require converting bound names, to avoid capturing v. We will in fact consider terms up to α-conversion, that is up to renaming of bound names.

The grammar given above defines only a subset of π^* as it was given in [5]. Namely, apart from the restricted usage of names, we replace the "floating definitions" $\langle x = R \rangle$ by the more "located" ones $(\text{def } x = R \text{ in } P)$, which in π^* were syntactic sugar for $(\nu x)(\langle x = R \rangle \mid P)$. This allows us to dispense with some odd structural manipulations we had in [5]. We can still regard the λ-terms as a particular kind of process, defining application as

$$(PQ) =_{\text{def}} (\text{def } x = Q \text{ in } Px)$$

provided that x is not free in P and Q. We will also use $\text{rec}\, x.P$ as syntactic sugar for $(\text{def } x = P \text{ in } x)$.

Now we describe how programs in our calculus compute. We define a reduction relation $P \to P'$, the main ingredient being "message passing", that is the transformation of $uz_1 \cdots z_n$ into $Rz_1 \cdots z_n$, where R is a resource found for u in the environment, either in a declaration or in a definition. The chemical metaphor (see [4]) would be perfect here, since we want to describe asynchronous computations, where no ordering is assumed on the messages for a given name. However, this style is difficult to maintain with typing purposes, therefore we use a more traditional style, with *evaluation contexts*. Nevertheless, we still informally distinguish a "heating phase" in the computing process,

$$(P \mid Q) \rightarrow (Q \mid P)$$
$$((\nu r)P \mid Q) \rightarrow (\nu r)(P \mid Q) \qquad\qquad r \notin \mathsf{fn}(Q)$$
$$((\mathsf{def}\ D\ \mathsf{in}\ P) \mid Q) \rightarrow (\mathsf{def}\ D\ \mathsf{in}\ P \mid Q) \qquad \mathsf{def}(D) \cap \mathsf{fn}(Q) = \emptyset$$
$$(\mathsf{def}\ D\ \mathsf{in}\ (\mathsf{def}\ D'\ \mathsf{in}\ P)) \rightarrow (\mathsf{def}\ D,\ D'\ \mathsf{in}\ P) \qquad \mathsf{fn}(D) \cap \mathsf{def}(D') = \emptyset$$
$$(\mathsf{def}\ D\ \mathsf{in}\ (\nu r)P) \rightarrow (\nu r)(\mathsf{def}\ D\ \mathsf{in}\ P) \qquad\qquad r \notin \mathsf{fn}(D)$$
$$(\mathsf{def}\ D\ \mathsf{in}\ P)x \rightarrow (\mathsf{def}\ D\ \mathsf{in}\ Px) \qquad\qquad x \notin \mathsf{def}(D)$$

———————————— **Table 1: Structural Rules** ————————————

which is described by the rules for structural manipulations, in Table 1. Structural transformations – as any other computing step – may be performed in any evaluation context, that is

$$P \rightarrow P' \ \Rightarrow\ \mathbf{E}[P] \rightarrow \mathbf{E}[P']$$

where evaluation contexts $\mathbf{E}$ are given by

$$\mathbf{E} ::= [] \mid (\mathbf{E}x) \mid (\mathbf{E} \mid P) \mid (P \mid \mathbf{E}) \mid (\nu r)\mathbf{E} \mid (\mathsf{def}\ D\ \mathsf{in}\ \mathbf{E})$$

and $\mathbf{E}[P]$ is defined in the obvious way.

Let us comment a little these rules: apart from the commutation of parallel components, the first two structural manipulations, for "scope migration", extract the binders (more precisely, restrictions and definitions) out of parallel composition, putting them on the top level. Then these are rearranged by means of the next two rules: the restrictions come first, then a compound definition (recall that everything is done up to α-conversion, so that the side conditions can always be met). In other words, any term P is transformed into another one having a "canonical form", namely:

$$P \xrightarrow{*} (\nu r_1 \ldots r_n)(\mathsf{def}\ D\ \mathsf{in}\ S)$$

where S is a "soup", the components of which do not immediately exhibit any binder other than an abstraction. Now, after this preliminary "heating phase", the "real" computation takes place. To state the "message passing" rules, δ and ϱ below, it is convenient to introduce another kind of context, consisting of a hole in a (special) soup:

$$\mathbf{P, Q, R} \ldots ::= [] \mid (\mathbf{P} \mid S) \mid (S \mid \mathbf{P})$$
$$S ::= A \mid (S \mid S) \qquad\qquad \textit{special soups}$$
$$A ::= (\lambda x)P \mid \langle r \Leftarrow P \rangle \mid M \qquad\qquad \textit{atoms}$$
$$M ::= u \mid (Mx) \qquad\qquad \textit{messages}$$

Reduction is not defined for soups containing components such as $(P \mid Q)x$, $\langle r \Leftarrow P \rangle z$ or $((\nu r)P)z$, but this is not really a restriction since these will be ruled out by the type system. For parallel systems $T = (T_1 \mid \cdots \mid T_k)$ where the T_i's

$$((\lambda x)P)z \rightarrow [z/x]P \qquad (\beta) \ (name \ instantiation)$$

$$(\text{def } D \text{ in } \mathbf{P}[xz_1 \cdots z_n]) \rightarrow (\text{def } D \text{ in } \mathbf{P}[Rz_1 \cdots z_n]) \quad \delta, \text{ where } x = R \in D$$

$$(\mathbf{P}[\langle r \Leftarrow R \rangle] \mid \mathbf{Q}[rz_1 \cdots z_n]) \rightarrow (Rz_1 \cdots z_n \mid (\mathbf{P} \mid \mathbf{Q}))^\diamond \quad \varrho \ (resource \ fetching)$$

Table 2: Reduction Rules
---

are either terms or the hole $[]$, we define $T^\diamond$ to be the result of shrinking the holes, using the law $(P \mid [])^\diamond = P = ([] \mid P)^\diamond$. Then the remaining reduction rules are given in the Table 2, and the reduction relation $\rightarrow$ is the least one containing all the rules and compatible with the evaluation contexts.

Clearly, the rule for resource fetching does not impose any order on the messages for a given name. Therefore, we can define a non-deterministic choice as follows:

$$P \oplus Q = (\nu pg)(\text{Buff} \mid (pP \mid (pQ \mid gI)))$$

where I is the identity function $(\lambda x)x$, and the "one-slot buffer" process is given by – writing simply p and g for the put and get operations:

$$\text{Buff} = \text{rec } x.\langle p \Leftarrow (\lambda z)\langle g \Leftarrow (\lambda y)(yz \mid x)\rangle\rangle$$

3. The Type System

The types are those of an applied λ-calculus, that is arrow types $\tau_1 \rightarrow \cdots \tau_n \rightarrow \sigma$, ending with a type variable (if any), or a basic type, among which are "process types", which we call *schedules*. These are basically products of modal types $\langle r \rangle \tau$, that give the type τ of a reference r. To define recursive schedules, we assume given a set Ξ of schedule variables. The syntax of types is then as follows:

$$\sigma, \tau, \zeta \ldots ::= \cdots \mid \psi \mid \tau \rightarrow \sigma \qquad \qquad types$$

$$\psi, \phi, \chi \ldots ::= \cdots \mid \xi \mid \mu\xi.\psi \mid \langle r \rangle \sigma \mid \mathbb{1} \mid (\psi \otimes \phi) \quad schedules$$

where $\xi \in \Xi$, and the $\cdots$ stand for any basic or variable type, of each kind. We denote by $\text{nm}(\sigma)$ the set of names occurring in σ, that is in a modal sub-type $\langle r \rangle \tau$, and we say that σ is *pure* if it contains no reference, i.e. $\text{nm}(\sigma) = \emptyset$, and no free schedule variable. We abbreviate $(\tau_1 \rightarrow (\cdots (\tau_n \rightarrow \sigma) \cdots))$ into $\tau_1 \cdots \tau_n \rightarrow \sigma$. We will always consider types up to α-conversion, that is up to the renaming of recursive schedule variables. In fact, we shall identify a recursive type τ with the infinite (regular) tree $\mathcal{A}(\tau)$ it determines, as it is standard (see [6] for instance). In particular, in the typing rules below, the equality of types is $\mathcal{A}(\tau) = \mathcal{A}(\sigma)$.

The type system we now introduce deals with sequents written in the style of Girard's LU [9]. In LU a sequent is $\Psi ; \Gamma \vdash \Delta ; \Phi$ where the central part Γ, Δ is *classical*, surrounded by the *linear* zones Ψ and Φ. Here the right-classical zone Δ will be empty, and the right-linear one Φ is a singleton. Then we actually deal with *intuitionistic* sequents, written $\Psi ; \Gamma \vdash P : \sigma$, where P is a term and σ a type. The classical zone Γ is, as usual, a mapping (exchange is implicit) from a

$$\frac{}{; \Gamma \vdash x : \tau} \; (^1) \qquad \frac{\Psi \,;\, x : \tau, \Gamma \vdash P : \sigma}{\Psi \,;\, \Gamma \vdash (\lambda x) P : \tau \to \sigma} \; (^2) \qquad \frac{\Psi \,;\, \Gamma \vdash P : \tau \to \sigma}{\Psi \,;\, \Gamma \vdash (Pz) : \sigma} \; (^3)$$

$$\frac{; \, x : \tau, \Gamma \vdash R : \tau \quad , \quad \Psi \,;\, x : \tau, \Gamma \vdash (\mathsf{def}\ D\ \mathsf{in}\ P) : \sigma}{\Psi \,;\, \Gamma \vdash (\mathsf{def}\ x = R,\, D\ \mathsf{in}\ P) : \sigma} \; (^4)$$

——————— **Table 3: the Type System (Classical Variables)** ———————

finite set $\mathsf{dom}(\Gamma)$ of names to types, with the restriction that the types assigned to variables are pure. This is written $u_1 : \tau_1, \ldots, u_k : \tau_k$, and whenever we write $u : \tau, \Gamma$ we implicitly mean $u \notin \mathsf{dom}(\Gamma)$. In this zone, we record in particular how, i.e. with which type, references can be used.

The linear zone Ψ is of the same kind, except that the types of the variables are not constrained here, and that we also allow here assumptions of the form $r : \sigma^\dagger$, where a type σ decorated with a † is what we call a *co-type*. These are used to record the fact that a declaration of a resource of type σ has been made for the reference r. Then Ψ is a mapping from a finite set of names to types and co-types. We denote by $\Psi^\dagger$ the part of Ψ which provides the co-types, and by $\mathsf{ref}(\Psi)$ the set of references that occur in a type (not a co-type) of the range of Ψ. The union of Ψ and Φ is denoted $\Psi + \Phi$, to emphasize the fact that this is only defined if Ψ and Φ coincide on the intersection of their domains. If they do not intersect, this is also denoted Ψ, Φ, as usual. We denote by $\Psi_{\lfloor u}$, and similarly for $\Gamma_{\lfloor u}$, the restriction of Ψ to $\mathsf{dom}(\Psi) - \{u\}$.

The type system will maintain some invariants, like for instance the fact that the variables declared in Ψ – the *linear variables* – are distinct from the variables in Γ – the *classical variables* (we should rather say: intuitionistic). Similarly, if $r : \sigma$ or $r : \sigma^\dagger$ occurs in Ψ, then the assumption $r : \sigma$ is also made in Γ. The linear variables are used to define recursive "objects" like the buffer process, while the classical ones are used in the λ-calculus part of the syntax. The references, even if they occur in the linear zone, are not, in a strict sense, linear, since several messages can be sent on these names, like in the buffer example. However, the type system will maintain, in the style of Amadio's π_1-calculus [2], a *unique location* principle for declarations (regarding replicated resources, the unique location principle is embodied in the standard $(\mathsf{def}\ D\ \mathsf{in}\ P)$ construct, as in the JOIN calculus [7]). This means that at any step of evaluation of a well-typed program, there is at most one declaration available for a given reference, which is then "linear" in this way. Then to type a term one must be able to properly sequentialize the messages sent to the references declared in a given (recursive) "object", following the "protocol" indicated by its type.

The rules of the type system are in Table 3 (continued on the next pages), annotated with side conditions given below, with comments. The first four rules deal with "classical variables". In these rules, the type τ is pure.

(^{1}) This is the "classical axiom", where $x \in \mathsf{dom}(\Gamma)$ and $\tau = \Gamma(x)$. It involves weakening for classical variables.

$$\frac{}{x:\sigma \,;\, \Gamma \vdash x:\sigma}\,(^5) \qquad \frac{x:\tau,\Psi^\dagger \,;\, \Gamma \vdash R:\tau \quad,\quad x:\tau,\Phi \,;\, \Gamma \vdash (\text{def } D \text{ in } P):\sigma}{\Psi^\dagger + \Phi \,;\, \Gamma \vdash (\text{def } x = R, D \text{ in } P):\sigma}\,(^6)$$

———————— **the Type System (Linear Variables)** ————————

(^{2}) The usual abstraction rule, introducing intuitionistic implication. Whenever the premise is provable, we have $x \notin \text{dom}(\Psi)$.

(^{3}) The application rule, where $z \in \text{dom}(\Gamma)$ and $\Gamma(z) = \tau$. The usual rule would use another premise $;\, \Gamma \vdash z:\tau$, but here this can only be an axiom.

(^{4}) This rule for (recursive) definitions is a kind of "linear/classical cut" (†). Recall that $(\text{def in } P) = P$. An obvious side condition we demand is that D does not capture any variable of $x = R$, that is $(\{x\} \cup \text{fn}(R)) \cap \text{def}(D) = \emptyset$. It can be checked that no free reference occurs in R, due to the assumption that the linear context in typing R is empty. We must make this assumption, since otherwise linear names could be duplicated by calling the definition several times.

These rules, where the linear context does not play any rôle, are quite standard. Now there are two rules regarding "linear variables", namely:

(^{5}) The linear axiom (for variables), involving weakening for classical names. We require that $x \notin \text{dom}(\Gamma)$.

(^{6}) The rule for "linear recursive definitions", which is a "linear/linear cut" (for variables). Whenever the premises are provable, we have $x \notin \text{dom}(\Gamma)$. Again, we assume that D does not capture any variable of $x = R$. The variable x is linear in both $(\text{def } D \text{ in } P)$ and in the body R of the definition. Then $x = R$ may be called several times (recursively, not simultaneously), and therefore we assume that R does not contain a call to any linear name other than x – namely, apart from $x:\tau$, the linear context for R is only made of co-types. Finally, we demand $\text{nm}(\tau) = \text{dom}(\Psi^\dagger)$ in this rule. This is easy to understand: for instance, a typing $\text{rec}\,x.R:\langle r \rangle \zeta$ is supposed to mean that $\text{rec}\,x.R$ offers a resource of type ζ on the name r. This could obviously be falsified – taking for instance $R = x$ – if we had not imposed the previous condition. Observe however that $;\, \Gamma \vdash \text{rec}\,x.x:\zeta$ is valid for any pure type ζ.

The last rules deal with references – except the rule for product, which is not specific to any particular kind of name. The first of them (^{7}), the linear axiom for references, is used to introduce references as the head of messages.

(^{8}) The rule for declarations introduces a resource type $\langle r \rangle \sigma$. As we said, we record with $r:\sigma^\dagger$ in the linear zone the fact that a declaration on r is made (possibly recursively). Since the classical zone records the type with which any name can be used, a side condition for this rule is $r \in \text{dom}(\Gamma)$ and $\Gamma(r) = \sigma$. For

---

(†) in LU there is no "classical/classical cut". For intuitionistic sequents the "classical/linear cut" is impossible, since the right-classical zone is empty. We shall see below two kinds of "linear/linear cut".

$$\frac{}{r:\sigma \; ; \; r:\sigma, \Gamma \vdash r:\sigma} \; (^7) \qquad \frac{\Psi \; ; \; \Gamma \vdash P:\sigma}{r:\sigma^\dagger + \Psi \; ; \; \Gamma \vdash \langle r \Leftarrow P \rangle : \langle r \rangle \sigma} \; (^8)$$

$$\frac{\Psi \; ; \; \Gamma \vdash P:\psi}{\Psi_{\lfloor r} \; ; \; \Gamma_{\lfloor r} \vdash (\nu r) P : (r) \psi} \; (^9) \qquad \frac{\Psi \; ; \; \Gamma \vdash P:\psi \;\;,\;\; \Phi \; ; \; \Gamma \vdash Q:\phi}{\Psi, \Phi \; ; \; \Gamma \vdash (P \mid Q), (Q \mid P):\psi \otimes \phi} \; (^{10})$$

$$\frac{\Psi \; ; \; \Gamma \vdash P:\chi \;\;,\;\; \Sigma, \Phi \; ; \; \Gamma \vdash Q:\phi}{\Psi, \Phi \; ; \; \Gamma \vdash (P \mid Q), (Q \mid P):\psi \otimes \phi} \; \chi \sim \psi \otimes \sigma, \;\; \partial(\sigma) = \Sigma \; (^{11})$$

──────────────── **the Type System (References)** ────────────────

technical reasons, we shall also assume that every reference in a declaration is itself declared, that is $\mathsf{dom}(\Psi) \cap \mathcal{R} = \mathsf{dom}(\Psi^\dagger)$.

(^{9}) Although this is perhaps not apparent, the rule for restriction is completely different from the one for a well-sorted $(\nu r)P$ in the π-calculus. The idea here is that one should not declare a reference r to be local to P unless we know for a fact that no demand on r is made in typing P, otherwise a deadlock could occur. That is, we require $r \notin \mathsf{ref}(\Psi) \cup \mathsf{dom}(\Psi - \Psi^\dagger)$ – whereas the usual rule would allow $r \in \mathsf{dom}(\Psi)$. In this rule the type ψ of P is supposed to be a schedule (not an arrow type). Since this type may record some offer on r – e.g. $\psi = \phi \otimes \langle r \rangle \sigma$ – we have to hide this in the resulting type for $(\nu r)P$. This is the purpose of the operation (r), which is the morphism on types determined by $(r)\langle r \rangle \sigma = \mathbb{1}$ (and $(r)\langle s \rangle \sigma = \langle s \rangle (r) \sigma$ if $r \neq s$, etc.).

We give two rules for parallel composition – though the first one is actually a special case of the second, we think this presentation is easier to understand. In these rules we use the following convention: the conclusion $(P \mid Q), (Q \mid P):\chi$ means that both $(P \mid Q):\chi$ and $(Q \mid P):\chi$ are valid.

(^{10}) This first rule simply introduces a product type $\psi \otimes \phi$. Notice that the components share the same classical context. That is, the use they make of references and classical variables is the same, as far as types are concerned. On the other hand, we have $\mathsf{dom}(\Psi) \cap \mathsf{dom}(\Phi) = \emptyset$, and in particular P and Q cannot both declare a given reference and cannot both use a given linear variable. To enforce the unique location principle, we require that

$$\big(\mathsf{ref}(\Psi) \cup \mathsf{dom}(\Psi)\big) \cap \big(\mathsf{ref}(\Phi) \cup \mathsf{dom}(\Phi)\big) = \emptyset \qquad (*)$$

The idea here is that, since an assumption $r:\sigma$ means that a resource for r, or any name in $\mathsf{nm}(\sigma)$, is assumed to be supplied by the environment, then by $(*)$ we enforce that the resource will not be supplied twice, and that it is not neglected if it is offered – e.g. if $r \in \mathsf{dom}(\Psi^\dagger)$.

(^{11}) This last rule is the most elaborate. It is a "linear/linear cut" rule (for references), which we call the *modal cut* rule. It allows for eliminating assumptions on references, namely $\Sigma = r_1 : \sigma_1, \ldots, r_k : \sigma_k$ in the rule (if $k = 0$, this is just the previous product rule). The type system ensures that $\Sigma \subseteq \Gamma$, therefore although some references may "disappear", we keep track of their type. Regarding the linear contexts, we still assume the same side condition $(*)$ as in the product rule. It just remains to explain $\chi \sim \psi \otimes \sigma$ and $\partial(\sigma) = \Sigma$. The relation $\sim$ is the least equivalence on schedules such that these types, equipped with $(\otimes, \mathbb{1})$, form a commutative monoid. The operation ∂ associates with schedules of the form $\langle r_1 \rangle \sigma_1 \otimes \cdots \otimes \langle r_k \rangle \sigma_k$, up to $\sim$, the context $r_1 : \sigma_1, \ldots, r_k : \sigma_k$ (the definition should be obvious).

One can see that a given reference r may occur free in both sides of a typable parallel system $(P \mid Q)$, for instance as the head of messages $r x_1 \cdots x_n$ and $r z_1 \cdots z_m$, with $r \in \mathrm{dom}(\Psi)$ and $r \in \mathrm{dom}(\Sigma, \Phi)$, but then a modal cut has to be made on this name from one component to the other, due to the condition $(*)$. This means that the type system ensures that there is a scheduling between the various messages to r. Let us see this with an example. If we let $\theta = \mu \xi . \langle p \rangle (\tau \to \langle g \rangle ((\tau \to \chi) \to (\chi \otimes \xi)))$ where τ is a given (pure) type, and χ a given (pure) schedule, and $\zeta = (\tau \to \chi) \to (\chi \otimes \theta)$ and $\sigma = \tau \to \langle g \rangle \zeta$, then one may check that for some appropriate Γ the following typing for the buffer process is valid:

$$p : \sigma^\dagger, \; g : \zeta^\dagger \; ; \; \Gamma \vdash \text{Buff} : \; \mu \xi . \langle p \rangle (\tau \to \langle g \rangle ((\tau \to \chi) \to (\chi \otimes \xi)))$$

Now regarding messages sent to the buffer object, one has for instance:

$$
\frac{
\dfrac{p : \sigma \; ; \; \Gamma \vdash p : \sigma}{p : \sigma \; ; \; \Gamma \vdash px : \langle g \rangle \zeta}
\qquad
\dfrac{g : \zeta \; ; \; \Gamma \vdash g : \zeta}{g : \zeta \; ; \; \Gamma \vdash gz : \chi \otimes \theta}
}{
p : \sigma \; ; \; \Gamma \vdash (gz \mid px) : \chi \otimes \theta
}
\qquad
\dfrac{p : \sigma \; ; \; \Gamma \vdash p : \sigma}{p : \sigma \; ; \; \Gamma \vdash py : \langle g \rangle \zeta}
$$

$$p : \sigma \; ; \; \Gamma \vdash ((gz \mid px) \mid py) : \chi \otimes \langle g \rangle \zeta$$

In this proof, there is a cut from px to gz: the "put" message px uses the hypothetical buffer, initially of type $\theta = \langle p \rangle \sigma$, and leaves it in a state of type $\langle g \rangle \zeta$, where a "get" can be performed. Then, after having accepted the put and the get, the (hypothetical) buffer object is in the state $(zx \mid \text{Buff})$ of type $\chi \otimes \theta$, which is precisely the type resulting from $(gz \mid px)$. Then another "put" py can be performed – that is, py can be cut from $(gz \mid px)$.

One can see that in this inference there is a "control thread", from px to gz, and then to py, along which the modal cuts are made. One could type the term $((gz \mid py) \mid px)$ in a similar way, but it is not possible to type $(gz \mid (px \mid py))$, because typing $(px \mid py)$ would require joining two similar assumptions for p, thus violating the condition $(*)$ in the rule for parallel composition (a cut is not possible here). Finally one can supply the buffer resource:

$$\vdots \qquad\qquad\qquad \vdots$$

$$\frac{p:\sigma^\dagger , \, g:\zeta^\dagger \, ; \, \Gamma \vdash \mathsf{Buff}: \langle p \rangle \sigma \qquad\qquad p:\sigma \, ; \, \Gamma \vdash ((gz \mid px) \mid py) : \chi \otimes \langle g \rangle \zeta}{p:\sigma^\dagger , \, g:\zeta^\dagger \, ; \, \Gamma \vdash (\mathsf{Buff} \mid ((gz \mid px) \mid py)) : \chi \otimes \langle g \rangle \zeta}$$

$$\frac{}{; \, \Gamma_{\lfloor p,g} \vdash (\nu pg)(\mathsf{Buff} \mid ((gz \mid px) \mid py)) : \chi}$$

One could have provided the resource immediately, thus inferring the same type for the system $((gz \mid (\mathsf{Buff} \mid px)) \mid py)$, but this must be done carefully: for instance $(((\mathsf{Buff} \mid gz) \mid px) \mid py)$ is *not* typable, since Buff declares g, but this declaration is not immediately available for "cutting" gz. This example shows that although some rearrangements are possible in a typing proof, this cannot be achieved by "local" means, like associativity of parallel composition: if for instance in typing $(P_0 \mid (P_1 \mid P_2))$ there must be a modal cut from P_2 onto P_1, and a cut from P_0 on P_2, then $((P_0 \mid P_1) \mid P_2)$ cannot be typed (using the rules we have adopted).

We christen our typing system $\mathcal{Z}$, and we write $\Psi \, ; \, \Gamma \vdash P : \sigma \, [\mathcal{Z}]$ to mean that this sequent is provable in the system. It is easy to see that, as far as λ-terms are concerned, typing in $\mathcal{Z}$ is the same as in the simple type system of Curry.

4. Type Safety

In this section we indicate, very briefly, how the subject reduction property is established.

THEOREM (SUBJECT REDUCTION) *If $P \to P'$ and $\Psi \, ; \, \Gamma \vdash P : \sigma \, [\mathcal{Z}]$ then $\Psi \, ; \, \Gamma \vdash P' : \sigma \, [\mathcal{Z}]$.*

It is immediate that, since $\mathcal{Z}$ is "compositional" – typing a term amounts to compose typings of its subterms – the "equitypability" relation is congruence. Therefore it is enough to consider the cases where $P \to P'$ is an instance of a structural rule, or of a rule among (β), δ or ϱ. All the cases, except the last one, are more or less straightforward, and the last three ones all amount to a form of cut elimination.

Regarding resource fetching, where $P = (\mathbf{P}[\langle r \Leftarrow R \rangle] \mid \mathbf{Q}[rz_1 \cdots z_n])$ and $P' = (Rz_1 \cdots z_n \mid (\mathbf{P} \mid \mathbf{Q}))^\circ$, the technique we use is rather unusual: as we suggested in the previous section, we have to show that some global reorganization of a typing proof can be done. The main steps are as follows. A preliminary fact to show is that a declaration $\langle r \Leftarrow R \rangle$ can be extracted out of a soup, that is:

CLAIM 1. *If $\Psi \, ; \, \Gamma \vdash \mathbf{P}[\langle r \Leftarrow R \rangle] : \psi \, [\mathcal{Z}]$ then $\Psi \, ; \, \Gamma \vdash (\langle r \Leftarrow R \rangle \mid \mathbf{P})^\circ : \psi \, [\mathcal{Z}]$.*

The proof relies on the fact that no modal cut can be made on a declaration, since no call on a reference is emitted from its body. This shows that supplying a resource can always be postponed up to the point where the corresponding name is declared to be local (this does not mean that we could restrict the syntax of declarations to "linear cuts" $(\nu r)(\langle r \Leftarrow R \rangle \mid P)$ – see the buffer example).

One can then see that in typing $(\langle r \Leftarrow R \rangle \mid (\mathbf{P} \mid \mathbf{Q}[rz_1 \cdots z_n])^\circ)$, the second component can only be typed by making an assumption about r, which is cut by the declaration. Then we show that making an assumption on r in typing a special soup means that there is a message on r that is the head of a "control thread", along which the modal cuts on r are made; this message can be extracted from the soup as the first one to serve. More precisely, we show:

CLAIM 2.   *Let S be a special soup. If $r : \sigma$, Φ ; $\Gamma \vdash S : \psi$ $[\mathcal{Z}]$ then there exist a (special) soup context $\mathbf{R}$ and variables $x_1, \ldots, x_n$ such that $S = \mathbf{R}[rx_1 \cdots x_n]$ and $r : \sigma$, Φ ; $\Gamma \vdash (rx_1 \cdots x_n \mid \mathbf{R})^\circ : \psi$ $[\mathcal{Z}]$ with a proof where not cut is made on $rx_1 \cdots x_n$.*

This crucial property is the most difficult to establish. It uses another fact, namely that all messages for a given reference in a soup have the same number (and type) of arguments, and therefore these messages (or rather, their arguments) can be exchanged without affecting the typing:

CLAIM 3.   *If Φ ; $\Gamma \vdash \mathbf{R}[rx_1 \cdots x_n] : \psi$ $[\mathcal{Z}]$, where ψ is a schedule, then $\Gamma(r) = \tau_1 \cdots \tau_n \to \phi$ for some $\tau_1, \ldots, \tau_n$ such that $\Gamma(x_i) = \tau_i$. Moreover for any $z_1, \ldots, z_n$ such that $\Gamma(z_i) = \tau_i$, we have Φ ; $\Gamma \vdash \mathbf{R}[rz_1 \cdots z_n] : \psi$ $[\mathcal{Z}]$.*

The type safety property has some immediate consequences, such as the *unique location of declarations* property: if $P \xrightarrow{*} P'$, and P is typable, then for any subterm $(Q \mid R)$ of P', the components Q and R do not declare a same reference. Similarly, P' cannot contain a subterm $(Q \mid R)x$, or $\langle r \Leftarrow R \rangle x$, or else $((\lambda x)Q \mid R)$, nor any immediately deadlocked subsystem like $(\nu r)rx_1 \cdots x_n$. The reader can easily check that the examples given in the introduction, namely $(\nu pg)(\mathsf{Buff} \mid gx)$ and $(\nu pg)((\mathsf{Buff} \mid px) \mid py)$ are also ruled out by our type system.

5. Conclusion

We have introduced a new type system for a calculus which is (a variant of) a direct extension of the π-calculus, and established the type safety property. Even if this is a crucial property for typed languages, this is clearly only a preliminary result. The underlying, untyped calculus is very expressive, but one should get some idea about how far this expressiveness is limited by the typing system. We shall return to this point below. As a matter of fact, our original motivation was (and still is) to show that the type system we propose guarantees a kind of *deadlock-freedom* property. What we have in mind is something like this: a term P is deadlock-free if, for any reduction – that puts it in a canonical form, but for typable terms this can always be done while preserving equitypability – that exhibits a message for a name whose scope is fixed, i.e.

$$P \xrightarrow{*} (\nu r_1 \ldots r_k)(\mathsf{def}\ D\ \mathsf{in}\ \mathbf{P}[uz_1 \cdots z_n])$$

where u is bound, then a corresponding resource will eventually be offered. In other words, in a well-typed process there should be no message which is forever not understood. It is easy to see that if u is a variable, then a definition for u actually exists in D, if P is well-typed. Then the only problem is with references. In this case, one has to show that, roughly speaking:

$$P \xrightarrow{*} (\mathbf{R}[\langle r \Leftarrow R \rangle] \mid \mathbf{Q})$$

We are currently working on this topic, using a realizability technique. Let us just say that using the modal types of HML seems to be a natural approach here.

Coming back to the expressivity question, one may notice that, for instance, the following attempt to write a *reference cell* (see [7,12,21]) "as usual", that is

$$\text{Cell } v = (\nu s)\big(\text{def read} = (\lambda y)\langle s \Leftarrow (\lambda u)(yu \mid su)\rangle,$$
$$\text{write} = (\lambda w)\langle s \Leftarrow (\lambda v)sw \rangle$$
$$\text{in } sv \mid \text{mkCell read write}\big)$$

fails to be typable. Indeed, this term is not deadlock-free in our sense: the private message sv representing the local state of the cell is not undertsood. One could try to restrict the notion of deadlock, but this looks difficult here, since there is no control on the classical names read and write. As a matter of fact, there is another standard way to write the cell, using the sum operator $P + Q$ (see [21], where Turner uses a synchronous π-calculus). Extending the calculus with "input guarded sums" $\langle r_1 \Leftarrow R_1 \rangle + \cdots + \langle r_k \Leftarrow R_k \rangle$, we can write a cell as follows:

$$\text{Cell} = \text{rec } x.(\lambda v)\big(\,\langle \text{read} \Leftarrow (\lambda y)(yv \mid xv)\rangle$$
$$+ \langle \text{write} \Leftarrow (\lambda w)xw \rangle\,\big)$$

To type this term we must extend the typing system, and a natural way is to use additive conjunction $\psi \& \phi$ (with a multiplicative management of the co-types) to type guarded sums. Moreover, we should extend the typing system with linear arrows $\tau \multimap \sigma$, in order to be able to type "synchronous output" like $(\nu r)(\text{read } r \mid \langle r \Leftarrow (\lambda v)P \rangle)$. We leave these possible extensions for further work.

REFERENCES

[1] S. ABRAMSKY, S. GAY, R. NAGARAJAN, *Interaction categories and the foundations of typed concurrent programming*, in Deductive Program Design (M. Broy, Ed), NATO ASI Series F (1995).

[2] R. AMADIO, *An asynchronous model of locality, failure, and process mobility*, INRIA Res. Report 3109 (1997) to appear in the Proceedings of the Conference COORDINATION'97.

[3] R. AMADIO, M. DAM, *Toward a modal theory of types for the π-calculus*, Formal Techniques in Real-Time and Fault Tolerant Systems'96, Lecture Notes in Comput. Sci. 1135 (1996).

[4]   G. BERRY, G. BOUDOL, *The chemical abstract machine*, Theoretical Comput. Sci. 96 (1992) 217-248.

[5]   G. BOUDOL, *The π-calculus in direct style*, POPL'97 (1997) 228-241.

[6]   F. CARDONE, M. COPPO, *Two extensions of Curry's type inference system*, in Logic and Computer Science (P. Odifreddi, Ed.), Academic Press (1990) 19-75.

[7]   C. FOURNET, G. GONTHIER, *The reflexive* CHAM, *and the join calculus*, POPL'96 (1996) 372-385.

[8]   J.-Y. GIRARD, *Linear Logic*, Theoretical Comput. Sci. 50 (1987) 1-102.

[9]   J.-Y. GIRARD, *On the unity of logic*, Annals of Pure and Applied Logic 59 (1993) 201-217.

[10] M. HENNESSY, R. MILNER, *Algebraic laws for nondeterminism and concurrency*, JACM 32 (1985) 137-161.

[11] N. KOBAYASHI, B. PIERCE, D. TURNER, *Linearity and the π-calculus*, POPL'96 (1996) 358-371.

[12] N. KOBAYASHI, *A partially deadlock-free typed process calculus*, Proceedings of LICS'97 (1997) 128-139.

[13] K. G. LARSEN, *Proof systems for satisfiability in Hennessy-Milner logic with recursion*, Theoretical Comput. Sci. 72 (1990) 265-288.

[14] M. MICULAN, F. GADDUCI, *Modal μ-types for processes*, LICS'95 (1995) 221-231.

[15] R. MILNER, J. PARROW, D. WALKER, *A calculus of mobile processes*, Information and Computation 100 (1992) 1-77.

[16] R. MILNER, *The polyadic π-calculus: a tutorial*, Technical Report ECS-LFCS-91-180, Edinburgh University (1991) Reprinted in *Logic and Algebra of Specification*, F. Bauer, W. Brauer and H. Schwichtenberg, Eds, Springer Verlag, 1993, 203-246.

[17] O. NIERSTRASZ, *Composing Active Objects*, In Research Directions in Concurrent Object-Oriented Programming (G. Agha, P. Wegner and A. Yonezawa Eds), MIT Press (1993) 151-171.

[18] O. NIERSTRASZ, *Regular Types for Active Objects*, Chapter 4 of Object-Oriented Software Composition (O. Nierstrasz and D. Tsichritzis, Eds), Prentice Hall (1995) 99-121.

[19] B. PIERCE, *Programming in the π-calculus – A Tutorial Introduction to Pict*, available electronically, Computer Science Department, Indiana University (1997).

[20] K. TAKEUCHI, K. HONDA, M. KUBO, *An interaction-based language and its typing system*, PARLE'94, Lecture Notes in Comput. Sci. 817 (1994).

[21] D. TURNER, *The Polymorphic Pi-calculus: Theory and Implementation*, Ph.D. Thesis, University of Edinburgh (1995).

[22] N. YOSHIDA, *Graph types for monadic mobile processes*, FST-TCS'96, Lecture Notes in Comput. Sci. 1180 (1996) 371-386.

An Imperative Language with Read/Write Type Modes

Paul Roe

Queensland University of Technology, Brisbane, Australia
p.roe@qut.edu.au

Abstract. Reading and writing of data is fundamental in computing, as is its control. However control of reading and writing has traditionally only been available at the level of file systems, and not programming language data structures. In this paper a simple imperative language is described which uses type modes to control reading and writing of data. A type may be labelled read-write or read-only; a read-only type is guaranteed by the type system not to be written. Furthermore a read-write type may be treated read-only in a sub-context. To achieve this implicit aliasing is prevented and the program heap is partitioned into collections. Collections form a unit of read-write control of heap allocated data, by isolating different heap regions. Collections were originally introduced in the Euclid and Turing programming languages for aliasing control; however this was rather restrictive and not strictly enforced. Controlling aliasing is beneficial in its own right since aliasing is a common source of programming errors.

1   Introduction

Reading and writing of data is fundamental in computing, as is its control. However control of reading and writing has traditionally only been available at the level of file systems, and not programming language data structures. Clearly it is desirable for a programming language to be capable of specifying and enforcing controls on the reading and writing of data. In particular this is useful for: documentation, software engineering (more rigorous programming), formal reasoning about programs and security eg for persistent systems or distributed computing (applets).

In this paper a simple imperative language is described which uses *type modes* to specify the read/write attributes of data. Only data of type read-write may be written; data of type read-only is guaranteed not to be written. These are strong guarantees, enforced by the programming language's type system. Furthermore the type system safely permits data of read-write type to be treated read-only in a sub-context. Languages such as C and Ada support constant parameter passing modes; however this is not guaranteed in the presence of aliasing and only operates at a shallow level. The language presented here overcomes these limitations.

To make strong guarantees concerning read-write attributes of data, implicit aliasing must be prevented. For example, a variable of type read-only must not be aliased to one of a writable type. However explicit aliasing via pointers is useful; to support this the program heap is partitioned into *collections*. Collections form a unit of read-write control of heap allocated data, by isolating different heap regions. Collections were originally introduced in the Euclid [9] and, its successor, Turing [6, 7] programming languages for aliasing control. However collections in these systems were rather restrictive and aliasing was not strictly enforced. Controlling aliasing is beneficial in its own right since unintentional aliasing is a common source of programming errors. The idea of statically controlling aliasing has been around for a long time, eg [4, 10].

The remainder of this paper is organised as follows: the next section informally describes the language, Section 3 formally describes the language's type system, the last sections describe related work and, conclusions and future work.

2 The Language: Informal Introduction

The philosophy taken was to create a small, first order, imperative language, similar to existing languages, other than its control of reading and writing. The language is only a toy one, but is sufficiently expressive to demonstrate key ideas. It could be easily extended with additional control constructs, data types, nested procedures, global variables etc. The most important omissions from the language are: modules and type abstraction; the latter is discussed in the final section.

2.1 Simple types

A program consists of a set of procedure definitions, one of which is called **main**, eg:

```
proc main
var i: *int
begin
  i := 42
  print(i)
end
```

The language supports basic data types (integers, booleans and pointers), and records. Each basic type has an associated mode: read-only denoted "-" or read-write "*". In the above example, the variable i may be assigned to because it has a read-write type (*). If it was declared as having type -int, assigning to i would be a type error. (As such i would be useless since it could not be written; however the language does not prevent the writing of such programs.) Note, the language has no global variables and procedures cannot be nested. To understand the subtleties of the programming language, assignment must be understood as a copying operation: it *copies* a value into a location.

Type modes subsume parameter passing mechanisms. For example the **print** procedure is declared thus:

```
proc print (i: -int)
begin
  ...
end
```

Thus **print** takes a single integer parameter which is read-only within the context of the procedure. A read-write type is compatible with a read-only formal parameter, but the converse does not hold.

Record types are not moded, but their fields, if of basic type, are eg:

```
proc recexample (r: rec i: *int, b: -bool end)
begin
  if r.b then r.i := 42 end
  print(r.i)
end
```

The boolean field, b, cannot be written, only read. In general using modes on basic types to control reading and writing necessitates the use of structural type equivalence.

Arrays are treated like single element variables. All elements of an array are identified with the array since an indexing operation may access any element of the array. Thus writing to any array element is equivalent to writing to all elements, eg:

```
proc arrayexample (a: array [100] *int)
var i: *int
begin
  i := 0
  while i#100 do
    a[i] := i
    i := i+1
  end
end
```

Arrays are indexed from zero, of statically known size, and type equivalent by structure including size. Arrays may be multidimensional.

Aliasing is only permitted of constant, read-only, types, eg:

```
proc foo(i: *int, j: *int)
begin end

proc bar(i: -int, j: -int)
begin end

proc main
var x: *int, y: *int
begin
  foo(x,y)     -- ok
```

```
  -- foo(x,x) -- error, aliasing actual to r/w formals
  bar(x,x)    -- ok, since formals are constant
end
```

Notice how a read-write typed actual parameter is compatible with multiple read-only formal parameters. Thus the language has some similarities with linear type systems. Read-write types are like linear types; a read-write value can only be bound to a single variable (identifier).

2.2 Complex Types: Pointers and Collections

Complex types involving pointers necessitate collections. Collections are used to partition the program heap. A collection consists of a bag of values of some type. All pointers point into some collection, and type recursion is only possible through collections. Pointers are only assignment compatible if they refer to the same collection. For example a collection representing list cells may be defined thus:

```
proc main
collection list = rec i: *int, n: *ptr list end
var l1 = *ptr list, l2 = *ptr list
begin
  new(l2)  l2^.i := 2  l2^.n := nil
  new(l1)  l1^.i := 1  l1^.n := l2
end
```

The keyword collection declares new collections, in much the same way as var declares local variables. Each collection contains one type of element. All elements of a collection are identified with the collection since a pointer may point to any element of the collection. Collections are rather like dynamically sized arrays.

Procedures may be parameterised on collections, eg. list length procedure:

```
proc len <list = rec i: -int, n: -ptr list end>
         (l: -ptr list, i: *int)
var t: *ptr list
begin
  i := 0   t := l
  while t # nil do
     i := i + 1
     t := t^.n
  end
end
```

Collection parameters are enclosed in angle braces. Actual collections are not supplied as explicit arguments. For example len may be invoked thus: len(l1,i).

The key point is that actual collections are matched against formal collections by structure. Thus len can be invoked on lists in different collections; this is in stark contrast to the Euclid and Turing languages. Formal collections are ignored if they are not used in formal parameters.

In the example above notice how a cursor (t) is used to traverse the read-only list structure. The type of the list collection guarantees that the list will not be changed by this procedure. Using cursors to traverse data structures like this is a common pattern of computation and the types provide a useful description of this.

Collection parameters can be aliased, like ordinary parameters. However in addition collections may be combined: multiple actual collections can be bound to one formal collection. In both cases, collection aliasing or combination, collections must have a read-only type. In the case of aliasing this prevents inconsistencies if collection aliases are treated differently, and in the case of collection combination it prevents implicit cross collection pointers from being formed.

Furthermore a value cannot be aliased by being bound to part of a collection formal parameter and by also being bound to a conventional formal parameter; unless it is constant in both situations. For example an invocation such as len(11,11^.n) is illegal (type incorrect) since the list collection formal parameter and formal parameter i are aliased, and i has a read-write type.

Another example, a procedure to concatenate two lists together, belonging to the same collection:

```
proc listconcat <list = rec i: -int, n: *ptr list end>
                (x: *ptr list, y: -ptr list)
var z: *ptr list
begin
   if x=nil then x := y else
      z := x
      while z^.n # nil do  z := z^.n  end
      z^.n := y
   end
end
```

The type of the list collection states that the list structure (pointers) may be changed, but the elements (integers) will not change.

List head and tail may be defined in a similar way:

```
proc head <list = rec i: -int, n: -ptr list end>
          (l: -ptr list, i: *int)
begin
   if l#nil then i := l^.i end
end
```

```
proc tail <list = rec i: -int, n: *ptr list end> (l: *ptr list)
begin
   if l#nil then l := l^.n end
end
```

Like list length, the type of list head guarantees that the list is not changed, and that the parameter n cannot be part of the list. List tail is more interesting, and reveals the nature of the restricted programming model which arises using collections and only explicit aliasing. As previously mentioned a read-write value cannot be bound to a formal parameter and be part of a collection formal parameter. Thus the parameter to tail cannot actually be part of the list structure itself. This is illustrated in the example below:

```
proc main
collection list = rec i: *int, n: *ptr list end
var l1 = *ptr list, l2 = *ptr list
begin
  new(l2)   l2^.i := 2   l2^.n := nil
  new(l1)   l1^.i := 1   l1^.n := l2
  -- tail(l1^.n) -- illegal, l1^.n is part of the list collection
  tail(l1)          -- ok since l1 is not part of the list collection
end
```

Effectively a style of programming arises where root, external, pointers to collections are distinguished from internal ones. This is rather restrictive, particularly for recursive algorithms. However, it is usually possible to copy an internal pointer to a local variable in order to overcome this restriction.

Therefore the type of tail can be rewritten thus, without loss of applicability:

```
proc tail <list = rec i: -int, n: -ptr list end> (l: *ptr list)
begin
    if l#nil then l := l^.n end
end
```

3 The Formal Type System

The abstract syntax for the language is shown in Figure 1 and the types in Figure 2. All basic types have an associated mode: -, * or !. The role of ! will be explained later. A special type () is used for commands.

The type rules are shown in Figures 3 and 4. The rules have the form: $\Gamma \vdash S : T$ where S is one of the categories of abstract syntax. The type of the environments used for type checking are: $\Gamma, \Delta : Id \mapsto T$. (The predicate *Check-ColPointers* is not shown, it checks that pointer types refer to collections which are in scope.)

Most of the type rules are straightforward. A few noteworthy ones are discussed. Assignment type compatibility is checked by the := relation (Figure 5) having form: $T := U$ where T and U are types. It requires the basic type components of an assignment target to have read-write modes. Thus if a record is assigned to, all its components must be writable.

The type of **new** is rather strange in that it only requires the pointer to be writable, but the collection could be read-only; however in such a context the new element could not be set.

Programs	*Prog*	$= Pd^*$
Procedure decls	*Pd*	$=$ **proc** *Id Cp Vp Cd Vd C*
Collection params/decls	*Cp, Cd*	$= (Col = T)^*$
Variable params/decls	*Vp, Vd*	$= (Id : T)^*$
Collections	*Col*	$= Id$
Commands	*C*	$= L := E \mid$ **new** *L*
		$\mid$ **skip** $\mid C_1 ; C_2$
		$\mid$ **if** E **do** C **end** $\mid$ **while** E **do** C **end**
		$\mid$ **call** *Id* E^*
Expressions	*E*	$= L \mid Integer \mid$ **nil**
		$\mid E_1 + E_2 \mid E_1 < E_2$
L-Expressions	*L*	$= Id \mid L.Lb \mid L^\wedge \mid L[E^*]$
Labels	*Lb*	
Identifiers	*Id*	

Fig. 1. Abstract Syntax

All of the complexity in the type system is involved in type checking procedure calls:

$$
\begin{array}{ll}
(1) & \Gamma(P) = proc\ CL\ (U_1 \dots U_n) \\
(2) & \Gamma \rightarrow \bigoplus_{i=0\dots n} \Gamma_i \quad \forall_{i=1\dots n} : \ \Gamma_i \vdash E_i : T_i \\
(3) & \Delta = \{Col \mapsto T \mid (Col = T) \in CL\} \\
(4) & \mathcal{C} \subseteq dom(\Gamma) \times dom(\Delta) \quad Check(\mathcal{C}, \Delta) \\
(5) & \forall_{i=1\dots n} : \ \mathcal{C} \vdash T_i \Rightarrow U_i \\
(6) & \forall(Col, Col') \in \mathcal{C} : \ \mathcal{C} \vdash \Gamma_0(Col) \Rightarrow \Delta(Col')
\end{array}
$$
$$\Gamma \vdash \textbf{call}\ P\ (E_1 \dots E_n) : ()$$

Line 1 simply looks up the procedure's type in the environment, but note the language is only first order. The general approach is similar to that taken for linear type systems; essentially the environment and its types are partitioned, using a three place relation $(X \rightarrow Y \oplus Z)$ (line 2, defined in Figure 6) such that if a value (a variable or collection in the environment) has a read-write type it only occurs in one partition. The special type mode ! is used in other partitions to denote that the type (value) is unavailable. Each actual parameter is checked in one of the environment partitions. Thus each actual parameter which must be used read-write can only be bound to one formal parameter, since it is only moded read-write in one environment partition (in others it is "!").

A mini-environment of formal collections is created, line 3, for actual to

$$
\begin{aligned}
\text{Types} \quad T, U, V = {} & M\,B \mid \\
& \mid\ rec\ (Lb : T)^* \\
& \mid\ array\ [Nat^*]\,T \\
& \mid\ proc\ (Col = T)^*\ T^* \\
& \mid\ ()
\end{aligned}
$$

$$
\text{Basic Types } B, B' = int \mid bool \mid nil \mid ptr\ Col
$$

$$
\text{Type Modes } M, ? = -\mid * \mid\,!
$$

Fig. 2. Types

Programs

$$
\Gamma' = \Gamma \uplus \biguplus_{i=1\ldots n}\{P_i \mapsto proc\ Cp_i\ (T|T \in Vp_i)\ where\ Pd_i = \mathbf{proc}\ P_i\ Cp_i\ Vp_i\ \text{---}\}
$$
$$
\forall_{i=1\ldots n}:\ \Gamma' \vdash Pd_i : ()
$$
$$
\overline{\Gamma \vdash Pd_1 \ldots Pd_n : ()}
$$

Procedures

$$
CheckColPointers(Cp,\ Vp,\ Cd,\ Vd)
$$
$$
\Gamma' = \{Col \mapsto T|(Col = T) \in Cp\} \uplus \{Id \mapsto T|(Id : T) \in Vp\} \uplus
$$
$$
\{Col \mapsto T|(Col = T) \in Cd\} \uplus \{Id \mapsto T|(Id : T) \in Vd\}
$$
$$
\Gamma' \vdash C : ()
$$
$$
\overline{\Gamma \vdash \mathbf{proc}\ Id\ Cp\ Vp\ Cd\ Vd\ C : ()}
$$

$$
X \uplus Y = if\ dom(X) \cap dom(Y) = \emptyset\ then\ X \cup Y\,else\ undefined
$$

Fig. 3. Type Checking: Programs and Procedures ($\Gamma \vdash Prog :\ T,\ \Gamma \vdash Pd :\ T$)

formal collection compatibility checking. In line 4 a map between actual and formal collections is created: $C : Col \times Col$. In addition the map is subject to the constraints imposed by *Check* (Figure 7). The *Check* predicate ensures that if actual and formal collections are not in a simple one to one correspondence then the formal collections involved must be constant.

Actual parameter types are checked for compatibility with formal parameter types (line 5) using the $\Rightarrow$ relation having form: $C \vdash T \Rightarrow U$. This relation, defined in Figure 8, checks that: types are the same, type modes are compatible, and that any collection mappings occur in C, and hence are valid. Note that

Commands

$$\frac{\Gamma \vdash LE : T \quad \Gamma \vdash E : U \quad T := U}{\Gamma \vdash LE := E : ()} \qquad \frac{\Gamma \vdash LE : *ptr\ Col}{\Gamma \vdash \mathbf{new}\ LE : ()}$$

$$\Gamma \vdash \mathbf{skip} : ()$$

$$\frac{\Gamma \vdash C_1 : () \quad \Gamma \vdash C_2 : ()}{\Gamma \vdash C_1 ; C_2 : ()} \qquad \frac{\Gamma \vdash E : ?bool \quad \Gamma \vdash C : ()}{\Gamma \vdash \mathbf{if/while}\ E\ \mathbf{do}\ C\ \mathbf{end} : ()}$$

$$\frac{\begin{array}{c} \Gamma(P) = proc\ CL\ (U_1 \ldots U_n) \\ \Gamma \to \bigoplus_{i=0\ldots n} \Gamma_i \quad \forall_{i=1\ldots n} : \Gamma_i \vdash E_i : T_i \\ \Delta = \{Col \mapsto T \mid (Col = T) \in CL\} \\ \mathcal{C} \subseteq dom(\Gamma) \times dom(\Delta) \quad Check(\mathcal{C}, \Delta) \\ \forall_{i=1\ldots n} : \mathcal{C} \vdash T_i \Rightarrow U_i \\ \forall(Col, Col') \in \mathcal{C} : \mathcal{C} \vdash \Gamma_0(Col) \Rightarrow \Delta(Col') \end{array}}{\Gamma \vdash \mathbf{call}\ P\ (E_1 \ldots E_n) : ()}$$

Expressions

$$\Gamma \vdash Integer : -int, \qquad \Gamma \vdash \mathbf{nil} : -nil$$

$$\frac{\Gamma \vdash E_1 : ?int \quad \Gamma \vdash E_2 : ?int}{\Gamma \vdash E_1 + E_2 : -int} \qquad \frac{\Gamma \vdash E_1 : ?int \quad \Gamma \vdash E_2 : ?int}{\Gamma \vdash E_1 < E_2 : -bool}$$

L-Expressions

$$\Gamma \vdash Id : \Gamma(Id)$$

$$\frac{\Gamma \vdash LE : rec \ldots (Lb : T) \ldots}{\Gamma \vdash LE.Lb : T} \qquad \frac{\Gamma \vdash LE : ?ptr\ Col \quad \Gamma(Col) = T}{\Gamma \vdash LE^\wedge : T}$$

$$\frac{\Gamma \vdash LE : array\ [N_1 \ldots N_n] T \quad \forall_{i=1\ldots n} : \Gamma \vdash E_i : ?int}{\Gamma \vdash LE[E_1 \ldots E_n] : T}$$

Fig. 4. Type Checking: Commands and Expressions $(\Gamma \vdash C : T, \ \Gamma \vdash E : T)$

the relation has no rules for ! moded types, hence such types are prohibited in actual parameter types. However importantly "!" moded types can be used during actual parameter evaluation.

In the final line (6) the types of actual collections are checked for compatibility with the types of formal collections using the $\Rightarrow$ relation. Thus for a procedure call, the transitive closure of all pairs of actual and formal collections which will become bound are checked for parameter type compatibility.

Note that the call type environment Γ is partitioned into $n + 1$ parts, where

$$*B := ?B, \qquad *ptr\ Col := ?nil$$

$$\frac{\forall_{i=1\ldots n}:\ T_i := U_i}{rec\,(Lb_1 : T_1)\ldots(Lb_n : T_n) := rec\,(Lb_1 : U_1)\ldots(Lb_n : U_n)}$$

$$\frac{T := U}{array\,[N_1\ldots N_n]\,T := array\,[N_1\ldots N_n]\,U}$$

Fig. 5. Assignment Type Compatibility $(T := U)$

Environments

$$\Delta_n \rightarrow \bigoplus_{i=0\ldots n} \Gamma_i\ =\ \Delta_i \rightarrow \Gamma_i \oplus \Delta_{i-1}, \qquad \Delta_0 = \Gamma_0$$

$$\{\} \rightarrow \{\} \oplus \{\}$$

$$\frac{T \rightarrow U \oplus V}{\{Id \mapsto T\} \rightarrow \{Id \mapsto U\} \oplus \{Id \mapsto V\}} \qquad \frac{\Gamma \rightarrow \Gamma_1 \oplus \Gamma_2 \quad \Delta \rightarrow \Delta_1 \oplus \Delta_2}{\Gamma \uplus \Delta \rightarrow (\Gamma_1 \uplus \Delta_1) \oplus (\Gamma_2 \uplus \Delta_2)}$$

Types

$$*B \rightarrow *B \oplus !B, \quad *B \rightarrow !B \oplus *B, \quad *B \rightarrow -B \oplus -B,$$
$$-B \rightarrow -B \oplus -B, \quad !B \rightarrow !B \oplus !B$$

$$\frac{\forall_{i=1\ldots n}:\ T_i \rightarrow U_i \oplus V_i}{rec\,(Lb_1 : T_1)\ldots(Lb_n : T_n) \rightarrow rec\,(Lb_1 : U_1)\ldots(Lb_n : U_n)\ \oplus}$$
$$rec\,(Lb_1 : V_1)\ldots(Lb_n : V_n)$$

$$\frac{T \rightarrow U \oplus V}{array\,[N_1\ldots N_n]\,T \rightarrow array\,[N_1\ldots N_n]\,U\ \oplus\ array\,[N_1\ldots N_n]\,V}$$

Fig. 6. Environment and Type Partitioning Relation $(X \rightarrow Y \oplus Z)$

there are n parameters; a separate environment partition is used for checking collection type compatibility. This ensures that a value in an actual collection cannot be simultaneously bound to a formal parameter and part of a formal collection; unless it is constant in both situations. For example it prevents procedure calls such as: `len(l1,l1^.n)` (see previous section).

An interesting feature of the formal description is that it supports mutual type recursion, via collections, often omitted in such descriptions.

$$Check(\mathcal{C}, \Delta) \;=\; \forall(a,b) \in \mathcal{C}: \forall(c,d) \in \mathcal{C}:\; [a{=}c \;\&\; b{\neq}d \Rightarrow con\,(\Delta(d)) \;\&\; con\,(\Delta(b))] \;\& \\ [a{\neq}c \;\&\; b{=}d \Rightarrow con\,(\Delta(d))]$$

$$con\,(-B) \qquad \frac{con\,(T_1)\,\ldots\,con\,(T_n)}{con\,(rec\,(Lb_1 : T_1)\ldots(Lb_n : T_n))} \qquad \frac{con\,(T)}{con\,(array\,[N_1 \ldots N_n]\,T)}$$

Fig. 7. Collection Aliasing and Combination Check

Modes

$$* \Rightarrow *, \qquad * \Rightarrow -, \qquad - \Rightarrow -$$

Types

$$\frac{M \Rightarrow M'}{\mathcal{C} \vdash M\,int \Rightarrow M'\,int} \qquad \frac{M \Rightarrow M'}{\mathcal{C} \vdash M\,bool \Rightarrow M'\,bool} \qquad \frac{M \Rightarrow M'}{\mathcal{C} \vdash M\,nil \Rightarrow M'\,ptr\,Col}$$

$$\frac{M \Rightarrow M' \quad (Col, Col') \in \mathcal{C}}{\mathcal{C} \vdash M\,ptr\,Col \Rightarrow M'\,ptr\,Col'}$$

$$\frac{\forall_{i=1\ldots n}: \;\mathcal{C} \vdash T_i \Rightarrow U_i}{\mathcal{C} \vdash rec\,(Lb_1 : T_1)\ldots(Lb_n : T_n) \Rightarrow rec\,(Lb_1 : U_1)\ldots(Lb_n : U_n)}$$

$$\frac{\mathcal{C} \vdash T \Rightarrow U}{\mathcal{C} \vdash array\,[N_1 \ldots N_n]\,T \Rightarrow array\,[N_1 \ldots N_n]\,U}$$

Fig. 8. Parameter Type Compatibility $(\mathcal{C} \vdash T \Rightarrow U)$

4 Related work

Euclid [9] and its successor Turing [6, 7] are Pascal-like languages, both of which support collections and control aliasing. Aliasing is controlled to aid formal reasoning, not for fine level control over reading and writing as it is in this approach. Aliasing is checked by a mixture of static and dynamic tests, the latter of which may be turned off by compilers, rather like array index checking. Collections are limited in these languages because they cannot be abstracted; they are type equivalent by name only. Thus no code can be shared to operate on different collections, even if of the same form, eg a separate list length function has to be written for each different collection.

The closest work to this is FX [2, 3]. FX is a programming language, based on

Scheme, with a sophisticated type system for controlling effects. Expressions have types and effects (such as reading, writing and allocating). FX has a larger class of effects than in the language presented here. Effects take place over regions, which play a similar role to the variables and collections used here. The FX language is polymorphic, thus generic types, effects and regions are supported. In general FX is a more powerful system than that described here, but at the expense of considerable complexity. One of the goals of the language presented here was to keep it simple, which FX is not.

The Standard ML and Haskell functional languages both use types to distinguish between constant and writable (reference) values. Both allow the encapsulation of state manipulating computations, and Haskell achieves this without loss of referential transparency [8]. However both Haskell and Standard ML divide values into two worlds: mutable types (references) and immutable types. Values in these worlds are not compatible and must be copied between them. For example a mutable list must be transformed, copied, into a immutable list structure in order to pass it to a immutable formal parameter. The philosophy taken here is not to have two separate worlds of mutable and immutable values, but to have one such world and simply mode values (types) as being writable or not according to context.

Some languages support read-only export of identifiers from modules, eg. Oberon-2. This is useful but not as general as the approach, described here, in particular it is rather coarse grained, and only allows clients to read not write values.

It is possible to use an ADT to control the reading and writing of values; however this again is rather coarse grained, and can necessitate copying of values cf. ML and Haskell. Using a technique similar to this Bancroft [1] has investigated deriving and reasoning about programs containing pointers. His technique relies on encapsulating complex data types into ADTs which export no pointers (references) to data structure elements. The ADTs encapsulate linear data structures, ie. ones with no sharing. It would be interesting to combine this with this work on collections; for example to support a tree with leaves in different collections. Similarly, Islands [5] aims to control object aliasing by grouping objects together in islands. These islands are only accessible from bridge objects. The thrust of this work is on support for encapsulation of object state.

Typestate [11] has been used in the NIL and Hermes languages. It enforces static invariants on the state of a program, at different program points. For example assignment before use of variables. Typestate is unable to check programs involving traditional pointers; instead it relies on higher level complex data structures such as Lisp s-expressions and ADT's supporting insert, delete and find.

The formal precursors to this work were that of Girard on linear logic [4], and Reynolds on "Syntactic Control of Interference" [10]. Since then there have been many developments in the formal area but few approaches have addressed traditional imperative languages or been as simple or practical as the one presented here.

5 Conclusions and Future Work

The language presented here has some limitations. It may be extended to add pure functions (which only have constant parameters), and even write only types (cf. out parameters). Global variables and nested procedures may also be added; aliasing between formals and non-locals can be controlled by treating non-locals as implicit formals. Support for procedure types and subtyping require further work.

The most serious deficiency of the language is the lack of type abstraction, ie abstract data types. At present all read/write control is at the level of basic types. Abstract data types require underlying representations to be hidden; thus ADTs themselves require type modes which transitively apply to the whole type. The interaction between transitive type modes and collections requires further investigation.

Read-write type modes are potentially very useful for concurrency control. For example to support different interaction paradigms such as single writer, multiple reader. In general it is possible to make the mode and type system arbitrarily sophisticated, and complex. For example it may be possible to use existential data types to model local collections, and hence to support data structures such as trees with leaves in different local collections. However, more practical experience is required to see what is really useful. The original goal was to devise a simple language in the Pascal tradition with control of reading and writing.

A prototype translator for this toy language has been written in Haskell; this translates the language into C. The lack of aliasing means that an implementation may safely pass large read-only (and read-write) parameters by reference and small, eg word sized, read-write parameters by value-result (copy in copy out). Naturally small read-only parameters may be passed by value.

The result of the research is a small programming language which controls reading and writing of data via type modes, at the expense of a more restricted programming model than usual. Further experience is needed to see how restrictive the programming model is, and therefore which aspects may require revision. Programs written in the language should be amenable to formal manipulation since all aliasing is explicit.

Acknowledgements

This work has been supported by the Programming Languages and Systems group at QUT and partially by Australian Research Council grants.

References

1. P G Bancroft and I J Hayes. Refinement in a type extension context. In *Proceedings of the Fifth Australian Refinement Workshop (ARW-96)*. Department of Computer Science, The University of Queensland, April 1996.

2. D Gifford, P Jouvelot, M Sheldon, and J O'Toole. Report on the FX-91 programming language. Technical Report TR-531 (revised version), LCS, MIT.

3. D K Gifford and J M Lucassen. Integrating functional and imperative programming. In *ACM Conference on Lisp and Functional Programming*, pages 28–38, 1986.

4. J-Y Girard. Linear logic. *Theoretical Computing Science*, (50):1–102, 1987.

5. J Hogg. Islands: Aliasing Protection in Object Oriented Languages. In *OOPSLA '91*, pages 271–285, 1991.

6. R C Holt and J R Cordy. The Turing Programming Language. *CACM*, 31(12):1410–1423, 1988.

7. R C Holt, P A Matthews, J A Rosselet, and J R Cordy. *The Turing Language: Design and Definition*. Prentice Hall, 1987.

8. S L Peyton Jones and J Launchbury. State in Haskell. *LASC*, 8(5):293–341, December 1995.

9. G J Popek, J J Horning, B W Lampson, J G Mitchell, and R L London. Notes on the Design of Euclid. *ACM SIGPLAN Notices*, 12(3), 1977.

10. J C Reynolds. Syntactic control of interference. In *5th ACM Symposium on Principles of Programming Languages*, pages 39–46, 1978.

11. R E Strom and S Yemini. Typestate a programming language concept for enhancing software reliability. *IEEE Transactions on Software Engineering*, SE-12(1):157–171, January 1986.

Efficient Goal Scheduling
in a Concurrent Logic Language
Using Type-Based Dependency Analysis

Kazuhiko OHNO[1], Masahiko IKAWA[2], Masahiro GOSHIMA[1],
Shin-ichiro MORI[1], Hiroshi NAKASHIMA[3] and Shinji TOMITA[1]

[1] Kyoto University, JAPAN
[2] Current affiliation : Mitsubishi Electric Corporation
[3] Current affiliation : Toyohashi University of Technology

Abstract. In the execution model of concurrent logic languages like
KL1, each goal is regarded as a unit of concurrent execution. Although
this fine-grained concurrency control enables flexible concurrent/parallel
programming, its overhead also causes inefficiency in its implementation. We propose an efficient goal scheduling scheme using the result of
static analysis. In this scheme, we obtain precise dependency relations
among goals using type-based dependency analysis. Then each set of
goals without concurrency is compiled into one thread, a sequence of
statically ordered goals, to reduce the overhead of goal scheduling. Since
stacks are used to hold goal environments for each thread, the number
of garbage collection is also reduced. The result of preliminary evaluation shows our scheme considerably reduces goal scheduling overhead
and thus it achieves 1.3–3 times speedup.

1   Introduction

Concurrent logic programming languages like KL1 [1, 2] has an important feature
in that they can express concurrency in a flexible fashion. In these languages,
implicit communication prevents synchronization bugs in parallel programming,
and networks of concurrent/parallel processes are easily represented.

However, these languages are not efficient enough in terms of the execution
speed, mainly because of the overhead of fine-grained concurrency control. Since
each goal is regarded as a unit of concurrency in these languages, every goal
including essentially sequential ones is dynamically scheduled. Reduction of such
dynamic scheduling overhead is necessary for efficient execution.

In this paper, we propose a new scheme for efficient goal scheduling. In our
scheme, we use type-based dependency analysis to obtain precise dependency
relations among goals. Using this information, goals whose execution order can be
statically determined, are compiled into a thread. By the dynamic scheduling of
threads, the essential concurrency is retained, reducing the scheduling overhead
of goals within each thread.

This paper is organized as follows: Sect. 2 gives an overview of KL1 and
its implementation named KLIC; Sect. 3 discusses performance problems of
conventional scheduling schemes and overviews our scheme; Sect. 4 describes
static analysis and how threads are generated; Sect. 5 evaluates the effect of this

scheme; Sect. 6 compares the scheme with related works; and Sect. 7 gives the conclusion.

2 Background

2.1 Overview of KL1

KL1 [2] is a concurrent logic programming language designed at the Institute for New Generation Computer Technology (ICOT).

Syntax of KL1. KL1 is based on a flat version of the Guarded Horn Clauses (GHC) [1], which is a member of so-called committed-choice logic programming language family.

A KL1 program consists of a set of clauses, which have the following form:

$$H : - G_1, \ldots, G_m \mid B_1, \ldots, B_n.$$

H, G_i, B_j are called clause head, guard goal, body goal, respectively. Guard and body goals represent calls of corresponding predicates. A predicate is defined by a set of clauses whose heads have the same name and arity. We use the notation '*name/arity*' for goals and predicates. For reason of efficiency, a guard goal is restricted to be a built-in predicate.

When a goal is executed, one clause with a matching head and satisfied guard goals is selected, and the original goal is replaced by the body goals of the clause. This operation is called goal reduction, and the execution is performed by repeating reductions. An initial goal main/0 is given at the beginning of the execution.

Data Structure of KL1. The data in KL1 is either atomic data such as symbolic atoms and integers, or structured data such as lists and functors. Structured data can contain logical variables which can refer to other data, which makes it possible to create nested structures easily.

Such logical variables are untyped and can be instantiated to any values. A variable does not have a value at initialization (unbound), and by unifying with a data above(instantiation), it holds the data as its value. The value of a variable cannot be altered after instantiation.

During execution of a goal g_i, a guard goal within the clause may unify with an unbound variable v_j. In such a case, the execution of g_i is suspended and another executable goal is scheduled. When v_j is instantiated by other goals, g_i is resumed (becomes executable), and scheduled again in time.

Process and Stream. One typical programming style of KL1 is that several processes run concurrently using streams as communication channels.

In logic languages, a unit of the execution is a goal, which terminates as soon as it is executed. So in KL1 programs, recursion is used to make a process that exists for a certain period. In this paper, we call a process that starts with the goal p/n as 'process p/n'.

```
main :- p(10000,S), c(S).
p(T,S) :- T>0 | S=[T|S0], T0:=T-1, p(T0,S0).
p(T,S) :- T=0 | S=[].
c(S) :- S=[T|S0] | c(S0).
c(S) :- S=[] | true.
```

Fig. 1. Process and Stream

A stream is a shared variable among processes, which is used to transmit values. As an instantiated variable cannot be updated, a stream variable is instantiated into a cons cell, whose car part transfers the value and cdr part is unbound. By using cdr part as a new shared variable, data transfer can be repeated.

Fig. 1 shows a simple example. The program consists of 2 processes; a producer $p/2$ and a consumer $c/1$. $p/2$ sends the value of its state variable T and terminates when T becomes 0. $c/1$ receives the value from the stream and terminates when the stream is terminated with a nil atom.

2.2 Overview of KLIC

KLIC [3, 4] is a portable implementation of KL1 developed at ICOT. KLIC translates KL1 programs into C programs and object codes are generated by a C compiler for a target machine. Thus, KLIC has high portability except for machine dependent modules like subroutines for message communication.

KLIC has a runtime kernel as a library, which provides facilities of goal scheduling, garbage collection(GC), etc. The C program, translated from user's KL1 program, performs data generation and goal reduction under the control of this kernel.

In KLIC, an instance of a goal is represented as a goal record that contains a pointer to the corresponding code and arguments. The runtime kernel has a goal queue for executable goals. The goal scheduler dequeues a goal record and executes the corresponding code, then enqueues the generated goal records. If a goal suspension occurs, the goal is hooked to the referenced variable. When the variable is instantiated, the hooked goal is enqueued to the goal queue again.

Because execution order of goals is dynamically determined, the goal records are stored in the heap and are target of GC like KL1 data.

3 Efficient Goal Scheduling

3.1 Problems in the Current Implementation

As we mentioned in Sect. 2.1, a goal is suspended at its reference to an unbound variable, and the goal scheduler switches to another executable goal. The suspended goal is resumed when the referring variable is instantiated, and continues its execution when it is scheduled again. Although this mechanism assures correct execution of the program, the overhead of suspending, switching and resuming of goals causes slow-down if it occurs frequently.

```
main :- p0([int(100)|L1],L2),p1(L1,L2).
p0(L1,L2) :- L1=[int(N)|NL1],N>0 | L2=[int(NN)|NL2],NN:=N-1,p0(NL1,NL2).
p0(L1,L2) :- L1=[int(N)|NL1],N=:=0 | L2=[].
p1(L1,L2) :- L2=[int(N)|NL2] | L1=[int(NN)|NL1],NN:=N-1,p1(NL1,NL2).
p1(L1,L2) :- L2=[] | L1=[].
```

Fig. 2. Program handshake

In the current implementations of KL1, every goal is scheduled dynamically. The goal scheduler selects the next goal based on a certain strategy. If the selected goal cannot be executed, the goal is suspended and the scheduler selects another goal. As a result, programs that match the strategy are efficiently executed, while other programs are inefficient because of the overhead.

Here we outline two scheduling schemes of the current implementations, and some program patterns that cause inefficiency.

Process-Oriented Scheduling. The KL1 implementation on Multi-PSI [5] and PIM [6] adopts this scheme. This strategy reduces goal switching by first scheduling subgoals of the executing goal. In this strategy, the scheduling order in the call-tree is depth-first as long as no suspension occurs. As a result, programs where the data flow is according to this fashion can be efficiently executed. However this scheme causes a large overhead in the following cases:

1. Once a goal of a concurrent process is selected, the process runs as long as its goals are executable. As a result, switching of processes is always accompanied by a goal suspension. This overhead cannot be ignored in fine-grained concurrent processes.
2. When a goal g_i is suspended, the runtime scheduler tries every other goals in depth-first order. If these goals refer to an output value of g_i, they are also suspended. Thus, such useless scheduling gives rise to unnecessary overhead.

Resumption-First Scheduling. The current version of KLIC [3] adopts this scheme. This strategy reduces the overhead caused by process-oriented scheduling. When a suspended goal is resumed by the instantiation of the referring variable, this goal is executed immediately after the current reduction finishes. In this scheme, the switching to the suspended concurrent processes is done without another suspension, because the switching occurs as soon as the suspended goal is resumed. Thus the overhead of process switching is reduced.

For example, consider a program named **handshake** shown in Fig. 2. In this program, two process p0/2 and p1/2 runs concurrently exchanging a counter value. In resumption-first scheduling, initially p0/2 is executed and this suspends at its first recursive call. So the switching from p1/2 to p0/2 is always done without suspending p1/2 as soon as p1/2 generates the value referred to by p0/2. Therefore the overhead of switching is reduced compared to process-oriented scheduling where each switching is accompanied by suspension.

However, this scheme causes another problem. Because the process switching occurs as soon as the suspending goal is resumed, the referred variable may not be completely instantiated if the value is a structured data. This may increase the

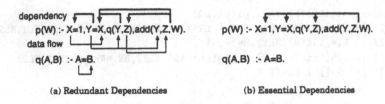

(a) Redundant Dependencies   (b) Essential Dependencies

Fig. 3. Data Flow and Dependencies

number of process switching. In handshake, =/2 in l. 4 instantiates the stream variable to [int(NN)|NL1], by which p0/2 is resumed and scheduled. But when :=/2, the child goal of p0/2, is executed, it refers to the value of NN, which is instantiated by :=/2 in l. 4. So the process is again switched to p1/2. [4]

3.2 Problems in Threading Goals

To decrease the scheduling overhead in the implementation of fine-grained languages, merging several scheduling units into one thread is effective. This scheme has been applied to the functional language Id90 and has obtained a reasonable performance [7].

Although the basic idea can be applied also to KL1, the following characteristics unique to logic languages cause some problems:

1. Logical data flow does not show accurate dependency among goals.
2. The data flow of a structured data may be bi-directional.

Goal Dependencies. In KL1 programs, input/output of goal arguments are not given explicitly. This information can be obtained by mode analysis [8], and static scheduling of goals in the order of the data flow reduces the number of suspensions.

However, goal ordering constraints given by logical data flow is too strict. In logic programs, data flow between two goals does not always mean a dependency. For example, consider a unification of two variables. In semantics, this unification represents a logical flow of the value from one variable v_i to the other variable v_j (or from v_j to v_i). But in execution, the value of v_i is not required in this unification and the unification goal can be executed even if v_i is unbound.

Fig. 3 is a small example. The goals seems to have dependencies shown in (a). But the necessary condition for the execution with no suspension is that 'other 3 goals must be executed before add/3 is scheduled'. Thus the essential dependencies are only those shown in (b).

We will give more precise definition of goal dependency in Sect. 3.3.

Data Flow in Structured Data. In logic languages, each element of a structured data can be instantiated individually. When a process p/n instantiates a

---

[4] This is not the case in the current KLIC which treats executable built-in body goals at the reduction of their parent goal. But the same problem occurs if these goals are user-defined.

```
main :- drive(100,S),stack(S,none).
drive(M,S) :- M=:=0 | S=[].
drive(M,S) :- M=\=0 | S=[push(M)|S0],S0=[pop(N)|S1],N0:=M-1,drive(N0,S1).
stack([]           ,D        ) :- true.
stack([push(X)|S],D          ) :- stack(S,p(X,D)).
stack([pop(X)|S] ,p(Y,D1)) :- X=Y,stack(S,D1).
```

Fig. 4. Bi-directional Communication

variable v_i to a functor $f(v_j)$, a process c/m that refers to $f(v_j)$ may instantiate v_j and the process p/n may refer to the value of v_j. Especially in KL1, bi-directional inter-process communication often uses this feature.

A simple example is shown in Fig. 4. The process **drive/2** uses a stream variable S to send messages to a stack process **stack/2**. When **drive/2** sends a **pop(N)** message with the variable N unbound, **stack/2** instantiates N to the popped value, to make bi-directional communication using a single stream.

In KL1, as shown above, structured data may contain elements whose data flow is opposite from that of the structure itself. Therefore, not only the mode information of goal arguments but also type information that represents these data structures is necessary.

3.3 Overview of Our scheme

Definition of Dependency. Here we define dependencies among KL1 goals.

In KL1, a goal is a call of a built-in/user-defined predicate. The execution model of KL1 goals can be regarded as follows: a built-in goal refers to some values of the arguments, then instantiates other arguments; a user-defined goal refers to some values of the arguments in the guard part, then creates body goals of a selected clause as its children goals. With this execution model, the following conditions must be satisfied for a goal g_i to be executable without suspension:

- **Control Dependency**
  To create the goal g_i, its parent goal g_p has to be executed. If g_i is a body goal, the guard goals of the clause containing g_i; $g_{g1}, \ldots, g_{gm}$ also have to be executed. Therefore, g_i depends on these goals. We call this kind of dependency *control dependency*.

- **Data Dependency**
  If g_i refers to the value of a variable v_j, the goal g_w that creates the referenced value, and consequently the unification goals $g_{u1}, \ldots, g_{ul}$ that are required to unify the created value with v_j, have to be executed before the execution of g_i. Therefore, g_i depends on these goals. We call this kind of dependency *data dependency*.

An example is shown in Fig 5. **add(Y,1,Z)** has control dependencies to **p(W,V)**, **X=Y**, **integer(Y)**, because it is not generated until all these goals are executed. It also has data dependencies to **W=1**, which creates the value of Y, and **X=Y**, which makes data flow path from W to Y.

The above conditions also define *direct dependency* of the goal g_i. If g_w has dependency to a goal g_q, g_q also have to be executed before the execution of g_i. So

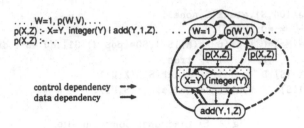

```
... , W=1, p(W,V), ...
p(X,Z) :- X=Y, integer(Y) | add(Y,1,Z).
p(X,Z) :- ...
```

control dependency --▶
data dependency ━━▶

Fig. 5. Goal Dependencies

g_i indirectly depends to g_q. We call this type of dependency *indirect dependency*.

The condition for a goal g_i to become executable without suspension is that 'all goals that g_i has direct or indirect dependency are executed'.

Definition of Thread.

Definition: A *thread* is a sequence of goals whose execution order can be statically determined without deadlock.

Using the result of dependency analysis, the execution order of body goals $b_1, \ldots, b_n$ in each clause is determined. The goals which belong to the same thread are scheduled in depth-first order. If b_i and its descendant goals do not depend to b_j and its descendant goals, b_j can be statically scheduled as a successor goal of b_i in the same thread.

In this scheduling scheme, b_j and its descendant are not scheduled until b_i and all its descendant goals are executed. Therefore, the goal environments of a thread can be managed in a stack as in sequential language systems like the WAM [9] for Prolog. This implementation reduces the number of GC and the overhead of enqueuing/dequeuing goals, thus the efficiency is more improved.

In the case that the above condition is not satisfied, a new thread is generated for b_j. Although a goal g_i in a thread T_k may have no dependency to any successor goals in T_k, g_i may be suspended because of dependency to a goal g_j in another thread T_l. In this case, T_k is suspended and another thread is executed. By the dynamic scheduling of these threads, the essential concurrency of the program due to the mutual goal dependencies is retained.

Using this scheme, the problems of the current implementation disappear. In our scheme, when a goal g_i is suspended, the thread g_i belongs to is also suspended. Because the goals that depends to g_i are the succeeding goals of g_i in the thread, they are not scheduled until g_i is executed. Not like the process-oriented scheduling, our scheme prevents the scheduling of unexecutable goals. Also in our scheme, the switching of threads do not occur until the currently running thread is suspended. Because concurrent processes are compiled into different threads, a process of the suspended thread is not scheduled until the process of the running thread is suspended. Therefore, enough amount of instantiations of structured data is expected. For example in **handshake**, the suspended thread of p0/2 will not be scheduled until the thread of p1/2 is suspended. As a result, :=/2 in p1/2 is executed before p0/2 is scheduled again, and thus the value referred to by :=/2 in p0/2 is already instantiated.

4 Compilation

In our scheme, we assume that target programs are *well-moded* [8]. In such programs, only one occurrence of the same variable is in output mode. Also, the mode of a goal (or a structure) argument depends on the position of appearance in the program, and is independent from the mode of its sibling arguments. We also assume that every pattern matching of clause head arguments are written as guard goals, and all of the head arguments are variables.

4.1 Dependency Analysis

Since the control dependency can be easily obtained, our major interest is how to derive data dependency. As we discussed in Sect. 3.2, we use type-based analysis to derive data dependency.

We first give a definition of *type-dependence set*, which is the intermediate result of our analysis, and we describe the algorithm to derive type-dependence sets of the program. Then we describe how to obtain dependency among goals using these sets, and how to compile goals into threads.

To simplify the discussion in this section, we regard target programs do not contain recursive calls nor multiple calls of a same user-defined predicate. In Sect. 4.3, we discuss how to handle such program structures.

Type-Dependence Set. Although a KL1 variable is not typed, it can be instantiated only once and thus its value is not modified throughout the execution. So we regard the type of this value as the type of the corresponding variable.

However, a same variable may be instantiated to different values according to the execution path. Generally, static analysis cannot determine a unique type of a variable, but a set of possible types of the variable is obtained. We also need information of dependent goals of each type, which shows the dependency of a goal that refers to the value of the type. We introduce a *type-dependence set* to represent these information of a variable.

Definition: A *type-dependence set* of a variable v_i is in the form:

$$T(v_i) = \{e_1, \ldots, e_n\}$$

Each element of the set e_j is one of the following items: a pair consisting of a type and its dependency goal set (t_j, G_j); a pair with a type variable and its dependency goal set (v_j, G_j); and an unknown type '*'.

We regard cons cells and vectors are functors with special name, and represent each type of these structured data in the form: $s(name, arity, (T_1, \ldots, T_{arity}))$. Because each argument of a structured data may also have several possible types, they are expressed in type-dependence sets T_k recursively.

A type variable represents a variable that literally appears in the program as an argument of a structured data. We do not expand the variable's type in the place and leave as a corresponding type variable. Thus the complexity of structured data types are limited to that of terms in the program, and recursive data structures do not cause infinite data types.

The dependency goal set G_j expresses the goals that must be executed before v_i can be instantiated to a value of type t_j; goals that generates the value and the unification goals that unify the value and v_i. In this paper, we number each goals as p/n^k or $add^l(X, Y, Z)$ and express G_j as a set of these numbers.

Here we define two operations on type-dependence sets for the analysis.

Definition: The result of AG (Append Goals) operation, which appends a dependency goal set G to a type-dependence set T: $T_{AG} = AG(T, G)$, is a minimum set satisfying the following conditions:

1. For each $(t_i, G_i) \in T$:

   if t_i is a atomic data type: $T_{AG} \ni (t_i, G_i \cup G)$

   if t_i is a structured data type $(s(f, n, (T_1, \ldots, T_n)), G_l))$:

   $T_{AG} \ni (s(f, n, (T_{AG,1}, \ldots, T_{AG,n})), G_l \cup G)$, where $T_{AG,k} = AG(T_k, G)$
2. For each $(v_j, G_m) \in T$: $T_{AG} \ni (v_j, G_m \cup G)$
3. If $* \in T$: $T_{AG} \ni *$

Definition: The result of OR operation of two type-dependence sets: $T_{OR} = OR(T_A, T_B)$ is a minimum set satisfying the following conditions:

1. If t_i is a atomic data type:

   $(T_A \ni (t_i, G_A)) \wedge (T_B \ni (t_i, G_B)) \rightarrow T_{OR} \ni (t_i, G_A \cup G_B)$

   If t_i is a structured data type:

   $(T_A \ni (s(f, n, (T_{A,1}, \ldots, T_{A,n})), G_A)) \wedge (T_B \ni (s(f, n, (T_{B,1}, \ldots, T_{B,n})), G_B))$
   $\rightarrow T_{OR} \ni (s(f, n, (T_{OR,1}, \ldots, T_{OR,n})), G_A \cup G_B)$, where $T_{OR,k} = OR(T_{A,k}, T_{B,k})$
2. $(T_A \ni (v_j, G_A)) \wedge (T_B \ni (v_j, G_B)) \rightarrow T_{OR} \ni (v_j, G_A \cup G_B)$
3. Any $(t_i, G_A) \in T_A, (v_j, G_A) \in T_A$ that does not satisfy (1), (2) are also included in T_{OR}. Similarly with T_B.

Analysis Algorithm. Let G, V denote sets of all goals and all variables in the program; $H_{p/n,m}, B_{p/n,m}$ denote sets of the mth arguments of clause heads p/n and body goals p/n; and s_j denote structured data.

The analysis algorithm is described as follows:

```
U ← ∅      /* Initialize update pool */
forall vi ∈ V {  T(vi) ← {*}  }
forall gi ∈ G
    if gi instantiates vj to a value of type tk
       {  T(vj) ← {(tk, {i})},  U ← U ∪ (vj, gi)  }
while  U ≠ ∅ {
    take out a tuple (vj, gi) from U
a.  forall (vj =l vk ∈ G) (l ≠ i)
       {  T(vk) ← AG(T(vj), {l}),  U ← U ∪ (vk, gl) if T(vk) is altered  }
b.  forall guard goal vj =l sm ∈ G (l ≠ i)
        forall vk which appears in sm
           {  get T'(vj) in T(vj) which corresponds to vk in sm,
              indirect_unify(vk, T'(vj), l)  }
c.  forall guard goal vk =l sm ∈ G (l ≠ i and vj appears in sm)
           {  get T'(vk) in T(vk) which corresponds to vj in sm,
              indirect_unify(vj, T'(vk), l)  }
```

d. **forall** $H_{p/n,m} \ni v_j$ $(g_i \neq p/n)$
   $\{ T_{HB} \leftarrow \emptyset$ /* Initialize */
     forall $v_h \in H_{p/n,m}$ $\{ T_{HB} \leftarrow OR(T_{HB}, T(v_h)) \}$
     forall $v_b \in B_{p/n,m}$ $\{ T(v_b) \leftarrow T_{HB}, U \leftarrow U \cup (v_b, g_l)$ if $T(v_b)$ is altered
               where g_l is the goal p/n with v_b as its mth arg. $\}\}$

e. **forall** $B_{p/n,m} \ni v_j$ $(g_i \neq p/n)$
   $\{ T_{BH} \leftarrow \emptyset$ /* Initialize */
     forall $v_b \in B_{p/n,m}$ $\{ T_{BH} \leftarrow OR(T_{BH}, T(v_b)) \}$
     forall non-variable term: $b_b \in B_{p/n,m}$, which type is t_b
              $\{ T_{BH} \leftarrow OR(T_{BH}, \{(t_b, \{\})\}) \}$
     forall $v_h \in H_{p/n,m}$ $\{ T(v_h) \leftarrow T_{BH}, U \leftarrow U \cup (v_h, g_l)$ if $T(v_h)$ is altered
               where g_l is the goal p/n with v_j as its mth arg. $\}\}\}$

A procedure *indirect_unify*(v, T, l), called in *(b),(c)*, traces indirect unification via structured data. The algorithm is as follows:

procedure *indirect_unify*(v, T, l) {
   if $(t_i, G_i) \in T(v)$ $(G_i \not\ni l)$ exists   /* flow from v */
     forall $(v_j, G_j) \in T$
       $\{ T(v_j) \leftarrow AG(T(v), \{l\}), U \leftarrow U \cup (v_j, g_l)$ if $T(v_j)$ is altered $\}$
   else $\{T(v) \leftarrow AG(T, \{l\}), U \leftarrow U \cup (v, g_l)$ if $T(v)$ is altered $\}$ }

Although we do not make mode analysis explicitly, our analysis follows the direction of data flow. In the above algorithm, *(a)* traces intra-clause type flow, and *(d),(e)* trace inter-clause type flow. Because KL1 does not allow instantiation of a head variable v_i in guards, v_i is input mode in a guard goal $v_i = t_k$. Also, v_i is output mode in a body goal $v_j = t_k$ in a well-moded program. If the program is not well-moded, it can be detected as a conflict during the update of $T(v)$.

The termination of our algorithm is assured because (1) each type-dependence set monotonically grows larger; (2) the set is finite because the structured data types are subset of types of all terms appearing in the program text; and (3) a tuple (v_i, g_i) is added to U only when $T(v_i)$ is altered.

A simple example of type-dependence analysis is shown in Fig. 6, 7.

Goal Dependency Analysis. Because the mode and referencing types of built-in predicates are known, we can derive direct data dependency of each goal from the obtained type-dependence sets as follows:

1. **built-in goal** b/m: For each v_i that occurs as an input arguments, if $(t_j, G_j) \in T(v_i)$ and the value of type t_j is referred to, b/m has direct data dependency on G_j.

2. **user-defined goal** u/n: For each v_i that occurs as an input argument in a guard goal in the definition clauses of predicate u/n, if $(t_j, G_j) \in T(v_i)$ and the value of type t_j is referred to, u/m has direct data dependency on G_j.

Because our scheme orders the body goals in each clause, we finally obtain ordering constraints among these body goals. Here we consider a clause with body

main : $-p^1(X), X =^2 Y, q^3(Y)$.
p(A) : $-A =^4 1$.
p(A) : $-A =^5 a$.
q(B) : $-integer^6(B)|true$.
q(B) : $-atom^7(B)|true$.

main : $-p^1(X), X =^2 Y, q^3(Y)$.
p(A) : $-A =^4 f(C), p1^5(C)$.
p1(E) : $-integer^6(E)|true$.
q(B) : $-B =^7 f(D)|D =^8 1$.

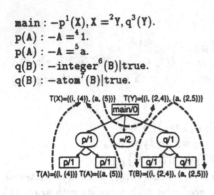

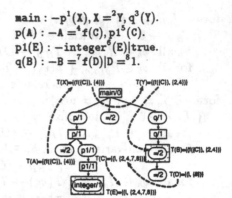

Fig. 6. Type-Dependence Analysis (1)   **Fig. 7.** Type-Dependence Analysis (2)

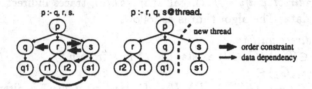

Fig. 8. Threading of Program

goals $b_1, \ldots, b_n$. We use the notations $D_c(b_i), D_d(b_i)$ for direct control/data dependencies of b_i. The preceding goals of b_i ; $Prec(b_i)$ is obtained by the following algorithm:

1. Initialize $Prec(b_i)$ with the direct data dependencies: $Prec(b_i) = D_d(b_i)$
2. Expand indirect dependencies: for each $b_k \in Prec(b_i)$;
   $Prec(b_i) \leftarrow Prec(b_i) \cup D_c(b_k) \cup D_d(b_k)$
3. The preceding goals of b_i's descendant $(Des(b_i))$ are also preceding goals of b_i: for each $b_l \in Des(b_i)$; $Prec(b_i) \leftarrow Prec(b_i) \cup Prec(b_l)$

For each goal $b_j \in Prec(b_i)$, a ordering constraint 'b_j must precede b_i' exists. We use a notation $prec(b_i, b_j)$ for this constraint.

4.2 Generation of Threaded Code

Using the ordering constraint, we generate threaded code.

For each clause of the program, we statically order the body goals. If two constraints $prec(b_i, b_j)$ and $prec(b_j, b_i)$ exist, these goals cannot be ordered. So a pragma to generate a new thread @thread is appended to b_j.

An example is shown in Fig. 8. The goals q, r are sequentialized in the same thread of p. And because s cannot be ordered in this thread, a new thread is generated and s is executed on it.

4.3 Analysis on Shared Predicates

If the target program has multiple body goals of same name and arity, our previous algorithm may obtain inaccurate dependency.

main : $-X =^1 0, p^2(X)$.
p(N) : $-N <^3 10|$add$^4(N, 3, N1)$,
        subtract$^5(N1, 2, N2), p^6(N2)$.
p(N) : $-N =^7 10|$true.

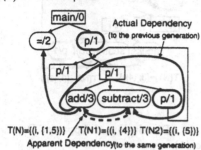

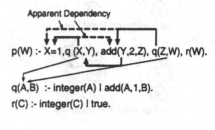

Apparent Dependency

p(W) :- X=1,q (X,Y), add(Y,2,Z), q(Z,W), r(W).

q(A,B) :- integer(A) | add(A,1,B).

r(C) :- integer(C) | true.

Fig. 9. Apparent Dependency(1)   **Fig. 10.** Apparent Dependency(2)

If the call-tree of the program has loop structure caused by a recursive call, it causes apparent dependencies (Fig. 9). This is because our algorithm does not distinguish loop generations, and the dependence of the goal on a previous generation in the example is treated as a dependence to the same generation. For example, although add/3 and subtract/3 seems to have mutual dependence in Fig. 9, add/3 actually depends on the subtract/3 of the previous generation.

Even if the call-tree has no loops, it may cause apparent dependencies if a shared subtree exists in the call tree. In the example shown in Fig. 10, two body goals q/2 exist. As our algorithm merges every dependence of each body goal q/2 as a dependence set of the predicate q/2, each body goal seems to have all of these dependence.

We call a predicate p/n, which multiple goals p/n exist, a *shared predicate*, and the goals *shared goals*. The loop structure caused by a recursive call of r/m can be regarded as a kind of shared predicate, because r/m must have multiple call (entry of the loop and a recursive call).

Consider a shared predicate s/n, a goal s/n^i, and two goals; $q/l \in Des(s/n^i)$ and $p/m \notin Des(s/n^i)$. The dependencies from/to q/l can be pushed up to its ancestor goal s/n^i without affecting the ordering constraint (Fig. 11). Therefore, to dissolve these apparent dependencies of shared predicates, our analysis is modified as follows:

1. In the analysis algorithm for type-dependence sets,
   - In *(d)*, replace every dependence set of T_{HB} with $\{b\}$, and update $T(v_b)$ with the new set instead of T_{HB}.
   - In *(e)*, replace every dependence set G_k of T_{BH} with $\{(b, G_k)\}$, and update $T(v_h)$ with the new set instead of T_{BH}.
2. In goal dependency analysis, if the reference to t_j by a goal g_i turns out and the dependence set of t_j has an element (l, G), append G to the dependence set of the goal l instead of appending to the dependence set of g_i.

The apparent dependency shown in Fig. 9 is dissolved as shown in Fig. 12.

With this modification, a recursive goal has the dependence of its descendant as its own dependence. Therefore, in goal dependency analysis, recursive goals can be regarded to have no descendant goals.

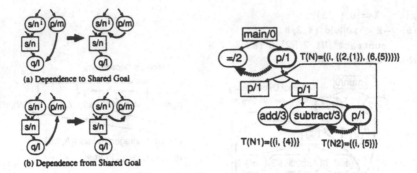

(a) Dependence to Shared Goal

(b) Dependence from Shared Goal

Fig. 11. Dependency of Shared Predicate

Fig. 12. Dissolution of Apparent Dependency(1)

Table 1. Result of Evaluation

	handshake		reverse		circle_to_square		12queen	
	original	threaded	original	threaded	original	threaded	original	threaded
Time (sec)	19.21	9.42	79.42	27.37	53.03	39.61	40.80	29.79
Suspension	1000000	500001	119	17	3	1	0	0
GC	24	7	2964000	92999	84	30	68	21

5 Evaluation

We have implemented the runtime system for our scheme on KLIC version 2.002, and evaluated our scheme on SPARC Station 20. We have done a preliminary comparison of our implementation with the original KLIC using four simple benchmark programs. Table 1 shows the execution time, the number of suspensions, and the number of GC. A more comprehensive evaluation is still underway.

Handshake is the program shown in Fig. 2, in which the switching of two concurrent processes is repeated (Body goals of p0/2, p1/2 are modified into user-defined goals). Because our scheme avoids the problem of resumption-first scheduling described in Sect. 3.1, the suspensions are reduced to 1/2. It also reduced the number of GC to 1/3 and a 2 times speedup is obtained.

Reverse is a program where two concurrent processes repeatedly update an Othello game board. Because the game board is represented with lists and functors, the program generates a lot of goal instances that check and update each element. This causes frequent GC. Using our scheme, the number of GC and suspensions are reduced to 1/32 and 1/7, and a 3 times speedup is obtained.

Circle_to_square is a program that computes size ratio of circle and square by counting grid points within the circle, and 12queen is a 12-queen problem solver. In these two programs, the suspension overhead can be ignored. However, our scheme reduced the number of GC to 1/3, and achieved 1.3–1.4 times speedup. This result shows that even in the programs whose scheduling are efficient enough in the original KLIC, static goal scheduling using a stack-based execution mechanism reduces GC and goal enqueuing/dequeuing overhead, and thus achieves considerable performance improvement.

6 Related Works

[10], [11] target logic languages with dynamic scheduling. They use abstract interpretation for dependency analysis, and the result is used to eliminate delay declarations, thus it reduces the overhead of dynamic scheduling.

[12] propose a threading scheme for a concurrent logic language. They analyze dependency using constraints in sequences of goals, and the threading scheme is similar to our scheme.

[13] propose a sequentialization scheme for Flat GHC. They target a class of fully-moded feedback-free programs, and statically sequentialize them using result of mode analysis. All mode of a program in this class must be statically determinable, and any cyclic body-goal dependencies must not exist. Their scheme cannot be applied to many existing programs that does not satisfy the latter condition. Our scheme do not requires the feedback-free condition, so such programs can also be optimized.

[14] propose a granularity optimization scheme for a committed-choice language Fleng [15]. They use two techniques; inline expansion, which replace a goal call with the definition of the goal, and goal fusion, which merges several goals in one clause. Although these techniques has advantage that the overhead of generating goal environment is also reduced, inline expansion may increase the code size if shared predicates exist. And these techniques cannot sequentialize a whole loop, which our scheme can compile into a single thread. Moreover, their dependency analysis is not so accurate because they use a subset of mode analysis [8]. Our scheme uses more precise analysis, which results in better sequentialization.

7 Conclusion

We proposed a new scheme for efficient goal scheduling of the concurrent logic language KL1.

We use type-based dependency analysis to obtain precise dependencies among goals, and compile goals into threads using these dependencies. In this scheme, static ordering of goals in each thread reduces the overhead of fine-grained dynamic goal scheduling. By managing goal environments of a thread with a stack, the overhead of GC and goal enqueuing/dequeuing are also reduced.

Our preliminary evaluation results are quite promising and show that our scheme can obtain 2-3 times speedup for programs that are not efficient in current KLIC. And even with programs that is relatively efficient in current KLIC, 30% improvement is achieved.

We are planning to do a more comprehensive evaluation of our scheme with larger and more practical KL1 programs. There are also a number of improvements which remain to be tried. The granularity control of threads and better thread scheduling scheme will be required, especially for efficient parallel execution. They will be our future works.

Acknowledgment

We would like to express our sincere appreciation to Dr. R. Yap for many helpful and detailed suggestions to improve the quality of this paper, as well as anonymous referees for their comments. We also would like to thank ICOT/AITEC and its KLIC task group for many technical information and advises.

References

1. K. Ueda. Guarded horn clauses. In *LNCS221 Logic Programming '85*, pp. 168–179. Springer-Verlag, 1986.
2. K. Ueda and T. Chikayama. Design of the kernel language for the parallel inference machine. *The Computer Journal*, Vol. 33, No. 6, pp. 494–500, 1990.
3. T. Chikayama, T. Fujise, and D. Sekita. A portable and efficient implementation of KL1. In *Proc. 6th Intl. Symp. PLILP'94*, pp. 25–39, 1994.
4. Takashi Chikayama. *KLIC User's Manual*. ICOT, March 1995.
5. K. Nakajima, Y. Inamura, N. Ichiyoshi, K. Rokusawa, and T. Chikayama. Distributed implementation of KL1 on the Multi-PSI/V2. In *Proc. 6th Intl. Conf. and Symp. on Logic Programming*, pp. 436–451, 1989.
6. T. Chikayama. Operating system PIMOS and kernel language KL1. In *FGCS'92*, pp. 73–88, 1992.
7. Klaus E. Schauser, David E. Culler, and Seth C. Goldstein. Separation constraint partitioning - a new algorithm for partitioning non-strict programs into sequential threads. In *POPL'95*, pp. 259–271, 1995.
8. K. Ueda and M. Morita. Moded Flat GHC and its message-oriented implementation technique. *New Generation Computing*, Vol. 13, No. 1, pp. 3–43, November 1994.
9. D. H. D. Warren. An abstract prolog instruction set. Technical Report 309, SRI International, 1983.
10. K. Marriott, M. Garcia de la Banda, and M. Hermenegildo. Analyzing logic programs with dynamic scheduling. In *POPL'94*, 1994.
11. G. Puebla and M. Hermenegildo. Automatic optimization of dynamic scheduling in logic programs. In *LNCS1140 PLILP'96*, pp. 475–476. Springer-Verlag, 1996.
12. A.King and P.Soper. Schedule analysis of concurrent logic programs. In *Proc. of the Joint Intl. Conf. and Symp. on Logic Programming*, pp. 478–492, 1994.
13. B. C. Massey and E. Tick. Sequentialization of parallel logic programs with mode analysis. In *4th International Conference on Logic Programming and Automated Reasoning*, pp. 205–216, 1993.
14. T. Araki and H. Tanaka. A static granularity optimization method of a committed-choice language Fleng(In Japanese). In *IPSJ 96-PRO-8*, pp. 109–114, August 1996.
15. M. Nilsson and H. Tanaka. Fleng prolog - the language which turns supercomputers into prolog machines. In *LNCS264*. Springer-Verlag, 1989.

An Analysis of Divisibility Orderings and Recursive Path Orderings

Ryu HASEGAWA

Graduate School of Mathematics, The University of Tokyo, 3-8-1 Komaba, Meguro-ku, Tokyo, 153 Japan

Abstract

We show that normal and analytic functors provide a foundation to the theory of divisibility orderings and recursive path orderings. These functors are used to give intrinsic definitions independent from particular syntactic presentations.

1 Introduction

To address the problem, we consider the set T of finite ordered trees generated by the following rule:

$$t \quad ::= \quad \mathsf{span}\overbrace{\langle t, \ldots, t \rangle}^{n} \qquad (n \geq 0).$$

Kruskal's theorem asserts that T is a well-partial-order with regard to the tree embedding [13, 18]. The theory of recursive path orderings is based on this theorem [3].

Since the lists $\langle t_1, \ldots, t_n \rangle$ are given recursively also by cons and nil, we can represent finite trees as binary trees by the translation $(-)^*$ defined as:

$$t = \mathsf{span}\langle t_1, t_2, \ldots, t_n \rangle \quad \rightsquigarrow \quad t^* = \mathsf{cons}(t_1^*, \mathsf{cons}(t_2^*, \cdots \mathsf{cons}(t_n^*, \mathsf{nil}) \cdots)).$$

In fact, this translation gives a bijection from the set of finite trees of n nodes (including leaves) onto the set of binary trees with n leaves.

This translation, however, affects the tree embedding relation. For instance, we consider two finite trees of the first line in Fig. 1.1. By the translation $(-)^*$, these trees are transformed into the two trees of the last line in Fig. 1.1 where cons is denoted by $*$ and nil by $\circ$. We denote by $\trianglelefteq_T$ the tree embedding on finite trees, and by $\trianglelefteq_B$ the tree embedding on binary trees. As shown in the figure, it may happen that $s \ntrianglelefteq_T t$ while $s^* \trianglelefteq_B t^*$.

This example shows that tree embedding relations (thus recursive path orderings) depend on syntactic presentations. If we take different presentations for finite trees, we obtain different tree embeddings. The difference lies especially in "subterms" of given terms. A subterm (i.e., subtree) of a binary tree may not remain a subterm after translated into finite trees. As Oyamaguchi pointed out to the author, the choice of a particular syntactic presentation entails the choice of a structure we equip with the set of objects.

Figure 1.1

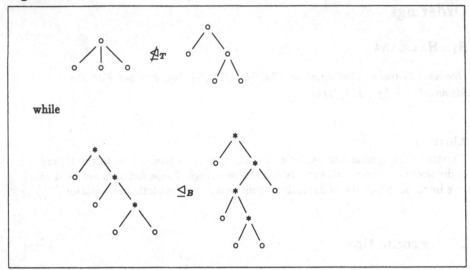

while

The use of syntax to endow a structure is, however, not always the best choice. First the notion of subterm is sensitive to a slight change of syntax. We prefer a stable definition induced from mathematical structures rather than from how to represent them in the form of terms. Second we have trouble if we generalize beyond ordinary tree embeddings. For example, Friedman's embedding with gap [20] provides an extension of tree embedding. But the definition of this extended embedding sounds ad hoc as far as we write it using the presentation as terms.

In this paper, we show that a certain functorial structure induces the natural definition of divisibility orderings (including tree embeddings) and recursive path orderings without relying on syntax. In sections 3 and 5, we demonstrate that Friedman's embedding and also Takeuti's ordinal diagrams are natural consequences of the structures derived from our functorial presentation.

The principal vehicles are normal functors and analytic functors. To introduce them, let us consider the set T of finite ordered trees and the set B of binary ordered trees. These sets can be represented as initial algebras (i.e., least fixpoints):

$$T = \mu X. \text{List}(X)$$
$$B = \mu X. 1 + X^2$$

where $\text{List}(X)$ is the set of all finite lists of members of a set X. The former is obtained since T is the least closure of spanning finite lists of members of T. The latter is obvious from the BNF generating binary trees, $t ::= \text{nil} \mid \text{span}\langle t, t \rangle$. We want to find a common structure between $\text{List}(X)$ and $1 + X^2$. First of all, these can be regarded as functors from the category **Set** of sets to **Set** with obvious extensions to functions. The crucial observation is that both $\text{List}(X)$ and $1 + X^2$

are represented as formal power series of X. The latter is indeed a polynomial. For the former, we have an isomorphism $\text{List}(X) \cong 1 + X + X^2 + X^3 + \cdots$, where X^n corresponds to the set of finite lists of length exactly n.

The normal functors introduced by Girard [7] are by definition those functors which can be represented as formal power series. We use also analytic functors by Joyal [11, 12] that generalize normal functors. The aim of this paper is to give the definitions of divisibility orderings and the recursive path orderings relying only on the structures as normal (or analytic) functors. Using these functors, we can give syntax-free definitions of these orderings, including many well-known examples in combinatorics, logic and theoretical computer science.

2 Preliminaries

A *quasi-order* is a set endowed with a binary relation $\leq$ satisfying reflexivity and transitivity. A *well-quasi-order* is a quasi-order A subject to the condition that every infinite sequence $a_1, a_2, \ldots$ from A has indices $i < j$ such that $a_i \leq a_j$. If, moreover, A is a partial order, it is called a well-partial-order. A *linearization* of a partial order $(A, \trianglelefteq)$ is a linear order $(A, <)$ such that the reflexive closure $\leq$ of $<$ contains $\trianglelefteq$.

2.1 Fact
If $(A, <)$ is a linearization of a well-partial-order $(A, \trianglelefteq)$, then the linear order $< $ on A is a well-order. $\square$

An *ordered tree* is generated by the form $\text{span}\langle t_1, \ldots, t_n \rangle$ where the order of the subtrees t_i matters. An *unordered tree* is such that the difference of the order of subtrees is ignored. We refer the reader to [13, 18, 9] for aspects of tree embedding.

We denote by **Set** the category of sets and functions, by **QO** the category of quasi-orders and order-preserving maps, and by **LO** the category of linear orders and strictly order-preserving maps. For a functor $F : \mathbf{C} \to \mathbf{Set}$ from some category $\mathbf{C}$, the *category* $\text{el}(F)$ *of elements* [15] has pairs (A, a) for an object A of $\mathbf{C}$ and $a \in FA$ as objects, and $(A, a) \xrightarrow{f} (B, b)$ for $A \xrightarrow{f} B$ such that $Ff(a) = b$ as morphisms.

For $F : \mathbf{Set} \to \mathbf{Set}$, a *finite normal form* of an object (A, a) of $\text{el}(F)$ is an initial object $(X, c) \xrightarrow{f} (A, a)$ in the slice category $\text{el}(F)/(A, a)$ where X is a finite set. We can generalize this definition to a functor $F : \mathbf{C} \to \mathbf{Set}$ from some category $\mathbf{C}$ by replacing finite sets with finitely presentable objects. The finite normal form is equivalent to the normal form in [7], though they are not literally the same.

2.2 Definition

A *normal functor* $F :$ **Set** $\to$ **Set** is defined by one of the following equivalence conditions:

(i) F is isomorphic to coproduct of functors represented by finite sets. Namely, $FA \cong \sum_{i \in I} \mathbf{Set}(X_i, A)$ for some family of finite sets X_i.

(ii) F preserves filtered colimits and pullbacks (including infinite ones).

(iii) Each object of the category $\mathrm{el}(F)$ of elements has a finite normal form.

Remark: In the assertion (ii), [7] contains also the condition that F preserves equalizers. But this is derived from other universal properties, since we can verify that every analytic functor preserving pullbacks is a normal functor. Hence the normal functor defined above is the same as the one in [7].

The functor $\mathrm{List}(X)$ is an example of normal functors we often use below. We define $\mathrm{List}(A)$ as the collection of all finite lists of members of a set A. An object of $\mathrm{el}(\mathrm{List})$ has the form $(A, \langle a_1, a_2, \ldots, a_n \rangle)$. Its finite normal form has the shape $(X, \langle x_1, x_2, \ldots, x_n \rangle) \xrightarrow{f} (A, \langle a_1, a_2, \ldots, a_n \rangle)$ where X is an n-point set $\{x_1, x_2, \ldots, x_n\}$ and f assigns a_i to x_i. The formal power series representation of $\mathrm{List}(X)$ is given by $1 + X + X^2 + X^3 + \cdots$.

Analytic functors contain normal functors as a special case. A *transitive object* in a category $\mathbf{C}$ is an object X satisfying that the homset $\mathbf{C}(X, A)$ is non-empty and transitive with regard to the action of $\mathrm{Aut}_{\mathbf{C}}(X)$ by composition for every object A. Here $\mathrm{Aut}_{\mathbf{C}}(X)$ is the group of all automorphisms on X. A transitive object is unique up to isomorphisms if it exists. An initial object is a special case of a transitive object where $\mathrm{Aut}_{\mathbf{C}}(X)$ is the unit group.

For a functor $\mathbf{C} \xrightarrow{F} \mathbf{Set}$ from some category $\mathbf{C}$, a *finite weak normal form* of an object (A, a) of $\mathrm{el}(F)$ is a transitive object $(X, c) \xrightarrow{f} (A, a)$ in the slice category $\mathrm{el}(F)/(A, a)$ where X is a finitely presentable object of $\mathbf{C}$.

2.3 Definition

An *analytic functor* $F :$ **Set** $\to$ **Set** is defined by one of the following equivalence conditions:

(i) F is isomorphic to a functor of the form $\sum_{i \in I} \mathbf{Set}(X_i, A)/G_i$ where X_i is a finite set and G_i is a subgroup of the symmetric group of all permutations on X_i.

(ii) F preserves filtered colimits and weak pullbacks (including infinite ones).

(iii) Each object of the category $\mathrm{el}(F)$ of elements has a finite weak normal form.

Remark: In [12], analytic functors are defined as those functors which preserve all ω^{op}-limits and, instead, which preserve only binary weak pullbacks. This is equivalent to our definition in Def. 2.3.

A leading example of analytic functors is the functor $\exp(X)$. For a given set A, we define $\exp(A)$ as the set of all finite multisets of members of A. For a finite multiset $\{a_1, a_2, \ldots, a_n\}$ of members of A, we have a weak normal form $(X, \{x_1, x_2, \ldots, x_n\}) \xrightarrow{f} (A, \{a_1, a_2, \ldots, a_n\})$ for an n-pointed set X of pairwise distinct $x_1, x_2, \ldots, x_n$. Here the function $X \xrightarrow{f} A$ is not unique, but is determined unique up to the action of S_n on X by permutation. So the functor $\exp(X)$ is isomorphic to $1 + X + X^2/S_2 + X^3/S_3 + \cdots$ where S_n is the symmetric group on n. The reason the functor is called $\exp(X)$ is that the power series above turns out to equal the Taylor series of the exponential if we identify the symmetric groups S_n with their orders $n!$.

We have a straightforward generalization of normal and analytic functors to those functors on $\textbf{Set}^n$.

3 Divisibility Ordering

Some of analytic functors can be regarded as functors on the category $\textbf{QO}$ of quasi-orders. For example, the functors represented by polynomials such as $1 + X^2$ works on $\textbf{QO}$ by reading + coproduct and $\times$ cartesian product. The functor $\text{List}(X)$ is lifted to $\textbf{QO}$ by ordering $\text{List}(A)$ with Higman embedding [10] for each quasi-order A. Also the functor $\exp(X)$ is lifted by ordering with the divisibility relation which is defined as follows: for multisets $\alpha, \beta \in \exp(A)$, we put $\alpha \trianglelefteq \beta$ iff there is a one-to-one function $\alpha \xrightarrow{f} \beta$ such that $x \leq f(x)$ for every $x \in \alpha$.

An *inclusion* between quasi-orders is an order-preserving map $A \xrightarrow{f} B$ such that $f(a) \leq f(a')$ implies $a \leq a'$. A functor $F : \textbf{QO} \to \textbf{QO}$ is a *lifting* of a functor $F_0 : \textbf{Set} \to \textbf{Set}$ if the square diagram

$$
\begin{array}{ccc}
\textbf{QO} & \xrightarrow{F} & \textbf{QO} \\
\downarrow & & \downarrow \\
\textbf{Set} & \xrightarrow{F_0} & \textbf{Set}
\end{array}
$$

commutes, where the vertical arrows are the forgetful functors. We often write simply F for F_0.

We notice the following fact: If a functor $F : \textbf{QO} \to \textbf{QO}$ preserving inclusions is a lifting of a functor on $\textbf{Set}$ preserving filtered colimits, then F preserves filtered colimits.

3.1 Definition
Let $F : \textbf{QO} \to \textbf{QO}$ be a functor preserving inclusions which is a lifting of an analytic functor on $\textbf{Set}$.

The *divisibility ordering* on an initial algebra μF is an ω-inductive limit in the category **QO** of $A_0 \xrightarrow{e_0} A_1 \xrightarrow{e_1} \cdots$ where A_0 is an empty quasi-order and e_0 is an empty map, and A_{n+1}, e_{n+1} are defined as follows:

(i) The underlying set of A_{n+1} is $F(A_n)$. The quasi-ordering of A_{n+1} is given as the transitive closure of the union of the following two relations: The first is the quasi-order of $F(A_n)$. The second is the collection of all $a^\circ \le a$ if $(X, z) \xrightarrow{f} (A_n, a)$ is a weak normal form in el(F) and a° is in the image of $X \xrightarrow{f} A_n \xrightarrow{e_n} A_{n+1}$.

(ii) $e_{n+1} : A_{n+1} \to A_{n+2}$ is given by $F(e_n)$. We can show that e_{n+1} is order-preserving.

Remark: (i) The underlying set μF of the divisibility ordering is simply the inductive limit $\operatorname{colim}_n F^n(\emptyset)$ where F is regarded as a functor on **Set**. Roughly speaking, μF is the union $\bigcup_n F^n(\emptyset)$. Since an analytic functor F preserves filtered colimits, there is a canonical bijection $\gamma : F(\mu F) \xrightarrow{\sim} \mu F$ in **Set**.

(ii) We may define the *subterms* of a member a of μF as follows: Let a be in A_{n+1} and we can take a finite set of a° as in (i) of Def. 3.1. We call each a° (regarded as a member of μF) a subterm of a.

We explain that tree-embeddings are special cases of the divisibility orderings, using a functor $FX = 1 + X^2$ as an example. The underlying set of μF is the collection of all binary ordered trees. The unique member of $A_1 = 1 + \emptyset^2 \cong 1$ is the tree consisting of a single node. For $A_{n+1} = 1 + A_n^2$, the first factor 1 is the same as A_1, and the second factor A_n^2 corresponds to the collection of the trees of the form $\operatorname{span}\langle t, t' \rangle$ where t and t' are members of A_n. In this way, the set A_n is the collection of all binary trees of height at most n. We have a natural embedding of A_n into A_{n+1}, corresponding to e_n in the definition.

Let us consider the quasi-order on A_{n+1}. We recall that the order is generated by the union of two quasi-orderings. The first one is induced from $1 + A_n^2$ where the ordering on A_n^2 is the componentwise comparison. Hence this ordering amounts to the following: ($\odot$) if $t \le u$ and $t' \le u'$ in A_n, then $\operatorname{span}\langle t, t' \rangle \le \operatorname{span}\langle u, u' \rangle$ holds in A_{n+1}. To understand the second one, we note that the normal form of $(A, \operatorname{span}\langle t, t' \rangle)$ in the category el(F) of elements has the shape $(X, \operatorname{span}\langle x, x' \rangle) \xrightarrow{f} (A, \operatorname{span}\langle t, t' \rangle)$ where $X = \{x, x'\}$ and f assigns t to x and t' to x'. So the image of $e_n f$ is the set of t and t' as subsets of A_{n+1}. Hence this orderings corresponds to ($\circledast$) $t \le \operatorname{span}\langle t, t' \rangle$ and $t' \le \operatorname{span}\langle t, t' \rangle$. The transitive closure of ($\odot$) and ($\circledast$) yields the tree-embeddings restricted to A_{n+1}. Hence, taking the colimit of all A_n, we see that the divisibility ordering on μF is exactly the tree-embedding on the set of binary ordered trees.

3.2 Theorem

*Let $F : \mathbf{QO} \to \mathbf{QO}$ be a functor preserving inclusions which is a lifting of an analytic functor on **Set**.*

If F sends well-quasi-orders to well-quasi-orders, then the divisibility ordering on an initial algebra μF is a well-quasi-order.

Remark: We can weaken the condition that the functor on **Set** is analytic in the theorem. What we need is that we have some sort of normal forms $(X, z) \xrightarrow{f} (A, a)$ such that the image of Ff is determined. We take analytic functors as a modest choice that are mathematically interesting and cover important examples.

The proof of theorem is a modification of standard minimal bad sequence argument. We first prove the following lemma.

3.3 Lemma

Let $\gamma : F(\mu F) \xrightarrow{\sim} \mu F$ be the canonical bijection in **Set**. Then γ is order-preserving, i.e., a morphism of **QO**.

(*Proof*) We may regard μF as the directed union $\bigcup A_n$. Since F preserves filtered colimits of quasi-orders, if $a \leq a'$ holds in $F(\mu F)$, then there is A_n such that $a \leq a'$ holds in $F(A_n)$. Hence $a \leq a'$ holds in A_{n+1}, which implies $a \leq a'$ in μF. (We note that the inverse μ^{-1} does not preserve quasi-orderings.) $\square$

(*Proof of Theorem*) We define $p(a)$ of $a \in \mu F$ by the least number n satisfying $a \in A_n$. Supposed that there is an infinite bad sequence, we take an infinite minimal bad sequence $a_0, a_1, a_2 \ldots$ in the following sense: for every infinite decreasing sequence $a_0, a_1, \ldots, a_{n-1}, b_n, b_{n+1}, \ldots$ ($n \geq 0$), it holds that $p(a_n) \leq p(b_n)$. (Note: there may be no infinite bad sequence for which the sequence $p(a_0), p(a_1), \ldots$ is minimal by the lexicographic order, since A_n may be infinite, preventing us from the use of König's lemma.)

For each i, we let $(X_i, z_i) \xrightarrow{f_i} (A_{p(i)}, a_i)$ be a weak normal form in el(F). We put the sub-quasi-order S of μF as the union $\bigcup \text{Im}(f_i)$. We claim that S is a well-quasi-order. Let us assume there is an infinite bad sequence b_i in S, for contradiction. Suppose that b_0 is in $\text{Im}(f_{i_0})$. Since $\text{Im}(f_0) \cup \cdots \cup \text{Im}(f_{i_0-1})$ is finite, we assume without loss of generality that no b_i belongs to this union. Now consider an infinite sequence $a_0, a_1, \ldots, a_{i_0-1}, b_0, b_1, b_2, \ldots$. This sequence must be good in μF since $p(b_0) < p(a_{i_0})$ while the sequence a_i is minimal. Thus there are $j < i_0$ and $k \in \omega$ such that $a_j \leq b_k$ in μF. We have $b_k \in \text{Im}(f_l)$ for some l and moreover $i_0 \leq l$ by the condition on b_i. Hence $a_j \leq a_l$ and $j < l$, contradicting the assumption that a_i is bad. Therefore S is a well-quasi-order.

Now $F(S)$ is a well-quasi-order by hypothesis on F. So the sequence a_i must be good in $F(S)$, and thus in $F(\mu F)$. By Lemma 3.3, the sequence a_i is good also in μF. This contradicts the assumption that a_i is bad. (*End of Proof*)

The functors we considered so far preserve well-quasi-orders. Disjoint sum + and cartesian product × preserve well-quasi-orders [2]. The functor exp(-) does so by ordering $\exp(X)$ by the divisibility relation. Moreover List(-) preserves well-quasi-orders as derived from Thm. 3.2, since $\text{List}(X)$ itself is a divisibility ordering on the initial algebra $\mu Y. 1 + XY$. Hence all of the examples in the following are well-quasi-orders (actually well-partial-orders).

3.4 Example
(i) For a quasi-order A, the divisibility ordering on $\text{List}(A) = \mu Y. 1 + AY$ is exactly the Higman embedding.

(ii) The divisibility ordering on $\mu X. \text{List}(X)$ is exactly the tree-embedding on ordered finite trees.

(iii) The divisibility ordering on $\mu X. \exp(X)$ is exactly the tree-embedding on unordered finite trees.

We want to deal with iterated applications of the initial algebra construction μ. For example, supposed $F : \mathbf{Set}^2 \to \mathbf{Set}$ is a 2-place analytic functor, we have a functor $\mu Y. F(X,Y)$ in a single variable X. In order to bind X with the operator μ, we must know that $\mu Y. F(X,Y)$ is analytic.

3.5 Lemma
The functor $\mu F : \mathbf{Set}^n \to \mathbf{Set}$ is analytic for each analytic functor $F : \mathbf{Set} \times \mathbf{Set}^n \to \mathbf{Set}$. Furthermore, μF is normal if F is normal.

(*Proof*) The functor μF is defined as the colimit of $A_n(Y)$ where $A_0(Y) = \emptyset$ and $A_{n+1}(Y) = F(A_n(Y), Y)$. We show that every object (B,b) of $\text{el}(\mu F)$ has a weak normal form. There are n and $b_0 \in A_n(B)$ such that $b = (\gamma_n)_B(b_0)$ where $\gamma_n : A_n \to \mu F$ is a natural transformation occurring as a part of the colimiting cone. Let us take a weak normal form $(Z, c_0) \xrightarrow{f} (B, b_0)$ in $\text{el}(A_n)$. But γ_n is a weak cartesian natural transformation, which is defined as a cartesian natural transformation [7] but the defining square diagrams being weak pullbacks rather than pullbacks. Since a weak cartesian natural transformation preserves weak normal forms, $(Z, (\gamma_n)_Z(c_0)) \xrightarrow{f} (B, b)$ is a weak normal form. $\quad\square$

For example, $F(X) = \mu Y. Y^2 + X$ is a normal functor with this lemma. The formal power series representation of this functor can be computed symbolically as follows: We consider an algebraic equation $Y = Y^2 + X$. The root of this equation subject to $Y(0) = 0$ is given by $Y = (1 - \sqrt{1 - 4X})/2$. Expanding the right hand side, we have $F(X) = X + X^2 + 2X^3 + 5X^4 + \cdots + C_{n-1}X^n + \cdots$ where C_n is the n-th Catalan number $(1/(n+1))\binom{2n}{n}$. Indeed, it is easy to see that this series is the unique one satisfying the algebraic equation.

As an example of iterated initial algebras, we consider $\mu X_1 \mu X_2 \cdots \mu X_n. \exp(X_1 + X_2 + \cdots + X_n)$. This example provides an embedding of trees with a gap condition. We decompose the iterated initial algebras into

$$D_1 = \mu X_1 . D_2[X_1]$$
$$D_2[X_1] = \mu X_2 . D_3[X_1, X_2]$$
$$\vdots$$
$$D_n[X_1, X_2, \ldots, X_{n-1}] = \mu X_n . D_\infty[X_1, X_2, \ldots, X_n]$$
$$D_\infty[X_1, X_2, \ldots, X_n] = \exp(X_1 + X_2 + \cdots + X_n).$$

We associate a canonical substitution $\eta = [D_1/X_1][D_2/X_2] \cdots [D_n/X_n]$. Let γ_k be the constructor associated to the operator μX_k, namely, the canonical isomorphism $[D_k/X_k]D_{k+1} \xrightarrow{\sim} D_k$ (see Remark (i) after Def. 3.1), and let $\overline{\gamma}_k t$ be a shorthand of an element $\gamma_k \gamma_{k+1} \cdots \gamma_n t$ of ηD_k where t is a member of ηD_∞. We note that every element of ηD_k has this form. An element t of ηD_∞ is a multiset $\{\overline{\gamma}_{k_1} t_1, \overline{\gamma}_{k_2} t_2, \ldots, \overline{\gamma}_{k_n} t_n\}$. It is convenient to write this an unorederd tree with edges labeled by natural numbers from $1, 2, \ldots, n$:

Let s be an element ηD_∞ given as $\{\overline{\gamma}_{j_1} s_1, \overline{\gamma}_{j_2} s_2, \ldots, \overline{\gamma}_{j_m} s_m\}$ and t as above. Then we can show that $s \trianglelefteq t$ holds with the divisibility ordering iff there is a one-to-one function $m \xrightarrow{e} n$ such that $j_i = k_{ei}$ and there is a path from the root of t_{ei} to some subterm t° (possibly t_{ei} itself) such that all labels l of the edges on the path satisfy $j_i \leq l$ and moreover $s_i \trianglelefteq t^\circ$ holds, for all $i = 1, 2, \ldots, m$. This is an edge-labeled version of Friedman's embedding with a gap condition [20]. We note that Thm. 3.2 an easy proof that this embedding forms a well-partial-ordering.

Remark: Let us define a class of algebras A by the following syntax:

$$A \quad ::= \quad \emptyset \mid 1 \mid X \mid A + A \mid A \times A \mid \mu X . A$$

Among these, X is a variable taken from a given countable set. The other symbols have obvious interpretations as partial orders. For instance, 1 is the partial order of a singleton, $A + B$ is the coproduct of two partial orders, and $\mu X . A$ is the divisibility ordering. By Thm. 3.2 and Lemma 3.5, all closed algebras (i.e., those without free variables) are well-partial-orders. This is a generalization of the class dealt in [9].

4   Recursive Path Ordering

We turn to the category **LO** of linear orders. Some of the functors that appear in the previous sections are regarded also as functors from **LO** to **LO**.

(1) The functors of the shape of polynomials such as $1 + X^2$. The sum $A + B$ of linear orders is defined by putting B over A. The product $A \times B$ is linearly ordered by the inverse lexicographic ordering. Namely we compare the second

component first. This is in order to accommodate to the convention in standard ordinal notations. Note that $1 + X^2$ is not isomorphic to $X^2 + 1$ in **LO**.

(2) The functor $\mathrm{List}(X)$. We have two linear orderings on $\mathrm{List}(A)$ where A is a linear order. According to $\mu Y. 1 + YA$ and $\mu Y. 1 + AY$, Def. 4.1 below yields two orderings. The former yields the kachinuki ordering, that is, the monadic recursive path ordering [19, 16], and the latter the ordering that compares two lists by lengths first, and by the inverse lexicographic ordering second.

(3) The functor $\exp(X)$ turns out to be a functor on **LO** by the multiset ordering [4]. The multiset ordering for $X = \{x_1 > \cdots > x_n\}$ corresponds to the lexicographic ordering as a term ordering on the set of power products $x_1^{k_1} x_2^{k_2} \cdots x_n^{k_n}$ in the theory of Gröbner bases [1]. Similarly to $\mathrm{List}(X)$, there is another linear order on $\exp(X)$ by comparing the number of elements in multisets first and then by comparing them by the multiset ordering. In words of term orders, this corresponds to the total degree-lexicographic ordering (*ibid.*).

4.1 Definition
Let a functor $F : \mathbf{LO} \to \mathbf{LO}$ be a lifting of an analytic functor F on **Set**.

The *recursive path ordering* on an initial algebra μF is an ω-inductive limit in the category **LO** of $A_0 \xrightarrow{e_0} A_1 \xrightarrow{e_1} \cdots$ where A_0 is an empty linear order and e_0 is an empty map, and A_{n+1}, e_{n+1} are defined as follows:

(i)   The underlying set of A_{n+1} is $F(A_n)$. The order on A_{n+1} is defined as the binary relation $<$ satisfying the following: Let a, b be members of A_{n+1} with weak normal forms $(X, z) \xrightarrow{f} (A_n, a)$ and $(Y, v) \xrightarrow{g} (A_n, b)$ in $\mathrm{el}(F)$. Then $a < b$ holds in A_{n+1} iff either
   (1) $a < b$ in $F(A_n)$ and moreover, for every a° in the image of $X \xrightarrow{f} A_n \xrightarrow{e_{n+1}} A_{n+1}$, it holds that $a^\circ < b$ in A_{n+1}; or
   (2) $a \le b^\circ$ in A_{n+1} for some b° in the image of $Y \xrightarrow{g} A_n \xrightarrow{e_{n+1}} A_{n+1}$.

(ii) $e_{n+1} : A_{n+1} \to A_{n+2}$ is given by $F(e_n)$. We can show that e_{n+1} is strictly order-preserving.

Remark: (i) The definition of the order on A_{n+1} is given by the induction on $p(a) + p(b)$. We define $p(a)$ of $a \in \mu F$ by the least number n satisfying $a \in A_n$. We can prove that A_{n+1} is a linear ordered set.   (ii) Let us note that $a < b$ in $F(A_n)$ does not imply $a < b$ in A_{n+1}.

4.2 Theorem
*Let $F : \mathbf{LO} \to \mathbf{LO}$ be a lifting of an analytic functor on **Set**.*

If F sends well-orders to well-orders, then the recursive path ordering on μF is a well-order.

(*Proof*)   For contradiction, suppose that there is an infinite decreasing sequence $a_0, a_1, \ldots$ in μF. Then it is immediate to see that there is a minimal infinite decreasing sequence in the following sense: $a_0, a_1, \ldots$ is minimal iff, for every infinite decreasing sequence $a_0, a_1, \ldots, a_{n-1}, b_n, b_{n+1}, \ldots$ $(n \geq 0)$, it holds that $p(a_n) \leq p(b_n)$ where p is defined as in the remark after Def. 4.1.

We put S to be the set of all subterms of a_n $(n \in \omega)$. We show that S is well-ordered as a suborder of μF. For contradiction, we assume that $b_0, b_1, \ldots$ is an infinite decreasing sequence. We let b_0 be a subterm of a_n. Then the sequence $a_0, a_1, \ldots, a_{n-1}, b_0, b_1, \ldots$ is an infinite decreasing sequence satisfying $p(a_n) \leq p(b_0)$. This contradicts minimality.

Since F preserves well-orders, $a_0, a_1, \ldots$ cannot be decreasing in $F(S)$, thus in $F(\mu F)$. So there is some n such that $a_n < a_{n+1}$ in $F(\mu F)$ while $a_n > a_{n+1}$ in μF. By definition of recursive path ordering, we must have some subterm a° of a_n such that $a^\circ \geq a_{n+1}$. Then $a_0, a_1, \ldots, a_{n-1}, a^\circ, a_{n+2}, \ldots$ is an infinite decreasing sequence with $p(a^\circ) < p(a_n)$. Contradiction. $\square$

Remark: In contrast with the corresponding proof of Thm. 3.2, the canonical mapping $F(\mu F) \to \mu F$ is not a morphism of **LO**. So we give a more direct proof instead.

We can employ Fact 2.1 to check the conditions of the theorem. The functors on **LO** given at the beginning of this section are linearization of functors on **QO**. Namely a functor **LO** $\xrightarrow{F}$ **LO** is associated with **QO** $\xrightarrow{F'}$ **QO** in such a way that, for each linear order A, the linear order $F(A)$ is a linearization of the partial order $F'(A)$. In this situation, if F' preserves well-quasi-orders, then F preserves well-orders by Fact. 2.1. Hence we can immediately derive that the recursive path orderings in the following example are well-orders.

4.3 Example
(i) If we order $\exp(X)$ by the multiset ordering, the recursive path ordering on $\mu X. \exp(X)$ is the multiset path ordering on the set of unordered finite trees that are regarded as terms generated by a single function symbol of variable arity.

(ii) The recursive path ordering on $\mu X \mu Y. 1 + XY$ corresponds to the relation $\prec_r$ in [5], although we must pad with virtually least element 0 to right rather than to left since we take the inverse lexicographic ordering.

(iii) The set $\mu X. 1 + X^2 + \exp(X) + X^3$ is generated by one constant a, one binary symbol f, one tertiary symbol g, and one symbol h of variable arity. The recursive path ordering on μF is the RPO with status [14, 17] where f and g are given a lexicographic status and h a multiset status. The precedence ordering is $a \prec f \prec h \prec g$.

5 Dilator

In the previous section, we considered a functor $F : \textbf{LO} \to \textbf{LO}$ which is a lifting of an analytic functor, and which preserves well-orders. We show that such a functor is actually a dilator [6]. A *dilator* is a functor from **LO** to **LO** preserving filtered colimits and binary pullbacks as well as preserving well-orders.

5.1 Proposition

Let $F : \mathbf{LO} \to \mathbf{LO}$ be a lifting of an analytic functor on **Set**.

If F sends well-orders to well-orders, then F is a dilator.

(*Proof*) Let F be a lifting of $F_0 : \mathbf{Set} \to \mathbf{Set}$. We must show that, if F_0 preserve weak pullbacks, then F preserves (binary) pullbacks. Note that F_0 preserves one-to-one functions since F_0 has a lifting, and that a weak pullback is a pullback if the projections are one-to-one. □

5.2 Example

(i) $F(X) = \mu Y. X + Y^2$ is the dilator of lexicographic path ordering on binary ordered trees the leaves of which are labeled with members of X.

(ii) $F(X) = \mu Y. (\exp Y) \times X$ is the dilator of multiset path ordering on finite unordered trees the nodes of which are labeled with members of X.

As a final example, we show that a slight variation of ordinal diagrams $O(n, A)$ by Takeuti [21] turns out to be naturally a dilator as a functor of linear order A with recursive path orderings. For a positive natural number n, let us put

$$O(n, A) = \mu X_1 \mu X_2 \cdots \mu X_n. \exp(X_1 A + X_2 A + \cdots + X_n A).$$

We define D_i $(i = 1, 2, \ldots, n, \infty)$ as in section 3 by replacing the right hand side of D_∞ with $\exp(X_1 A + \cdots + X_n A)$. By Prop. 5.1, this $O(n, A)$ is a dilator as a functor of A. In particular, $O(n, A)$ is well-ordered if so is A.

We show that $O(n, A)$ behaves almost as ordinal diagrams. We follow the notation in section 3. If $t = \{\overline{\gamma}_{k_1}\langle t_1, a_1\rangle, \ldots, \overline{\gamma}_{k_m}\langle t_m, a_m\rangle\}$ is a member of ηD_∞, we associate an ordinal diagram t^o given as the natural sum $(k_1 - 1, t_1^o, a_1) \,\sharp\!\!\!\sharp\, \cdots \,\sharp\!\!\!\sharp\,$ $(k_m - 1, t_m^o, a_m)$. If m equals 0, we put $t^o = 0$. We do not distinguish an ordinal diagram from its permutation of the summands with respect to $\sharp\!\!\!\sharp$. Moreover, we regard $0 \,\sharp\!\!\!\sharp\, s$ to equal s (this is a minor difference from the original definition). In the following, we do not distinguish s from the associated ordinal diagram s^o.

In order to define linear orders on ordinal diagram, Takeuti introduces i-sections for $i = 0, 1, \ldots, n - 1$. We have a natural interpretation of i-sections in terms of analytic functors. Let u be a member of ηD_∞. For each occurrence $\overline{\gamma}_{k+1}\langle t, a\rangle = (k, a, t)$ in the multiset u, let

$$(Z_1, \ldots, Z_k, c) \xrightarrow{(f_1, \ldots, f_k)} (\eta D_1, \ldots, \eta D_k, \overline{\gamma}_k\langle t, a\rangle)$$

be a finite weak normal form in $\mathrm{el}(D_{k+1})$. Then t is a k-section of u and, furthermore, if (i, a, s) is in the image of $Z_{i+1} \xrightarrow{f_{i+1}} \eta D_{i+1}$ $(i = 0, 1, \ldots, k - 1)$ then s is an i-section of u.

$n + 1$ orderings $<_i$ (where $i = 0, 1, \ldots, n - 1, \infty$) on the set of ordinal diagrams are defined almost in the same way as in [21]. A difference is in that we read $(s_1 \natural \cdots \natural s_m) <_i (t_1 \natural \cdots \natural t_n)$ as the multiset ordering (i.e., as natural sums) only if $i = \infty$. Accordingly we apply the rule for $<_i$ ($i \neq \infty$) to all ordinal diagram, not only those of the shape (j, b, t) (connected diagrams).

We show that the orders $<_i$ for $i = 0, 1, \ldots, n - 1$ correspond to the recursive path orderings on D_{i+1}, and that the order $<_\infty$ corresponds to the induced multiset ordering on D_∞:

5.3 Proposition
Let s and t be ordinal diagrams.

(i) *$s <_\infty t$ holds iff $s < t$ by the multiset path ordering on ηD_∞.*

(ii) *$s <_i t$ holds iff $\overline{\gamma}_{i+1} s < \overline{\gamma}_{i+1} t$ by the recursive path ordering on ηD_{i+1}, for all $i = 0, 1, \ldots, n - 1$.* $\square$

We emphasize that complicated syntactic definitions of i-sections and linear orders $<_i$ are naturally interpreted using analytic functors and recursive path orderings. Moreover, our notation with iterated initial algebras clearly suggests the reason we need subsidiary orderings $<_1, \ldots, <_{n-1}, <_\infty$ to define the principal one $<_0$.

Hence iterated initial algebras give a method to obtain the functorial notations of big ordinals, more succinctly than other approaches [8, 22]. In fact, we can achieve all ordinals less than the proof-theoretical ordinal of Π_1^1-CA_0 with only $+$, $\times$ and the operator μ.

References

1. T. Becker and V. Weispfenning, *Gröbner Bases*, Graduate Texts in Mathematics 141, (Springer, 1993).

2. D. H. J. de Jongh and R. Parikh, Well-partial orderings and hierarchies, *Indagationes Math.* **39** (1977) 195–207.

3. N. Dershowitz, Orderings for term-rewriting systems, *Theoretical Computer Sci.* **17** (1982) 279–301.

4. N. Dershowitz and Z. Manna, Proving termination with multiset orderings, *Communications ACM* **22** (1979) 465–476.

5. N. Dershowitz and M. Okada, Proof theoretic techniques for term rewriting theory, in: *Third Annual Symposium on Logic in Computer Science*, 1988, Edinburgh, Scotland, (IEEE, 1988) pp.104–111.

6. J.-Y. Girard, Π_2^1-logic, part I; dilators, *Ann. Math. Logic* **21** (1981) 75–219.

7. J.-Y. Girard, Normal functors, power series and λ-calculus, *Ann. Pure Applied Logic* **37** (1988) 129–177.

8. J.-Y. Girard and J. Vauzeilles, Functors and ordinal notations II: A functorial construction of the Bachmann-hierarchy, *J. Symbolic Logic* **49** (1984) 713–729.

9. R. Hasegawa, Well-ordering of algebras and Kruskal's theorem, in: *Logic, Language and Computation, Festschrift in Honor of Satoru Takasu*, N. D. Jones, M. Hagiya,

M. Sato, eds., Lecture Notes in Computer Science 792, (Springer, 1994) pp. 133–172.

10. G. Higman, Ordering by divisibility in abstract algebras, *Proc. London Math. Soc., Third Series* **2** (1952) 326–336.

11. A. Joyal, Une théorie combinatoire des séries formelles, *Advances Math.* **42** (1981) 1–82.

12. A. Joyal, Foncteurs analytiques et espèces de structures, in: *Combinatoire Enumérative*, Proceedings, Montreal, Québec, Canada, 1985, G. Labelle, P. Leroux, eds., Lecture Notes in Mathematics 1234, (Springer, 1986) pp. 126–159.

13. J. B. Kruskal, Well-quasi-ordering, the tree theorem, and Vazsonyi's conjecture, *Transactions American Math. Soc.* **95** (1960) 210–225.

14. P. Lescanne, Uniform termination of term rewriting systems, recursive decomposition ordering with status, in: *Ninth Colloquium on Trees in Algebra and Programming*, 1984, Bordeaux, France, B. Courcelle ed., (Cambridge University Press, 1984) pp. 181–194.

15. S. Mac Lane and I. Moerdijk, *Sheaves in Geometry and Logic, A First Introduction to Topos Theory*, (Springer, 1992).

16. U. Martin and E. Scott, The order types of termination orderings on monadic terms, strings and multisets, in: *Proc. Eighth Annual IEEE Symposium on Logic in Computer Science*, 1992, Montreal, Canada, (IEEE, 1993) pp. 356–363.

17. A. Middeldorp and H. Zantema, Simple termination of rewrite systems, *Theoretical Computer Sci.*, **175** (1997) 127–158.

18. C. St. J. A. Nash-Williams, On well-quasi-ordering finite trees, *Proc. Cambridge Philosophical Soc.* **59** (1963) 833–835.

19. K. Sakai, Knuth-Bendix algorithm for Thue system based on kachinuki ordering, ICOT Technical Memorandum: TM-0087, ICOT, Institute for New Generation Computer Technology, Dec. 1984.

20. S. G. Simpson, Nonprovability of certain combinatorial properties of finite trees, in: *Harvey Friedman's research on the foundations of mathematics*, L. A. Harrington, M. D. Morley, A. Scedrov, S. G. Simpson, eds., (North-Holland, 1985) pp. 87–117.

21. G. Takeuti, *Proof Theory*, Studies in Logic and the Foundations of Mathematics, Vol. 81, (North-Holland, 1975).

22. A. Weiermann, A functorial property of the Aczel-Buchholz-Feferman function, *J. Symbolic Logic*, **59** (1994) 945–955.

Share-Where Maintenance in Visual Algebraic Specifications

T. B. Dinesh[1] and Susan M. Üsküdarlı[2,3]

[1] CWI, P.O. Box 94079, 1090 GB Amsterdam, The Netherlands. dinesh@cwi.nl
[2] Current address: Philips Research Palo Alto, 1070 Arastradero Road, Palo Alto, CA 94304-1336, USA. susan@prpa.philips.com
[3] Work done while at: WINS, University of Amsterdam, The Netherlands.

Abstract. Algebraic specifications whose signatures (abstract-syntax) have a mapping to pictures (two-dimensional concrete syntax) along with equations which are defined in terms of these pictures are introduced as visual algebraic specifications. The visual signatures are specified using visual lexicals which may be user-defined. The semantic rules are a set of equations which are defined using the language's own syntax. Signatures, semantic rules, and terms (programs) are all defined with interactive editors. The usual notion of term construction in an editor is extended by allowing subterm sharing which is necessary for two-dimensional representations. As is usual for algebraic specifications, we use term rewriting to provide a prototyping environment for these visual algebraic specifications. This work addresses the problem of presenting output terms after rewriting (visual pretty printing). We introduce a technique called "Share-Where Maintenance" which is used to preserve layout information and demonstrate its use as well as its limitations.

1 Introduction

Algebraic specification formalisms are useful in describing the syntax and semantics of a language and have been popularized by [5–7]. These formalisms can also be used to provide meta-environments that help not only in developing such specifications for a given language, but also in prototyping the language environment itself [3]. This is possible since the (conditional) equations used to specify the semantics can be oriented into a term rewriting system which reduces a program to its result. Also, a mapping from the signature of the algebra to a concrete syntax for the language can be used to generate syntax directed editors that become part of the language environment. When a program is constructed with such an editor, the corresponding (abstract syntax) terms can be reduced by the term rewriting system. The result of which is pretty printed using the mapping back to concrete syntax [2].

We focus on developing such an environment for visual languages, i.e., languages where the mapping from abstract syntax to a concrete syntax results in pictures instead of text [11]. Accordingly, we extend the usual notion of syntax directed program construction to permit the sharing of similar program constructs as dictated by sort information. This sharing is present only at the editor level. It is not reflected to the abstract syntax as we still consider term rewriting as our operational semantics.

After rewriting the term we must present it to the user. In doing so we must try to preserve the similarity of the appearance of the common terms between the initial and final terms (residuals). Furthermore, we must find some way of presenting the terms introduced during rewriting. If we were to simply rely on the mapping from abstract syntax to visual syntax to construct the final presentation we would loose all the presentation choices the user has made in the initial term—such as placement and sizes. This would result in a picture that could confuse the user, where they may not be able to recognize the similar pictures in the output term. The use of visual syntax is very powerful in presenting relationships. However, jumbling up a picture into a semantically equivalent one often is not be perceived as equivalent. Thus maintaining consistency in visual presentations is very important.

In order to tackle the pretty printing problem, we track the origin of a (sub)picture and use as much information from it as possible. Origins can either be in the initial term or in an equation which is responsible for the creation of new symbols. Both such origins have visual presentations in our VAS (Visual Algebraic Specification) formalism [12]. We annotate the abstract syntax trees with information on which terms were shared and where the corresponding pictures were created. We then transform the term rewriting system to another one which maintains these annotations as the term reduces. The semantics of the original term rewriting system is not altered. The annotations present in the result of such a reduction help when building a concrete picture by allowing one to inspect the properties of the originating picture.

In Section 2 we explain how the syntax and semantics of two dimensional visual languages can be specified using our VAS formalism. In Section 3 we illustrate sharing in a term editor. In Section 4 we consider the problem of pretty printing and discuss Share-Where maintenance. Finally, in Section 5 there is a discussion of related work and concluding remarks.

2 VAS specification

A VAS specification consists of three parts. The first part concerns the definition of the visual lexicals for the language. This is achieved with a language called VODL (Visual Object Definition Language) [13] which defines graphical elements. We refer to these definitions as vods (visual object definitions). The second part specifies the context-free syntax of the visual language using the lexicals defined in the first part. This phase constructs a mapping from abstract syntax constructs to the vods. This is analogous to the classical BNF and SDF [7] approach used for 1-dimensional (textual) languages and gives a specification of allowable visual terms. The third part defines the semantics of the language using the syntax of the language itself. We will illustrate this specification process with a small language for a deterministic finite state automata which we will call *FSA*.

	vod	Description
1	v (in a circle)	a *vod* contained within a circle.
2	v (in a double circle)	a *vod* contained within double circle.
3	$\Rightarrow v$	arrow followed by a *vod*.
4	$v_1 \xrightarrow{\ v_2\ } v_3$	an arrow connected to two *vods* with a *vod* above.
5	$v_1\ v_2$	two unconstrained *vods*
6	$\begin{array}{c} v_1 \\ v_2 \end{array}$	one *vod* above another *vod*.
7	v (with a rectangle above it)	a *vod* with a rectangle above it.
8	$\boxed{v}$	*vod* in a rectangle.

Fig. 1. Some *vods* of interest.

2.1 Visual lexicals

Figure 1 shows some of the *vods* that are used when defining the syntax of our *FSA* language. These *vods* are all parameterized composite *vods*, where a parameter is represented with a *v*, possibly subscripted. The first five *vods* will be used to represent some syntactic construct of *FSA*: 1) normal state; 2) final state; 3) start state; 4) transition; 5) transition set. The fifth *vod* defines a *vod* consisting of two *vods* with no constraints between them, thus it is used only for relating them together. The last two *vods* are used in the definition of the dynamic semantics of the language: 6) used in defining *vod* 7 and defining the output configuration of the FSA (*FSA-OUT-CONF* in Figure 3); 7) current state; 8) variable definition. These *vods* are used in the next two sections where sorts serve as the parameters for these *vods*.

2.2 Syntax definition

The syntax of finite state automata is defined in the module *FSA* shown in Figure 2. An automaton consists of a set of transitions along with a starting state and a collection of final states. The imported module *Strings* defines upper-case characters (*UChar*) and lower-case characters (*LChar*). Upper case letters are used as state labels and lower case letters are used for input characters. The sort *L* is a parameter for *vods* 1 and 2. The sort *STATE* is a parameter

---

module FSA

imports Strings

sorts   *L FSA STATE SSTATE FSTATE TRAN TRAN-C ALPHA*

context-free syntax

UChar	→ *L*
LChar	→ *ALPHA*
Ⓛ	→ *STATE*
ⓛ	→ *FSTATE*
⇒*STATE*	→ *SSTATE*
STATE $\xrightarrow{ALPHA}$ *STATE*	→ *TRAN*
FSTATE	→ *STATE*
TRAN∗ ◁ {}	→ *TRAN-C*
TRAN-C SSTATE	→ *FSA*

Fig. 2. The syntax specification for *FSA* language.

for *vod*s 3 and 4 (twice for 4). The sort *ALPHA* is a parameter for *vod* 4. The *TRAN-C* defines a collection of transitions, which is used in the definition of *FSA* along with a *SSTATE*. Note that these representations follow from the constraint definitions which have no physical appearance themselves. For example, the fifth *vod* is shown as a composition of one *vod* beside another. In fact, there is no constraint dictating this presentation and thus a picture where one *vod* is above another could also be an instance of it. Such concreteness of visual notation is somewhat problematic in that it can mislead the reader to infer relationships that do not exist. This syntax will be used in term construction as well as semantic specification. Each such definition has a corresponding abstract syntax with an association between the two permitting moving from one level to the other. All term rewriting is done at the abstract level.

2.3   FSA Semantics

To specify the dynamic semantics of *FSA* we first specify a syntax for the functions involved in specifying the semantics. Figure 3 shows the chosen syntax for *FSA* and defines a set of variables that may be used in the equations. Figure 4 shows the semantic equations. The current state is represented with a rectangle

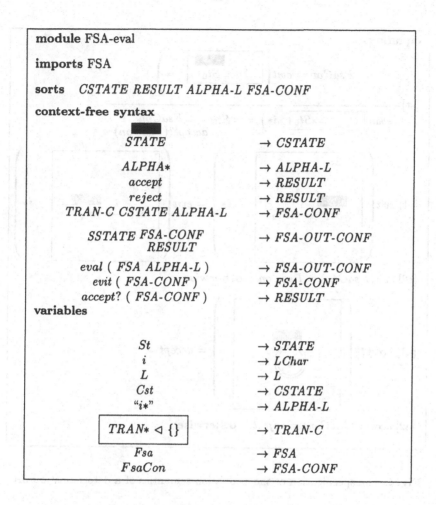

module FSA-eval

imports FSA

sorts   *CSTATE RESULT ALPHA-L FSA-CONF*

context-free syntax

STATE	→ *CSTATE*
ALPHA∗	→ *ALPHA-L*
accept	→ *RESULT*
reject	→ *RESULT*
TRAN-C CSTATE ALPHA-L	→ *FSA-CONF*
SSTATE FSA-CONF RESULT	→ *FSA-OUT-CONF*
eval (FSA ALPHA-L)	→ *FSA-OUT-CONF*
evit (FSA-CONF)	→ *FSA-CONF*
accept? (FSA-CONF)	→ *RESULT*

variables

St	→ *STATE*
i	→ *LChar*
L	→ *L*
Cst	→ *CSTATE*
"i∗"	→ *ALPHA-L*
TRAN∗ ◁ {}	→ *TRAN-C*
Fsa	→ *FSA*
FsaCon	→ *FSA-CONF*

Fig. 3. The specification of the syntax for the evaluation semantics of an *FSA*.

above a state. The input list is zero or more *ALPHA*s. The *eval* function takes an *FSA-CONF*, which is an *FSA*, current state *CSTATE* and an input list *ALPHA-L* and returns the final configuration *FSA-OUT-CONF* with the *RESULT* (*accept* or *reject*) under it. The function *evit* iteratively processes the input string list as far as possible. This function *accept?* returns *accept* if an *FSA-CONF* has the current state on a final state; *reject* otherwise[1].

The declarations involving *TRAN∗* ◁ {} are specified using the predefined collection data type. *TRAN-C* is a collection of zero or more transitions (*TRAN∗*) with no constraining operations between the items in the collection (◁ {}). A collection variable matches a collection. Here for example, $\boxed{Tr}$ matches a

---

[1] The equations marked by the keyword **otherwise** are default equations which can be avoided by using auxiliary functions [3]. Note that by "equations" we mean (conditional) rewrite rules.

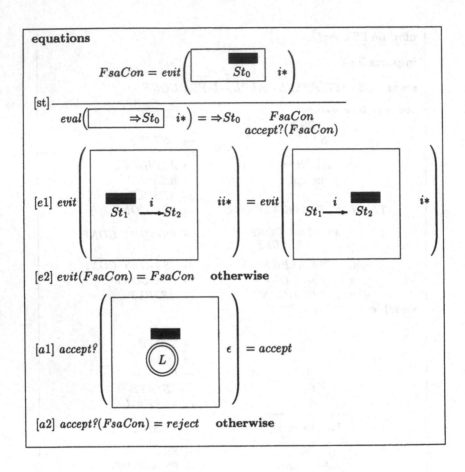

Fig. 4. The specification of the evaluation semantics of a deterministic *FSA*.

collection with at least one transition Tr, where ☐ matches the rest of the collection other than Tr.

The *eval* function starts processing the input string by replacing the start state with the current state and applying the *evit* function, the result of which is combined with the start state again. The reason for putting back the start state is in order to present it back in the result of evaluating the *FSA*. Otherwise it is not necessary. The *accept?* function decides whether the *FSA* configuration is in an acceptable state. The resulting term consists of the *FSA* configuration along with the string *accept* or *reject* positioned below the *FSA*.

In equation [*st*] the evaluation of the *FSA* begins by setting up an *FSA-CONF* by making the start state a current state. The result of iterative evaluation (*evit*) of this *FSA-CONF* is assigned to a variable *FsaCon*. This is used in constructing a presentable *FSA-OUT-CONF* by putting the start state back along with the result of *accept?* under it. The equations [*e1*] and [*e2*] step through the input string moving the current state marker when a transition occurs. In an *FSA-CONF* term

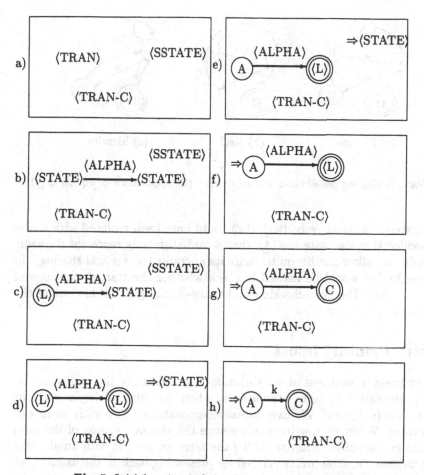

Fig. 5. Initial actions of the construction of an *FSA* sentence. In frame f) the sharing of Ⓐ happens — Ⓐ is selected as the ⟨STATE⟩ which visually shares the already existing Ⓐ with the newly created subterm Ⓐ of the start state.

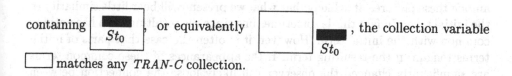

containing [▮ St_0], or equivalently [St_0], the collection variable [ ] matches any *TRAN-C* collection.

3 FSA Term Construction

FSA terms are constructed by providing a collection of transitions and a start state:⟨TRAN-C⟩ ⟨SSTATE⟩. According to the syntax definition the start state, *SSTATE*, may appear anywhere since it is unconstrained. We can, however, choose to make it share the representation of a particular state in the *FSA*. Figure 5 shows a construction sequence where such a (pseudo) sharing is chosen. We call it pseudo sharing, since it is only at the editor level. The sharing choice

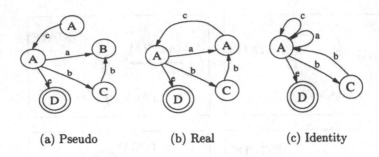

| (a) Pseudo | (b) Real | (c) Identity |

Fig. 6. Various sharing possibilities resulting from the application of equation [p1].

is made in step f. Alternatively, ⟨SSTATE⟩ could have been replaced with a new state. Provided that the state was (A), they would abstractly represent the same term. We do not allow a subterm to share its ancestor (no vertical sharing). In fact a type-checker would be needed to check whether the start state is one of the states of *FSA*. The type-checking and share-checking issues are out of the scope of this paper.

4 Pretty Printing Issues

One of the main advantages of multi-dimensional syntax is the ability to use shared representation in term presentation when depicting multiple relations that exist on a (sub)term. We have already demonstrated how such terms can be constructed. When we rewrite terms we use the abstract syntax of the term constructed in the editor. After rewriting the term we are left with an abstract syntax term that must be pretty printed for presenting back to the user.

The syntax definition of the language provides us with the information we need to obtain a visual term corresponding to the abstract term. However, there are some problems. First of all the *vod* definitions are typically under constrained and thus correspond to many pictures. Even if we choose some criteria to select among these pictures, it is likely that what we present will bear little similarity to the initial term. In fact this is sometimes fine since the resulting term has nothing common with the initial term. However, it is often the case that parts of initial terms remain in the resulting term. If the appearances of these common terms are significantly changed the observer will likely loose the connection between these terms – which is unacceptable. We will focus on this aspect and propose a method whereby we maintain information not only from the initial term but also from the instance where they were created during rewriting. This information is then used to aid in the presentation of the final term.

We refer to the sharing discussed in Section 3 as *pseudo sharing*. The effect of pseudo sharing can be illustrated by the equation:

$$[p1]\ f\left(\boxed{St_1 \xrightarrow{\ c\ } St_2}\right) = \boxed{\text{A}\xrightarrow{\ c\ } St_2}$$

when f is applied the term:

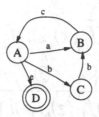

Depending on the underlying representation and interpretation there are choices to be made as how to present the term. The resulting term could be, among others, any of the terms shown in Figure 6. Pseudo sharing is used in work presented in this paper. Real sharing is commonly found in graph grammar approaches. Identity sharing is obtained by giving a meta-level directive that all similar states should be shared. Such sharing requirements are specifiable in context-sensitive formalisms [9]. The sub-figure (a) illustrates the effect of pseudo-sharing and the application of function f. This rewrites a transition labeled "c" and ending in some state St_2 to a transition labeled "c" that begins in state "A" and ends in St_2. Note that all "B" states are not affected but only one which matched the rule is rewritten into "A". After the rewrite it is not clear where to print the "A" state created by application of the rule. Using the approach we discuss below, it would be possible to print it close to (B) with an appropriate constraint solver. Although from the FSA perspective, we would want the two (A)'s of Figure 6(a) to be visually shared, we cannot infer this either from the initial term or from the rule [$p1$].

4.1 Share-Where maintenance

This method annotates terms and propagates created annotations as a result of applying rewrite rules to the term. The underlying rewriting semantics itself is not influenced, since the annotations are not used for determining when a term matches another. Every $f(\cdots)$ is annotated as $f_{[l,t_i:p]}(\cdots)$ where f is an abstract syntax function name, l is a label, t_i is an identifier of a term editor or an equation editor, and p is a path. When a term is initially created by a user, each node gets a unique label l; t_i is the name of the term editor that created the term and p is the path to the node in that editor where the term was created. However when some subterms are shared the share annotation of the sharer is copied to the sharee. This allows the (re)creation of shared representation when displaying the term.

The idea is to maintain information regarding how terms are created and where the creator resides. Having this information gives us a starting point for presenting terms according to the manner in which they originate. One of the major problems in pretty printing is how to treat newly created subterms. This is addressed by preserving references to the equations that create the terms. Thus, newly introduced terms will appear as in equations as much as possible. Such information provides good starting points for presenting the terms. We say starting point, since clearly, the chosen representations may result in constraint

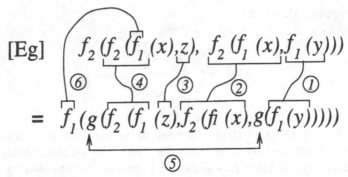

$$[Eg] \quad f_2\,(f_2\,(f_1\,(x),z),\ f_2\,(f_1\,(x),f_1\,(y)))$$

⑥ ④ ③ ② ①

$$= \ f_1(g\,(f_2\,(f_1\,(z),f_2\,(fi\,(x),g(f_1\,(y)))))$$

⑤

①·③ : common subterm
② : common subterm in a common sub-context
④ : common sub-context (maximal)
⑤ : introduced symbols
⑥ : arbitrary choice (common sub-context)

Fig. 7. Various Share-Where relations in an equation.

violations in a larger term. However, they still give excellent starting points, or "hints", to the solver indicating where the subterms should approximately be placed.

Here, we consider some heuristics of "basic" Share-Where maintenance, and in Section 4.2 discuss "dependence labeling". Share-Where maintenance consists in analyzing the equations for propagation of Share-Where information using the following four rules in order (Figure 7 may be used as a reference example):

1. *Common Subterm in maximal common sub-context:* Corresponding nodes of the common subterms (common to both left hand side and right hand side of an equation) are related. If a subterm on the right hand side can be related to more than one on the left hand side (e.g. $f_1(x)$) then look for maximal sub-context[2] in which they appear, in order to arbitrate.

2. *Common sub-context (maximal):* Look for sub-contexts on the right hand side that correspond to similar sub-contexts on the left and relate them by giving priority to larger matches.

3. *Introduced symbols:* The new symbols introduced on the right hand side get new share annotations (e.g. $g(-)$). If these are explicitly shared in the (equations) editor then they get the same annotation.

4. *Trivial arbitration:* These are common variables and function symbols that remain unrelated by the above rules. These could then be arbitrarily related to one of the choices on the left[3].

---

[2] A (sub)context is a (sub)term with holes in it. E.g., given a term $h_1(h_2, h_3)$; $h_1(\bullet, \bullet)$, $h_1(h_2, \bullet)$ and $h_1(\bullet, h_3)$ are contexts where $\bullet$ represents a hole.

[3] For function symbols (the f_1 case in figure) this could lead to same share information between a parent (ancestor) and a child, however this does not imply pseudo sharing. These cases could also be better handled by dependence labeling.

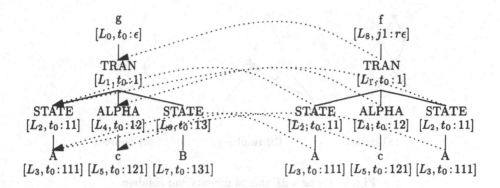

Fig. 8. Share-Where annotations for a term and propagation after rewriting.

To see how the Share-Where information is determined and propagated we consider the simple term:

$g\left(\text{(A)} \xrightarrow{c} \text{(B)}\right)$ and a simple equation: $[j1]\ g(\ S_1 \xrightarrow{i} S_2) = f(\ S_1 \overset{i}{\curvearrowleft})$

Figure 8 shows the Share-Where annotations for the initial term and equation [j1] is used to rewrite it. The dotted lines show how the shared subterms on the right-side have the same origin for their representations. The Where information "$t_0 : 12$" means that the node was created in term t_0 at occurrence 12 (second child of first child of top node). The *ALPHA* and *STATE* subterms are unchanged and thus get their Share-Where annotations from the left side (common variable rule). The "TRAN" node also has the same annotation due to common sub-context rule. The symbol f is a new symbol created by the equation. The new annotation $[uid(), j1 : r\epsilon]$ says: a unique label[4] is generated (by $uid()$) for the Share part and the Where part tells that this f was created in equation [j1] at the right-hand side (r) top (ϵ) occurrence. Note that if instead of the shared S_1s on the right, they were introduced constants, they would both share the same $uid()$s every time the rule is applied.

4.2 Dependence labeling

The "basic" *Share* maintenance does not accommodate sharing of the symbols introduced in the equations (unless they are shared in the right-hand sides of the equations). This often results in undesirable effects in the output picture. For example, Figure 9-b shows the effect of equation [eg1] b = c on the sentence in Figure 9-a. Whereas one would desire that the generated "c" symbols are also shared in the output picture as in Figure 9-c.

To address this problem, we introduce dependence labeling, where the share labeling in the introduced symbols depend on some the labels of symbols on the

---

[4] New Share annotations need an unique identifier, otherwise too many symbols would be shared while rewriting. However, unique identifiers cause too many symbols being non-shared. See Section 4.2.

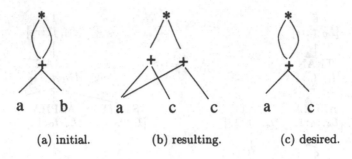

(a) initial.　　　　(b) resulting.　　　　(c) desired.

Fig. 9. Terms with shared parents and children.

left-hand side. In [eg1] the labeling of c could be made to depend on the label of b. Then the following (a) term, could after rewriting be presented as (b):

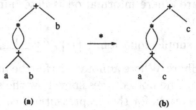

(a)　　　　　　　　　**(b)**

Dependence labeling appropriately replaces the "introduced symbols" rule above with two new cases:

- *redex-contractum case:* the labeling of the introduced symbols depend on the labeling of the top symbol of the redex and a label associated with the occurrence of the symbol. If an occurrence is shared, then the associated labels are identical. In

$$[eg3] \qquad \overset{+}{\wedge}_{a \quad 0} \quad = \quad \overset{*}{\wedge}_{a \quad 1}$$

the labels of * and 1 depend on the label of +.

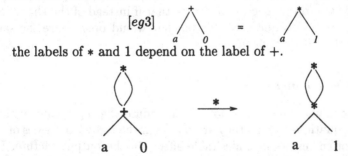

- If the common sub-context rule can narrow down the dependency to a more specific subterm then the labeling of the introduced symbol depends on that subterm. For example, in the equation

$$[eg4] \qquad \overset{+}{\underset{a \quad s}{\wedge}} \quad = \quad \overset{+}{\underset{a \quad 0}{\wedge}}$$

$$\overset{|}{x}$$

the label of 0 depends on the label of s. Thus:

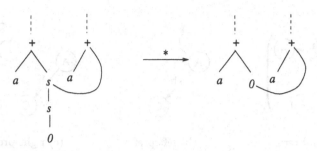

Dependence labeling removes the need for generating unique identifiers ($uid()$) during the rewriting process.

4.3 Discussion

For our FSA language we have enough information to present the result without surprises. E.g.,

Now let's consider a case which introduces complications. Let an equation $[j2]$ be defined as follows:

$$[j2] \; id\left(\boxed{S_1 \xrightarrow{\;i\;} S_1}\right) = \boxed{S_1 \circlearrowleft^{i}}$$

Figure 10(a) shows the initial term and the parts (b) and (c) show two possible pretty printing results depending on which S_1 from left-hand side passes the Share-Where annotations to the S_1 on the right. Although these two terms look considerably different their abstract syntax is equivalent and thus share the same semantic behavior. We may consider the representation in Figure 10(c) visually undesirable as it gives the appearance of a disconnected *FSA* although its behavior is correct. The problem here is determining which Ⓐ from the left side is to be chosen as being the representation corresponding to the Ⓐ on the right side.

Clearly, the Share-Where information can be used more extensively (i.e. during matching) and more sophisticated Share-Where information can be collected for better pretty printing results. One of the immediate applications of this information is their use in pretty printing rules which could be specified by the language designer as a separate module and could be used to pretty print the terms in a language-specific preference. The pretty printing issues addressed in this paper would then be considered as default pretty printing. Such a pretty printer would be able to track colored (marked) input constructs and help in debugging specifications by indicating where a certain part of the output term originated from.

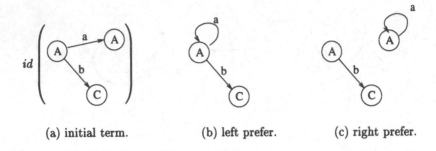

| (a) initial term. | (b) left prefer. | (c) right prefer. |

Fig. 10. Pretty printing results based on two different annotations of same term.

5 Related Work and Conclusions

Typically visual languages are syntactically very complex. The sharing of sub-terms among several terms leads one to consider context-sensitive grammars for specifying visual languages. Most approaches to syntax specification have adopted context-sensitive formalisms considering context-free specifications not useful in dealing with realistic languages. This point can be observed in [9] which details formal approaches to visual language specification. These approaches tend to define other language aspects such as type-checking and semantics along with the syntactic definition. Contrary to this approach we wish to examine a language specification style that separates these two aspects clearly and pushes the definition of semantics, type-checking and so on to the domain of semantic specification.

The work on constraint multi-set grammars [9] and graph grammars [10] provide alternative approaches to the algebraic specification approach we have considered. Our approach is an exercise in using the traditional algebraic specification formalisms to define visual languages by allowing two-dimensional lexicals. Our approach has led us to simulate sharing with pseudo-sharing and maintain Share annotations to preserve sharing in the output term. The use of real sharing would alleviate this problem but that would be a different formalism. The Where annotations are useful in any case and similar techniques could be used by other formalisms for maintaining consistency of presentation.

The ASF+SDF Meta-environment [7] has been the source of inspiration for our work on the VAS formalism. The work on origin-tracking [3, Chapters 7 and 9] and error reporter generation [3, Chapter 4] in the ASF+SDF context has further inspired the maintenance of Share-Where information. Our Share-Where information is in some ways more general than origin-tracking due to the presence of the Where information; as the labels used in Share annotations could help provide "primitive" origins in the absence of sharing. These techniques are related to residuals and descendants as can be found in [8] and subject-tracking as defined in [1]. Our dependence labeling is comparable to dependence tracking of [4] and underlined/overlined labelings of Levi [8]. It is simpler than these since the dependence is on the labels and not on function symbols as we are only interested in share-ability hints.

We have, by means of an example, elaborated on the utility of visual algebraic specifications for defining visual languages. We have introduced Share-Where maintenance which uses the creation information both in the initial term and dynamic instances, as examples, to present the result of computation back to the user. Although for the general case there is a need for additional pretty print specification (Section 4.3), Share-Where maintenance can nevertheless assist a constraint solver produce desirable solutions.

Acknowledgments: Comments of the referees has greatly improved the paper.

References

1. Y. Bertot. A canonical calculus of residuals. In G. Huet and G. Plotkin, editors, *Logical Environments.* Cambridge University Press, 1993.
2. M. G. J. van den Brand and E. Visser. Generation of formatters for context-free languages. *ACM Transactions on Software Engineering and Methodology,* 5(1):1–41, January 1996.
3. A. van Deursen, J. Heering, and P. Klint. *Language Prototyping. An Algebraic Specification Approach.* AMAST series in Computing. World Scientific, 1996.
4. J. Field and F. Tip. Dynamic dependence in term rewriting systems and its application to program slicing. In M. Hermenegildo and J. Penjam, editors, *Proceedings of the Sixth International Symposium on Programming Language Implementation and Logic Programming,* volume 844 of *Lecture Notes in Computer Science,* pages 415–431. Springer-Verlag, 1994.
5. J. A. Goguen, J. W. Thatcher, and E. G. Wagner. Abstract data types as initial algebras and correctness of data representation. In *Proc. Conference on Computer Graphics Pattern Recognition and Data Structure,* pages 89–93, 1975.
6. J. V. Guttag and J. J. Horning, editors. *Larch: Languages and Tools for Formal Specification.* Texts and Monographs in Computer Science. Springer-Verlag, 1993. With S. J. Garland, K. D. Jones, A. Modet, and J. M. Wing.
7. P. Klint. A meta-environment for generating programming environments. *ACM Transactions on Software Engineering and Methodology,* 2(2):176–201, 1993.
8. J.W. Klop. Term rewriting systems. Technical Report Report CS-R9073, CWI, Amsterdam, 1990.
9. K. Marriott and B. Meyer. Towards a hierarchy of visual languages. In *Workshop on Theory of Visual Languages,* May 1996.
10. A. Schürr, A. Zündorf, and A. Winter. Visual programming with graph rewriting systems. In *Proc. 1995 IEEE Symposium Visual Languages,* September 1995.
11. S. M. Üsküdarlı. Generating visual editors for formally specified languages. In *Proc. 1994 IEEE Symposium Visual Languages,* pages 278–285, St. Louis, Illinois, October 1994.
12. S. M. Üsküdarlı. *Algebraic Specification of Visual Languages.* PhD thesis, University of Amsterdam, March 1997.
13. S. M. Üsküdarlı and T. B. Dinesh. Towards a visual programming environment generator for algebraic specifications. In *Proc. 1995 IEEE Symposium Visual Languages,* September 1995.

A Fault Tolerant Broadcast Scheme in Star Graphs

Satoshi Fujita

Department of Electrical Engineering
Faculty of Engineering, Hiroshima University
Kagamiyama 1-4-1, Higashi-Hiroshima, 739 Japan
E-mail: fujita@se.hiroshima-u.ac.jp

Abstract. In this paper, we propose a simple and nonadaptive fault tolerant broadcast scheme in star graphs under the single-port communication model. The proposed scheme can tolerate up to $n-2$ vertex and/or edge faults in the star graph with $n!$ vertices, and in the full-duplex communication mode, it takes at most $4n-3$ more time units than an optimal nonadaptive broadcast scheme.

1 Introduction

The star graph is a member of the class of Cayley graphs, and is known to have many attractive features as an underlying topology of interconnection networks [1]. In the past decade, the star graph has been extensively studied from various aspects, which includes the development of parallel algorithms, point-to-point routing schemes, and information dissemination schemes [1, 2, 3, 5, 11, 14, 15]. Fault tolerant routing and broadcasting in star graphs have also been investigated by many researchers: for example, Letifi [8], Gargano et al. [9], and Rouskov and Srimani [13] independently studied the *fault diameter* of star graphs; Baherzadeh et al. [4] proposed an *adaptive* fault tolerant broadcast scheme based on the depth first search technique; and Fragopoulou and Akl [6] proposed an efficient fault tolerant broadcast scheme under the all-port communication model, which is based on the construction of edge-disjoint spanning trees.

In this paper, we propose a simple and nonadaptive fault tolerant broadcast scheme in star graphs under the single-port communication model. The proposed scheme can tolerate up to $n-2$ vertex and/or edge faults in the star graph with $n!$ vertices. Recently, Mei et al. [10] proposed a nonadaptive fault tolerant broadcast scheme under the same model, which was later extented by Hamada et al. [7] to the case of Byzantine faults [12]. Although Mei et al.'s scheme can tolerate the same number of faults with our scheme and completes a broadcast in an asymptotically optimal time, it is too complicated to be efficiently implemented and the coefficient of the leading term of the broadcast time is strictly greater than 1. Our scheme proposed in this paper is much simpler than Mei et al.'s scheme, and the coefficient of the leading term exactly meets the lower bound 1. Furthermore, it is proved that in the full-duplex communication mode, the proposed scheme takes at most $4n-3$ more time units than an optimal nonadaptive broadcast scheme, and takes at most $8n - 7$ more time units in the half-duplex communication mode.

The remainder of this paper is organized as follows. In Section 2, we give a formal definition of the star graph and the communication modes considered in this paper. Section 3 describes the proposed broadcast scheme, and in Section 4, the correctness and the time complexity of the scheme are proved. Section 5 concludes the paper with some future directions of research.

2 Preliminaries

Let V_n be the set of $n!$ permutations of symbols $\{1, 2, \ldots, n\}$. We denote $u(i)$ the ith digit of permutation u. For $2 \leq i \leq n$, a **generator** g_i is defined as follows: for given permutation $u = u(1)u(2) \ldots u(n)$ $(\in V_n)$,

$$g_i(u) = \underline{u(i)}u(2) \ldots u(i-1)\underline{u(1)}u(i+1) \ldots u(n),$$

i.e., g_i is a function that interchanges the symbol $u(i)$ with the symbol $u(1)$. A **star graph** on n symbols, denoted by $S_n = (V_n, E_n)$, is an undirected graph with a vertex set V_n and an edge set E_n, where

$$E_n = \{\{u, g_i(u)\} \mid u \in V_n, \ 2 \leq i \leq n\}.$$

For $1 \leq i \leq n$, let $V(i)$ $(\subset V_n)$ denote the set of vertices with suffix i (in what follows, "suffix" and "prefix" imply those of length one, respectively, unless otherwise stated). It is well known that $V(i)$ induces a subgraph of S_n which is isomorphic to S_{n-1} [1].

In this paper, we consider the fault tolerant broadcast problem in star graphs under the **single-port** communication model, i.e., we assume each vertex can access at most one incident edge in each time unit. The source vertex of a broadcast is assumed to be fault-free, and during a broadcast, the set of faulty vertices and edges can not be changed. Each edge in E_n can be used in a bidirectional manner according to one of the following two communication modes: in the **full-duplex** mode, each edge can carry at most two messages one in each direction in each time unit, and in the **half-duplex** mode, each edge can carry at most one message in each time unit.

3 Broadcast Scheme

In this section, we propose a fault tolerant broadcast scheme in S_n which can tolerate up to $n - 2$ vertex and/or edge faults. In what follows, without loss of generality, we let $s = 123 \ldots n$ $(\in V(n) \subset V_n)$ be the source of a broadcast; i.e., $s(i) = i$ for all $1 \leq i \leq n$. The proposed scheme proceeds as follows:

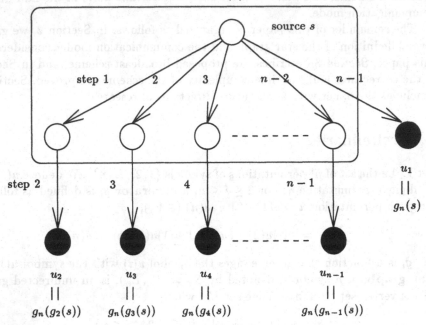

Fig. 1. Phase 1 (vertices u_i's are painted gray).

Scheme FBSimple

Phase 1: { Broadcast to $n-1$ vertices in different substars }

Let M be the message to be broadcast. In the tth time unit for $1 \leq t \leq n-2$, the source vertex, s, sends message M to vertex $g_{t+1}(s)$ which forwards the received message to vertex $u_{t+1} = g_n(g_{t+1}(s))$ in the $(t+1)$st time unit. In the $(n-1)$st time unit, vertex s sends message M to vertex $u_1 = g_n(s)$. See Figure 1 for illustration. Note that for each $1 \leq i \leq n-1$, $u_i \in V(i)$.

Phase 2: { Broadcast in each substar S_{n-1} }

For $1 \leq i \leq n-1$, vertex u_i broadcasts the message received in Phase 1 (if any) to all vertices in $V(i)$ along an optimal broadcast tree in the subgraph of S_n induced by $V(i)$.

Phase 3: { Exchange messages among substars }

Phase 3 consists of four stages of an *identical* structure:

Stage: In the first time unit, each vertex u ($\in V_n$) sends the message received so far (if any) to vertex $g_n(u)$, and in the tth time unit ($2 \leq t \leq n-1$), vertex u sends the message received so far (if any) to vertex $g_t(u)$. The objective of the first stage is to inform message M to all non-faulty vertices in $V(n)$ ($= V(s(n))$) with prefix 1 ($= s(1)$) correctly, that of the second stage is to inform message M to all non-faulty vertices in $V(1)$ ($=

$V(s(1)))$ correctly, that of the third stage is to inform message M to all non-faulty vertices in $V(n)$ correctly, and that of the fourth stage is to inform message M to all non-faulty vertices in $V_n - V(n)$ correctly. □

4 Correctness

In this section, we show that scheme FBSimple can tolerate up to $n - 2$ faults and that under the full-duplex (resp. half-duplex) mode, it takes at most $4n - 3$ (resp. $8n - 7$) more time units than an optimal nonadaptive broadcast scheme. We start this section with a lemma concerned with the delivery paths in Phases 1 and 2.

Lemma 1. *For any two vertices $u \in V(i)$ and $v \in V(j)$ such that $1 \le i < j \le n - 1$, the delivery paths in Phases 1 and 2 from the source vertex to vertices u and v are vertex-disjoint.*

Proof. In Phase 1, vertices $u_1, u_2, \ldots, u_{n-1}$ are connected with vertex s by a set of mutually vertex-disjoint paths (see Figure 1). In Phase 2, vertex u_i ($\in V(i)$) broadcasts the message received in Phase 1 to all vertices in $V(i)$ along an optimal broadcast tree with vertex set $V(i)$. Finally, since $V(i) \cap V(j) = \emptyset$ for any $1 \le i < j \le n - 1$, the lemma follows. □

It should be worth noting here that if no fault occurs, at the end of Phase 2, any vertex $u \in V_n - V(n)$ receives exactly one (copy of) message M.

In the following, for convenience, for any $u \in V_n$, we denote $u^{-1}(y) = x$ if $u(x) = y$. It is enough to show that at the end of Phase 3, any non-faulty vertex v correctly receives message M, provided that there are at most $n - 2$ faults. First, let us consider the delivery of the message to vertices in $V(n)$ with prefix 1.

Lemma 2. *In the first stage of Phase 3, any non-faulty vertex $v \in V(n)$ with prefix 1 receives message M correctly, provided that there are at most $n - 2$ faults.*

Proof. Let v be a vertex in $V(n)$ with prefix 1, and suppose no fault occurs. Then, in the first stage of Phase 3, vertex v receives message M from the following $n - 1$ distinct vertices:

$$w_2 = g_{v^{-1}(2)}(v)$$
$$w_3 = g_{v^{-1}(3)}(v)$$
$$\vdots$$
$$w_n = g_{v^{-1}(n)}(v) = g_n(v),$$

where the receipt of a message from vertex $g_n(v)$ ($= w_n \in V(1)$) takes place in the first time unit. Since $w_i(1) = i$ for all $2 \le i \le n$, in the first time

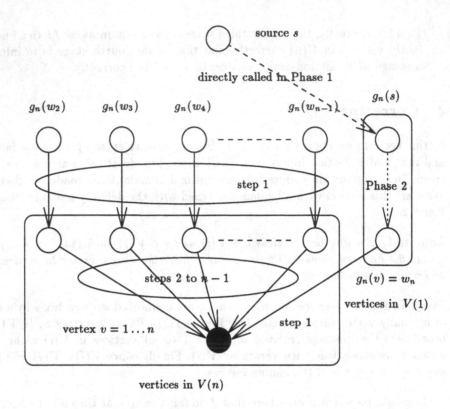

Fig. 2. The first stage of Phase 3.

unit, vertex w_i $(2 \leq i \leq n - 1)$ receives message M from a "unique" vertex $g_n(w_i)$ in $V(i)$, and in one of the succeeding $n - 2$ time units, it forwards the received message to vertex v. See Figure 2 for illustration. Vertex v and vertices $g_n(w_2), g_n(w_3), \ldots, g_n(w_{n-1}), g_n(v)$ are connected by a set of mutually vertex-disjoint paths, and since $s(1) = v(1)$ and $s(n) = v(n)$, by Lemma 1, $n - 1$ delivery paths passing through vertices $w_2, w_3, \ldots, w_n$ are mutually vertex-disjoint. Hence the lemma follows. $\qquad \square$

Next, we consider the delivery paths in the second and third stages.

Lemma 3. *In the second stage of Phase 3, any non-faulty vertex $v \in V(1)$ receives message M correctly, provided that there are at most $n - 2$ faults.*

Proof. If there are no faults, in the second stage, vertex $v \in V(1)$ receives message M as is shown in Figure 3. Since $n - 2$ vertices painted gray in the figure belong to distinct subsets $V(i)$ for $2 \leq i \leq n - 1$, by Lemma 1, $n - 2$ delivery paths passing through those gray vertices are mutually vertex-disjoint. On the other hand, by Lemma 2, if it is operational, vertex $g_n(g_{v^{-1}(n)}(v))$ with prefix 1 and suffix n, which is painted black in the figure, can correctly receive message

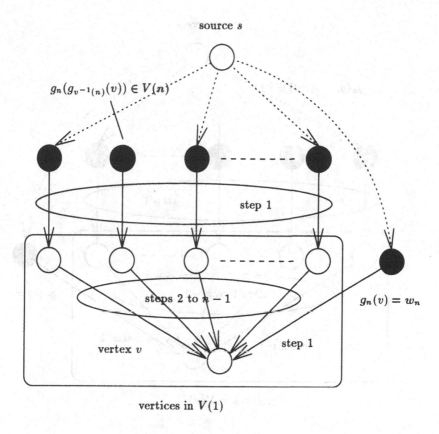

Fig. 3. The second stage of Phase 3 (the black vertex is the one directly calling vertex v when the prefix of v is n).

M in the first stage provided that there are at most $n-2$ faults. Since the path connecting $g_n(g_{v^{-1}(n)}(v))$ ($\in V(n)$) and v ($\in V(1)$) is mutually vertex-disjoint with any of the above $n-2$ delivery paths, the lemma follows.   □

Lemma 4. *In the third stage of Phase 3, any non-faulty vertex $v \in V(n)$ receives message M correctly, provided that there are at most $n-2$ faults.*

Proof. By Lemma 2, without loss of generality, we may assume $v(1) \neq 1$. If there are no faults, in the third stage, vertex v receives message M as is shown in Figure 4. Since $s(n) = v(n)\ (= n)$, $n-2$ delivery paths passing through gray vertices in the figure are mutually vertex-disjoint. On the other hand, by Lemma 2, if it is operational, vertex $g_n(g_{v^{-1}(1)}(v))$ in $V(1)$, which is painted black in the figure, can correctly receive message M in the second stage provided that there are at most $n-2$ faults. Since the path connecting $g_n(g_{v^{-1}(1)}(v))$ ($\in V(1)$) and v ($\in V(n)$) is mutually vertex-disjoint with any of the above $n-2$ delivery paths, the lemma follows.   □

318

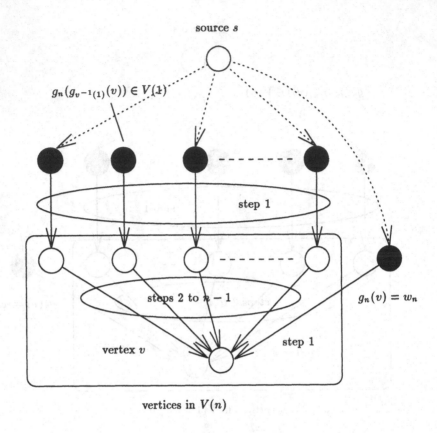

source s

$g_n(g_{v^{-1}(1)}(v)) \in V(1)$

step 1

steps 2 to $n-1$

$g_n(v) = w_n$

vertex v

step 1

vertices in $V(n)$

Fig. 4. The third stage of Phase 3 ($v(1) \neq 1$).

By using a similar argument to Lemma 3, we can easily show that in the fourth stage, any non-faulty vertex $v \in V_n - V(n)$ receives message M correctly, provided that there are at most $n-2$ faults. Hence we have the following theorem.

Theorem 5. *Scheme* FBSimple *can tolerate up to $n-2$ vertex and/or edge faults.*
□

Finally, let us consider the broadcast time of the proposed broadcast scheme. Let $t(n)$ denote the optimal broadcast time in (fault-free) S_n under the single-port model. Note that $t(n) \geq \lceil \log_2(n!) \rceil = \lceil \sum_{i=2}^{n} \log_2 i \rceil$ and $t(n) \leq \sum_{i=2}^{n} \lceil \log_2 i \rceil$ [15]. Since Phase 1 takes $n-1$ time units in both communication modes, and since Phase 3 takes $4(n-1)$ (resp. $8(n-1)$) time units in the full-duplex (resp. half-duplex) mode, we immediately have the following theorem on the broadcast time.

Theorem 6. *In the full-duplex mode, scheme* FBSimple *completes a broadcast in $t(n-1) + 5(n-1)$ time units, and in the half-duplex mode, it completes a broadcast in $t(n-1) + 9(n-1)$ time units.*
□

Corollary 7. *In the full-duplex mode, scheme* FBSimple *takes at most* $4n - 3$ *more time units than an optimal nonadaptive broadcast scheme, and in the half-duplex mode, it takes at most* $8n - 7$ *more time units than an optimal scheme.*

Proof. Fix an optimal fault tolerant broadcast scheme, and consider a situation in which all vertices receiving the first $n - 2$ messages from the source vertex are faulty. In such a situation, the actual broadcast, which takes at least $t(n)$ time units, starts in the $(n - 1)$st time unit. Since $t(n) \geq t(n - 1)$ clearly holds, the broadcast time of the optimal scheme is at least $t(n - 1) + n - 2$. Hence the corollary follows. □

5 Concluding Remarks

In this paper, we proposed a simple and nonadaptive fault tolerant broadcast scheme in star graphs under the single-port communication model. The proposed scheme can tolerate up to $n - 2$ vertex and/or edge faults in the star graph with $n!$ vertices, and in the full-duplex (resp. half-duplex) communication mode, it takes at most $4n - 3$ (resp. $8n - 7$) more time units than an optimal nonadaptive broadcast scheme. An interesting direction of future research is to generalize this result to a wider class of Cayley graphs; e.g., the class of *hierarchical* Cayley graphs. It should also be interesting if we could fill the gap between the upper and lower bounds by proposing a noble technique for improving the lower bound.

Acknowledgements: The author thanks Dr. P. Fragopoulou who pointed out an error in an early version of the paper. This research was partially supported by the Ministry of Education, Science and Culture of Japan (Grant #08680372), and Research for the Future Program from Japan Society for the Promotion of Science (JSPS): Software for Distributed and Parallel Supercomputing (JSPS-RFTF96P00505).

References

1. S. B. Akers and B. Krishnamurthy. A group-theoretic model for symmetric interconnection networks. *IEEE Trans. Comput.*, 38(4):555–566, April 1989.
2. S. G. Akl and K. Qiu. Fundamental algorithms for the star and pancake interconnection networks with applications to computational geometry. *Networks*, 23:215–225, 1993.
3. S. G. Akl and K. Qiu. A novel routing scheme on the star and pancake networks and its applications. *Parallel Computing*, 19:95–101, 1993.
4. N. Bagherzadeh, N. Nassif, and S. Latifi. A routing and broadcasting scheme on faulty star graphs. *IEEE Trans. Comput.*, 42(11):1398–1403, November 1993.
5. P. Fragopoulou and S. G. Akl. Optimal communication algorithms on star graphs using spanning tree constructions. *Journal of Parallel and Distributed Computing*, 24:55–71, 1995.
6. P. Fragopoulou and S. G. Akl. Edge-disjoint spanning trees on the star network with applications to fault tolerance. *IEEE Trans. Comput.*, 45(2):174–185, February 1996.

7. Y. Hamada, A. Mei, F. Bao, and Y. Igarashi. Broadcasting in star graphs with byzantine failures. *Technical Report of IEICE*, COMP96-27:47–56, July 1996.

8. S. Latifi. On the fault-diameter of the star graph. *Inform. Process. Lett.*, 46:143–150, June 1993.

9. L.Gargano, U. Vaccaro, and A. Vozella. Fault tolerant routing in the star and pancake interconnection networks. *Inform. Process. Lett.*, 45:315–320, April 1993.

10. A. Mei, F. Bao, Y. Hamada, and Y. Igarashi. Optimal time broadcasting in faulty star networks. In *Proc. WDAG'96*, LNCS 1151, pp.175–190, 1996.

11. V. E. Mendia and D. Sarkar. Optimal broadcasting in the star graph. *IEEE Trans. Parallel and Distributed Systems*, 3:389–396, July 1992.

12. A. Pelc. Reliable communication in networks with Byzantine link failures. *Networks*, 22:441–459, 1992.

13. Y. Rouskov and P. K. Srimani. Fault diameter of star graphs. *Inform. Process. Lett.*, 48:243–251, 1993.

14. J.-P. Sheu, C.-T. Liaw, and T.-S. Chen. A broadcasting algorithm in star graph interconnection networks. *Inform. Process. Lett.*, 48:237–241, 1993.

15. J.-P. Sheu, C.-T. Liaw, and T.-S. Chen. An optimal broadcasting algorithm without message redundancy in star graphs. *IEEE Trans. Parallel and Distributed Systems*, 6(6), June 1995.

Calculus of Classical Proofs I

Ken-etsu Fujita

Kyushu Institute of Technology, Iizuka, 820, Japan

Abstract. We introduce a simple natural deduction system of classical propositional logic called λ^v_{exc}, and prove the computational properties of the system based on a call-by-value strategy. We show (1) a strict fragment of λ^v_{exc} that is complete with respect to classical provability, and the computational meaning of the existence of such a fragment; (2) a simple exit mechanism by the use of a proof of Peirce's law, and some examples using classical proofs as programs; (3) the Church-Rosser property; (4) the CPS-translation from λ^v_{exc} to $\lambda^{\to}$, and its correctness with respect to conversions; (5) a computational use of the logical inconsistency in λ^v_{exc}, extended with a certain signature.

1 Introduction

The computational meaning of proofs has been investigated by many researchers not only in intuitionistic logic [17][16][23] and constructive type systems [24], but also in classical logic [14][22][27][4][32] and modal logic [19]. Algorithmic contents of proofs can be used to obtain correct programs which satisfy logical specifications. In this paper, our motivation is to study a computational aspect of a simple classical natural deduction system that is a consequence of our observations of the existence of a special form of cut-free LK [34][36] proofs for each tautology, which we called LJK proofs with invariants [11][12]. In LJK proofs, the succedent of each sequent is such that every occurrence in the succedent, except for at most one occurrence, is the same as the invariant throughout the proof. Following the proof theoretical result, we have presented a classical natural deduction system λ_{exc} [13] by using the law of the *exc*luded middle. In this paper, we investigate the computational properties of classical proofs in a call-by-value version of λ_{exc}. We also briefly studied a simple call-by-value variant of Parigot's $\lambda\mu$-calculus [27] in [10] from a point of classical substructural logics. Here, however, based on the Curry-Howard-De Bruijn isomorphism [17][37], we demonstrate that classical proofs can be used for practical programs involving an exit mechanism.

In Section 2, we introduce the natural deduction system λ^v_{exc} of classical propositional logic, where the computation is based on a call-by-value strategy. We investigate a strict fragment of λ^v_{exc}, which is complete with respect to classical provability, and show that the existence of such a fragment is useful as a guide to writing proofs as programs. In Section 3, we prove that a nontrivial subset of λ^v_{exc} has the Church-Rosser property. In Section 4, we define the CPS-translation of λ^v_{exc}-terms and show the correctness of the translation with respect to conversions. In Section 5, we extend λ^v_{exc} with a signature so that a computation in type-free λ-calculus can be simulated in a system that becomes logically inconsistent. In Section 6, we briefly investigate the relation to some existing systems: $\lambda_{exn}^{\rightarrow}$ of de Groote [7] and Felleisen's λ_c [8][9].

2 Call-by-Value Language λ_{exc}^v based on Classical Logic

We introduce a simple natural deduction system λ_{exc}^v of classical propositional logic, in which the reduction rules are based on a call-by-value strategy[1].

The terms are defined by two kinds of variables x's and y's, where y's are used only for negation types $\neg A$ defined as $A \rightarrow \bot$. $FV(M)$ stands for the set of free variables in M.

λ_{exc}^v:

Types   Contexts

$A ::= \alpha \mid \bot \mid A \rightarrow A$ $\Gamma ::= \langle\rangle \mid x : A, \Gamma \mid y : \neg A, \Gamma$

Terms

$M ::= x \mid \lambda x.M \mid MM \mid yM \mid \mathrm{raise}(M) \mid \{y\}M$

Type Assignment

$$\Gamma \vdash x : \Gamma(x) \qquad \frac{\Gamma \vdash M : A}{\Gamma \vdash yM : \bot}\ (\bot I)\ if\ \Gamma(y) \equiv \neg A \not\equiv \neg\bot$$

$$\frac{\Gamma, x : A \vdash M : B}{\Gamma \vdash \lambda x.M : A \rightarrow B}\ (\rightarrow I) \qquad \frac{\Gamma \vdash M_1 : A \rightarrow B \quad \Gamma \vdash M_2 : A}{\Gamma \vdash M_1 M_2 : B}\ (\rightarrow E)$$

$$\frac{\Gamma \vdash M : \bot}{\Gamma \vdash \mathrm{raise}(M) : A}\ (\bot E)\ if\ A \not\equiv \bot \qquad \frac{\Gamma, y : \neg A \vdash M : A}{\Gamma \vdash \{y\}M : A}\ (exc)$$

The side conditions of the inference rules exclude trivial reasoning.

The classical rule (exc) is a variant of the law of the *excluded middle* [33]. This rule is introduced independently of $(\bot E)$, which is in contrast to the double-negation elimination rules, such as $(\bot_C)$ which infers $\Gamma \vdash A$ from $\Gamma, \neg A \vdash \bot$, and (C) which infers $\Gamma \vdash A$ from $\Gamma \vdash \neg\neg A$. We call the rule (exc) a rule of local *exception-handling*. The type A in (exc) is called a type of *exceptional parameter*.

Note the similarity of $(\bot I)$ with $(\rightarrow E)$, but also note that $\Gamma \not\vdash y : \neg A$ even if $\Gamma(y) = \neg A$. The negative assumption of the form $y : \neg A$ can be discharged only by (exc) in this system. This style of proof is called a regular proof in Andou [1]. In λ_Δ-calculus [32], not only regular but also non-regular proofs are considered. However, from a non-regular proof, we can simply construct a regular proof that has the same assumptions and the same conclusion.

The notion of values is defined as variables, λ-abstractions, and terms of the form yM, where the variable y works as a value-constructor like an exception constructor of ML [21][7]. On the other hand, since a term of the form $\{y\}M$, like a packet opened by (ev4-1) below, is not regarded as a value, $(\lambda x.M_1)(\{y\}M_2)$

---

[1] Since there is an isomorphism between Parigot's $\lambda\mu$-calculus [27] and the call-by-name version λ_{exc} [13], λ_{exc}^v can be regarded, in some sense, as a call-by-value variant of $\lambda\mu$-calculus

will not be a β-contractum, but will be a contractum of (ev5-2) below, which is dual to the structural reduction in Parigot [27], and can be considered as a logical permutative reduction in the sense of Prawitz [31] and Andou [1].

Values

$V ::= x \mid \lambda x.M \mid yM$

Term reductions

(ev1) $(\lambda x.M)V \; \rhd^v_{exc} \; M[x := V]$;

(ev2-1) (raise M)$N \; \rhd^v_{exc} \;$ (raise M);   (ev2-2) V(raise M) $\rhd^v_{exc} \;$ (raise M);

(ev3-1) y(raise V) $\rhd^v_{exc} \; V$;   (ev3-2) $y(\{y_1\}M) \; \rhd^v_{exc} \; yM[y_1 := y]$;

(ev4-1) $\{y\}M \; \rhd^v_{exc} \; M$ if $y \notin FV(M)$;   (ev4-2) $\{y\}$(raise yM) $\rhd^v_{exc} \; \{y\}M$;

(ev5-1) $(\{y\}M)N \; \rhd^v_{exc} \; \{y\}((M[y \Leftarrow N])N)$;

(ev5-2) $V(\{y\}M) \; \rhd^v_{exc} \; \{y\}(V(M[V \Rightarrow y]))$,

where $M[y \Leftarrow N]$ is defined as the term obtained from M by replacing each subterm of the form yM' in M with $y(M'N)$, that is,

$x[y \Leftarrow N] = x$; $(\lambda x.M)[y \Leftarrow N] = \lambda x.M[y \Leftarrow N]$;

$(yM)[y \Leftarrow N] = y(M[y \Leftarrow N]N)$; $(y'M)[y \Leftarrow N] = y'(M[y \Leftarrow N])$ if $y' \not\equiv y$;

$(M_1 M_2)[y \Leftarrow N] = (M_1[y \Leftarrow N])(M_2[y \Leftarrow N])$;

(raise M)$[y \Leftarrow N] = $ raise$(M[y \Leftarrow N])$; $(\{y'\}M)[y \Leftarrow N] = \{y'\}(M[y \Leftarrow N])$.

The term $M[N \Rightarrow y]$ is similarly defined as the term obtained from M by replacing each subterm of the form yM' in M with $y(NM')$.

We identify $\{y\}\{y_1\} \cdots \{y_n\}M$ with $\{y\}M[y_1, \cdots, y_n := y]$ for technical simplicity. The binary relation $\rhd^{v*}_{exc}$ is defined by the reflexive transitive closure of $\rhd^v_{exc}$, and the congruence relation generated by $\rhd^v_{exc}$ is denoted by $=^v_{exc}$. The relation $\rhd_{\beta_V}$ is defined as usual. We sometimes write the term $\{y : \neg A\}M$ for $\{y\}M$, where $\Gamma, y : \neg A \vdash M : A$ for some Γ.

Proposition 1. *There exists a term M such that $\Gamma \vdash_{\lambda^v_{exc}} M : A$ iff A considered as a formula is classically provable from Γ.*

Proposition 2 (Subject Reduction). *Let $\Gamma \vdash_{\lambda^v_{exc}} M : A$. If $M \rhd^v_{exc} N$, then $\Gamma \vdash_{\lambda^v_{exc}} N : A$.*

Although λ^v_{exc} is simple, data types of pair and case-analysis are naturally implemented by the definability of conjunction and disjunction in classical logic.

Let a context $\mathcal{E}[\,]$ with a hole $[\,]$ be as follows:

$\mathcal{E}[\,] ::= [\,] \mid V(\mathcal{E}[\,]) \mid (\mathcal{E}[\,])M$.

We denote by $\mathcal{E}[M]$ the term obtained by replacing $[\,]$ in $\mathcal{E}[\,]$ with the term M. Then we have $\mathcal{E}[\text{raise } M] \; \rhd^{v*}_{exc} \;$ raise M and $\mathcal{E}[\{y\}\text{raise}(yM)] \; \rhd^{v*}_{exc} \; \{y\}\text{raise}(y\mathcal{E}[M])$ where $y \notin FV(M)$. Here, by the permutative reductions (ev5-1) and (ev5-2), the continuation $\mathcal{E}$ of $\{y\}\text{raise}(yM)$ is accumulated as an argument of y.

Example 1 (Exit Mechanism by the use of a Proof of Peirce's Law). Let $\mathcal{P}_1$ be $\lambda x_1.\{y\}x_1(\lambda x_2.\text{raise}(yx_2))$ of the type $Peirce \equiv ((A \to B) \to A) \to A$. We consider the following two cases. The first case is called a normal case, and the second is an exceptional case.

(1) Case of $k \notin FV(M)$:

$\mathcal{P}_1(\lambda k.M) = (\lambda x_1.\{y\}x_1(\lambda x_2.\text{raise}(yx_2)))(\lambda k.M) \; \rhd^{v*}_{exc} \; \{y\}M \; \rhd^v_{exc} \; M$.

(2) Case of $k \notin FV(\mathcal{E}[V])$:
$$\mathcal{P}_1(\lambda k.\mathcal{E}[kV]) \, \triangleright^{v*}_{exc} \, \{y\}\mathcal{E}[\text{raise}(yV)] \, \triangleright^{v*}_{exc} \, \{y\}\text{raise}(yV) \, \triangleright^{v}_{exc} \, \{y\}V \triangleright^{v}_{exc} \, V.$$

In the second case, the context $\mathcal{E}[\,]$ is abandoned, and the value V to be passed on has the same type as that of the exceptional parameter of $\mathcal{P}_1$. This is the reason why the type A in the definition of (exc) is called the type of exceptional parameter[2]. The second case can be applied to implement a simple exist mechanism. Now we discuss which subformulæ of the given formula can be the type of exceptional parameters.

Definition 3 (Candidates for Types of Exceptional Parameter). Given a type A, candidates for types of exceptional parameter denoted by $EP(A)$ are defined as a collection of strictly positive subformulæ of A with respect to $\rightarrow$. In other words, when A is decomposed by the following rule $\Rightarrow$ starting from $([\,], A)$, $EP(A)$ is a collection of the second elements of all the pairs appearing in the decomposition process:
$$([\Gamma], A \rightarrow B) \Rightarrow ([\Gamma, A], B) \quad \text{if } B \not\equiv \bot.$$
For each $A_i \in EP(A)$, we will write $\text{Assume}(A_i, A)$ for the first element $[\Gamma]$ of the pair $([\Gamma], A_i)$ appearing in the decomposition of A by $\Rightarrow$.

For instance, $EP(Peirce) = [Peirce, A]$, and $\text{Assume}(A, Peirce) = [(A \rightarrow B) \rightarrow A]$. Since the provability of negations is the same between classical and intuitionistic propositional logic, $A \rightarrow \bot$, i.e., $\neg A$ is not further decomposed.

Next we will show that a strict fragment of λ^v_{exc}, in which a single use of (exc) is allowed, is complete with respect to classical provability. The terms of the fragment M_C are defined as follows:
$$M_C ::= \{y\}M_I \mid \lambda x.M_C; \qquad M_I ::= x \mid \lambda x.M_I \mid M_I M_I \mid yM_I \mid \text{raise}(M_I).$$

For example, we have $\mathcal{P}_1 : Peirce$ with $A \in EP(Peirce)$, and $\mathcal{P}_2 \equiv \{y\}\lambda x_1.x_1(\lambda x_2.\text{raise}(y\lambda v.x_2)) : Peirce$ with $Peirce \in EP(Peirce)$. To prove $Peirce$ we have only two ways to apply (exc) to a subformula of $Peirce$.

The following proposition shows that the restricted terms M_C that represent some standard form of classical proofs are complete with respect to classical provability, and that the existence of candidates allows an effective way to determine which type has to be assumed in writing classical proofs as programs.

Proposition 4. *Let A, as a formula, be classically provable from Γ and $A_i \in EP(A)$. Then there exists a λ^v_{exc}-term M_C such that $\Gamma \vdash M_C : A$ and the type of exceptional parameter is A_i.*

Proof. Since A is classically provable from Γ and $A_i \in EP(A)$, A_i is also provable from $\Gamma \cup \text{Assume}(A_i, A)$. By Glivenko's theorem in propositional logic,

---

[2] Although we can write the ML program `fun Peirce(w) = let exception y of '1α in w(fn z => raise(y z)) handle (y x) => x end` as $\mathcal{P}_1$, whose type can be inferred as `(('1α -> 'β) -> '1α) -> '1α` by the ML system, the correspondence is *informal* in the sense that the occurrence of `y` in `exception y` is treated as a name of an exception rather than a variable, like in $\{y\}M$. See also section 5.

A_i is intuitionistically provable from $\Gamma \cup \mathrm{Assume}(A_i, A) \cup \{\neg A_i\}$. Thus we have a term M_C such that $\Gamma \vdash M_C : A$ is provable in λ^v_{exc} by applying (exc) once with A_i as the type of exceptional parameter. $\square$

The proposition means that it is possible to restrict the application of (exc) only for a strictly positive and atomic subformula of the conclusion, which is a respective property of Theorem 1 on page 39 of [31].

When an exception arises, we often use an exception handler to continue the computation. We show three examples below, including programs for normal and exceptional cases.

(1) $\mathcal{L} \equiv \lambda x g.\{y\}g(x(\lambda k.\mathrm{raise}(yk))) : ((A \to B) \to C) \to (C \to A) \to A$
$\mathcal{L}V_1V_2$ provides the computation below: Following the case-analysis in Example 1, if $V_1 \equiv \lambda k.M$ where $k \notin FV(M)$ (normal case), then the result of $\mathcal{L}V_1V_2$ is V_2M. If $V_1 \equiv \lambda k.\mathcal{E}[kV]$ where $k \notin FV(\mathcal{E}[V])$ (exceptional case), then the entire result becomes V. That is, $\mathcal{L}$ computes a composition of V_2 and V_1 of a normal case. A substitution instance of this type is known as Hosoi's law.

(2) $\mathcal{H} \equiv \lambda x f.\{y\}x(\lambda k.\mathrm{raise}(y(fk))) : ((A \to B) \to C) \to (A \to C) \to C$
$\mathcal{H}V_1V_2$ gives the following computation: If $V_1 \equiv \lambda k.M$ where $k \notin FV(M)$ (normal case), then the whole result is M. If $V_1 \equiv \lambda k.\mathcal{E}[kV]$ where $k \notin FV(\mathcal{E}[V])$ (exceptional case), then the result of $\mathcal{H}V_1V_2$ becomes V_2V. Thus, $\mathcal{H}$ can be regarded as a handler of an exception.

(3) $\mathcal{G} \equiv \lambda x g f.\{y\}g(x(\lambda k.raise(y(fk))))$
$$: ((A \to B) \to C) \to (C \to D) \to (A \to D) \to D$$
$\mathcal{G}$ is obtained by combining the roles of $\mathcal{L}$ and $\mathcal{H}$ into one program.

To demonstrate a simple example we assume the constants used below, and the reduction rules and the inference rules are also assumed as usual:

fix $f.M \triangleright M[f := \mathrm{fix}f.M]$;

infer $\Gamma \vdash \mathrm{fix}f.\lambda x.M : A \to B$ from $\Gamma, f:A \to B, x:A \vdash M : B$, etc.

Let prod be

$\lambda l'.\lambda exit.(\mathrm{fix}f.\lambda l.$ if l=nil then 1

else if car(l)=0 then $(exit\ 0)$ else $*\ (\mathrm{car}(l))\ (f(\mathrm{cdr}(l)))\ )l'$

with the type int list $\to$ (int $\to$ int) $\to$ int.

To compute the product of all integers in the integer list l, using Example 1 we define Prod as $\lambda l.\mathcal{P}_1(\mathrm{prod}\ l)$ with the type int list $\to$ int. Then Prod(l) makes it possible to return 0 immediately as an exception if l contains 0. For instance, we compute neither $*\ 1\ 2$ nor $*\ 0\ 3$ in the following:

Prod$[1,2,0,3] \triangleright^* \{y\}(\mathrm{fix}f.\cdots)[1,2,0,3] \triangleright^* \{y\}*\ 1\ (*\ 2\ (\mathrm{fix}f.\cdots)[0,3])$
$\triangleright^* \{y\}*\ 1\ (*\ 2\ (\mathrm{raise}\ (y\ 0))) \triangleright^* \{y\}\mathrm{raise}\ (y\ 0) \triangleright^* 0$.

Instead of $\mathcal{P}_1$, when we use $\mathcal{G}$ in the above, the program $\mathcal{G}(\mathrm{prod}\ l)$ f g computes g 0 if l contains 0, otherwise f n where n is the product of l.

3 Church-Rosser Property of λ^v_{exc}

In this section, we prove that the non-trivial subset of λ^v_{exc} without (ev3-2) has the Church-Rosser property by the well-known method of parallel reductions [2][30][35] and the Lemma of Hindley-Rosen, see [2].

Proposition 5 (Church-Rosser Theorem). *For λ_{exc}^v without* (ev3-2),
if $M \rhd_{exc}^{v*} N_1$ and $M \rhd_{exc}^{v*} N_2$, then $N_1 \rhd_{exc}^{v*} M'$ and $N_2 \rhd_{exc}^{v*} M'$ for some M'.

To prove this proposition, first define two parallel reductions, $\gg_1$ and $\gg_2$,
on λ_{exc}^v-terms, for commutativity of the two parallel reductions.
(1) $x \gg_1 x$;
(2) if $M \gg_1 N$, then $\lambda x.M \gg_1 \lambda x.N$;
(3) if $M \gg_1 N$, then raise $M \gg_1$ raise N;
(4) if $M_i \gg_1 N_i$ $(i = 1, 2)$, then $M_1 M_2 \gg_1 N_1 N_2$;
(5) if $M \gg_1 N_1$ and $V \gg_1 N_2$ then $(\lambda x.M)V \gg_1 N_1[x := N_2]$;
(6) if $M_1 \gg_1 N_1$, then (raise $M_1)M_2 \gg_1$ raise N_1 for any M_2;
(7) if $M_1 \gg_1 N_1$, then $V($raise $M_1) \gg_1$ raise N_1 for any V;
(8) if $M_i \gg_1 N_i$ $(i = 1, 2)$, then $(\{y\}M_1)M_2 \gg_1 \{y\}((N_1[y \Leftarrow N_2])N_2)$;
(9) if $V \gg_1 N_1$ and $M \gg_1 N_2$, then $V(\{y\}M) \gg_1 \{y\}(N_1(N_2[N_1 \Rightarrow y]))$;
(10) if $M \gg_1 N$, then $\{y\}M \gg_1 \{y\}N$;
(11) if $M \gg_1 N$, then $yM \gg_1 yN$.

Lemma 6. *If $V \gg_1 M$, then M is a value.*
If $M \gg_1 N_1$ and $V \gg_1 N_2$, then $M[x := V] \gg_1 N_1[x := N_2]$.
If $M_i \gg_1 N_i$ $(i = 1, 2)$, then $M_1[y \Leftarrow M_2] \gg_1 N_1[y \Leftarrow N_2]$.
If $M \gg_1 N_1$ and $V \gg_1 N_2$, then $M[V \Rightarrow y] \gg_1 N_1[N_2 \Rightarrow y]$.

Lemma 7. *For any M, there exists M^{*1} such that for any N, $N \gg_1 M^{*1}$ whenever $M \gg_1 N$.*

Proof. By induction on the derivation of $\gg_1$. Here, M^{*1} can be inductively
given as follows:
1) $x^{*1} = x$;;   2) $(\lambda x.M)^{*1} = \lambda x.M^{*1}$;;   3) (raise $M)^{*1} =$ raise(M^{*1});;
4-1) $((\lambda x.M)V)^{*1} = M^{*1}[x := V^{*1}]$,
4-2) $(($raise $M)N)^{*1} =$ raise(M^{*1}),
4-3) $(V($raise $M))^{*1} =$ raise(M^{*1}),
4-4) $((\{y\}M)N)^{*1} = \{y\}((M^{*1}[y \Leftarrow N^{*1}])N^{*1})$,
4-5) $(V(\{y\}M))^{*1} = \{y\}(V^{*1}(M^{*1}[V^{*1} \Rightarrow y]))$,
4-6) $(MN)^{*1} = M^{*1}N^{*1}$;;
5) $(\{y\}M)^{*1} = \{y\}M^{*1}$;;   6) $(yM)^{*1} = yM^{*1}$. $\square$

To cover (ev4-1) and (ev4-2), we define $\gg_2$ inductively as follows:
(1) $x \gg_2 x$;
(2) if $M \gg_2 N$, then $\lambda x.M \gg_2 \lambda x.N$;
(3) if $M \gg_2 N$, then raise $M \gg_2$ raise N;
(4) if $M_i \gg_2 N_i$ $(i = 1, 2)$, then $M_1 M_2 \gg_2 N_1 N_2$;
(5) if $M_1 \gg_2 N_1$, then (raise $M_1)M_2 \gg_2$ raise N_1 for any M_2;
(6) if $M_1 \gg_2 N_1$, then $V($raise $M_1) \gg_2$ raise N_1 for any V;
(7) if $M \gg_2 N$, then $\{y\}M \gg_2 \{y\}N$;
(8) if $M \gg_2 N$, then $\{y\}M \gg_2 N$ where $y \notin FV(M)$;

(9) if $M \gg_2 N$, then $\{y\}(\text{raise } yM) \gg_2 \{y\}N$;

(10) if $M \gg_2 N$, then $yM \gg_2 yN$.

Lemma 8. *For any M, there exists M^{*2} such that for any N, $N \gg_2 M^{*2}$ whenever $M \gg_2 N$.*

Proof. By induction on the derivation of $\gg_2$ as done in Lemma 7. With respect to $\gg_2$, we can also obtain the respective properties to Lemma 6. $\square$

It is clear that $M \gg_1 M$ and $M \gg_2 M$. Let $\gg_1^*$ and $\gg_2^*$ be the transitive closures of $\gg_1$ and $\gg_2$, respectively. Now we can obtain that $\gg_1^*$ and $\gg_2^*$ commute, i.e., if $M \gg_1^* M_1$ and $M \gg_2^* M_2$, then $M_1 \gg_2^* N$ and $M_2 \gg_1^* N$ for some N. For this, it is enough to show the following lemma [2].

Lemma 9. *If we have $M \gg_1 M_1$ and $M \gg_2 M_2$, then $M_2 \gg_1 N$ and $M_1 \gg_2^* N$ for some N.*

Proof. By induction on the derivations of $\gg_1$ and $\gg_2$. We show one of the essential cases.

Case 1. $(\{y\}M_1)M_2 \gg_1 \{y\}N_1[y \Leftarrow N_2]N_2$ from $M_1 \gg_1 N_1$ and $M_2 \gg_1 N_2$; and $(\{y\}M_1)M_2 \gg_2 R_1 R_2$ from $\{y\}M_1 \gg_2 R_1$ and $M_2 \gg_2 R_2$:

There are three cases for the derivation of $\{y\}M_1 \gg_2 R_1$.

Case 1-1. $\{y\}M_1 \equiv \{y\}(\text{raise } yM_3) \gg_2 R_1 \equiv \{y\}R_3$ from $M_3 \gg_2 R_3$:

We have $M_1 \equiv (\text{raise } yM_3) \gg_1 N_1 \equiv (\text{raise } yN_4)$ from $M_3 \gg_1 N_4$. By the induction hypotheses, for some S_1 and S_2 we have $N_4 \gg_2^* S_1$ and $R_3 \gg_1 S_1$; and $N_2 \gg_2^* S_2$ and $R_2 \gg_1 S_2$. Then, $(yN_4)[y \Leftarrow N_2] \gg_2^* (yS_1)[y \Leftarrow S_2]$, and $(\text{raise}((yN_4)[y \Leftarrow N_2]))N_2 \gg_2^* \text{raise}((yS_1)[y \Leftarrow S_2])$ are obtained. From this we have $\{y\}(\text{raise}((yN_4)[y \Leftarrow N_2]))N_2 \gg_2^* \{y\}\text{raise}((yS_1)[y \Leftarrow S_2])$. Here, $\{y\}\text{raise}((yS_1)[y \Leftarrow S_2]) \equiv \{y\}\text{raise}(y(S_1[y \Leftarrow S_2]S_2)) \gg_2 \{y\}(S_1[y \Leftarrow S_2]S_2)$. On the other hand, $R_1 R_2 \equiv (\{y\}R_3)R_2 \gg_1 \{y\}(S_1[y \Leftarrow S_2]S_2)$.

Case 1-2: $\{y\}M_1 \gg_2 R_1$ from $M_1 \gg_2 R_1$ where $y \notin FV(M_1)$; and Case 1-3: $\{y\}M_1 \gg_2 R_1 \equiv \{y\}R_3$ from $M_1 \gg_2 R_3$ can be easily confirmed. $\square$

From Lemmata 7 and 8, we obtain that $\gg_1$ and $\gg_2$ have the diamond property, and so have $\gg_1^*$ and $\gg_2^*$. Moreover, from Lemma 9 and the Lemma of Hindley-Rosen, $(\gg_1 \cup \gg_2)^*$ has the diamond property. Since we have $(\gg_1 \cup \gg_2)^* = (\triangleright_{exc}^v - (\text{ev3-1,2}))^*$, it can be proved that λ_{exc}^v without (ev3-1,2) has the diamond property.

Secondly to cover (ev3-1), define $\gg_3$ similarly to $\gg_2$. Then we can also prove that $\gg_3$ has the diamond property and $(\gg_1 \cup \gg_2)^*$ commutes with $\gg_3^*$. For the commutativity, we can prove the respective properties to Lemma 6, e.g., if $M_i \gg_3 N_i$ $(i = 1, 2)$, then $M_1[y \Leftarrow M_2] \gg_3^* N_1[y \Leftarrow N_2]$ where $\gg_3^*$ is the *transitive* relation of $\gg_3$[3]. Thus, from the Lemma of Hindley-Rosen, Proposition 5 (Church-Rosser) can be confirmed for λ_{exc}^v without (ev3-2).

---

[3] Here, "if $M_i \gg_3 N_i$ $(i = 1, 2)$, then $M_1[y \Leftarrow M_2] \gg_3 N_1[y \Leftarrow N_2]$" is not true. Counterexample: $y(\text{raise}(yx)) \gg_3 yx$ can be derived, but not $(y(\text{raise}(yx)))[y \Leftarrow N] \equiv y((\text{raise}(y(xN)))N) \gg_3 (yx)[y \Leftarrow N] \equiv y(xN)$. This observation shows that the same proof method of Church-Rosser could not work for the system with (ev3-2).

4 CPS-Translation of λ_{exc}^v-Terms

We define the translation from the full λ_{exc}^v to $\lambda^\to$, which logically induces Kuroda's translation and is applied to show the strong normalization property with respect to some fragment of λ_{exc}^v. This translation, with an auxiliary function Ψ for values, comes from Plotkin [30] and de Groote [7]. It is proved that the translation is sound with respect to conversions.

Definition 10 (CPS-translation from λ_{exc}^v to $\lambda^\to$). $\overline{x} = \lambda k.kx$;
$\overline{\lambda x.M} = \lambda k.k(\lambda x.\overline{M})$; $\quad \overline{yM} = \lambda k.k(\overline{M}y)$; $\quad \overline{MN} = \lambda k.\overline{M}(\lambda m.\overline{N}(\lambda n.mnk))$;
$\overline{\mathrm{raise}(M)} = \lambda k.\overline{M}(\lambda x.x)$; $\quad \overline{\{y\}M} = \lambda y.\overline{M}y$.
$\Psi(x) = x$; $\qquad\qquad\qquad \Psi(\lambda x.M) = \lambda x.\overline{M}$; $\quad \Psi(yM) = \overline{M}y$.

Lemma 11. *For any value V, $\overline{V} = \lambda k.k\Psi(V)$.*

Lemma 12. *For any term M and value V, $\overline{M[x := V]} = \overline{M}[x := \Psi(V)]$.*

Lemma 13. *For any term M where $k \notin FV(M)$, $\lambda k.\overline{M}k \triangleright_\beta \overline{M}$.*

The above three lemmata can be proved by straightforward induction.

Lemma 14. *For any terms M and N, $\overline{M[y \Leftarrow N]} \triangleright_\beta^* \overline{M}[y := \lambda m.\overline{N}(\lambda n.mny)]$.*

Proof. By induction on the structure of M. $\square$

Lemma 15. *For any term M and value V, $\overline{M[V \Rightarrow y]} \triangleright_\beta^* \overline{M}[y := \lambda n.\Psi(V)ny]$.*

Proof. By induction on the structure of M. Only the case of yM is shown:
$\overline{(yM)[V \Rightarrow y]} = \lambda k.k((\lambda k'.\overline{V}(\lambda m.\overline{M[V \Rightarrow y]}(\lambda n.mnk')))y)$
$\triangleright_\beta \lambda k.k((\lambda k''.k''\Psi(V))(\lambda m.\overline{M[V \Rightarrow y]}(\lambda n.mny)))$
$\triangleright_\beta^* \lambda k.k(\overline{M[V \Rightarrow y]}(\lambda n.\Psi(V)ny)) \triangleright_\beta^* \lambda k.k(\overline{M}[y := \lambda n.\Psi(V)ny](\lambda n.\Psi(V)ny))$
$= \lambda k.k(\overline{M}y)[y := \lambda n.\Psi(V)ny] = \overline{yM}[y := \lambda n.\Psi(V)ny]. \square$

Lemma 16. *If $M \triangleright_{exc}^v N$, then $\overline{M} =_\beta \overline{N}$.*

Proof. By induction on the derivation of $M \triangleright_{exc}^v N$. Only the case of (ev5-2) $V(\{y\}M) \triangleright_{exc}^v (\{y\}M)[V \Rightarrow y]$ is shown:
$\overline{V(\{y\}M)} = \lambda k.\overline{V}(\lambda m.(\lambda y.\overline{M}y)(\lambda n.mnk))$
$\triangleright_\beta \lambda k.(\lambda k_1.k_1\Psi(V))(\lambda m.\overline{M}[y := \lambda n.mnk](\lambda n.mnk))$
$\triangleright_\beta^* \lambda k.\overline{M}[y := \lambda n.\Psi(V)nk](\lambda n.\Psi(V)nk) = \lambda y.\overline{M}[y := \lambda n.\Psi(V)ny](\lambda n.\Psi(V)ny)$
$=_\beta \lambda y.\overline{M[V \Rightarrow y]}(\lambda n.\Psi(V)ny) =_\beta \lambda y.(\lambda m.\overline{M[V \Rightarrow y]}(\lambda n.mny))\Psi(V)$
$=_\beta \lambda y.(\lambda k.\overline{V}(\lambda m.\overline{M[V \Rightarrow y]}(\lambda n.mnk)))y = \overline{\{y\}V(M[V \Rightarrow y])}. \square$

We have confirmed the soundness of the translation in the sense that equivalent λ_{exc}^v-terms are translated into equivalent λ-terms.

Proposition 17 (Soundness of the CPS-Translation). *If we have $M =_{exc}^v N$, then $\overline{M} =_\beta \overline{N}$.*

The translation logically establishes the double-negation translation of Kuroda.

Definition 18 (Kuroda's Translation). $A^q = A$ where A is atomic;
$(A \to B)^q = A^q \to \neg\neg B^q.$ $\quad (x{:}A, \Gamma)^q = x{:}A^q, \Gamma^q; \quad (y{:}\neg A, \Gamma)^q = y{:}\neg A^q, \Gamma^q.$

Proposition 19. *If we have* $\Gamma \vdash_{\lambda^v_{exc}} M : A$, *then* $\Gamma^q \vdash_{\lambda \to} \overline{M} : \neg\neg A^q.$

It is also derived that λ^v_{exc} is consistent in the sense that there is no closed term M of $\vdash_{\lambda^v_{exc}} M : \bot$, and hence no closed term of the form $\text{raise}(M)$ either.

5 λ^v_{exc} with Signature

From the programming side we extend λ^v_{exc} with a signature. The signature is used to introduce constants or to declare global variables, such as exception constructors (names of exceptions) in ML or special variables in LISP. In the following, the term $\{c\}M$ is treated as a packet which can be opened by a reduction. We show that λ^v_{exc} with a certain signature can simulate computations of type-free λ-calculus.

$\lambda^v_{exc} + \Sigma$:
$A ::= \alpha \mid \bot \mid A \to A;$
$\Gamma ::= \langle \, \rangle \mid x{:}A, \Gamma \mid y{:}\neg A, \Gamma; \qquad \Sigma ::= \langle \, \rangle \mid c{:}A, \Sigma;$
$M ::= x \mid c \mid \lambda x.M \mid MM \mid yM \mid \text{raise}(M) \mid \{y\}M \mid \{c\}M;$
$V ::= x \mid c \mid \lambda x.M \mid yM \mid cV;$

$$\Gamma \vdash_\Sigma c : \Sigma(c) \qquad \Gamma \vdash_\Sigma x : \Gamma(x) \qquad \frac{\Gamma \vdash_\Sigma M : A}{\Gamma \vdash_\Sigma yM : \bot} \text{ if } \Gamma(y) \equiv \neg A \not\equiv \neg\bot$$

$$\frac{\Gamma, x{:}A \vdash_\Sigma M : B}{\Gamma \vdash_\Sigma \lambda x.M : A \to B} (\to I) \qquad \frac{\Gamma \vdash_\Sigma M_1 : A \to B \quad \Gamma \vdash_\Sigma M_2 : A}{\Gamma \vdash_\Sigma M_1 M_2 : B} (\to E)$$

$$\frac{\Gamma \vdash_\Sigma M : \bot}{\Gamma \vdash_\Sigma \text{raise}(M) : A} \text{ if } A \not\equiv \bot \qquad \frac{\Gamma, y{:}\neg A \vdash_\Sigma M : A}{\Gamma \vdash_\Sigma \{y\}M : A} (exc)$$

$$\frac{\Gamma \vdash_\Sigma M : A}{\Gamma \vdash_\Sigma \{c\}M : A} (Exc) \text{ if } \Sigma(c) \equiv \neg A$$

(ev1), (ev2-1), (ev2-2), (ev3-1), (ev3-2), (ev4-1), (ev4-2), (ev5-1), (ev5-2) and (ev6-1) $\{c\}(\text{raise } cV) \vartriangleright^v_{exc} V$;
(ev6-2) $\{c\}(\text{raise } c'V) \vartriangleright^v_{exc} \text{raise}(c'V)$ if $c \not\equiv c'$; $\qquad$ (ev6-3) $\{c\}V \vartriangleright^v_{exc} V$.

Since the occurrence c in the definition of the reduction rules is treated as if it were a global variable, we computationally call (Exc) a rule of global exception handling. In terms of ML, based on the correspondence of $\bot$ with exn (type of exceptions in ML), `let exception c of A in M handle (c x) => x end` may be regarded as the term $\{c{:}\neg A\}M$ rather than $\{y{:}\neg A\}M$, see also footnote 2. Among the reduction rules, (ev6-1) under the call-by-value computation is essentially used for encoding type-free λ-calculus in this section.

We show that the computation of $\vartriangleright_{\beta v}$ in type free λ-calculus can be simulated in λ^v_{exc} with the following signature. This simulation would be regarded as a computational use of logical inconsistency.

Definition 20 (*lam* and *app*). Let $\star$ be $(\alpha \to \alpha) \to \alpha \to \alpha$. Let Σ_e be $E :$
$\neg(\star \to \star)$. Let F be $\lambda x_1 x_2.x_2$ and *id* be $\lambda x.x$.
$lam = \lambda x v.\text{raise}(Ex) : (\star \to \star) \to \star;$
$app = \lambda x_1 x_2.(\{E\}F(x_1 \ id))x_2 : \star \to \star \to \star.$

For a term of type free λ-calculus:
$M ::= x \mid \lambda x.M \mid MM$
the following encoding into $\star$ is defined by using *lam* and *app*.

Definition 21 (Encoding of Type-Free λ-Calculus in $\lambda_{exc}^v + \Sigma_e$). The encoding $\lceil \ \rceil : Terms \to \star$ is defined as follows:
$\lceil x \rceil = x; \qquad \lceil \lambda x.M \rceil = lam(\lambda x.\lceil M \rceil); \qquad \lceil MN \rceil = app\lceil M \rceil \lceil N \rceil.$

Proposition 22. *Let V be a value, i.e., a variable or a λ-abstraction.*
(1) $\lceil M[x := N] \rceil \equiv \lceil M \rceil [x := \lceil N \rceil].$ *(2)* $\lceil V \rceil$ *is also a value.*
(3) $app(lam(V)) \triangleright_{exc}^{v*} \lambda v.Vv$ *where v is fresh.*
(4) If we have $M \triangleright_{\beta_V} N$ in the type-free λ_v-calculus à la Plotkin [30], then
$\lceil M \rceil \triangleright_{exc}^{v*} \lceil N \rceil$ *in $\lambda_{exc}^v + \Sigma_e$.*

Proof. We verify only (4):
$\lceil (\lambda x.M)V \rceil \equiv app(\lambda v.\text{raise}(E(\lambda x.\lceil M \rceil))))\lceil V \rceil \triangleright_{exc}^v (\{E\}F(\text{raise}(E(\lambda x.\lceil M \rceil)))))\lceil V \rceil$
$\triangleright_{exc}^v (\{E\}\text{raise}(E(\lambda x.\lceil M \rceil)))\lceil V \rceil \triangleright_{exc}^v (\lambda x.\lceil M \rceil)\lceil V \rceil \triangleright_{exc}^v \lceil M[x := V] \rceil. \ \square$

In the above proof, (ev6-1) with the call-by-value computation is essentially necessary. For instance, Turing's fixed point combinator
$$Y \equiv (\lambda x f.f(xxf))(\lambda x f.f(xxf))$$
can be simulated as $\lceil YV \rceil \triangleright_{exc}^{v*} \lceil V(YV) \rceil$ for any V. This encoding would be regarded as a counterpart of [20], in which Lillibridge established simulation of recursive types with exceptions of ML.

Now the system λ_{exc}^v with the signature becomes logically inconsistent, so that $\lambda\ast$ [3] with Girard's paradox [5][18] can also be interpreted in this system by a similar method. Of course, this encoding is impossible in λ_{exc}^v with empty signatures, which is logically consistent.

6 Comparison with Related Work and Concluding Remarks

We briefly compare λ_{exc}^v with some of the existing call-by-value styles: $\lambda_{exn}^{\to}$ of de Groote [7], and λ_c of Felleisen [8][9]. The comparison reveals some similarities and distinctions between them.

6.1 Relation to $\lambda_{exn}^{\to}$ of de Groote

Based on classical propositional logic, P.de Groote [7] introduced the simply typed λ-calculus $\lambda_{exn}^{\to}$ for formalizing the exception-handling mechanism as in

ML. At first appearance, λ^v_{exc} is a small subsystem of $\lambda^{\to}_{exn}$, and the two systems seem similar; however, different permutative reduction rules are used in them.

In the following, we consider a simplified version of $\lambda^{\to}_{exn}$ [7]. The term is defined by two distinct variables x's (λ-variables) and y's (exception variables only with negation type):
$$M ::= x \mid y \mid \lambda x.M \mid MM \mid (\text{raise } M) \mid \langle y.M|x.M \rangle.$$
The value is defined as follows:
$$V ::= x \mid y \mid \lambda x.M \mid yV.$$
The typing rules are $(\to I)$, $(\to E)$, $(\bot E)$, and the following excluded middle:
infer $\Gamma \vdash \langle y.M|x.N \rangle : B$ from $\Gamma, y : \neg A \vdash M : B$ and $\Gamma, x : A \vdash N : B$.
The reduction rules[4] are $\rhd_{\beta_V}$; (ev2-1); (ev2-2); and

(**handle**$_{\text{simple}}$) : $\langle y.V|x.N \rangle \rhd_{exn} V$ if $y \notin FV(V)$;
(**handle/raise**) : $\langle y.(\text{raise } yV)|x.N \rangle \rhd_{exn} \langle y.N[x := V]|x.N \rangle$;
(**handle**$_{\text{left}}$) : $V\langle y.M|x.N \rangle \rhd_{exn} \langle y.VM|x.VN \rangle$;
(**handle**$_{\text{right}}$) : $\langle y.M|x.N \rangle O \rhd_{exn} \langle y.MO|x.NO \rangle$.

Now we have the following natural translation from $\lambda^{\to}_{exn}$ to λ^v_{exc}.

Definition 23 (Translation from $\lambda^{\to}_{exn}$ to λ^v_{exc}). $(x)^\circ = x$; $(y)^\circ = \lambda k.yk$;
$(\lambda x.M)^\circ = \lambda x.M^\circ$; $(MN)^\circ = M^\circ N^\circ$;
$(\text{raise } M)^\circ = \text{raise}(M^\circ)$; $(\langle y.M \mid x.N \rangle)^\circ = \{y'\}(\lambda y.M^\circ)(\lambda x.y'N^\circ)$.

Proposition 24. *If we have $\Gamma \vdash M : A$ in $\lambda^{\to}_{exn}$, then $\Gamma \vdash_{\lambda^v_{exc}} M^\circ : A$.*

Lemma 25. *If we have $M \rhd_{exn} N$ in $\lambda^{\to}_{exn}$, then $M^\circ =^v_{exc} N^\circ$.*

In terms of the inverse translation, λ^v_{exc} can be regarded as a fragment of $\lambda^{\to}_{exn}$. However, (ev5-1) and (ev5-2) could not be interpreted in $\lambda^{\to}_{exn}$. (**handle**$_{\text{left}}$) and (**handle**$_{\text{right}}$) are simple permutative reductions. On the other hand, (ev5-1) and (ev5-2) are types of permutations, but the segment, in terms of Prawitz [31], is separated, and we have to shift the lower rule up to both the immediately higher one and the separated ones.

Definition 26 (Translation from λ^v_{exc} to $\lambda^{\to}_{exn}$). $(x)^+ = x$;
$(\lambda x.M)^+ = \lambda x.M^+$; $(MN)^+ = M^+N^+$; $(yM)^+ = yM^+$;
$(\text{raise } M)^+ = \text{raise}(M^+)$; $(\{y\}M)^+ = \langle y.M^+ \mid x.x \rangle$.

Proposition 27. *If we have $\Gamma \vdash_{\lambda^v_{exc}} M : A$, then $\Gamma \vdash_{\lambda^{\to}_{exn}} M^+ : A$.*

Comparing with (ev4-1), (ev4-2) and (**handle**$_{\text{simple}}$), (**handle/raise**), the latter rules are restricted to a value[5]. This restriction to a value breaks down the Church-Rosser property of $\lambda^{\to}_{exn}$. For example, $(\{y\}x_1)x_2$ leads to x_1x_2 and $\{y\}x_1x_2$ in λ^v_{exc}[6] under the restriction, and similarly in $\lambda^{\to}_{exn}$. In contrast, the value restriction makes it possible to simulate (ev4-1) and (ev4-2) by the rules of Felleisen's λ_c as described in the next subsection.

---

[4] Here, we take an important subset of the reduction rules from the original $\lambda^{\to}_{exn}$ to discuss the relation.

[5] This restriction seems to be not essential in $\lambda^{\to}_{exn}$, by personal communication from P.de Groote.

[6] This example has been given by Y.Akama.

6.2 Relation to Felleisen's λ_c

For reasoning about a call-by-value language, Felleisen et al. [8][9] introduced λ_c-calculus by extending the type-free λ_v-calculus of Plotkin [30] with the control operator C and the abort operator A. By Griffin [14] the λ_c-calculus has been applied to extend the Curry-Howard-De Bruijn isomorphism to classical logic from a computational viewpoint. It is a distinct point that λ_c uses the usual reduction rules (compatible) and the computation rules (non-compatible) only at the top-level, which bring the computation of the top-level continuation to a stop. We observe that the computation rules in λ_c are necessary to simulate some of the reduction rules in λ_{exc}^v [7].

According to observations in Rehof and Sørensen [32], we consider a variant of λ_c as follows. The terms and values are defined as usual.
$M ::= x \mid \lambda x.M \mid MM \mid \mathcal{F}M$
The reduction rules are $\triangleright_{\beta_V}$, (F_L), (F_R), and (F_{top}) as follows:
(F_L): $(\mathcal{F}M)N \triangleright_c \mathcal{F}(\lambda k.M(\lambda f.k(fN)))$; (F_R): $V(\mathcal{F}M) \triangleright_c \mathcal{F}(\lambda k.M(\lambda f.k(Vf)))$;
(F_{top}): $\mathcal{F}M \triangleright_c \mathcal{F}(\lambda k.M(\lambda f.kf))$.
The operator $\mathcal{F}$ has the type $\neg\neg A \to A$, which is a variant of and can be defined by Felleisen's C, see [32]. In addition, the computation rule is (F_T): $\mathcal{F}M \triangleright_T M\lambda x.x$, which is applied only at the top-level.

Definition 28 (Translation from λ_c to λ_{exc}^v). $\underline{x} = x$;
$\underline{\lambda x.M} = \lambda x.\underline{M}$; $\underline{M_1 M_2} = \underline{M_1}\ \underline{M_2}$; $\underline{\mathcal{F}M} = \{y\}\mathrm{raise}(\underline{M}(\lambda x.yx))$.

Proposition 29. If $\Gamma \vdash_{\lambda_c} M : A$, then $\Gamma \vdash_{\lambda_{exc}^v} \underline{M} : A$.

With regard to the reduction rules, (F_{top}) can be translated such that
$\underline{\mathcal{F}(\lambda k.M(\lambda f.kf))} = \{y\}\mathrm{raise}((\lambda k.\underline{M}(\lambda f.kf))(\lambda x.yx)) \triangleright_{exc}^{v*} \{y\}\mathrm{raise}(\underline{M}(\lambda f.yf)) = \underline{\mathcal{F}M}$. However, (F_L) and (F_R) could not be simulated in λ_{exc}^v. The reason may be explained by the definition of (ev5-1) and (ev5-2). In the definition, the permutations $[y \Leftarrow N]$ and $[N \Rightarrow y]$ can be replaced with the substitutions $[y := \lambda x.y(xN)]$ and $[y := \lambda x.y(Nx)]$, respectively (denoted by (ev5-1'), (ev5-2')). Then (F_L) and (F_R) can be simulated in λ_{exc}^v. In a call-by-name system, the above replacement gives no mismatch, since we have $M[y := \lambda x.y(xN)] \triangleright_\beta^* M[y \Leftarrow N]$ and $M[y := \lambda x.y(Nx)] \triangleright_\beta^* M[N \Rightarrow y]$. However, in a call-by-value system, the situation is not exactly the same. We do not know whether the CPS-translation in section 4 can also be established, even with (ev5-1') and (ev5-2').

A proof of double-negation elimination is used to interpret $\mathcal{F}$ in the above and C in de Groote [6]. We often adopt the following operational semantics [8][9]: $\mathcal{E}[CM] \triangleright M(\lambda x.A(\mathcal{E}[x]))$. This rewriting rule can be simulated in part by a proof of Peirce's law $\mathcal{P}_1$, instead of a double-negation elimination. Consider the case M of $\lambda k.\mathcal{E}'[kV]$ where $k \notin FV(\mathcal{E}'[V])$. Then $\mathcal{E}[C(\lambda k.\mathcal{E}'[kV])] \triangleright^* \mathcal{E}'[A(\mathcal{E}[V])] \triangleright^* \mathcal{E}[V]$, and $\mathcal{E}[\mathcal{P}_1(\lambda k.\mathcal{E}'[kV])] \triangleright_{exc}^{v*} \{y\}\mathrm{raise}(y\mathcal{E}[V]) \triangleright_{exc}^{v*} \mathcal{E}[V]$. When $k \notin FV(M)$, we have that $\mathcal{E}[C(\lambda k.M)] \triangleright^* M$, and $\mathcal{E}[\mathcal{P}_1(\lambda k.M)] \triangleright_{exc}^{v*} \mathcal{E}[M]$. In this sense, $\mathcal{P}_1$ behaves like call/cc, for instance see Harper et al. [15], rather than C.

---

[7] Of course, no reduction rules in λ_{exc}^v are restricted to the top-level use.

Definition 30 (Translation from λ_{exc}^v to λ_c). $\langle x \rangle = x$;

$\langle \lambda x.M \rangle = \lambda x.\langle M \rangle$; $\qquad \langle M_1 M_2 \rangle = \langle M_1 \rangle \langle M_2 \rangle$; $\qquad \langle yM \rangle = y\langle M \rangle$;

$\langle \text{raise } M \rangle = \mathcal{F}(\lambda v.\langle M \rangle)$; $\qquad \langle \{y\}M \rangle = \mathcal{F}(\lambda y.y\langle M \rangle)$.

Proposition 31. *If* $\Gamma \vdash_{\lambda_{exc}^v} M : A$, *then* $\Gamma \vdash_{\lambda_c} \langle M \rangle : A$.

With respect to the reduction rules, (ev2-1) and (ev2-2) can be simulated by (F_L) and (F_R), respectively. In contrast, the reduction rules (ev4-1) and (ev4-2) with the restriction to a value, as mentioned in the previous subsection, can be simulated by the use of the non-compatible (F_T). λ_c can simulate (ev5-1') and (ev5-2'), but with a value restriction such that the term before the reduction has the form $(\{y\}V)N$ and $V(\{y\}V')$, respectively. Finally, the remaining rules (ev3-1) and (ev3-2) with the value restriction of $(y\{y_1\}V)$ can be simulated in λ_c by using the following reduction rule (F_R''): $y(\mathcal{F}M) \triangleright_c M(\lambda x.yx)$, where the type of y is of the form $\neg A$. This rule is a special form of C_R'' in Barbanera and Berardi [4]. Here, $\underline{y(\mathcal{F}M)} \triangleright_{exc}^{v*} \underline{M}(\lambda x.yx)$. Moreover, using (F_{top}) and (F_R''), we have that $\underline{\langle \mathcal{F}M \rangle} =_c \mathcal{F}\langle M \rangle$. We also have that $\underline{\langle \{y\}V \rangle} \triangleright_{exc}^{v*} \{y\}\langle V \rangle$, and $\langle \text{raise } M \rangle \triangleright_{exc}^{v*}$ raise $\langle M \rangle$. From the above observations, λ_{exc}^v with the value restrictions and λ_c with (F_R'') have, in some sense, an isomorphism with respect to conversions.

6.3 Final Remarks

We have provided the call-by-value calculus λ_{exc}^v, based on classical propositional logic. There is a strict fragment of the form M_C in λ_{exc}^v, which represents some standard form of classical proofs. We also observed that every strictly positive subformula with respect to $\rightarrow$ can be the type of value to be passed on, and the use of $\mathcal{P}_1$ makes it possible to implement a simple exit mechanism. To model the exception-handling of ML, we have extended λ_{exc}^v with a signature, so that the computation of type-free λ-calculus can be simulated in it.

To find similarity between λ_{exc}^v and λ_c, we placed a value restriction on λ_{exc}^v. The notion of values has to be reconsidered. The term of the form yV is regarded as a value in de Groote [7], which is based on some analogy of exceptions in ML. However, the mechanism of exception handling in $\lambda_{exn}^{\rightarrow}$ and λ_{exc}^v is different from that in ML, which has great resemblance to the global exception in $\lambda_{exc}^v + \Sigma$. A simple exit mechanism can be implemented mainly by (ev4-1) and (ev4-2). Here, in (ev4-2): $\{y\}(\text{raise } yM) \triangleright \{y\}M$, the term M that is passed on and is an argument of y is not restricted to a value for establishing the Church-Rosser property[8]. Without the loss of the Church-Rosser property, this observation may lead to the assumption of another point such that yM is a value instead of yV. Nevertheless, the CPS-translation of λ_{exc}^v-terms has been obtained and moreover, we can obtain that $\overline{M} \triangleright_\beta^+ \overline{N}$ if $M \triangleright_{exc}^v N$ without (ev5-1,2), since β-conversions $=_\beta$ are necessary only for simulating (ev5-1,2) in the proof of Lemma 16[9]. Here, $\triangleright_\beta^+$ denotes the transitive closure of $\triangleright_\beta$.

---

[8] Instead of (ev4-2), if we had $\{y\}(\text{raise } yV) \triangleright \{y\}V$, then $(\{y\}(\text{raise } yx_1))x_2 \triangleright^*$ $\{y\}(\text{raise } y(x_1x_2))$ and x_1x_2 (not confluent).

[9] From Proposition 19 and the Strong Normalization of $\lambda^{\rightarrow}$, this implies the Strong Normalization of the strict fragment of λ_{exc}^v, with neither (ev5-1) nor (ev5-2).

Besides the Strong Normalization of the full λ_{exc}^v, there are other open problems to be considered. $\lambda_{exc}^v + \Sigma_e$ can interpret $\lambda*$ as in section 5. In turn, similar to the CPS-translation in section 4, we can obtain that if $\Gamma \vdash_{\Sigma_e} M : A$ in $\lambda_{exc}^v + \Sigma_e$, then $\Gamma^q \vdash M' : \neg\neg A^q$ in $\lambda*$, where the constant E in Σ_e can be interpreted using the proof of Girard's paradox of the type $\bot$. Here, is there a translation such that if $M \triangleright_{exc}^v N$ in $\lambda_{exc}^v + \Sigma_e$, then $Tr(M) =_\beta Tr(N)$ in $\lambda*$? The positive answer could show simulation of the Y combinator in $\lambda*$.

Recently, we have become aware of the work by Ong and Stewart [26]. They extensively studied a call-by-value programming language based on a call-by-value variant of Parigot's $\lambda\mu$-calculus [27]. We also have to relate their work to ours, since the call-by-name version λ_{exc} [13] is isomorphic to $\lambda\mu$-calculus.

Acknowledgements I am deeply grateful to M. Horai-Takahashi, M. Dezani-Ciancaglini, P. de Groote, M. Lillibridge, Y. Andou and Y. Akama for helpful discussions and/or communication. I would also like to thank the referees for most helpful comments. This work has been partially supported by the Saneyoshi Scholarship Foundation.

References

1. Andou, Y.: A Normalization-Procedure for the First Order Classical Natural Deduction with Full Logical Symbols. Tsukuba Journal of Mathematics **19** 1 (1995) 153–162
2. Barendregt, H.P.: The Lambda Calculus Its Syntax and Semantics (revised edition). North-Holland (1984)
3. Barendregt, H.P.: Lambda Calculi with Types. Handbook of Logic in Computer Science Vol. II. Oxford University Press (1992) 1–189
4. Barbanera, F. and Berardi, S.: Extracting Constructive Context from Classical Logic via Control-like Reductions. LNCS **664** (1993) 45–59
5. Coquand, T.: An Analysis of Girard's Paradox. Proc. 1st Logic in Computer Science (1986) 227–236
6. De Groote, P.: On the Relation between the $\lambda\mu$-Calculus and the Syntactic Theory of Sequential Control. LNAI **822** (1994) 31–43
7. De Groote, P.: A Simple Calculus of Exception Handling. LNCS **902** (1995) 201–215
8. Felleisen, M., Friedman, D.P., Kohlbecker, E. and Duba, B.: Reasoning with Continuations. Proc. Annual IEEE Symposium on Logic in Computer Science (1986) 131–141
9. Felleisen, M. and Hieb, R.: The Revised Report on the Syntactic Theories of Sequential Control and State. Theoretical Computer Science **103** (1992) 131–141
10. Fujita, K.: On Embedding of Classical Substructural Logics. Proc. Theory of Rewriting Systems and Its Applications Kyoto University RIMS **918** (1995) 178–195
11. Fujita, K.: μ-Head Form Proofs and its Application to Programming. Computer Software **14** 2 (1997) 71–75
12. Fujita, K.: μ-Head Form Proofs with at Most Two Formulas in the Succedent. Transactions of Information Processing Society of Japan **38** 6 (1997) 1073–1082
13. Fujita, K.: Calculus of Classical Proofs from Programming Viewpoint. Kyoto University RIMS **1010** (1997) 7–34

14. Griffin, T.G.: A Formulae-as-Types Notion of Control. Proc. 17th Annual ACM Symposium on Principles of Programming Languages (1990) 47–58
15. Harper, R., Duba, B.F. and MacQueen, D.: Typing First-Class Continuations in ML. J. Functional Programming **3** (4) (1993) 465–484
16. Hayashi, S. and Nakano, H.: PX A Computational Logic. The MIT Press (1988)
17. Howard, W.: The Formulae-as-Types Notion of Constructions. To H.B.Curry: Essays on combinatory logic, lambda-calculus, and formalism. Academic Press (1980) 479–490
18. Howe, D.J.: The Computational Behaviour of Girard's Paradox. Proc. 2nd Logic in Computer Science (1987) 205–214
19. Kobayashi, S.: Monads, Modality and Curry-Howard Principle. Proc. 10th Japan Society for Software Science and Technology (1993) 225–228
20. Lillibridge, M.: Exceptions Are Strictly More Powerful Than Call/CC. Carnegie Mellon University CMU-CS-95-178 (1995)
21. Milner, R., Tofte, M. and Harper, R.: The Definition of Standard ML. The MIT Press (1990)
22. Murthy, C.R.: An Evaluation Semantics for Classical Proofs. Proc. 6th Annual IEEE Symposium on Logic in Computer Science (1991) 96–107
23. Nakano, H.: Logical Structures of the Catch and Throw Mechanism. PhD thesis University of Tokyo (1995)
24. Nordström, B., Petersson, K. and Smith, J.M.: Programming in Martin-Löf's Type Theory An Introduction. Clarendon Press (1990)
25. Ong, C.-H.L.: A Semantic View of Classical Proofs: Type-Theoretic, Categorical, and Denotational Characterizations. Linear Logic '96 Tokyo Meeting (1996)
26. Ong, C.-H.L. and Stewart, C.A.: A Curry-Howard Foundation for Functional Computation with Control. Proc. 24th Annual ACM SIGPLAN-SIGACT Symposium of Principles of Programming Languages (1997)
27. Parigot, M.: $\lambda\mu$-Calculus: An Algorithmic Interpretation of Classical Natural Deduction. LNCS **624** (1992) 190–201
28. Parigot, M.: Classical Proofs as Programs. LNCS **713** (1993) 263–276
29. Parigot, M.: Strong Normalization for Second Order Classical Natural deduction. Proc. 8th Annual IEEE Symposium on Logic in Computer Science (1993)
30. Plotkin, G.: Call-by-Name, Call-by-Value and the λ-Calculus. Theoretical Computer Science **1** (1975) 125–159
31. Prawitz, D.: Natural Deduction: A Proof-Theoretical Study. Almqvist&Wiksell (1965)
32. Rehof, N.J. and Sørensen, M.H.: The λ_Δ-Calculus. LNCS **789** (1994) 516–542
33. Seldin, J.P.: Normalization and Excluded Middle I. Studia Logica XLVIII 2 (1989) 193–217
34. Szabo, M.E.: The Collected Papers of Gerhard Gentzen. North-Holland (1969)
35. Takahashi, M.: Parallel Reductions in λ-Calculus. J. Symbolic Computation **7** (1989) 113–123
36. Takeuti, G.: Proof Theory (second edition). North-Holland (1987)
37. Tonino, H. and Fujita, K.: On the adequacy of representing higher order intuitionistic logic as a pure type system. Annals of Pure and Applied Logic **57** (1992) 251–276

Tracing the Evaluation of Lazy Functional Languages: A Model and Its Implementation

Richard Watson[1] and Eric Salzman[2]

[1] Department of Mathematics and Computing,
University of Southern Queensland,
Toowoomba, QLD 4350, Australia
rwatson@usq.edu.au
[2] Department of Computer Science,
The University of Queensland, QLD 4072, Australia
eric@it.uq.edu.au

Abstract. We address the problem of producing a trace of the evaluation of a program written in a lazy functional language. To avoid ambiguities and possible misunderstandings it is essential that the trace structure is defined with respect to a formally described model of program evaluation.

We provide such a formal semantics for lazy evaluation of a simple lazy language, based closely on the work of Launchbury. The trace corresponds to the sequence of expression reductions defined by the evaluation model.

We also present a scheme to generate a concrete trace of the evaluation of programs written in the target language, based on its semantic rules. We employ a two-step transformational approach: first transform the program so that, on execution, it generates a call-by-name trace as result, then further transform this trace to a call-by-need trace.

Keywords: functional programming, debugging, lazy evaluation, program transformation

1 Introduction

While there has been much progress over recent years in the design and implementation of lazy functional languages, the development of tools to enable debugging of programs written in these languages is not as well advanced. To debug a program, one must be able to observe its behaviour. In this paper we describe a technique for generating an *evaluation trace* for a program written in a lazy functional language. The trace is a history of the computational steps carried out in evaluating (executing) the program, so can form the basis of a debugging system.

Although the current work is motivated by the need for debugging tools, our focus is only on trace generation. We describe elsewhere (Watson and Salzman, 1997) an example of such a debugging tool, which we call a trace browser.

We also recognise that execution tracing provides but one possible path to understanding program behaviour; for instance, the use of execution profilers (see e.g. Runciman and Wakeling, 1993; Sansom and Peyton Jones, 1995) can reveal the time and space consumption of the functions in a program.

Before building a trace generation system, two questions must be addressed: (1) what form should the trace take, and (2) how can the trace be generated? The answers to these questions define the current work, and serve to contrast it with previous work. We have chosen to generate a *reduction* trace by *transforming* a program so that, on evaluation of the transformed program, a trace is generated as the result of the program. (Actually we generate a pair — the result of the original program together with its evaluation trace.) While others have described how a trace of reductions can be generated (see e.g. Snyder, 1990; Goldson, 1994) and how a transformed (instrumented) program can be used to produce a trace (O'Donnell and Hall, 1988; Kishon, 1992; Sparud, 1996), our work is unique in that we combine these two features together with a *formal semantic model* of lazy evaluation which serves to define the reduction steps that the trace reports. Our transform system, for which we provide a set of simple rules, uniformly handles difficult-to-implement language features such as higher-order functions; other transformational approaches have employed special rules depending on the type of a function argument (Sparud, 1996) or failed to satisfactorily address how curried application is traced (Naish and Barbour, 1996).

Our model is a big step operational semantics based very closely on the work of Launchbury (1993). To our knowledge, only Gibbons and Wansbrough (1996) have built a tracing system based on a formally defined reduction model (in their case, the lazy lambda calculus of Ariola et al. (1995)); we believe the Launchbury-style of operational model is superior to that of Ariola et al. as a means of trace definition because it is simpler, with fewer rules, and just one rule for each kind of expression in the language.

The remainder of the paper is organised as follows. In section 2 we provide a background to the problems of tracing non-strict higher-order functional programs, and refer to past attempts at their solution. In section 3 we introduce a simple lazy functional language, its semantic model, and a trace structure based on the model. In section 4 we describe the transformational tracing scheme that we have developed. In section 5 we evaluate the significance of the work reported, and suggest future research directions.

2 The tracing problem

In this section we identify the challenges associated with tracing lazy functional programs, then address the questions raised in the introduction, namely "what should a trace look like and how can it be created?".

The properties of pure, higher-order, non-strict functional languages impose a number of interesting constraints on the task of trace generation:

- *purity* precludes the production of a trace as a side-effect.

- *higher-orderness* requires that we must be able to trace the partial application of a function, and identify the resulting abstraction.
- the *non-strict* property prevents us from reporting an argument's value at application time. However we assume that the reader of the trace will wish to know the argument value, and so must devise a technique of associating the possible eventual evaluation of the argument with its corresponding application instance.

Our tracing system solves all these problems; it can present a user-oriented view of the evaluation trace within the constraints of the language paradigm.

Two kinds of trace have been described in the literature (the terminology is our own): an *operational* trace, which describes a sequence of actions in the order that they were performed to evaluate a program, and a *declarative* trace, which describes the result of function application (argument and result values) but places the information in a trace structure corresponding to the declarative structure of the program.

We have adopted an operational style of trace, because it supports the style of debugging which has proved effective in the imperative language domain. The programmer compares expected program behaviour with that reported in the trace — a divergence between the two indicates a potential error. The declarative trace is appealing mainly because it supports the use of the *algorithmic debugging technique* (Shapiro, 1982) which can detect program errors in a semi-automatic manner. See the work of Nilsson and Fritzson (1994), Sparud (1996), and Naish and Barbour (1996) for application of the technique to lazy functional languages. We reject the declarative trace because we believe that it does not fit well with the programmer's mental model of lazy functional computation; reduction models are usually used to teach and explain the way functional programs work (see e.g. Bird and Wadler, 1988), so an operational trace should closely match a programmer's concept of how functional languages are evaluated.

Three approaches to trace generation have been reported (representative work is cited):

1. modify the standard program translator to produce compiled code which, on execution, will generate a trace (Snyder, 1990; Nilsson and Fritzson, 1994).
2. build a special purpose interpreter which reports its evaluation steps (Goldson, 1994; Augustson, 1995; Gibbons and Wansbrough 1996).
3. transform the original program so that evaluation of the instrumented program generates a trace (O'Donnell and Hall, 1988; Sparud, 1996; Naish and Barbour 1996).

While all these schemes have their merits, we have chosen to employ the program instrumentation approach. This yields a portable scheme, applicable to different languages and implementations.

The program instrumentation aims to *simulate* an evaluation sequence as defined by some abstract model of evaluation. That is, rather than monitoring the activity of an evaluation machine, the original program is augmented so that the evaluation of this instrumented program will generate both a resulting value

$k \in Const$
$x \in Var$
$e \in Expr \ ::= \lambda x.e \mid e_1\ e_2 \mid x \mid k \mid let\ d_1 \ldots d_n\ in\ e$
$d \in Decl \ ::= x = e$

Fig. 1. Abstract syntax of normalised language

---

and a simulated trace of its evaluation. We must be absolutely clear about what we are simulating; hence we adopt a formal operational model to describe the semantics of the language being traced.

3   A model for lazy evaluation

The lazy language we describe exhibits *call-by-need* semantics. That is, the language is non-strict (as defined by call-by-name semantics), and the evaluation of expressions is shared where possible. In our model, only those expressions bound to variables are shared: once a variable is evaluated to a whnf value, further references to that variable yield the value directly. More extensive sharing is possible *via* program transformation (Peyton Jones, 1987, Chapter 15), but is beyond the scope of this work.

We use a formal evaluation model based on Launchbury's operational semantics for lazy evaluation (Launchbury, 1993). Our model is very similar, so in the following we will present the model with little explanation but focus on the differences between our model and Launchbury's. Looking ahead, the trace structure that we will generate includes one object for each judgement present in the semantic rules, so our justification for departure from the original model is to provide a better basis for trace description.

We describe here a very simple lazy language. We have developed a model and tracing system for a larger language including algebraic data types, **case** expressions, and primitive operators (see Watson (1997) for a description of the extended language and semantics), but don't present it for lack of space, and because tracing the extended language does not greatly extend the technique presented here.

3.1   A simple language

Figure 1 shows the abstract syntax of the language. A program is a list of declarations. Programs in this language differ from the concrete programs in two respects: (1) variables appearing in the original program are systematically renamed so that all names are unique (thus lexical scope need not be modelled by the semantic rules) and (2) function definitions in the original program take the form $x\ x_1 \cdots x_n = e$ which is normalised to $x = \lambda x_1 \cdots \lambda x_n.e$.

This simple language is identical to Launchbury's with the important exception that we allow the general form of application expressions $e_1\ e_2$, rather than the normalised form $let\ x = e_2\ in\ e_1\ x$.

Constant	$(\Gamma, n) : k \Downarrow (\Gamma, n) : k$
Abstraction	$(\Gamma, n) : \lambda x.e \Downarrow (\Gamma, n) : \lambda x.e$

Application
$$\frac{(\Gamma, k) : e_1 \Downarrow (\Delta, m) : \lambda x.e \quad (\Phi, n) : \hat{e}[x^n/x] \Downarrow (\Theta, o) : z}{(\Gamma, k) : e_1\ e_2 \Downarrow (\Theta, o) : z}$$
$$\text{where } n = m + 1$$
$$\Phi = \Delta \cup \{x^n \mapsto e_2\}$$

Variable
$$\frac{(\Gamma, k) : e \Downarrow (\Delta, l) : z}{((\Gamma,\ x^n \mapsto e), k) : x^n \Downarrow ((\Delta, x^n \mapsto z), l) : z}$$

Let
$$\frac{(\Delta, k) : e \Downarrow (\Phi, l) : z}{(\Gamma, k) : let\ x_1^r = e_1 \cdots x_n^r = e_n\ in\ e \Downarrow (\Phi, l) : z}$$
$$\text{where } \Delta = \Gamma \cup \{x_1^r \mapsto e_1, \cdots, x_n^r \mapsto e_n\}$$

Fig. 2. Call-by-need semantic rules

3.2 Dynamic rules

The rules appear in figure 2. The following naming conventions are used:
$$\Gamma, \Delta, \Phi, \Theta \in Heap = Var \twoheadrightarrow Expr$$
$$z \in Val ::= \lambda x.e \mid k$$

Judgements are of the form $(\Gamma, k) : e \Downarrow (\Delta, l) : z$, which means: "After k applications have occurred, the expression e, in the context of the set of bindings in Γ, evaluates to the value z. Following the evaluation, l applications will have occurred, and the new heap is Δ."

Variables in the rules appear either as x, a statically declared program variable name (see the application rule), or as x^n, a dynamically created instance of the program variable x. The instance x^n is created due to the nth invocation of the application rule. This explicit dynamic renaming, which subsumes the limited renaming required under Launchbury's rules, is a key element of our rules; it also explains the presence of the application counter that is paired with the heap in the rules.

The $\hat{e}$ notation is conditional α-conversion: it denotes renaming of all let-bound variable *names* defined within expression e, except those defined in the body of an abstraction, to specific variable *instances*. Note that, while Launchbury only performs renaming of variables when required to avoid name capture, we rename *all* variables. The $\hat{e}$ operation, and the $[x^n/x]$ substitution, are *dynamic variable renaming*, but an equivalent and more appropriate term is *instance creation*. The use of $\hat{e}$ captures the intuitive notion that a let-bound variable within the body of a lambda abstraction is a dynamic object in that its value is (potentially) dependent upon the value of a formal parameter, which is itself dynamically bound by function application.

Apart from the adoption of an explicit and universal variable renaming scheme, we differ from Launchbury primarily in the application and variable rules. We bind a renamed formal parameter on the heap rather than perform a β-substitution. This corresponds to the operational semantics described briefly by Ariola et al. (1995). Launchbury himself also proposes it as a viable alternative. We carry out dynamic renaming of variables (instance creation) in the application rule while Launchbury does so in the variable rule. We believe our approach is intuitively more appealing as it reflects the notion that instances are created due to application, not as a consequence of variable evaluation. Launchbury uses β-substitution, effectively removing any reference to formal parameters from a reduction proof, yet his use of a normalisation step to replace argument expressions by an extra variable effectively re-introduces it; our scheme uses formal variables directly, hence our claim to a nicer rule set because we don't need to introduce the extra pseudo-parameter to an application. Our argument binding approach allows the use of the general form of application expressions (in Launchbury's semantics, argument expressions must be variables), though at the cost of dynamic parameter renaming, a larger heap, and an extra reduction step for each evaluated argument.

3.3 An abstract trace

An abstract trace is a representation of the sequence of semantic rules applied to reduce an expression to normal form. There are a number of possible forms that this trace can take; for instance, Launchbury shows an example which depicts the trace as a linear textual form of a natural deduction proof tree. We adopt a *sequential* trace structure, which mirrors the sequence of rule applications, and corresponds to the concrete trace structure described in the next section.

The rules for generating the sequential reduction trace, called rt_{seq}, appear in figure 3. There are three rules; the choice of rule depends upon the number of precedent judgements in the semantic rule. The abstract trace is a sequence of *objects*, each of which is either an expression or, in the case of the application rule, an (expression,trace) pair. Note that the care with which we have constructed the semantics is reflected in the simplicity of the trace. Because the terminal value of the rightmost judgements for each rule is the same (for each rule, examine the rightmost expression above and below the horizontal line), we only need report initial expressions of a rule. This simplification is not possible using Launchbury's rules.

As a simple example, consider the sequential trace of a let expression.

$$[\ let\ a = 1, f = \lambda x.x\ in\ f\ a,$$
$$(f\ a,\ [f,\ \lambda x.x]),$$
$$x,$$
$$a,$$
$$1\ ]$$

In the second line, the trace object for the application $f\ a$ includes a trace of the evaluation of its function f to an abstraction. This is a single step here but may

$$rt_{seq}\,((\Gamma,k):e \Downarrow (\Delta,l):z) \;=\; [e] \qquad\qquad \text{Const, Abs}$$

$$rt_{seq}\left(\frac{J_1}{(\Gamma,k):e \Downarrow (\Delta,l):z}\right) = e:rt_{seq}(J_1) \qquad\qquad \text{Var, Let}$$

$$rt_{seq}\left(\frac{J_1 \quad J_2}{(\Gamma,k):e \Downarrow (\Delta,l):z}\right) = (e,rt_{seq}(J_1)):rt_{seq}(J_2) \qquad \text{App}$$

Fig. 3. Sequential trace rules

---

in general consist of many reductions (see the example in figure 5). The final object in a function reduction is always an abstraction, and the object following an application (here line three) is the body of that abstraction, with one or more lambda variables bound to arguments.

3.4 A concrete trace

A concrete trace, which provides a basis for the trace generation scheme described in the following section, can be derived from the rt_{seq} trace, and is described by the following Haskell data definitions:

```
type Trace = [Step]
data Step  = Ks String              -- constant
           | Abs String             -- abstraction
           | App Trace              -- application
           | VP String | VL String  -- variable
           | LExp String [String]   -- let expression
```

Each trace object is "tagged" by a data constructor to indicate its expression class, and the constructor arguments describe which particular expression is being described. Apart from the Ks object, which simply reports a constant value, all other objects rely on the systematic generation of a unique "name" for all variables and abstractions. These names are derived from the lexical structure of the original program and take the form $level_1.level_2.\cdots.name$ where $level_1.\cdots.level_n$ describes the declaration level at which $name$ appears. New levels are "created" by declarations and application expressions.

This unique naming, used only in the trace objects, is how we solve the problem of reporting lambda abstractions in a trace, thus enabling higher order functions to be traced.

The application object does not directly indicate the expression (say $e_1\ e_2$) it denotes, but it does include a trace of evaluation of e_1, from which e_1 can be determined. To preserve non-strict semantics, the evaluation of e_2 cannot be generated at application time, though it may well appear later in the trace if the argument is evaluated. Associating this argument evaluation with its binding application is a major challenge — see section 4.4.

The let expression object LExp takes two arguments: the first is the name of the abstraction in which it occurs, and the second is the list of variables defined within the expression. This information is vital in performing the trace transform from call-by-name to call-by-need, which we sketch in the section 4.4.

As a final note on trace objects, we observe that the distinction between let-bound and formal parameter variables, traced respectively by VL and VP, is unnecessary from a trace generation perspective, but serves only to aid in trace interpretation by the reader.

4 A tracing transform

In this section we describe how a call-by-need evaluation trace can be produced by firstly generating a raw call-by-name trace as the result of executing an instrumented program, and then how the raw trace can be transformed to call-by-need. We consider the general approach to program instrumentation in sections 4.1 and 4.2, before presenting the instrumentation (§4.3) and the trace transform (§4.4). Example traces appear in section 4.5.

4.1 Approaches to program instrumentation

Simply stated, our aim is to transform some original program (written in the simple language just described) into a Haskell program that on execution will produce a reduction trace. This *concrete* reduction trace should be equivalent to the rt_{seq} *abstract* trace that would be produced by application of the call-by-need semantic rules to the original program.

The one-to-one correspondence between the expression types of our language and the reduction rules we wish to simulate suggests an expression-based transform. For all expressions e in the original program:

$$\mathcal{TE}[e] = (e', object: trace)$$

where e' is the tracing analogue to e, *object* describes e, and *trace* is the trace of evaluation of e. For whnf expressions, *trace* is empty, and for applications, *object* includes the trace of evaluation of the function which is applied. This mirrors precisely the rt_{seq} trace format.

This approach is *bottom-up* in the sense that a complete trace is assembled by building sub-traces and gluing them together. An alternative *top-down* scheme looks like:

$$\mathcal{TE}[e] = \lambda trace.(e', \ trace + [object])$$

where $+$ is the list concatenation operator. Here the trace is built by adding to the end of the sequence; of necessity a state (the trace so far) must be carried through the computation. The encapsulation of e' within an abstraction results in a less efficient instrumented program, as the amount of sharing carried out by the implementation language system is reduced. For this reason we have adopted the bottom-up approach.

4.2 Call-by-name, call-by-need, and transform state

We show in this section that a stateless, bottom-up transform cannot provide a call-by-need trace — it can only manage call-by-name. On the other hand, inclusion of suitable state (specifically: the evaluation status of variables) can enable the creation of a call-by-need trace. This is an important result as it justifies the two-step call-by-need trace generation scheme we will describe.

We sketched above a simple, stateless, bottom-up transform. Consider the use of this kind of transform to instrument the declaration

$$e = \ldots x \ldots x \ldots$$

where we assume both the x variables occur in the same scope. The instrumented code becomes

$$\mathcal{TE}[e] = \ldots \mathcal{TE}[x] \ldots \mathcal{TE}[x] \ldots$$

Now assuming both variables x are evaluated, then by referential transparency both $\mathcal{TE}[x]$ terms must evaluate to the same (result,trace) pair. That is, two identical traces of evaluation of x will be produced. This does not reflect the notion of sharing inherent in call-by-need semantics, whereby we would expect one of the variable evaluation traces to be shorter as it would show reduction directly to a normal form because the evaluation of the other x variable had already taken place.

So how can we implement call-by-need instrumentation? We could use some form of static strictness analysis to determine the ordering of variable evaluations and then apply a different transform to the two sub-expressions, one resulting in a complete trace and the other generating a trace of just the resulting value. There is a more straightforward and reliable method. The idea is to carry information about the evaluation status of variables and then decide *at evaluation time* to generate an abbreviated trace if necessary. The transformed version of our earlier example might be

$$\mathcal{TE}[\ldots x \ldots x \ldots] = \texttt{let} \quad (z,t) = \mathcal{TE}[x]$$
$$x' = \text{if } x \text{ has been evaluated } then \ (z,[z])$$
$$else \ (z,t)$$
$$\texttt{in} \quad \ldots x' \ldots x' \ldots$$

Clearly our transformed program must maintain a *runtime* state to be able to determine if a variable (x in our example) has been previously evaluated.

4.3 Call-by-name program instrumentation

Figure 4 shows the transformation rules. Before these transformations can be applied, all function declarations are normalised to create explicit lambda abstractions. Transforms are written as

$$\mathcal{TE}[e] = \text{`a Haskell expression'}$$

Each transform maps from the abstract syntax of the original program (inside [ ] brackets) to concrete Haskell syntax (shown in `typewriter` font). In practice,

$$\mathcal{TD}\,[x = e] = x \,=\, \mathcal{TE}[e]$$

$$\mathcal{TE}[k] = (k,\ [\text{Ks "}k\text{"}])$$
$$\mathcal{TE}[\lambda x.e] = (\backslash x\ \text{->}\ \mathcal{TE}[e],\ [\text{Abs } absName])$$
$$\mathcal{TE}[e_1\ e_2] = \text{let (fun, funTr)} = \mathcal{TE}[e_1]$$
$$\text{(app, appTr)} = \text{fun } \mathcal{TE}[e_2]$$
$$\text{in (app, App funTr: appTr)}$$
$$\mathcal{TE}[x] = \text{let (var, varTr)} = x$$
$$\text{in (var, \{VP|VL\}}\ varName\text{: varTr)}$$
$$\mathcal{TE}[let\ decls\ in\ e] = \text{let } map\ (\mathcal{TD})\ decls$$
$$\text{in let (letE, letTr)} = \mathcal{TE}[e]$$
$$\text{in (letE, LExp } abstraction\ bv\text{: letTr)}$$

Fig. 4. Minimal, bottom-up, call-by-name instrumentation

---

the transform functions also take as argument an environment which is used to calculate the names of abstraction and variable trace objects, and which also holds a symbol table to track variable names and their class.

The transform rules are straightforward so deserve little comment. Note that the application expression transform respects non-strict argument evaluation: transformed argument expression $\mathcal{TE}[e_2]$ is not evaluated but rather passed as argument to the (non-strict) function fun. The terms $varName$, $absName$, and $abstraction$ are unique manufactured names, and bv is the list of let-bound variables. Their values are determined by consulting the environment, which is also updated as the original program is traversed. Details of the environment, rules for its maintenance, and the precise form of the naming convention used in the concrete trace objects can be found in Watson (1997).

4.4 Conversion to call-by-need

The raw trace created by the instrumented program is not quite what we want. There are two problems. The non-strict property of the language results in variable evaluation appearing at some possibly distant point in the trace from where it was bound by function application. This leads to problem one: the raw trace provides no link between function application and corresponding variable evaluation, so it is very difficult to interpret the trace. Secondly, the simple, stateless program transform can only provide a call-by-name view of the trace (§4.2).

We remedy this situation by transforming the raw call-by-name trace to a call-by-need trace. This trace transform performs three tasks as it traverses the trace:

1. application objects are numbered in the order dictated by the semantic rules.
2. variable trace objects are numbered with the number of the application that caused their instantiation.
3. when the evaluation of a variable instance is repeated (generating identical duplicate sub-traces), all but the initial evaluation sub-trace are replaced by a single-element sub-trace showing direct reduction to whnf.

The first two actions allow unambiguous identification of variable instances, and the final one converts the trace to call-by-need. Application numbering and duplicate trace removal are straightforward, with the caveat that identification of the duplicate traces relies on instance identification (step 2 above), which is not so simply achieved.

The structure of the trace alone cannot be used to guide the instance identification process as there is no inherent relationship between application order and the order of variable evaluation. We seek to do this: on traversing the raw trace, when we encounter a variable trace object we must be able to determine its instance number (the application number of its binding application, as defined by the semantic rules). We resort to consideration of the scope of variable instances to do so. We maintain a transform state as we traverse the raw trace, which lists the variable instances currently in scope; hence determining the correct instance requires a simple lookup operation. Maintaining the in-scope list is the key to this procedure. We present elsewhere (Watson, 1997) a scopeful semantics which formally describes the way in-scope lists are created.

Notice that, after eschewing state considerations in developing a simple call-by-name trace, we are now resorting to a state-based scheme to create a call-by-need trace. This is consistent with our argument in section in section 4.2, but we must answer the queston: why did we not produce a call-by-need trace directly, using a runtime state? The answer is twofold. Firstly the two-step approach is more efficient, and secondly it allows more flexibility in that a call-by-name trace may in fact be sufficient for some purposes.

4.5 An example

Figure 5 shows three traces of evaluation of the expression

```
let  f x y = x (x y)
     id a  = a
     g     = f id
  in  g g 1
```

The first (leftmost) trace is the raw call-by-name trace produced by evaluating the transformed expression. The tracing names are seen in the formal parameter and abstraction trace objects: for example the second argument to f is labelled as f'' as is its binding abstraction. Alongside is the call-by-need version whose variable and application objects have been annotated with an application number. The vertical space in this trace shows where repeated evaluations (for g [object VL 0 g] and parameter x [object VP 1 f']) have been removed.

The remaining column shows an *expression trace*, which is a sequence of successively simplified expressions. Excepting the initial expression, each expression is formed from its predecessor by reducing a sub-expression (the redex) as defined by the call-by-need trace of reductions. Unevaluated (argument) expressions appear italicised. This expression trace can be automatically generated from the

Raw call-by-name	Call-by-need	Expression
[Let z f id g,	[Let z f id g,	let ...
App [App [VL g,	App 5 [App 2 [VL 0 g,	g g 1
App [VL f,	App 1 [VL 0 f,	f id g 1
Abs f'],	Abs f'],	(\x y -> x(x y)) id g 1
Abs f''],	Abs f''],	(\y -> x(x y)) g 1
App [VP f',	App 3 [VP 1 f',	x (x y) 1
VL id,	VL 0 id,	id (x y) 1
Abs id'],	Abs id'],	(\a -> a) (x y) 1
VP id',	VP 3 id',	a 1
App [VP f',	App 4 [VP 1 f',	x y 1
VL id,		
Abs id'],	Abs id'],	(\a -> a) y 1
VP id',	VP 4 id',	a 1
VP f'',	VP 2 f'',	y 1
VL g,	VL 0 g,	g 1
App [VL f,		
Abs f'],		
Abs f''],	Abs f''],	(\y -> x(x y)) 1
App [VP f',	App 6 [VP 1 f',	x (x y)
VL id,		
Abs id'],	Abs id'],	(\a -> a) (x y)
VP id',	VP 6 id',	a
App [VP f',	App 7 [VP 1 f',	x y
VL id,		
Abs id'],	Abs id'],	(\a -> a) y
VP id',	VP 7 id',	a
VP f'',	VP 5 f'',	y
Ks 1]	Ks 1]	1

Fig. 5. Trace example

call-by-need trace and is used as the basis of a trace browser described in Watson and Salzman (1997).

To relate the expression trace to the reduction trace consider the reduction trace and expression trace for the application expression e_1 arg:

```
App [ o1,            e1 arg
      o2,            e2 arg
      ...            ...
      om ],          em arg
    on               en
    ...              ...
```

The trace objects $o_1, o_2 \ldots o_n$ denote expressions $e_1, e_2 \ldots e_n$. Observe how a single App object represents a sequence of successively simplified expressions. The expression e_n is the body part of the lambda abstraction e_m, with argument arg bound to the lambda variable in e_m.

We show just one possible representation here. The expression trace can be further simplified by removing the abstractions when they obviously derive from a named function, and by removing from the trace the evaluation of "trusted" functions. Or information can be added: we could show instance numbers for variables and also include heap binding information.

4.6 Implementation

A prototype implementation of the transformation system has been carried out using the Gofer language. A series of performance tests were performed which compared, for a set of test programs, the cost of evaluating the original and transformed versions of the programs.

The relative cost of producing the call-by-name trace is approximately 60 times the cost of running the original program. If only the result of the computation is required (but not the trace), then the cost ratio is about 45. While these figures indicate a significant but perhaps manageable overhead, especially given that we are dealing with a prototype implementation, the cost of generating call-by-need traces is much worse, with a slowdown factor of between two and three orders of magnitude. Much of the cost of producing a call-by-need trace arises from the requirement to maintain a runtime state (the evaluation status of each variable); in our simple prototype the heap was implemented as a linear list, which is clearly not an efficient scheme.

5 Discussion and conclusions

In summary we consider that the approach we have outlined has a number of advantages over comparable schemes:

+ it is based on a simple, explicit, and intuitive model for lazy evaluation

+ it employs a simple trace structure, which allows straightforward transformation into other user views of the evaluation history

+ the transform scheme is very simple and uniform, yet handles curried function application and higher order functions.

These advantages must be partially offset against the major disadvantage of the cost of trace generation. In defence, we offer the following comments:

− While our measurements indicate poor absolute performance, we are unable to compare our approach to others, due to the lack of available data. How efficient are other schemes? Could it be that tracing (without resort to meddling with the internals of a compiler) is an inherently costly undertaking? We note that very recent work by Sparud and Runciman (1997) has reported relatively low cost of trace generation but does rely on support from the language translator.

− Our implementation is a prototype, and its design was dictated by speed of development, not speed of execution. We anticipate significant reductions in execution cost if alternate implementations based on the existing transform scheme are developed.

- The production of a call-by-need trace is much more costly than a call-by-name trace. Perhaps programmers would be content with the call-by-name view of computation, which is semantically equivalent? If so then we achieve an enormous saving!
- If traces could be selectively generated, only for functions which the user considers of interest, then the other parts of the program could execute at full speed. This seems an important avenue for future investigation, as suggested by Hall et al. 1990.

There are a number of possible directions of future research based on the work reported here.

While the program instrumentation is seen to offer advantages of simplicity and portability, an alternative trace generation scheme based on a lazy abstract machine for the language semantics could be a viable approach. Initial investigations have shown that a straightforward implementation of an interpreter for the semantic rules yields a trace generator which is comparable in speed to our instrumentation approach, though it exhibited very poor space utilisation. Implementation of an abstract machine for the semantics in the style of Sestoft (1997) could be a much more promising proposition.

Although we have demonstrated how the fundamental features of lazy languages can be traced, a usable debugging system would require that advanced language features such as pattern matching, input/output, and list comprehensions be traced also. We have already extended the semantics and tracing mechanism to encompass eager primitive functions, algebraic data types, and simple pattern matching (Watson, 1997). We believe that the transformation scheme can be further extended to the other features, especially if these language features are amenable to description using an extended version of our language semantics.

In conclusion, we summarise our work as follows. We have presented a transformational approach to trace generation for lazy functional programs. The key features of the scheme are its simplicity, that it handles adequately the fundamental problems of tracing non-strict higher-order languages, and that it is based on an intuitive formal model for lazy evaluation. The transformational scheme we have presented to produce a concrete trace can be considered as a first step toward a "industrial strength" tracing system; while exhibiting poor absolute performance it may well form the basis of a more advanced and efficient trace generator.

References

Z. Ariola, M. Felleisen, J. Mariast, M. Odersky, and P. Wadler. A call-by-need lambda calculus. In *Proceedings of the 22nd ACM Symposium on Principles of Programming Languages*, pages 233–246, 1995.

M. Augustson and J. Reinfelds. A visual Miranda machine. In *Proceedings, Software Education Conference SRIG-ET'94, Ed. M. Purvis, IEEE Computer Society Press, Los Alamitos California*, pages 198–203, 1995.

R. Bird and P. Wadler. *Introduction to Functional Programming*. Prentice Hall, 1988.

J. Gibbons and K. Wansbrough. Tracing lazy functional languages. In *Proceedings of Computing: The Australasian Theory Symposium"*, 1996.

D. Goldson. A symbolic calculator for non-strict functional languages. *The Computer Journal*, 37(3):177–187, 1994.

C. Hall, K. Hammond, and J. O'Donnell. An algorithmic and semantic approach to debugging. In *Proceedings of the 1990 Glasgow Workshop on Functional Programming*, pages 44–53, 1990.

A. Kishon. *Theory and Art of Semantics-Directed Program Execution Monitoring*. PhD thesis, Department of Computer Science, Yale University, 1992.

J. Launchbury. A natural semantics for lazy evaluation. In *Proceedings of the 20th ACM Symposium on Principles of Programming Languages*, pages 144–154, 1993.

L. Naish and T. Barbour. Towards a portable lazy functional declarative debugger. In *Proceedings of the 19th Australian Computer Science Conference*, 1996. Also available as Technical Report 95/27, Department of Computer Science, University of Melbourne.

H. Nilsson and P. Fritzson. Algorithmic debugging for lazy functional languages. *Journal of Functional Programming*, 4(3):337–369, 1994.

J. T. O'Donnell and C. V. Hall. Debugging in applicative languages. *Lisp and Symbolic Computation*, 1(2):113–145, 1988.

S. L. Peyton Jones. *The Implementation of Functional Programming Languages*. Prentice-Hall, 1987.

C. Runciman and D. Wakeling. Heap profiling for lazy functional programs. *Journal of Functional Programming*, 3(2):217–245, 1993.

P. M. Sansom and S. L. Peyton Jones. Time and space profiling for non-strict higher-order functional languages. In *Proceedings of the 22nd ACM Symposium on Principles of Programming Languages*, pages 355–366, 1995.

P. Sestoft. Deriving a lazy abstract machine. *Journal of Functional Programming*, 7 (3), 1997. To appear.

E. Shapiro. *Algorithmic Program Debugging*. MIT Press, 1982.

R. M. Snyder. Lazy debugging of lazy functional programs. *New Generation Computing*, 8:139–161, 1990.

J. Sparud. *A Transformational Approach to Debugging Lazy Functional Programs*. Licentate thesis, Department of Computer Science, Chalmers University of Technology, 1996.

J. Sparud and C. Runciman. Tracing Lazy Functional Computations Using Redex Trails. In *Proceedings of the Ninth International Symposium on Programming Languages, Implementations, Logics, and Programs (PLILP97)*, 1997.

R. Watson. *Tracing Lazy Evaluation by Program Transformation*. PhD thesis, School of Multimedia and Information Technology, Southern Cross University, 1997.

R. Watson and E. Salzman. A trace browser for a lazy functional language. In *Proceedings of the Twentieth Australian Computer Science Conference*, pages 356–363, 1997.

Basic Results in Automatic Transformations of Shared Memory Parallel Programs into Sequential Programs

Yosi Ben-Asher and Esti Stein

Dept. of computer science, Haifa University, Haifa Israel

Abstract. We study the problem of developing a set of syntax-driven transformations for automatic translation of shared memory parallel programs into sequential programs. The result is a sequential program that is a "refinement" (its execution is consistent with one possible execution of the parallel program) of the original program. Consequently, the problem of debugging parallel programs is reduced to the problem of debugging sequential programs. Moreover, the efficiency of parallel programs can be increased by sequentializing code segments that include extra parallelism.

The main difficulty in developing such a system is to preserve the fairness property of any actual parallel execution, which states that no process can wait forever unserved. Thus, non termination of the sequential version (namely an infinite loop) is allowed only if there is at least one **fair** parallel execution that does not halt as well (i.e., a process that executes an infinite loop whose termination is not dependent on any other process).

We show that it is sufficient to consider the case of two sequential programs executed in parallel in order to solve the general case. We then describe several types of transformations and check their ability to preserve fairness. The results, with regards to the existence of such a transformation for general parallel programs are not conclusive; however, we do show that restricted cases (which are likely to appear in the reality) can be sequentialized using this set of transformations. The problem of detecting bad execution sequences is discussed in the last section. In particular, wrong versions of mutual exclusion algorithms are discussed. It is shown that synchronous type of transformations might overlook bad execution sequences of these algorithms. A new type of transformation, which works by nesting parallel while-loops, is developed. Indeed, it is shown that the transformed program reveals the known bug of Hyman's algorithm for mutual exclusion.

1 Introduction

In this work we consider the problem of transforming parallel programs into sequential programs, such that the sequential version will be a "refinement" (its execution is consistent with one possible execution of the parallel program) of the original program. We seek to find a syntax driven transformation ϕ, such that for a given parallel program R, $\phi(R)$ will be its sequential version. This sequential version should satisfy three

requirements: *correctness, fairness* and *similarity*. These requirements will be explained next and formally defined in section2.

The underlying model supports shared memory parallel programs with the "par block" statement $[R_1||\ldots||R_k]$ to create k parallel processes, as described in [1]. The transformation is done at source level, so that it uses the same syntax as the original program, excluding parallelism. For example, consider two possible sequential versions of the following program:

$x = 0;$
$[\ int\ i;$ $x = 0;$ $x = 0;$
$\quad for\ i = 0\ldots 10\ do\ x++;$ $int\ i, j;$ $int\ i;$
$||\ int\ j;$ $\Longrightarrow$ $for\ i = 0\ldots 10\ do\ x++;$ $for\ i = 0\ldots 10\ do\ \{$
$\quad for\ j = 0\ldots 10\ do\ x--;$ $for\ j = 0\ldots 10\ do\ x--;$ $x++;$
$]$ $x--;$
                    $\}$

Clearly, both versions are refinements of the original program, as they describe two possible execution orders of it. This reflects the fact that there can be many possible execution orders of the same parallel program. However, the set of all possible execution orders of a given program must be identical to the set of all possible interleavings of the program [7]. Thus, the first requirement of the sequential version is that it will be "correct", that is its execution should be consistent with a possible execution order of the original program.

In addition, we assume that the parallel machine that executes the parallel program is "fair"; i.e., at some time during the execution, a finite time delay will advance every servable process by at least one instruction. Thus, no process is blocked forever due to lack of resources. Clearly, in the reality, all parallel machines support fair execution if they allow dynamic creation of processes (i.e., generating more processes than processors). Thus, the second requirement of ϕ is that it will preserve fairness, i.e., for all R, the execution of $\phi(R)$ must be equivalent to some fair execution order of R. Consider, for example, the program $R \equiv x = 1; [while(x); || x = 0;]$. Clearly, any fair execution of the above program will terminate, as there must be a time that the second process $x = 0;$ will be advanced to stop the busy-wait of the first process $while(x);$. However, choosing $\phi(R) \longrightarrow x = 1; while(x); x = 0;$ is incorrect, as it will never terminate. Choosing $\phi(R) \longrightarrow x = 1; x = 0; while(x);$ is the correct decision, as it will terminate, and thus preserve the fairness of the original program.

The third requirement, *similarity*, requires that $\phi(R)$ must "resemble" R. This requirement is hard to formalize; however, we can maintain that: A) the editing distance between $\phi(R)$ and R will be small; and B) $\phi(R)$ should be obtained using a set of re-write rules that works according to the syntax or the grammar rules of R. For example, realizing $\phi(R)$ using a simulator [4] that simulates the parallel execution of R contradicts both A) and B). The need for similarity will be motivated by the potential uses of $\phi(R)$ given next.

If successful, $\phi(R)$ can be used to develop a tool that automatically transforms a parallel program into a sequential one. Possible applications of such a tool include:

– Debugging $\phi(R)$ using existing sequential debuggers on sequential machines, saving the need to develop special systems for debugging parallel programs. This is based on the similarity of $\phi(R)$ to R, so that any bug found in $\phi(R)$ can be easily translated to a bug in R.

Usually, debugging of parallel programs requires us to execute them. This can be done either on the target parallel machine [5, 9, 12], or by simulating the parallel execution on a sequential host [4]. Both methods are subject to many flaws, including:

- Parallel execution requires heavy display system, allowing the user to view the parallel execution as a two dimensional drawing, e.g., visualizing the activity graph, simultaneous access to shared variables, and breakpoints in the different activities.

- Simulation of parallel programs is a slow process, mainly due to the overhead needed to manage processes, simulate context-switches [6, 3] and collect time statistics.

- Parallel execution is also complicated, as we have to sample the execution without being too intrusive [2]. This requires a fast sampling mechanism which is faster than the underlying parallel machine [8, 13].

– ϕ can be used to sequentialize sub-components or parts of a parallel program. This can increase the granularity of R, by decreasing the number of processes it creates (as some of them have been transformed into sequential code). This in turn, decreases the overhead involved in a parallel execution of R. The relation between efficient execution and granularity is described in [10], in particular the reduction of overhead involved in creating new processes. The requirement of similarity guarantee that the additional instructions added by ϕ to R will be minimal, so that the work involved in executing $\phi(R)$ will be the same as for R.

– Alternative ways (rules) of transforming R can be used to generate different sequential versions of R. Upon execution, these programs will be used as tests to find bugs that are dependent on the execution order (the actual scheduling in which R will be executed). Clearly, any sequentializing transformation can be viewed as a realization of a particular execution order. Thus we can use alternatives rules to generate different types of execution orders. We are mainly concerned with two natural types of execution orders generated by the scheduling policy of the underlying machine. The scheduling is usually determined by the way in which the underlying machine managed its Ready Queue, which hold all the processes that are ready to run. The first scheduling is called "synchronous", and is generated by a FIFO policy, namely each processor takes a process from the head of the ready queue, executes it for a while and returns it to the tail of the ready queue. The other type of execution order is called "asynchronous", and is generated by a LIFO scheduling. It is shown that testing these two types of execution orders is useful to detect bugs that are dependent on scheduling.

– An additional motivation for the tool could be its use to run legacy parallel programs on sequential systems (when parallel machine is not available).

2   Transformation system guidelines

As explained in the introduction, we seek to find a set of re-write rules or transformations whose application can transform a parallel program into a sequential one. The syntax of the parallel programs is given by the following BNF rules (where S/E stands for statement/expression and key-words are in lowercase letters): [1]

$$
\begin{aligned}
S &\longrightarrow Variable = E & assignment \\
S &\longrightarrow if\ (E)\ S_1\ else\ S_2 & conditional\ statement \\
S &\longrightarrow while\ (E)\ S & while-loop \\
S &\longrightarrow \{S_1; S_2; \ldots; S_k\} & sequential\ block \\
S &\longrightarrow [S_1 \| S_2 \| \ldots \| S_k] & parallel\ block \\
S &\longrightarrow & empty\ statement
\end{aligned}
$$

The semantics of the execution is operational [14] and is defined to be any "execution-order" produced by an "arrow-machine".

For a given parallel program R, let $\hat{R}$ denote a parallel program obtained by adding arrows $\uparrow$ before some of the statements in R, e.g., $\{x = 0; [while(x == 0) \uparrow k + +; \| \uparrow x = 1;]\}$. Let $\hat{R} = \alpha \uparrow S\beta$ be a decomposition of $\hat{R}$ such that S is a statement as described above, and $\uparrow S$ (a program counter) indicates that S might be executed next. Let M denote the "memory state", the value of all variables used in R. The next step in the execution of $\hat{R}$ with the memory state M, $(\hat{R} : M)$ is a new program $\hat{R}'$ and a new memory state M' obtained by one of the following transitions:

$$
\begin{aligned}
&\alpha \uparrow Var = E; \beta : M \longrightarrow \alpha \uparrow \beta : M' & &M'\ memory\ state\ after\ Var = E \\
&\alpha \uparrow if\ (E)\ S_1\ else\ S_2\beta : M \longrightarrow \alpha \uparrow S_1\beta : M & &E = true \\
&\alpha \uparrow if\ (E)\ S_1\ else\ S_2\beta : M \longrightarrow \alpha \uparrow S_2\beta : M & &E = false \\
&\alpha \uparrow while\ (E)\ S\beta : M \longrightarrow \alpha \uparrow S\ while\ (E)\ S\beta : M & &E = true \\
&\alpha \uparrow while\ (E)\ S\beta : M \longrightarrow \alpha \uparrow \beta : M & &E = false \\
&\alpha \uparrow [S_1 \| \ldots \| S_k]\beta \longrightarrow \alpha[\uparrow S_1 \| \ldots \| \uparrow S_k]\beta \\
&\alpha[\uparrow \| \ldots \uparrow \| \uparrow]\beta \longrightarrow \alpha \uparrow \beta & &synchronization\ point \\
&\alpha \uparrow \{S_1 \ldots S_k\}\beta \longrightarrow \alpha\{\uparrow S_1 \ldots S_k\}\beta \\
&\alpha\{\uparrow\}\beta \longrightarrow \alpha \uparrow \beta
\end{aligned}
$$

Definition 1. An execution of a parallel program R, with initial memory state M, is a sequence of steps made by an arrow machine:

$$
R : M \equiv \uparrow R : M \longrightarrow \hat{R}_1 : M_1 \longrightarrow \ldots \longrightarrow \hat{R}_t : M_t \ ,
$$

such that each transition $\hat{R}_i : M_i \longrightarrow \hat{R}_{i+1} : M_{i+1}$ is a legal step of an arrow machine.

The arrows in an execution sequence are usually labeled for identification, to determine which arrow has been moved at the next step. The labels themselves are generated by concatenating numbers to previous labels:

$$
\alpha \uparrow_{lb} [S_1 \| \ldots \| S_k]\beta \longrightarrow \alpha[\uparrow_{lb\cdot 1} S_1 \| \ldots \| \uparrow_{lb\cdot k} S_k]\beta
$$

---

[1] we ignore declaration of shared variables and assume that all variables in the program have been declared. We also assume that the input is given by initial values of the variables.

$$\alpha[\uparrow_{lb\cdot 1} \| \cdots \| \uparrow_{lb\cdot k}]\beta \longrightarrow \alpha \uparrow_{lb} \beta$$

Note that an execution sequence of a given program might be infinite, as is shown by the execution sequence $\mathcal{R} \{x = 0; [while(x == 0)k + +; \|x = 1;]\}$:

$$
\begin{aligned}
&\uparrow_0 \{x = 0; [while(x == 0)k + +; \|x = 1;]\} : M \longrightarrow \\
&\{\uparrow_0 [while(x == 0)k + +; \|x = 1;]\} : M_1 \longrightarrow \\
&\{[\uparrow_1 while(x == 0)k + +; \| \uparrow_2 x = 1;]\} : M_2 \longrightarrow \\
&\{[\uparrow_1 k + +; while(x == 0)k + +; \| \uparrow_2 x = 1;]\} : M_2 \longrightarrow \\
&\{[\uparrow_1 while(x == 0)k + +; \| \uparrow_2 x = 1;]\} : M_3 \longrightarrow \\
&\{[\uparrow_1 k + +; while(x == 0)k + +; \| \uparrow_2 x = 1;]\} : M_3 \longrightarrow \\
&\{[\uparrow_1 while(x == 0)k + +; \| \uparrow_2 x = 1;]\} : M_4 \longrightarrow
\end{aligned}
$$

$$
\begin{aligned}
&\{[\uparrow_1 k + +; while(x == 0)k + +; \| \uparrow_2 x = 1;]\} : M_n \longrightarrow \\
&\{[\uparrow_1 while(x == 0)k + +; \| \uparrow_2 x = 1;]\} : M_{n+1} \longrightarrow
\end{aligned}
$$

Sometimes, we use the short notation $M \longrightarrow M_1 \longrightarrow \cdots \longrightarrow M_t$ to denote a given execution order where $\longrightarrow M_i$ includes only the steps that involve assignments and a possible change of the memory state. It is also possible to mark which assignment (say $x + +$ of $w3$) of the underlying program is used for the next step, in which case we add a reference above the arrow of the form $M_i \xrightarrow{x++;(w3)} M_{i+1}$. A termination of the program is denoted by $\longrightarrow$ *done* at the end of the execution sequence.

Definition 2. An arrow $\uparrow_i$ is "moved" in the t'th step if it participates in the t'th transition An execution sequence $\uparrow R : M$ is fair iff for every arrow $\uparrow_i$ that is moved in the t'th step of $\uparrow_0 R : M$, there is a pre-fixed number k such that $\uparrow_i$ is moved in the next k steps after step t.

Accordingly, the above execution sequence of $\mathcal{R}$ is not fair, as $\uparrow_2$ is never advanced. By definition, any finite execution sequence is always fair.

Practically, every parallel machine can use preemption [2] and a FIFO queue to store preempted activities. Hence, in reality, an execution of a parallel program is **always fair**, and the programmer can (and usually will) rely on that fact. Note that some systems do not use preemption, let their processes run-to-completion. However, this lack of fairness severely impairing the ability to write general parallel programs. The challenge in developing sequentializing transformations is to preserve the fairness given by actual machines. If the underlying parallel machine uses preemption, then $\mathcal{R}$ always terminates : The first process $while(x == 0)k + +;$ will be preempted after a finite delay, $\uparrow_2$ will be advanced and x will be set to zero, terminating the program. In this case, any fair execution

---

[2] Preemption indicates that the execution of a given process can be stopped by an interrupt from the clock, thus moving the process to the end of a FIFO-queue.

sequence will be finite and of the form:

$$\uparrow_0 \{x = 0; [while(x == 0)k + +; || x = 1;]\} : M \longrightarrow$$
$$\{\uparrow_0 [while(x == 0)k + +; || x = 1;]\} : M_1 \longrightarrow$$
$$\{[\uparrow_1 while(x == 0)k + +; || \uparrow_2 x = 1;]\} : M_1 \longrightarrow$$
$$\{[\uparrow_1 k + +; while(x == 0)k + +; || \uparrow_2 x = 1;]\} : M_1 \longrightarrow$$
$$\{[\uparrow_1 while(x == 0)k + +; || \uparrow_2 x = 1;]\} : M_2 \longrightarrow$$

....

....

$$\{[\uparrow_1 while(x == 0)k + +; || \uparrow_2 x = 1;]\} : M_k \longrightarrow$$
$$\{[\uparrow_1 while(x == 0)k + +; || \uparrow_2]\} : M_{k+1} \longrightarrow$$
$$\{[\uparrow_1 || \uparrow_2]\} : M_{k+1} \longrightarrow$$
$$\{\uparrow\} : M_{k+1}$$

Recall that the goal of this work is to find and study sequentializing transformations that work on source level. Clearly, the transformed program is a sequential one and should preserve the semantics of the original program. Using the above definition, we can formally define the requirements from such transformations:

Definition 3. Let ϕ be a system of re-write rules that transforms any parallel program R to another program $\phi(R)$, then $\phi(R)$ is *correct* (as a sequentializing transformation) if:

1. $\phi(R)$ is a sequential program, i.e., any execution sequence of $\phi(R)$ uses one arrow.
2. $\phi(R)$ is a refinement of the original program, i.e., for any execution sequence (possibly infinite) $X = \uparrow \phi(R) : M \longrightarrow M_1 \longrightarrow \ldots \longrightarrow M_t$ of $\phi(R)$ there is an execution sequence of the original program (called the induced execution sequence) $Y = \uparrow R : M \longrightarrow M_{i_1} \longrightarrow \ldots \longrightarrow M_{i_k}$ that is obtained by eliminating all steps of X that are not part of the original program R.

We say that a transformation $\phi(R)$ is *fair* if the induced execution sequence Y is also fair.

Consider, for example, the following transformation that attempts to sequentialize two parallel while loops by executing them alternatively (10 times each), so that when one of the loops has terminated the second is continued.

$$\phi([while(E_1)S_1 || while(E_2)S_2]) \equiv$$

$$\{ k = 0; while(E_1 \&\& E_2)\{while(E_1 \&\& (k\%10 \neq 0))\{S_1; k + +; \};$$

$$while(E_2 \&\& (k\%10 \neq 0))\{S_2; k + +; \}; \} while(E_1)S_1; while(E_2)S_2; \}$$

This transformation adds instructions $(k++;)$ to the original program. Consider, for example, the transformed program of $R \equiv [while(x \leq 0)x + +; || while(x \geq 0)x - -;]$, where $\phi(R) \equiv$

$$\{ k = 0; while_0(x \leq 0 \&\& x \geq 0)\{while_1(x \leq 0 \&\& (k\%10 \neq 0))\{x + +; k + +; \}$$

$while_2(x \geq 0 \&\&(k\%10 \neq 0))\{x--; k++; \}; \}while_3(x \leq 0)x++; while_4(x \geq 0)x--; \}$

The execution sequence of $\phi(R)$, starting with $M_{x=0,k=0}$ (where only the transitions involving memory change are depicted) is now given :

$$\phi(R): M_{x=0,k=0} \xrightarrow{x++(w_1)} M_{x=1,k=0} \xrightarrow{k++(w_1)}$$

$$M_{x=1,k=1} \xrightarrow{exit(w_1)} M_{x=1,k=1} \xrightarrow{x--(w_2)}$$

$$M_{x=0,k=1} \xrightarrow{k++(w_2)} M_{x=0,k=2} \xrightarrow{x--(w_2)} M_{x=-1,k=2}$$

$$\xrightarrow{k++(w_2)} M_{x=-1,k=3} \xrightarrow{exit(w_2)} M_{x=-1,k=3} \xrightarrow{x++(w_3)} M_{x=0,k=3} \xrightarrow{x++(w_3)} M_{x=1,k=3} \xrightarrow{exit(w_3)}$$

$$M_{x=1,k=3} \xrightarrow{x--(w_4)} M_{x=0,k=3} \xrightarrow{x--(w_4)} M_{x=-1,k=3} \xrightarrow{exit(w_4)} M_{x=-1,k=3} \longrightarrow done$$

The induced execution sequence in this case is obtained by removing all the instructions that are not related to R, namely, the steps that perform $k++;$. Thus, the induced execution sequence is:

$$M_{x=0,k=0} \xrightarrow{x++(w_1)} M_{x=1} \xrightarrow{x--(w_2)} M_{x=0} \xrightarrow{x--(w_2)} M_{x=-1}$$

$$\xrightarrow{x++(w_3)} M_{x=0} \xrightarrow{x++(w_3)} M_{x=1} \xrightarrow{x--(w_4)} M_{x=0} \xrightarrow{x--(w_4)} M_{x=-1} \longrightarrow done .$$

Indeed, this induced execution sequence can be obtained as a correct execution sequence of the original program, namely

$$[while_1(x \leq 0)x++; || while_2(x \geq 0)x--]: M_{x=0,k=0} \xrightarrow{x++(w_1)} M_{x=1} \xrightarrow{x--(w_2)}$$

$$M_{x=0} \xrightarrow{x--(w_2)} M_{x=-1} \xrightarrow{x++(w_1)} M_{x=0} \xrightarrow{x++(w_1)} M_{x=1} \xrightarrow{exitw_1} M_{x=1} \xrightarrow{x--(w_2)}$$

$$M_{x=0} \xrightarrow{x--(w_2)} M_{x=-1} \xrightarrow{exitw_2} M_{x=-1} \longrightarrow done .$$

The notion of an induced execution sequence can be used to show that any transformation that works for two sequential programs executed in parallel $\phi([R_i^s || R_{i+1}^s])$ can be extended to work for several sequential programs $\phi([R_1^s || \ldots || R_k^s])$ as well:

Lemma 4. *Let R^s denote a sequential program which does not contain any $||$ symbols. Assume that ϕ is correct for any two sequential programs executed in parallel $[R_1^s || R_2^s]$, and that for more than two sequential programs ϕ is defined by*

$$\phi([R_1^s || \ldots || R_k^s]) = \phi(\phi([R_1^s || \ldots || R_{k-1}^s]) || R_k^s) ,$$

then ϕ is correct for $[R_1^s || \ldots || R_k^s]$ as well.

Proof: Let $M \longrightarrow M_1/M_2 \longrightarrow M_3/M_4 \longrightarrow \ldots \longrightarrow M_{t-2}/M_{t-1} \longrightarrow M_t$ denote an execution sequence with replacements of memory states, where $M_i \longrightarrow M_{i+1}/M_{i+2}$ denotes a step $M_i \longrightarrow M_{i+1}$, followed by an arbitrary change in memory state from M_{i+1} to M_{i+2} (such that M_{i+2} allows the next step to be executed).

As replacing the memory states is consistent with the next step, such an execution sequence may also be an execution sequence of the original program. Moreover, if $\phi(R)$ is correct for regular execution sequences (without replacements), and X is an execution sequence of $\phi(R)$ with replacements, then X is also an execution sequence of R. Consider, by negation, the first step $M_{i-1}/M_i \longrightarrow M_{i+1}$ in the induced sequence $\phi(R) : M$ at a stage where this step is not possible for the parallel program $R : M$ (e.g., $M_i \longrightarrow M_{i+1}$ is a 'then' part of an 'if' statement in $\phi(R)$, where R would choose to execute the 'else' part of the statement). Both execution sequences share the memory state M_{i-1}, yet $M_i \longrightarrow M_{i+1}$ is possible for $\phi(R)$ but not for R. It is clearly possible to add a sequence of assignments to R, such that it will change M_{i-1} to M_i directly (omitting the memory replacement M_{i-1}/M_i). Let R' be the modified program, then the step $M_i \longrightarrow M_{i+1}$ is allowed in $\phi(R') : M$ however forbidden in $R' : M$. Hence, if we consider the part of R' that yields the execution sequence until M_{i+1}, we have an execution sequence with no memory replacements that contradicts the correctness of ϕ.

Now, consider the following recursive modification of ϕ:

$$\phi([R_1^s || R_2^s || \ldots || R_k^s]) = \phi([\phi([R_1^s || R_2^s || \ldots || R_{k-1}^s]) || R_k^s])$$

Let $X = M \longrightarrow M_1 \longrightarrow \ldots \longrightarrow M_t$ be the induced execution sequence of $\phi([R_1^s || R_2^s || \ldots || R_k^s]) : M$. Clearly X can be partitioned into two execution sequences with replacements X_1 and X_2 such that X_1 contains all the steps (in the original order) of $\phi([R_1^s || R_2^s || \ldots || R_{k-1}^s])$ and X_2 all the steps of R_k^s. The replacements of the memory states in X_1 and X_2 reflect the fact that the control in $[\phi([R_1^s || R_2^s || \ldots || R_{k-1}^s]) || R_k^s] : M$ alternates between $\phi([R_1^s || R_2^s || \ldots || R_{k-1}^s])$ and R_k^s. For example, the replacement M_i/M_j represents the state before the control (arrow movement) moved from $\phi([R_1^s || R_2^s || \ldots || R_{k-1}^s])$ to R_k^s, and then the memory state after it returned to $\phi([R_1^s || R_2^s || \ldots || R_{k-1}^s])$.

Assume by induction that $\phi([R_1^s || R_2^s || \ldots || R_{k-1}^s])$ is correct. It then follows that $\phi([R_1^s || R_2^s || \ldots || R_{k-1}^s])$ is also correct for execution sequences with replacements, yielding that X_1 is an induced execution sequence for $[R_1^s || R_2^s || \ldots || R_{k-1}^s]$ as well. Thus, the original execution sequence X is also an execution sequence of $[R_1^s || R_2^s || \ldots || R_k^s]$. The base case of the above induction is obtained by the assumption that ϕ is correct for any two sequential programs that are executed in parallel $[R_1^s || R_2^s]$. ∎

A simple corollary of the above lemma is that it is sufficient to construct ϕ such that it will work for the case of two sequential programs:

Theorem 5. *Let R^s denote some sequential program which does not contain any $||$ symbols. If for any two sequential programs R_1^s, R_2^s, $\phi([R_1^s || R_2^s])$ is correct according to def. 3, then $\phi(R)$ is correct for any general program R like $R = [R_1^s || if(..) [R_2^s || R_3^s] else [R_4^s || R_5^s]]$.*

Proof: Clearly, there must be at least one statement in R of the form $[R_1^s || \ldots || R_k^s]$, where R_i^s is purely sequential. Lemma 4 allows us to replace it by $\phi([R_1^s || \ldots || R_k^s])$

and obtain a program that is a "refinement" of the original R. This process can be repeated until the whole program is replaced by an equivalent (refinement) sequential program $\phi(R)$. The goal is to show that the induced execution of $\phi(R) : M$ is an execution sequence of $R : M$, yielding that ϕ is correct for any general program. The induced execution sequence of $\phi(R) : M$ will be constructed inductively, following the above replacement process. We will also use the assumption that for any sequential program R^s, $\phi(R^s) = R^s$.

The same argument used in lemma 4 will work here. Let $X = M \longrightarrow M_1 \longrightarrow \ldots \longrightarrow M_t$ be the induced sequence of $\phi(R) : M$, where $\phi(R)$ is obtained by the above process. Consider the innermost parallel construct selected by the above process $[R_1^s || \ldots || R_k^s]$. Let $X_{R_1^s}, \ldots, X_{R_k^s}$ be the sub-sequences (with replacements) of X induced by $R_1^s, \ldots, R_k^s$; i.e., $X_{R_i^s}$ is the sequence of steps induced by R_i^s. As in lemma 4, $X_{R_1^s}, \ldots, X_{R_k^s}$ can be merged to form an execution sequence for $[R_1^s || \ldots || R_k^s]$. Following the bottom-up order selected by the above process, we can show that the induced sequence of X is an execution sequence of R ∎

The argument of Lemma 4 and Theorem 5 can be repeated for fair transformations; the assumption that $\phi([R_1^s || R_1^s])$ preserves fairness yields that ϕ preserves fairness for general programs as well.

Corollary 6. *Let R^s denote a sequential program which does not contain any $||$ symbols. If for any two sequential programs R_1^s, R_2^s, $\phi([R_1^s || R_2^s])$ is correct and fair, then $\phi(R)$ is correct and fair for any general program R.*

Proof: By definition, any composition of fair execution sequences is also fair, hence the proof of theorem 5 also applies here. ∎

Thus, the basic case of two sequential programs that are executed in parallel is sufficient to test the validity of a proposed transformation.

3 Simple realization of $\phi([R_1^s || R_2^s])$ using merge-like operations

At this point we know that it is sufficient to solve the problem of transforming two sequential programs $[R_1^s || R_2^s]$, in order to solve the problem of transforming general programs. It is also clear that the problematic cases must involve two while-loops that are executed in parallel. If one of the two programs (say R_1^s) does not contain a while-loop, then it is finite, and hence can be safely executed first, i.e., $\phi^s([R_1^s || R_2^s]) \longrightarrow \{R_1^s; R_2^s\}$.

Lemma 7. *Let R_1^s and R_2^s be two sequential programs, where R_1^s does not contain while-loops, then $\phi^s([R_1^s || R_2^s]) \longrightarrow \{R_1^s; R_2^s\}$ is correct and fair.*

Proof: Since $\uparrow R_1^s : M$ is finite, then $\uparrow \{R_1^s; R_2^s\} : M$ can be divided into two parts, where the first part contains all the instructions of R_1^s and the second those of R_2^s:

$$\uparrow\{R_1^s; R_2^s\} : M \xrightarrow{R_1^s} M_1 \ldots \xrightarrow{R_1^s} M_k \xrightarrow{R_2^s} M_{k+1} \ldots \xrightarrow{R_2^s} M_n \xrightarrow{R_2^s} \ldots .$$

Since k is finite, the induced execution sequence is clearly correct and fair

$$[\uparrow_1 R_1^s \| \uparrow_2 R_2^s] : M \xrightarrow{\uparrow_1} \dots \xrightarrow{\uparrow_1} [\uparrow_1 \| \uparrow_2 R_2^s]M_k \xrightarrow{\uparrow_1} [\uparrow_2 R_2^s]M_k$$

$$\xrightarrow{\uparrow_2} M_{k+1} \dots \xrightarrow{\uparrow_2} M_n \xrightarrow{\uparrow_2} \dots .$$

∎

However, ϕ^s might not preserve fairness, if both R_1^s and R_2^s contain while-loops that are mutually dependent, i.e., the termination of the while-loop in R_1^s depends on some statement in R_2^s and vice-versa. Consider, for example, the following program:

$$R \equiv \{i = 1; x = 1; [while(i\&\&x)\{x++; i++;\} i = 0; \| while(i)x = 0;]\} \ .$$

Any fair execution sequence of R will terminate once the second loop executes a step : x will be reset to zero, terminating the first loop so that its arrow must execute $i = 0$, which then terminates the second loop. All these events must occur in this order since the execution sequence is fair and there is a finite number k in which every arrow is advanced at least once. However, any application of ϕ^s's rules must yield one of the following two programs:

$$\phi^s(R) \longrightarrow \{i = 1; x = 1; \{while(i\&\&x)\{x++; i++;\} i = 0; \ while(i)x = 0;\}\}$$

or

$$\phi^s(R) \longrightarrow \{i = 1; x = 1; \{while(i)x = 0; while(i\&\&x)\{x++; i++;\} i = 0;\}\} \ .$$

Evidently, both programs yield infinite execution sequences whose induced execution sequences are not fair. Thus, any type of transformation which works in a similar way to ϕ^s will fail.

In this section we consider a simple way of overcoming the above problem, namely, to merge the bodies of two while-loops that are executed in parallel until one of the loops terminates, as follows: [3]

$$\phi^m([\{while(E_1)S_1; S_3\} \| \{while(E_2)S_2; S_4\}]) \longrightarrow$$

$$\{while(E_1\&\&E_2)\phi([S_1 \| S_2]); \ if(E_1)\phi^s([\{while(E_1)S_1; S_3\} \| S_4]) \ else$$

$$\phi^s([\{while(E_2)S_2; S_4\} \| S_3])\}$$

If we apply this transformation on the above program we get that:

$$\phi^m(\{i = 1; x = 1; [\{while(i\&\&x)\{x++; i++;\} i = 0;\} \| while(i)x = 0;]\}) \longrightarrow$$

$$\{i = 1; x = 1; \{while(i\&\&x\&\&i)\phi^s([\{x++; i++;\} \| x = 0;]);$$

$$if(i\&\&x)\phi^s([\{while(i\&\&x)\{x++; i++;\} i = 0;\} \|])\}$$

---

[3] Since we use C-like syntax then a semicolon is always part of a statement and a statement sequence is just a sequence of statements with no separators; however, for clearance reasons we sometimes leave the semicolon, e.g., $\{S_1; S_2\}$.

$$else\ \phi^s([while(i)x = 0; ||i = 0;])\}\} \longrightarrow$$

$$\{i = 1; x = 1; while(i\&\&x\&\&i)\{x + +; i + +; x = 0;\};$$

$$if(i\&\&x)\ while(i\&\&x)\{x + +; i + +; i = 0;\}\ else\{while(i)x = 0; i = 0;\}\ \}$$

Note that the execution will never reach the last term $while(i)x = 0; i = 0;$. Clearly, the last program terminates and it is easy to see that its induced execution sequence is fair as well.

The merging operation can be used to define a complete set of transformations $\phi^m([R_1^s||R_2^s])$, where S_i might be a block $\{S_1; \ldots; S_k\}$ or a sequence $S_1; \ldots; S_k$. Note that by Theorem 5 it is sufficient to define ϕ^m for $[R_1^s||R_2^s]$.

$$\phi^m([\{S_1\}||S_2]) \xrightarrow{\ 0\ } \{\phi^m([S_1||S_2])\}$$

$$\phi^m([A_1; S_1||S_2]) \xrightarrow{\ 1\ } \{A_1; \phi^m([S_1||S_2])\}$$

$$\phi^m([F_1; S_2||F_3; S_4]) \xrightarrow{\ 2\ } if(E_1)\phi^m([S_1^t; S_2||F_3; S_4])\ else\ \phi^m([S_1^f; S_2||F_3; S_4])$$

$$\phi^m([F_1; S_2||W_3; S_4]) \xrightarrow{\ 3\ } if(E_1)\phi^m([S_1^t; S_2||W_3; S_4])\ else\ \phi^m([S_1^f; S_2||W_3; S_4])$$

$$\phi^m([W_1; S_3||W_2; S_4]) \xrightarrow{\ 4\ } while(E_1\&\&E_2)\phi^m([S_1||S_2]); if(E_1)\phi^m([(while(E_1)S_1; S_3)||S_4])$$
$$else\ \phi^m([while(E_2)S_2; S_4||S_3])$$

$$\phi^m([S||]) \xrightarrow{\ 5\ } S$$

$$\phi^m([S_1||S_2]) \xrightarrow{\ 6\ } \phi^m([S_2||S_1])$$

As will be shown next, merge-like operations do not always work; hence, there are cases where $\phi^m([R_1^s||R_2^s])$ will not preserve fairness. The advantage of ϕ^m is that the resulting program is similar to the original, and the programmer can easily identify the original program parts. Another advantage of ϕ^m is that the number of additional statements that are added to the original program is minimal, generating the efficiency of the resulting program. These claims should be compared to the efficiency and similarity of the alternatives to ϕ^m that will be described next. Finally, it remains to characterize the class of programs for which ϕ^m is fair, so that an automatic system can use ϕ^m whenever possible to transform suitable sub-parts of a given program.

Lemma 8. *Let R_a^s and R_b^s be two sequential programs that do not contain nested while-loops, then $\phi^m([R_a^s||R_b^s])$ is correct and fair.*

Proof: Let R_a^s/R_b^s contain k_a/k_b while-loops, such that:

$$R_a^s = \alpha_1^a W_1^a \alpha_2^a W_2^a \ldots \alpha_{k_a}^a W_{k_a}^a = \sum_{i=1}^{k_a} \alpha_i^a W_i^a \quad R_b^s = \alpha_1^b W_1^b \alpha_2^b W_2^b \ldots \alpha_{k_b}^b W_{k_b}^b = \sum_{i=1}^{k_b} \alpha_i^b W_i^b .$$

Assume by induction that ϕ^m is fair for all sequential programs R_a^s and R_b^s such that $k_a + k_b < k$. It is easy to see that ϕ^m will first merge two first non-while parts of the programs, so that it can merge the first while-loops of each :

$$\phi^m([R_a^s||R_b^s]) = \phi^m([\alpha_1^a||\alpha_1^b]); while(E_1^a\&\&E_1^b)\phi^m([S_1^a||S_1^b]); if(E_1^1)$$

$$\phi^m([W_1^a \sum_{i=2}^{k_a} \alpha_i^a W_i^a || \sum_{i=2}^{k_b} \alpha_i^b W_i^b])\ else\ \phi^m([\sum_{i=2}^{k_a} \alpha_i^a W_i^a || \sum_{i=1}^{k_b} \alpha_i^b W_i^b]) .$$

The sub execution sequence induced by $\phi^m([\alpha_1^a || \alpha_1^b])$ is fair since it involves two finite components which do not contain a while-loop. The sub execution sequence induced by the second component $while(E_1^a \&\& E_1^b)\phi^m([S_1^a || S_1^b])$ is also fair, as every iteration of $while(E_1^a \&\& E_1^b)$ advances both arrows of $[\uparrow_a R_a^s || \uparrow_b R_b^s] : M$. The third component contains $k - 1$ while-loops; therefore, by the induction hypothesis, its induced execution sequence is also fair. Consequently, if the induced execution sequence of $\phi^m([R_a^s || R_b^s])$ is fair for $k - 1$ while loops, then it is also fair for programs with k while-loops.

The base case of the induction is for $k = 1$, where one of the programs contains no while-loop. Let R_b^s be the program without while-loops; then $\phi^m([R_a^s || R_b^s])$ will merge the two programs such that R_b^s will be inserted before the while loop of R_a^s. The induced execution sequence is fair since $\uparrow_b$ in $[\uparrow_a R_a^s || \uparrow_b R_b^s] : M$ will be removed in a finite number of steps, and an execution sequence with one arrow (the remaining $\uparrow_a$) is always fair. ∎

4 Dealing with nested while-loops

In this section we discuss nested while loops that are executed in parallel, and describe two types of transformations that can handle such cases. We proved in Lemma 8 that ϕ^m does work for parallel programs that do not contain nested while loops. Unfortunetly, for programs with nested while-loops, ϕ^m might also fail to preserve the fairness requirement. Consider, for example, the following program :

$$R_{bad} \equiv \{x = 0; [while(x < 10)\ x + +; || while(x < 10)\ while\ (x < 10);]\}$$

The trick with this example is that "merging" the left while-loop with either the outer right while-loop or the inner right while-loop will not yield a correct transformation.

Clearly, any **fair** execution sequence of $R_{bad} : M$ will terminate, as, once the loop on the left process has been executed 10 times, it will terminate the nested while-loops of the right process. All these events must occur in this order since the execution sequence is fair and there is a finite number k in which every arrow is advanced at least once. However, applying ϕ^m on R_{bad} will generate the following program :

$$\phi^m(x = 0;\ [while(x < 10)\ x + +; || while(x < 10)\ while(x < 10);]) \longrightarrow$$
$$x = 0;\ \phi^m([while(x < 10)x + +; || while(x < 10)\ while(x < 10);]) \longrightarrow$$
$$x = 0;\ while(x < 10\ \&\&\ x < 10)\ \phi^m([\ x + +; || while(x < 10);]) \longrightarrow$$
$$x = 0;\ while(x < 10)\{\ x + +;\ while(x < 10);\ \}.....$$

The body of the merged while loops $(x + +;\ while\ (x < 10);)$ yields an infinite execution sequence. The induced execution sequence of $\phi(R) : M$, $[\uparrow_1 while\ (x < 10)\ x + +; || \uparrow_2 while(x < 10)\ while(x < 10);] : M$ is therefore not fair, as the body of the right while loop is executed infinitely, so that (in the original program) the arrow pointing to the body of the left while- loop is never advanced.

An immediate solution is to "flatten" nested while-loops into a single while-loop, so that ϕ^m can be applied. Consider, for example, parallel execution of programs with a single nested while -loop:

$$[R_a^s || R_b^s] \equiv [while(E_1) \{\alpha_1; while(E_2) \ \alpha_2; \beta_1\} || \ while(E_3) \ \{\alpha_3; while(E_4) \ \alpha_4; \beta_3\}] \ .$$

Once, the nested while-loops in R_a^s and R_b^s have been flattened (using a transformation $F(R^s)$), then ϕ^m can be applied:

$$\phi([R_a^s || R_b^s]) = \phi^m([F(R_a^s) || F(R_b^s)]) \ .$$

The flattening itself is done using an external while-loop that simulates the effect of nested while-loops using if statements and flags. Each inner while loop is converted into an if construct. In addition, flags are placed before and after each converted inner loop, in order to mark which block of statements is to be executed next:

$$\phi([while(E_1) \ \{\alpha_1; while(E_2) \ \alpha_2; \beta_1\} \ || \ while(E_3) \ \{\alpha_3; while(E_4) \ \alpha_4; \beta_3\}]) \longrightarrow$$

$$\phi^m(F(while(E_1) \ \{\alpha_1; while(E_2) \ \alpha_2; \beta_1\}) \ ||$$

$$F(while(E_3) \ \{\alpha_3; while(E_4) \ \alpha_4; \beta_3\})) \longrightarrow$$

$$\phi^m \left(\left[\begin{array}{l} fl_1 = 1; fl_2 = fs_1 = 0; e_1 = E_1; \\ while(e_1) \ \{ \\ \quad if(fl_1)\{\alpha_1; fl_1 = 0; fl_2 = 1;\} \\ \quad if(fl_2 \&\& E_2) \\ \quad\quad \{\alpha_2; if(!E_2) \ fl_2 = 0; fs_1 = 1;\} \\ \quad if(fs_1) \\ \quad\quad \{\beta_1; fs_1 = 0; fl_1 = 1; e_1 = E_1;\} \\ \} \end{array} \right\| \begin{array}{l} fl_3 = 1; \ fl_4 = fs_3 = 0; \ e_3 = E_3; \\ while(e_3) \ \{ \\ \quad if(fl_3)\{\alpha_3; fl_3 = 0; fl_4 = 1;\} \\ \quad if(fl_4 \&\& E_4) \\ \quad\quad \{\alpha_4; if(!E_4) \ fl_4 = 0; fs_3 = 1;\} \\ \quad if(fs_3) \\ \quad\quad \{\beta_3; fs_3 = 0; fl_3 = 1; e_3 = E_3;\} \\ \} \end{array} \right] \right) \longrightarrow$$

Indeed, flattening will work for the bad example given at the beginning of this section:

$$\phi^m(x = 0; [\ F(while(x < 10)x + +;) || \ F(while(x < 10) \ while(x < 10);) \ ]) \longrightarrow$$
$$x = 0; fl = 0; while(x < 10)\{x + +; fl = 1; if(fl \ \&\& \ x < 10)if(!(x < 10))fl = 0; \})$$

Clearly, the transformed program terminates and it is easy to see that its induced execution sequence is fair as well.

The flattening mechanism can be generalized to any type of nested while-loops; however, the resulting program will be complex, using many extra flags and conditional statements. The main disadvantage of the flattening method is the dissimilarity between the original code of the parallel program, and the code of the transformed sequential program.

Another type of solution (ϕ^c), which will preserve the similarity better than flattening, is to insert the nested loops of one of the processes inside the inner while-loop of the other process. The innermost while loop is executed for K iterations, after which control is passed to the external loop and so forth. In this way, the induced execution sequence advances the arrows in both processes alternately. Application of this method on the initial bad example is performed as follows:

$\phi^c(\{x = 0; [while(x < 10)x + +; ||while(x < 10)\ while(x < 10);]\}\ ) \longrightarrow$
$x = 0; k = 0; f = 0;\ while(x < 10)\{x + +;\ if(f)\{f = 0; goto\ 1; \}$
$\quad while(x < 10)\{\ 1 : k + +; while((x < 10)\&\&(k\%K \neq 0))k + +; if(x < 10)goto\ 2; \}$
$\quad 2 : f = 1;\ \})$

Clearly, the transformed program also terminates and it is easy to see that its induced execution sequence is fair as well.

The formal definition of ϕ^c is omitted and is available in the final version of this paper.

5 Detecting bad execution sequences

We use the well known mutual exclusion problem [11] as a leading example to study the need for producing asynchronous execution sequences. Consider, for example, a simple erroneous code for mutual exclusion of two processes, along with a sequential version which lets the two processes execute the critical section at the same time.

process 0 :	process 1 :	
$turn = 0;$	$turn = 1;$	$turn = 0;\ while(turn! = 0);$
$while(turn! = 0);$	$while(turn! = 1);$ $\implies$	$turn = 1;\ while(turn! = 1);$
$critical\_sec0;$	$critical\_sec1;$	$critical\_sec0;$
$turn = 1;$	$turn = 0;$	$critical\_sec1;$
		$turn = 1;\ turn = 0;$

Applying ϕ^m causes no problem. The sequential version $\phi^m : M$ will merge the two processes such that they never enter into the critical section at the same time. The proposed transformation for this case is ϕ^i that transforms two parallel while-loops by inserting one loop inside the body of the other. The inserted inner loop is executed K times every iteration of the outer loop. The general mechanism of ϕ^i is given next; however, it will work only if $E_1 = true$ as long as $E_2 = true$ is true (the full version of this rule which takes into account all possible cases has been omitted).

$[while(E_1)S_1 || while(E_2)S_2] \implies while(E_1)\{S_1; while(E_2\&\&((k++\ \%\ K)\ ==0))S_2\}$

Thus, the execution sequences generated by ϕ^c allows one arrow to move K times before the other arrow moves (full details of ϕ^c have been omitted).

The power of ϕ^c can be demonstrated by applying it to Hyman's incorrect solution for mutual exclusion, as described in [11]. There are two processors, P0 and P1, which compete for access to the critical section as follows:

flag0 = flag1 = 0;	
turn = rand()%2;	
Process 0:	Process 1:
0.1- flag0 = 1;	1.1- flag1 = 1;
0.2- while(turn != 0){	1.2- while(turn != 1){
0.3- while(flag1);	1.3- while(flag0);
0.4- turn = 0;	1.4- turn = 1;
0.5- }	1.5- }
0.6- critical_sec0;	1.6- critical_sec1;
0.7- flag0 = 0;	1.7- flag1 = 0;

The bug in Hyman's algorithm manifests itself when merging the two processes using ϕ^i:

```
flag1 = 1;
int k, fL = 1, fA = 1;
while(turn! = 1 && fL) { k = 0;
    if(!flag0){
        if(fA){ flag0 = 1; fA = 0;
        if(!(turn! = 0 && k < K)) {
            if(!(turn! = 0)) {
                fL = 0;
                turn = 1; }
            }else...
    } }else ....
if(!fL && !(turn! = 1))
    φ ( critical_sec0; flag0 = 0; || critical_sec1; flag1 = 0; )
```

Finally, we wish to note that alternative rules (such as ϕ^m and ϕ^c) might be useful to generate a large set of different sequential versions of the same program. This set can be used as an approximation for the actual set of all possible execution orders that might be generated by a real parallel machine. Thus, an actual tool for sequentializing parallel programs should contain many types of alternative rules for every construct in the grammar. The selection of alternative rules can be made at random allowing us to generate a random sampling of the set of all possible sequential versions that can be generated by the tool. Random sampling of execution orders (actually an approximation of such a set) might be useful as a criterion for the validity of a debugged program.

6 Acknowledgment

This paper has been greatly improved by the detailed comments from the Program Committee and anonymous referees. In particular, we wish to thank Prof. Yeda and Prof. Shyamasundar whose detailed comments improved the paper significantly.

References

1. K. R. Apt and E.-R. Olderog. *Verification of Sequential and Concurrent Programs*. Springer-verlag, 1991.
2. Ziya Aral and Ilya Gertner. Non-intrusive and interactive profiling in Parasight. In *Proc. ACM/SIGPLAN PPEALS (Parallel Programming: Experience with A pplications, Languages and Systems)*, pages 21–30, Jul 1988.
3. M. J. Bach and S. J. Buroff. Multiprocessor UNIX operating systems. *AT&T Bell Labs Tech. J.*, 63(8, part 2):1733–1749, Oct 1984.
4. Y. Ben-Asher and G. Haber. On the usage of simulators to detect inefficiency of parallel programs caused by bad schedulings: the simparc approach. In *HiPC (High performance computing)*, New Delhi, India,, 1995.
5. Aaron J. Goldberg and John L. Hennessy. Mtool: An integrated system for performance debugging shared memory multiprocessor applications. *IEEE Trans. Parallel & Distributed Syst.*, 4(1):28–40, Jan 1993.

6. Phillip Krueger and Miron Livny. A comparison of preemptive and non-preemptive load distributing. In *Intl. Conf. Distributed Comput. Syst.*, number 8, pages 123–130, Jun 1988.
7. Leslie Lamport. How to make a multiprocessor computer that correctly executes multiprocess programs. *IEEE Transactions on Computers*, C-28(9):690–691, Sep 1979.
8. Allen D. Malony. Event-based performance perturbation: A case study. In *Symp. Principles & Practice of Parallel Programming*, number 3, pages 201–212, Apr 1991.
9. Charles E. McDowell and David P. Helmbold. Debugging concurrent programs. *ACM Computing Surveys*, 21(4):593–622, Dec 1989.
10. Constantine D. Polychronopoulos. *Parallel programming and compilers*. Kluwer academic, 1988.
11. M. Raynal. *Algorithms for Mutual Exclusion*. The MIT Press, 1986.
12. Zary Segall and Larry Rudolph. PIE: A programming and instrumentation environment for parallel pro cessing. *IEEE Software*, 2(6):22–37, Nov 1985.
13. Jeffrey J. P. Tsai, Kwang-Ya Fang, and Horng-Yuan Chen. A noninvasive architecture to monitor real-time distributed systems. *Computer*, 23(3):11–23, Mar 1990.
14. Glynn Winskel. *The Formal Semantics of Programming Languages-An Introduction*. MIT press, 1993.

Recurrent Oscillatory Self-organizing Map: Adapting to Complex Environmental Periodicities

Mauri Kaipainen
University of Helsinki, Cognitive Science Program
PL 13, 00014 Helsingin yliopisto, Finland
kaipaine@helsinki.fi

Pantelis Papadopoulos
Indiana University, Computer Science Department, Cognitive Science Program,
406 Lindley Hall Bloomington, Indiana 47405 USA,
pantelis@cs.indiana.edu

Pasi Karhu
University of Helsinki, Cognitive Science Program
PL 13, 00014 Helsingin yliopisto, Finland
pasi.karhu@helsinki.fi

A Recurrent Oscillatory Self-Organizing Map (ROSOM) is introduced. It is used for periodicity detection and synchronization using a non-time-windowed stream of data. The architecture, a modification of Kohonen's self-organizing map, assumes oscillatory states, assigned to all units, indicating their "readiness-to-fire" and constituting thereby an internal timing mechanism. The networks's input vector is a conglomeration of the standard external input vector and an internal feedback vector consisting of all units' states. This causes the units to recognize and adapt not only to current input but also to the entire history of activations encoded by the states. The ROSOM is capable of detecting consistently repetitive sequences from uni- or multi-dimensional input streams. The model translates these sequences into real-time periodicities to which the model can then automatically adapt and phase-lock. In the self-organizing process relying on the detected periodicity, different units of the network become responsive to different phases of the period.

Our results indicate that the network can synchronize to what it detects as a salient periodicity among multiple subperiodicities of the data, provided that the initial cycle duration parameter of the model is set close enough to the cycle duration of the data period and the data period does not exceed the number of units in the network. Without relying on ad-hoc time-windowing, the model is capable of distinguishing between datapoints that do not differ but with respect to their context, i.e. their position in a hierarchical sequence structure, such as As in sequence ABACABAD. Large enough networks can also distinguish multiple repetitive periods (As) from other subsequent repetitive periods (Bs), as in sequence AAAABBBB.

Furthermore, the network has the capability of carrying on activity in the absence of any input, suggesting applicability in complex coordination tasks in artificial life simulations. Diagnostic use for periodic multidimensional data should also be considered. This might be accomplished by examining the ways in which the original data deviates from its own ROSOM-developed representation, which can be seen as a kind of normalization of the periods in the original data.

Basic Binary Decision Diagram Operations for Image Processing

C. Lursinsap[1], K. Kanchanasut[2], T. Siriboon[3]

[1] Department of Mathematics and Computer Science, Chulalongkorn University, Bangkok, Thailand
[2] Computer Science and Information Management, Asian Institute of Technology, Patumthani, Thailand
[3] Department of Computer Engineering, Chulalongkorn University, Bangkok, Thailand

(Extended Abstract)

1 Introduction

Binary decision diagram (BDD) was first introduced by Akers [1] and later it was applied to circuit design problems. Commonly used BDD's are Ordered Binary Decision Diagrams or OBDD [3] which represent a Boolean function as a rooted directed acyclic graph with two terminals which are *one* and *zero* terminals. In this paper, we apply the BDD to problems in image processing applications where only the *one* terminals are needed. We show that image operations can be applied directly on the compact image representation with polynomial time complexities.

2 BDD Representation for Bitmapped and Gray-Scaled Image

Typically an image can be viewed as a matrix of size $n \times m$ whose entries correspond to pixels having either value 0 or 1 for bitmapped images or any value between 0 and 255 for gray-scaled images. Processing these images by matrix computations could take $O(nm)$ in time which may not be tolerated when the image is large.

To transform a bitmapped image to a BDD, we assign a set of Boolean variables to each co-ordinate of the image matrix and consider each pixel as a minterm, as shown in Figure 1. Thus for an $n \times m$ image matrix we need $\lceil log_2(n) \rceil + \lceil log_2(m) \rceil$ Boolean variables. Next we apply the Boolean minimization to group these minterms and to derive a Boolean function in a sum-of-product form. Once we have the canonical form we can apply the algorithm and transformation rules proposed by Bryant and other researchers' [2] to create a reduced OBDD. We then delete all edges connecting the *zero* terminal and the variable vertices.

Gray-scaled images can be represented by multiple BDDs because the value of each pixel, $a_{i,j}$, is represented by $log_2 a_{i,j}$ bits separable to bit planes where each plane is represented by one BDD.

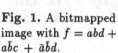

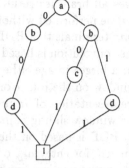

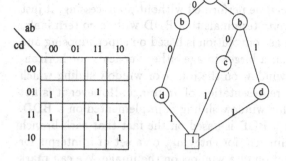

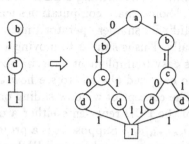

Fig. 1. A bitmapped image with $f = abd + a\bar{b}c + \bar{a}\bar{b}d$.

Fig. 2. A BDD for a bitmapped image in Figure 1.

Fig. 3. Inserting the missing verices.

Unlike the case of logic syhthcsis, variables and their ordering relate to the coordinates of the non-zero pixels in an image. Thus in our case the same set of variables, their ordering and the orientation of the BDDs must be kept uniform on all images. This difference has made our proposed Boolean operations simpler than those of Bryant [2]. Preprocessing of BDD by inserting missing vertices, as shown in Figure 3; must be performed on BDD prior to performing image operations.

3 Image Operations

The main operation in image processiong is convolution of two images which consists of additions and multiplications of the two matrices representing the two images. Multiplications can be implemented as a set of recursive additions which are in turn transformable to a set of Boolean operations AND, OR, exclusive-OR (XOR) and NOT.

In performing a binary operation on any two images we perform the operation on the two coresponding pixels of the two operator images. We call a path from the root to the *one* terminal node is a *branch* on the BDD. Each branch correspond to a pixel or a set of pixels in the original image. A binary Boolean operation on any two BDDs correspond to superimposing corresponding branches of the two operator BDDs. A superimposition is *perfect* if the matching process sucessfully matches the two branches entirely from the roots to the terminal vertices. This occurs when both branches are identical. Otherwise, when successive matching of vertices and edges starting from the root vertices fails before a terminal vertex is reached, we say that the superimposition is *partial*. An AND operation either returns no branch at all or the superimpostion of the two identical branches when a perfect suprimposition exists. An OR operation returns the result of a partial superimposition together with the remaining differences or unmatched portions for the two operand branches. To get an XOR, we need one more step which simply removes all branches resulting from a perfect superimposition. A NOT operation can be performed without prepocessing, it just simply transforming a BDD with *one* terminals to a BDD with *zero* terminals.

Some image computation such as convolution is based on superimposing and sliding a smaller operator image on a larger image either vertically or horizontally. This is similar to moving a window on the image or window sliding which is easy to implement on a matrix representation of an image. However it is not so easy and obvious to see how this window sliding is implemented on a BDD. The concept of window sliding on a BDD is based on the fact that each branch of the BDD represents either a minterm for entry $a_{i,j}$ or a set of minterms for $\bigcup_{some\ i,j} a_{i,j}$. Suppose A is a projection of a window on the image. We can mark on a preprocessed image's BDD all branches which belong to A and subsequently remove all branches which do not.

4 Discussion and Related Works

Performances of image operations on BDDs depend on the size of the BDDs. With larger blocks of the one pixels, the smaller the size of the minterms and subsequently the shorter the branches. Thus BDD provide compact representations with fast operations for images with few large blocks. Degenrate case occurs when an image consists of a large number of small blocks of one pixels, particularly when one minterm cover only one pixel. BDD can degenerate and become exponentially large. However, the size of the BDD is still $(\lceil log_2(n) \rceil + \lceil log_2(m) \rceil)^2$ which is still a substantial reduction from $n \times m$ number of pixels from the original image.

References

1. S.B. Akers, "Binary Decision Diagram", IEEE Transactions on Computers, Vol. C-27, No. 6, June 1978, pp. 509-516.
2. R.E. Bryant, "Graph-Based Algorithms for Boolean Function Manipulation", IEEE Transactions on Computers, Vol. C-35, No. 8, August 1986, pp. 677-691.
3. R.E. Bryant, "Symbolic Boolean manipulation with ordered binary decision diagrams", ACM Computing Surveys, Vol 24., No. 3 (September, 1992), pp. 293-318.

Adaptive Object Storage System for Mobile Computing Environments

Tatsuo Nakajima

Japan Advanced Institute of Science and Technology
1-1 Asahidai Tatsunokuchi Ishikawa 923-12 JAPAN

This paper describes an adaptive object storage system for mobile computing environments. The object storage system adopts the object graph framework[1], and changes the configuration of its structure according to computing environments.

The power management has become an important consideration in the design of new hardware and software. The disk is a promising candidate for power management because it is a device with which the user does not interact with directly. With proper management by the operation system, the disk may be spun up and down without the user noticing much difference in performance or reliability.

However, if the portable computers have connected to an AC power supply, spinning down of a disk is not necessary, and *performance* is more important than *energy consumption*. On the other hand, if remaining battery is not sufficient, the *reliability* of modified objects becomes more important since the computer may be shutdown at any moment when the battery becomes empty. Therefore, three metrics, *performance, reliability, battery consumption* should be taken into account for object storage systems in mobile computing environments. When a portable computer is connected to an AC power supply, *performance* is the most important. However, when the computer is driven by the battery, *battery consumption* is the most important. On the other hand, if remaining battery is not sufficient, *reliability* is the most important. The adaptive object storage system should take into account the tradeoff between the three metrics.

Our object storage system is constructed by an object graph that consists of four objects. The object *OF* is an object that implements the interface of the object storage system and mechanisms for managing objects. The adaptive object *MM* contains memory management policies that determines which objects should be cached in physical memory.

The adaptive object *PS* contains policies for moving modified objects to the object DM. The adaptive object changes the object processing messages from other objects according to computing environments. The object that currently receives messages is called an *active object*. Two objects are contained in *PS* by considering the tradeoff between *reliability* and *performance*. PS_1 copies objects whenever objects are modified for ensuring the consistency of objects that reside in physical memory and a disk. This policy increases the *reliability* by sacrificing the *performance*. PS_2 copies objects to a disk periodically for decreasing the number of disk accesses. The object sacrifices the *reliability* for increasing the *performance*.

The next adaptive object DM manages the movement of modified objects from physical memory to a disk. DM_1 copies modified objects in a flash memory as described in the previous section. In the policy, the energy consumption is more important. Since the movement of modified objects can be delayed, the storage system can stop a disk for a long time. On the other hand, DM_2 copies objects to a disk directly. DM_1 requires to copy objects twice. Thus, the performance may be degraded when DM_1 is used. However, the storage system may spin up a disk whenever an object is copied to a disk since DM_2 requires to copy objects to a disk. Thus, the policy sacrifices the energy consumption.

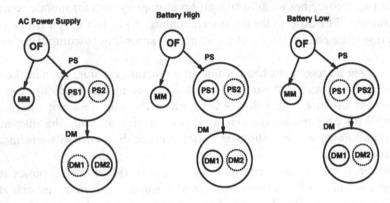

The above figure shows the configuration of the object graph of our object storage system. If the computer is connected to an AC power supply, MM_2, PS_1, and DM_2 are active objects of the adaptive object MM, PS, and DM respectively. In this case, the *performance* is considered the most important metric. If the AC power supply is disconnected, but the enough capacity remains in a battery, MM_1, PS_1, and DM_1 are active objects. In the configuration, the *battery consumption* is the most important. However, the capacity of a battery is low, MM_1 and PS_2, and DM_1 are active objects. In this case, the *reliability* is the most important metric.

A prototype implementation of the adaptive object storage system has been build on Real-Time Mach[3]. We implemented the prototype by modifying the Texas persistent storage system[2]. The storage system was implemented as a library that is linked to a program.

References

1. A.Hokimoto, K.Kurihara, T.Nakajima, "An Approach for Constructing Mobile Applications using Service Proxies", The 16th International Conference on Distributed Computing Systems(ICDCS'96), May, 1996.
2. V. Singhal, S. Kakkad, and P. Wilson, "Texas: An Efficient, Portable Persistent Store", In Persistent Object Systems: Proceedings of the Fifth International Workshop on Persistent Object Systems, 1992.
3. H.Tokuda, T.Nakajima, P.Rao, "Real-Time Mach: Towards a Predictable Real-Time System", the USENIX Mach Workshop, October, 1990.

Structure of User Interface Module for Practical Internet Messages

Morioka Tomohiko

JAIST, Hokuriku; 1-1 Asahidai, Tatsunokuchi, Nomi, Ishikawa, 923-12, Japan
E-mail: morioka@jaist.ac.jp

MIME offers structures like "multipart"[2] for messages. Structured messages may form a tree and in that case the node of the tree is called "entity"[1]. Each entity has a type known as "media-types"[1] for representing the data type. Conventional MUAs (Message User Agent; mail reader, news reader, etc.) provide the features necessary for message navigation. However, they do not provide any feature for navigating the entities and therefore, some kind of mapping between the message and the entity hierarchy is required. Moreover, as the conventional MUAs can not process the entities itself, the MIME module has to be employed for processing the entities. The processing is normally defined by a mapping between media-type and program. However, entity processing is not depended on media-type alone. Hence, a simple mapping between media type and program is not adequate. In the present study, the notion of "acting situation model" is proposed to overcome the above mentioned problems of the conventional MUAs. Instead of the simple mapping between media-type and program; a generlaized MIME processing module is designed based on the "acting situation model". The proposed system is implemented on GNU Emacs and its variants, namely "tm"[3] and "SEMI"[4].

1 Mapping between a message and its entities

Traditional Internet messages are limited to plain text. Hence, conventional MUAs do not require complex message processing. They ignore the internal structure and simply manage messages. Therefore, the proposed MIME processing module must provide the adequate features to process and manage the hierarchy of entities, and at the same time it has to offer an interface between a message and its structure. In the present approach, SEMI and tm employ the *"preview"* function for supporting these functions. Entity related information are embedded for allowing the user to navigate entities in *preview*. Tm and SEMI manage the mapping between a message and its *preview*. The interface modules between MIME processing module and MUAs replace the display for a message of original MUAs by its *preview*. *Preview* functions as a message display for MUAs and therefore, MIME processing features are added to the message features of the original MUAs.

2 Acting situation model

An "Acting situation" consists of (1) information of entities specified by the header (ex. Content-Type[1]), (2) conditions related to program execution, (3) operation type and (4) information related to MUA type. "Acting situation" is generated by the operation on entity. In case of tm and SEMI, an acting situation is represented by the association list: $((t_1.v_1)(t_2.v_2)...(t_n.v_n))$. An acting situation consists attributes with type t_i and value v_i. During an operation on entity, tm or SEMI generates the draft for acting situation with the help of (1), (3) and (4) (They are unique and therefore they are simply appended). Finally the appropriate condition is retrieved from (2) and it is compared with the draft of acting situation. For example, if the draft for action situation is:

```
((media-type . message)(media-subtype . partial)("number" . "2")
("total" . "3")("id" . "foo@tsukuyomi.jaist.ac.jp")
(mode . play)(major-mode . gnus-original-article-mode))
```

and

```
((media-type . message)(media-subtype . partial)
(method . mime-combine-message/partials-automatically)
(major-mode . gnus-original-article-mode)
(summary-buffer-exp . gnus-summary-buffer))
```

is matched with the list of conditions (2), then

```
((media-type . message)(media-subtype . partial)
("number" . "2")("total" . "3")
("id" . "foo@tsukuyomi.jaist.ac.jp")
(mode . play)(major-mode . gnus-original-article-mode)
(method . mime-combine-message/partials-automatically)
(summary-buffer-exp . gnus-summary-buffer))
```

will be generated as the acting situation. Next, the program specified by the 'method' attribute is executed. The remaining attributes are to be referenced by the program.

3 Conclusion

The proposed MIME processing module employs *preview* for providing an adequate mapping mechanism between a message and its hierarchy of entities. The functions of the proposed MIME processing module should be consistent with the original functions of MUAs. The acting situation model allows the user to specify conditions along with various factors. In the proposed method the acting situation is generated dynamically, hence it is flexible. However present implementation of the model might generate wrong acting situation. Therefore, the subject is to be farther investigated.

References

[1] Freed, N. and Borenstein, N., "Multipurpose Internet Mail Extensions (MIME) Part One: Format of Internet Message Bodies", RFC 2045, 1996-02-12.

[2] Freed, N. and Borenstein, N., "Multipurpose Internet Mail Extensions (MIME) Part Two: Media Types", RFC 2046, 1996-12-02.

[3] ftp://ftp.jaist.ac.jp/pub/GNU/elisp/mime/

[4] ftp://ftp.jaist.ac.jp/pub/GNU/elisp/mime/alpha/

[5] Borenstein, N., "A User Agent Configuration Mechanism For Multimedia Mail Format Information", RFC 1524, 1993-09-23.

Software Specification Using *LASS*

Mihal Badonski, Mirjana Ivanović, Zoran Budimac
Institute of Mathematics, Faculty of Science, University of Novi Sad,
Trg D. Obradovića 4, 21000 Novi Sad, Yugoslavia
e-mail: {mihal, mira, zjb}@unsim.ns.ac.yu

Abstract. The paper introduces a new agent-oriented programming language named *LASS*. *LASS* is aimed for agent-oriented programming in multi-agent systems.

1 Introduction

Multi-agent systems are a new and promising area in the field of distributed artificial intelligence, as well as in the mainstream computer science. These systems are compound of relatively autonomous and intelligent parts, called *agents*. Agent-oriented programming (AOP) languages are programming languages developed for the programming of agents. AOP introduces new concepts such as mental categories, reactivity, pro-activeness, concurrent execution inside and between agents, communication, meta-level reasoning, etc.

This paper presents an AOP language named *LASS*. Agent programmed with *LASS* possesses *intentions*, *beliefs* and *plans* for its *public* and *internal services*. Besides deliberative properties, agent specified with *LASS* can behave reactively as well. *LASS* introduces the usage of *behaviors* - programming primitives enabling agent to react immediately when it is necessary. *LASS* enables powerful communication between agents which is based on agents' public services. Services are used similarly like remote procedure calls. Most of the concepts in *LASS* are already seen in other programming languages. However, the usage of all of them in one computer language is unique.

This paper introduces *LASS* by comparing it with other AOP languages. The full account to the language is given in [2], while some of its applications are described in [1].

2 How *LASS* Differs?

The first AOP language that uses mental categories is AGENT0. Agents programmed in AGENT0 have their initial beliefs and capabilities to perform private and communicative actions. The main part of AGENT0 program are the commitment rules. Each commitment rule determines the new commitments and other mental changes that will occur if particular message is received. The language is loosely coupled with modal temporal logic. This logic is used for the specification of the language. Unlike AGENT0, *LASS* is intended for practical usage. AGENT0's purpose was to introduce new concepts in an elegant manner. *LASS* is not bound to any logic. It uses some procedural constructs and its expressive power is greater than it is in AGENT0. Agents programmed in *LASS* do not use clocks and references to time points to synchronize their actions. `ask_service_wait` can be used for synchronization. While AGENT0 possesses some elements of logic programming, *LASS* is more oriented to procedural constructs.

PLACA is the descendant of AGENT0. PLACA introduces planning capabilities of agents. Agent in PLACA uses plans to achieve the desired state of the world. Agents in *LASS* also use plans, but plans cannot be generated at run-time as they can be in PLACA.

In Concurrent MetateM, MAS is specified with the logic. The logic is modal and linear temporal. Specification of MAS is directly executed. Concurrent MetateM is only in experimental stage and so far it has no common features with *LASS*.

HOMAGE is the language for agent specification with two levels. The lower level uses objects of Java, Common Lisp and C++ instead of mental categories. Higher level contains constructs for organization of objects from the lower level into agent's program. Agents in HOMAGE communicate and received messages are handled with rules similar to those in AGENT0 and PLACA. *LASS* does not allow the use of other languages. However, two types of primitives in *LASS* can be identified. Primitives that are specific for AOP languages (communicative actions, services, plans, intentions, behaviors, etc.) correspond to higher level in HOMAGE. Primitives inherited from procedural languages correspond to lower level in HOMAGE.

The AOP language with the greatest influence on our research is AgentSpeak. Creators of AgentSpeak aimed to join object oriented programming and MAS concepts such as: mental categories, reactive and proactive properties, distribution over wide area network, real-time response, communication with speech acts, concurrent execution of plans in and between agents and meta-level reasoning. The main difference between *LASS* and AgentSpeak is in communication. We believe that *LASS* introduces more powerful communicative primitives than those existing in languages enlisted above. Speech acts can be easily implemented in *LASS* using services. Services act like remote procedure calls and enable more efficient and simpler transfer of information.

None of the above languages possess such a powerful construct for agent's reactivity such as behaviors. Behavioral approach to artificial intelligence is developed at MIT, by R. Brooks. Behaviors in *LASS* are organized in the similar manner.

3 Conclusion

Most of the concepts used in *LASS* are already seen in other programming languages. The significance of *LASS* is in the inclusion of all these concepts into one practical programming language.

References

1. Badonski, M., *LASS in Action*. In Proc. of Abstracts of XI Conf. on Applied Mathematics "Prim '97" (Palić, Yugoslavia), 1997, to appear.
2. Badonski, M., Ivanović, M., *LASS - a Language for Agent-Oriented Software Specification*. In Proc. of VIII Int. Conf. on Logic and Computing "Lira '97" (Novi Sad, Yugoslavia), pp. 9-18, 1997.

Nepi^2: A Two-Level Calculus for Network Programming Based on the π-Calculus*

Eiichi Horita[1] and Ken Mano[2]

[1] NTT Software Laboratories, E-mail: horita@slab.ntt.co.jp
[2] NTT Communication Science Laboratories, E-mail: mano@cslab.kecl.ntt.co.jp

We propose a two-level calculus, Nepi^2, for network programming that is based on the π-calculus [4, 5]; one level treats *local* (or *intra-process*) concurrency and the other treats *global* (or *inter-process*) concurrency. We give the operational semantics and a distributed implementation of this calculus.

Nepi^2 evolved from Nepi [1], a network programming language based on the π-calculus that does not distinguish between local and global concurrency. In Nepi, any two agents (or threads) can communicate with each other only via a single *global communication manager* (*GCM*). This method of inter-agent communication has two problems related to performance and scalability: (i) For two agents residing within a local system, this method entails unnecessary global interactions. (ii) A substantial part of the load of managing inter-agent communication is concentrated on the GCM, which can be a bottleneck when the overall system is scaled up.

A major reason for introducing two levels in Nepi^2 is our desire to alleviate these problems. There are, however, other reasons for differentiating the two levels: (i) There are no problems in introducing locally defined datatypes that are used only within a local system, even when it consists of multiple threads, but datatypes used across different local systems need to have their specifications advertised globally. (ii) Mutable data objects and pointers can be used within a local system, but it is very hard to use them across different local systems with their original semantics preserved.
Apart from these inherent differences, we have kept the differences between the treatments of local concurrency and global concurrency as small as possible from the viewpoints of programming and semantics.

The language of Nepi^2 consists of the following two levels. The first-level language is a programming language defining the syntactic category of *process expressions*. It is used for representing *local systems* as processes (each possibly consisting of multiple agents) of the form $(P_1 \parallel \cdots \parallel P_n)$, with P_i representing an agent $(i = 1, \ldots, n)$ and $\parallel$ being the *parallel operator in the first level*. We have two kinds of communication primitives for sending and receiving data. One kind is for *local* (or *intra-process*) communication and the other for *global* (or *inter-process*) communication. The second-level language is defined on top of the first-level and defines the syntactic category of *system expressions* of the form $(P_{1,1} \parallel \cdots \parallel P_{1,n(1)}) \prod \cdots \prod (P_{k,1} \parallel \cdots \parallel P_{k,n(k)})$, with $\prod$ being the *parallel operator in the second level*. This level is used for analyzing global systems consisting of the processes described in the first-level language.

---

* This paper is an extended abstract of [2].

The operational semantics of Nepi[2] is defined along the lines of the polyadic π-calculus [4] by using a Plotkin-style transition system, which is in turn defined using a two-level version of the *structural congruence* [4] among process and system expressions.

The main technical contribution of our work is the development of the distributed implementation of Nepi[2] on a network. This implementation is based on the following two theoretical results, which constitute the main theoretical contributions of our work: **(i)** We introduce another calculus called the $\nu\pi$-calculus, which is more suited for distributed implementation, and establish the *weak bisimilarity* (an equivalence at an appropriate level of abstraction) between the π-calculus and our $\nu\pi$-calculus. The main reason that the $\nu\pi$-calculus is suited for distributed implementation is that the $\nu\pi$-calculus instantiates every *restricted* channel variable into a fresh channel constant, and thereby obviating the need for the highly costly procedure of searching and constructing structurally congruent (typically α-congruent) system configurations in a distributed environment. **(ii)** We propose a new protocol for decentralized implementation of channel-based communication with choice and prove that it is free from deadlock and livelock [3]. This protocol uses dynamically-created *local communication managers* (LCMs) in addition to a predefined set of GCMs, and assigns priorities to the GCMs and the LCMs so that any contention among two or more communication managers for an agent's commitment to a communication alternative can be resolved according to their priorities.

We have developed a distributed programming system for Nepi[2] by implementing the $\nu\pi$-calculus on a network, using the above mentioned new protocol and standard Unix facilities such as TCP/IP protocols and thread libraries.

Pierce and Turner developed *Pict*, another language based on the π-calculus, and implemented it on a uniprocessor [6]. As they pointed out [6], multi-processor implementations of any language based on the π-calculus remain for future research. Our development of Nepi[2] is an effort in this direction.

References

1. E. Horita and K. Mano: Nepi: a network programming language based on the π-calculus. In *Proceedings of the 1st International Conference on Coordination Models, Languages and Applications 1996*. Lecture Notes in Computer Science, Vol. 1061, pp. 424–427, Springer, 1996.
2. E. Horita and K. Mano: *Nepi[2]: a Two-Level Calculus for Network Programming Based on the π-Calculus*. ECL Technical Report, Vol. 14296, NTT Software Laboratories, 1997.
3. E. Horita and K. Mano: *A Decentralized Protocol for Channel-Based Communication with Choice*. Technical Report of IEICE, SS97-18, July, 1997.
4. R. Milner: *The Polyadic π-Calculus: a Tutorial*. Technical Report ECS-LFCS-91-180, LFCS, Department of Computer Science, Univ. of Edinburgh, 1991.
5. R. Milner, J. Parrow and D. Walker: A calculus of mobile processes, I and II. *Information and Computation*, Vol. 100, pp. 1–40 and 41–77, 1992.
6. B. C. Pierce and D. N. Turner: Concurrent objects in a process calculus. In *Proceedings of International Workshop TPPP'94*. Lecture Notes in Computer Science, Vol. 907, pp. 187–215, Springer, 1994.

On Semantics of Reactive Rule-Based Systems[*]

Man Lin[1], Jacek Malec[12], Simin Nadjm-Tehrani[1]

[1] Department of Computer and Information Science
Linköping University
S-581 83 Linköping, Sweden
linma,jam,snt@ida.liu.se

[2] Department of Computer Engineering
Mälardalens Högskola
Box 883, S-721 23 Västerås, Sweden

Extended Abstract

1 Overview

The Rule-based paradigm for knowledge representation appears in many disguises within computer science. Issues connected to the rule-based paradigm of programming appear in production systems, parallel program design (e.g. Unity), default reasoning within AI, logic programming, rewriting, active and deductive databases, and logics for action and change. Although there are many differences in the contexts in which this paradigm is employed there are also common problems and patterns of reasoning which are easily recognized by any rule-programmer.

Our work combines results from the three areas of rule-based knowledge representation, (real-time) reactive systems, and formal verification. The combination of rules and reactive behaviour, which entails dealing with environment feedback, together with a formal analysis of this behaviour is thus the main contribution of our work. Different approaches for specification of real-time and reactive systems range over automata-based, temporal logics, Petri nets, action systems, and process algebras. In our view a rule-based language with a formal semantics shares the benefits of these specification languages. In addition, it has a special appeal: it mimics the natural mode of reasoning by humans in many applications. Therefore, it can be considered as a powerful tool for capturing expert knowledge and formally analysing it. Moreover, rules can be executed and can therefore be seen as both a specification and a programming language.

The synchronous family of high-level programming languages for real-time systems (Lustre, Esterel, Statecharts) share the above characteristic. They too can be used both for capturing high level design and as executable code. Though very different in syntax and style of programming, adding reactiveness to our rules leads to formal semantics which is reminiscent of a couple of the proposed semantics for Statecharts and Esterel.

[*] This research has been supported by Volvo Research Foundation, Volvo Educational Foundation, the Center for Industrial Information Technology (CENIIT), and the Swedish Research Council for Engineering Sciences.

2 Rules and Reactiveness

In order to address the issues arising during design of reactive systems we have developed a rule language RL. The language has been successfully used for developing a reactive application: a driver-support system.

RL programs consist of event-condition-action rules of the form

> WHEN A *= a IF B *= b AND NOT C |= c THEN D := d;

read as "When A changes to a then if B changes simultaneously to b and C has not been c then D obtains value d". The characteristics of this language are:

- The meaning of a reactive program is independent of the ordering of the rules (in case of larger systems rule ordering is a cumbersome and error-prone process; the semantics of such programs is unclear and easy to distort). In our approach a program can be enhanced by simply adding new rules to the existing rule base;
- The language allows for taking account of concurrent events (in the example rule events A *= a and B *= b occur simultaneously);
- The language distinguishes time flow without introducing metric time (C |= c means "C has had value c before", while C *= c means "C has value c at the current reaction");
- The language includes usual logical operations, including negation;
- The language assumes finite domains for variables (i.e. is a datalog-type language) allowing a finite model of the domain.

3 Contributions

The technical results obtained in our research are the following:

- We have defined a rule-based language RL that allows for taking explicit account of concurrency and time in the simplest possible way;
- For this language we have defined a declarative semantics providing causal and deterministic outcome of computations;
- We have defined a number of correctness criteria for reactive programs. They ensure termination of rule firings at each reaction, consistency of the fired rules and a unique reaction for each new set of parallel stimuli to the system;
- We have defined and implemented an operational semantics, based on three-valued evaluation of rules, that guarantees the correct results of computations for correct programs;
- We have developed a static procedure for checking the correctness of programs;
- For a subclass of stratified programs we have developed a simpler operational semantics and implemented it;
- We have proven soundness of the obtained results.

The immediate topic for future research is completeness of our algorithms.

The Non-standard Semantics of Esterel

Jean-Raymond Gagné[1] and John Plaice[2]

[1]Département d'informatique,
Université Laval, Sainte-Foy (Québec) Canada G1K 7P4.
Email: gagne@ift.ulaval.ca

[2]School of Computer Science and Engineering,
University of New South Wales, Sydney 2052, Australia.
Email: plaice@acm.org

Synchronous programming formalisms, such as Esterel, Lustre, RLucid, Signal or Statecharts, have been used for the programming of reactive systems for the last ten years. The semantics of these formalisms assumes that the reaction to an input event is *instantaneous*. This assumption, realistic in many situations, greatly simplifies the programming of reactive systems.

For each of these formalisms, it is understood in the standard semantics that 'time' corresponds to a sequence of *instants*, labeled either by integers (as in Esterel or Lustre) or by real numbers (as in RLucid). Within each instant, things are supposed "to happen instantaneously or simultaneously". But we know that this is not quite true: within a given instant, some things must happen before others. This point of "infinitely fast but ordered" was raised by Gérard Berry in the mid-eighties when he was working on the semantics of Esterel, but he did not formalize it.

This concept can be formalized using *non-standard numbers*, which were first invented by Leibniz for the calculus, and resurrected by Robinson. An instant, as perceived by synchronous languages, becomes a *macro-instant*. Each macro-instant is then subdivided into a set of *micro-instants*, which can be used as needed to differentiate different steps in computing the reaction to an input event. For our purposes, the set of micro-instants is just a countable, discrete set, as in the integers. Therefore, the micro-instant $\langle r, z \rangle$ can be considered to be $r + \epsilon z$, where ϵ is a fixed infinitesimal value.

This time domain, presented in [2], was introduced for dealing with problems of time granularity in temporal databases: no matter what time granularity is used for data, a finer *infinitesimal* granularity is needed for computations over the data.

A new synchronous language, Blizzard, was also defined over the non-standard time domain. Key to the design of Blizzard is that *every* micro-instant has a unique previous and a unique next instant, which is not the case for the time model $\mathbf{R} \times \mathbf{N}$, used in much discussion about hybrid systems.

Using this approach, it is possible to redefine the semantics of Esterel, in such a manner that in the statement $p;q$, the signals emitted by q no way influence the possible behaviors of p.

We begin with the assumption that $p;q$ means "do p, then do q". The intuition is, for most people, that q's behavior cannot affect p's behavior. However,

Berry's semantics assumes that if q emits a signal s, then s must be seen by all components running in the same instant, in particular by p if it passed control to q in the same instant, as in $(s?!o,0);!s$, which emits both o and s. In some sense, this assumption is reasonable because a reaction is supposed to take place *instantaneously*, which has been interpreted as "it takes no time".

Following this assumption, two separate incarnations of a local signal can mutually interact, and the "second" one can communicate information to the "first" one. Key to this point is the definition of the constructive behavioral semantics' *Must* predicate [1, p.65], which states when a signal must be emitted:

$$M(p;q, E) = \begin{cases} M(p, E), & M_k(p, E) \neq \{0\}, \\ \langle M_s(p, E) \cup M_s(q, E), \ M_k(q, E) \rangle, & M_k(p, E) = \{0\}. \end{cases}$$

Berry himself [1, p.123] states that many of these examples are pathological, but that there are situations where multiple incarnations are useful, referring to the example shown below:

```
loop
   ACTIVE_BUTTON := GET_MENU_BUTTON(?MENU, ?MOUSE);
   signal BUTTON(BUTTON), BUTTON_OUT in
      trap CHANGE_BUTTON in
         [
            emit BUTTON(ACTIVE_BUTTON);
            copymodule BUTTON;
            exit THE_END
         ||
            await BUTTON_OUT do exit CHANGE_BUTTON end
         ]
      end
   end
end
```

But in this example, each incarnation of the BUTTON module is independent, and there is no need to send information "to the past". We surmise that this is the case for most useful programs taking advantage of this feature.

We therefore take a different approach, and assume that "it takes no time" can in fact mean that it takes *infinitesimal* time. Each infinitesimal step corresponds to advancing the program by emitting all directly emissable signals, then labeling as absent all signals not having been emitted. The next micro-instant begins, and all signals emitted in previous micro-instants remain visible. As a result, the semantics for Esterel is greatly simplified.

References

1. G. Berry. The constructive semantics of Esterel, draft version 2.0. ftp://ftp-sop. inria.fr/meije/esterel/papers/constructiveness.ps.gz, 22 May 1996.
2. J.R. Gagné and J. Plaice. A non-standard temporal deductive database system. *Journal of Symbolic Computation*, 22:649–664, 1996.

Hybrid Support for Lenient Implementation of Array-Comprehension

Shigeru Kusakabe, Kentaro Inenaga, and Makoto Amamiya

Dept. of Intelligent Systems, Kyushu University
Kasuga Fukuoka 816, Japan

1 Introduction

Array-comprehensions of non-strict functional programming languages provide both expressiveness and efficiency. Array-comprehensions define the contents of different regions of the array using different computation rules, and create all elements at once, avoiding the overhead of incremental array creation.

We employ a lenient evaluation approach because combination of non-strictness and lenient evaluation provides high degree of implicit parallelism, as well as high expressive power[2]. During the execution of a program with array-comprehensions, a lot of instances of the filling function may created, and require frequent dynamic scheduling. On machines without hardware support for fine-grain dynamic scheduling, naive implementation may incur heavy overhead.

In order to reduce overhead of lenient implementation of array-comprehensions, we develop a hybrid runtime mechanism, which speculatively uses a stack frame for a filling function invocation, while supporting suspension of the function instance.

2 Hybrid Runtime Mechanism

Non-strict data-structures such as I-structures[1] are effective to realize lenient array-comprehensions. However, a filling function of an array-comprehension may be suspended by a non-strict data-structure access. Accordingly, non-strict data-structure accesses may increase the complexity of static analysis to avoid frequent dynamic scheduling at a fine-grain level. We use a relaxed analysis rule, assuming the runtime mechanism described below, in order to reduce the static scheduling complexity and enlarge execution granularity. We use different types of function invocation for filling functions:

1. Regular stack-based invocation for a function which has neither a certain nor a potential suspension point.
2. Suspensive stack-based invocation for a function which has potential suspension points.
3. Heap-based invocation for a function which has certain suspension points.

Heap-based invocation is provided to support fine-grained flexible dynamic scheduling. Regular stack-based invocation may be as efficient as usual C function invocation. Suspensive stack-based invocation speculatively uses a stack frame for invoking a function. If it is suspended, the stack frame will be changed into a heap frame and managed as the same as the heap frame. Otherwise, if the function terminates without suspension, the behavior is almost the same as regular stack invocation, and the performance would be as efficient as the performance of regular stack-based invocation.

3 Evaluation and Related Works

As an example, we consider a simple program, matmul, which multiplies two matrices. In this program, instances of filling functions may request non-strict data-structure accesses. Table 1 shows the experimental results on an engineering workstation. In "suspensive" version, all filling functions are invoked with

	Suspensive	By-hand	Sisal	C
Elapsed time(sec)	3.7×10^{-2}	4.1×10^{-2}	3.7×10^{-2}	1.6×10^{-2}

Table 1.: Elapsed time of matmul(size20)

suspensive stack-based frame, while in "by-hand" version, all filling functions are serialized by hand-coding and invoked with regular stack frames even if the filling functions include data-structure accesses. From the elapsed time of these two versions, we can say that static analysis can be imperfect by paying the reasonable penalty. The penalty to provide the care for the dynamic scheduling is about 10%. Table 1 also shows the elapsed time of Sisal and C program. Sisal is a dataflow functional language efficiently implemented on stock machines, but it has a strict semantics and does not provide non-strict array-comprehensions. As seen from the table, by speculatively using stack frame, a non-strict program can execute almost as fast as a strict Sisal program. Since C is not so high level language as dataflow functional languages, the C program runs about two time faster than ours.

4 Conclusion

We tried to efficiently implement array-comprehensions on commodity machines. As a runtime support, we provided a hybrid runtime mechanism, which can dynamically change a suspended stack frame into a heap frame when a filling function suspends and requires dynamic scheduling due to suspending factors such as non-strict data-structure accesses.The results of the preliminary performance evaluation indicated that we can implement array-comprehensions with practical performance even on stock machines.

References

1. Arvind et al. "I-structures: Data Structures for Parallel Computing" TR-87-810, Cornel University, 1987.
2. S. Kusakabe et al. "Dataflow-Based Lenient Implementation of a Functional Language, Valid, on Conventional Multi-processors", Proc. of PACT'94.
3. K. E. Schauser et al. "Separation Constraint Partitioning - A New Algorithm for Partitioning Non-strict Programs into Sequential Threads" In Proc. of POPL'95.

Solver for Hierarchical CSP Containing Several Constraint Types and Multi-output Constraints

Mouhssine Bouzoubaa

Department of Optimisation, SINTEF, Applied Mathematics
Postboks 124 , N-0314, Blindern
Oslo, Norway

e-mail: mbo@math.sintef.no

Abstract :*We describe an algorithm (Latif) for solving a hierarchy of constraints in which the last level is associated with a global comparator and all the other levels are associated with a local comparator. Latif uses local propagation techniques to determine parts of constraint hierarchy that can be solved simultaneously.*

1. Introduction

Borning et al. proposed a theory of constraint hierarchies to cope with the over-constrained CSPs [Borning et al., 1992]. Hosobe in [Hosobe et al., 1994,1996] present an extended theory of the one described by Borning, and an efficient algorithm named *Detail*. *Detail* handles multi-way constraints with single-output. Moreover, it handles hierarchies where the first *n-1* levels are associated with the *Locally-predicate-better* criterion and the last level is associated with the *Least-squares-better* criterion. However, the restriction imposed by *Detail* is that the constraints must be single-output. In many situations this restriction is undesirable since multi-output constraints are useful in solving cycles and also are indispensable for modelling some situations in user interface design, document formatting, etc. In this paper we relax this restriction by accommodating an extended definition in order to solve constraint hierarchies such that : 1) the constraints can be multi-output. 2) the errors combination mode of each level of the hierarchy can be different : the last level of the hierarchy is associated with the *Least-squares-better* criterion or with the *Worst-case-better* criterion, and the other levels are associated with a local criterion.

2. Latif System

2.1 General View of Latif System

In order to solve a constraint graph that comprises of a hierarchy, Latif subdivides the constraint graph into constraint cells by creating successively, an admissible graph and a solution graph (there are no cycle in the reduced admissible graph). After this first step, Latif solves each cell locally by using a specific subsolver and propagates the values of it's variables to the other cells. Latif creates a partial order between cells in order to propagate values of variables between cells. Each cell is solved by one or several subsolvers depending on the type of constraints included. Latif is an incremental algorithm: on each operation, a new solution graph is obtained, and the cells comprising this solution graph are solved. The modelling of cells is done by using conditions that favour the creation of an admissible graph. More conditions are added in order to obtain a solution graph. This later gives a solution to the hierarchy after solving the set of cells in the solution graph.

2.2 Cell Modelling

In order to handle constraints with multi-output variables, Latif uses a new definition of constraint cells : given a constraint cell $p=(V_p, C_p)$, p must not be under-constrained (the value of each variable in V_p can be determined by at least one constraint in C_p). Moreover, each sub-set of variables in V_p is must not be under-constrained. We say that p is an over-constrained cell if and only if the value of at least one variable in V_p is determined by more the one constraint in C_p and each sub-set of variables in V_p is not under-constrained.

2.3 Admissible Graphs

Given a constraint graph $B=(V, C, E)$ and a set P of constraint cells in B, a quadruple $B_S=(V, C, E, P)$ is an admissible graph of B if and only if : 1) each variable and constraint in V and C respectively belongs to only one constraint cell in P. 2) there are no cyclic dependencies among constraint cells in P.

2.4 Solution Graphs

To define a solution graph that give a solution to the hierarchy we will use the following definitions : 1) *Internal Strength of a Cell p* : is *weakest* if $C_p = \emptyset$, or the minimum among strengths of constraints in C_p otherwise). 2) *p* is *Adjacent to p' Cells* : if *p* contains at least one variable constrained by a constraint in the cell *p'*. 3) *Walkabout Strength of a Cell p*: is the weakest among *p*'s internal and walkabout strength of cells adjacent to *p*.

The following theorem is based on the previous cell modelling definitions. This theorem helps us to prove the correctness of Latif.

Theorem 1: let *p* be an over-constrained cell where any pairs of the set of its variables and the set of its constraints (whose strength is different from the internal strength of the cell) is not a constraint cell. Let *p'* be adjacent to *p*. *a)* If (the internal strength of *p* = the strength of the last level of the hierarchy = the walkabout strength of *p'*) then merging *p* with *p'* may create a better valuation. b) If (the internal strength of *p* = the strength of the last level of the hierarchy < the walkabout strength of *p'*) then merging *p* with *p'* does not create a better valuation.

A graph is a solution graph if and only if : 1) for each constrained cell with multiple constraints, any pair of the set of its variables and the set of its constraints (where the strength is different from the internal strength of this cell) is not a constraint cell. 2) For each over-constrained cell that contains constraints of the last level in the hierarchy, its internal strength is weaker than the walkabout strength of any other adjacent cells.

The first condition means that constraint cells must use the weakest constraints to determine the values of their variables. We then obtain a solution with a minimal error. The second condition is based on Theorem 1. If this condition is satisfied that it is impossible to create better solution graph by merging such over-constrained cells with others.

2.5 Algorithm

When a new constraint *c* is added to the hierarchy, Latif puts this constraint *c* in a new cell, and finds the adjacent cell with the weakest walkabout strength. If this walkabout strength is weaker than the strength of *c* then the procedure follows the path in the graph of the constraint cells from *c* to this adjacent cell and reverses the dependency between these cells. After this process, the constraint *c* becomes active. Latif eliminates cycles in constraint cells generated by the previous process by merging cyclic cells depending on *c*, and updates the walkabout strength correctly. By considering the definition of the solution graph and the theorem, Latif merges over-constrained cells with others, so that they can minimize the errors of their constraints. Finally Latif solves each cell by calling an adequate subsolver and applies local propagation to propagate the values of the variables computed in the cells.In order to remove a constraint *c*. Latif works in the similar way as for adding constraints[1].

3. Conclusion

The Latif solver can be seen as a generalisation of the *Detail* algorithm. Latif incrementally solves multiple solution types of constraints in single constraint hierarchies by grouping together cyclic or conflicting constraints into constraint cells. Moreover, it supports constraints with multi-output methods. Latif can be used as the constraint solver in geometric layout, user interface design, algorithm animation, and design and analysis of mechanical devices.

Acknowledgments

Firstly, many thanks to Dr. Bouzoubaa Taoufik for his enthusiastic help. The four reviewers were full of constructive criticism which have helped shape the paper.

References

[Borning et al., 1992] Borning, A., Freeman-Benson, B., & Wilson, M., *Constraint hierarchies*, Lisp and Symbolic Computation, Vol. 5, pp. 221-268, 1992.
[Hosobe et al., 1994] Hosobe, H., Miyachita, K., Takahashi, S., Matsuoka, S., & Yonezawa, A., *Locally Simultaneous Constraint Satisfaction LNCS 874: PPCP,* Nov. 1994.
[Hosobe et al., 1996] Hosobe, H., Satoshi, M. & Akinori, Y., *Generalized Local Propagation: ,A framework for solving constraint hierarchies, LNCS 1118: PPCP,* Nov. 1996.

---

1. because , when a constraint c is removed, it may create one or more constraint cells with an equal or weaker walkabout strength. Latif reverses the dependency between the cell with such constraints and the cell that contained the removed constraint c.

Author Index

Amamiya, M. 383
Ayache, N. 4
Badonski, M. 375
Ben-Asher, Y. 351
Boudol, G. 239
Bouzoubaa, M. 385
Bryant, R. E. 18
Budimac, Z. 375
Burns, A. 72
Büssow, R. 46
Chin, Y. H. 83
Codognet, P. 136
Cortesi, A. 225
Dang, V. H. 166
Davis, R. 72
Dinesh, T. B. 297
Fujita, K. 321
Fujita, S. 312
Gagné, J.-R. 381
Georget, Y. 136
Goebel, V. 151
Goshima, M. 268
Grieskamp, W. 46
Harao, M. 197
Hasegawa, R. 283
Horita, E. 377
Huang, Z. 98
Igarashi, S. 110
Ikawa, M. 268
Inenaga, K. 383
Inuzuka, N. 212
Itoh, H. 212
Ivanović, M. 375
Kaipainen, M. 367
Kanchanasut, K. 368
Karhu, P. 367
Khatib, L. 121
Kusakabe, S. 383
Lakhnech, Y. 181
Le Charlier, B. 225
Leclère, C. 225
Lei, W.-J. 98

Li, X. 166
Lin, M. 379
Lursinsap, C. 368
Malec J. 379
Mano K. 377
Merz S. 32
Mikk E. 181
Mizutani, T. 110
Mori, S. 268
Morioka, T. 373
Nadjm-Tehrani, S. 379
Nakajima, T. 371
Nakashima, H. 268
Ohno, K. 268
Papadopoulos, P. 367
Plagemann, T. 151
Plaice, J. 381
Punnekkat, S. 72
Rabin, M. O. 1
Ramanujam, R. 57
Roe, P. 254
Rossi, F. 136
Rossi, S. 225
Salzman, E. 336
Sattar, A. 98, 121
Seki, H. 212
Shio, M. 110
Siegel, M. 181
Siriboon, T. 368
Stein, E. 351
Sun, C. 98
Tomita, K. 110
Tomita, S. 268
Tseng, S.-M. 83
Üsküdarlı, S. M. 297
Velev, M. N. 18
Watson, R. 336
Wetprasit, R. 121
Yang, W.-P. 83
Zheng, T. 166

Lecture Notes in Computer Science

For information about Vols. 1–1274

please contact your bookseller or Springer-Verlag

Vol. 1275: E.L. Gunter, A. Felty (Eds.), Theorem Proving in Higher Order Logics. Proceedings, 1997. VIII, 339 pages. 1997.

Vol. 1276: T. Jiang, D.T. Lee (Eds.), Computing and Combinatorics. Proceedings, 1997. XI, 522 pages. 1997.

Vol. 1277: V. Malyshkin (Ed.), Parallel Computing Technologies. Proceedings, 1997. XII, 455 pages. 1997.

Vol. 1278: R. Hofestädt, T. Lengauer, M. Löffler, D. Schomburg (Eds.), Bioinformatics. Proceedings, 1996. XI, 222 pages. 1997.

Vol. 1279: B. S. Chlebus, L. Czaja (Eds.), Fundamentals of Computation Theory. Proceedings, 1997. XI, 475 pages. 1997.

Vol. 1280: X. Liu, P. Cohen, M. Berthold (Eds.), Advances in Intelligent Data Analysis. Proceedings, 1997. XII, 621 pages. 1997.

Vol. 1281: M. Abadi, T. Ito (Eds.), Theoretical Aspects of Computer Software. Proceedings, 1997. XI, 639 pages. 1997.

Vol. 1282: D. Garlan, D. Le Métayer (Eds.), Coordination Languages and Models. Proceedings, 1997. X, 435 pages. 1997.

Vol. 1283: M. Müller-Olm, Modular Compiler Verification. XV, 250 pages. 1997.

Vol. 1284: R. Burkard, G. Woeginger (Eds.), Algorithms — ESA '97. Proceedings, 1997. XI, 515 pages. 1997.

Vol. 1285: X. Jao, J.-H. Kim, T. Furuhashi (Eds.), Simulated Evolution and Learning. Proceedings, 1996. VIII, 231 pages. 1997. (Subseries LNAI).

Vol. 1286: C. Zhang, D. Lukose (Eds.), Multi-Agent Systems. Proceedings, 1996. VII, 195 pages. 1997. (Subseries LNAI).

Vol. 1287: T. Kropf (Ed.), Formal Hardware Verification. XII, 367 pages. 1997.

Vol. 1288: M. Schneider, Spatial Data Types for Database Systems. XIII, 275 pages. 1997.

Vol. 1289: G. Gottlob, A. Leitsch, D. Mundici (Eds.), Computational Logic and Proof Theory. Proceedings, 1997. VIII, 348 pages. 1997.

Vol. 1290: E. Moggi, G. Rosolini (Eds.), Category Theory and Computer Science. Proceedings, 1997. VII, 313 pages. 1997.

Vol. 1291: D.G. Feitelson, L. Rudolph (Eds.), Job Scheduling Strategies for Parallel Processing. Proceedings, 1997. VII, 299 pages. 1997.

Vol. 1292: H. Glaser, P. Hartel, H. Kuchen (Eds.), Programming Languages: Implementations, Logigs, and Programs. Proceedings, 1997. XI, 425 pages. 1997.

Vol. 1293: C. Nicholas, D. Wood (Eds.), Principles of Document Processing. Proceedings, 1996. XI, 195 pages. 1997.

Vol. 1294: B.S. Kaliski Jr. (Ed.), Advances in Cryptology — CRYPTO '97. Proceedings, 1997. XII, 539 pages. 1997.

Vol. 1295: I. Prívara, P. Ružička (Eds.), Mathematical Foundations of Computer Science 1997. Proceedings, 1997. X, 519 pages. 1997.

Vol. 1296: G. Sommer, K. Daniilidis, J. Pauli (Eds.), Computer Analysis of Images and Patterns. Proceedings, 1997. XIII, 737 pages. 1997.

Vol. 1297: N. Lavrač, S. Džeroski (Eds.), Inductive Logic Programming. Proceedings, 1997. VIII, 309 pages. 1997. (Subseries LNAI).

Vol. 1298: M. Hanus, J. Heering, K. Meinke (Eds.), Algebraic and Logic Programming. Proceedings, 1997. X, 286 pages. 1997.

Vol. 1299: M.T. Pazienza (Ed.), Information Extraction. Proceedings, 1997. IX, 213 pages. 1997. (Subseries LNAI).

Vol. 1300: C. Lengauer, M. Griebl, S. Gorlatch (Eds.), Euro-Par'97 Parallel Processing. Proceedings, 1997. XXX, 1379 pages. 1997.

Vol. 1301: M. Jazayeri, H. Schauer (Eds.), Software Engineering - ESEC/FSE'97. Proceedings, 1997. XIII, 532 pages. 1997.

Vol. 1302: P. Van Hentenryck (Ed.), Static Analysis. Proceedings, 1997. X, 413 pages. 1997.

Vol. 1303: G. Brewka, C. Habel, B. Nebel (Eds.), KI-97: Advances in Artificial Intelligence. Proceedings, 1997. XI, 413 pages. 1997. (Subseries LNAI).

Vol. 1304: W. Luk, P.Y.K. Cheung, M. Glesner (Eds.), Field-Programmable Logic and Applications. Proceedings, 1997. XI, 503 pages. 1997.

Vol. 1305: D. Corne, J.L. Shapiro (Eds.), Evolutionary Computing. Proceedings, 1997. X, 307 pages. 1997.

Vol. 1306: C. Leung (Ed.), Visual Information Systems. X, 274 pages. 1997.

Vol. 1307: R. Kompe, Prosody in Speech Understanding Systems. XIX, 357 pages. 1997. (Subseries LNAI).

Vol. 1308: A. Hameurlain, A M. Tjoa (Eds.), Database and Expert Systems Applications. Proceedings, 1997. XVII, 688 pages. 1997.

Vol. 1309: R. Steinmetz, L.C. Wolf (Eds.), Interactive Distributed Multimedia Systems and Telecommunication Services. Proceedings, 1997. XIII, 466 pages. 1997.

Vol. 1310: A. Del Bimbo (Ed.), Image Analysis and Processing. Proceedings, 1997. Volume I. XXII, 722 pages. 1997.

Vol. 1311: A. Del Bimbo (Ed.), Image Analysis and Processing. Proceedings, 1997. Volume II. XXII, 794 pages. 1997.

Vol. 1312: A. Geppert, M. Berndtsson (Eds.), Rules in Database Systems. Proceedings, 1997. VII, 214 pages. 1997.

Vol. 1313: J. Fitzgerald, C.B. Jones, P. Lucas (Eds.), FME '97: Industrial Applications and Strengthened Foundations of Formal Methods. Proceedings, 1997. XIII, 685 pages. 1997.

Vol. 1314: S. Muggleton (Ed.), Inductive Logic Programming. Proceedings, 1996. VIII, 397 pages. 1997. (Subseries LNAI).

Vol. 1315: G. Sommer, J.J. Koenderink (Eds.), Algebraic Frames for the Perception-Action Cycle. Proceedings, 1997. VIII, 395 pages. 1997.

Vol. 1316: M. Li, A. Maruoka (Eds.), Algorithmic Learning Theory. Proceedings, 1997. XI, 461 pages. 1997. (Subseries LNAI).

Vol. 1317: M. Leman (Ed.), Music, Gestalt, and Computing. IX, 524 pages. 1997. (Subseries LNAI).

Vol. 1318: R. Hirschfeld (Ed.), Financial Cryptography. Proceedings, 1997. XI, 409 pages. 1997.

Vol. 1319: E. Plaza, R. Benjamins (Eds.), Knowledge Acquisition, Modeling and Management. Proceedings, 1997. XI, 389 pages. 1997. (Subseries LNAI).

Vol. 1320: M. Mavronicolas, P. Tsigas (Eds.), Distributed Algorithms. Proceedings, 1997. X, 333 pages. 1997.

Vol. 1321: M. Lenzerini (Ed.), AI*IA 97: Advances in Artificial Intelligence. Proceedings, 1997. XII, 459 pages. 1997. (Subseries LNAI).

Vol. 1322: H. Hußmann, Formal Foundations for Software Engineering Methods. X, 286 pages. 1997.

Vol. 1323: E. Costa, A. Cardoso (Eds.), Progress in Artificial Intelligence. Proceedings, 1997. XIV, 393 pages. 1997. (Subseries LNAI).

Vol. 1324: C. Peters, C. Thanos (Eds.), Research and Advanced Technology for Digital Libraries. Proceedings, 1997. X, 423 pages. 1997.

Vol. 1325: Z.W. Raś, A. Skowron (Eds.), Foundations of Intelligent Systems. Proceedings, 1997. XI, 630 pages. 1997. (Subseries LNAI).

Vol. 1326: C. Nicholas, J. Mayfield (Eds.), Intelligent Hypertext. XIV, 182 pages. 1997.

Vol. 1327: W. Gerstner, A. Germond, M. Hasler, J.-D. Nicoud (Eds.), Artificial Neural Networks - ICANN '97. Proceedings, 1997. XIX, 1274 pages. 1997.

Vol. 1328: C. Retoré (Ed.), Logical Aspects of Computational Linguistics. Proceedings, 1996. VIII, 435 pages. 1997. (Subseries LNAI).

Vol. 1329: S.C. Hirtle, A.U. Frank (Eds.), Spatial Information Theory. Proceedings, 1997. XIV, 511 pages. 1997.

Vol. 1330: G. Smolka (Ed.), Principles and Practice of Constraint Programming - CP 97. Proceedings, 1997. XII, 563 pages. 1997.

Vol. 1331: D. W. Embley, R. C. Goldstein (Eds.), Conceptual Modeling - ER '97. Proceedings, 1997. XV, 479 pages. 1997.

Vol. 1332: M. Bubak, J. Dongarra, J. Waśniewski (Eds.), Recent Advances in Parallel Virtual Machine and Message Passing Interface. Proceedings, 1997. XV, 518 pages. 1997.

Vol. 1333: F. Pichler. R.Moreno-Díaz (Eds.), Computer Aided Systems Theory - EUROCAST'97. Proceedings, 1997. XII, 626 pages. 1997.

Vol. 1334: Y. Han, T. Okamoto, S. Qing (Eds.), Information and Communications Security. Proceedings, 1997. X, 484 pages. 1997.

Vol. 1335: R.H. Möhring (Ed.), Graph-Theoretic Concepts in Computer Science. Proceedings, 1997. X, 376 pages. 1997.

Vol. 1336: C. Polychronopoulos, K. Joe, K. Araki, M. Amamiya (Eds.), High Performance Computing. Proceedings, 1997. XII, 416 pages. 1997.

Vol. 1337: C. Freksa, M. Jantzen, R. Valk (Eds.), Foundations of Computer Science. XII, 515 pages. 1997.

Vol. 1338: F. Plášil, K.G. Jeffery (Eds.), SOFSEM'97: Theory and Practice of Informatics. Proceedings, 1997. XIV, 571 pages. 1997.

Vol. 1339: N.A. Murshed, F. Bortolozzi (Eds.), Advances in Document Image Analysis. Proceedings, 1997. IX, 345 pages. 1997.

Vol. 1340: M. van Kreveld, J. Nievergelt, T. Roos, P. Widmayer (Eds.), Algorithmic Foundations of Geographic Information Systems. XIV, 287 pages. 1997.

Vol. 1341: F. Bry, R. Ramakrishnan, K. Ramamohanarao (Eds.), Deductive and Object-Oriented Databases. Proceedings, 1997. XIV, 430 pages. 1997.

Vol. 1342: A. Sattar (Ed.), Advanced Topics in Artificial Intelligence. Proceedings, 1997. XVII, 516 pages. 1997. (Subseries LNAI).

Vol. 1343: Y. Ishikawa, R.R. Oldehoeft, J.V.W. Reynders, M. Tholburn (Eds.), Scientific Computing in Object-Oriented Parallel Environments. Proceedings, 1997. XI, 295 pages. 1997.

Vol. 1344: C. Ausnit-Hood, K.A. Johnson, R.G. Pettit, IV, S.B. Opdahl (Eds.), Ada 95 - Quality and Style. XV, 292 pages. 1997.

Vol. 1345: R.K. Shyamasundar, K. Ueda (Eds.), Advances in Computing Science - ASIAN'97. Proceedings, 1997. XIII, 387 pages. 1997.

Vol. 1346: S. Ramesh, G. Sivakumar (Eds.), Foundations of Software Technology and Theoretical Computer Science. Proceedings, 1997. XI, 343 pages. 1997.

Vol. 1347: E. Ahronovitz, C. Fiorio (Eds.), Discrete Geometry for Computer Imagery. Proceedings, 1997. X, 255 pages. 1997.

Vol. 1348: S. Steel, R. Alami (Eds.), Recent Advances in AI Planning. Proceedings, 1997. IX, 454 pages. 1997. (Subseries LNAI).

Vol. 1349: M. Johnson (Ed.), Algebraic Methodology and Software Technology. Proceedings, 1997. X, 594 pages. 1997.

Vol. 1350: H.W. Leong, H. Imai, S. Jain (Eds.), Algorithms and Computation. Proceedings, 1997. XV, 426 pages. 1997.

Vol. 1355: M. Darnell (Ed.), Cryptography and Coding. Proceedings, 1997. IX, 337 pages. 1997.